THE LAW DICT

Anderson Publishing Co.
Featured Publications

■ SOFTWARE

Anderson's Ohio Law on Disc
Anderson's Bankruptcy Filing System
Anderson's Ohio EPA on CD-ROM
Kentucky Instructions to Juries on Disk
Ohio Jury Instructions on CD-ROM

■ OHIO PUBLICATIONS

Page's Ohio Revised Code Annotated
Anderson's Ohio Case Locator
Anderson's Ohio Civil Practice with Forms
Anderson's Ohio Criminal Practice
and Procedure
Anderson's Ohio Family Law
Anderson's Ohio Probate Practice
and Procedure
Baker's Ohio School Law Guide
Couse's Ohio Form Book
Ohio Corporation Law
Ohio Criminal Law Handbook
Ohio EPA Laws and Regulations
Ohio Evidence
Ohio Jury Instructions
Ohio Liquor Laws and Rules
Ohio Manual of Criminal Complaints
and Indictments
Ohio School Finance
Ohio Securities Law and Practice
Ohio Workers' Compensation Law
Rules Governing the Courts of Ohio
Sixth Circuit Federal Practice Manual

■ OHIO PRACTICE MANUAL SERIES

Publications on appellate practice, domestic
relations, elder law, creditors' rights, pretrial
litigation, real estate transactions, the simple
will and others

■ NATIONAL PUBLICATIONS

Alternative Sentencing
Anderson's Estate Planning Forms
and Clauses
Anderson's Manual for Notaries Public
Federal Antitrust Law
Federal Civil Procedure Litigation Manual
Federal Evidence
Law of Oil and Gas
Law of Premises Liability
Legal Liability and Risk Management for
Public and Private Entities
Uninsured and Underinsured
Motorist Insurance

■ KENTUCKY PUBLICATIONS

Anderson's Kentucky Corporation
Record Book
Kentucky Family Law
Kentucky Instructions to Juries
Kentucky Criminal Code Handbook

■ EVIDENCE COURTROOM MANUALS

Alabama, California, Colorado, Federal,
Florida, Illinois, Indiana, Kentucky,
Michigan, New Jersey, New York,
North Carolina, Ohio, Pennsylvania,
and Tennessee, and others

■ CRIMINAL JUSTICE PUBLICATIONS

Career Planning in Criminal Justice
Criminal Justice Internships: Theory
into Practice
Criminal Justice Research Sources

■ PARALEGAL PUBLICATIONS

Alternative Dispute Resolution
for Paralegals
Effective Interviewing for Paralegals
A Guide to a Successful Legal Internship
Legal Research and Writing for Paralegals
Legal Research Workbook
The Paralegal Resource Manual

■ LAW SCHOOL PUBLICATIONS

Alternative Dispute Resolution: Strategies
for Law and Business
American Legal Systems: A Resource and
Reference Guide
Basic Accounting Principles for Lawyers:
With Present Value and Expected Value
Elements of Law
Introduction to the Study of Law: Cases
and Materials
ADA Handbook:
Statutes, Regulations and Related Materials
Preventative Law: Materials on a Non
Adversarial Legal Process
Science in Evidence

THE LAW DICTIONARY

Pronouncing Edition
A Dictionary of Legal Words and Phrases

With

*Latin and French Maxims of the Law
Translated and Explained*

Abbreviations Found in Legal Publications

Seventh Edition

Revised by
AMY B. BRANN, J.D.
Senior Legal Editor, Anderson Publishing Co.

ANDERSON PUBLISHING CO.
CINCINNATI

THE LAW DICTIONARY, Seventh Edition

© 1888, 1892 by Robert Clarke & Company
© 1924, 1956, 1973 by The W. H. Anderson Company
© 1986, 1997 by Anderson Publishing Co.

2035 Reading Road / Cincinnati, Ohio / 45202-1416
513 421-4142   800 582-7295
Fax: 513 562-8110   *E-Mail:* andpubco@aol.com
World Wide Web: http://www.legalpubs.com

Library of Congress Cataloging-In-Publication Data

The Law dictionary : pronouncing edition : a dictionary of legal words and phrases with Latin and French maxims of the law, translated and explained. -- 7th ed. revised by Amy B. Brann.
       p.   cm.
    Abbreviations found in legal publications.
    ISBN 0-87084-517-9 (paperback)
    1. Law--United States--Dictionaries.   I. Brann, Amy B.
KF156.L37   1997
349.73'03--dc21   96-45448
                                                                        CIP

CONTENTS

FOREWORD

When we use a law lexicon, we ought to consider what some of the wise members of the legal profession, who have gone before us, have had to say about dictionaries and words. Justice Robert H. Jackson said that a dictionary was the last resort of the baffled judge.[1] Justice Lucius Q. C. Lamar said that words are the common signs that mankind make use of to declare their intention to one another.[2] Perhaps the most foreboding statement about words was by Lord William Mansfield.[3]

"Most of the disputes in the world arise from words."

Lord Mansfield's statement should be a warning to people who write dictionaries, and persons who use them should also consider the advice of Justice Oliver Wendell Holmes, Jr.:[4]

"A word generally has several meanings, even in the dictionary. You have to consider the sentence in which it stands to decide which of those meanings it bears in the particular case, and very likely will see that it there has a shade of significance more refined than any given in the wordbook."

Similarly, Judge Learned Hand said that words are chameleons, which reflect the color of their environment.[5] At another time he developed the same theme to a greater degree.[6]

"Of course it is true that the words used, even in their literal sense, are the primary, and ordinarily the most reliable, source of interpreting the meaning of any writing: be it a statute, a contract, or anything else. But it is one of the surest indexes of a mature and developed jurisprudence not to make a fortress out of the dictionary; but to remember that statutes always have some purpose or object to accomplish, whose sympathetic and imaginative discovery is the surest guide to their meaning."

---

[1] Jordan v. DeGeorge, 341 U.S. 223, 234 (1951).

[2] Lake County v. Rollins, 130 U.S. 662, 671 (1889).

[3] Morgan v. Jones, Loft 160, 176, 98 Eng. Rep. 587, 596 (K.B. 1773).

[4] Holmes, *The Theory of Legal Interpretation*, 12 HARV. L. REV. 417 (1899).

[5] Commissioner v. National Carbide Corp., 167 F.2d 304, 306 (2d Cir. 1948).

[6] Cabell v. Markham. 148 F.2d 737, 739 (2d Cir. 1945).

Perhaps one of the best known statements concerning this very point was from Justice Holmes, when he argued that it was not necessarily true that the word, "income," means the same thing in the Constitution and in a statue:[7]

> ". . . A word is not a crystal, transparent and unchanged, it is the skin of a living thought and may vary greatly in color and content according to the circumstances and the time in which it is used."

It is the character of human language that no word conveys to the mind one single definite idea in all situations. Almost all written work contains words which, if taken in their rigorous sense, would convey a meaning different from that which is obviously intended.[8] In law and elsewhere, words of many-hued meanings derive their scope from the use to which they are put.[9] Words express whatever meaning convention has attached to them.[10]

---

[7] Towne v. Eisner, 245 U.S. 418, 425 (1918).
[8] Chief Justice John Marshall, in M'Culloch v. Maryland, 17 U.S. (4 Wheat.) 316, 414 (1819).
[9] Justice Felix Frankfurter, in Powell v. U.S. Cartridge Co., 339 U.S. 497, 529 (1950).
[10] Justice Holmes, in Trimble v. Seattle, 231 U.S. 683, 688 (1914).

PREFACE

It is the aim of this book to give, in condensed form, the meaning and application of all such words, phrases, maxims, abbreviations and references to reports, as a student of the law will be likely to encounter in his reading, and which the ordinary knowledge of the English language might not enable him to understand. The long dissertations on the law, which appear in older and larger dictionaries, and which, useful as they are in works approaching the magnitude of an encyclopedia, are incompatible with the objects of this book, have been avoided yet, where an example, or illustration of the use of a word could be stated in brief, so as to help the student to a fuller understanding of its meaning and application, it has been supplied.

To bring the work within the required compass, a large number of obsolete words and phrases, whose meaning is a matter of curiosity rather than importance, and many words of current English usage, which cannot be said to have any special significance in connection with the law, have been omitted. Where one form of a word is used it has not been deemed necessary to introduce other forms; the given meaning of the *verb*, for instance, being quite sufficient to enable the student of ordinary intelligence to understand *nouns*, *adjectives*, or *participles*, derived from the same root.

Condensation and facility of reference have been further secured by arranging in one paragraph phrases beginning with the same word, and compound words having the same stem; by using **boldface type** to point out with distinctness the successive words or phrases defined; and by the frequent use of cross-references. While intended primarily for the student, it is hoped that the book may also prove a serviceable desk companion for the practicing lawyer; and, in this connection, special attention is called to the very full table of abbreviations and references to the reports, contained in Appendix A.

This seventh edition of *Cochran's Law Lexicon* has been thoroughly revised in order to make it reflect the words and definitions which are characteristic of law in the last years of the twentieth century. A great number of new definitions were added. A few older definitions were also added because they have timely significance. A major portion of the definitions in this edition reflect the influence of the Uniform Commercial Code, other uniform laws, the Model Penal Code, the Restatements, the Federal Rules of Evidence, the Federal Rules of Civil Procedure, and the Federal Rules of Criminal Procedure.

Many definitions which are chiefly of historical significance, and those which pertain to English law, have been retained in order to record their meaning, but have been trimmed in order to delete the details which do not seem relevant to the American law of today. The number of cross references has been greatly enlarged. The Latin and French maxims have been verified, corrected, and interfiled with the definitions.

This edition is built on the work of the earlier authors and revisers of *Cochran's Law Lexicon*, including Wesley Gilmer, Jr. and W.C. Cochran, who were remarkably accurate and knowledgeable, particularly concerning the historic English and early American terms. As times change, old words should be defined in terms of current usage and contemporary examples, however. This was the goal of this seventh edition.

LATIN PRONUNCIATION

The pronunciation of French, French-English, Anglicized Latin, and unusual English words is indicated. In the case of the purely Latin terms it seemed best to indicate the stressed syllable and allow the reader to make use of either the Roman method of pronunciation, now generally taught in American schools and colleges, or of the English method formerly used both in England and in the United States and consequently frequently employed in legal circles.

The general rules for the Roman pronunciation of Latin are as follows:

VOWELS

a as	*a*	in	ah
e "	*e*	"	they
i "	*i*	"	pique
o "	*o*	"	hole
u "	*u*	"	rule

The short vowels have nearly the same sounds as the long ones mentioned above, but occupy only half as much time in utterance.

DIPHTHONGS

ae as	*ai*	in	aisle
oe "	*oi*	"	coin
au "	*ou*	"	out
eu "	*eu*	"	feud
ui "	*we*	"	suite

CONSONANTS

c as	*c*	in	come
ch "	*ch*	"	chemist
g "	*g*	"	get
i "	*y*	"	yet

r	"	r	"	rumor
s	"	s	"	son
t	"	t	"	time
v	"	w	"	we
qu	"	qu	"	quit
b	"	p	"	before s and t

According to the English pronunciation, the vowels have approximately the same sounds as in English.

DIPHTHONGS

ae	as	e	in	Caesar
oe	"	e	"	Oedipus
au	"	au	"	author
eu	"	eu	"	neuter
ui	"	ui	"	pronounced as a diphthong

CONSONANTS

c   as *k*

c   before *e* and *i* as *s*

c   before *e* and *i*, preceded by an accented syllable and followed by a vowel as *sh*

g   as *g* in go

s   before *e* and *i* as *j*

s,   *t* and *x* before *i*, preceded by an accented syllable and followed by a vowel as *sh*

t   after *s, t* or *x*, before *i*, preceded by an accented syllable and followed by a vowel as *t*

s,   final, as *z*

s   as *z* in certain words following the analogy of the English words: Caesar, causa, musa, miser, etc.

x,   initial, as *z*

DEFINITIONS

with

Latin and French Maxims of the Law Translated and Explained

NOTE—Abbreviations used in the text are:

      Amend., Amendment;

      Cf., Compare;

      e.g., for example;

      Fed. R. Civ. P., Federal Rules of Civil Procedure;

      Fed. R. Crim. P., Federal Rules of Criminal Procedure;

      Fed. R. Evid., Federal Rules of Evidence;

      fr., French;

      i.e., that is;

      l., Latin;

      L. fr., Law French; *(q.v.),* which see;

      (Rom.), Roman or Civil Law;

      (Sc.), Scotch;

      scil., being understood;

      Stat., United States Statutes at Large;

      U.C.C., Uniform Commercial Code;

      U.S.C., United States Code;

      U.S. Const., Constitution of the United States.

For other abbreviations, see *Table of Abbreviations,* post.

A

a (ä, as in ah), or **ab,** *l.,* from; by; in; of; at.

a (*a,* as in *ash*), *fr.,* of; at; to; for; in; with.

ab an'te, in advance.

ab anteceden'te, beforehand.

ab anti'quo, from ancient time.

ab assuetis non fit injuria, from that which has grown customary no legal wrong can arise.

ab ex'tra, from without.

ab ini'tio, from the beginning.

ab intesta'to, from one who died without making a will.

ab invi'to, unwillingly.

ab ira'to, by one who is angry.

a cancel'lis, at the cancelli; the chancellor.

a coelo usque ad centrum, *l.,* from the heavens to the center of the earth; formerly descriptive of the vertical extent of an owner's right in land.

a communi observantia non est recedendum, common usage or observance should not be departed from.

a fortio'ri, for a stronger reason; another proposition, included within an established proposition, is true for a greater reason; all the more.

a jure suo cadunt, they fall from, or lose, their right.

a l'impossible nul n'est tenu, no one is bound to do an impossible thing.

a men'sa et tho'ro, from bed and board; a kind of divorce (*q.v.*).

a non posse ad non esse sequitur argumentum necessarie negative, licet non affirmative, from impossibility to nonexistence the argument follows necessarily; but existence cannot be argued from possibility.

a piratis et latronibus capta dominium non mutant, the ownership of things taken by pirates and thieves does not change.

a posterio'ri, a priori, see *argument.*

a prendre (å prôn dr), to take, as from the soil.

a quo, from which.

a rendre (á rôn dr), to render, or yield, as services or rent.

a re'tro, from back; in arrears.

a tempore cujus contrarii memoria non existit, from a time of which memory to the contrary does not exist.

a verbis legis non est recedendum, from the words of the law there must be no departure, *i.e.,* statutes must be literally construed. Cf. *legislative intent.*

a vin'culo matrimo'nii, from the bond of marriage; a complete divorce (*q.v.*).

abandon, to forsake one's interest in property.

abandonment, desertion, by husband or wife. (2) Relinquishment, or surrender of property, or rights. (3) Leaving a vessel and giving it up as a total loss. (4) Surrendering to the underwriters all interest in the thing insured.

aban'dum, or **abandun,** any thing abandoned, forfeited, or confiscated.

abate, to put an end to; to nullify.

abatement, a making less, or destroying; a suspension or termination of an action for want of proper parties, or a defect in the writ or the service of process. (2) A reduction of rent, interest, or an amount due. (3) A removal or cessation of a nuisance. (4) A diminution of a freehold by the entry of a stranger upon the lands after the death of the former owner and before the heirs or devisees take possession. (5) The reduction of a legacy when an estate is insufficient to pay all debts and legacies. (6) A reduction of duties on account of damage to imported goods, or a decrease in the amount of taxes assessed upon a particular person or property. See *rebate.*

abator, or **abater,** one who abates a nuisance. (2) One who enters into a house or land vacant by the death of the former possessor, and not yet taken possession of by his heir or devisee. See *disseisin; intrusion.*

abbreviationem ille numerous et sensus accipiendus est, ut concessio non sit inanis, in abbreviations, the number and sense is to be interpreted, that the grant be not made void.

abbreviations, see *Table of Abbreviations,* post.

abbroach, to monopolize goods or forestall a market.

abdicate, to give up or renounce. (2) To renounce the throne or government.

abduction, the crime of forcibly, fraudulently or by persuasion, taking away a female person or a child. (2) Kidnaping (*q.v.*).

abet, to aid, encourage, or incite another to commit a crime.

abettor, one who is present inciting the principal. See also, *abet.*

abeyance, in expectation. (2) The condition of an estate or right where there is no person presently entitled to it. (3) Suspension.

abide, to submit to, or conform to, something, such as an order of court or an award of arbitrators.

abjudicate, to give away or transfer by judgment.

abjuration, a renunciation of allegiance upon oath. An oath, formerly taken by a felon who had claimed sanctuary, to forsake the realm forever.

abnegation, denial; renunciation.

abnormally dangerous activity, the essential question is whether the risk created is so unusual, either because of its magnitude or the circumstances surrounding it, as to justify the imposition of strict liability for the harm that results from it, even though it is carried on with all reasonable care. Because of the interplay of various factors, it not possible to reduce the phrase to a definition. Restatement (Second) of Torts § 520, Comment f.

abode, a settled place of residence.

aborticide, the killing of the fetus (*q.v.*) in the uterus.

abortion, a miscarriage or premature expulsion of the fetus (*q.v.*).

abortive trial, a trial terminated without reaching a verdict.

abridgment, or **abridgement,** a condensation, abstract, or digest of writing, *e.g.*, a law book.

abrogate, to annul or repeal a former law by the passage of a new one. Abrogation may be by express words, or by necessary implication.

abscond, to leave one's usual residence or to conceal one's self in order to avoid legal proceedings.

absence, nonappearance; being away from one's domicile. When continued for seven years, without the person being heard from, a presumption of death arises.

absence beyond seas, *i.e.*, from the United Kingdom and the adjacent (including the Channel) islands, was a disability (*q.v.*), and still in some cases entitles a person to an extension of time for pleading or appealing. The operation of statutes of limitation (*q.v.*) is generally suspended or modified as against a person who absents himself from the country or state in which a cause of action arises.

absolute, complete; unconditional; not relative or qualified. (2) A rule absolute is an order which can be forthwith enforced, in contradistinction to the rule nisi, which commands the opposite party to appear on a day therein named, and show cause why he should not perform the act, or submit to the terms therein set forth. In default of his appearance or showing good cause, the rule is made absolute.

absolution, the dismissal of a charge, declaration of a person's innocence, or remission of sins or penalties.

abs'que, *l.*, without.

absque a'liquo in'de redden'do, without reserving any rent therefrom; used of a grant by the crown.

absque hoc, without this; technical words of exception formerly used in a special traverse.

absque impetitio'ne vas'ti, without impeachment of waste; terms indicating the tenant's freedom from liability for waste.

abstention, a judge-made doctrine in the federal courts that sanctions postponement of an immediate decision in narrowly limited special circumstances, *e.g.,* a case where a challenged state statute is susceptible of a construction by the state courts that would avoid or modify the necessity of reaching a federal constitutional question. The doctrine serves to minimize federal-state friction and avoids premature and perhaps unnecessary constitutional adjudication. It contemplates that deference to state-court adjudication only be made when the issue of state law is uncertain. (2) Keeping an heir from possession. (3) The tacit renunciation of a succession by an heir. (4) A voluntary doing without.

abstract, a summary, epitome, or brief statement of essential points; (2) a history of the title to a particular tract of land.

abstract of title, a summary of all the deeds, wills, and legal proceedings which show the nature of a person's right to a piece of real property, together with the mortgages, judgments, liens and other encumbrances thereon.

abundans cautela non nocet, extreme care does no mischief.

abuse, ill-use; improper treatment of a thing. (2) Words or acts contrary to good order. (3) Rape.

abuse of discretion, a vague term descriptive of a judicial act that causes injustice; variously, an unjustified, unsound, unreasonable, or arbitrary action by a court or judge; a decision against reason and evidence. See also, *discretion.*

abuse of distress, using an animal or chattel distrained, which makes the distrainer liable as for a conversion.

abuse of process, the improper use of some regular civil or criminal legal proceeding to obtain a result which the proceeding was not intended to effect. If damage results, a tort is committed. Accord, Restatement (Second) of Torts § 682.

abutting, see *bounding.*

accede, to attain an office or position. (2) To enter into the duties of an office. (3) To agree.

Accelerated Cost Recovery System, ACRS; depreciation methods which increase the depreciation deductions in the early years of an asset's useful life and decrease them in later years.

acceleration, the shortening of the time for the vesting in possession of an expectant interest, the performance of a contract, or the payment of a note.

acceptance, the receipt of a thing, offered by another, with the intention of retaining it. (2) Of an offer (*q.v.*), a manifestation of assent (*q.v.*) to the terms of an offer, made by the offeree in a manner invited or required by the offer. Restatement (Second) of Contracts § 50(1). (3) The agreeing to terms or proposals by which a bargain (*q.v.*) is concluded and the parties are bound. (4) An agreement by the person, on whom a draft or bill of exchange is drawn, to pay the same according to its terms, generally expressed by writing the word "accepted" across the face and signing his name under it. (5) A drawee's (*q.v.*) signed engagement to honor a draft as presented. It must be written on the draft, and may consist of his signature alone. It becomes operative when completed by delivery or notification. U.C.C. § 3-410(1). (6) Of goods, occurs when the buyer (a) after a reasonable opportunity to inspect the goods signifies to the seller that the goods are conforming or that he will take or retain them in spite of their nonconformity, (b) fails to make an effective rejection, but such accep-tance does not occur until the buyer has had a reasonable opportunity to inspect them, or (c) does any act inconsistent with the seller's ownership, but if such act is wrongful as against the seller it is an acceptance only if ratified by him. U.C.C. § 2-606(1). (7) Concerning goods, acceptance of a part of any commercial unit is acceptance of the entire unit. U.C.C. § 2-606(2).

acceptance of goods, see *acceptance (6), (7)*.

acceptance of offer, see *acceptance (2)*.

acceptance supra protest, the acceptance, by a person not named in the bill or liable thereon, of a bill which has been protested, for the honor of the drawer or a particular indorser.

access, approach or the means of approaching, *e.g.*, an access road to real property. (2) The presumption of a child's legitimacy is rebutted, if it be shown that the husband did not have access to his wife within such a period of time before birth, as admits of his having been the father.

accessary, or **accessory,** one who is not the actual perpetrator of a felony, but is in some way concerned with the perpetration of it. He may be an accessory (a) before the fact, *e.g.*, by inciting or counseling, or (b) after the fact, by relieving or assisting the felon.

accessory after the fact, one who knowingly assisted a felon in escaping and avoiding punishment.

accessory before the fact, one who aided or encouraged the commis-sion of a felony without being actually or constructively present at the time of perpetration.

accession, the right to all which one's own property produces, *e.g.,* the fruit of trees or the young of animals, and to that which becomes added to or incorporated with it either naturally or artificially, *e.g.,* land formed by gradual deposit of soil (see *alluvion*) and buildings erected on, or trees, vines, etc., planted in one's ground. (2) The right, upon paying for the materials, to an article manufactured out of materials belonging to another, *e.g.,* bread made from flour or wine made from grapes, where the conversion was effected innocently, the person believing the materials to be his own. See also, *adjunction* and *specificatio.* (3) Coming into the enjoyment of an office or dignity.

accessorium non ducit sed sequitur suum principale, that which is the accessory (or incident) does not lead (or carry), but follows its principal.

accessorius sequitur naturam sui principalis, an accessory follows the nature of his principal [and therefore cannot be guilty of a higher crime].

accessory, see *accessary.*

accident, such an unforeseen event, misfortune, act, or omission as is not the result of negligence or misconduct in any party. (2) Something which happens without any human agency. See also, *act of God.* A recognized ground for equitable relief.

accomen'da, a contract made by an individual with the master of a vessel, to whom he entrusts personal property to be sold for their joint account.

accommodation paper, a promissory note or bill of exchange which a party makes, indorses, or accepts without consideration, for the benefit of another who receives money on it and is to provide for its payment when due. The want of consideration is a valid defense to an action brought on such paper by the person accommodated, but is no defense to an action by a third person who is a bona fide holder for value.

accommoda'tum, see *commodatum.*

accomplice, one concerned or involved with others in the commission of a crime. Cf. *particeps criminis.*

accompt, see *account.*

accord, an agreement between two (or more) persons, one of whom has a right of action against the other, that the latter should do or give, and the former accept, something in satisfaction of the right of action. When the agreement is executed, and satisfaction has been made, it is called accord and satisfaction, and operates as a bar to the right of action. Accord, Restatement (Second) of Contracts § 281(1).

accord and satisfaction, see *accord.*

account, or **accompt,** an account is a contract of deposit of funds between a depositor and a financial institution (*q.v.*), and includes a checking account, savings account, certificate of deposit, share account, and other like arrangement. Uniform Probate Code § 6-101(1). (2) A detailed statement of receipts and payments of money, or of trade transactions which have taken place between two or more persons. Accounts are either (a) open or current, where the balance is not struck, or is not accepted by all the parties; (b) stated, where it has been expressly or impliedly acknowledged to be correct by all the parties (accord, Restatement (Second) of Contracts § 282(1)); or (c) settled, where it has been accepted and discharged. (3) To make a rest in an account, or an account with rests is, at stated periods, to strike a balance, so that interest may thence forward be computed on the sum actually due, not merely on the original principal or debt.

account book, a book in which business transactions are entered, which if regularly kept as a book of original entry, may be admitted evidence.

account settled, see *account (2)(c)*.

account stated, see *account (2)(b)*.

accountable receipt, a written acknowledgment of the receipt of money or goods to be accounted for by the receiver, as distinguished from an ordinary receipt or acquittance for money paid in discharge of a debt.

accounts payable, amounts which are due to trade vendors and/or others for goods or services received for which payment has not been made.

accounts receivable, amounts owed to the entity which have not been paid.

accredit, to acknowledge; to send a diplomatic agent with proper credentials.

accretion, addition to property by operation of natural causes, *e.g.*, gain of land by gradual deposit of soil washed up from the sea or river. See also, *alluvion*.

accrual, accruer, a right accrues when it vests in a person, especially when it arises without his active intervention, *e.g.*, by lapse of time, or determination of a previous right. For cases of accruer, see also, *accession, alluvion,* and *survivorship*.

accrual basis, a basis of accounting under which revenues are recorded when earned. Expenditures are recorded as soon as they result in liabilities regardless of when the revenue is actually received or the payment is actually made.

accrue, to grow to; to be added to, as interest to principal. (2) To arise; to happen or come to pass, as a cause of action.

accrued interest, interest which has accumulated between interest dates but which is not yet due.

accumulative sentence, one passed before the first has expired, to commence upon its expiration.

accusare nemo se debet, no one is bound to accuse himself.

accusation, the charge that one has been guilty of a crime or misdemeanor, made to a proper officer.

accusator post rationabile tempus non est audiendus, nisi se bene de omissione, excusaverit, an accuser ought not to be heard after reasonable time, unless he has made a good excuse for his delay.

Acid Precipitation Act of 1980, title VII of the Energy Security Act (*q.v.*) concerning an interagency task force, comprehensive program, comprehensive research plan, and its implementation. 42 U.S.C. §§ 8901 *et seq.*

acknowledgment, the act of going before a competent officer or court and declaring the execution of a deed or other instrument. The acknowledgment is certified by the officer, and his certificate is some times called the acknowledgment. Acknowledgment of deeds, mortgages, and instruments conveying an interest in real property is required by the laws of most of the states, to entitle them to be recorded and to dispense with other proof of their execution.

acquets, (Rom.) property obtained during marriage by a husband or wife.

acquiescence, silent assent, or neglecting to speak when one wishing to object or stand on his rights would naturally speak or act. Conduct from which consent may be implied, as distinguished from express consent (*q.v.*).

acquittal, a release or discharge, especially by verdict of a jury.

acquittance, a release or written discharge of a sum of money due.

act, something done or established. (2) Laws passed by Congress and the legislatures of the states are styled Acts. These may be (a) general or public, affecting the whole community; (b) private or special, affecting only particular persons and places and private concerns. (3) An external manifestation of the will of an actor (*q.v.*); it does not include any of its results. Restatement (Second) of Torts § 2. See also, *action (2)*.

act in pais (ăkt ĭn pă eš), a thing done out of court, and not a matter of record.

act of bankruptcy, formerly, certain actions specified by Bankruptcy Act § 3 (a) (1898), 11 U.S.C. § 21 (a), relative to the property of a debtor, which if performed by the debtor, could be used to force the debtor into bankruptcy court and have him adjudged to be a bankrupt. Under the Bankruptcy Reform Act (*q.v.*), the concept of acts of bankruptcy is abolished; the only basis for an involuntary case is the failure of the debtor to meet its debts as they mature, or the appointment of a custodian within the 120-day period preceding the filing of an involuntary petition to take charge of the property of the debtor. 92 Stat. 2559, tit. I, § 101 (1978); 11 U.S.C. § 303(h).

act of God, an inevitable event, one which occurs without human intervention, and for which, therefore, no one is to be blamed, *e.g.*, hurricane, tornado or flood. On this ground carriers are released from liability for loss, and a person is in some cases discharged from his covenant or contract.

act of honor, an instrument drawn up by a notary public, after protest of a bill of exchange, when a third party is desirous of paying or accepting a bill for the honor of any or all of the parties to it.

act of state doctrine, the principle that the courts will not examine the validity of a taking of property by a foreign government within its own territory, if the foreign government is extant and recognized by the United States at the time of the suit, in the absence of a treaty or other unambiguous agreement regarding controlling legal principles, even if the complaint alleges that the taking violates customary international law. The act in question must be public, and not commercial in nature. Expropriation claims may be heard as set-offs (*q.v.*) in some circumstances, however.

act on petition, a summary mode of proceeding to obtain an adjudication on questions in divorce, probate, and ecclesiastical matters.

acta exteriora, indicant interiora secreta, outward acts show the inward intent.

ac'tio, *l.*, an action.

actio ad exhiben'dum (Rom.), an action instituted for the purpose of compelling production of documents or testimony.

actio aestimato'ria, actio quan'ti mino'ris (Rom.), an action which lay on behalf of a buyer to reduce the contract price proportionately to the defects of the object; not to cancel the sale.

actio arbitra'ria (Rom.), an action depending on the discretion of the judge.

actio bo'nae fide'i (Rom.), an action which the judge decided according to equity, acting as arbiter with a wide discretion.

actio calum'niae (Rom.), an action for malicious prosecution.

actio commoda'ti contra'ti contra'ria (Rom.), an action by a borrower against a lender, to enforce the contract.

actio commoda'ti direc'to (Rom.), an action by a lender against a borrower.

actio commu'ni dividun'do (Rom.), an action for a division of property held in common.

actio conduc'tio inde'biti (Rom.), an action for the recovery of a sum of money paid by mistake.

actio confesso'ria (Rom.), an affirmative action for the enforcement of a servitude.

actio dam'ni inju'ria (Rom.), an action for damages.

actio de do'lo ma'lo (Rom.), an action of fraud.

actio de pecu'lio (Rom.), an action concerning or against the peculium or separate property of a party.

actio de pecu'nia constitu'ta (Rom.), an action for money due under a promise.

actio de tig'no junc'to (Rom.), an action by the owner of material built into his building.

actio depo'siti contra'ria (Rom.), an action which a depositary has against a depositor, to compel him to fulfill his engagement.

actio depo'siti direc'ta (Rom.), an action brought by a depositor against a depositary, to get back the thing deposited.

actio ex conduc'to (Rom.), an action by a bailor for hire against a bailee, to compel him to deliver the thing hired.

actio ex loca'to (Rom.), an action which one who lets may have against one who hires.

actio fami'liae eriscun'dae (Rom.), an action for the division of an inheritance.

actio furti (Rom.), an action of theft.

actio instito'ria (Rom.), an action against the owner of a shop served by his slave.

actio judica'ti (Rom.), an action to obtain execution of a judgment.

actio manda'ti (Rom.), an action founded on a mandate.

actio non accre'vit infra sex annos (Rom.), the action did not accrue within six years.

actio non datur non damnificato, no action is given to one who is not injured.

actio non ulter'rius, a name given in English pleading to the distinctive clause in the formal plea against further maintenance of the action; introduced in place of the plea puis darrein continuance.

actio personalis moritur cum persona (Rom.), a personal action dies with the person. Statutes have modified this concept in many instances.

actio pigneriti'tia (Rom.), an action for a thing pledged after payment of a debt.

actio poenalis in haerendem non datur, nisi forte ex damno locupletior haeres factus sit, a penal action is not given against an heir, unless such heir is benefited by the wrong.

actio pro so'cio (Rom.), an action by which a partner could compel his copartners to perform the partnership contract.

actio redhibito'ria (Rom.), an action brought by a purchaser to recover the price, for breach of implied warranty on the sale.

actio u'tilis (Rom.), an equitable action.

actio vendi'ti (Rom.), an action by a seller to secure the performance of a contract of sale. See *action.*

action, a lawsuit; a proceeding taken in a court of law. Its chief classifications are: civil, to enforce a right; criminal, to punish an offender. Under the modern rules of civil procedure adopted in the United States courts and many state courts, and the codes of civil practice in most other states, the common law forms of action are abolished and one form of action, known as a *civil action,* is established. The following classifications are, therefore, significant mainly from a historical viewpoint. In rem (against a thing), to bind a thing; in personam (against a person), to bind a person; real, to recover lands, tenements, or hereditaments; personal, to recover money, damages, or specific personal property; mixed, which partake of the nature of both real and personal actions as actions of partition, actions to recover possession of property and damages, etc., ex contractu, those which arise out of contract; and ex delicto, those which arise out of tort or the fault of the defendant. In common law pleading actions ex contractu were classed as follows:—(a) covenant, being on a deed alone; (b) assumpsit, being on a simple contract only; (c) debt, being indifferently on a deed or simple contract; (d) scire facias, being on a judgment; (e) account, to compel an account and enforce the payment of the balance found due; (f) annuity, to enforce the payment of an annuity. Actions ex delicto were classed as follows:—(a) trespass quare dausum fregit, to real property, or de bonis asportatis, to personal property; (b) case, being for torts which had no special writ or remedy, prior to 13 Edw. 1. c. 24, and for which, by that statute, special writs were to be framed, according to the circumstances of each case, on the lines of those already existing, such as torts committed without force, injuries resulting from negligence, abuse of legal process, etc., and injuries to reversionary, incorporeal and relative rights; (c) trover, to recover damages for the wrongful appropriation or conversion of property; (d) detinue, for the wrongful detention of property lawfully taken, and (e) replevin, to recover specific personal property, unlawfully taken. (2) Act or action means a bodily movement whether voluntary or involuntary. Model Penal Code § 1.13 (2).

action in rem, see *rem, action in.*

actionable, something which may be the subject of an action. Often used concerning spoken or written words which constitute slander or libel.

actionary, one who owns shares in a European joint-stock company.

actio'nes nomina'tae, *l.,* writs for which there were precedents in the English chancery, prior to 13 Edw. 1. c. 24, as distinguished from Actiones innominatae, for which there were none. See also, *trespass.*

action of a writ, a phrase formerly used when a defendant pleaded that the plaintiff had no right to the writ sued upon, although it might be that he was entitled to another writ or action for the same matter.

actor, *l.,* a manager, an advocate, an agent. (2) The plaintiff or active claimant in a case. (3) Either a person whose conduct is in question, as subjecting him to liability toward another, or as precluding him from recovering against another whose tortious (*q.v.*) conduct is a legal cause of the actor's injury. Restatement (Second) of Torts § 3. (4) Includes, where relevant, a person guilty of an omission (*q.v,*). Model Penal Code § 1.13 (6).

actor do'minae, manager of the estate.

actor eccle'siae, the manager of church property.

actor sequitur forum rei, a plaintiff must bring action in the court which has jurisdiction over the defendant or the subject of the dispute.

actore non probante reus absolvitur, when the plaintiff does not prove his case the defendant is acquitted.

actori incumbit onus probandi, the burden of proof lies on a plaintiff.

actual, that which is real or existing, as opposed to something merely possible, or to something which is presumptive or constructive.

actual authority, authority expressly or impliedly conferred by a principal upon his agent to act in his behalf.

actual bias, a prepossession on the part of a juror which leads to a just inference that he will not act with entire impartiality.

actual cash value, the price in money which something will bring when it is offered for sale by one who desires to sell but is not compelled to do so, and is purchased by someone who desires to buy but is not compelled to do so. (2) The fair or reasonable cash price for which something could be sold in the market, in the ordinary course of business, and not at a forced sale.

actual compulsion, forcibly compelling a person to do an act.

actual damages, damages awarded as compensation for a loss or injury actually sustained.

actual delivery, the surrender of control and possession of property by the vendor and the assumption of possession by the vendee.

actual force, personal violence; any force, of whatever degree, inflicted during a robbery directly upon the person robbed, sufficient to compel that person to part with his property.

actual fraud, any intentional false representation or contrivance which misleads another to his hurt.

actual knowledge, facts which are within one's knowledge; notice or information of circumstances putting one on an inquiry which, if followed, would lead to knowledge.

actual malice, ill will, malevolence, grudge, spite, wicked intention or enmity toward an individual, as distinguished from constructive or fictitious malice. (2) In the law of libel and slander, a test that requires that a plaintiff prove that a defamatory statement concerning a public figure (*q.v.*) was made with knowledge that it was false or with reckless disregard of whether it was false or not.

actual notice, see *actual knowledge.*

actual residence, the place where one actually lives or resides.

actual service, service of process made either by reading the process to the defendant or by delivering to him a copy thereof.

actuary, a person who calculates insurance risks and premiums. (2) A registrar or clerk.

actus legis nemini facit injuriam, the act of the court does wrong to no one.

actus me invito factus, non est meus actus, an act done by me against my will is not my act.

actus non facit reum, nisi mens sit rea, an act does not make a man guilty, unless he be so in intention.

actus reus, evil act; a deed, an act, an offense or an omission of conduct; the wrongful act which renders one criminally liable if combined with mens rea.

ad, *l.,* at; by; for; near; on account of; to; until; upon.

ad abundantio'rem caute'lam, for greater caution.

ad a'liud exa'men, to another tribunal.

ad cu'riam, at court.

ad custa'gia, or **ad cus'tum,** at the costs.

ad dam'num, to the damage; that part of a pleading or writ which states the amount of the plaintiff's loss or injury.

ad di'em, at the day.

ad ea quae frequentis accidunt jura adaptantur, the laws are adapted to those cases which most frequently arise.

ad exhaeridatio'nem, to the disinheriting; a term used in the old writ of waste against a tenant.

ad fi'dem, in allegiance.

ad fi'lum a'quae, or **vi'ae,** to the thread or center line of the stream, or road.

ad fi'nem, at or near to the end.

ad hoc, for this case only. (2) As to this. (3) Special.

ad ho'minem, To the man; argument adapted especially to the person spoken to.

ad i'dem, to the same point, essential agreement.

ad infini'tum, without limit.

ad inquiren'dum, for inquiry; a judicial writ commanding inquiry to be made into matters related to the suit pending.

ad in'terim, in the meantime.

ad ju'ra re'gis, for the king's rights; a writ which was brought by a clerk who had been presented to a royal living, against those who endeavored to eject him to the prejudice of the king's title.

ad lar'gum, at large.

ad li'bitum, at pleasure.

ad li'tem, for the lawsuit.

ad lon'gum, at length.

ad nocumen'tum, to the hurt or injury. (2) To the nuisance.

ad o'pus, to the work.

ad os'tium eccle'siae, at the church door. See also, *dower.*

ad proximum antecedens fiat relation, nisi impediatur sententia, the relative should be referred to the next, or last, antecedent, unless the sense forbid.

ad quem, to which; correlative to a quo, from which.

ad questiones facti non respondent judices; ad questiones legis non respondent puratores, [in trial by jury] the judges do not decide questions of fact; nor the jury, questions of law.

ad quod dam'num, to what injury.

ad ratio'nem po'nere, to cite a person to appear.

ad responden'dum, for answering.

ad satisfacien'dum, to satisfy.

ad sec'tam, at the suit of.

ad ter'minum anno'rum, for a term of years.

ad ter'minum qui prae'teriti, a writ of entry which lay for the owners of the reversion upon a lease, when the lease had expired.

ad tunc et ibi'dem, then and there; technical words in the old form of indictment.

ad valo'rem, according to the value, *e.g.,* a tax or duty based on the value of property.

ad ven'trem inspicien'dum, inspection of the womb; a writ issued for the purpose of ascertaining whether a woman condemned to death, or from whom an heir might be born, is pregnant.

ad vi'tam, for life.

ad vi'tam aut cul'pam, for life, or until bad behavior.

Adamson Act, an act establishing an eight-hour day for employees of carriers engaged in interstate and foreign commerce. 45 U.S.C. § § 65, 66.

ADA, see *Americans with Disabilities Act.*

addict, a person who habitually or compulsively uses something, especially drugs, to such an extent that he no longer has his self-control.

addic'tio (Rom.), the giving up to a creditor of his debtor's person or goods.

addition, the title or place of residence of a person, written after his name for certainty of identification.

additional servitude, or **new servitude,** making a different use than that for which the land was originally taken under eminent domain proceedings, and requiring a new condemnation to justify its taking.

additur, in some states, a remedy granted by an appellate court by which a new trial is denied to the plaintiff on the express condition that the defendant agree to a specified increase in the amount of the plaintiff's judgment. Cf. *remittitur.*

adduce, to bring forward; to offer; to present; to introduce, *e.g.,* to adduce testimony at a trial.

ADEA, see *Age Discrimination in Employment Act.*

adeemed by extinction, property specifically described by the testator in the will and not in the estate at death.

ademption, a revocation, or a taking away of a legacy. Where a testator, having given a specific thing by his will, parts with it before his death, he adeems the legacy. See also, *satisfaction.*

ademption by satisfaction, the testator makes a inter vivos gift of property to a devisee in the will with the intention of rendering the testamentary gift inoperative.

adequate remedy, one that affords complete relief with reference to the matter in controversy, and which is appropriate to the circumstances of the case.

adhesion contract, a standard form printed agreement prepared by one party and submitted to the other party for acceptance or rejection, but not for negotiation. There is often no equality of bargaining power in such transactions, and adhesion contracts are often construed accordingly.

adit, in mining law, a lateral way or passage to a mine, horizontal or nearly so.

adjacent, next to, or near.

adjective law, rules of procedure or administration as distinguished from rules of substantive law (*q.v.*).

adjourn, to put off the hearing or meeting to another day.

adjourned term, a continuance of a previous or regular term of court.

adjudicate, to determine judicially.

adjudication, a judgment or decision. (2) Of bankruptcy, the declaring a debtor bankrupt. See also, *bankrupt.*

adjunction, the attachment or permanent union of something belonging to one, to that which belongs to another, by which the right of property passes to the person owning the principal, *e.g.*, the building of a house on another's ground, setting a diamond in another's ring, using the buttons of one to make another's coat. See also, *accession.*

adjuration, a swearing or binding upon oath.

adjusted gross income, AGI; income adjusted for federal tax purposes.

adjustment, the settlement of an insurance claim.

admanuensis, one who swears by laying his hand on the Testament.

admeasurement, writ of, of dower, lay where a widow took or had assigned to her a larger dower than rightly belonged to her; (2) Of pasture, lay where anyone having common of pasture surcharged the common—to correct the excess in either case. See *surcharge.*

adminicular evidence, explanatory, or in support.

administer, to give, to direct, or cause, to be taken. (2) To act as the personal representative of a deceased person in an estate settlement.

administration, the carrying out of the executive's duties in a government or other organization. (2) The management and disposal, under legal authority, of the estate of a deceased person. If the deceased left a will and nominated a person to manage his estate, such person, when appointed by the court, is called an executor. If the deceased left no will, the court appoints a person who is called an administrator.

administration in general, relating to the whole management and closing up of the estate; or special, *e.g.*, ad colligen'dum, for collecting and preserving goods which are perishable or liable to loss, when for any reason regular probate and administration cannot be granted at once. **an'cillary,** subordinate to the principal administration, for collecting assets in another state or a foreign country. **cum testamen'to annex'o,** with the will annexed, when no executor is named in the will, or the person named is unable or unwilling to serve. **de bonis non,** concerning the goods not administered, when the first administrator dies without having fully administered. **duran'te mino're aeta'te,** or **absen'tia,** where the sole executor is a minor or beyond seas. **penden'te li'te,** while a suit is pending respecting the will, to take care of the estate only until the suit is ended. The mode of appointing administrators, their duties and powers, and the judicial supervision of their acts and accounts, are regulated by various state statutes.

administrative law judge, a public official in the federal government who performs the duties and exercises the authority of a hearing examiner (*q.v.*). The title of such officials in the federal government was changed from hearing examiner to administrative law judge. 92 Stat. 183 (1978).

Administrative Procedure Act, an act to establish a uniform system of administering laws by and among the agencies of the United States government, and to provide for administrative and judicial review of the decisions of those agencies. 5 U.S .C. § § 551 *et seq.*, 701 *et seq.*

administrator, or **administratrix,** one to whom letters of administration have been granted by a court, and who administers an estate. See also, *administration.*

administrator cum testamento annexo, an administrator appointed by the court where the will does not name an executor or the executor named does not serve.

administrator cum testamento annexo de bonis non, an administrator appointed by the court if an executor fails to complete the administration.

administrator de bonis non, an administrator appointed by the court where the administrator of an intestate fails to complete the administration for some reason.

admiralty, the jurisdiction exercised by United States courts over maritime contracts, torts, injuries and seizures, including cases arising on the navigable lakes and rivers. U.S. Const. Art. III, Sec. 2. In England, this jurisdiction is exercised by the Probate, Divorce and

Admiralty Division of the High Court of Justice, and is confined to cases arising on the high seas and those portions of rivers and sounds in which the tides rise and fall.

admission, the act by which attorneys and counselors become officers of a court and are licensed to practice law. The requirements for admission vary greatly in different states. (2) A voluntary statement or acknowledgment, made by a party, which is admissible in evidence against that party. (3) A statement (*q.v.*) which is offered against a party and is (a) his own statement, in either his individual or a representative capacity, (b) a statement of which he has manifested his adoption or belief in its truth, (c) a statement by a person authorized by him to make a statement concerning the subject, (d) a statement by his agent or servant concerning a matter within the scope of his agency or employment, made during the existence of the relationship, or (e) a statement by a coconspirator of a party during the course and in furtherance of the conspiracy. Fed. R. Evid. 801(d)(2). (4) An express or implied acknowledgment that an allegation in the pleading of the opposing party is true.

admixture, the mingling of goods by confusion or accession.

admonition, a caution given by a court to jurors concerning the rules for their conduct while they are participating in a lawsuit. (2) A warning, rebuke, or reprimand.

admortization, the reduction of property in lands or tenements to mortmain, in the feudal custom.

adolescence, variously, the period commencing at 12 in females, and 14 in males, and ending at 21 years of age; the period between childhood and maturity; the period of youthfulness.

adoption, the act by which a person takes the child of another into his family and makes him, for all legal purposes, his own child. The formalities, effect and validity are controlled by the statutes and court decisions of the respective states. (2) The affirmation or acceptance of a contract which one is at liberty otherwise to repudiate, *e.g.*, a contract made by an infant during his minority.

adoption by reference, the statement in a writing by which another statement in a separate writing is incorporated into the former. Statements in a pleading may be adopted by reference in a different part of the same pleading, or in another pleading or in a motion.

ADR, see *alternative dispute resolution*.

adstipula'tor (Rom.), an accessory party to a promise, who received the same promise, in whole or in part, as his principal did, and could equally exact fulfillment, even after death of the principal.

adult, of full age. In civil law, a male who has reached the age of 14, a female who has reached the age of 12. In common law, a person who has attained the age of 21. By statute in many states, a person who has attained the age of 18.

adulteration, the act of mixing cheap or inferior substances with another substance.

adultery, the voluntary sexual intercourse of a married person with someone other than his spouse. It was not an indictable offense at common law, but was left to the ecclesiastical courts for punishment. It is made punishable by fine and imprisonment by the statutes of most of the states, and is a generally recognized ground for an absolute divorce.

advancement, a gift by a parent to a child with the intent to vest in him the whole or part of what he would otherwise inherit on the death of the parent, the amount of which is deducted from the distributive share of such child. The purchase of land by the parent in the name of the child, or the settlement of a portion on him, is presumed to be an advancement. Money paid out for the maintenance or education of a child is not.

advances, payments made to the owner of goods by the factor or consignee who is to have possession of the goods for the purpose of selling them. An agent is entitled to a lien on the goods and the proceeds of their sale for the amount of such advances, and a right of action against the principal for the balance, if the proceeds are insufficient to cover the advances.

adventure, the sending to sea of a ship or goods at the risk of the sender to be sold by an agent for the benefit of the owner.

adverse, opposing; conflicting; contrary to.

adverse enjoyment, or **user,** the possession or exercise of an easement or privilege under a claim of right as against the owner of the land.

adverse possession, the actual holding and enjoyment of land under a claim of right which is opposed to or inconsistent with the rights of the true owner.

adversus extraneos vitiosa possessio prodesse solet, prior possession is a good title of ownership against all who cannot show a better.

advisory, informative; not conclusive; not binding.

advisory opinion, in some jurisdictions, the formal opinion of a higher court concerning a point at issue in a lower court. (2) The formal opinion of a legal officer, *e.g.,* Attorney General, concerning a question of law submitted by a public official. (3) In some jurisdictions, the opinion of a court concerning a question submitted by a legislative body.

advocate, an attorney who speaks or writes, or both, in support of his client's cause.

advoca'tus dia'boli, devil's advocate.

advow'try, continuous living in adultery.

aedeficare in tuo proprio solo non licet quod alteri noceat, it is not lawful to build on your own land what may injure another.

aedificatum solo, solo cedit, that which is built upon the land goes with the land.

aequitas agit in personam, equity acts upon the person. An equitable decree is enforced against the person and not against the property.

aequitas est quasi aequalitas, equity is as it were equality.

aequitas nunquam contravenit leges, equity never contravenes the laws.

aequitas sequitur legem, equity follows the law; equity has no jurisdiction to change the rights of parties which are clearly defined and established by statute.

ae'quum et bo'num, reasonable.

aestimatio praeteriti delicti ex post facto nunquam crescit, the estimation of a crime committed is never increased by what happens afterward.

affectus punitur licet non sequatur effectus, the intention is punished, although the consequence does not follow.

affiance, a promise to marry; an engagement.

affiant, one who makes oath to a written statement; one who signs an affidavit.

affida'tus, a tenant by fealty, a retainer; an ally.

affidavit, a written statement of fact, signed and sworn to before a person having authority to administer an oath.

affiliation, an association or membership. (2) The fixing of the paternity of a bastard child upon one legally bound to support it.

affinis mei affinis non est mihi affinis, one related by marriage to one related to me by marriage has no affinity to me.

affinity, relationship by marriage between the husband and the blood relations of the wife, and between the wife and the blood relations of the husband. Cf. *consanguinity.*

affirm, to make firm; to establish. (2) To ratify or confirm the judgment of a lower court. (3) To ratify or confirm a voidable contract. (4) To declare or verify as a substitute for an oath. See also, *affirmation.*

affirmanti, non neganti, incumbit probatio, the proof lies upon him who affirms, not upon him who denies.

affirmation, a solemn declaration without oath. The privilege of affirming in judicial proceedings is now generally extended to all persons who object to taking an oath.

affirmative action, programs which are designed to remedy past discriminatory practices in the employment of minorities.

affirmative defense, a response to a claim for relief which states information not otherwise before the court, *e.g.,* a plea of payment in response to a claim that a promissory note was executed and delivered. (2) A justification or avoidance.

affirmative pregnant, an affirmative allegation implying some negative in favor of the adverse party.

affirmative proof, evidence of the truth of the matters asserted tending to establish them.

affixed to the realty, so fastened to the land or imbedded in the land or permanently resting upon the land as to pass with the land.

affranchise, to make free.

affray, the fighting of persons in a public place to the terror of the people.

affreightment, the contract by which a ship is hired to carry goods.

aforesaid, contained in an earlier part of the same document.

aforethought, planned beforehand; premeditated.

after-acquired property, property acquired by a person after some particular date or event, *e.g.,* acquired by a person after the date on which he gave a mortgage.

after-born child, a person born subsequent to the making of a testator's will, or after his death.

aftermath, the second crop of grass. (2) The right to have the last crop of grass or pasturage.

age, the period of time that someone has been alive. (2) Majority. Usually a person becomes of age on the day preceding his or her eighteenth birthday. These matters are regulated by various statutes in force in the respective states.

Age Discrimination in Employment Act of 1967, an act to prohibit age discrimination in employment. 29 U.S.C. §§ 621 *et seq.,* amended, 5 U.S.C. §§ 3322, 8335, 8339.

agency, the fiduciary relationship which results from the manifestation of consent by one person to another that the other shall act on his behalf and be subject to his control, and consent by the other to so act. Restatement of Agency, Second § 1.

agency shop, a factory, store or other place of employment where an employee does not have to become a member of the union, but any employee electing not to join must pay to the union an amount equal to the customary initiation fee and the periodic dues required of members.

agenda, the program of business to be brought up at a meeting.

agent, a person authorized by another (the principal), to do an act or transact business for him, and to bind the principal within the limits of that authority. An agent may be general, to do all business of a particular kind; or special, to do one particular act. The agent's power to bind the principal is according to the scope of his authority. See also, *deputy.*

agentes et consentientes pari poena plectentur, acting and consenting parties are liable to the same punishment.

aggravated assault, attempting to cause serious bodily injury to another, or causing such injury purposely, knowingly, or recklessly under circumstances manifesting extreme indifference to the value of human life. (2) Attempting to cause, or purposely, or knowingly causing bodily injury to another with a deadly weapon. Model Penal Code § 211.1(2).

aggravation, that which adds to the enormity of a crime or a tort, or is a ground for increasing the damages awarded for an injury. See also, *exemplary damages.*

aggressor, a person who initiates a quarrel, dispute, or fight.

AGI, see *adjusted gross income.*

agist (a jist'), or **agistment,** the feeding of other persons' cattle on one's land for reward. (2) The profit of such feeding.

agister's lien, a contract or statutory right to retain possession of an animal that belongs to another person, as security for unpaid compensation for the care of the animal.

agistment, see *agist.*

agnation, kinship by the father's side.

agno'men, a name added to the Christian and surname as a mark of distinction; usually derived from some personal characteristic or achievement, *e.g.,* Richard the Lion-Hearted. (2) A nickname.

agreed judgment, or **agreed order,** see *consent decree.*

agreement, the concurrence of two or more minds in anything done or to be done. Accord, Restatement (Second) of Contracts § 3. (2) A contract. Agreements may be executed, *i.e.,* complete, performed; or executory, where something remains to be done by one or both of the parties; express, where the terms are stated orally or in writing; and implied, which the law presumes the parties have made from their acts and surrounding circumstances, though the terms were not expressed. (3) The bargain of the parties in fact as found in their language or by implication from other circumstances, including course of dealing or usage of trade or course of performance as provided in the U.C.C. U.C.C. § 1-201(3).

agreement of rescission, an agreement (*q.v.*) under which each party agrees to discharge all of the other party's remaining duties of performance under an existing contract (*q.v.*). Restatement (Second) of Contracts § 283 (1). See also, *rescission.*

aid and abet, to knowingly assist, encourage, or urge on someone to commit a crime. (2) To similarly associate with someone who commits a tort.

aider by verdict, the presumption which arises after verdict, whether in a civil or criminal case, that those facts without proof of which the verdict could not have been found were proved, though they were not distinctly alleged.

aids (auxilia), were originally free gifts from the tenant to his lord, but came afterward to be regarded as a right. See *writ in aid.*

air, the gaseous substance which surrounds the earth. The right to free access of air is the natural right of everyone, interference with which by interruption or pollution, unless by virtue of an acquired easement (*q.v.*), is actionable. An easement to light and air over the land of another cannot be acquired by prescription in the United States, though the rule is otherwise in England.

air pollution, the making of the air in the earth's atmosphere unclean or impure with an unnatural concentration of material, *e.g.*, gasoline engine exhaust and burned waste. Air pollution is often identified by the accumulation of smog, offensive odors, and hazy skies.

Air Quality Act of 1967, an act to amend the Clean Air Act (*q.v.*), to authorize planning grants to air pollution control agencies; expand research provisions relating to fuels and vehicles; provide for interstate air pollution control agencies or commissions; authorize the establishment of air quality standards, and for other purposes. 42 U.S.C. §§ 1857-1857l; 81 Stat. 485 (1968).

a.k.a., also known as.

Alcohol Abuse and Alcoholism Act, see *Comprehensive Alcohol Abuse and Alcoholism Prevention, Treatment, and Rehabilitation Act.*

alcohol blood test law, see *implied consent law.*

Alcohol Fuels Act, see *Biomass Energy and Alcohol Fuels Act of 1980.*

alderman, a member of the legislative body in some cities. (2) Formerly a municipal officer having the powers of a civil magistrate or justice of the peace.

a leatory contract, an agreement in which performance by one or more of the parties is made to depend upon an event, the occurrence of which is uncertain, *e.g.,* an insurance policy.

alia, other things.

alia enor'mia, *l.,* other wrongs; words used in the conclusion of a declaration in trespass.

aliamen'ta, a liberty of passage, open way, watercourse, etc., for the tenant's accommodation.

a'lias, *l.* (otherwise), (*Scil.,* dictus), a second name applied to a person. (2) A second or further writ or process, which is issued after a former writ or process has failed to accomplish its intended purpose.

al'ibi, *l.* (elsewhere), a defense resorted to where the party accused, in order to prove that he could not have committed the crime with which he is charged, offers evidence that he was in a different place at the time the offense was committed.

alien, a person of foreign birth who is not a citizen. (2) A person who is a citizen or subject of a foreign state or who owes allegiance to a foreign government. (3) To transfer property, *i.e.,* alienate.

alien ami (ā lē ĕn á mē), or **amy** (friend), a subject of a nation which is at peace with this country.

alien enemy, a subject of a nation which is at war with this country.

alienage, the status or circumstances of a person who is an alien.

alienate, or **aliene,** to transfer property. Alienor is one who transfers to an alienee. (2) To cause the loss or transfer of a wife's or husband's affections.

alienation clause, a clause in a fire insurance policy voiding the policy in the event of transfer of ownership by the insured.

alienatio rel praefertur juri accrescendi, alienation is favored by the law rather than accumulation.

ailene, see *alienate.*

alie'ni ju'ris, *l.,* under another's authority, *e.g.,* a committee or guardian; incapable of acting for one's self. See also, *sui juris.*

alienist, a person qualified to examine and render an opinion as to the mental condition of a defendant.

alimen'ta, *l.,* things necessary to support life, *e.g.,* food, clothing, and shelter.

alimony, the allowance made to a wife out of her husband's estate for her support, either during a matrimonial suit, which is called alimony pendente lite, or at its termination; when she proves herself entitled to a separate maintenance, the fact of marriage being established. Alimony is not ordinarily granted to a husband, but under the statutes in some states, it may be awarded to the husband and ordered to be paid by the wife.

alimony in gross, a gross sum, rather than a periodic allowance, awarded to a spouse by a decree of divorce or separation; lump sum alimony.

alimony pendente lite, temporary alimony designed to provide support for a spouse during the divorce action.

alimony trust, a situation where the divorce or separation agreement requires the payor to transfer a specified amount of property to a trust under the terms of which the income is to be paid to the payee for the payee's life or until the payee's remarriage with provision for distribution of the remainder to the payor or to others upon the payee's death or remarriage.

a'lio intu'itu, *l.*, with another view or object.

aliquid conceditur ne injuria remanerit impunita, quod alias non concederetur, something is conceded, which otherwise would not be, lest an injury remain unredressed.

aliquis non debet esse judex in propria causa, quia non potest esse judex et pars, one ought not to be a judge in his own case, for it is not possible for one to be both judge and suitor.

aliquot, a part or fraction of a whole.

a'liter, *l.*, otherwise; otherwise held or decided.

aliud est celare, aliud tacere, it is one thing to conceal; another to be silent.

aliun'de, *l.*, from elsewhere, from another source, *e.g.*, proof aliunde.

all fours, a precedent case is said to be on all fours with a problem case when they are substantially similar in their material facts.

All Writs Act, section 1651 of Ch. 111 of Part V of an act to revise, codify and enact into law title 28 U.S.C. entitled "Judicial Code and Judiciary." It provides that the U.S. Supreme Court and all courts established by act of Congress may issue all writs necessary or appropriate in aid of their respective jurisdictions agreeable to the usages and principles of law, and that an alternative writ or rule nisi (*q.v.*) may be issued by a justice or judge of a court which has jurisdiction. 28 U.S.C. § 1651.

allegans contraria non est audiendus, a person making contradictory allegations is not to be listened to.

allegans suam turpitudinem non est audiendus, a person alleging his own infamy is not to be listened to.

allegari non debuit quod probatum non relevat, something which if proved, would not be relevant, ought not to be alleged.

allegation, a statement of fact made in a legal proceeding, which the person stating it intends to prove. An allegation is a bare assertion, as compared with proof, which is a substantiation of the allegation.

allegiance, loyalty and obedience due from the citizen to the government. It may be (a) natural by birth; (b) acquired by naturalization, or (c) local, during residence in a country.

Allen charge, instructions frequently given to a jury that reports that it is deadlocked and unable to reach a verdict, to the effect that in a large proportion of cases absolute certainty cannot be expected; that although the verdict must be the verdict of each individual juror and not a mere acquiescence in the conclusion of his fellows, yet they should examine the question submitted with candor and with a proper regard and deference to the opinions of each other; that it is their duty to decide the case if they can conscientiously do so; that they should listen, with a disposition to be convinced, to each other's arguments; that if much the larger number are for conviction, a dissenting juror should consider whether his doubt is a reasonable one which made no impression upon the minds of so many jurors, equally honest, equally intelligent with himself; and that if upon the other hand the majority is for acquittal, the minority ought to ask themselves whether they might not reasonably doubt the correctness of a judgment which was not concurred in by the majority.

aller sans jour (å lā sôn zhur), *fr.,* to go without day, *i.e.,* to be finally dismissed from the court, no further day being assigned for appearance. Said formerly of a successful defendant.

alley, a thoroughfare through the middle of a square or block giving access to the rear of lots or buildings.

allocation, something set apart for a particular purpose. (2) An allowance made upon accounts in the English exchequer.

allograph, a document or signature made for a party by someone else; opposed to autograph.

allonge (å lônzh'), *fr.,* a piece of paper firmly affixed to a bill of exchange or promissory note, on which indorsements may be written for which there is no room on the instrument itself. Accord, U.C.C. § 3-202(2), Official Comment 3.

allot, to assign a share, *e.g.,* of land on partition or inclosure, or of stock in a company.

allotment, the share of land or stock allotted. (2) The act of allotting; partition. (3) An allowance made by a member of the armed forces by which he assigns a part of his future earnings to a dependent.

allu'vion, or **allu'vio,** land gradually gained from the sea or a river by the washing up of sand and soil. The new land belongs to the owner of that to which it is annexed and whereof it forms part. See also, *avulsion, derelict,* and *aqua cedit solo.*

ally', a nation which has entered into a mutual association with another nation for a common purpose, often for the conduct of a war; a citizen of such a nation.

alter ego doctrine, doctrine holding that where a sole owner, or several dominant owners of shares have managed their corporation in such a way as not to separate their personal affairs from those of their corporation, they have made themselves liable for the corporate debts and other liabilities.

alteration, a change or modification. Concerning negotiable instruments, as against any person other than a subsequent holder in due course, a fraudulent and material alteration by the holder discharges any party whose contract is thereby changed, unless that party assents or is precluded from asserting the defense. A material alteration is one which changes the contract of any party thereto in any respect, including any such change in the number or relations of the parties, or an incomplete instrument, by completing it otherwise than authorized, or the writing as signed, by adding to it or removing any part of it.

alternative dispute resolution, procedures for settling disputes other than litigation, *e.g.,* arbitration, mediation, etc.

alternative writ, one which commands the defendant to do the thing required, or show cause why he should not do it.

amalgamation, the union of two incorporated companies or societies by one's being merged in the other. (2) The marriage of people of different races, as of whites with blacks.

amanuensis, a person who writes for another person. (2) A stenographer or secretary.

ambassador, a representative sent by one sovereign or country to another, with authority to deal with affairs of state. His person is protected from civil arrest, and his goods from seizure. His is the highest rank among diplomatic officials.

ambidex'ter, *l.* (one who uses both hands), an attorney or juror who takes bribes from both parties. See also, *embracery.*

ambigua responsio contra proferentem est accipienda, an ambiguous answer is to be taken against him who makes it.

ambiguis casibus semper praesumitur pro rege, in doubtful cases the presumption is always in favor of the crown.

ambiguitas verborum latens verificatione suppletur; nam quod ex facto oritur ambiguum verificatione facti tollitur, latent ambiguity may be corrected by evidence; for an ambiguity which arises from an extrinsic fact may be removed by proof of the fact.

ambiguitas verborum patents nulla verificatione excluditur, a patent ambiguity cannot be removed by proof.

ambiguity, the quality or state of being subject to two or more different interpretations. There are two species of ambiguity: (a) patent, *i.e.,* apparent on the face of the instrument, which may occasionally be supplied or explained by extrinsic evidence, *i.e.,* evidence not contained in the instrument itself; (b) latent, where, the instrument being apparently free from obscurity, a doubt arises in carrying it into execution, *e.g.,* from a name used in it being applicable to two persons or things. In such a case, extrinsic evidence is often admissible. See also, *parol evidence rule.*

ambiguum pactum contra venditorem interpretandum est, an ambiguous contract ought to be construed against the seller.

ambiguum placitum interpretari debet contra proferentem, an ambiguous plea ought to be interpreted against the pleader.

ambit, a boundary line.

ambulance chaser, an attorney who violates the ethics of the legal profession by soliciting law practice, especially personal injury claims. (2) A person who is not an attorney and solicits personal injury claims for an attorney.

ambulatoria est voluntas defuncti, usque ad vitae supremum exitum, the will of a deceased person is ambulatory (*q.v.*), until the last moment of life.

ambulatory, alterable; shifting; capable of revocation.

amendment, a change, correction, or alteration of any pleading, or statement in a cause. (2) An addition to, or modification of, an existing constitution, law, contract, or other document.

amentia, insanity, idiocy.

amercement, or **amerciament,** a fine.

Americans with Disabilities Act, ADA; a disability discrimination law whose purpose is (1) to provide a clear and comprehensive national mandate for the elimination of discrimination against individuals with disabilities, (2) to provide clear, strong, consistent, enforceable standards addressing discrimination against individuals with disabilities, (3) to ensure that the Federal Government plays a central role in enforcing the standards established in this chapter on behalf of individuals with disabilities, and (4) to invoke the sweep of congressional authority, including the power to enforce the fourteenth amendment and to regulate commerce, in order to address the major areas of discrimination faced day-to-day by people with disabilities. 42 U.S.C. § 12101 *et seq.*

ami, or **amy,** usually called prochein ami (pro shen a mi), *fr.*, the next friend, as distinguished from the guardian, suing on behalf of an infant. (2) A friend.

amicable action, a lawsuit which is litigated by agreement of the parties in order to resolve a dispute.

ami'cus cu'riae, *l.* (friend of the court), an attorney who, by leave of court, intervenes in pending litigation, especially arguments on appeal, in order to influence the decision in the litigation, which as a precedent is likely to affect the attorney's client. (2) A stander by, not being a party to, or interested in the cause, who informs the court of any decided case, statute, or other fact, of which it can take judicial notice.

amnesty (non-remembrance), an act by which crimes against the government up to a date therein named are pardoned or forgiven, so that they can never thereafter be made the subject of a charge. An amnesty may be general, to all concerned in the offense, or particular, to one or more.

amortization, or **amortisement,** the payment of bonds, mortgages or other indebtedness in installments; (2) An alienation of lands in mortmain (*q.v.*).

amotion, or **amove,** to remove from possession; (2) from a post or office.

ampliation, an enlargement of time; a deferring of judgment till the cause be further examined.

amy, see *ami.*

analytical jurisprudence, a school of juristic thought, founded by John Austin, chiefly characterized by its effort to analyze law and legal institutions.

anarchy, absence of government; political disorder.

ancestor, a forefather; one from whom another has descended lineally. (2) More strictly, in law, he from whom another inherits real estate.

ancestral, such as come to the possessor by descent.

ancient, old or very old.

ancient documents, or **ancient writings,** documents (*q.v.*) more than 30 years old. These are presumed to be genuine without express proof, when coming from the proper custody. (2) Ancient documents, documents (*q.v.*) in existence 20 years or more, the authenticity of which is established. Fed. R. Evid. 803(16).

ancient lights, windows which have had uninterrupted access of light and air for twenty years and upward. In England, windows which have been used for light and air without obstruction for twenty years or more acquire a prescriptive right and may not thereafter be obstructed by an adjoining landowner. In most of the United States no such right can be acquired by prescription.

ancient writings, see *ancient documents.*

an'cillary, that which is subordinate to, or assists, some other thing, *e.g.,* ancillary administration.

ancillary jurisdiction, jurisdiction assumed by federal courts that extends beyond the judicial power expressly conferred upon them by the Constitution or by federal statutes. Under the concept of ancillary jurisdiction, a federal district court acquires jurisdiction over issues that otherwise would be determinable only in a state court as an incident of disposition on a closely related federal matter that is properly before such federal court. This type of jurisdiction is largely granted as a result of general convenience to the parties in question.

animal, any animate being, except a human, endowed with the power of voluntary motion. Animals are either (a) mansuetae, tame or domesticated, or (b) ferae naturae, wild. (2) A domestic animal is by custom devoted to the service of mankind at the time and in the place in which it is kept; a wild animal is not by custom devoted to the service of mankind at the time and in the place in which it is kept. Restatement (Second) of Torts § 506.

a'nimo cancellan'di, with intent to cancel.

a'nimo capien'di, with intent to take.

a'nimo furan'di, with intent to steal.

a'nimo lucran'di, with intent to profit.

a'nimo manen'di, with intent to remain.

a'nimo moran'di, with intent to remain or delay.

a'nimo recipien'di, with intent to receive.

a'nimo republcan'di, with intent to republish.

a'nimo reverten'di, with intent to return.

a'nimo revocan'di, with intent to revoke.

a'nimo signandi, with intent to sign.

a'nimo testan'di, with intent to make a will.

animus, mind; will; intention.

animus ad se omne jus ducit, all law applies to the intention, *e.g.*, on a question of domicile, the intention of remaining in the new residence (animus manendi), or of returning to the old one (animus revertendi) is controlling.

animus hominis est anima scripti, a man's purpose is the soul of his writing, *e.g.*, a written agreement.

an'ni nu'biles, *l.*, the age at which a girl is, by law, fit for marriage; under common law, the age of 12. In the United States, regulated by various state statutes.

anno domini, in the year of our Lord.

annuity, a periodical payment of money, either bequeathed as a gift, or secured by the personal covenant or bond of the grantor. (2) A form of insurance, often used for retirement income. (3) An arrangement under which one buys a right to future money payments.

annul, to make void or cancel, *e.g.*, a marriage, contract, or deed. See also, *nullity of marriage.*

annulment of marriage, see *nullity of marriage.*

answer, in pleading, a statement of the defenses on which a party defending a lawsuit intends to rely. (2) A statement under oath, in response to written interrogatories, *i.e.* questions, or oral questions.

ante, *l.* (before), a word used to refer to a previous part of the same book or statement.

ante litem motam, before suit brought.

antedate, to date an instrument before the day of its execution.

antena'ti, ante natus, or **antenatus,** persons born before a certain period, *e.g.*, before the Declaration of Independence.

antenuptial, before marriage. See also, *settlement.*

antenuptial agreement, see *prenuptial agreement.*

anticipation, doing a thing before its proper time, *e.g.*, dealing with or distributing property, income, etc., before the time fixed by the deed, or will conveying the same.

anticipatory breach, the act of one party to a contract in repudiating the contract prior to the time of performance. In such event the other party may bring suit immediately.

antig'raphy, a copy or counterpart of a deed.

anti-trust acts, or **antitrust acts,** various federal and state statutes intended to protect trade and commerce from unlawful restraints and monopolies.

apices juris non sunt jura, the niceties of the law are not the law.

apostle, in Admiralty, a summary statement of a case received by a higher court from a lower one.

apparatus, tools, equipment or other things provided and adapted as a means to some end; any complex instrument or appliance for a specific action or operation.

apparent authority, in agency, that authority which, although not actually given, a principal knowingly permits his agent to exercise.

apparent easement, one which is open, visible or easily ascertainable.

appeal, an application to a higher court to correct or modify the judgment of a lower court. The person initiating the appeal is called an appellant, or petitioner, and the opposite party is called an appellee, or respondent. The manner of taking appeals, and the cases which may be appealed, are regulated by various state and federal statutes.

appeal bond, security in an amount required by statute to be posted by an appellant, as a requirement for perfecting an appeal.

appearance, the initial court response by a defendant in a lawsuit. (2) A formal submission to the jurisdiction of the court by a party to a suit. It can be made in person, or by an attorney, guardian, or next friend. Appearance by guardian or next friend is limited to cases where the party is an infant or under some other disability.

appellant, a person who initiates an appeal from one court to another.

appellate court, see *court.*

appellate jurisdiction, the authority of a superior court to review and modify the decision of an inferior court.

appellee´, the party in a lawsuit against whom an appeal has been taken.

appilcatio est vita regulae, application is the life of the rule.

appointee, a person selected for a particular purpose. (2) The person in whose favor a power of appointment (*q.v.*) is executed.

appointment, the selection of a person for a particular office. (2) A gift or distribution of property made by a person (called the donee of the power, or appointor), under a power given him by some instrument. Such powers may be general, *i.e.,* authorizing the donee to appoint to any one he pleases, or particular, *i.e.,* limited to certain specified persons. An appointment is exclusive if limited to certain individuals out of the particular class specified by the power.

apportionment, the division of assets or liabilities according to the respective interests of the various parties.

appraisement, a valuation; generally required by law to be made of the goods of an intestate, or insolvent, or of goods attached or replevied.

apprehend, to seize a person; to arrest.

apprentice, a person who is learning or beginning a craft or skilled occupation. (2) Formerly, a person bound by indentures to serve a tradesman, or artificer, who covenanted in turn to teach him his trade, art, or business.

appropriation, the setting apart of money or goods for a particular purpose. (2) The application of a payment made by a debtor to his creditor to the whole or partial discharge of a particular debt, as requested by the debtor at the time payment is made, or in default of that, as the creditor may wish. (3) Statutory provision of a specified sum of money for the support of the government or for particular governmental purposes.

approved indorsed notes, notes indorsed by a person other than the maker, for additional security, the indorser being satisfactory to the payee.

approver, or **prover,** an accomplice in crime, who, while confessing himself guilty, accuses others of the same offense and is admitted as a witness, at the discretion of the court, to give evidence against his companions in guilt.

appurtenance, something which belongs to something else, so that when the latter is transferred, the former will automatically be transferred with it, *e.g.,* a passageway to a piece of land, *i.e.,* an easement, is an appurtenance to the land.

appurtenant, pertaining to, or belonging to, something else; something which is an appurtenance.

a'qua, *l.,* water.

aqua cedit solo, water passes with the soil. In the eyes of the law, water is land covered with water. The ownership of water, therefore, goes with that of the soil beneath. Where a river divides properties belonging to different persons, the center of the stream is usually taken to be the boundary line.

ar'biter, an arbitrator. (2) Formerly a person who decided according to the rules of law and equity.

ar'bitrage, buying stocks and bonds in one market and selling them in another, for the sake of the profit arising from a difference in price in the two markets.

arbitrary punishment (Sc.), such as is left to the discretion of a judge, and not defined by statute.

arbitration, the voluntary submission of a matter in dispute to the nonjudicial judgment of one, two, or more disinterested persons, called arbitrators, whose decision, called an award, is binding upon the parties.

Arbitration Act, various state and federal laws providing for arbitration (*q.v.*). U.S.C. tit. 9 is the federal arbitration act; 61 Stat. 669, c. 392 (1947), as amended.

arbitration and award, the voluntary settlement of a controversy by mutually agreeing to submit the controversy to arbitration, so that the decision in the arbitration is binding on the parties. (2) An affirmative defense which seeks to avoid a claim because it was previously submitted to arbitration and an award was established.

arbitrator, a private nonjudicial person who is selected by the agreement of contesting parties and is authorized by them to finally settle a controversy.

archetype, the original type, or pattern.

Architectural Barriers Act, an act to insure that certain buildings financed with federal funds are so designed and constructed as to be accessible to the physically handicapped. 42 U.S.C. §§ 4151 *et seq.*

archives, a chamber or place where ancient records, charters, etc., are kept. (2) The records, etc., themselves.

arguendo, by way of argument.

argument, the formal or informal presentation to a court, judge, or jury, of opposing counsel's reasons why they suggest that their respective clients should prevail in a lawsuit. (2) An attempt to persuade a court, judge, or jury. (3) A process of reasoning.

argumentative, the quality of a pleading, affidavit, or oral statement to a jury which states, not merely the facts, but the conclusions to be drawn from them.

argumentum ab inconvenienti plurimum valet in lege, an argument drawn from inconvenience is very forcible in law.

arma in armatos sumere jura sinunt, the laws permit the taking up of arms against armed persons.

armed neutrality, a state of neutrality between hostile nations, which the neutral nation is prepared to maintain by force of arms.

ar'mistice, an agreement between belligerents for a temporary cessation of hostilities for political purposes; a truce.

arms, weapons. (2) Any thing carried for defense, or used to inflict injury on the person of another, including every thing with which one strikes, or which one may throw.

arraign, to bring an accused person to court for the purpose of having him answer the charge against him.

arraignment, the initial court appearance of a person who is charged with a crime. It consists of three parts: (a) calling the defendant by name, (b) reading him the indictment, (c) asking him if he is guilty or not guilty. He may plead "guilty" or "not guilty," or stand mute, which is in effect the same as pleading "not guilty"

array, the entire group of persons summoned into court for jury duty.

arrears, or **arrearages,** money, *e.g.,* interest or rents, which is overdue and unpaid.

arrest, the seizing of a person and detaining him in custody by lawful authority. (2) Taking of another into the custody of the actor (*q.v.*) for the actual or purported purpose of bringing the other before a court, or of otherwise securing the administration of the law. Restatement (Second) of Torts § 112. (3) The seizure and detention of personal chattels, especially ships and vessels libeled in a court of admiralty.

arrest of judgment, the refusal of a court to give judgment, notwithstanding a verdict, which may occur when there is some substantial error appearing on the face of the record which vitiates the proceeding, or when it appears on the face of the record that the plaintiff is not entitled to it. The critical requirement is that a judgment can be arrested only on the basis of error appearing on the face of the record and not on the basis of proof offered at trial.

arson, the crime of purposely setting fire to a house or other building. (2) Starting a fire or causing an explosion with the purpose of destroying a building or occupied structure of another, or destroying or damaging any property, whether his own or another's, to collect insurance for such loss. It is an affirmative defense that the actor's conduct did not recklessly endanger any building or occupied structure of another or place any other person in danger of death or bodily injury. Model Penal Code § 220.1(1).

article, a portion of a document, *e.g.,* a clause or paragraph in a constitution or contract.

articled clerk, in English law, the pupil of a solicitor. The solicitor undertook to instruct the pupil in the principles and practice of law, in consideration of the pupil's services.

articles of agreement, a written memorandum of the terms of contract.

articles of association, the regulations of a company.

Articles of Confederation, the compact of union adopted by the thirteen original states March 1, 1781, which was superseded by the Constitution (*q.v.*) of the United States. 1 Stat. 4 (1861).

articles of impeachment, the written statement of charges which are relied upon as grounds for removing a person from office.

articles of incorporation, the instrument filed with the appropriate governmental agency, usually the secretary of state, upon the incorporation of a business. Contents of the articles of incorporation typically include: (1) the name of the corporation, (2) the location of the principal office, (3) the corporate purpose, (4) the number and par value per share of shares with par value which the corporation is authorized to issue, (5) the authorized number of shares without par value, (6) the express terms, if any, of the authorized shares, if the authorized shares are classified, the designation of each class, the authorized number and par value per share, if any, of the shares of each class, and the express terms of the share of each class, and, (7) the amount of the initial stated capital.

articles of partnership, the written terms on which two or more persons associate as partners.

articles of the peace, a complaint on oath made to a court that the applicant is in fear of his life or of bodily harm from the threats of another person. The object of such a complaint is to have the court require of the defendant that he make bond with surety to keep the peace or upon failure to make such bond, that defendant be jailed. See also *peace bond.*

articles of war, the code of laws formerly used for the government of the army. See also, *Uniform Code of Military Justice.*

articulo mortis, at the moment of death.

artificial, made by the art of man or created by law; opposite of natural.

artificial insemination, impregnation of a female through the injection of semen from a donor other than her husband and other than through sexual intercourse.

artificial person, an entity created under law which is given some of the legal characteristics of a natural person, *e.g.,* rights and duties. (2) A corporation. (3) Occasionally, the estate of a bankrupt or a deceased person.

artisan's lien, a possessory lien of an artisan which allows him to keep possession of the object of personal property that he has worked on until he has been paid for such labor.

Asbestos School Hazard Detection and Control Act of 1980, an act to establish a program for the inspection of schools to detect the presence of hazardous asbestos materials, to provide loans to states or local educational agencies to contain or remove hazardous asbestos materials from schools and to replace such materials with other suitable building materials, and for other purposes. 20 U.S.C. § § 3601 *et seq.*

ascendants, the ancestors of a person in a direct line.

asportation, carrying away or removing goods. In all larcenies, there must be both a taking and a carrying away.

assault, strictly speaking, threatening to strike or harm. (2) A threatening gesture, with or without verbal communication. If a blow is struck, it is battery (*q.v.*). (3) Attempting to cause or purposely, knowingly, or recklessly causing bodily injury to another, or negligently causing bodily injury to another with a deadly weapon, or attempting by physical menace to put another in fear of imminent serious bodily injury; also called simple assault. Model Penal Code § 211.1(1).

assay, the testing of ore.

assembly, the meeting of a number of persons in the same place.

assent, approval of something done. It may be express, *i.e.*, openly declared; or implied, *i.e.*, presumed by law, as when the thing done is for the person's benefit and he makes no express dissent.

assess, to ascertain the value of property for taxation. (2) To charge a proportion of the cost of a public improvement on persons or property peculiarly benefited thereby. (3) To fix the amount to be paid on each share of stock of an incorporated company for the purposes of the corporation. (4) To fix the amount of damages to which the prevailing party in a suit is entitled.

assessor, the government official responsible for the evaluation of all taxable properties located within a taxing unit.

assets, anything of value that a person may own. (2) Things of value that pass into the possession of a fiduciary, *e.g.*, administrator or executor. (3) Property available for the payment of debts.

assign, to transfer property, especially rights in action. The person making the assignment is called the assignor; the person receiving it, the assignee. (2) To allot or set off, *e.g.*, a widow's dower (*q.v.*). (3) To point out or specify, *e.g.*, the errors complained of on the trial of a case in the court below.

assignatus utitur jure auctoris, an assignee enjoys the rights of his assignor.

assignment for benefit of creditors, the transfer by a debtor of his property to an assignee in trust for the payment of his debts.

assignment of dower, the act by which a widow's share in her deceased husband's real estate is ascertained and set apart to her.

assisa, *l.*, **assise,** or **assize** (as ē za, as sēz, as sīz), ancient homonyms with myriad meanings, *e.g.*, a session of court. (2) A jury. (3) A writ to determine the right of possession to land. (4) An ordinance or statute. In modern usage, an assize is the periodic session of the judges of the English High Court of Justice, which is held in the various counties.

assi'sa armo'rum, a statute ordering the keeping of arms.

assi'sa ca'dere, to be non-suited, as when there is such a plain legal insufficiency in an action that the plaintiff cannot successfully proceed any further in it.

assi'sa continuan'da, an ancient writ addressed to the justices of the assize for the continuation of a cause, when certain facts put in issue could not have been proved in time by the party alleging them.

assi'sa de fores'ta, a statute regulating conduct in and about the king's forests.

assi'sa pa'nis, a law regulating the price of bread. (2) A sitting together; a session of the court; legal proceedings.

assistance, writ of, a writ issued to the sheriff to carry out a decree of the court by putting the parties in possession of property. .

assi'sus, rented or farmed out for certain assessed rent in money or. provisions.

assize, see *assisa.*

Assize of Clarendon, a statute of 1166 concerning persons of bad character who were required to leave the kingdom.

assize of novel disseisin (a sēz ŏu nŏvel di sē zin), a real action which lay when one had recently been disseised.

assize of nuisance, an action which lay when something had been done which worked an injury to plaintiff's freehold, to abate the nuisance and recover damages.

assize of u'trum, an action by a parson to recover lands which his predecessor had allowed the church to be deprived of improperly.

associate, an attorney who is practicing law with another attorney or a law firm, but who is not a partner or member of the firm. (2) A colleague or co-worker. (3) Formerly an officer in the English Courts of Common Law.

association, a collection of persons who have joined together for a common purpose. (2) A company or society. (3) In English law, a writ or patent sent by the crown to the justices appointed to take assizes, to have others associated with them; it is usual where a judge becomes unable to attend to his circuit duties, or dies.

assump'sit, *l.,* (he has undertaken), formerly the name of an action which lay for damage for breach of a simple contract, *i.e.,* one not under seal. It was a species of action on the case (*q.v.*). See also, *indebitatus assumpsit.*

assumption of mortgage, a promise made by the purchaser of land on which there is a mortgage that the purchaser will pay the mortgage debt and will be personally liable for a deficiency on foreclosure.

assumption of risk, a defense to a claim for negligent injury to a person or property, *i.e.,* a person who voluntarily exposes himself or his property to a known danger may not recover for injuries thereby sustained. Accord, Restatement (Second) of Torts § 496A.

assurance, or **common assurance,** the legal evidence of the transfer of property. See also, *conveyance.* (2) See *insurance.*

assured clear distance ahead, a statutory requirement providing that no person shall drive a motor vehicle upon public roads at a rate of speed greater than will permit him to bring it to a stop within the assured clear distance ahead. It applies to anything in the line of vision of the motorist in the assured clear distance ahead which is static or present long enough for him to observe it and stop his car.

assurer, one who undertakes to indemnify another, called the assured, against risks or dangers; an underwriter. See also, *insurance.*

asylum, a place of refuge for fugitive offenders, sick people, or persons who have suffered misfortune. (2) Sanctuary.

at arms length, at a distance; not on familiar or confidential terms. One holding confidential or fiduciary relations toward another is bound to put himself at arms length, *i.e.,* to divest himself entirely of that influence, authority, or advantage which he possesses by reason of such relation before he can make a binding contract with such other. This applies especially to the relations of attorney and client, guardian and ward, trustee and cestui que trust.

at large, free; out of prison, or bounds; without restraint. See also, *Statutes at Large.*

at maturity, at the time when payment or other performance on a contract falls due.

atheist, a person who does not believe in the existence of a God.

attaché (å tå shā), *fr.,* one attached to an embassy or legation.

attachment, the seizure and taking into custody of the law of the person or property of a party to the suit, either in an action already begun, *e.g.,* to punish for contempt of court, or at the beginning of an action to acquire jurisdiction, to secure possession of property which is in controversy or to create security for a debt which is in controversy. When debts are attached, the process is called garnishment (*q.v.*) or trustee process (*q.v.*). (2) The writ or order in pursuance of which the seizure is effected.

attachment of privilege, in English law, when a person by virtue of his privilege, calls another into that court to which he himself belongs, to answer some action. (2) A power to apprehend a person in a privileged place.

attainder, the extinction of civil rights which formerly resulted from a sentence of death or outlawry for treason or felony. The chief consequences were forfeiture of the criminal's property, corruption of his blood, so that no property could pass through him, and incapacity to sue. See also, *bill of attainder.*

attaint, stain or disgrace, *e.g.,* under attainder. (2) Writ of, issued to inquire whether a jury gave a corrupt verdict, so that the judgment following thereupon might be reversed.

attempt, an intent to commit a crime, combined with an act which falls short of accomplishment of the thing intended.

attentat, a proceeding wrongfully attempted by a judge in a suit, which has been removed from his court to a higher court by appeal.

attestation, evidence by witnesses to the execution of an instrument. Usually the witnesses observe the act of signing, which is done by a party to the instrument, and then sign their names below the party's signature as witnesses.

attestation clause, the sentence subscribed to a written instrument, signed by the witnesses to its execution, stating that they have witnessed it. They are then attesting witnesses, and can be called at any future time to identify the instrument and prove its due execution.

attested copy, a verified reproduction of a document, which is assured to be correct by an official signature.

attested will, a will signed by the testator and witnesses.

attesting witness, a person who signs his name to an instrument, at the request of the parties to the instrument, in order to prove it or identify it.

attorn (a tŭrn), to turn over, transfer or assign. See also, *attornment.*

attorney, an attorney at law (*q.v.*). (2) A person appointed by another to act in his place, *i.e.,* an attorney in fact (*q.v.*).

attorney at law, a person licensed by a court to practice the profession of law. Such a license authorizes him to appear in court, give legal advice, draft written instruments, and do many other things which constitute the practice of law (*q.v.*).

attorney in fact, a person appointed to act for another in a private matter, or for a special purpose designated in the instrument of appointment called a Power of Attorney (*q.v.*). (2) Agent.

attorney general, the chief legal officer of the United States or of a state. The office is created by a constitution or a statute, which defines the authority and responsibility of the officer. (2) An officer appointed by the President, whose duties are to appear for the United States in all suits in the Supreme Court to which the United States is a party, and to give his opinion on questions of law when requested by the President or the heads of departments. He is a member of the Cabinet of the United States (*q.v.*), and the head of the Department of Justice. (3) In English law, the chief legal representative of the Crown who conducts prosecutions on behalf of the Crown, represents the Crown in civil matters, advises concerning the drafting of statutes and advises government departments on legal matters.

attornment, the acknowledgment by a tenant of a new owner of land. The tenant thereby agrees to become the tenant of the purchaser, to pay the rent to him and to perform the covenants for him.

attractive nuisance doctrine, a principle which imposes liability for injury to children who are incapable of perceiving the risk of danger, even though they may be trespassers, when the injuries result from the failure of the person in charge to take measures to prevent injuries from equipment or conditions which attract children. Judicial opinion concerning this principle is not uniform.

auction, a public sale of property to the highest bidder, usually conducted by a person licensed for that purpose, who is called the auctioneer, and who is regarded in law as the agent of both vendor and purchaser, for the purpose of binding them by his memorandum of sale. See also, *without reserve.*

audi alteram partem, hear the other side.

audience court, formerly an English ecclesiastic court held by the archbishop, or learned deans on his behalf.

audit, the examination of records and accounts as well as the securing of other evidence for one or more of the following purposes: (a) determining the propriety of proposed or completed transactions, (b) ascertaining whether all transactions have been recorded, and (c) ascertaining whether transactions are accurately recorded in the accounts and in the statements reflecting the accounts.

au'dita quere'la, *l.,* an equitable action whereby a person against whom judgment had been given might prevent execution, on the ground of some matter of defense which there was no opportunity of raising in the original action. Now generally abolished by statute, and super- seded by proceedings on motion to set aside the judgment in the court which rendered it.

auditing, the verification of the accuracy and completeness of financial records of an organization as well as the appraisal of the legality, efficiency, and effectiveness of the financial management of the organization.

auditor, one who examines accounts. (2) The officer of the government charged with the duty of examining the accounts of officers who have received and disbursed public moneys. (3) An officer appointed by the court to take and state an account between parties to a suit.

aula, *l.,* a hall or palace.

aula eccle'siae, the nave of a church, where temporal courts were anciently held.

aula re'gis, or **re'gia,** formerly a court, established by William the Conqueror; it was composed of the great officers of state, and followed the king's household in all his expeditions. Out of this grew the Court of King's Bench, Court of Common Pleas, and Court of Exchequer (*q.v.*).

Australian ballot, a system of voting, first used in Australia, whereby secrecy is compulsorily maintained and the ballot used is an official one furnished by the government. With local variations, the Australian ballot has been adopted in the United States, England, Western Europe and other nations.

auter, *l.,* or **autre,** *fr.,* another.

authentic act, that which has been executed before a notary or other public officer, duly authorized, or which is attested by a public seal, or has been rendered public by the authority of a competent magistrate, or which is certified as being a copy of a public register.

authentication, an attestation made by a proper officer, by which he certifies that a record is in due form of law, and that the person who certifies it is the officer appointed so to do.

authentics, a collection of the Novellae Constitutiones (additions to the Code) of Justinian, made by an anonymous author.

authority, power or right conferred on a person; usually by another to act on his behalf. See also, *agent.* (2) A public officer or body having certain powers of jurisdiction. (3) Constitutions, statutes, precedent cases, opinions of text writers, and other material, cited in arguments.

auto da fe (ō tō da' f ā), (act of faith), public announcement and execution of the sentences of the Inquisition; the burning of heretics.

automatism, automatic behavior by an individual who possesses the requisite capacity; the state of a person who is capable of action but is not conscious of what he is doing.

automobile, a self-propelled vehicle for use on streets and highways to transport persons or articles of commerce, and not dependent upon tracks or an outside source of power. Judicial opinions and legislative enactments in this sphere are not uniform. See also, *motor vehicle.*

Automobile Dealers Day-In-Court Act, or **Automotive Dealers Franchise Act,** an act to supplement the antitrust acts (*q.v.*) in order to balance the power weighted in favor of automobile manufacturers, by enabling franchise automobile dealers to bring suit to recover damages sustained by reason of the failure of manufacturers to act in good faith in complying with the terms of franchises or in terminating or not renewing franchises with dealers. 15 U.S.C. §§ 1221 *et seq.*

automobile guest statute, statutes which provide that the driver of an automobile is liable to one who is riding as a gratuitous guest in his car only for some form of aggravated misconduct.

Automobile Information Disclosure Act, an act to require the full and fair disclosure of certain information, including the manufacturer's suggested retail price, in connection with the distribution of new automobiles in commerce, and for other purposes. 15 U.S.C. § § 1231 *et seq.*, 72 Stat. 325 (1958).

Automobile Price Law, see *Automobile Information Disclosure Act.*

Automobile Safety Act, see *National Traffic and Motor Vehicle Safety Act of 1966.*

automobile title state, see *title state.*

autonomy, self-government or independence.

autopsy, examination of a dead body to determine the cause of death.

autre, see *auter.*

autre action pendant (ó tr ak sjôn pôn dôn), a plea that another suit for the same cause is already pending.

autre droit (ó tr drŵȧ), in right of another, *e.g.*, a trustee holds in the right of his cestui que trust.

autre vie (ó tr vē), for or during the life of another, *e.g.*, an estate for the life of another.

autrefois (ó tr fwȧ), *fr.*, formerly.

autrefois acquit, a plea in a criminal case that the defendant has already been acquitted on the same charge.

autrefois attaint, a plea in a criminal case that the defendant has already been attained, so that he cannot be prosecuted for another felony.

autrefois convict, a plea in a criminal case that the defendant has already been convicted on the same charge, which is not good if the former judgment was reversed for error.

auxi'lium, *l.*, an aid.

auxi'lium cu'riae, an order of court summoning a person at the suit of another to appear and warrant something.

auxi'lium re'gis, the king's aid; money levied in former times, when the sovereign provided out of his privy purse for many departments of the public service.

auxi'lium vicecomi'ti, a duty formerly paid to sheriffs for the better support of their offices.

avails, profits or proceeds.

aval (á vål), *fr.*, (at the bottom), the signature of a surety on a note, bond, or bill.

aver (a věr), to allege as true (in pleadings), whence averment.

average, a contribution, or adjustment of loss, made by merchants when goods have been thrown overboard for the safety of a ship. It is either general, *i.e.*, where the loss having been incurred for the general benefit, the owners of the ship and all that have cargo on board contribute proportionately toward making good the loss; or particular, where the loss has been accidental, or not for the general benefit, and therefore there is no general contribution. An average bond is an instrument executed by the several persons liable to contribute, empowering an arbitrator to assess the amount of their contributions. (2) Petty average, a small duty paid to masters of ships over and above the freight; known also as primage and average. (3) Formerly a service which an English tenant owed to his lord by doing work with his work beasts.

aver'sio, a turning away; (2) A sale in gross or in bulk.

aver'sio peri'culi, a turning away of peril; used of a contract of insurance.

avoidance, a pleading which affirmatively sets forth new matter for the purpose of avoiding the claim previously filed. See also, *affirmative defense*. (2) The making of a transaction or instrument void, or of no effect.

avoucher, the calling upon a warrantor to fulfill his undertaking.

avowal, in trial procedure, an offer of proof out of the hearing of the jury, made with the objective of recording for appeal the testimony that would have been given by a witness, if he had been allowed to testify.

avowry, a pleading in an action of replevin brought to recover property taken in distress, in which the defendant acknowledges the taking, and setting forth the cause thereof, justifies his right to do so.

avulsion, the sudden and forcible separation of land from other land of which it formed part, by a flood, earthquake, or change in the course of a river. The title to such land is not changed. See also, *alluvion*.

award, to adjudge or assess, *e.g.,* award damages. (2) A determination or decision which emanates from an arbitrator, a workers' compensation board, or a commissioner in admiralty. (3) The selection and announcement of the best competitive bid on a public contract. (4) The designation of the person who is entitled to the custody of a child in a matrimonial dispute.

away-going (or way-going) crops, those sown during the last year of a tenancy, but not ripe until after its expiration. The right which an out-going tenant has to enter, cut and take an away-going crop when ripe is sometimes given to him by the express terms of the contract; but where that is not the case, he is generally entitled to do so by the custom of the country.

B

back water, water checked or turned back in its flow by a dam or other obstruction. At common law, a riparian proprietor had no right to obstruct the flow of water, unless he acquired it by grant or prescription, and was liable to an action for damages for flooding lands above his own, or diminishing the flow of water through lands below.

backadation, a consideration given to retard the delivery of corporate stock when the price is lower for time than for ready money.

backing, indorsing.

backing a warrant, indorsing a warrant issued by a justice in another county, so as to authorize its service in the county to which it is sent.

backside, a yard at the back part of or behind a house.

backwardation, see *backadation.*

BACT, see *best available control technology.*

bad, in addition to the ordinary meanings commonly attributed to this adjective, it is a technical word for unsoundness in pleading.

bad debt, a worthless account receivable; an unpaid bill which the creditor perceives to be uncollectible.

bad faith, an imprecise term denoting a state of mind which affirmatively operates to mislead or deceive another. (2) A deliberate failure to comply with a plain and well understood obligation. (3) Arbitrary action or inaction without a reasonable excuse or for frivolous reasons.

bad title, see *title (1).*

badge of fraud, an infinite number of suspicious circumstances which justify an inference of fraud (*q.v.*) when they are not satisfactorily explained. Usually applied to the circumstances under which a debtor's assets are transferred beyond the reach of his creditors.

badger, to persistently torment or harass someone, *e.g.,* an adverse witness or opposing counsel. (2) Formerly a person who bought merchandise in one location and took it to another location for a profitable resale.

baggage, clothing and such other articles as are necessary to the comfort and convenience of a traveler, and are carried with him in bags or trunks, as distinguished from merchandise. The distinction is important in the law of common carriers.

bail, to set at liberty a person arrested or imprisoned, on written security taken for his appearance on a day, and at a place named. The term is applied, as a noun, to the persons who become security for the defendant's appearance; to the act of delivering such defendant to his bondsmen; and also to the bond given by the sureties to secure his release. A person who becomes someone's bail is regarded as his jailer, to whose custody he is committed. The word "bail" is never used with a plural termination. See also, *bailable.*

bail bond, a written undertaking, signed by a surety at the time of the release of a person who has been arrested, conditioned for the due appearance of such defendant.

bail court, sometimes called the Practice Court, was an auxiliary of the Court of Queen's Bench, wherein points connected with pleading and practice and common motions were determined.

bail jumping, failing to appear at a specified time and place without lawful excuse by a person set at liberty by court order, with or without bail, upon condition that he would subsequently appear at that time and place. This does not apply to obligations to appear incident to release under suspended sentence or on probation or parole. Model Penal Code § 242.8.

bailable, an arresting process is said to be bailable when the person arrested may obtain his liberty on giving bail, *e.g.,* a capias on mesne process is bailable; a capias ad satisfaciendum is non-bailable.

bailable offense, a crime for which a person who is accused, but not convicted, is entitled to be set free if bail *(q.v.)* is given. Generally, all crimes except capital crimes *(q.v.)* are bailable offenses.

bailee, a person to whom personal property *(q.v.)* is intrusted for a specific purpose. See also, *bailment.*

bailie (Sc.), a magistrate.

bailiff, an officer of a court who executes arrest process; a courtroom attendant; a sheriff's officer.

bailiwick, a geographical area in which an officer, *e.g.,* a bailiff, exercises his jurisdiction. (2) Sometimes a county. (3) Formerly, a liberty exempted from a sheriff, over which a bailiff was appointed by the lord, with such powers as an under-sheriff exercised.

bailment, a broad expression which describes the agreement, undertaking, or relationship which is created by the delivery of personal property by the owner, *i.e.*, the bailor, to someone who is not an owner of it, *i.e.*, the bailee, for a specific purpose, which includes the return of the personal property to the person who delivered it, after the purpose is otherwise accomplished. In a bailment, dominion and control over the personal property usually pass to the bailee. The term is often used to describe, *e.g.*: (1) The gratis loaning of an automobile for the borrower's use. (2) The commercial leasing of an automobile for a fee. (3) The delivery of an automobile to a repairman for the purpose of having it repaired. (4) The delivery of an automobile to a parking attendant for storage, when the keys are left with the attendant.

bailor, or **bailer,** a person who commits goods to another person (the bailee) in trust for a specific purpose.

bailpiece, a record containing the names of special bail, with other particulars, which is signed by a judge and is filed in the court in which the action is pending.

balance of power, in international relations, a distribution and opposition of armed forces, so that no nation shall be in a position, either alone or united with others, to impose its will on any other nation or to interfere with its independence.

ballastage, a toll paid for the privilege of taking up ballast from the bottom of a port or harbor.

balloon mortgage, a mortgage payable and due, in total, within a very short span of time, ordinarily between one and five years. However, the nature of the mortgage permits a favorable amortization schedule usually between 20 and 30 years serving best the commercial investment market.

ban, a proclamation, public notice, summons, or edict, whereby a thing is commanded or forbidden. See also, *banns of matrimony*.

banc, or **bancus,** *fr.*, a bench; the seat of government. The sitting together of all the judges of a court, or a quorum thereof, is termed sitting in banc, as distinguished from their separate sittings, sittings in chambers, or sittings in panels.

Bancus Reginae, or **Bancus Regis,** the Court of Queen's Bench or King's Bench, respectively.

Bancus Superior, the Upper Bench, or Superior Court.

bandit, a person outlawed, put under the ban of the law. Sometimes, a robber.

banishment, a punishment by which a convicted person is forced to leave the country. (2) Exile. (3) See *abjuration.*

bank, an institution, usually incorporated, authorized to receive deposits of, and to lend, money.

bank check, an instrument employed by a depositor for withdrawing funds from a bank. See also, *check.*

Banking Act of 1935, an act to create a Federal Deposit Insurance Corporation to insure the deposits of all banks entitled to the benefits of insurance thereunder. 12 U.S.C. §§ 1811 *et seq.*

bankrupt, broken up; ruined; insolvent. Generally, someone who has failed in business, or is unable to pay his debts as they become due. Technically, a person is not a bankrupt until a bankruptcy court adjudges him to be one.

bankruptcy, jurisdiction exercised by United States courts and created by federal statute. It concerns the affairs of insolvent debtors and includes voluntary petitions of natural persons, wage earner plans (*q.v.*), and corporate reorganizations. Bankruptcy existed in Roman law and in English law. Congress is empowered to establish uniform laws on the subject of bankruptcies. U.S. Const. Art. I, Sec. 8. (2) Occasionally, insolvency.

Bankruptcy Reform Act, an act to establish a uniform law on the subject of bankruptcies. 11 U.S.C. §§ 101 *et seq.*

banns of matrimony, public notice or proclamation of a matrimonial contract.

bar, the whole body of the legal profession. A person is admitted to the bar when he is authorized by a court to practice law before it. (2) A low partition or railing running across a courtroom which separate the judges, licensed attorneys, court officers and attendants, parties and witnesses from the public. It separates the portion of the courtroom in which the proceedings are held from the place where the spectators sit. (3) A legal obstacle, *e.g.,* statute of limitations (*q.v.*).To bar something is to destroy its legal effectiveness. (4) A place where drinks are served and consumed.

bar association, a voluntary or compulsory organization composed of licensed attorneys who share common interests. Usually bar associations are organized according to geographic areas, *e.g.,* American Bar Association, Ohio Bar Association or The Association of the Bar of the City of New York. Occasionally they are organized according to particular courts, *e.g.,* Federal Bar Association, or the character of the practice of the members, *e.g.,* American Trial Lawyers Association.

bar, plea in, a pleading showing some ground for barring or defeating an action at common law.

bare trustee, or **dry trustee,** one whose active duties as a trustee (*q.v.*) have come to an end, so that he can be compelled by the beneficiary (cestui que trust) to convey the property according to his direction.

bargain, an agreement (*q.v.*) to exchange promises or to exchange a promise (*q.v.*) for a performance or to exchange performances. Restatement (Second) of Contracts § 3.

bargain and sale, a transaction or agreement concerning the disposal of real property or personal property, in which, for a valuable consideration, the property is immediately transferred to the new owner. (2) A form of conveyance of real property.

bargain collectively, see *collective bargaining.*

barleycorn, one-third of an inch. (2) In conveyancing, a nominal consideration or rent.

baron, the lowest degree of English nobility. (2) A judge of the English Court of Exchequer. (3) A husband.

baron et feme, a husband and wife; seldom used.

Baron of the Cinque Ports (sink), a member of the English Parliament from one of the Cinque Ports (*q.v.*).

baronage, the entire nobility of England of all ranks.

baronet, an English dignity descendible to male issue, originally created in 1611.

barony of land, a quantity of land amounting to 15 acres. In Ireland, a subdivision of a county.

barrator, a person who commits barratry.

bar'ratry, or **bar'retry,** the offense of constantly stirring up quarrels and suits, either at law or otherwise. (2) Any illegal or fraudulent conduct by the master or crew of a ship by which the freighter or owner is injured. (3) In Scotland, the crime of a judge who is induced by bribery to pronounce a judgment.

barrier, the wall of coal left between two contiguous mines. (2) An obstruction.

barrister, an English attorney who tries cases in court.

barter, a contract by which parties exchange goods for goods, differing from sale, in which they exchange goods for money.

base-estate, land held by an English tenant, who performed certain prescribed menial services for his lord.

base-fee, otherwise called a fee qualified or conditional, is an estate in land conditioned to terminate on the occurrence of some particular event, which may or may not occur, *e.g.*, the failure to have male heirs.

base line, a line to which all other measurements are referred; the reference line in a triangulation.

basil'ica, an abridgement of the Corpus Juris Civilis of Justinian, a legal work completed about A.D. 880.

basis of accounting, the policy governing when revenues or expenditures are counted in an organization's accounting records; possibilities include cash basis (which lists financial events only when money is actually received or paid out) and accrual basis (which counts changes when the organization knows the events will occur).

bastard, a person born out of wedlock. (2) An illegitimate child. Defined by various statutes in the respective states.

bastard-eigne (*ā nyā*), If a man have a natural son, and afterward marry the mother, and by her have a legitimate son, the latter is called mulier puisné, and the elder son bastardeigné.

bastardize, to judicially declare one a bastard. (2) To give evidence in proof of bastardy.

bastardy, the offense of begetting a bastard child. The condition of a bastard.

bastardy action, or **process,** a statutory mode of proceeding against the father of an illegitimate child, for the purpose of compelling the father to support his child.

battel, wager of, an ancient form of trial by combat abolished by statute. 59 George III. c. 46.

battered child syndrome, a term used to characterize a clinical condition in young children who have received serious physical abuse, generally from a parent or foster parent

battered woman syndrome, a condition in which a woman who is subjected to continued physical and or mental abuse by her husband or companion refuses to tell anyone of the situation, and based on a fear of increased aggression against herself, often engages in an act of physical violence against her husband or companion in the name of self-defense.

battery, an unlawful touching, beating, wounding, or laying hold, however trifling, of another's person or clothes without his consent.

batture, *fr.,* shoals; shallows; an elevation of the bed of a river under the surface of the water.

bawd, a person who keeps a house of prostitution, or bawdy house, and procures opportunities for illicit intercourse.

bear, (stock exchange), one who speculates for a fall in prices. (2) To carry.

bearer, a person who carries something. (2) A person in possession of an instrument, document of title or security that is payable to bearer or indorsed in blank.

bearer paper, commercial paper that can be negotiated by delivery without indorsement.

bearing date, showing a date on its face.

belief, a conviction based upon some evidence that a fact exists, an act was done, or that a statement is true.

belligerency, the status of de facto (*q.v.*) statehood attributed to a body of insurgents, by which their hostilities are legalized. (2) The condition of being at war.

belligerent, engaged in lawful war.

bello parta cedunt repubilcae, things acquired in war go to the state.

bellum, *l.,* war.

belonging to, a flexible term which can mean various degrees of ownership, *e.g.,* an unqualified or absolute title, or less.

bench, a tribunal of justice. (2) Judges as a group, distinguished from the bar (*q.v.*). See also, *banc.*

benchbook, a reference book used by a judge as a ready source of frequently needed information concerning his judicial duties.

benchers, seniors in the English inns of court, intrusted with their government or direction.

bench warrant, an order issued at the direction of a court or judge for the arrest of an individual, *e.g.,* for contempt or where an indictment has been found.

beneficial interest, profit, benefit, or advantage resulting from a contract or estate, as distinct from legal ownership or control.

beneficiary, a person who is entitled to the benefits of a trust which is administered by a trustee. Sometimes called a cestui que trust. As it relates to trust beneficiaries, includes a person who has any present or future interest, vested or contingent, and also includes the owner of an interest by assignment or other transfer. As it relates to a charitable trust, includes any person entitled to enforce the trust. Uniform Probate Code § 1-201(2). (2) A person named in a trust account as one for whom a party to the account is named as trustee. Id. § 6-101(2). (3) A person to whom life insurance is payable at the death of the insured. (4) A person other than a promisee who will benefit from the performance of a promise. Restatement (Second) of Contracts § 2(4).

beneficiary trustee, a trustee who is also a beneficiary under the trust.

benefi'cium, any favor or privilege.

benefi'cium abstinen'di, the power of an heir to decline an inheritance.

benefi'cium cedenda'rum actio'num, the right of the surety to demand from the creditor, before paying him, the choses in action of his principal.

benefi'cium competen'tiae, the privilege of retaining the necessaries of life out of something granted pursuant to a gratuitous obligation in Scottish law, and the similar privilege of an insolvent debtor on making cession of his property for the benefit of his creditors, in Roman law.

benefi'cium divisio'nis, the right of surety to contribute only ratably with his solvent co-sureties.

benefi'cium inventa'rii, the privilege which an heir had, by having an inventory taken of the testator's property before he entered into possession of it, to protect himself from liability beyond the amount of the property inventoried.

benefi'cium or'dinis, a privilege by which a surety could call on a creditor to sue the principal debtor first, and only to sue the sureties for that which he could not recover from the principal.

benefi'cium separatio'nis, (Rom.), the privilege, sometimes granted to creditors, of having the goods of an heir separated from those of the testator, *e.g.*, if the heir were insolvent.

benefit of clergy, a privilege originally granted to the English clergy, and subsequently extended to all persons who could read, whereby they were exempted from capital punishment and trial for criminal offenses by the secular courts of England. Finally abolished by 7 and 8 Geo. IV. c. 28. In the United States, the privilege was recognized in some early cases, but in others it was not recognized. In some United States jurisdictions it was expressly abolished by statute.

benevolence, an act of kindness or charity. (2) In English law, nominally a voluntary gratuity made by subjects to the sovereign, which came to be a forced loan or tax.

benigne faciendae sunt interpretationes, propter simplicitatem laicorum, ut res magis valeat quam pereat; et verba intentioni, non e contra, debent inservire, [in construing written instruments], some latitude of interpretation must be allowed on account of the want of technical knowledge in the general public, so that the instrument may rather be upheld than come to nought; and the words ought to subserve the intention, not the reverse.

benignior sententia, in verbis generalibus seu dubiis, est praeferenda, the more liberal meaning of general, or doubtful words is to be preferred.

bequeath, to make a bequest, or gift of personal property by will. See also, *legacy*.

bequest, a gift of personal property by will.

berca'ria, a sheep-fold, or other inclosure to keep sheep.

bertillon system (bĕr tē yôn), a system for the identification of persons by bodily measurements and photographs which was used in France and other countries until it was superseded by fingerprint identifi-cation.

best available control technology, BACT; an emission limitation based on the maximum degree of reduction which the permitting authority determines is achievable taking into account energy, environmental and economic impacts and other costs.

best evidence, the proof which provides the greatest certainty of the fact to be proven; the most reliable evidence. Under the best evidence rule, which is ordinarily applied to documents sought to be proven, usually the highest degree of proof, *i.e.*, the original document, must be presented if it is available.

best interests of the child, an analysis the court makes in custody actions which determines the best provider for the disposition, care, and maintenance of a child or children. What is in the best interest of the child is the determinative factor in deciding which parent, or in some cases nonparent will be awarded custody.

bestiality, carnal intercourse by a human with the lower animals.

bet, an agreement between two or more that a sum of money, or some valuable thing, in contributing which all agreeing take part, shall become the property of one or some of them, on the happening in the future of an event at the present uncertain.

betrothment, a contract for future marriage.

betterments, improvements made to real property which render it better than mere repairs would do.

between, as between two dates, all days except the first and the last are included.

between merchants, in any transaction with respect to which both parties are chargeable with the knowledge or skill of merchants. U.C.C. § 2-104(3). See also, *merchant*.

beyond the jurisdiction of the court, beyond reach of process of court.

beyond the seas, out of the United States; out of the state; out of the United Kingdom and the Channel islands. See also, *absence*.

BFOQ, see *bona fide occupational qualification*.

bica'meral system, the division of a legislative body into two chambers, *e.g.*, House of Representatives and Senate.

bicycle, a vehicle propelled with foot pedals, usually with two wheels.

bid, an offer of a price for something which is being sold by auction. (2) An offer of a price for which a public contract, *e.g.*, street construction, will be performed by the bidder.

bigamy, the offense of having two husbands or two wives at the same time. (2) A married person contracting or purporting to contract another marriage, unless at the time of the subsequent marriage: (a) the actor believes that the prior spouse is dead; (b) the actor and the prior spouse have been living apart for five consecutive years throughout which the prior spouse was not known by the actor to be alive; (c) a court has entered a judgment purporting to terminate or annul any prior disqualifying marriage, and the actor does not know that judgment to be invalid; or (d) the actor reasonably believes that he is legally eligible to remarry. Model Penal Code § 230.1(1). (3) Contracting or purporting to contract marriage with another, knowing that the other is thereby committing bigamy. Model Penal Code § 230.1(3). Cf. *polygamy.*

bilateral contract, an agreement in which two parties mutually promise to fulfill obligations reciprocally toward each other, *e.g.*, one party promises to convey a house and lot and the other party promises to pay the agreed price for it.

Bilingual Education Act, title VII of an act to strengthen, improve, and extend programs of assistance for elementary and secondary education, and for other purposes. Formerly 20 U.S.C. §§ 880b *et seq.*, revised, now similar provisions, 20 U.S.C. §§ 3222, 3223.

bill, a written statement of one's claim or account against another. (2) An unconditional, written, and signed, order to pay a sum certain in money to someone, drawn by a person on a third party, *e.g., a bill of exchange,* also called a draft. If it is drawn on a bank and payable on demand, it is a check. U.C.C. § 3-104. (3) The original draft of a law presented to a legislative body for enactment. It is a bill until passed, and then becomes an act, or statute. The term is applied to some special acts after their passage; *e.g., bill of attainder, bill of indemnity,* etc. (4) A document evidencing the receipt of goods for shipment, *i.e., a bill of lading,* issued by a person engaged in the business of transporting or forwarding goods. U.C.C. § 1-201. (5) The written statement of an offense charged against a person, which is presented to a grand jury. If satisfied by the evidence that the charge is probably true, it is endorsed, "a true bill," and called an indictment.

bill for foreclosure, a written statement filed by the mortgagee against the mortgagor, for the purpose of having the property sold.

bill in aid of execution, a written statement which seeks to carry the principle of a decree into execution.

bill in equity, the written statement of his cause of complaint, made by a party initiating a suit in equity.

bill of adventure, a writing signed by a person who takes goods on board a vessel, wholly at the risk of the owner, and agreeing to account solely for the proceeds of the goods when sold.

bill of attainder, a legislative act which inflicts punishment on named individuals or members of an easily ascertainable group without a judicial trial. In determining whether a particular statute is a bill of attainder, the analysis requires an inquiry into whether the three definitional elements—specificity in identification, punishment, and lack of a judicial trial—are contained in the statute. Strictly defined, in English law a bill of attainder directed punishment by death, and a bill of pains and penalties directed punishment of a lesser degree. The U.S. Const. forbids Congress and the states to pass bills of attainder and the courts have interpreted the prohibition to also forbid them to pass bills of pains and penalties. U.S. Const. Art. I, Secs. 9, 10.

bill of certiora'ri, an application for a writ of certiorari (*q.v.*) to remove a cause from an inferior court to a superior one.

bill of conformity, an application filed by an executor or administrator, when the affairs of the deceased were so involved that he could not safely administer the estate, except under the direction of a court.

bill of costs, a statement of the items which form the total amount of the taxable court costs in a suit or action.

bill of credit, paper issued by the authority of the state, on the faith of the state, and designed to circulate as money.

bill of discovery, an application to a court which asks for the discovery of facts resting within the knowledge of the person against whom the bill is filed, or of deeds, writings, or other things, in his custody or control, and material to enable the party filing the bill to prosecute or defend some action at law. Under modern rules of practice, this procedure is less formal and is usually called discovery (*q.v.*).

bill of exceptions, a written statement of objections to decisions of the trial court upon questions of law arising during the progress of the trial, so as to put the decision objected to on record for the information of the court having cognizance of the cause in error.

bill of exchange, see *bill (2)*.

bill of health, a certificate by the proper officer, usually a consul, that a vessel therein named comes from a place where no contagious diseases prevail, and that none of her crew were affected with any such disease at the time of her departure.

bill of indemnity, formerly an act of the English Parliament, passed every session until 1869, for the relief of those who had unwittingly or unavoidably neglected to take the oaths required for the purpose of qualifying them to hold their respective offices.

bill of interpleader, a written statement filed in court by a person who has money or property in his possession, which is claimed by two or more persons, asking that they be required to interplead and set up their claims, and that the court adjudge to which of them he shall pay or deliver. Often called interpleader (*q.v.*).

bill of lading, see *bill (4)*.

Bill of Middlesex, a fiction by which the English court of King's Bench acquired jurisdiction in ordinary civil suits.

bill of pains and penalties, see *bill of attainder*.

bill of particulars, a statement of the factual details concerning a claim, cause of action, set-off, or counterclaim.

bill of peace, a claim for relief which is filed when a person has a right which may be controverted by various persons, in order to have his right established against them all on one suit, and thus prevent a multiplicity of suits.

bill of privilege, formerly, the form of proceeding against an attorney of the court who was not liable to arrest.

bill of review, a claim filed in court in order to have a decree of the court reviewed, modified, or reversed, analogous to a petition for rehearing (*q.v.*).

bill of revivor, a method by which the legal representative of a deceased party can continue litigating a lawsuit which has been abated because of the death of the party. In some forms of modern practice this is accomplished by a motion and order for the substitution of parties. Fed. R. Civ. P. 25.

bill of revivor and supplement, a bill of revivor (*q.v.*) which also supplies any defects in the original proceedings arising from subsequent events.

Bill of Rights, the first ten amendments to the United States Constitution. (2) A statement of personal rights and privileges in the state constitutions of many of the United States. (3) In English law, a declaration enacted in Parliament, declaring illegal certain acts of the former king, and setting forth the rights and privileges of the people.

bill of sale, an agreement or instrument in writing, by which one transfers his right to, or interest in, goods and personal chattels to another. The transfer of a motor vehicle or a ship is usually evidenced by a bill of sale.

bill qui'a ti'met, see *luia timet.*

bill to perpetuate testimony, a petition filed in court to record and preserve the testimony of witnesses with reference to some matter which is not in litigation, but may become so.

bill to take testimony de bene esse, a petition or motion filed in court to take and record the testimony of witnesses to facts material to a case already pending, when there is cause to believe that, on account of the age, infirmity, or intended absence of the witnesses, the testimony may otherwise be lost before the time of trial.

billa casse'tur, *l.,* that the bill may be quashed or made void.

bind, to oblige, constrain, or hold by legal obligation or contract, *e.g.,* to bind over a party accused of a crime to appear before a grand jury or court having jurisdiction of the offense charged.

binder, a writing which evidences a temporary contract of insurance.

Biomass Energy and Alcohol Fuels Act of 1980, title II of the Energy Security Act (*q.v.*) concerning general biomass energy development, municipal waste biomass energy, rural, agricultural, and forestry biomass energy, and the use of gasohol. 7 U.S.C. §§ 341, 342, 427, 1435, 3129, 3154; 15 U.S.C. §§ 753, 3391a; 16 U.S.C. §§ 590h, 1642; 42 U.S.C. §§ 8801 *et seq.*

bipar'tite, of two parts.

birre'tum, in English law, the cap or coif of a judge or sergeant-at-law.

birth, the act of coming into life and having an independent circulation.

bis dat qui cito dat, he gives double who gives promptly.

bishop, the chief of the English clergy within his diocese. (2) A clergyman of high rank.

bishopric, a diocese.

bishop's court, an ecclesiastical court.

bissex'tile (tĭl), the day added every fourth year, *i.e.,* leap year, to the month of February; the 29th of February.

black acre, a term used to signify a hypothetical parcel of land.

Black Book of the Admiralty, an ancient book considered the highest authority in matters concerning admiralty.

black cap, cap worn by an English judge when passing sentence of death.

black list, a flexible term describing a compilation of names of persons who are disliked or unfavorably regarded, *e.g.,* bad debtors, untrustworthy persons, or persons who are friendly with one's enemy or opponent.

Black Lung Benefits Act, also known as the Federal Coal Mine Health and Safety Act and the Black Lung Benefits Reform Act of 1977, various acts to provide for the protection of the health and safety of persons working in the coal-mining industry, and for other purposes. Among other things, it provides for health and safety standards, inspections and investigations, enforcement, black lung benefits, and administration. 30 U.S.C. §§ 901 *et seq.*

black rents, rents payable in labor or farm products, as distinguished from white rents payable in silver.

black rod, an usher in English Parliament.

blackmail, a crime, sometimes called extortion, by which money is obtained from someone by threats of ill treatment, libelous accusations, or exposure of faults. (2) Historically, rent formerly paid by inhabitants in the north of England and south of Scotland to men allied to robbers and marauders to be protected by them from theft and violence.

blanch-holding (Sc.), an ancient tenure, the duty payable being nominal.

blank, a space left in writing or printing, to be filled up with a word or words to complete the sense. (2) A printed paper containing the formal parts of a deed or other instrument, with vacant spaces left to be filled in with the names of the parties and other appropriate information.

blank acceptance, a drawee's signed engagement to honor a draft, written on the draft before it is made and delivered, which will bind him to the extent of any amount that may afterward be written in. U.C.C. § 3-410.

blank bar, common bar, a plea in an action of trespass used to compel the plaintiff to name the place where the alleged trespass was committed.

blank indorsement, an indorsement (*q.v.*) which does not specify a particular indorsee (*q.v.*) in whose favor it is made. It causes an instrument, which otherwise is payable to order (*q.v.*), to become payable to bearer (*q.v.*) and negotiable by delivery alone. U.C.C. § 3-204(2).

blanket insurance, a flexible term denoting broad coverage.

blanket mortgage, a mortgage which covers more than one piece of property and is generally utilized in the commercial end of the real estate business.

blasphemy, in England, the offense of speaking against God, Jesus Christ, the Bible, or the book of Common Prayer, with intent to excite contempt against the established religion, or to promote immorality. In some of the United States, the offense is defined and made penal by statute.

blockade, the maintenance of armed force outside a nation, port, or city so as to prevent ingress or egress.

blockage theory, a theory of valuation of corporation stock in computing gift taxes, based on the reasoning that a large block of stock ordinarily cannot be marketed as readily as a few shares without depressing the market; evidence of sales of small blocks of stock is not a true measure of the value of a large block of the same stock.

blood, that quality or relationship which enables a person to succeed to the property of another by descent. Brothers and sisters are said to be of the whole blood, if they have the same father and mother; of the half blood, if they have only one parent in common.

blood feud, avenging the slaughter of kin on the person who slaughtered him, or on his belongings.

blood test for alcohol law, see *implied consent law.*

blue law, see *Sunday law.*

Blue Sky Law, a popular name for statutes providing for the regulation and supervision of investment companies and securities.

board, a group of people elected or appointed to take the care and management of a public trust or institution, or conduct the business of a municipal or private corporation, *e.g.,* a board of health, a board of trade, a board of directors. (2) Food and lodging furnished under a contract, express or implied, for a stipulated compensation.

Board of Health, a governmental body charged with the supervision of public health, and often vested with large discretionary powers for the purpose.

Board of Supervisors, a county board of representatives having charge of fiscal affairs.

Board of Trade, an organization of business people for the promotion of trade and commerce.

body, a person; a natural or artificial person created by law, as a body corporate, or corporation; a body politic, or state. (2) A mass or collection of individual things in a general system, *e.g.,* a body of laws; a body of divinity. (3) The main part of any instrument; in deeds, it is spoken of as distinguished from the recitals and introductory parts and from the signatures; in affidavits, from the title and jurat.

bogus, spurious, pretended or deceptive.

boilerplate, standard language in a legal document that appears in all instruments of like nature..

boiler-room transaction, high pressure sales of investments of questionable value.

bo'na, *l.* goods; personal property; in Roman law, all kinds of property, real, personal, and mixed.

bona confisca'ta, or **forisfac'ta,** goods confiscated or forfeited to the imperial fisc or treasury.

bona fide, in good faith (*q.v.*); honestly; without fraud or unfair dealing.

bona fide occupational qualification, BFOQ; discriminatory treatment on the basis of religion, sex, or national origin, but not race or color, may be justified when the criterion is a bona fide occupational qualification reasonably necessary to the normal operation of the particular business or enterprise. When the essence of the business would be undermined or safe and efficient job performance would be severely impaired, the BFOQ defense will be recognized.

bona fide purchaser, one who bought real property or personal property in good faith (*q.v.*), for a valuable consideration and without notice of any adverse claims against the property. Accord, Uniform Probate Code § 2-202(3).

bona fi'des, *l.,* good faith (*q.v.*).

bona fides exigit ut quod convenit fiat, good faith requires that what is agreed upon should be done.

bona fides non patitur, ut bis idem exigatur, good faith does not suffer that payment should be twice exacted for the same thing.

bona gestu'ra, good behavior.

bona gra'tia, voluntarily.

bona mobi'lia; immobi'lia, goods movable; immovable.

bona notabi'lia, notable goods, *i.e.,* goods sufficient in amount to require probate or administration.

bona pa'tria, an assize of countrymen or good neighbors.

bona peritu'ra, perishable goods.

bona vacan'tia, goods in which no one claims property, *e.g.,* shipwrecks and treasure trove.

bona wavia'ta, goods thrown away by a thief in his flight, for fear of being apprehended.

bond, a written obligation. (1) In court, bonds constitute undertakings or promises by parties, usually with surety, that the party will perform the orders and judgments of the court. If the undertaking or promise is violated, the bond is forfeited and the sum of money for which the bond is made must be paid to the officer or person who is the obligee of the bond. The execution of such bonds is usually a statutory prerequisite to some privilege granted a party, *e.g.,* repossession before judgment (replevin bond), release from custody pending trial (bail bond, *q.v.*) and to refrain from paying a judgment until an appeal has been decided (supersedas bond, *q.v.*). (2) Public officials execute similar bonds with surety, undertaking or promising that they will faithfully perform the duties of their office, *e.g.*, turn over to the proper officer or board such money as they collect or not make false arrests. (3) An instrument of indebtedness issued by governments and corporations.

bondage, the state of being under restraint; involuntary servitude; slavery.

bonded warehouse, a building in which goods, on which taxes are unpaid, are stored under bond in the joint custody of the owner and the tax officials.

bondsman, a surety; one who is bound or gives security for another.

boni judicis est ampliare jurisdictionem, it is the duty of a good judge to enlarge his jurisdiction, *i.e.*, to amplify the remedies of the law.

boni judicis est causas litium dirimere, it is the duty of a good judge to prevent litigation.

bonis non amoven'dis, *l.*, (that the goods be not removed), a writ addressed to the sheriff, commanding that the person against whom judgment is obtained be not allowed to remove his goods until a writ of error be tried and determined.

bono et malo, *l.*, (for good and bad), formerly a writ of jail delivery, which issued for every prisoner.

bonum necessarium extra terminos necesitatis non est bonum, a thing good from necessity is not good beyond the limits of necessity.

bonus, an imprecise word denoting an extraordinary payment.

bonus judex secundum aequum et bonum judicat, et aequitatem stricto juri praefert, a good judge decides according to equity and right, and prefers equity to strict law.

bonus shares, shares for which nothing was paid.

bookmaking, the practice of receiving and recording bets made on the results of horse races and other events; often illegal.

book value, the net worth of all corporate assets, less all liabilities, and with no allowance for good will not clearly shown to be of certain value.

boon-days, in English law, days on which copyhold tenants were bound to perform certain services for the lord.

bootleg, to illegally manufacture, deal in, or deliver a commodity, e.g, whiskey.

booty, the personal property of an enemy captured by a land army.

bordage, in English law, tenure by which lands were held; the rents were paid in eggs, poultry, and small items for the table.

borough, a town; part of a township organized for municipal purposes; in England, a town that sends a burgess or burgesses to parliament.

borough courts, local English tribunals, held by prescription, charter or act of parliament

borough-English, or **postremo geniture,** an English practice by which the youngest son formerly inherited all the realty which belonged to his father, situated within such borough.

bote, necessaries for housekeeping or husbandry. (2) Reparation for injury.

bottomry, or **bummaree,** a species of mortgage or hypothecation of a ship, by which the ship is pledged as security for the repayment of a sum of money. If the ship be totally lost, the lender loses his money; but if the ship arrives safely, he recovers his principal, together with the interest agreed upon, which is at a high rate corresponding to the risk. The contract may be called a bottomry bill or a bottomry bond. See also, *respondentia.*

bought and sold notes, documents delivered by a broker to the parties on the conclusion of a sale of stock, containing a record of the transaction.

bound, or **boundary,** the limit or dividing line of two pieces of land. Boundaries may be natural, *e.g.,* a lake, river, or sea shore, or artificial, *e.g.,* a fence, highway, or imaginary line drawn from fixed stakes, stones (called monuments), or trees, to other like objects.

bounding, or **abutting,** lands which adjoin or touch something, *e.g.,* a lake, highway, or someone else's land.

bounds, boundaries, both natural and artificial, such as streams or streets.

bounty, a premium paid by a government in order to encourage particular activities.

boycott, to withhold or abstain from dealing with someone, *e.g.,* an employer or merchant.

brain death, see *death (2).*

branding, a method of marking animals for recognition. (2) Formerly, a mode of punishment, by inflicting a mark on an offender with a hot iron.

brawling, the offense of quarreling or creating a disturbance.

breach, a breaking or violation.

breach of close, an unwarrantable entry on another's land. See also, *trespass.*

breach of contract, a flexible term for the wrongful failure to perform one or more of the promises which a person previously undertook when he made a contract, *e.g.*, failure to deliver goods.

breach of covenant, a violation of an agreement contained in a deed, either to do or not to do some act; it is a civil injury.

breach of peace, a flexible term, occasionally defined by statute, for a violation of public order; an act calculated to disturb the public peace. (2) A breach of the peace is a public offense done by violence, or one causing or likely to cause an immediate disturbance of public order. Restatement (Second) of Torts § 116.

breach of pound, the breaking of a place where distrained cattle or goods are deposited, in order to rescue them.

breach of prison, an escape by a prisoner lawfully in prison.

breach of promise of marriage, a violation of a promise to marry, which gives rise to an action for damages, unless the breach was justifiable. In some states this action has been abolished by statute.

breach of trust, the willful misappropriation, by a trustee, of a thing which has been committed to him in trust for certain purposes, and was lawfully in his possession.

breaking, parting or dividing by force; bursting through or removing an obstruction. See also, *burglary.*

breaking bulk, opening a box, bale, or package and removing part of the contents.

breve (brēv), *l.*, a writ; used more frequently in the plural brevia.

breve de recto, writ of right.

breve judiciale non cadit pro defectu formae, a judicial writ fails not through defect of form.

bre've origina'le, *l.*, an original writ.

brevet (brē vet′ or brĕv′ĕt), a commission conferring on an army officer a rank above that which he holds, without giving him increased pay.

bribery, the offense of giving or receiving a gift or reward intended to influence a person in the exercise of a judicial or public duty. (2) The Model Penal Code treats various kinds of bribery, *e.g.*, commercial bribery (§ 224.8), bribery in official and political matters (§ 240.1), compensation for past official behavior (§ 240.3).

bridewell, a house of correction; workhouse; prison.

brief, a printed or typewritten statement of a party's view of his case, submitted as an argument to the judge or judges of a court. The form, content, and length are governed by the rules of the court in which submitted. Usually an appellate brief is a printed pamphlet, about 6" x 9¼", containing a table of contents, a table of cases, a statement of the issues, a statement of the facts, and an argument of law.

bright line distinction, a test where the result is objectively, rather than subjectively, determined; an effort by an appellate court to provide clear guidance to lower courts in resolving an issue by making the presence or absence of a particular factor or factors determinative of the outcome.

brocage, or **brokerage,** the wage or commission of a broker. The trade or occupation of a broker.

broc'ards, law maxims.

broker, an agent employed to make contracts in matters of trade, and to find persons who may be willing to enter into such contracts. He is paid by a commission, or brokerage. See also, *stockbroker, insurance broker,* and *factor.*

brothel, a house kept for purposes of prostitution; a common habitation of prostitutes.

brother, a male born of the same parents as another. A half-brother is one who has but one parent in common with another. A brother-in-law is the brother of one's wife, or the husband of one's sister. A stepbrother is the son of one's step-parent by a former or subsequent marriage.

bucket shop, a gambling institution, ostensibly for stock brokerage, in which no purchases are made.

Buckley Amendment, a section of an act to extend and amend the Elementary and Secondary Education Act of 1965, and for other purposes. It concerns the protection of the rights and privacy of parents and students. 20 U.S.C. § 1232g.

buggery, sodomy and bestiality.

building association, a cooperative organization, usually incorporated, established for the purpose of accumulating and loaning money on real estate security.

building restrictions, private limitations on the use of property, contained in the deeds to several portions of an original tract, creating easements in favor of all the lot owners.

Bulk Sales Acts, various state statutes which provide that the sale of all or any portion of a stock of merchandise, other than in the normal course of business, shall be fraudulent as against the seller's creditors, unless the purchaser receives from the seller a list of the seller's creditors and the purchaser notifies such creditors of the proposed sale, or pays them from its proceeds. The various state statutes have been replaced in most instances by U.C.C. §§ 6-101 to 6-111.

bulk zoning, zoning that regulates the size and shape of the buildings to be erected and their location on the land. The purpose of this type of zoning is to control population density, open space, and access to daylight and air.

bull, (stock exchange), one who speculates for a rise in the market.

burden of proof (onus probandi), the duty of proving facts disputed on the trial of a case. It commonly lies on the person who asserts the affirmative of an issue, and is sometimes said to shift when sufficient evidence is furnished to raise a presumption that what is alleged is true. The shifting of the burden of proof is better characterized as the creation of a burden of going forward with the evidence, however, because the total burden of proof is not thereby changed, and the burden of going forward with the evidence is apt to revert to the other party and change from time to time. See also, *evidence; proof.*

bureau, a department or office of government for the transaction of public business.

Bureau of Standards Act, an act to establish the National Bureau of Standards. 15 U.S.C. §§ 271-278.

bureaucracy, government by nearly autonomous bureaus or departments.

burgage-tenure, a right by which houses and lands in ancient boroughs were held. See also, *borough-English.*

bur'gess (jĕss), an inhabitant of a borough. (2) A representative of a borough in Parliament. (3) A magistrate of a borough, discharging duties similar to those of a mayor of a city.

burgh (bur´ō) (Sc.), equivalent to the English borough (*q.v.*).

burglar, a person who commits burglary (*q.v.*).

burglary, a breaking and entering by night into a dwellinghouse with intent to commit a felony. Breaking includes entering a house by fraud, threats, or collusion. Often defined by state statute. (2) Entering a building or occupied structure, or separately secured or occupied portion thereof, with purpose to commit a crime therein, unless the premises are at the time open to the public or the actor is licensed or privileged to enter. It is an affirmative defense that the building or structure was abandoned. Model Penal Code § 221.1(1). Cf. *housebreaking.*

burning in the hand, when a layman was admitted to benefit of clergy (*q.v.*) he was burned "in the brawn of the left thumb" in order that he might not claim the benefit twice.

business, every trade, occupation, or profession. Uniform Partnership Act § 2. See also, *doing business.*

business judgment rule, a rule that immunizes directors from liability in corporate transactions undertaken within the power of the corporation and the authority of the director where there is a reasonable basis indicating that the transaction was made in good faith and with due care.

business or **corporate trust,** a trust in which the managers of the company are the principals and the shareholders are the beneficiaries.

business visitor, see *invitee (2).*

buyer, a person who buys or contracts to buy goods. U.C.C. § 2-103 (1)(a).

by-bidding, bidding at an auction for the purpose of advancing the price, by a person who does not intend to buy. See also, *puffer.*

by bill, in former procedure, actions commenced by capias (*q.v.*) instead of by original writ (*q.v.*).

bylaws, by-laws of, or **bye-laws,** rules and regulations promulgated by a corporation or unincorporated association, concerning the conduct of its internal and external affairs.

C

C. & F., cost of the goods and freight are included in the seller's price. U.C.C. § 2-320.

cabal, a small faction, sometimes political.

cabinet, an advisory board, usually composed of the heads of principal departments of the United States government, of state governments and of other organizations, to consult with and aid the chief executive in his administration.

Cabinet of the United States, a group of high officials which assembles for the purpose of advising the President, composed of department heads. As a collective body, it exists by custom, rather than by law, and is a response to the President's need for advice. It has no collective power, and if the President chooses to disregard the advice of the Cabinet, he may do so. Its membership has changed over the years, varying from 4 to 13 members.

cachet, lettres de (*lĕtr du cà shā´*), letters formerly issued under the private seal of kings of France, and countersigned by a secretary of state, authorizing the arrest, imprisonment, or exile of a person.

cadastre, appraised property values in an area used to determine tax assessments.

calendar, a list or enumeration of cases arranged for trial in court; a program or agenda.

call, a lender's demand for payment of a promissory note that is due. (2) A corporation's demand for payment of money by its shareholders. (3) The direction and length of a boundary line given in a deed or survey, or the monuments (*q.v.*) between which it runs.

callable bonds, see *redeemable bonds.*

calling to the bar, conferring the degree or dignity of barrister upon a member of the English Inns of Court.

calum'nia (Rom.), malicious prosecution.

calum'niae jusjuran'dum, an oath formerly taken by both parties to an action that the same was brought or defended in good faith, and that the facts alleged by them were true; used principally in divorce cases. The verification (*q.v.*) of pleadings, required by the codes of practice of some of the states corresponds to this oath.

Calvo Doctrine, the doctrine that foreign governments are not justified in intervening by force to secure the claims of their citizens for injuries sustained in consequence of domestic disturbances.

ca'mera, a chamber; the judge's private room adjoining the courtroom. Cases are sometimes heard there, especially in divorce matters. See also, *chambers.*

Ca'mera Stella'ta, the Star Chamber, an English court originally created to prevent the obstruction of justice in the inferior courts by undue influence. Its authority was enlarged and it subsequently fell into abuse. It was later abolished.

cancella'ria; cancella'rius, *l.,* chancery; the English Court of Chancery; the chancellor.

cancellation, an invalidation or revocation of a written instrument, often accomplished by drawing lines across it *(cancelli)*, by tearing the signatures or by writing on it "canceled."

canon, an entry or item in a compilation of rules or precepts, which are collectively called canons. Often applied to the rules of a governing body of a church, the rules for construction of statutes and the rules governing the legal profession. See also, *Canons of Ethics.*

canon law, a body of Roman ecclesiastical law, first codified by Gratianus in 1139. This and five subsequent collections form the *Corpus Juris Canonici.* In England, the canon law (or Canons of the Church) consists of certain ecclesiastical laws or constitutions.

Canons of Ethics, various rules which governed the legal profession during the years 1908-1969. The legal profession is principally governed at present by the Code of Professional Responsibility (*q.v.*)

which has been adopted by many state courts and contains within it a subdivision called canons. In 1983 the American Bar Association adopted Model Rules of Professional Conduct (*q.v.*) which are presently being considered for adoption by courts of various states.

capacity, a flexible term denoting legal ability to contract, to take, hold, and convey property, to sue and be sued and to otherwise engage in legal relationships. (2) A natural person who manifests assent to a transaction has full legal capacity to incur contractual duties thereby, unless he is under guardianship, an infant (*q.v.*), mentally ill or defective, or intoxicated. Restatement (Second) of Contracts § 12(2).

ca'pe (*kå pā*), formerly a judicial writ concerning lands or tenements.

ca'pias (*that you take*), a generic name for writs (usually addressed to the sheriff), ordering the person to whom they are addressed to arrest a person therein named. See also, *mesne process.*

ca'pias ad audien'dum judi'cium, formerly, a writ issued in case the defendant be found guilty of a misdemeanor, to bring him to the court to receive sentence.

ca'pias ad computan'dum, a writ issued in the action of account, to compel the defendant to come before the auditors and account.

ca'pias ad responden'dum, a writ issued for the arrest of a person against whom an indictment for misdemeanor was found. (2) It formerly issued against an absconding debtor, who was then made to give special bail.

ca'pias ad satisfacien'dum, or **ca. sa.,** formerly a writ by which a civil defendant, against whom judgment had been recovered, was arrested and imprisoned until payment was made. Such imprisonment has been abolished in most of the United States.

ca'pias in wither'nam, formerly a writ directing the sheriff to take other goods of the distrainor equal in value to those he has taken in distress and removed or concealed, so that the sheriff could not take them when directed to do so in an action of replevin (*q.v.*).

ca'pias pro fi'ne, a writ issued against a defendant who has failed to pay his fine.

ca'pias utlaga'tum, formerly a writ directing the arrest of an outlaw.

ca'pita, *l.,* heads. See also, *per capita.*

capital, a flexible term relating to the head; chief; principal. (2) Wealth; the principal invested in a business.

capital crime, or **capital offense,** a misdeed which is punishable by death, *e.g.,* first degree murder, armed robbery, or high treason.

capital punishment, a penalty which results in the loss of the convict's life. Abolished in several states.

capital stock, the sum of money which is invested in a corporation, in exchange for which stock certificates are issued to the investors.

capital surplus, all surplus other than earned surplus.

capitation tax, a tax imposed upon a person at a fixed rate, regardless of the taxpayer's ability to pay, occupation, assets, or income, *i.e.,* a tax levied by the head.

ca'pite, see *tenure in capite.*

capi'tula, collections of laws and ordinances drawn up under heads or divisions.

capitulation, a treaty which contains the terms of surrender.

"Captain of the Ship," a doctrine or rule under which a physician who has authority or control over other medical personnel respecting a specific medical procedure may be subject to vicarious liability for the conduct of such personnel during the procedure, although he or she would not otherwise be liable for their conduct.

caption, a heading which labels or identifies a legal document. In pleadings, court orders and judgments, it usually sets forth the name of the court, the title of the action including the names of the parties and their adversary posture, the file number and a designation of the nature of the document, *e.g.,* complaint, answer, or judgment.

cargo, the entire load of a ship, steamboat, or other vessel, usually applied to goods (*q.v.*) only and not to passengers.

Carlisle Tables, mortality tables (*q.v.*) which were published in 1815 and formerly used by actuaries. Superseded by later statistics.

carnal knowledge, sexual intercourse.

carrier, one who transports persons or merchandise for hire via land, water, air, or pipeline. If he does so as his regular business, he is a common carrier; if by special contract, a private carrier (*q.v.*). A common carrier is bound to carry for any one who offers to pay his hire, and is liable for loss or injury to them. Often defined and regulated by statute.

carta, a deed or charter.

carte blanche (cart blônsh), the signature of one or more individuals on a blank paper, with a sufficient space left above it to insert writing.

cartel, an association of companies having common interests. Often used in a sense that connotes monopoly, restraint of trade, or illegal purpose.

carucate, or **carve of land,** formerly the amount of land that a man could cultivate in a year and a day with a single plow (caruca).

case, a lawsuit or item of legal work. A case previously decided is a precedent case and a case on which a lawyer or judge is presently working is a problem case. (2) An abbreviation for trespass on the case. See also, *leading case* and *trespass (3)*.

case law, judicial precedent generated as a by-product of the decisions which courts have made in resolving unique disputes, as distinguished from statutes and constitutions. Case law concerns concrete facts. Statutes and constitutions are written in the abstract.

case method, the studying and teaching of law by the examination and discussion of the facts of precedent cases and the manner in which the courts resolved the disputes therein.

case of first impression, see *first impression.*

case reserved, a decision rendered as a matter of form so that the opinion of a higher court might be obtained.

case system, see *case method.*

cases and controversies, a generic phrase denoting bona fide disputes or lawsuits in which something is decided either affirmatively or negatively. Controversy is usually descriptive of civil proceedings and cases usually include both criminal prosecutions and civil proceedings. Article III of the United States Constitution uses the terms, cases and controversies, to define the judicial power of the United States. (2) The difference between an abstract question and a case or controversy is one of degree and is not discernible by any precise test. The basic inquiry is whether the conflicting contentions of the parties present a real, substantial controversy between parties having adverse legal interests, a dispute definite and concrete, not hypothetical or abstract.

cash, that which circulates as money.

cash basis, the basis of accounting under which revenues are recorded only when actually received. Only cash disbursements are recorded as expenditures.

cash dividend, a distribution, ordinarily in cash, to shareholders of a portion of the profits or surplus assets of a corporation.

cash sale, a sale of goods to be paid for at the time of purchase or delivery.

cashworthiness doctrine, a holding adopted by a majority of the courts, that because an automobile manufacturer's duty of design and construction extends to producing a product reasonably fit for its intended use, and free of hidden defects rendering it unsafe for such use, the manufacturer is under a duty to use reasonable care in the design of its vehicle to avoid subjecting the user to an unreasonable risk of injury.

cassa're, to quash, to render void, to break.

casse'tur billa, *l.,* let the bill be quashed.

casting vote, the decisive vote of a presiding officer when the votes of the assembly are equally divided.

casual elector, formerly, the nominal defendant in the old action of ejectment (*q.v.*).

casualty, an accident. An unforeseen circumstance occasioning loss or damage, *e.g.*, a fire, storm, or wreck.

ca'su consi'mili, or **ca'su provi'so,** *l.*, formerly writs of entry for the benefit of a reversioner.

casus, *l.*, a case; event; occurrence.

ca'sus be'lli, an act giving rise to or justifying war.

ca'sus foe'deris, a case stipulated by treaty, or which comes within the terms of a compact.

casus fortu'itus, an accidental occurrence not foreseen.

casus fortuitus non est sperandus et nemo tenetur divinare, a fortuitous event is not to be foreseen, and no person is bound to foretell it.

casus omis'sus, a case not provided for by contract or statutes intended to govern like cases.

casus omissus et oblivioni datus dispositioni communis juris relinquitur, a case omitted and forgotten [in framing a law] is left to the disposal of the common law.

catching bargain, a transaction with an expectant heir (*q.v.*) or reversioner, for inadequate consideration.

caucus, a meeting of the leaders of a party or faction to decide on the candidates or policies to be supported by their followers.

causa, *l.*, a cause; a reason; a writ of action pending.

causa causae est causa causati, the cause of a cause is the cause of the effect.

causa causans, the immediate or operating cause.

causa mortis, by reason of, or in view of, death.

causa proxima, the direct cause.

causa proxima, non remota spectatur, the immediate, not the remote, cause is to be regarded.

causa remota, the remote cause.

cause of action, a flexible term, the definition of which is occasionally controversial. (1) An aggregation of facts which will cause a court to grant relief, and therefore entitles a person to initiate and prosecute a lawsuit. (2) The concurrence of a right belonging to a plaintiff, and a wrong committed by a defendant, which breaches the right and results in damage. Under modern rules of civil procedure, the term has been partly superseded by claim for relief (*q.v.*). See also, *count (1)*.

cautio; caution, a species of bail or security given for the performance of an obligation. The surety is termed the cautioner.

ca'veat, *l.*, (let him take heed), a warning. (2) Notice entered in the court records to prevent a particular act from being done, *e.g.*, probate of a will without informing the caveator. (3) A legal notice filed in the patent office, that the caveator has invented a certain thing, describing it, the effect of which is to prevent the granting of a patent to another for the same thing, without giving him an opportunity to establish his priority of invention.

caveat conductus, let the one who has been hired beware.

ca'veat emp'tor (let the buyer beware), a principle of law which imposes on a purchaser the risk of defects in title or quality of the thing purchased, unless there is an express or implied warranty, or some fraud or misrepresentation on the part of the seller. The significance of this principle is declining, because courts tend to imply warranties.

caveat emptor; qui ignorare non debuit quod jus alienum emit, let the buyer beware; who ought not to be ignorant that he is buying another's rights.

caveat venditor, let the seller beware.

ca'veat via'tor, let the traveler beware.

cd-rom, compact discs with read only memory which employ optical disc technology that can only be "read" and not written to. They typically contain digitally coded texts and can store vast quantities of information.

cede, to assign or transfer.

cedent (Sc.), an assignor.

census, a count of the population. Although the most prominent census is the federal census which is taken every ten years in the United States, censuses may also be made at other times for local purposes.

ce'pi cor'pus, *l.*, I have taken the body. Formerly used by a sheriff in making a return upon an attachment or capias, when he had arrested the person against whom the writ was issued.

ce'pit in a'lio lo'co, *l.*, formerly a plea in replevin, when the defendant took the goods in another place than that mentioned in the declaration.

certainty, clearness, confidence, definiteness.

certificate, a statement in writing, signed by a person having some official status, relative to a matter within his official knowledge or authority.

certificated security, shares which are represented by an instrument issued in bearer or registered form.

certificate of deposit, an acknowledgment by a bank of receipt of money with an engagement to repay it. The maker of a certificate of deposit is usually a financial institution. The payee is usually the individual or institution to whom the proceeds of the deposit plus corresponding interest must be paid upon its expiration or termination.

certificate of public convenience and necessity, a permit which is issued by a public body that is charged with the supervision of public facilities, *e.g.*, carriers or public utilities, authorizing the holder of the permit to operate such a public facility within a particular area. The issuance is made after application, notice, and hearing.

certificate of stock, see *stock certificate.*

certification proceeding, a nonadversary, fact-finding proceeding conducted by the National Labor Relations Board to ascertain the will of the employees as to representation.

certified check, a draft, *i.e.*, an order for the payment of money on demand, drawn on a bank, upon which the bank signs its engagement to honor, *i.e.*, pay, the draft as presented. The engagement must be written on the draft. When the holder procures such certification, the drawer and all prior endorsers are discharged. U.C.C §§ 3-411, 3-410, 3-104.

certified copy, a paper which is verified to be a faithful replica of a document which is in the custody of the officer making the certification. It is signed by the officer and usually has an official seal affixed to it.

certified public accountant, an accountant whose proficiency is certified by public authority.

certiora'ri (to be more fully informed), an original writ or action whereby a cause is removed from an inferior to a superior court for review. The record of the proceedings is then transmitted to the superior court. (2) A discretionary appellate jurisdiction that is invoked by a petition for certiorari, which the appellate court may grant or deny in its discretion. A dominant avenue to the United States Supreme Court. 28 U.S.C. §§ 1257(3), 2103.

certum est quod certum reddi potest, that is certain which can be rendered certain.

cessante causa, cessat effectus, the cause ceasing, the effect ceases.

cessante ratione legis cessat ipsa lex, the reason of the law ceasing, the law itself ceases.

cessa'vit, formerly an action which was used when a tenant ceased to pay rent or perform services for two years.

cesser, coming to an end.

cess'et execu'tio, a stay of execution.

cess'et process'us, a stay of proceedings.

cess'io bono'rum (Rom.) (a surrender of goods), the voluntary assignment by a debtor of all his effects to his creditors. It operated as a discharge pro tanto of a man's debts and exempted him from imprisonment.

cession, a yielding up, *e.g.*, of territory by one nation to another.

cessionary (Sc.), an assignee.

cessor, one who ceases or neglects so long to perform a duty that he thereby incurs the danger of the law.

cestui que trust (sĕt'ē kĭ trust), see *beneficiary (1)*.

cestui que use (sĕt'ē kĭ use), (orig., cestui a que use), formerly equivalent to a cestui que trust in regard to real property. Currently inconsequential. See also, *use*.

cestui que vie (sĕt'ē kĭ vē), the person for whose life real property is held by someone else. Upon the death of the cestui que vie, the holder's title terminates.

chain of title, the successive instruments conveying real property, commencing with the original grant or other source and including the conveyance to the person claiming title.

challenge, an exception or objection. Challenge of jurors may be (i) to the array, *i.e.*, to the whole jury, on account of partiality in the officer who arrayed the panel, or some error in forming the same; or (ii) to the polls, *i.e.*, to individual jurymen. Challenges may be (a) for cause, which under the law disqualifies the jury or juror from sitting; and (b) peremptory, those made without assigning any reason, and which the court must usually allow. The number of peremptory challenges allowed to each party is usually prescribed by statute. (2) A request by one person to another to fight a duel. Sending or carrying a challenge is severely punished by the laws of most states.

chambers, a private office, usually adjoining a courtroom, in which a judge studies, holds hearings concerning motions, and attends to other court business which does not require a jury. See also, *camera*.

cham'perty, a bargain by the terms of which a person, having no interest in the subject matter of an action, undertakes to carry on the suit at his own expense, in consideration of receiving a share of the property recovered or deriving some benefit therefrom, in the event of success. Such a contract cannot be enforced in most states. See also, *maintenance*.

champion, he who fights for another, or who takes his place in a quarrel. (2) One who fights his own battles.

chance, the happening of an event not ascertainable through foresight or ingenuity; fortuity; risk.

chancellor, a judge who presides over a court of chancery, *i.e.*, a court of equity.

Chancellor of the Exchequer, an English officer in charge of the treasury.

chance-medley, a sudden affray, not prearranged or intended. The term is sometimes applied to a homicide committed in such an affray or in self-defense.

chancery, equity. (2) A court exercising equitable jurisdiction. The terms equity and chancery are used synonymously in the United States. Under modern rules of civil procedure and some codes of civil practice, there is no longer any distinction between actions at law and suits in equity.

chance verdict, a decision by a jury which is arrived at by means of casting lots or by other similar device.

change of venue, see *venue*.

chapter, a subdivision of a legislative act or code of statutes. Chapters are further subdivided into sections. (2) A community or corporation composed of the prebends and other clergymen belonging to a cathedral or collegiate church, and presided over by the dean.

chapter XIII proceedings, see *wage earners' plan*.

character evidence, testimony concerning the reputation of a person in his community, *i.e.*, among those persons who know him best, regarding a particular trait, *e.g.*, reputation for truth and veracity. (2) The credibility of a witness may be attacked or supported by evidence in the form of opinion or reputation, but subject to these limitations: (a) the evidence may refer only to character for truthfulness or untruthfulness, and (b) evidence of truthful character is admissible only after the character of the witness for truthfulness has been attacked by opinion or reputation evidence or otherwise. Fed R. Evid. 608 (a).

charge, the instructions given by the court to a grand jury before it enters upon its investigations, or to a petit jury at the close of a trial as to the principles of law which should guide it in arriving at a verdict. (2) An accusation. (3) A duty or obligation imposed upon some person; or a lien, incumbrance, or claim to be satisfied out of a particular estate.

charge d' affaires (shår zhã då får'), *fr.*, a diplomatic representative who has charge of his country's affairs in a foreign country in the absence of the ambassador or minister.

charge off, a deduction from income or assets, *e.g.,* expenses, depreciation, or bad debts.

charitable corporation, a corporation organized and operated exclusively for religious, charitable, scientific, testing for public safety, literary, or educational purposes, exclusively for the prevention of cruelty to children or animals, or exclusively for a home for the aged.

charitable trust, a trust set up for the benefit of a named charity, whether a religious institution, non-profit agency or other worthy cause.

charitable use, charitable purpose; charitable trust; charity; *e.g.,* the establishment of colleges, schools, and hospitals and the carrying on of religious and missionary enterprises. See also, *public charity.*

charity, see *public charity.*

charta, *l.,* a charter, deed or writing. See also, *Magna Charta.*

charter, the basic document, containing grants of authority and restrictions on authority, under which a private corporation is organized. The relationship of the corporation to its charter is analogous to the relationship of a nation or state to its constitution. (2) The portion of the state statutes which pertains to a particular private corporation or to a particular municipal corporation. (3) A certificate of in corporation.

charter-party, the written contract by which the owner of a ship or other vessel hires her out to another person for a particular period or voyage.

chattel mortgage, an instrument in writing which transfers the title to personal property as security for a debt. The term is falling into disuse. See also, *security agreement.*

chattel paper, a writing or writings which evidence both a monetary obligation and a security interest in or a lease of specific goods.

chattels, any property, except a freehold of real property. It includes personal property, *e.g.,* furniture, automobiles, animals, leases and other interests in land which are less than a freehold.

chattels real, see *personal chattels.* Cf. *chattels.*

cheat, a flexible term for the fraudulent obtaining of another's property by deceit.

check, or **cheque,** an unconditional order to pay a sum certain in money to order or to bearer, drawn on a bank and payable on demand, which is signed by the drawer. U.C.C. § 3-104.

check kiting, a type of fraud in which the kiter creates a continuous exchange of overdrafts between accounts in at least two banks. Kiting depends upon the combination of two circumstances: first, the willingness of depositary banks to allow the kiter immediate credit when he deposits checks drawn on other banks and, second, the period of time between the deposit of those checks and their presentment to the drawees.

chief, principal; one put over others; head of a department.

chief clerk, the principal clerk in a court or a department of government, who supervises the keeping of records and other matters of routine and carries out the orders of the head of the department.

Chief Justice, the presiding judge of a supreme court or court of appeals.

Chief Justice of the United States, the highest judicial officer of the United States. He presides over the United States Supreme Court and the Judicial Conference of the United States. He is responsible for assigning judges from one United States court to another.

child, includes any individual entitled to take as a child under the Uniform Probate Code by intestate succession from the parent whose relationship is involved, and excludes any person who is only a stepchild, a foster child, a grandchild, or any more remote descendant. Uniform Probate Code § 1-201(3).

Child Abuse Prevention and Treatment Act, an act to provide financial assistance for a demonstration program for the prevention, identification, and treatment of child abuse and neglect, to establish a National Center on Child Abuse and Neglect, and for other purposes. 42 U.S.C. §§ 5101 *et seq.*

Child Abuse Prevention and Treatment and Adoption Reform Act of 1978, an act to promote the healthy development of children who would benefit from adoption by facilitating their placement in adoptive homes, to extend and improve the provisions of the Child Abuse Prevention and Treatment Act (*q.v.*), and for other purposes. 42 U.S.C. §§ 5105 *et seq.*

Child Kidnapping Act, see *Parental Kidnapping Prevention Act of 1980.*

Child Sexual Exploitation Act, see *Protection of Children Against Sexual Exploitation Act of 1977.*

chirographum apud debitorem repertum praesumitur solutum, a bond found with the debtor is presumed to be paid.

Chivalry, Court of, formerly an English court of honor held before the Lord High Constable and Earl Marshal.

choate lien, a lien in which all requisites for perfection are met (*i.e.,* identity of lienor, property subject to lien, and amount of lien).

chose (*shōz*), *fr.,* a thing; personal property.

chose in action, a right to sue for a debt or sum of money.

chose in possession, personal property of which one has the actual possession and enjoyment.

C.I.F., cost of the goods, insurance, and freight are included in the seller's price. U.C.C. § 2-320.

cinque ports (sink), the ports of England which lie toward France, *i.e.,* Dover, Sandwich, Romney, Hastings, Hythe, Rye and Winchelsea.

circuit court, various courts in different jurisdictions which are inferior to supreme courts. Some of them are intermediate appellate courts and some of them are trial courts. (2) Formerly United States courts established for the relief of the Supreme Court, to which cases decided in the district courts were taken on error or appeal. See also, *United States Court of Appeals.*

Circuit Court of Appeals, see *United States Court of Appeals.*

circuits, judicial divisions of the United States or a state, originally so called because the judges traveled from place to place within the circuit, holding court in various locations. The practice of traveling from place to place continues today in rural areas.

circuitus est evitandus, circuity is to be avoided.

circuity of action, the bringing of more than one action to accomplish something that could be accomplished by a single action.

circumstantial evidence, evidence from which a fact is reasonably inferred, although not directly proven. It is often introduced when direct evidence is not available.

citation, a reference to a constitution, statute, precedent case, or other persuasive material used in legal writing. (2) A summons to appear in court. (3) A compliment or award.

cite, to give or issue a citation (*q.v.*).

citizen, a flexible term descriptive of a person who has the freedom and privileges of a city, county, state, or nation. (2) A person who is a member of a body politic, owes allegiance to its government, and may claim the protection of its government.

Citizen of the United States, any person born in the United States, or born out of the United States, if his parents were citizens, or one of foreign birth and parentage who has become naturalized. All persons born or naturalized in the United States, and subject to the jurisdiction thereof, are citizens of the United States and of the State wherein they reside. U.S. Const. Amend. XIV, Sec. 1.

city, or **municipal corporation,** a public corporation established as a subdivision of a state for local governmental purposes, with various powers of government vested in its own officials.

civil, a flexible term pertaining to a person's relationship to his fellow citizens.

civil action, a lawsuit which has for its object the protection of private or civil rights or compensation for their infraction.

civil court, see *court.*

civil death, in some states, persons convicted of serious crimes are considered civilly dead meaning that certain civil rights and privileges are forfeited.

civil law, or **Roman law,** the law compiled by the Roman jurists under the auspices of the Emperor Justinian, which is still in force in many of the nations in Europe.

civil officer, any officer of the United States who holds his appointment under the national government, whether his duties are executive or judicial, in the highest or lowest departments of the government, with the exception of officers of the army and navy.

civil remedy, the remedy which an injured party has against a party who committed the injury, as distinguished from a criminal proceeding by which the wrongdoer is made to expiate the injury done to society.

civil rights, the rights of citizens of the United States guaranteed by the Constitution of the United States, particularly Amendments I, XIII, XIV and XV. (2) The rights of a citizen. See also, *1983.*

Civil Rights Act of 1957, an act to provide means of further securing and protecting the civil rights of persons within the jurisdiction of the United States. 42 U.S. C. §§ 1971, 1975, 1975 a-e, 1995; 5 U.S.C., § 5319 (19); 28 U.S.C. §§ 1343, 1861; 71 Stat. 634 (1957).

Civil Rights Act of 1960, an act to enforce constitutional rights, and for other purposes. 42 U.S.C. §§ 1971, 1974-1974e, 1975d; 18 U.S.C. §§ 837, 1074, 1509; 20 U.S.C. §§ 241, 640; 74 Stat. 86 (1960).

Civil Rights Act of 1964, an act to enforce the constitutional right to vote, to confer jurisdiction upon the district courts of the United States to provide injunctive relief against discrimination in public accommodations, to authorize the Attorney General to institute suits to protect constitutional rights in public facilities and public education, to extend the Commission on Civil Rights, to prevent discrimination in federally assisted programs, to establish a commission on Equal Employment Opportunity, and for other purposes. 28 U.S.C. § 1447; 42 U.S.C. §§ 1971, 1975a-d, 2000a-2000h-6; 78 Stat. 241 (1964). See also, *Equal Employment Opportunity Act.*

Civil Rights Commission Act of 1978, an act to extend the Commission on Civil Rights for five years, to authorize appropriations for the

Commission, to effect certain technical changes to comply with changes in the law, and for other purposes. 42 U.S.C. §§ 1975b-1975e, 92 Stat. 1067 (1978).

Civil Service, government employees other than military, naval, legislative, and judicial. Such employees who are in the lower pay classifications often have specific rights of tenure and promotion.

Civil Service Commission, various groups of officials in the United States, state, and city governments, respectively, which supervise the appointment, tenure, and promotion of government employees in the lower pay classifications, pursuant to statutory directives.

civilian, a student, practitioner, or professor of the civil law (*q.v.*). (2) A person who is not in the military service.

claim, the assertion of a right; a demand. (2) The possession by a settler or miner of a tract of wild or mineral land which he intends to acquire from the government. (3) The tract of wild or mineral land staked out and held by such settler or miner. See also, *claims.*

claim and delivery, see *replevin.*

claim for relief, under modern rules of civil procedure, a short and plain statement showing that the pleader is entitled to relief. It should give fair notice of the character of the claim asserted so as to enable the adverse party to answer and prepare for trial. It must contain a distinctive group of facts which distinguish the action from all other controversies so that the matter at issue can be later identified as res judicata (*q.v.*). Fed. R. Civ. P. 8(a).

claimant, a person who makes a claim. (2) The plaintiff in the old action of ejectment. (3) In admiralty practice, the person admitted to defend a libel *in rem,* so called because he claimed the property seized.

claims, in respect to a protected person (*q.v.*), includes liabilities of the protected person, whether arising in contract, tort, or otherwise, and liabilities of the estate which arise at or after the appointment of a conservator (*q.v.*), including expenses of administration. Uniform Probate Code § 5-103(1). See also, *claim.*

Clarendon, Constitutions of, 16 articles which defined the relationship between the church and the state in England. They were promulgated in 1164 to limit the pretensions of the clergy.

class action, or **representative action,** a lawsuit initiated or defended by a person, who brings it or defends it for himself and on behalf of all other persons similarly situated. If persons constituting a class are so numerous as to make it impracticable to bring them all before the court, such of them, one or more, as will fairly insure the adequate representation of all may, on behalf of all, sue or be sued in certain instances, depending upon the character of the right sought to be enforced. Fed. R. Civ. P. 23.

clausula generalis de residuo non ea complectitur quae non ejusdem sint generis cum iis quae speciatim dicta fuerant, a general clause concerning the residue does not comprehend those things which are not of the same kind with those which have been specially expressed.

clausula quae abrogationem excludit ab initio non valet, a clause [in a law] which precludes its repeal is invalid from the beginning.

clausulae inconsuetae semper inducunt suspicionem, unusual clauses always excite suspicion.

clausum, close; an inclosure.

Clayton Act, an act to supplement earlier laws, including the Sherman Act (*q.v.*), against unlawful restraints and monopolies. 15 U.S.C. §§ 12 *et seq.*; 18 U.S.C. §§ 402 *et seq.*, 29 U.S.C. §§ 52, 53.

Clean Air Act, an act to improve, strengthen, and accelerate programs for the prevention and abatement of air pollution, as amended, 42 U.S.C. §§ 7401 *et seq.*; 77 Stat. 392 (1963), 79 Stat. 992 (1965), 80 Stat. 954 (1966), 81 Stat. 485 (1967), 83 Stat. 283 (1969), 84 Stat. 1676 (1970), 91 Stat. 685 (1977). See also, *Air Quality Act of 1967.*

clean hands, a principle that may be invoked to preclude affirmative equitable relief to someone who seeks it, and has himself been guilty of inequitable conduct, concerning the matter in which he seeks relief.

clear and convincing, a flexible term concerning the degree of proof required for certain issues in some civil cases. It is less than the degree required in criminal cases, but more than required in the ordinary civil action.

clear days, a period of days calculated by excluding the first day and excluding the day on which a thing must be done.

clear title, ownership free from encumbrance, burden, or limitation.

clearance, a certificate given by the collector of a port to the master of a vessel, that his vessel has been entered and cleared according to law. A permission to sail. The act of clearing.

clearing-house, or **clearinghouse,** an office where banks exchange checks and drafts drawn on each other, and settle their balances.

clearly erroneous, firmly viewed on the entire record by a reviewing court as definitely mistaken. (2) A showing that the evidence and reasonable inferences from it, viewed as a whole, can only lead to a decision contrary to that of the trial court. (3) Unsupported by substantial, credible evidence in the record. (4) Erroneous as a matter of law. (5) The reviewing court on the entire evidence is left with the definite and firm conviction that a mistake has been committed, although there is evidence to support the finding. See Fed. R. Civ. P. 52(a).

clergy, ecclesiastical ministers as distinguished from the laity. See also, *benefit of clergy.*

clergyable, formerly allowing of, or entitled to, the benefit of clergy (*q.v.*); descriptive of crimes or persons.

clerical error, a mistake made in transcribing, or in the performance of other clerical operations.

cle'ricus, *l.,* a clerk; a clergyman.

clerk, an officer of a court who files pleadings, motions, orders, and judgments, who issues the process of the court, and who keeps the records of legal proceedings. (2) A person employed to sell goods or attend to business in the store or office of another.

client, a person who employs an attorney to appear in court, give advice, draft a written instrument, or do any other thing which constitutes the practice of law (*q.v.*).

Clifford trust, a trust established for a minimum of ten years and one day under which title to the income producing assets is transferred and then reclaimed when the trust expires. The objective was to shift income from high tax bracket parents to children in a lower bracket. The Tax Reform Act of 1986 repealed such rules for transfers made after March 1, 1986 and the income of the trust is now taxed at the grantor's rate.

close, a piece of land.

close corporation, a corporation (*q.v.*), *i.e.,* an artificial person or legal entity, in which the ownership is in a few hands and is only rarely bought and sold. (2) One wherein a major part of the persons to whom the corporate powers have been granted have the right to fill vacancies arising among them. (3) One in which the owners are so few in number that each owner personally, or his representative, is a member of the board of directors.

closed season, a time of the year when the taking of game is prohibited by statute.

closed shop, a factory, store, or other place of employment which refuses to employ nonunion workmen.

cloud on title, an invalid, but ostensible, evidence of title, lien, or claim, in whole or in part, to property which gives the appearance of a limitation on ownership.

cluster housing, individual homes, usually party-wall row houses, or apartment buildings, that are grouped together on relatively small plots of land.

Coal Mine Health and Safety Act, see *Black Lung Benefits Act.*

coassignee, one of two or more persons to whom an assignment has been made.

COBRA, Consolidated Omnibus Budget Reconciliation Act of 1986; 42 USC §§ 1396a *et seq.*

Cochran-Patterson Acts, acts to forbid the transportation of any person in interstate or foreign commerce who is kidnapped, or otherwise unlawfully detained, and to make such act a felony. 18 U.S.C. §§ 10, 1201.

code, or **statutes,** a classified and indexed compilation of legislative acts in effect in a particular jurisdiction as of a given date, regardless of the date of the enactment of the acts. (2) A collection or system of laws. (3) The collection of laws and constitutions, made by order of Emperor Justinian in 528, is called *The Code.*

Code of Judicial Conduct, proposed standards that judges should observe. It consists of seven statements of norms denominated canons, accompanying text setting forth specific rules, and commentary. Adopted by the House of Delegates of the American Bar Association on August 16, 1972.

Code of Professional Responsibility, the rules which in the main govern the legal profession, consisting of nine canons, ethical considerations and disciplinary rules. Adopted by the House of Delegates of the American Bar Association on August 1, 1969, and subsequently amended. Cf. *Model Rules of Professional Conduct.*

codex, a volume or roll; The Code of Justinian was the Codex.

cod'icil (cŏd), a written instrument which supplements or modifies a prior will. It must be executed with the same formalities as a will.

coercion, constraint; compulsion; compelling a person by physical force or by threats to do what he would otherwise not do. See also, *criminal coercion.*

cogitationis poenam nemo patitur, no one suffers punishment for his thoughts.

cogna'ti, relations by the mother's side.

cog'nizance, or **con'usance,** acknowledgment; recognition; jurisdiction; hearing a matter judicially. A judge is bound to take judicial cognizance of certain matters without having them proved in evidence, *e.g.,* the statutes of the state in which he holds court, and the extent of his jurisdiction.

cogno'men, the surname or family name.

cogno'vit (actio'nem), *l.*, a defendant's written confession of judgment in an action brought against him, *i.e.*, his admission that he has no defense, and consents to judgment being entered against him.

cognovit note, a promissory note which contains a provision authorizing the confession of judgment on the note. The decisions of various courts concerning the validity of such provisions are not uniform.

cohabit, to live together in the same house as man and wife. Accord, Model Penal Code § 230.2.

coheir, or **co-heir,** one of several persons to whom an inheritance descends.

coif, a white silk cap, the badge of English sergeants at law. See also, *Order of the Coif.*

collateral, property which is subject to a security interest. U.C.C. § 9-105 (1) (c). (2) Property which is pledged as security for the satisfaction of an indebtedness, *e.g.*, real property which is mortgaged as security for a promissory note. (3) By the side of; indirect.

collateral attack, an attempt to defeat the operation of a valid judgment in a separate proceeding, which only incidentally generates such an issue.

collateral estoppel, once a court has decided an issue of fact or law necessary to its judgment, that decision may preclude relitigation of the issue in a suit on a different cause of action involving a party to the first case. It relieves parties of the cost and vexation of multiple lawsuits, conserves judicial resources, and by preventing inconsistent decisions, encourages reliance on adjudication. Cannot apply when the party against whom the earlier decision is asserted did not have a full and fair opportunity to litigate the issue in the earlier case. Cf. *res judicata.*

collateral facts, those not directly connected with the issue or matter in dispute.

collateral inheritance tax, a tax levied upon the collateral devolution of property by will or under the intestate law.

collateral issue, a question of law or fact which is foreign to the general issue in the case.

collateral limitation, one which makes the enjoyment of an estate depend upon the happening of some event not related to or depending upon the parties.

collateral relationship, as opposed to lineal, is that of persons descended from a common ancestor, *e.g.*, cousins.

collateral security, see *collateral (1), (2).*

collateral source rule, a rule under which any evidence of a plaintiff's alternative or additional sources of payment for expenses or losses for which damages are sought in a civil action, such as insurance coverage, is excluded as irrelevant.

collateral warranty, a guarantee concerning real property which was made by an ancestor. It is not enforceable against the heirs in all jurisdictions, but where it is enforceable, the heirs of a person who has made a covenant, warranty or guarantee are answerable for it to the extent of the real property which descended to them.

collaterals, relatives who trace relationship to an intestate through a common ancestor but who are not in the lineal line of ascent or descent.

collaterals of the half-blood, persons related to an intestate through only one common ancestor.

collation, the comparison of a copy with its original to ascertain its correctness. (2) The gathering and assembly in correct order of sheets of typed, printed, or copied material on paper.

collective bargaining, a procedure looking toward the making of an agreement between an employer and the accredited representative of his employees concerning wages, hours, and conditions of employment.

colleg'atary, a person who has a legacy left to him in common with other persons.

collision, a broad term meaning striking together or striking against each other, by two or more objects. (1) In the context of motor vehicle insurance, the force may be applied via human agency or natural energy. The object with which collision occurs can be another motor vehicle, a ditch, an embankment, a boulder, water, and many other things. Both objects may be in motion, or one may be in motion and the other stationary. (2) The act of ships or other vessels striking together or of one vessel running into or foul of another.

collo'quium (a talking together), the statement in a complaint or declaration for libel or slander that the libelous or slanderous imputation had reference to the plaintiff.

colloquy, a checklist used by trial judges for the purpose of informing a defendant who proposes to plead guilty concerning his constitutional rights. It is made a permanent part of the court record after it has been performed and executed.

collusion, a secret agreement between persons apparently hostile, to do some act in order to defraud or prejudice a third person, or for some improper purpose.

colony, a group of citizens or subjects who have left their country to people another, and who remain subject to the mother country.

color, a prima facie right or title; semblance; appearance.

colorable, that which is not what it purports or professes to be; deceptive.

color of office, a pretense of official right to do an act made by one who has no such right.

color of right, semblance of right.

color of title, apparent ownership of land founded upon a written instrument, *e.g.*, a deed or decree of court.

comaker, one of two or more persons who signs a negotiable instrument on its face, and thereby makes himself primarily liable for its payment.

combination, a union of people for the purpose of violating the law, as in restraint of trade.

comes, an earl, or count.

comita'tus, or **county,** is derived from comes, the earl to whom its government was intrusted. His authority was usually exercised through the vice-comes, or shire-reeve (hence, our sheriff).

com'ity, the practice by which one court follows the decision of another court on a like question, though not bound by the law of precedents to do so.

comity of nations, the obligation granted by courtesy to the laws of one nation within the territories of another, when they do not conflict with the laws of the latter.

commandite (*kom môn dē'*), *fr.*, or **in commen'dam,** a form of partnership in France (Societe en Commandite) in which certain of the partners (commandataires) take no active share in the business, but merely lend money to it, and are only liable to the extent of such money.

commenda'tus, formerly a person who put himself under the protection of a superior lord.

Commerce Clause, the provision in the United States Constitution which grants to Congress the power to regulate commerce with foreign nations, among the several states and with the Indian tribes. U.S. Const. Art. I, Sec. 8.

Commerce Court, formerly a United States court created to handle interstate commerce matters.

commercia belli, agreements by belligerents, made in time of peace to take effect in event of war, or made during the war itself, by which arrangement is made for non-hostile trade.

commercial, relating to trade or commerce.

commercial agency, or **credit bureau,** an organization for the purpose of furnishing information as to the financial standing of persons engaged in business or seeking credit, or both.

commercial agent, a person who sells goods through catalogs or by sample.

commercial code, see *Uniform Commercial Code.*

commercial law, that branch of the law which concerns the relationships of persons engaged in business or doing business.

commercial impracticability, a contract can be defended, discharged or excused if certain events or conditions make its performance utterly impracticable. This doctrine is predicated upon the theory that the parties to a contract made their bargain with specific circumstances in mind; that their basic assumptions about the world in which the contract was negotiated was thereafter upset by a failed contingency or condition. Performance under the contract becomes commercially impracticable and legally excused.

commercial paper, negotiable instruments (*q.v.*), *e.g.,* checks and promissory notes.

commission, an authorization or order to do some act, *e.g.,* to take depositions or to hold an inquest of lunacy. (2) The evidence of an officer's appointment and authority to discharge the duties of his office. (3) A body of persons appointed with necessary powers to do certain things. (4) The act of perpetrating an offense. (5) The compensation of a person employed to sell goods, usually a percentage on the amount realized from the sale.

commission form of government, government by a body called a commission in which are vested all the powers of municipal government.

commissioner, a court officer who is authorized to perform certain judicial or administrative functions and report his actions to the court for ratification. (2) The title given by law to the heads of bureaus in certain departments of the United States government and to state officials charged with special duties.

Commissioner, United States, see *United States Commissioners.*

commisso'ria lex, *l.,* (Rom.), the privilege of a vendor to rescind a sale if the purchaser did not pay his purchase money at the time agreed upon.

commitment, the sending of a person to prison. (2) The sending of a person to a hospital because of mental disorder.

committee, one or more members of a legislative body, corporate board of directors, or association, appointed to consider and report upon certain matters or to carry out the resolutions of that body. (2) A fiduciary (*q.v.*) appointed by a court to administer the assets of an incompetent person, analogous to a guardian (*q.v.*).

commoda'tum (Rom.), the loan of a thing to be used for a definite time and then to be returned, without pay or reward; the thing lent.

Commodities Clause, a clause in the Hepburn Amendment to the Interstate Commerce Act (*q.v.*) prohibiting railroad companies from producing the commodities they carry.

commodum ex injuria sua nemo habere debet, no person ought to derive benefit from his own wrong.

common, a use which a person has of the land of another, jointly with him and others. Except in the case of a copyhold (*q.v.*), it can not be claimed by custom, but only by grant or prescription. (2) Land subject to the right of common. See *tenancy.* (3) General; ordinary; pertaining to all.

common assurance, see *assurance* (1).

common bench, the English *Court of Common Pleas* (*q.v.*).

common carrier, see *carrier.*

common council, a municipal legislative body.

common counts, allegations in old forms of pleading which were made for the purpose of preventing a defeat of justice by a variance of the evidence.

common informer, a person who, without special authority or being under no duty to do so, gives information which leads to the prosecution of offenders.

common intent, the natural sense given to words.

common law, an ambiguous term. (1) A system of jurisprudence founded on principles of justice which are determined by reasoning and administration consistent with the usage, customs, and institutions of the people and which are suitable to the genius of the people and their social, political, and economic condition. The rules deduced from this system continually change and expand with the progress of society. (2) That system of law which does not rest for its authority upon any express statutes, but derives its force and authority from universal consent and immemorial usage, and which is evidenced by the decisions of the courts of law, technically so called, in contradistinction to those of equity and the ecclesiastical courts.

common-law marriage, an agreement by man and woman to presently enter into the marriage relation without ecclesiastical or civil ceremony, followed by the assumption of marital duties and cohabitation.

common-law wife, see *common-law marriage.*

common nuisance, see *nuisance.*

common pleas, (communia placita), an old term descriptive of such actions as were brought by man against man or by the government when the cause of action was of a civil nature. See also, *Court of Common Pleas.*

common seal, the seal used by a corporation.

common shares, shares with the following characteristics: (1) the right to receive dividends contingent upon an apportionment of the profits, (2) negotiability, (3) the ability to be pledged or hypothecated, (4) the conferring of voting rights in proportion to the number of shares owned, and (5) the capacity to increase in value.

commons, the people of England as distinguished from the king and nobility. See also, *Houses of Parliament.*

commorancy, residency within a certain district.

commorien'tes, *l.,* persons who perish at the same time and by a common calamity, *e.g.,* airplane crash or shipwreck.

Communications Act of 1934, an act to provide for the regulation of interstate and foreign communication by wire, radio, or television. 18 U.S. C. §§ 1304,1464, 47 U.S.C. §§ 151-609.

communis error facit jus, a common error makes (or becomes) law.

Communist Control Act of 1954, an act concerning the proscription of the Communist Party, its successors and subsidiary organizations, the application of the Internal Security Act of 1950 (*q.v.*) to members of the Communist Party and other subversive organizations, determination by jury, and the like. 50 U.S.C. §§ 841 *et seq.*; 68 Stat. 775 (1954).

community of interest, an interest common to all parties, *i.e.* an identity of interest, in benefits and responsibilities.

community property, property acquired by a husband and wife, or either of them, during coverture (*q.v.*). This concept was unknown to English common law. It was introduced in the United States via the French and Spanish colonies and is in effect in only a minority of the states, *i.e.,* Arizona, California, Idaho, Louisiana, New Mexico, Nevada, Texas, Washington and to a limited extent, Oklahoma.

commutation, the modification of a sentence so as to make the punishment to which a person has been condemned less severe. (2) An ad hoc exercise of executive clemency; a governor may commute a sentence at any time for any reason without reference to any standards. Cf. *parole.* (3) The conversion of a right to receive installment payments into one fixed or gross payment.

compact, contract; generally used with reference to formal and serious engagements, *e.g.,* compacts between two states respecting their common boundary.

company, a flexible term. (1) A corporation. (2) An unincorporated association organized for commercial purposes.

comparative fault, see *comparative negligence.*

comparative jurisprudence, or **comparative law,** a course of study in which different legal systems are compared, *e.g.,* a comparison of the German, Russian and American legal systems.

comparative negligence, or **comparative fault,** a doctrine in tort law which allows proportionate recovery if both the plaintiff and defendant were negligent and thereby contributed to the cause of an injury. This doctrine is in effect in 42 states, Puerto Rico, and the Virgin Islands.

compensatory damages, see *damages.*

competency, the legal fitness or capacity of a witness to testify on the trial of a case. (2) Freedom from mental illness or defect because of which a person is unable to understand in a reasonable manner the nature and consequences of a transaction, or he is unable to act in a reasonable manner in relation to the transaction. Restatement (Second) of Contracts § 15(1). (3) The quality of evidence offered which makes it proper to be received.

competent, legally qualified or capable.

competent evidence, see *competency.*

complainant, a person who makes a complaint; the plaintiff.

complaint, the charge made before a proper officer that an offense has been committed by a person named or described. (2) Under modern rules of civil procedure, a pleading which must be filed to commence an action.

complicity, the acts of actively planning the crime, but not being present at the time of the commission; of being with the criminal at the time of commission of the crime; and, of giving aid and comfort to a criminal, knowing that a crime was committed, but having no part in its perpetration.

com'pos men'tis, *l.,* (sound of mind), capable of transacting business.

composition, an agreement between a debtor and his creditors, by which the latter agree to accept a certain proportion of their debts in satisfaction of the whole.

compound interest, interest upon interest, *i.e.,* when the simple interest on a sum of money is added to the principal as it becomes due, and then bears interest, becoming a sort of secondary principal. See also, *account.*

compound larceny, see *mixed larceny.*

compounding, accepting or agreeing to accept a pecuniary benefit in consideration of refraining from reporting to law-enforcement authorities the commission or suspected commission of an offense, or information relating to an offense. It is an affirmative defense that the pecuniary benefit did not exceed an amount which the actor believed to be due as restitution or indemnification for harm caused by the offense. Model Penal Code § 242.5. See also, *compounding a felony.*

compounding a debt, making a composition (*q.v.*).

compounding a felony, to enter into an agreement for a valuable consideration not to prosecute a felon. See also, *compounding.*

Comprehensive Alcohol Abuse and Alcoholism Prevention, Treatment, and Rehabilitation Act, an act of 1970 and amendment of 1974, to provide a comprehensive federal program for the prevention and treatment of alcohol abuse and alcoholism. It deals with a national institute, federal assistance for state and local programs, admission to hospitals, confidentiality of records, and the like. 42 U.S.C. § 2900 *et seq.*

Comprehensive Employment and Training Act of 1973, an act to assure opportunities for employment and training to unemployed and underemployed persons. 29 U.S.C., § § 801 *et seq.* Cf. *Job Training Partnership Act.*

compromise, settlement of an action or matters in dispute by agreement.

comptroller, or **controller,** a public official appointed to examine accounts settled by the auditors and to perform other duties defined by law.

compulsion, force brought to bear to make a person do what he would otherwise not do. See also, *coercion; duress.*

compurga'tor, formerly, a person who, on oath, asserted another's innocence. Under the early Saxons, a person accused of a crime was acquitted if twelve or more compurgators (juratores or justificatores) came forward, and swore to a veredictum (or true statement) that they believed him innocent. This procedure was called wager of law.

concealed weapon, a flexible term for arms (*q.v.*) so placed that they cannot readily be seen under ordinary observation. The courts are not in agreement concerning the application of this concept in unique factual situations.

concealers, formerly, persons used to find out lands which had been privily kept from the crown, by persons without title.

concealment, in the law of contracts, the improper suppression of any fact or circumstance, by which one of the parties is induced to enter into the contract. (2) The fraudulent hiding of one's property so that creditors may not levy on it to satisfy debts. (3) Covering up or keeping secret the evidence of a crime.

conces'si, *l.,* (I have granted), a term formerly used in deeds, equivalent to grant, lease, and release.

concessio versus concedentem latam interpretationem habere debet, a grant ought to have a liberal interpretation against the grantor.

conciliation, an attempt to settle a dispute amicably before trial.

conci'lium, or **consi'lium,** *l.,* consultation; determination; formerly applied to the order setting a case down for argument on demurrer or in proceedings on a writ of error.

concise, expressing much in a few words.

conclude, to end; close up; determine.

conclusive, that which cannot be gainsaid or doubted.

conclusive presumption, an inference which the law will not allow to be overcome by the introduction of evidence to the contrary.

concord, an agreement of settlement. (2) Formerly an agreement between parties who intended to levy a fine of lands concerning how and in what manner the lands should pass.

concordat (*kŏn kor dǎ´*), a convention, a pact; an agreement between independent governments.

concubine, a woman who cohabits with a man as his wife, without being married.

concurrent jurisdiction, the authority of two or more courts to entertain a particular suit. Often the choice as to which court will hear the suit is optional with the party who initiates it.

concurrent negligence, the failure to exercise care by two or more persons, each of whom acts independently, which combines to produce a single indivisible injury.

concurrent writ, a writ of summons of the same tenor as an original, which remains in force; used where there are several defendants or it is advisable to try to serve the same defendant in different places.

condemnation, the taking of private property for a public or quasi-public use, in return for fair compensation, *e.g.,* for a highway or urban renewal. (2) The declaration of a competent tribunal that a building is in a dangerous condition or that a ship is unfit for use. (3) The judgment or decree by which property seized for a violation of the revenue or navigation laws is forfeited to the government. (4) A judgment that a captured ship is a lawful prize.

conditio illicita habetur pro non adjecta, an unlawful condition is held as not annexed.

conditio praecedens adimpleri debet priusquam sequatur effectus, a condition precedent must be fulfilled before the effect can follow.

condition, a qualification, restriction, or limitation annexed to a grant or agreement, by which it is deprived of its absolute character and may be defeated, suspended, or canceled on the happening of a certain event or the performance by the grantee, of certain things, *e.g.*, the provision in a bond that it shall be void if the principal does certain things, or the provision in a mortgage that the conveyance, otherwise absolute in form, shall be void if the mortgagor pays certain specified notes. (2) An event, not certain to occur, which must occur unless its non-occurrence is excused, before performance under a contract becomes due. Restatement (Second) of Contracts § 224. See also, *precedent condition* and *subsequent*.

condition precedent, see *precedent condition*.

condition subsequent, see *subsequent*.

conditional fee, see *base-fee*.

conditional limitations, a right concerning real property, wherein a condition subsequent is followed by a limitation over, in the event of noncompliance with, or breach of, the condition. It is both a condition and a limitation.

conditional sale, a form of security device for sales on credit in which the vesting of title is made to depend upon future payment of the purchase price; falling into disuse.

conditiones quaelibet odiosae; maxime autem contra matrimonium et commercium, any conditions are odious; but especially those against marriage and commerce.

condominium, the fee simple (*q.v.*) ownership of an apartment, rooms, office space, or other unit in a multiple-unit building, and an undivided ownership of the common elements of the real property, *e.g.*, the land, foundations, main walls, roofs, halls, and stairways. Frequently defined by various state statutes.

condonation, a pardoning by a spouse of a conjugal offense by the marriage partner, which prevents the offense from being made the subject of legal proceedings at any future time.

conduct, an action or omission and its accompanying state of mind, or where relevant, a series of acts and omissions. Model Penal Code § 1.13 (5).

confederacy, a combination of two or more persons to damage or do injury to another or to commit some other unlawful act. See also, *conspiracy*. (2) A loose union of two or more states or nations.

conference, a meeting of committees appointed by the two houses of Congress or a state legislature to reconcile differences about proposed legislation.

confessio facta in judicio omni probatione major est, a confession made in court is of greater effect than any proof.

confession, an admission by a person accused of crime that he has committed the offense charged. It may be judicial, *i.e.*, made before a court or examining magistrate, or extrajudicial, *i.e.*, made outside of court.

confession and avoidance, a plea admitting certain facts alleged by the opponent's preceding pleading, but avoiding their legal effect by alleging new matter. See also, *affirmative defense and avoidance (1)*.

confession, judgment by, see *cognovit*.

confidential communications, statements made by one person to another when there is a necessary relation of trust and confidence between them, which the person receiving them cannot be compelled to disclose, *e.g.*, the statements made by a husband to his wife, or a client to his attorney.

confirmare nemo potest priusquam jus ei acciderit, no one can confirm before the right accrues to him.

Confirma'tio Charta'rum, *l.*, the 1297 English statute which reenacted Magna Charta with some additions.

confirmatio omnes supplet defectus, licet id quod actum est ab initio non valuit, confirmation supplies all defects though that which was done was not valid at the beginning.

confirmation, a conveyance by which a voidable estate is made valid or by which a particular estate is increased.

confiscation, the appropriation of property taken from an enemy, or seized for a violation of law, to the use of the government.

conflict of laws, the variance between the laws of two states or countries relating to the subject matter of a suit brought in one of them, when the parties to the suit, or some of them, or the subject matter, belong to the other. See also, *lex loci*.

confrontation, bringing witnesses face to face with the accused; cross-examination. The absolute right of cross-examination, *i.e.*, confrontation of witnesses, is basic to the American judicial system.

confusion, a mixing together of the goods of two or more persons, so that the several portions can no longer be distinguished, *e.g.*, fungible grain or cured tobacco.

conge' (*kôn zha*), leave; permission; license.

conge' d'accorder (*dà' cor dà*), leave to accord or agree.

conge' d'emparier (*dôm pår lā́*), leave to imparl or talk together with the opposite party.

congeable (*kô j 'ābl*), lawful; done with permission.

Congress, or **Congress of the United States,** the name of the legislative body of the United States, composed of the Senate and House of Representatives. U.S. Const. Art. I, Sec. 1, *et seq.*

conjoints, persons married to each other.

con'jugal rights, the rights arising from the relation of husband and wife.

conjuration, a compact made by persons combining by oath to do public harm. (2) The attempt to have conference with evil spirits.

conni'vance, guilty knowledge of, or assistance in, a crime. (2) Consent, express or implied, by one spouse to the adultery of the other.

consanguin'eus fra'ter (Rom.), a brother who has the same father.

consanguin'ity, or **kindred,** the connection or relationship of persons descended from some common ancestor. It is either lineal, as that of father and son, or collateral, as that of brothers or cousins.

consecutive sentence, see *cumulative sentence.*

consensus facit legem, consent makes the law, *i.e.,* the agreement of the parties is the law between them.

consensus, non concubitus, facit matrimonium, consent, not cohabitation, constitutes marriage.

consensus tollit errorem, consent removes, or obviates, mistake.

consent, willingness in fact that an act or an invasion of an interest (*q.v.*) shall take place. Restatement (Second) of Torts § 10A.

consent agreement, the meeting of minds. It presupposes mental capacity to act. It may be express, *i.e.,* by word of mouth or in writing, or implied from acts, inaction, or silence which are consistent only with assent. If obtained by fraud or duress, it is not binding.

consent decree, a judgment or order entered in a suit by consent of the parties; an agreed order or an agreed judgment.

consentientes et agentes pari poena plectantur, those consenting and those perpetrating are liable to equal punishment.

consequential damages, those losses or injuries which are a result of an act but are not direct and immediate. Consequential damages resulting from a seller's breach of contract include any loss resulting from general or particular requirements and needs of which the seller at the time of contracting had reason to know and which could not reasonably be prevented by cover or otherwise, and injury to person or property proximately resulting from any breach of warranty. U.C.C. § 2-715 (2).

conservator, a person who is appointed by a court to manage the estate of a protected person (*q.v.*) and includes a limited conservator. Uniform Probate Code §§1-201(6), 5-103(3).

conservatorship, a statutory creation that provides for a guardian in situations where a petitioner is physically infirm but not mentally incompetent.

conservators of the peace, officers appointed to preserve the public peace, *e.g.*, judges, sheriffs, and coroners.

consideration, the price, motive, or matter of inducement of a contract (*q.v.*), which must be lawful in itself. (2) The term is flexible and includes that which is bargained for and paid in return for a promise, the benefits to the party making the promise and the loss or detriment to the party to whom the promise is made. (3) A performance or a return promise which is bargained for. Restatement (Second) of Contracts § 71(1). (4) A contract derives its binding force from the existence of a valuable consideration between the parties. Consideration may be executed, *i.e.*, past or performed; executory, *i.e.*, to be performed; or continuing, *i.e.*, partly both. See also, *good consideration, meritorious consideration,* and *valuable consideration.*

considera'tum est per cu'riam, *l.*, it is considered by the court.

consign, to send goods to a factor or agent to sell. The person sending the goods is called the consignor, the person to whom they are sent, the consignee, and the goods themselves, the consignment.

consignee, see *consign.*

consignment, see *consign.*

consignor, see *consign.*

consilium, see *concilium.*

consistory court, an English ecclesiastical court.

consolidated fund, the English public revenue.

consolidation, the joining of several independent suits, which involve common questions of law or fact, for the purpose of a joint hearing or trial. (2) The fusing of many acts of a legislative body into one act.

consols (*kôn sŏl*), *fr.*, a consolidated fund for the payment of the public debt.

consor'tium, *l.*, marital fellowship, company, companionship. The duties and obligations which, by marriage, the husband and wife take upon themselves toward each other.

conspiracy, an unlawful combination or agreement between two or more persons to carry into effect a purpose hurtful to some individual, or class, or the public at large. (2) An inchoate offense, the essence of which is an agreement to commit an unlawful act. Traditionally the law has considered conspiracy and the completed substantive offense to be separate crimes. The conspiracy to commit an offense and the subsequent commission of the crime normally do not merge into a single punishable act. (3) With the purpose of promoting or facilitating the commission of a crime, (a) agreeing with another person or persons that they or one or more of them will engage in conduct which constitutes the crime or an attempt or solicitation to commit the crime, or (b) agreeing to aid such other person or persons in the planning or commission of the crime or of an attempt or solicitation to commit the crime. Model Penal Code § 5.03(1). (4) Frequently defined by various federal and state statutes. Cf. *Wharton's Rule.*

constables, officers appointed to keep the peace, serve writs, and levy executions.

constablewick, the jurisdiction of a constable.

constat, *l.* (it appears), a certificate of that which appears on the record.

constituent, a principal; one who appoints an agent or attorney. (2) A voter or member of an electorate.

constitution, the fundamental and basic law of a state or nation which establishes the form and limitations of government and secures the rights of the citizens. (2) The Constitution of the United States was adopted in a convention of representatives of the people, at Philadelphia, September 17, 1787, and became the law of the land on the first Wednesday in March, 1789. 1 Stat. 10 (1861). (3) Each of the states composing the United States has a constitution of its own.

constitutional, in accordance with the constitution. Laws which are unconstitutional, *i.e.*, which contravene the constitution, are null and void; they will not be enforced by the courts.

constitutional convention, an assembly or meeting held for the purpose of drafting and proposing a new or revised constitution.

constructio legis non facit injuriam, the construction of the law does, *i.e*, should be made to do, no injury.

construction, the interpretation of a statute or written instrument. See also, *legislative intent.*

constructive, implied by law though not actual in fact, *e.g.*, delivery, notice, and trust.

constructive annexation, doctrine that holds that certain objects, though in no way attached to a building, are to be regarded as so strongly connected with the building that they are fixtures (*i.e.*, keys, electronic garage door opener, etc.).

constructive eviction, the surrender of possession of premises by a tenant on justifiable grounds. (2) Some act which is done by a landlord with the intention and effect of depriving a tenant of the enjoyment of the premises, or a part of it, or obstructing or interfering with the enjoyment, to which the tenant submits by abandoning the premises.

constructive trust, a trust implied by law though not actual in fact against one who by actual or constructive fraud, by duress, or any other unconscionable conduct or questionable means, has obtained or holds the legal title to property which he is not equitably entitled to.

construe, to engage in construction (*q.v.*).

consuetudo debet esse certa, custom ought to be certain.

consuetudo est optimus interpres legum, custom is the best expounder of the laws.

consuetudo ex certa causa rationabili usitata privat communem legem, a custom founded on a certain and reasonable ground supersedes the common law.

consuetudo loci observanda est, the custom of the place is to be observed.

consul, an official appointed by a government to reside in a foreign country and there to look after the interests of the subjects of the country which appoints him, *e.g.*, by attending to commercial affairs, giving assistance or advice, or taking charge of the effects of a deceased citizen.

consular court, a court held by a consul within the territory of the nation to which he is accredited, pursuant to treaty authorization, for the trial of civil cases between the citizens of the country he represents.

Consumer Credit Protection Act, an act to safeguard the consumer in connection with the utilization of credit by requiring full disclosure of the terms and conditions of finance charges in credit transactions or in offers to extend credit; by restricting the garnishment of wages; and by creating the National Commission on Consumer Finance to study and make recommendations on the need for further regulation of the consumer finance industry; and for other purposes. 15 U.S.C. §§ 1601-1613, 1631-1641, 1661-1665, 1671-1677, 1681-168lt, 18 U.S.C. §§ 891-896. See also, *Fair Credit Billing Act, Fair Credit Reporting Act, Fair Debt Collection Practices Act,* and *Truth in Lending Act.*

consumer price index, CPI; an index measuring the change in the cost of the purchase of goods and services by a typical wage-earner. The cost is expressed as a percentage of these same goods and services in some base period. The concept is also known as the "cost of living."

Consumer Product Safety Act, an act to protect consumers against unreasonable risk of injury from hazardous products, and for other purposes. 5 U.S.C. §§ 5314, 5315, 15 U.S.C. §§ 2051 *et seq.*

Consumer Product Warranty Act, see *Magnuson-Moss Warranty—Federal Trade Commission Improvement Act.*

Consumer Protection Act, various state laws dealing with unfair, unconscionable, false, misleading, or deceptive actions or practices in the conduct of trade or commerce. Among other things, they tend to deal with contracts, combinations, and conspiracies in restraint of trade, provide for investigation and enforcement by the state attorney general, and for restoration of property.

consummation, the due completion of something.

contan'go, the interest in a bargain consisting of a sale of stock for cash and a repurchase of the same stock for resettlement two weeks ahead at the same price.

contemner (kŏn tĕm′ nĕr), or **contemnor,** one who has committed contempt (*q.v.*) of court.

contemporanea expositio est optima et fortissima in lege, a contemporaneous interpretation is the best and most authoritative in the eye of the law.

contempt, a wilful disregard or disobedience of public authority. Courts may punish one who disobeys the rules, orders, or process, or wilfully offends against the dignity and good order of the court, by fine or imprisonment. Similar authority is exercised by each house of the Congress of the United States, by state legislatures and in some instances by administrative agencies. The contempt power is usually subject to judicial review. See also, *purge.*

contentious jurisdiction, authority to hear and determine matters between adversaries in an action or other judicial proceeding.

contesta'tio li'tis, *l.,* (Rom), the statement of the plaintiff and answer or plea of the defendant, by which a case is brought before the judge. (2) The joinder of issue.

contest of will, or **will contest,** a proceeding instituted for the purpose of disputing whether a particular paper is a valid will and divesting named legatees and devisees of rights thereunder.

context, those parts of a writing which precede and follow a phrase or passage in question, and which may be looked at to explain the meaning of the phrase or passage.

contiguous, a flexible term. (1) Actual contact or touching, as contiguous lands. (2) Close.

contingency, an unforeseeable but possible event; a fortuity.

contingency with a double aspect, a fortuity which arises when two events are expressly named, or evidently implied, upon the happening of either of which an estate will vest.

contingent, conditional; doubtful; dependent upon the happening of an uncertain event, *e.g.*, a contingent estate (*q.v.*).

contingent estate, a right in property which depends for its effect upon an event which may or may not happen.

contingent fee, a frequent form of employment by which an attorney is engaged to represent a plaintiff in an adversary proceeding for compensation in an amount equal to a specified percentage of the amount recovered by the attorney for his client, *e.g.*, 25% or 33⅓%.

contingent legacy, a legacy contingent upon the happening of an event or one that is vested but not paid until an event occurs.

contingent liabilities, potentialities which may become liabilities as a result of conditions undetermined at a given date, such as pending law suits, judgments under appeal, and unsettled disputed claims.

contingent remainder, an expectant right in property limited to an uncertain person or upon an uncertain event, by which no present interest passes. See also, *remainder.*

continuance, the adjournment of a cause from one day to another in the same or a subsequent term.

continuan'do, formerly, to lay the action with a continuando, was to allege that the defendant's trespass was a continuing one.

continuing guaranty, see *guaranty.*

continuing offer, a proposal to do something which remains open for a specified period of time or until it is either withdrawn by the offeror or accepted by the offeree.

contra, *l.,* against; contrary to.

contra bonos mores, against good morals.

con'tra for'mam collatio'nis, against the form of the gift.

con'tra for'mam statu'ti, contrary to the form of the statute.

contra non valentum apre nulla currit praescriptio, no prescription runs against a person under disability.

con'tra pa'cem, against the peace.

con'tra proferen'tem, against the one putting it forth.

contraband, goods exported or imported in violation of law. (2) Goods the possession of which constitutes a violation of law. (3) In international law, those goods which a neutral may not carry to a belligerent, *e.g.,* munitions of war.

contract, an agreement between competent parties, upon a legal consideration, to do or to abstain from doing some act. It is usually applied to simple or parol (*q.v.*) contracts, including written as well as verbal ones. Contracts may be express, in which the terms are stated in words; or implied, *i.e.,* presumed by law to have been made from the circumstances and the relations of the parties; mutual and dependent, in which the performance by one is dependent upon the performance by the other; independent, when either promise may be performed without reference to the other; entire, in which the complete performance by one is a condition precedent to demanding performance of the other; severable, in which the things to be performed are capable of separation, so that on performance of part the party performing may demand a proportionate part of the consideration from the other; executed, in which the things each agrees to perform are done at the time the contract is made; executory, in which some act remains to be done by one or both of the parties; personal, *i.e.*, depending on the skill or qualities of one of the parties; contracts of beneficence, by which only one of the contracting parties is to be benefited, *e.g.*, loans and deposits. (2) The total legal obligation which results from the parties' agreement as affected by the U.C.C. and any other applicable rules of law. U.C.C. § 1-201 (11). (3) A promise or a set of promises for the breach of which the law gives a remedy, or the performance of which the law in some way recognizes as a duty. Restatement (Second) of Contracts. § 1. See also, *adhesion contract, agreement,* and *consideration.*

contract for deed, a contract for the sale of land that provides for a down payment, with the balance of the purchase price payable in monthly installments. The buyer receives his deed when all the installments have been paid or when the unpaid balance of the purchase price has been reduced to a certain agreed figure, whereupon the buyer is to receive a deed and give the seller a purchase money mortgage for the balance of the purchase price.

contracts of record, a lien, release, satisfaction, accord, documentation relating to judgments and documentation relating to bail and bond.

contracts under seal, promissory notes, mortgages, or other documentation which is left with a lasting impression of some sort such as a legal ring seal imprinted with wax, a signature or a corporate seal or impression made on paper.

contractus ex turpi causa, vel contra bonos mores, nullus est, a contract arising out of a base consideration, or against morality, is null.

contrariorum contraria est ratio, the reason of contrary things is contrary.

contravention, an act done in violation of a legal obligation.

contribution, the payment by each of two or more persons, *e.g.*, sureties who are jointly liable, of their respective shares of the liability. (2) The satisfaction by a devisee or legatee of his share of the debts or liabilities imposed by the will of the testator, or by law, upon the estate devised or bequeathed to him. (3) In maritime law, average contribution is the amount to be contributed by each person toward making good a loss at sea. It is proportioned to the value of goods he may have shipped. See also, *average*.

contributio'ne facien'da, *l.*, formerly a writ to compel contribution among tenants in common.

contributory, a person liable to contribute to the assets of a joint stock company in the event of the same being wound up.

contributory negligence, the failure to exercise care by a plaintiff, which contributed to the plaintiff's injury. Even though a defendant may have been negligent, in a minority of jurisdictions, contributory negligence will bar a recovery by the plaintiff. (2) Conduct on the part of a plaintiff which falls below the standard to which he should conform for his own protection, and which is a legally contributing cause co-operating with the negligence of the defendant in bringing about the plaintiff's harm. Restatement (Second) of Torts § 463. Cf. *comparative negligence.*

Controlled Materials Law, an act to provide for the acquiring of stocks of strategic and critical materials essential in times of national emergency and to encourage the further development of such materials within the United States. 50 U.S.C. §§ 98 *et seq.*

controlled substance, various drugs or other substances classified into Schedules I, II, III, IV, and V according to their potential for abuse, currently accepted medical use in treatment in the U.S., accepted safety for use of the drug or other substance, and consequences of its abuse. 21 U.S.C. § 812. Analogous provisions have been enacted by 33 states.

controller, see *comptroller.*

controversy, see *cases and controversies.*

contumacy, a refusal to appear in court when legally summoned; disobedience to the rules and orders of a court.

con'usance, see *cognizance.*

con'usant (zănt), knowing, or aware of.

conven'tio in u'num, *l.*, agreement between two parties upon the sense of the contract proposed.

conventio vincit legem, an agreement prevails against any implication of law.

convention, a coming together; an assembly of delegates for the purpose of framing or amending a constitution, making a political platform and nominating candidates, or any other purpose, except legislation, for which a representative body may be called. (2) An agreement with a foreign nation, *e.g.*, as to the extradition of fugitive offenders.

conventional estate, a right in property which is created by the express acts of the parties, in contradistinction to one which is legal and arises by operation of law.

conversion, a flexible term. (1) The wrongful appropriation of the goods of another. See also, *trover*. (2) An intentional exercise of dominion or control over a chattel which so seriously interferes with the right of another to control it that the actor (*q.v.*) may justly be required to pay the other the full value of the chattel. Restatement (Second) of Torts § 22A(1). (3) Equitable conversion is the changing of the nature of property, which may be (a) actual, *e.g.*, by converting land into money by selling it, or vice versa; or (b) constructive, where such an operation is assumed to have, though it has not actually, taken place, *e.g.*, when an owner has agreed to sell land, and dies before executing the conveyance, the executors are entitled to the money, and not the heirs. Property constructively converted assumes the same qualities as if the operation had been actually carried out.

conveyance, the transfer of the title to property from one person to another. (2) The instrument for affecting such transfer. (3) Every assignment, lease, mortgage, or encumbrance. Uniform Partnership Act § 2.

conveyancer, a person who prepares an instrument to effect a transfer of title to property.

conveyancing, the portion of the practice of law which involves the transfer and alienation of property by means of appropriate instruments. It also includes the examination of titles and the preparation of abstracts of title.

convict, the act of proving a person to be, or finding him to be, guilty of a crime or misdemeanor. (2) A person found guilty of a crime or misdemeanor. (3) Often applied to persons who are sentenced to imprisonment or death.

convoy, warships which accompany merchant ships to protect them from the enemy.

cooperative, apartment ownership similar to a condominium in which the buyer receives shares of stock in the building corporation and a lease or assignment of the seller's lease of the apartment being sold.

copar'cenary, a right in property which arises when an inheritable estate descends from the ancestor to several persons possessing an equal title to it, *e.g.*, to children generally. Such persons are called coparceners or parceners.

Copeland Act, an act to prohibit the movement in interstate commerce of adulterated and misbranded food, drugs, devices, and cosmetics. 21 U.S.C. §§ 301-392.

copies, in the copyright (*q.v.*) law, material objects, other than phonorecords, in which a work is fixed by any method now known or later developed, and from which the work can be perceived, reproduced, or otherwise communicated, either directly or with the aid of a machine or device. The term includes the material object, other than a phonorecord, in which the work is first fixed. 17 U.S.C. § 101. See also, *copy.*

copulatio verborum indicat acceptationem in eodem sensu, the coupling of words together indicates that they are to be understood in the same sense.

copy, a transcript of an original document. See also, *attested copy, certified copy,* and *copies.*

copyhold, in English law, a base tenure founded upon immemorial custom; held by copy of the court rolls.

copyright, subject to various limitations provided for by law, the exclusive rights to do and to authorize any of the following: (a) to reproduce the copyrighted work in copies or phonorecords; (b) to prepare derivative works based upon the copyrighted work; (c) to distribute copies or phonorecords of the copyrighted work to the public by sale or other transfer of ownership, or by rental, lease, or lending; (d) in the case of literary, musical, dramatic, and choreographic works, pantomimes, and motion pictures and other audiovisual works, to perform the copyrighted work publicly; and (e) in the case of literary, musical, dramatic, and choreographic works, pantomimes, and pictorial, graphic, or sculptural works, including the individual images of a motion picture or other audiovisual work, to display the copyrighted work publicly. 17 U.S.C. § 106. Generally treated in tit. 17 U.S.C. See also, *fair use.*

co'ram, *l.,* before; in the presence of.

co'ram no'bis, before us; formerly a manner of appeal; applied to writs of error.

co'ram non ju'dice, before one not the (proper) judge; applied to the acts of a court which has no jurisdiction over the person, the subject matter or the process. Such acts are wholly void.

co'ram pa'ribus, before his peers.

co'ram vo'bis' before you; a writ of error directed to the court which tried the cause; to correct an error in fact.

corespondent, or **co-respondent,** a party who is accused of having committed adultery with the accuser's spouse. Sometimes such a person is named as a party to a divorce suit.

coronato're eligen'do, or **exoneran'do,** *l.,* formerly writs issued to the sheriff commanding him to elect or remove a coroner.

coroner, an official possessing judicial and ministerial authority. In the former capacity, his chief duty is to hold inquests (*q.v.*). In the latter, he acts as the sheriff's substitute when there is a vacancy in the office of sheriff or when the sheriff is incapacitated by interest or otherwise.

coroner's jury, a group of citizens summoned for the purpose of holding an inquest (*q.v.*).

corporate domicile, the state of incorporation of a corporation.

corporate opportunity doctrine, if an officer or director of a corporation acquires information concerning an investment or other business opportunity which is within the corporation's line of business, the officer or director cannot appropriate the opportunity for his or her individual gain; instead, the corporation must be allowed to acquire and develop the opportunity, at least if it would be advantageous to the corporation and the corporation is financially able to exploit it.

corporation, an artificial person composed of individuals. It usually has a corporate name and perpetual duration. Sometimes its duration is a fixed term of years. It substitutes for the individuals who compose it. See also, *municipal corporation* and *professional service corporation.*

corporation by estoppel, a corporation by estoppel exists where parties, by their agreements or conduct, estop themselves from denying the existence of the corporation.

corporation de facto, a corporation de facto exists where there has been a colorable attempt to incorporate under the laws of the governing state, although compliance sufficient to form a de jure corporation is lacking, and the organization has functioned as a corporation; such a corporation will be treated as a legal entity separate from its incorporators and shareholders insofar as personal liability for its obligations is concerned.

corporation de jure, a corporation formed in full compliance with the laws of its governing state; it exists as a legal person for all purposes and its incorporators and shareholders will not be subject to personal liability for its obligations.

corpo'real, having a body; material; tangible.

corpo'real heredit'aments, such rights in real property as are tangible and capable of being inherited, *e.g.,* houses and lands. Cf. *incorporeal hereditaments.*

cor'pus, *l.,* body; the person; the whole.

corpus comita'tus, the whole county.

corpus delic'ti, the body of the offense; the proof that a crime has been committed.

corpus humanum non recipit aestimationem, a human body is not susceptible of appraisement.

corpus ju'ris civi'lis, the body of the civil law; the Institutes, Pandects, Code and Novels of Justinian.

correction, punishment.

corroborative evidence, additional testimony to reinforce a point which was previously the subject of proof.

Corrupt Practices Act, see *Foreign Corrupt Practices Act of 1977.*

corruption, a flexible term for gross dishonesty or illegality; sometimes applied to influencing a judge, juror, or public officer to do wrong or to disregard his duty.

corruption of blood, see *attainder.*

cosening (*kusĕnĭng*), or **cozening,** cheating.

cosinage, or **cousinage,** consanguinity.

cost accounting, a method of accounting which provides for the gathering and recording of all the elements of costs incurred to accomplish a purpose, to carry on an activity or operation, and/or to complete a unit of work or a specific job.

cost plus contract, an agreement providing for the payment of actual material and labor costs, plus a fixed percentage of such costs.

costs, the official fees incurred by the parties in the prosecution and defense of an action at law. In some cases attorney's fees are taxed, *i.e.,* charged, against the losing party or the fund which is the subject of litigation, by statutory authority.

co-surety, or **cosurety,** a fellow-surety.

cotenancy, an undivided right to possession by one or more persons but without the right of survivorship. See also, *tenancy in common.*

cotland, formerly land held by a cottager.

couchant (*kōō*), lying down.

council, the legislative body of a municipal corporation. Its acts are usually termed ordinances (*q.v.*).

Council on Environmental Quality, a part of the Executive Office of the President consisting of three members appointed by the President to serve at his pleasure, by and with the advice and consent of the Senate. One of its principal functions is to assist and advise the President in the preparation of an annual environmental quality report to

Congress. 42 U.S.C. § § 4341-4347. Established by National Environmental Policy Act of 1969 (*q.v.*).

counsel, a person who gives legal advice; an attorney-at-law. Often used as a collective noun applied to all attorneys who are united in the management of a cause or in advising with reference to a particular matter.

counselor-at-law, an attorney-at-law (*q.v.*).

count, the statement of a cause of action (*q.v.*). A complaint has as many counts as there are causes of action, or different statements of the same cause of action. (2) In criminal law, each part of an indictment which charges a distinct offense. See also, *common counts.*

counter, contrary; opposed to.

counter affidavit, a sworn statement in writing made in opposition to another already made.

counter bond, a bond (*q.v.*) given to indemnify a surety for signing one's bond.

counter deed, a secret writing which invalidates or alters another.

counterclaim, the defendant's claim against the plaintiff, which most courts permit him to set up in his response to the complaint.

counterfeit, an imitation made without lawful authority and with a view to defraud.

countermand, to revoke or recall.

counter-offer, an offer (*q.v.*) made by an offeree to his offeror relating to the same matter as the original offer, and proposing a substituted bargain (*q.v.*) differing from that proposed by the original offer. Restatement (Second) of Contracts § 39(1).

counterpart, the corresponding part or duplicate. Where an instrument, *e.g.,* a contract, is executed by the parties in several copies, one of them is the original and the others are counterparts. (2) The key of a cipher.

counter-security, or **countersecurity,** a security given to one who has entered into a bond or become surety for another.

countersign, the signature of a secretary, agent, or other officer to a writing in order to vouch for the authenticity of it. (2) An identification signal, *e.g.,* a spoken word.

countor, formerly an English sergeant-at-law (*q.v.*); an advocate.

county, a civil division of a state for judicial, administrative, and political purposes.

county commissioners, officers entrusted with the governmental and quasi-governmental affairs of a county.

county court, a flexible term, often a tribunal with limited jurisdiction. Usually defined by various state constitutions and statutes.

county rate, a tax levied on real property or the occupiers of lands for local purposes.

coupled with an interest, descriptive of the power of an agent to perform under a contract of agency, which continues despite the death of the principal or attempted revocation of the contract, *i.e.*, where the agency power is related to an interest in the subject of the agency which the agent acquires with the power.

cour de cassation (*koor du kås så si ôn'*), *fr.*, the highest court of appeal in France.

course of dealing, a sequence of previous conduct between the parties to a particular transaction, which is fairly to be regarded as establishing a common basis of understanding for interpreting their expressions and other conduct. U.C.C. § 1-205(1). Accord, Restatement (Second) of Contracts § 223(1).

course of employment, a flexible term for the performance by an employee of his contract of employment, applied in questions of agency and worker's compensation.

courses and distances, a boundary description of land, established by a survey, in which magnetic or true compass readings and exact measurements from fixed landmarks are recorded. See also, *metes and bounds.*

court, an institution for the resolving of disputes. (2) A place where justice is administered. (3) The judge or judges when performing their official duties. (4) Courts may be classified as courts of record, *i.e.*, those in which a final record of the proceedings is made, which imports verity and cannot be collaterally impeached, and courts not of record, *i.e.*, those in which no final record is made, though it may keep a docket and enter in it notes of the various proceedings; courts of original jurisdiction, in which suits are initiated, and which have power to hear and determine causes in the first instance, and appellate courts, which take cognizance of causes removed from other courts; courts of equity or chancery, which administer justice according to the principles of equity, and courts of law, which administer justice according to the principles of the common law; civil courts which give remedies for private wrongs; criminal courts, in which public offenders are tried, acquitted or convicted and sentenced; ecclesiastical courts, which formerly had jurisdiction over testamentary, and matrimonial causes; courts of admiralty, which have jurisdiction over maritime causes, civil and criminal; courts-martial, which have jurisdiction of offenses against the military or naval laws, committed by persons in that service. In numerous instances, the various classifications of courts have been consolidated. The same court may serve as a court of equity, a court of law, a civil court, a criminal court, and a court of admiralty. It may qualify as a court of record and be a court of original jurisdiction.

Court-Baron, an English court which, although not one of record, is incident to every manor, and may be held at anyplace within the same, on giving due notice.

Court for Crown Cases Reserved, formerly an English court for the decision of points of law arising in criminal trials which were reserved by the judge or justices.

Court for Divorce and Matrimonial Causes, formerly an English court established to take exclusive jurisdiction over such causes.

Court-Leet, an English court of record, sometimes held once a year for the purpose of hearing charges of petty offenses.

Court-Martial, see *court*.

court not of record, see *court*.

court of admiralty, see *court*.

Court of Ancient Demesne, a court formerly held by a bailiff appointed by the English king.

Court of Appeals, the highest court of New York, Maryland, Virginia, and prior to 1976, Kentucky. (2) An intermediate appellate court in many states. (3) A division of the *English Supreme Court of Judicature* (*q.v.*) is known as the Court of Appeal.

Court of Appeals, United States, see *United States Court of Appeals*.

Court of Chancery, see *court*.

Court of Claims, a United States court established for the purpose, among other things, of hearing and determining claims against the United States founded upon Acts of Congress, upon any regulation of an executive department, upon any contract, express or implied, with the government of the United States, and all set-offs, counterclaims, and demands on the part of the government against any person making claim against the government in that court.

Court of Commerce, see *Commerce Court*.

Court of Common Pleas, formerly one of the three English Superior Courts of Common Law. Its seat was fixed at Westminster by virtue of the 11th clause of the Magna Charta. It derived its name from the fact that the causes of the common people were heard there. By the Judicature Act of 1873, it was made a division of the High Court of Justice (*q.v.*). (2) In some states of the United States, the name of a court of original and general jurisdiction.

Court of Equity, see *court*.

Court of Exchequer, formerly an English superior court of record which had jurisdiction of revenue cases, and later took jurisdiction of all actions between private persons, except real actions. By the Judicature Act, 1873, it was made the Exchequer Division of the High Court of Justice, and by order in council it was, in 1881, merged in the Queen's Bench Division.

Court of Exchequer Chamber, formerly an English court for the correction and prevention of errors of law in the three superior common law courts. It consisted of the judges of two of the courts sitting together to decide questions appealed from the other. Questions of unusual difficulty and importance were reserved for the decision of the full court, consisting of all the judges of the three courts, and sometimes the Lord Chancellor. By the Judicature Act, 1873, this court was abolished, and its jurisdiction transferred to the Court of Appeal.

court of first instance, see *first instance, court of.*

Court of King's or Queen's Bench, formerly the supreme court of common law in England. Its jurisdiction was formerly confined to the trials of crimes and misdemeanors which amounted to a breach of the peace, and trespasses committed vi et armis (*q.v.*), but was gradually extended to all actions of case, actions where fraud was alleged, and finally to all personal actions and the action of ejectment. Its chief judge was, and is still, called the Lord Chief Justice of England, and there were four judges. By the Judicature Act, 1873, it became a division of the High Court of Justice (*q.v.*).

court of last resort, see *resort, court of last.*

court of law, see *court.*

Court of Ordinary, a tribunal having jurisdiction of the probate of wills and the regulation of the management of decedent's estates.

court of original jurisdiction, see *court.*

Court of Orphans, an English tribunal having charge of orphans whose parents died in London and were free of the city.

Court of Oyer and Terminer, courts of criminal jurisdiction in several states. See also, *oyer and terminer.*

Court of Passage, an English tribunal with jurisdiction over causes of action arising within the borough of Liverpool; and also in admiralty matters.

Court of Pie Powder, Py-Powder, Pipowder, Pie Poudre, or Pied Poudre, formerly a commercial court.

Court of Probate, the Probate, Divorce, and Admiralty Division of the English High Court of Justice (*q.v.*). See also, *probate court.*

Court of Queen's Bench, see *Court of King's Bench.*

Court of Record, see *court.*

Court of Session, the supreme civil court of Scotland.

Court of the Star Chamber, see *Camera Stellata.*

court reporter, see *reporter (1).*

Courts, Christian, ecclesiastical courts.

courts of assize and nisi prius (*nē′sē prē′ŭs*), English courts composed of two or more judges of assize, sent twice a year to the various circuits to try by a jury of the respective counties such matters of fact as were then under dispute.

Courts of Conscience, see *Courts of Request.*

Courts of Request, or **courts of conscience,** formerly English courts for the recovery of debts not exceeding forty shillings. In 1846 they were abolished and their jurisdiction was transferred to the county courts.

Courts of Survey, English tribunals that hear appeals from orders for the detention of ships.

cousinage, see *cosinage.*

cousin german, a first cousin, or child of one's uncle or aunt.

covenant, an agreement or unilateral contract such as is contained in a deed. See also, *agreement* and *contract.* The principal covenants in a deed conveying land are seisin, right to convey, for quiet enjoyment, against encumbrances, and for further assurances. A covenant is said to run with the land (or the reversion) when the benefit or burden of it passes to the assignee of the land. See also, *title.* (2) Formerly one of the forms of action.

coverture, the situation or condition of a woman during her marriage.

covin, fraud, collusion.

cozening, see *cosening.*

credit bureau, see *commercial agency.*

creditor, a person who gives credit, opposite of debtor; a person who has a claim against another, based on contract. The term includes a general creditor, a secured creditor, a lien creditor and any representative of creditors, including an assignee for the benefit of creditors, a trustee in bankruptcy, a receiver in equity and an executor or administrator of an insolvent debtor's or assignor's estate. U.C.C. § 1-201 (1) (12). See also, *secured creditor* and *secured party.*

creditors' bill, an extraordinary proceeding by one or more creditors, which seeks court assistance in reaching, and subjecting to the payment of their debts, such assets and rights of the debtor as cannot be the subject of the usual execution, levy, and sale.

cretio (Rom.), the period within which an heir must formally declare his intention to accept an inheritance.

crim. con., see *criminal conversation.*

crime, a flexible term for violations of law which are punished by the state or nation because of their effect on the public. See also, *felony* and *misdemeanor.*

crimen, *l.,* a crime.

crimen falsi (Rom.), a flexible term for forgery, perjury, counterfeiting, alteration of instruments, and other frauds.

crimen lae'sae majesta'tis (Rom.), treason.

crimen omnia ex se nata vitiat, crime vitiates all that springs from it.

crimen repetunda'rum (Rom.), bribery.

crime of omission, a crime which takes the form of a failure to perform a required action, rather than the doing of a prohibited act.

criminal, a person who is guilty of committing a crime. (2) Involving an offense against law; relating to crime.

criminal attempt, acting with the kind of culpability otherwise required for commission of the crime, if the person acting (a) purposely engages in conduct which would constitute the crime if the attendant circumstances were as he believes them to be; or (b) when causing a particular result is an element of the crime, does or omits to do anything with the purpose of causing or with the belief that it will cause such result without further conduct on his part; or (c) purposely does or omits to do anything which, under the circumstances as he believes them to be, is an act or omission constituting a substantial step in a course of conduct planned to culminate in his commission of the crime. Model Penal Code § 5.01(1).

criminal coercion, threatening with purpose unlawfully to restrict another's freedom of action to his detriment, to commit any criminal offense, or accuse anyone of a criminal offense, or expose any secret tending to subject any person to hatred, contempt, or ridicule, or to impair his credit or business repute, or take or withhold action as an official, or cause an official to take or withhold action. Model Penal Code § 212.5.

criminal conspiracy, see *conspiracy.*

criminal conversation, or **crim. con.,** unlawful intercourse with a married person; adultery.

criminal court, see *court.*

criminal homicide, purposely, knowingly, recklessly, or negligently causing the death of another human being; *i.e.,* murder, manslaughter, or negligent homicide. Model Penal Code § 210.1.

criminal information, a proceeding brought against a person accused of a crime, by a public prosecutor, without a previous indictment or presentment to the grand jury.

criminal law, jurisprudence concerning crimes and their punishment.

criminal letters (Sc.), a form of criminal process, similar to a summons in a civil action.

criminal mischief, damaging tangible property of another purposely, recklessly, or by negligence in the employment of fire, explosives, flood, avalanche, collapse of building, release of poison gas, radioactive material, or other harmful or destructive force or substance, or by any other means of causing potentially widespread injury or damage. (2) Purposely or recklessly tampering with tangible property of another so as to endanger person or property. (3) Purposely or recklessly causing another to suffer pecuniary loss by deception or threat. Model Penal Code § 220.3(1).

criminal proceedings, any proceeding in which a government seeks to prosecute a person for an offense and to impose upon him a penalty of a criminal character. Restatement (Second) of Torts § 654(1).

criminal solicitation, commanding, encouraging, or requesting another person to engage in specific conduct which would constitute a crime or an attempt to commit the crime, or which would establish his complicity in its commission or attempted commission, with the purpose of promoting or facilitating its commission. Model Penal Code § 5.02(1).

criminal trespass, see *trespass (4).*

criminology, the interdisciplinary and interprofessional study of the cause, prevention, and correction of criminal behavior. It is often a part of studies in sociology, law, or medicine.

criteria pollutants, air pollutants which the EPA has determined endanger the public health or welfare *and* which result from numerous and adverse sources. EPA must establish national primary and secondary ambient air quality standards for each such pollutant. In conjunction with the establishment of these standards, EPA must also issue air quality criteria for each of these pollutants which reflect the latest scientific knowledge regarding their impact on the health and welfare of the public.

cross-action, cross complaint, or **cross demand,** the responsive allegation by a defendant of a claim against a plaintiff, who has initiated a lawsuit against the defendant. Often called a counterclaim (*q.v.*) and often used interchangeably with cross-claim (*q.v.*).

cross-bill, in equity practice, a response by a defendant against a plaintiff, or against other defendants in the same suit, or against both, analogous to a counterclaim (*q.v.*) or a cross-claim (*q.v.*).

cross-claim, the claim by a party to a lawsuit against a coparty, which arises out of the transaction or occurrence that is the subject matter of the original action or of a counterclaim in the original action, or relating to property that is the subject matter of the original action. Fed. R. Civ. P. 13(g).

cross-examination, the questioning of a witness by the party opposed to the party which called the witness for direct examination. This usually occurs after the direct examination but on occasion may be otherwise allowed. The form of the questions on cross-examination is designed for the purpose of eliciting evidence from a hostile witness. (2) Cross-examination should be limited to the subject matter of the direct examination and matters affecting the credibility of the witness. The court may, in the exercise of discretion, permit inquiry into additional matters as if on direct examination. Fed. R. Evid. 611(b).

Crown, The, the English sovereign, *i.e.*, King or Queen. (2) Relating to or connected with the sovereign.

crown law, English criminal law, the Crown being the prosecuting party.

cruelty, in family law, acts which imperil the life, health, or physical comfort of a husband or wife. Often defined by state statute when it is a ground for divorce. (2) Cruelty to animals, *i.e.*, abuse or mistreatment, is an indictable offense by the laws of many states.

cui licet quod majus non debet quod minus est non licere, he who has authority to do the more important ought not to be prohibited from doing that which is less important.

cui pater est populus non habet ille patrem, he to whom the people is a father has no father.

cuicunque aliquis quid concedit, concedere videtur et id, sine quo res ipsa esse non potuit, whoever grants anything to another is supposed to grant that also without which the thing itself would be of no use. See *e.g.*, *way of necessity*.

cuilibet in arte sua perito est credendum, every skilled person is to be believed with reference to his own art.

cujus est commodum ejus debet esse incommodum, he who has the advantage should also bear the disadvantage.

cujus est divisio alterius est electio, when one party has the division, the other has the choice.

cujus est instituere ejus est abrogare, he that legislates may also abrogate.

cujus est solum ejus est usque ad coelum, *l.,* formerly, he who owns the soil owns it to the sky.

cujus est solum ejus est usque ad coelum et ad inferos, formerly, he who owns the soil owns it to the sky and to the center of the earth.

cul de sac, a dead end street. Sometimes, a circular area at the end of a street with no outlet, which is large enough for a vehicle to turn around in.

culpa (Rom.), fault; neglect.

culpa lato dolo aequiparatur, gross negligence is held equivalent to intentional wrong.

culpa tenet suos auctores, a fault binds its own authors.

culpable, variously, censurable, blamable, blameworthy, deserving punishment, criminal.

culpae poena par esto, let the punishment be proportioned to the crime.

cum, *l.,* with. .

cum confitente sponte mitius est agendum, one confessing willingly should be dealt with more leniently.

cum duo inter se pugnantia reperintur in testamento ultimum ratum est, where two things repugnant to each other are found in a will, the last prevails.

cum o'nere, with the burden; subject to the incumbrance, *i.e.,* a purchaser of land with knowledge of an incumbrance takes it cum onere.

cum testamen'to annex'o, with the will annexed. See also, *administration.*

cumulative, additional, increased, made larger.

cumulative evidence, testimony that is offered to prove what has already been proven by other evidence.

cumulative sentence, or **consecutive sentence,** an additional judgment given against one who has been convicted, to take effect after the execution of the first has expired.

cumulative voting, a shareholder is entitled to a total number of votes determined by multiplying the votes to which he is entitled by virtue of the shares he owns by the number of directors to be elected. At the meeting at which the directors are to be elected, he may then cast the total number of votes so determined for one candidate or may allocate them on any basis he desires between or among two or more candidates.

cur. adv. vult, see *curia advisare vult.*

curative act, a law passed by a legislature, which is intended to correct irregularities in a law which it previously passed.

curator, a fiduciary (*q.v.*) who performs the duties of a guardian (*q.v.*). He may perform such duties for: (a) a minor; (b) a person who is mentally incompetent; (c) property ad interim, called curator bonis; or (d) by conducting a suit for a minor, called curator ad litem.

cu'ria, *l.,* the court.

cu'ria advisa're vult, the court wishes to consider the matter; an entry reserving judgment until some subsequent day.

cu'ria re'gis, the king's court. Applied especially to the aula regis (*q.v.*).

current account, see *account (2)(a)* and *open account.*

currit tempus contra desides et sui juris contemptores, time runs against the slothful and those who neglect their right.

curtesy, the estate which a husband has in his wife's fee simple or fee tail estates, general or special, after her death. In many jurisdictions, the extent and nature of this right are modified and defined by various statutes. Under the common law, the husband had an estate for his life. Three things were necessary to this estate: A legal marriage, seisin of the wife, and birth of issue capable of inheriting, alive and during the mother's life.

curtilage, a yard, piece of ground, or garden which adjoins a dwelling house. (2) The land immediately surrounding and associated with the home.

custo'dia le'gis, or in custodia legis, *l.,* in the custody of the law.

custody, care; in criminal law, detention.

custom, unwritten law established by long usage.

customary freehold, is one held by privilege of frank tenure, *i.e.,* by custom, and not by the will of the lord, wherein it differs from copyholds. Otherwise, it resembles them.

custom-house, the office where goods are entered for import or export, and customs (*q.v.*) are paid.

custom-house broker, a person who is authorized to act for others in the entry or clearance of ships and the transaction of general business.

custom of merchants, see *law merchant.*

customs, taxes levied on merchandise which is imported or exported.

cus'tos rotulo'rum (the keeper of the rolls or records), the principal justice of the peace within an English county.

cy-pres (*sē prā'*), *fr.,* (as near as), a flexible principle or doctrine concerning wills which express both a general intention and a particular method of accomplishing that intention. If the general intention is found to exist, but it is impossible to accomplish via the particular method specified in the will, the courts may give effect to the general intention via another method that closely approximates the one specified.

D

damage, an injury to person, property, or reputation, occasioned by the wrongful act or negligence of another, or by accident. It may occur as a result of tort or breach of contract.

damage feasant, or **faisant** (doing damage), the act of animals going upon land, feeding, tramping down grass, and injuring growing crops.

damages, a flexible term for the reparation in money which is allowed by law on account of damage (*q.v.*). Accord, Restatement (Second) of Torts § 12A. These may be general, such as necessarily and by implication of law arise from the act complained of; special, such as under the peculiar circumstances of the case arise from the act complained of, but are not implied by law; compensatory, sufficient in amount to cover the loss actually sustained; exemplary, punitive, or vindictive, when in excess of the loss sustained and allowed as a punishment for torts committed with fraud, actual malice, or violence nominal, when the act was wrong, but the loss sustained was trifling; substantial, when the loss was serious. Accord, Restatement (Second) of Torts §§ 902-908. See also, *hedonic damages, liquidated damages*

dame, the legal title of the wife of an English knight or baronet.

damnum absque injuria, *l.*, loss or damage for which there is no legal remedy.

dangerous instrumentality, devices which are designed to do harm, *e.g.*, firearms, but does not include devices such as automobiles which become dangerous only when operated negligently.

dans et retinens nihil dat, giving and retaining [possession] gives nothing.

darrein (där ān´), last.

date, from *l.*, datum, given. The designation of the time when an instrument was executed.

day, the space of time which elapses between two successive midnights. (2) That portion of such time during which the sun is shining. Often time is computed in days for legal purposes, but fractions of days, *i.e.*, hours and minutes, become material in some cases, *e.g.*, priorities in filing liens. See also, *time* and *Uniform Time Act of 1966.*

day in court, the right of a person to appear in court and be heard concerning his complaint or his defense.

days of grace, see *grace, days of.*

daysman, an arbitrator; an elected judge.

d.b.a., "doing business as."

de, *l.,* of; for; about; concerning; from; out of.

de an'nuo re'ditu, formerly, a writ to recover an annuity.

de ave'riis replegian'dis, formerly, a writ to replevy cattle.

de be'ne es'se, a technical phrase applied to a thing done provisionally and out of due course, *e.g.,* evidence taken in advance of a trial, where there is danger that it may be lost owing to the age, infirmity, or intended absence of the witness.

de bonis asporta'tis, formerly, an action in trespass for the unlawful taking of personal property.

de bo'nis non, see *administration.*

de bo'nis pro'priis, a judgment against an administrator or executor to be satisfied out of his own property.

de di'e in di'em, from day to day, continuously.

de do'te un'de ni'hil ha'bet, formerly, a writ for a widow when no part of her dower had been assigned to her.

de estove'riis haben'dis, formerly, a writ for a woman divorced a mensa et thoro, to recover her alimony.

de fac'to, in fact; actually.

de facto corporation, see *corporation de facto.*

de ho'mine replegian'de, formerly, a writ to take a man out of prison or out of the custody of a private person.

de inju'ria, the replication by which the plaintiff in an action of tort denies the sufficiency of the excuse or justification set up by the defendant.

de jure, by right; lawful.

de jure corporation, see *corporation de jure.*

de jure judices, de facto juratores, respondent, the judges answer concerning the law, the jury concerning the facts.

de luna'tico inquiren'do, formerly, a writ for ascertaining whether a party charged is a lunatic.

de majore et minore non varlant jura, concerning the greater and the lesser, laws do not vary.

de manucaptia're, formerly, a writ commanding the sheriff to take sureties for a prisoner's appearance and to set him free.

de medieta'te lin'guae, see *medietatis linguae.*

de melio'ribus dam'nis, the liberty granted to a plaintiff, who has sued several defendants and had damages assessed severally against each, of electing which he will take.

de minimus non curat lex, the law does not concern itself with trivial matters.

de non apparentibus et non existentibus eadem est ratio, concerning things which do not appear, the law is the same as concerning things which do not exist.

de no'vo, anew; afresh. A trial de novo is a trial which is held for a second time, as if there had been no former decision.

de o'dio et a tia, formerly, a writ commanding the sheriff to inquire whether a person charged with murder was committed upon just cause of suspicion, or merely on account of some one's hatred and ill will.

de partitio ne facien'da, formerly, a writ for the partition of lands held by tenants in common.

de ple'giis acquientan'dis, formerly, a writ against a principal, in behalf of a surety who had been compelled to pay.

de reparatio'ne facien'da, formerly, a writ for one tenant in common to compel another to aid in repairing common property.

de similibus ad similia eadem ratione procedendum est, from similars to similars we proceed by the same rule.

de son tort (*dŭ sôn tôr*), of his own wrong; often applied to a person who, not being appointed an executor, takes it upon himself to act in that capacity.

de u'na par'te, of one part, applied to a written instrument in which only one party gives, grants, or binds himself to do a thing, as opposed to a deed inter partes (*q.v.*).

de ven'tre inspicien'do, formerly, a writ to inspect the body, when a woman claimed to be pregnant.

dead freight, money paid by a person who has chartered a ship and only partly loaded her, in respect of the part left empty.

Dead Man's Act, various state laws providing that no person may testify for himself concerning any oral statement of, or any transaction with, or any act done or omitted to be done by, one who is dead when the testimony is offered to be given, except for the purpose and to the extent of affecting one who is living, subject to certain exceptions.

deadly force, force (*q.v.*) which the actor uses with the purpose of causing or which he knows to create a substantial risk of causing death or serious bodily harm. Purposely firing a firearm in the direction of another person or at a vehicle in which another person is believed to be constitutes deadly force. A threat to cause death or serious bodily harm, by the production of a weapon or otherwise, so long as the actor's purpose is limited to creating an apprehension that he will use deadly force if necessary, does not constitute deadly force. Model Penal Code § 3.11(2).

deadly weapon, any firearm, or other weapon (*q.v.*), device, instrument, material or substance, whether animate or inanimate, which in the manner it is used or is intended to be used is known to be capable of producing death or serious bodily injury. Model Penal Code § 210.0(4).

death, ceasing to live. Definitions of this concept vary: (1) In the past it has been the cessation of all vital signs, which is a factual determination of a physician from clinical facts. (2) The Uniform Determination of Death Act provides that an individual who has sustained either (a) irreversible cessation of circulatory and respiratory functions, or (b) irreversible cessation of all functions of the entire brain, including the brain stem, is dead. A determination of death must be made in accordance with accepted medical standards. Uniform Determination of Death Act § 1. (3) The Uniform Anatomical Gift Act leaves the determination of the time of death to the attending or certifying physician. No attempt is made to define the uncertain point in time when life terminates. The real question is when have irreversible changes taken place that preclude return to normal brain activity and self-sustaining bodily functions. Uniform Anatomical Gift Act § 7, Comment. (4) Approximately 30 states have adopted some type of statute recognizing brain death; in the absence of such statutes, the courts have been open to current medical opinion on the matter.

death by accidental means, the termination of life by an unexpected and fortuitous event.

debenture, a form of instrument issued by a corporation as evidence of an obligation to pay money, which often enjoys a priority for its satisfaction. (2) A certificate issued to an importer, by the collector of a port, for the deduction or refund of duties on merchandise imported and then exported by him.

debet esse finis litium, there ought to be an end of lawsuits.

debet quis juri subjacere ubi delinquit, everyone ought to be subject to the law of the place where he offends.

debita sequuntur personam debitoris, debts follow the person of the debtor.

debitor non presumitur donare, a debtor is not presumed to give. A man must be just before he is generous.

debitum et contractus sunt nullius loci, debts and contracts are of no particular place.

de'bitum fun'di, *l.* (Sc.), a charge on land.

debt, a flexible term for a sum certain in money due from one person (the debtor) to another (the creditor). (2) Formerly the common law form of action to recover a sum certain.

decedent, a deceased person. (2) A deceased individual; includes a stillborn infant or fetus. Uniform Anatomical Gift Act § 1(b).

deceit, a type of fraud in which facts are withheld, misrepresented, or falsely intimated to be true, by which a person is misled to his injury. (2) Formerly, a common-law action to recover damages for loss caused by misrepresentation or fraud.

decipi quam fallere est tutius, it is safer to be deceived than to deceive.

decision, the determination or judgment of the court, as opposed to the reasoning of the court in its opinion.

declarant, a person who makes a declaration (*q.v.*). (2) A person who makes a statement (*q.v.*). Fed. R. Evid. 801(b).

declaration, a public proclamation, *e.g.*, the Declaration of Independence, 1 Stat. 1 (1861); a declaration of war. (2) The written statement by a plaintiff of his claim for relief or cause of action. (3) A statement made by one of the parties to a transaction or event, frequently admissible in evidence, *e.g.*, when it is against the pecuniary interest of the party making it, when it is part of the res gestae (*q.v.*), or when it is made by a dying person, in cases of homicide. See also, *dying declaration.*

declaration of intention, the formal statement by an alien that he renounces his allegiance to the sovereign of the country of which he is then a citizen, and will become a citizen of the United States, made before the proper court, with a view to naturalization (*q.v.*).

declaration of invalidity of a marriage, see *nullity of marriage (2).*

declaration of trust, an acknowledgment, usually in writing, by a person having the possession of and legal title to property, that he holds it for the use of another.

declaratory, that which explains or fixes the meaning of something which was previously doubtful or uncertain, *e.g.*, a declaratory statute.

declaratory judgment, or **declaratory decree,** a determination or decision by a court which states the rights of the parties to a dispute, but does not order or coerce any performance relative to those rights. The procedural and substantive conditions of the usual action must be present. The relief which the court grants is the distinguishing characteristic.

Declaratory Judgments Act, an act to empower United States courts, in cases of actual controversy, to declare rights and other legal relations whether or not further relief is or could be requested. 28 U.S.C. §§ 2201, 2202. Most of the states have adopted various similar acts, which are sometimes known by the same or a similar name.

declining balance depreciation, a depreciation method under which a uniform rate is applied to the unrecovered basis of the asset. Since the basis is always reduced by prior depreciation, the rate is applied to a constantly declining basis. The salvage value is not deducted from the basis prior to applying the rate, since under this method at the expiration of useful life there remains an undepreciated balance which represents salvage value.

decree (Sc. decreet), a determination made by the court in a suit in equity or libel in admiralty. It is interlocutory if it does not finally dispose of the case, *e.g.*, an order directing an accounting or a sale or appointing a receiver, or final, when it does dispose of the case. (2) Often used as a generic term for any judgment or order issued by a court.

decree nisi, a court determination which is at first conditional, but becomes absolute, unless within a given time the party against whom it is rendered shows good cause why it should not be. (2) Often used to indicate an interlocutory divorce judgment.

decree of dissolution of marriage, see *divorce (2)*.

decreet arbitral (Sc.), the award of an arbitrator.

decretal order, a determination made by a court of equity.

de'di, *l.*, I have given.

de'di et conces'si, I have given and granted.

dedicate, or **dedication,** the act of an owner who devotes or appropriates his land to some public use, *e.g.*, to make a private way public, or to set apart ground for a public park. The act may be express, *i.e.*, made by deed or declaration, or implied, *i.e.*, to be presumed from the action or inaction of the owner, *e.g.*, acquiescence in the public use.

dedi'mus potesta'tem, *l.* (we have given the power), formerly a writ or commission empowering the persons to whom it is directed to do a certain act.

dedition, the act of yielding up something; relinquishment.

deed, a written instrument designed for the purpose of conveying real property from a present owner to a new owner. (2) Sometimes any written instrument.

deed absolute, where a landowner borrows money and gives as security a quitclaim or warranty deed to the land.

deed of trust, a mortgage in which the borrower conveys the land, not to the lender, but to a third party, a trustee, in trust for the benefit of the holder of the note or notes that represent the mortgage debt.

deed poll, a written instrument which is executed by one party only, as opposed to an indenture (*q.v.*), *e.g.*, a conveyance or assignment.

defamation, a flexible term for the uttering of spoken or written words concerning someone, which tend to injure that person's reputation and for which an action for damages may be brought. (2) To create liability for defamation there must be (a) a false and defamatory statement concerning another, (b) an unprivileged publication to a third party, (c) fault amounting at least to negligence on the part of the publisher, and (d) either actionability of the statement irrespective of special harm or the existence of special harm caused by the publication. Restatement (Second) of Torts § 558. See also, *libel* and *slander*.

defamatory communication, bringing an idea to the perception of someone that tends so to harm the reputation of another as to lower him in the estimation of the community or to deter third persons from associating or dealing with him. Restatement (Second) of Torts § 559, Comment a.

default, a flexible term for the omission of that which a person ought to do. (2) The failure to plead or otherwise defend an action, by a party against whom a judgment for affirmative relief is sought.

default judgment, see *judgment.*

defeasance, a condition, providing that upon the performance of a certain act or the occurrence of a certain event, an estate or interest created shall be defeated and determined, *e.g.*, a mortgage is a deed that contains a clause of defeasance.

defeasible, something which may be defeated, determined, or divested.

defect, a lack of perfection or completeness; an imperfection, flaw, or failing. (2) To change one's loyalty or to desert.

defect of parties, a failure to name necessary parties in a lawsuit.

defec'tus san'guinis, *l.*, failure of issue, *i.e.*, lack of children.

defendant, a person against whom an action is brought, a warrant is issued, or an indictment is found.

defende'mus, *l.* (we will defend), formerly used in grants and donations to bind the donor and his heirs to indemnify the donee against encumbrances.

defense, a forcible resistance of an attempt to injure or to otherwise commit a felony. (2) A broad term for any fact or argument of law which exonerates a person from a criminal prosecution or from the claims asserted against him in a civil lawsuit. (3) The conduct of a trial on behalf of a defendant.

deference, respect and esteem for a superior or elder.

defiant trespass, see *trespass (5).*

deficiency judgment, in an action to enforce or foreclose a mortgage, a personal judgment against the mortgagor for the amount still due the mortgagee after sale. (2) In a lawsuit to collect a debt secured by a security interest on personal property, *e.g.,* an automobile, a personal judgment against the debtor for the amount still due the creditor after the sale of the personal property.

definitive, descriptive of court action which terminates a suit, *e.g.,* the final judgment of a court, in opposition to provisional or interlocutory judgment.

deforcement, a broad term for the holding of real property to which another person has a right; used especially to denote keeping out of possession one who has never had possession.

deforceor, one who withholds possession wrongfully.

defraud, a flexible term for acts, omissions, or concealments which involve a breach of duty, trust, or confidence, and are injurious to another, or by which an undue and unconscionable advantage is taken of another. (2) To cheat, trick, or dupe.

degree, a step from generation to generation in the distance between kindred.

dehors *(dŭ ôr ˊ), fr.,* out of; without; foreign to.

del cre'dere commission, an undertaking by which an agent or factor guarantees prompt payment on the part of the persons to whom he sells his principal's goods.

delectus personae, a latin phrase for the principle that a partnership may not be obtained except with the consent of all the partners.

delectus personarum, see *delectus personae.*

delegate, a person authorized to act for another. (2) A person elected to represent others in a deliberative assembly, *e.g.,* a political convention.

delegation, the body of delegates representing a particular nation, state, district, or county in a legislative or other assembly, or at the court of a foreign power.

delegatus non potest delegare, a delegate cannot delegate, *i.e.,* an officer or agent cannot devolve his duty upon another without express authority.

deletion, erasure, obliteration, or removal.

delicatus debitor est odiosus in lege, a luxurious debtor is odious in the eye of the law.

delictum, *l.,* a crime, tort, or wrong.

delivery, a flexible term for the act of transferring possession. It may be actual, or constructive, *i.e.,* implied by law from the acts of the parties, *e.g.,* handing to the buyer the key of the warehouse where his goods are stored. (2) In conveyancing, the transfer of a deed from the grantor to the grantee, or someone acting in his behalf, which is absolute, when the deed is intended to take effect immediately; or conditional, when the deed is handed by the grantor to a third person, to be by him handed to the grantee when certain specified conditions shall be performed. (3) With respect to instruments, documents of title, chattel paper, or securities, it means voluntary transfer of possession. U.C.C. § 1-201(14).

delusion, an extravagant belief to which a person adheres against evidence, argument and reason.

demand, a broad term for a claim, including any right of action. (2) A request to pay money, or do some act, made under a claim of right to have it paid or done. (3) A requirement, desire, or want. See also, *prayer.*

demand instrument, or **demand note,** negotiable paper payable at sight or on presentation, and that in which no time for payment is stated. U.C.C. § 3-108. Payment must be demanded before suit can be brought.

demandant, formerly, the term for a plaintiff in a real action (*q.v.*).

demesne (*du mān*), own; private.

demise, a transfer or conveyance. (2) A conveyance in fee, for life, or for years.

demonstrative legacy, a gift created by a will which is payable out of a particular fund or thing. If the fund or thing from which it is payable is insufficient to pay it, the gift is paid from the general estate.

demur, to stay or abide. To object formally to a pleading. See also, *demurrer.*

demurrage, a payment made to the owners of a ship by the freighter for detaining her in port longer than the period agreed upon. (2) The detention itself.

demurrer, a formal response to a pleading, which admits the allegations to be true for the purposes of argument, but asserts that no cause of action or defense is stated by the allegations of the pleading. It imports that the party demurring will stay, and not proceed, until the court decides whether he is bound to do so. Demurrers are either general, where no particular cause is assigned and the insufficiency of the pleading is stated in general terms, or special, where some particular defects are pointed out. Demurrers may be to the whole or any part of a pleading. Under modern rules of civil procedure, the demurrer has been replaced by a motion to dismiss for failure to state a claim. Fed. R. Civ. P. 12(b).

denizen, an alien who has some of the privileges of a citizen. (2) An inhabitant or resident.

department, an administrative subdivision of a nation or of a government.

Department of Energy Organization Act, an act to establish a Department of Energy in the executive branch of the United States government by the reorganization of energy functions within the federal government in order to secure effective management to assure a coordinated national energy policy, and for other purposes. 42 U.S.C. §§ 7101 *et seq.*

departure, in maritime law, a deviation from the course prescribed in the policy of insurance. (2) In pleading, a statement of matter in a subsequent pleading which is inconsistent with, or not pursuant to, the ground taken by the same party in his previous pleading. (3) In agency law, such a deviation from the usual and authorized manner of proceeding as to remove the acts of a servant from within the scope of his employment. Cf. *deviation.*

depo'nent, a person who gives testimony under oath, which is reduced to writing for use on the trial of a cause. (2) Occasionally, a person who makes an affidavit.

deportation, the forcible removal of an alien from a country.

depose, to give testimony under oath. (2) To oust a person from public office.

deposit, something of value, *e.g.,* money or property, lodged by one person with another as a pledge or security, *e.g.,* that he will complete a purchase, or repay a loan. (2) A bailment of goods to be kept for the depositor without a reward, and to be returned when he shall require it. (3) Money placed in bank for safekeeping, the bank undertaking to return not the specific money, but other money equal in amount.

Deposit Insurance Act, an act to create a Federal Deposit Insurance Corporation to insure the deposits of all banks entitled to the benefits of insurance thereunder. 12 U.S.C. §§ 1811 *et seq.*

dep'osition, a written record of oral testimony, in the form of questions and answers, made before a public officer for use in a lawsuit. Depositions are used for the purpose of discovery of information, or for the purpose of being read as evidence at a trial, or for both purposes.

depraved heart murder, intentionally performing an act that results in the death of another person under circumstances manifesting an extreme indifference to the value of human life.

depreciation, the reduction in the value of capital assets through wear and tear or obsolescence.

depreciation reserve, an accounting technique whereby a fund is built up over a period of time from annual contributions, which are charged as an expense of operation, to offset and equal the ultimate total loss through depreciation.

derivative action, a shareholder's suit on behalf of all shareholders to enforce a corporate cause of action. The suit, analogous to a class action, represents a last resort remedy to alter the conduct of the corporation.

deputy, a person who acts for, or instead of, another in the administration of a public office. The deputy usually has power to do any act which his principal might do, and acts in the name of his principal.

derelict, abandoned; especially used to describe a vessel forsaken at sea and land left permanently uncovered by the receding of water from its former bed.

derivativa potestas non potest esse major primitiva, the derivative power cannot be greater than the primary source.

derogate, to lessen; impair.

descendants, a person's children and grandchildren and their descendants ad infinitum.

descent, the transfer of real property to a new owner by operation of law, when the former owner dies intestate (*q.v.*). The person or persons to whom the property is transferred are specified by various state statutes. See also, *heir*.

desecration, defacing, damaging, polluting, or otherwise physically mistreating any object of reverence or sacred devotion (*i.e.*, U.S. flag, any public monument, any historical or commemorative marker, a place of worship, a work of art or a museum piece, etc.).

desertion, intentional or deliberate abandonment of an obligation, *e.g.*, to serve in the armed forces, or to live with one's spouse. Often defined by various statutes or court decisions.

design patent, a patent (*q.v.*) granted for giving a new and attractive appearance to a manufactured article.

detainer, the wrongful keeping of a person's real property or goods, although the original taking may have been lawful. See also, *forcible entry* and *forcible detainer*. (2) Lawful detention of a person for the purpose of turning him over to other authorities. Often done for the purpose of insuring that a prisoner will answer other charges when he is released from his current term of imprisonment.

determinable, liable to come to an end on the happening of some contingency, *e.g.,* an estate devised to a widow during life or until she remarries.

detinue, formerly, a personal action for the recovery of goods or their value.

deus solus haeredem facere potest, non homo, God alone, and not man, can make an heir, *i.e.,* heirship is a matter of birth, not of grant.

devasta'vit (he has wasted), a misapplication or waste of the property of a deceased person by an executor or administrator, for which he is liable.

devest, see *divest.*

deviation, by a ship, is departure from her proper course. This, when without necessity or just cause, invalidates her insurance policies. (2) A variance by an agent from the usual and authorized manner of proceeding, which does not necessarily remove him from the scope of his employment. Cf. *departure.*

devisa'vit vel non, *l.,* formerly, an issue sent from the Court of Equity to be tried in a court of law, to determine whether a paper purporting to devise certain lands is the valid will of the testator.

devise, a gift by will, usually applicable to real property, but sometimes also used to describe personalty. (2) When used as a noun, means a testamentary disposition of real or personal property; when used as a verb, means to dispose of real or personal property by will. Uniform Probate Code § 1-201(7). Cf. *legacy.*

devisee, a person who is given real property under a will. (2) Any person designated in a will to receive a devise (*q.v.*); in the case of a devise to an existing trust or trustee, or to a trustee on trust described by will, the trust or trustee is the devisee and the beneficiaries are not devisees. Uniform Probate Code § 1-201(8).

dic'tum, or **obiter dictum,** *l.,* a statement by a judge concerning a point of law which is not necessary for the decision of the case in which it is stated. Usually, dictum is not as persuasive as is its opposite, *i.e.,* holding (*q.v.*).

di'em clau'sit extre'mum, *l.,* (he has died), formerly an English writ directing the sheriff, on the death of a Crown debtor, to inquire when and where he died, and what assets he had at the time of his decease, and to seize them.

di'es, *l.,* a day.

di'es a quo, the day from which.

dies dominicus non est juridicus, Sunday is not a judicial day.

di'es gra'tiae, days of grace.

dies inceptus pro completo habetur, a day begun is held as complete.

digest, a methodically arranged and indexed compilation of abstracts of decisions, intended to aid an attorney in finding precedent cases which are relevant to his problem cases. (2) Formerly, a textbook concerning the law. See also, *Pandects.*

dilationes in lege sunt odiosae, delays in law are odious.

dilatory plea, a response to a lawsuit which has the object of delaying the action, without responding to the merits of the lawsuit.

diligence, care or persistence. Cf. *negligence.*

diminished capacity, a psychiatric defense in which psychiatric testimony is admissible to show that the defendant lacks the capacity to premeditate or to form malice aforethought.

diminution, decrease or reduction.

direct, straightforward; not collateral.

direct attack, an application or motion to amend, vacate, or appeal a judgment.

direct contempt, words spoken or acts done in the presence of a judge or judges, while court is in session, tending to embarrass or prevent justice.

direct evidence, testimony or other proof which expressly or straightforwardly proves the existence of a fact; opposite of circumstantial evidence (*q.v.*).

direct examination, the initial questioning of a witness by the party who calls him.

direct tax, a tax demanded from the very person who is intended to pay it (*e.g.,* a tax at a flat rate on all persons).

directed verdict, a determination by a jury made at the direction of the court, in cases where there has been a failure of evidence, an overwhelming weight of the evidence, or where the law, as applied to the facts, is for one of the parties.

direction, see *jury instructions.*

director, a person elected to manage or control the affairs of a corporation.

directory statute, an enactment of a legislative body, the strict fulfillment of which is not necessary to the validity of a proceeding, but with which there is a duty to comply as nearly as practicable; one with which substantial compliance is acceptable. Cf. *mandatory.*

disability, incapacity to do some legal act, *e.g.,* to sue or contract, as in the case of minors or persons of unsound mind. (2) In cases of personal injury, a person's inability to perform occupationally, physiologically, and socially. (3) In worker's compensation cases, the inability to work or the loss of earning power. (4) Cause for a protective order. (a) Appointment of a conservator (*q.v.*) or other protective order may be made in relation to the estate and affairs of a minor if the court determines that a minor owns money or property requiring management or protection that cannot otherwise be provided or has or may have business affairs that may be jeopardized or prevented by minority, or that funds are needed for support and education and that protection is necessary or desirable to obtain or provide funds. (b) Appointment of a conservator (*q.v.*) or other protective order may be made in relation to the estate and affairs of a person if the court determines that (i) the person is unable to manage property and business affairs effectively for such reasons as mental illness, mental deficiency, physical illness or disability, advanced age, chronic use of drugs, chronic intoxication, confinement, detention by a foreign power, or disappearance; and (ii) the person has property that will be wasted or dissipated unless property management is provided or money is needed for the support, care, and welfare of the person or those entitled to the persons' support and that protection is necessary or desirable to obtain or provide money. Uniform Probate Code §§ 5-103(4), 5401(b), (c).

disagreement, a dispute, difference, or variance.

disbar, to cancel or withdraw an attorney's license or privilege to practice law on account of his misconduct.

discharge, a flexible term that connotes finality, *e.g.*, cancellation, rescission, or nullification. (2) The court order by which a person held to answer a criminal charge is set free. (3) The court order by which a jury is relieved from further consideration of a case.

discharge in bankruptcy, the order by which a bankrupt is released from liability for his debts, which were incurred prior to the adjudication in bankruptcy. It is used as a defense to any lawsuit that might be filed to collect those debts.

disclaimer, a disavowal or renunciation. (2) A refusal to accept something, *e.g.*, an office by an executor who declines to prove a will, or an estate by one to whom it was conveyed or devised. (3) A denial as a tenant of his landlord's title. (4) A renunciation by defendants of all claim to the thing demanded by the plaintiff.

discontinuance, the failure to proceed in, or the voluntary dismissal of, a case.

discount, an allowance or deduction. (2) Sometimes an advance payment of interest or a charge for the negotiation of a promissory note.

discount shares, shares issued for less than par value.

discovert, descriptive of an unmarried woman or a widow.

discovery, a plaint method by which the opposing parties to a lawsuit may obtain full and exact factual information concerning the entire area of their controversy, via pre-trial depositions, interrogatories, requests for admissions, inspection of books and documents, physical and mental examinations, and inspection of land or other property. The purpose of these pre-trial procedures is to disclose the genuine points of factual dispute and facilitate adequate preparation for trial. Either party may compel the other party to disclose the relevant facts that are in his possession, prior to the trial. Fed. R. Civ. P. 26-37.

discredit, to cast doubt on a witness's testimony by assailing his reliability as an accurate source of information.

discretion, the use of private and independent judgment. (2) The authority of a trial court which is not controlled by inflexible rules, but can be exercised one way or the other as the trial judge believes to be best in the circumstances. It is subject to review, however, if it is abused. See also, *abuse of discretion.* (3) Ability to distinguish between good and evil.

discretionary trust, a trust (*q.v.*) giving to the trustee discretion (*q.v.*) as to the investment or use of the trust funds in satisfaction of a general trust intent, which is expressed as broad guidelines.

discrimination, the unfair treatment or denial of normal privileges to individuals based on their race, age, sex, national origin, handicap, or religion.

disentailing deed, an assurance by which an English tenant in tail may convert it into an estate in fee.

disfranchisement, the act of depriving a person of a right or privilege, particularly the right to vote.

dishonor, to refuse to accept or pay a draft or to pay a promissory note when duly presented. An instrument (*q.v.*) is dishonored when a necessary or optional presentment is duly made and due acceptance or payment is refused, or cannot be obtained within the prescribed time, or in case of bank collections, the instrument is seasonably returned by the midnight deadline; or presentment is excused and the instrument is not duly accepted or paid. U.C.C. § 3-507(1).

disme (dēm), a tenth or tithe; whence our word dime.

dismiss, to send a defendant or an action out of court. Dismissal may be final, *i.e.,* made after a full hearing on the merits, or without prejudice, *i.e.*, when the plaintiff is at liberty to bring another action for the same cause.

disorderly conduct, with purpose to cause public (*q.v.*) inconvenience, annoyance, or alarm, or recklessly creating a risk thereof, (a) engaging in fighting or threatening, or in violent or tumultuous behavior, (b) making unreasonable noise or offensively coarse utterance, gesture, or display, or addressing abusive language to a person present, or (c) creating a hazardous or physically offensive condition by an act which serves no legitimate purpose of the actor. Model Penal Code § 250.2(1).

disparagement, to discredit, degrade, belittle, or reduce in esteem. (2) Disparagement of property or merchandise, or of title, is actionable when false and malicious oral or written statements are made concerning a person's property or goods for sale, and special damages result. Cf. *slander of title.* (3) A statement which is understood to cast doubt upon the quality of another's land, chattels, or intangible things, or upon the existence or extent of his property in them, and (a) the publisher intends the statement to cast the doubt, or (b) the recipient's understanding of it as casting the doubt was reasonable. Restatement (Second) of Torts § 629. (4) Disparagement of a person's performance of his occupation is actionable if it imputes fraud, lack of integrity, or dishonesty. (5) In England, matching an heir in marriage beneath his degree or against decency.

disparate impact, a plaintiff challenges a rule or test that on its face is nondiscriminatory, but in its effect discriminates against individuals on the basis of their race, color, religion, sex, national origin, handicap, or veteran's status.

disparate treatment, intentional discrimination where plaintiff is singled out for different treatment because of his or her race, color, religion, sex, national origin, handicap, or veteran's status.

dispauper, to prevent a person suing any longer in forma pauperis (*q.v.*), if it appear during the action that he has property.

dispensation, an exemption from some law; permission to do something forbidden.

dispossession, intentionally (a) taking a chattel from the possession (*q.v.*) of another without the other's consent, (b) obtaining possession of a chattel from another by fraud or duress, (c) barring the possessor's access to a chattel, (d) destroying a chattel while it is in another's possession, or (e) taking a chattel into the custody of the law. Restatement (Second) of Torts § 221.

disseisee (*dĭs sē zē´*), a person wrongfully turned out of possession, or disseised.

disseisin (*dĭs sē′ zĭn*), a wrongful putting out of him that is entitled to possession of the freehold.

dissenting opinion, a judicial opinion disagreeing with that of the majority of the same court, given by one or more of the members of the court.

dissolution, a legal severance or breaking up. This may take place in cases of (a) partnership by death of a partner, by the withdrawal or expulsion of a partner, by agreement or by order of a court; (b) corporations by compliance with statutory formalities; (c) marriage by decree of divorce; (d) an attachment by an order of court releasing the goods taken, on giving bond, or proving that the writ was improperly issued.

dissolution of marriage, see *divorce (2).*

dissolution of a partnership, the change in the relation of the partners caused by any partner ceasing to be associated in the carrying on, as distinguished from the winding up, of the business. Uniform Partnership Act § 29.

distrain, to make seizure of goods or chattels by way of distress (*q.v.*).

distress, a taking of a personal chattel from the possession of a wrong-doer without legal process, to enforce payment, *e.g.*, of rent. It is limited to a taking of personal property for purposes of security.

distribution, the division among the legatees or the heirs of a deceased person of the residue of the estate remaining after paying the inheritance and estate taxes, debts, and costs of administration.

district, a geographic subdivision of a political entity, *e.g.*, a state or the United States, for administrative, political, or judicial purposes. Each state is divided into congressional districts, corresponding in number to the number of representatives it is entitled to send to the United States House of Representatives in each of which a congressman is elected by the qualified voters thereof. In a similar manner the states are divided into districts for the election of members of the state legislature. There are numerous and various other districts in the states and the United States, *e.g.* Federal Reserve District, judicial districts, and revenue districts.

district attorney, an officer appointed for each judicial district of the United States, whose duty it is to prosecute in the district all persons charged with violating the laws of the United States, and to represent the United States in all civil actions pending in the district to which the United States is a party.

District Courts, United States trial courts established in the respective judicial districts into which the whole United States is divided. Some states constitute a single district each, but the larger states are divided into two or more. (2) Courts of some of the states established for the purpose of hearing and deciding causes in limited districts to which their jurisdiction is confined. In some of the states their jurisdiction is chiefly appellate, in others it is original.

distrin'gas (that you distrain), formerly a writ addressed to the sheriff, directing him to distrain (*q.v.*) in order to compel the performance of a duty or the delivery of a chattel.

diversity, a plea by a prisoner alleging that his identity is mistaken.

diversity jurisdiction, to insure the just resolution of cases between plaintiffs and defendants from competing and different states, the federal courts are permitted to exercise jurisdiction strictly based on diversity. Diversity jurisdiction is often criticized as promoting forum shopping and glutting the federal courts with cases only because of residencies rather than federal questions.

diversity of citizenship, the coincidence of the parties on the opposite sides of a lawsuit being domiciled in different states, which is one of the grounds to invoke the jurisdiction of United States district courts, when the case also involves a controversy concerning $10,000.00 or more in value. 28 U S.C. § 1332. Its purpose is to provide out-of-state litigants an impartial court. The definition is deceivingly simple in appearance, but the concept is very intricate because of, *e.g.*, the mobility of parties, multiple plaintiffs and multiple defendants, nominal parties, the representative character of some actions and the interstate operations of corporations which result in their having multiple citizenship. Innumerable factors influence a court's determination as to whether diversity of citizenship exists in any particular case.

divest, or **devest,** to take something away from a person, *e.g.*, an estate or interest which has already vested.

dividend, a pro rata distribution among stockholders of the net earnings of a corporation, or of a portion of the capital if creditors are not prejudiced. (2) A flexible term for a share or division, *e.g.*, the pro rata payment made to an unsecured creditor in a bankruptcy proceeding or a receivership.

dividen'da, formerly an indenture or one part of an indenture.

divisible divorce concept, a concept under which full faith and credit is given to a divorce decree as to dissolution of a marriage but not as to property and support rights.

division of opinion, a disagreement between the judges constituting a court which prevents any judgment from being rendered in a matter before them.

divorce, a judicial severance of the tie of matrimony. It may be an absolute divorce (a vinculo matrimonii), or nullity of marriage, which is complete; or a legal separation (a mensa et thoro), which does not entitle the parties to marry again. (2) A decree of dissolution of marriage is the term used in lieu of divorce by Uniform Marriage and Divorce Act § 302. Cf. *nullity of marriage.*

DNA testing, a way of determining distinctive patterns in genetic material which allows the identification of the source of a biological specimen of blood, tissue, hair, or semen. DNA testing is used primarily to identify or rule out a crime suspect or to identify or rule out the father of a child.

dock, a place in some courts where a prisoner is put during his trial.

dock warrant, a type of document of title (*q.v.*) issued by a dock owner stating that the goods mentioned in it are deliverable to a person therein named, or to his assigns by indorsement.

docket, variously, an agenda for the proceedings of a court, an abstract or brief written entry in a court of record, or a book in which brief entries of acts done in court are made.

doctrine, a principle of law, often developed through court decisions; a precept or rule.

doctrine of secondary meaning, see *secondary meaning.*

document, a flexible term for a deed, agreement, letter, receipt, or other instrument in writing used to prove a fact. (2) In civil law, evidence delivered in due form, of whatever nature such evidence may be.

document of title, any document (*q.v.*), which in the regular course of business or financing is treated as adequately evidencing that the person in possession of it is entitled to receive, hold, and dispose of the document and the goods it cover, *e.g.*, bill of lading, dock warrant, dock receipt, warehouse receipt, or order for the delivery of goods. It must purport to be issued by, or addressed to, a bailee (*q.v.*) and purport to cover goods in the bailee's possession, which are either identified or are fungible portions of an identified mass. U.C.C. § 1-201(15).

Doe, John, one of the forms used to designate a party to a civil suit or criminal prosecution whose name is not known.

doing business, a highly splintered term with various meanings. (2) In a general sense, activities which apply assets and labor to the production of financial gain. (3) Pursuit of the objective of earning money. (4) Regularly engaging in an occupation or employment for livelihood or gain. (5) Exercise by a corporation of some of the functions for which the corporation was created. See also, *business.*

dole, a share.

do'li ca'pax, *l.,* capable of distinguishing between right and wrong.

doli incapax, *l.,* incapable of distinguishing between right and wrong.

dolosus versatur in generalibus, he who wishes to deceive deals in generalities.

do'lus, *l.,* an act which deceives another to his harm or violates a confidence. Used generally in the sense of wilful deceit, fraud, *i.e.,* dolus malus. See also, *misrepresentation.*

dolus auctoris non nocet successori, the fraud of a predecessor prejudices not his successor.

dolus circuitu non purgatur, fraud is not purged by circuity.

domain, a nation that is subject to a government; dominion; possession; the right to dispose of a possession at pleasure.

Domesday, or **Doomsday Book,** the description of England, a record of surveys, and a partial census of a large portion of England, made in 1085-1087, which became legal authority and was often quoted in court. It served the purpose of title deeds for those who held real property without written documentation.

domestic, a flexible term relating to the home, household, or one's state or nation.

domestic animal, see *animal.*

domestic corporation, when referred to in, or by, a particular state, a corporation (*q.v.*) created by or under the laws of the state, or located in the state and created by or under the laws of the United States.

domestic violence, knowingly or recklessly cause or attempt to cause physical harm to a family or household member.

domicile, the place where a person has his legal home or place of permanent residence (*q.v.*). It depends on the fact of residing and on the intention of remaining. Domicile is acquired by birth, by choice, or by operation of law, *e.g.,* the domicile of an infant is the same as that of his parents, though they are temporarily absent from it at the time of his birth.

dominant estate, or **dominant tenement,** an estate (*q.v.*) or tenement (*q.v.*) to which a servitude or easement is due, or for the benefit of which the service is constituted. See also, *easement.*

dominium, control; property or ownership.

do'minus, proprietor.

domus sua cuique est tutissimum refugium, to everyone his own house is the safest refuge. Every man's house is his castle.

dona clandestina sunt semper suspiciosa, clandestine gifts are always suspicious.

dona'tio, *l.,* a gift. A voluntary transfer of the title and possession of real or personal property to another without consideration.

donatio non praesumitur, a gift is not presumed.

donatio perficitur possessione accipientis, a gift is perfected by possession of the receiver.

donee, a person to whom a gift is made or a power of appointment is given.

donor, a person who makes a gift or confers a power of appointment.

Doomsday Book, see *Domesday.*

dormant, sleeping; silent; not acting.

dormant claim, a claim (*q.v.*) in abeyance; not enforced.

dormant judgment, a judgment (*q.v.*) on which execution has not been issued for so long a time that it cannot be enforced without further proceedings to revive it.

dormant partners, members of a partnership (*q.v.*) who do not take any active part as partners, but who nevertheless share in the profits and losses of the business, and thereby incur the responsibilities of partners.

dormiunt aliquando leges, nunquam moriuntur, the laws sometimes sleep, never die.

double citizenship, see *dual citizenship.*

double entry, an accounting and bookkeeping term used to designate books of account which show the debit and credit of every transaction.

double insurance, insurance effected in two or more companies upon the same property or interest and in excess of its value.

double jeopardy, a second time of danger or peril; a defense to a prosecution for crime, raising the claim that the defendant is being placed on trial for a second time for the same offense for which he has previously been tried. No person may be subject to be twice put in jeopardy of life or limb for the same offense. U.S. Const., Amend. V, and various state constitutions.

double or **treble damages,** an increase of the damages found by the jury, made by the court in giving judgment in some cases, *e.g.,* in case of a malicious infringement of a patentee's rights.

double waste, the actions of a tenant, who is obligated to repair, when he suffers a house to be wasted, and then unlawfully fells timber to repair it.

doubtful title, see *title (1)*.

dowable, entitled to dower.

dowager, a widow endowed.

dower, the common law life estate which a widow has in one-third of all the lands of which her husband was seized in fee simple, or fee tail, at any time during coverture. Dower is modified and defined by various state statutes.

dowress, a widow entitled to dower.

draft, a preliminary or rough copy of a legal document. (2) See *bill (2)*.

draft environmental impact statement, DEIS. 40 C.F.R. § 404.12.

draft law, see *Military Selective Service Act*.

draft-registration educational-benefits law, see *Solomon Amendment*.

draftsman, a person who composes or authors a legal instrument. Cf. *scrivener*.

dramshop, a bar, saloon, or other establishment where liquors are sold to be consumed on the premises.

dramshop liability, liability imposed upon dramshops for serving alcoholic beverages to someone who is already intoxicated or deemed otherwise incapable of protecting himself from the effects of the intoxicating drink who then injures a third party as a result of the intoxication.

drawee, a person to whom a bill or draft is directed, *e.g.*, the drawee of a check is the bank on which it is drawn. See also, *bill (2)*.

drawer, the person who draws a bill or draft, *e.g.*, the drawer of a check is the person who signs it. See also, *bill (2)*.

droit (drwå), *fr.*, law; a right.

droit ne poet pas morier, right cannot die.

drug, for purposes of the Food, Drug and Cosmetic Act (*q.v.*), (a) articles recognized in the official *United States Pharmacopeia*, official *Homoeopathic Pharmacopoeia of the United States*, or official *National Formulary*, or any supplement to any of them, (b) articles intended for use in the diagnosis, cure, mitigation, treatment, or prevention of disease in man or animals, (c) articles, other than food, intended to affect the structure or any function of the body of man or animals, and (d) articles intended for use as a component of any article specified above. It does not include devices or their components, parts, or accessories. 21 U.S.C. § 321(g)(1). (2) For purposes of drug- abuse prevention and control, the term has the same meaning. 21 U.S.C. § 802(12). See also, *controlled substance*.

drug addiction, the condition of a person who habitually or compulsively uses narcotics to such an extent that he does not have self-control.

drug-courier profile, an abstract of characteristics found to be typical of persons transporting illegal drugs. There is no consistent amalgam of traits that ineluctably leads to a stop of a suspect. The combination of factors looked for not only varies among law-enforcement agents, but varies from airport to airport as well. The U.S. Supreme Court has not condoned, or even specifically addressed, the use of the profile to justify investigative stops of suspects in all cases.

drunkenness, the condition of a person whose mind is affected by the use of alcoholic beverages; intoxication; inebriation. Some courts consider the lack of self-control or the overpowering effect of the drink as a material part of the definition.

dry mortgage, a seldom-used security device containing a provision against personal liability of the mortgagor beyond the value of the mortgaged property.

dry rent, rent without clause of distress.

dry trustee, see *bare trustee.*

dual capacity doctrine, a doctrine stating that while an employer is normally shielded from tort liability by exclusive remedy of workers' compensation law, he may become liable to his employee if he occupies, in addition to his capacity as employer, a second capacity that confers an obligation on him independent of that of an employer.

dual citizenship, dual nationality, or **double citizenship,** the result of the inconsistent provisions of the nationality laws of various countries, which overlap so that a person may be a citizen of two countries with conflicting duties. (2) The status of citizens of the United States who reside within a state. All persons who are born or naturalized in the United States, and subject to the jurisdiction thereof, are citizens of the United States and of the state wherein they reside. U.S. Const., Amend. XIV, Sec. 1.

dual purpose doctrine, a doctrine that states that if an employee's work requires him to travel, he is in the course of employment while doing that work even though at the same time he is serving some purpose of his own.

du'ces te'cum, a type of subpoena (*q.v.*).

due, a debt matured because the time for payment has arrived. (2) Sometimes, owing, regardless of whether the time for payment has arrived.

due process of law, a flexible term for the compliance with the fundamental rules for fair and orderly legal proceedings, *e.g.*, the right to be informed of the nature and cause of the accusation, to be confronted with the witnesses against you, to have compulsory process for obtaining witnesses in your favor, to have the assistance of counsel for your defense, and to have a fair and impartial jury. (2) Legal proceedings which observe the rules designed for the protection and enforcement of individual rights and liberties. No person shall be deprived of life, liberty, or property without due process of law, U.S. Const., Amend. V. No state shall deprive any person of life, liberty, or property without due process of law, U.S. Const., Amend. XIV, Section 1. Similar or analogous provisions are found in state constitutions.

dum, *l.*, while.

dumb bidding, in sales at auction, a minimum price.

dunnage, wood or other material placed in the hold of a ship, under or between the cargo.

duo non possunt in solido unam rem possidere, two cannot each possess one [*i.e.*, the same] thing in its entirety.

duplicate, one of two documents which are the same; an executed copy. Leases and contracts are usually executed in duplicate, so that each party may have evidence of it. (2) A counterpart produced by the same impression as the original, or from the same matrix, or by means of photography, including enlargements and miniatures, or by mechanical or electronic re-recording, or by chemical reproduction, or by other equivalent techniques which accurately reproduces the original (*q.v.*). Fed. R. Evid. 1001(4). See also, *tax duplicate.*

duplicity, deception or double-dealing. (2) Formerly the union of more than one cause of action or defense in a single pleading.

durable power of attorney, a power of attorney (*q.v.*) by which a principal designates another his attorney in fact in writing and the writing contains the words, "This power of attorney shall not be affected by subsequent disability or incapacity of the principal," or "This power of attorney shall become effective upon the disability or incapacity of the principal," or similar words showing the intent of the principal that the authority conferred shall be exercisable notwithstanding the principal's subsequent disability or incapacity. Uniform Probate Code § 5-501.

durable power of attorney for health care, a power of attorney in which the attorney-in-fact is authorized to make health care decisions for the principal to the same extent the principal could make the decisions if not incapacitated.

durance vile, jail or prison.

duran'te, *l.,* during.

duress, imprisonment; compulsion; coercion. (2) Threats of injury or imprisonment.

Durham test, test applied in some states for the defense of insanity; under this test an accused is not responsible for an unlawful act if the act was the product of mental disease or defect.

during coverture, during the period of the marriage.

dutch auction, the setting up of property for sale by auction at a price above its value, and gradually lowering the price till some person takes it.

duty, a flexible term for an obligation; the correlative to a right. (2) That which a person is obliged to do or refrain from doing. (3) A responsibility which arises from the unique relationship between particular parties. (4) What one should do, based on the probability or foreseeability of injury to a party. (5) The fact that an actor (*q.v.*) is required to conduct himself in a particular manner at the risk that if he does not do so he becomes subject to liability to another to whom the duty is owed for any injury sustained by the other, of which the actor's conduct is a legal cause. Restatement (Second) of Torts § 4. (6) A tax.

dwelling, any building or structure, though movable or temporary, or a portion thereof, which is for the time being the actor's home or place of lodging. Model Penal Code § 3.11(3).

Dyer Act, an act to punish the transportation of stolen motor vehicles in interstate or foreign commerce. 18 U.S.C. §§ 10, 2311-2313.

dying declaration, hearsay (*q.v.*) evidence of what a person said when he was aware that his death was imminent. Under particular circumstances and in certain cases, it is competent evidence in some courts. (2) In a prosecution for homicide or in a civil action or proceeding, a statement made by a declarant (*q.v.*) while believing that his death was imminent, concerning the cause or circumstances of what he believed to be his impending death. It is not excluded by the hearsay rule if the declarant is unavailable as a witness. Fed. R. Evid. 804(b)(2).

E

e, or **ex,** *l.,* from; out of.

e conver'so, on the other hand.

EA, see *environmental assessment.*

eadem est ratio, eadem est lex, the same reason, the same law.

eagle, formerly, a gold coin of the United States of the value of ten dollars.

earl, an English title of nobility, next below a marquis and above a viscount. They formerly had the civil government of a shire or county.

Earl Marshal of England, formerly, a high English officer of state.

earned premium, the portion of an advance payment on an insurance contract, which the payee is entitled to retain in the event of a premature cancellation of the contract.

earned surplus, the net balance of a corporation's net profits, income, gains, and losses from the date of incorporation, or from the latest date on which a deficit in earned surplus was eliminated by application of capital surplus or otherwise, after deducting distributions to shareholders (including dividends) and transfers to stated capital and capital surplus, to the extent that the distributions and transfers were made out of earned surplus; a historical record (from either the date of its incorporation or the latest date in which a deficit in earned surplus was eliminated) of its net profits and gains, less (1) its losses; (2) distributions to shareholders; and (3) transfers to other shareholders' equity accounts made from earned surplus.

earnest, or **earnest money,** the sum paid by the buyer of goods in order to bind the seller to the terms of the agreement; a deposit or down payment.

earnings, a flexible term for compensation, its exact meaning depending upon the context in which it is used.

Earthquake Hazards Reduction Act of 1977, an act to reduce the risks of life and property from future earthquakes in the U.S. through the establishment and maintenance of an effective earthquake hazards reduction program. 42 U.S.C. §§ 7701 *et seq.*

earwitness, a person who attests to something that he has heard himself. Cf. *eyewitness.*

easement, a privilege or intangible right which the owner of one parcel of real property, called the dominant tenement, has concerning another parcel of real property, called the servient estate, by which the owner of the latter is obligated not to interfere with the privilege. The most common easements are in the nature of passageways, *e.g.*, road, walkway, railroad, pole line, or pipeline. It is technically classified as an incorporeal hereditament.

easement appurtenant, an easement created for the benefit of a tract of land. There must always be two tracts of land owned by different persons for an easement appurtenant to exist. These two tracts are called the dominant tenement and the servient tenement.

easement of necessity, when the owner of land sells a part thereof that has no outlet to a highway except over his remaining land or over the land of strangers, a right of way by necessity is created by implied grant over the remaining land of the seller.

e'at in'de si'ne di'e, *l.,* words sometimes used on the acquittal of a defendant, that he may go thence without a day, *i.e.,* be [finally] dismissed.

ecclesiastical, connected with, or set apart for, the church, as distinguished from lay or civil. See also, *courts.*

ecology, a comprehensive biological science which deals with zoology and botany and concerns the interrelationships between, and community of, living things and their surroundings.

Economic Stabilization Act of 1970, title II of an act to amend the Defense Production Act of 1950, and for other purposes, by which the President is authorized to issue such orders and regulations as he deems appropriate, accompanied by a statement of reasons for such orders and regulations, to stabilize prices, rents, wages, and salaries at levels not less than those prevailing on May 25, 1970, except that prices may be stabilized at levels below those prevailing on such date if it is necessary to eliminate windfall profits or if it is otherwise necessary to carry out the purposes of the title, and stabilize interest rates and corporate dividends and similar transfers at levels consistent with orderly economic growth. 12 U.S.C. § 1904.

ecumenical, general or universal.

edict *(l.,* edictum), a law ordained by a sovereign.

educational-benefits draft-registration law, see *Solomon Amendment.*

effects, a highly flexible term. (2) Usually, property of all sorts, except real property. (3) Sometimes, property of all sorts, including real property.

effectus sequitur causam, the effect follows the cause.

egress, see *ingress.*

ei incumbit probatio, qui dicit, non qui negat, the proof lies upon him who affirms, not upon him who denies.

eire, or **eyre** (ār), a journey.

EIS, see *environmental impact statement.*

ejectment, formerly a mixed action at common law, which depended on fictions in order to escape the inconveniences in the ancient forms of action. It was a mixed action, because it sought to recover both possession of land (a real claim), and also damages (a personal claim). Various statutory proceedings for the recovery of land, some of which bear the same name, have taken its place in most of the United States.

ejus est non nolle qui potest velle, he may consent tacitly who may consent expressly.

ejus est periculum cujus est dominium aut commodum, he who has the dominion or advantage has the risk.

ejus nulla culpa est cui parere necesse sit, he is not in any fault who is bound to obey.

ejusdem ge'neris, *l.,* of the same kind or nature.

ejusdem generis rule, a rule of construction under which a provision containing specifically enumerated items followed by general language referring to other items is construed to refer only to other items of the same kind.

election, the making of a choice or selection, *e.g.,* the choice of a public official.

election of remedies, the act of choosing between two or more alternative or inconsistent kinds of redress.

election of rights, the act of choosing between two alternative or inconsistent prerogatives.

elector, a person who has the right to vote.

Electors, Presidential, persons elected by the people of the several states, whose duty it is to meet and vote for President and Vice-President of the United States. Lists of the persons thus voted for are certified and forwarded to the president of the Senate, to be opened and counted in the presence of both houses of Congress. U.S. Const., Amend. XII.

elective share, a method of protecting the spouse against disinheritance recognized by statutes affording the surviving spouse an election to take a statutory share rather than the provision, in any, made in the decedent's will. Most states have elective share statutes. The elective share is typically one-third.

eleemos'ynary corporation, or **institution,** a corporation (*q.v.*), constituted for the perpetual distribution of alms or bounty, usually having the objective of welfare, charity, or other public good, *e.g.,* hospitals, colleges, or universities.

ele'git, he has chosen, so called because the creditor formerly could choose between this writ and a writ of fieri facias, formerly a writ of execution by which the sheriff gave the judgment creditor possession of the real property of the judgment debtor, to be held by him until the money due on the judgement was fully paid.

elicit, to bring out.

elisors, persons appointed to perform the duties of the sheriff and coroner when they have been challenged for interest or partiality.

eloign *(ě loin ΄),* to remove; to take to a distance.

elonga'ta, a return sometimes made by a sheriff in replevin, meaning that the personal property sought is not to be found, or has been removed to a place unknown to him.

elonga'tus, sometimes a sheriff's return to a writ, meaning that the person is out of the sheriff's jurisdiction.

emancipation, the freeing of a minor child from parental control. Emancipation normally occurs when a child reaches the age of majority, marries, or enters the armed services.

Emancipation Proclamation, an order and declaration by President Abraham Lincoln, issued January 1, 1863, that all persons held as slaves within the states and parts of states that he designated as in rebellion henceforth shall be free, and that the executive government of the U.S. would recognize and maintain the freedom of those persons. 12 Stat. 1268 (1863).

embargo, the detention of vessels in port, by order of the government prohibiting their departure, usually issued in time of war or threatened hostilities.

embezzlement, the appropriation to his own use, by an agent or employee, of money or property received by him for and on behalf of his employer. It differs from larceny, in that embezzled property is not at the time in the actual or legal possession of the owner. It was not an offense punishable at common law, but is made so by the statutes of the United States, and the several states.

emblements, or **fructus industriales,** growing crops obtained by labor and cultivation. It does not pertain to crops which do not represent labor expended, *e.g.*, orchard fruit.

embraceor, or **embracery,** an attempt to corruptly influence a jury in favor of one party in a trial. The person making the attempt is called an *embraceor.*

Emergency Highway Energy Conservation Act, an act to conserve fuel during periods of current and imminent fuel shortages through the establishment of a national, maximum highway speed limit, *i.e.*, 55 m.p.h. 23 U.S.C. § 154.

eminent domain, the right which a government retains over the property of individuals to take it for public use (*q.v.*), in return for a fair compensation. It is often exercised for ordinary governmental purposes, *e.g.*, public highways and public buildings, and for certain private purposes, *e.g.*, pipelines and railroads.

emotional distress, a form of injury (*q.v.*) resulting from tortious (*q.v.*) conduct; it is not in itself a tort (*q.v.*). (2) Variously, mental suffering, mental anguish, nervous shock, and includes all highly unpleasant mental reactions, *e.g.*, fright, horror, grief, shame, embarrassment, anger, chagrin, disappointment, and worry; it is only when emotional distress is extreme that possible liability arises. Cf. *outrage*.

empanel, see *impanel*. See also, *panel*.

empirical, based upon facts gathered from observation, experience, or experiment.

empirical research, investigation or inquiry which is based on empirical (*q.v.*) facts.

employ, a flexible term for the personal relationship in which one engages or uses another as an agent or substitute in transacting business, or the performance of some service; it may include skilled or unskilled labor or professional services.

employee, a flexible term for a person who does work for someone else. See also, *employ*.

Employee Retirement Income Security Act of 1974, an act to provide for pension reforms. It deals with, among other things, protection of employee benefit rights, amendments to the Internal Revenue Code (*q.v.*) relating to retirement plans, jurisdiction, administration, enforcement, and plan-termination insurance, including the Pension Benefit Guaranty Corporation. 29 U.S.C. §§ 1001 *et seq.*

employer, a flexible term for a person who hires another person or persons to do work for him. See also, *employ*.

employers' liability acts, various state and federal statutes which enlarge the rights of employees and reduce the defenses available to employers, in cases of personal injuries to employees. Usually, the employer must be shown to have been negligent. See also, *Federal Employers' Liability Act*. Cf. *workers' compensation*.

employment-at-will, absent an express contract establishing the terms and conditions of employment, an employment relationship is presumed to be at will, allowing either party to terminate the relationship for any or no reason.

Employment Opportunities for Handicapped Individuals Act, Title II of an act to amend the Rehabilitation Act of 1973 to extend certain programs established in that act, to establish a community service employment program for handicapped individuals, and to provide comprehensive services for independent living for handicapped individuals, and for other purposes, also known as the Rehabilitation, Comprehensive Services, and Developmental Disabilities Amendments of 1978. 29 U.S.C. §§ 795 *et al.*

emptio, the act of buying.

emptor, a purchaser.

emptor emit quam minimo potest, venditor vendit quam maximo potest, the buyer buys for as little as possible; the seller sells for as much as possible.

en *(ôn), fr.,* in.

en autre droit *(ô tr drwä),* in the right of another.

en demeure *(dû mẽr),* in default.

en owel main, in equal hand.

en ventre sa mere *(vôn tr så mâr),* in its mother's womb.

enabling act, or **statute,** an act of a legislature, which removes a restriction or disability. (2) A statute which gave tenants in tail and others power to make leases for life, or for twenty-one years, which they could not do before.

enact, to establish by law; to decree.

enceinte (ôn sănt'), pregnant; with child.

enclosure, see *inclosure.*

encroachment, an unlawful extension of possession to the prejudice of another's property, *e.g.,* by taking in adjoining land.

encumbrance, see *incumbrance.*

Endangered Species Act, ESA; an Act passed to provide a means whereby the ecosystems upon which endangered species and threatened species depend may be conserved, to provide a program for the conservation of such endangered species and threatened species, and to take such steps as may be appropriate to achieve the purposes of the treaties and conventions the United States has pledged itself to. 16 U.S.C. §§ 1531 *et seq.*

endorsee, see *indorsee.*

enemy alien, see *alien enemy.*

Energy Assistance Act, see *Low-Income Home Energy Assistance Act of 1981.*

Energy Conservation Act, or **Energy Conservation Bank Act,** see *Solar Energy and Energy Conservation Act of 1980.*

Energy Department, see *Department of Energy Organization Act.*

Energy Security Act, an act to extend the Defense Production Act of 1950, and for other purposes. It concerns synthetic fuel, biomass energy and alcohol fuels, energy targets, renewable energy initiatives, solar energy and energy conservation, acid precipitation program, carbon dioxide study, and strategic petroleum reserve. 42 U.S.C. §§ 7361-7364; 12 U.S.C. §§ 3601 *et seq.*

endorsement, see *indorsement.*

enfeoffment *(fĕf),* see *feoffment.*

enfranchise, to make free, or incorporate a person into a privileged society. (2) To invest with the privilege of voting.

engross, to copy in a final draft; to prepare a deed for execution.

engrossed bill, a legislative proposal which has been put into final form and is ready to be enacted into law.

enjoin, to command; to require; to give an order that something shall or shall not be done, which may be enforced by fine or imprisonment. See also, *injunction.*

enjoyment, the beneficial use of property.

enlarge, a broad term for make larger, increase, or expand, *e.g.,* to enlarge an abstract principle of law is to increase or expand the scope of its meaning, so that the principle shall control more concrete cases.

enlargement, or **enlarger l'estate** (*ôn lär zhä lĕs tāte*), a type of release which consists of a conveyance of the interest of a remainderman or reversioner to the tenant.

Enoch Arden laws, laws attempting to deal with the social and legal problems created by the return of a long absent spouse in the context of remarriage.

enor'mia, *l.,* see *alia enormia.*

enroll, to record; to register; to enter on the records of the legislature or a court any act, order, or judgment.

entail, real property, or money directed to be invested in real property, which is settled on a man and the heirs of his body. See also, *tail.*

enter, to enroll (*q.v.*). (2) To take possession of land by going on it or occupying it.

entire contract, an indivisible contract (*q.v.*); one wherein everything required to be done on one side must be fully performed before the consideration is due from the other. This is opposed to an apportionable or severable contract.

entireties, tenants by, in some states, when real property is conveyed or devised to a man and his wife, during coverture, they are tenants by entireties, *i.e.,* each is seized of the whole estate, and neither can alien alone, so that in default of joint alienation, the estate goes to the survivor.

entirety, the whole, as distinguished from moiety, *i.e.,* the half or part.

entrapment, measures improperly employed by law enforcement officers to encourage persons suspected of engaging in criminal practices to commit a crime. In many jurisdictions it is a defense which may be raised by a person accused of a crime.

entry, see *enroll* and *enter* (2). (2) A memorandum in an account book of a sale or other transaction. (3) A listing of imported goods for the payment of duties at the customhouse. (4) The written order of a court in proceedings pending before it.

entry of satisfaction, see *satisfaction, entry of.*

enumerators, persons appointed to take the census.

enure, see *inure.*

environmental assessment, EA; an analysis required by the National Environmental Policy Act (NEPA), whereby all federal agencies are required to assess the environmental impact of a proposed "major federal action"; the EA shall include brief discussions of the need for the proposal, of alternatives, of the environmental impacts of the proposed actions and alternatives, and a listing of agencies and persons consulted. C.F.R. § 1508.9.

environmental impact statement, EIS; an analysis required by the National Environmental Policy Act (NEPA), whereby all federal agencies are required to prepare detailed statements on the environmental impacts whenever taking "major federal action significantly affecting the quality of the human environment."

environmental law, the resolution of disputes, usually between the national or state government and someone whom it accuses of violating its laws, concerning the conditions surrounding mankind and affecting his comfort and well-being, *e.g.*, air pollution, water pollution, heat pollution, noise pollution, solid waste disposal, and weather modification.

Environmental Protection Agency, an administrative agency of the United States government, created by the President's Reorganization Plan No. 3 of 1970.

e'o instan'te, at that instant.

EPA, see *Environmental Protection Agency.*

Equal Access to Justice Act, title II of an act to, among other things, provide for the payment of the United States of certain fees and costs incurred by prevailing parties in federal agency adjudications and in civil actions in courts of the United States. 5 U.S.C. § 504, 28 U.S.C. § 2412, 42 U.S.C. § 1988.

Equal Credit Opportunity Act, title V of an act relating to, among other things, deposit insurance and electronic fund transfers, as amended by an act concerning discrimination and the Consumer Credit Protection Act (*q.v.*). 15 U.S.C. §§ 1961 *et seq.*

Equal Employment Opportunity Act, title VII of the Civil Rights Act of 1964 (*q.v.*). It deals with discrimination by an employer because of race, color, religion, sex, or national origin, other unlawful employment practices, the Equal Employment Opportunity Commission, the prevention of unlawful employment practices, investigations, inspections, and the like. 42 U.S.C. §§ 2000e *et seq.*

Equal Pay Act of 1963, an act which generally prohibits covered employers from paying unequal wages to male and female employees who perform substantially the same jobs; also prohibits labor unions from causing or attempting to cause covered employers to violate the act. Employers are generally covered if they conduct business in interstate commerce.

equal protection of the laws, a flexible term for the guaranty of uniformity of treatment under state law, of all persons in like circumstances. U.S. Const., Amend. XIV. It usually is applied to civil and political rights.

equality, the condition of persons when one has no unfair advantage over another. (2) Coequality, uniformity, or likeness.

equitable, an abstract term for fair, reasonable, or proper. (2) Pertaining to rights and duties which historically were enforced only in a court of equity. (3) Pertaining to preventive and remedial justice which is appropriate under the unique facts of the problem case, and which is rendered by a court, in contradistinction to common-law justice. See also, *equity.*

equitable adoption, the provision of some judicial remedy for an unperformed contract for legal adoption.

equitable conversion, see *conversion (3).*

equitable estate, a right or beneficial interest in land, the legal title to which is in another, and which can be enforced only in a court of equity.

equitable estoppel, a rule that if one person has induced another to take a certain course of action in reliance upon the representations or promises of the former, the former person will not be permitted to subsequently deny the truth of the representations, or revoke such promises, upon which such action has been taken. See also, *estoppel.*

equitable mortgage, any instrument in writing by which the parties show their intention that real estate be held as a security for the payment of a debt.

equity, fairness. (2) A type of justice that developed separately from the common law, and which tends to complement it. The current meaning is to classify disputes and remedies according to their historical relationship and development. Under modern rules of civil procedure, law and equity have been unified. Fed. R. Civ. P. 2. (3) Historically, the courts of equity had a power of framing and adapting new remedies to particular cases, which the common-law courts did not possess. In doing so, they allowed themselves latitude of construction and assumed, in certain matters such as trusts, a power of enforcing moral obligations which the courts of law did not admit or recognize. (4) A right or obligation attaching to property or a contract. In this sense, one person is said to have a better equity than another. See also, *equitable.*

equity of a statute, the spirit and intent of a statute, as opposed to the strict letter. A statute may be construed according to its spirit and intent, rather than according to its strict letter. (2) Formerly, an English doctrine that extended statutes to cases which were not within their express words, on the ground that such an extension would serve the purposes of the statute.

equity of redemption, the right which the mortgagor of real property has to redeem it, following a judicial sale of the property in a foreclosure (*q.v.*) action.

equity to a settlement, formerly, the claim of a wife to have some portion, usually one-half, of property coming to her husband in her right during the coverture settled on herself.

erasure, or **rasure,** rubbing out or obliteration.

ERISA, see *Employee Retirement Income Security Act.*

errant, wandering, formerly descriptive of judges traveling a circuit.

error, a mistake in judgment. (2) An incorrect ruling or instruction made by a judge in the trial of a case. See also, *harmless error,* and *writ of error.*

ESA, see *Endangered Species Act.*

escape, the departure of a prisoner from custody before he is released by lawful authority. (2) Unlawfully removing oneself from official detention (*q.v.*) or failing to return to official detention following temporary leave granted for a specific purpose or limited period. Model Penal Code § 242.6(1).

escheat', a transfer of property to the state government by operation of law, because of its abandonment or lack of a private owner, *e.g.,* upon the intestate death of the owner without heirs or next of kin. Usually provided for, and often defined, by various state statutes. (2) The property itself, which is so transferred. (3) Formerly, a species of reversion of any estate of inheritance to the crown or the lord of the fee from whom, or from whose ancestor, the estate was originally derived, upon the determination of the estate.

escrow' (scroll or writing), a writing delivered to a third person, to be delivered by him to the person whom it purports to benefit, when certain specified conditions shall have been performed or satisfied. Until that time, the delivery is not effective.

escrow deposit, a sum of money intrusted to a real estate mortgagee for the purpose of paying the mortgagor's property taxes and hazard insurance. It is usually increased each month and paid simultaneously with the installment payments on the mortgage.

Esq., or **Esquire,** a title given to members of the bar and others, as a matter of courtesy.

essence, that which is essential or a necessary element.

essoin, essoign (*ĕ soin*), an excuse for nonappearance in court when summoned.

estate, the condition and circumstance in which a person stands with regard to those around him and his property. (2) The quantum or quality of the interest which a person has in property. Estates in property may be: legal or equitable; real or personal; vested or contingent; in possession or in expectancy; absolute, determinable, or conditional; sole, joint, or in common; of freehold or less than freehold. (3) Includes the property of a decedent, trust, or person whose affairs are subject to the Uniform Probate Code, as originally constituted and as it exists from time to time during administration. Uniform Probate Code § 1-201(11).

estate at will, a lease (*q.v.*) of property held at the will of the lessor.

estate by entireties, an estate (*q.v.*) in property held by husband and wife with right of survivorship.

estate by purchase, an estate (*q.v.*) in property acquired by any means, including gift, other than by descent.

estate by sufferance, an estate (*q.v.*) in property acquired by lawful means, but thereafter held without lawful title.

estate by the curtesy, an estate (*q.v.*) in property acquired by the widower on account of his marriage to his deceased spouse.

estate for years, an estate (*q.v.*) in property which will be terminated after a period of years fixed in advance.

estate from year to year, an estate (*q.v.*) in property held for an uncertain term of years.

estate in common, an estate (*q.v.*) in property wherein two or more persons hold an undivided part interest without right of survivorship.

estate in coparceny, an estate (*q.v.*) in property created by the descent of lands to two or more persons.

estate in expectancy, an estate (*q.v.*) in property which shall not vest in possession until the termination of a prior estate.

estate in fee conditional, an estate (*q.v.*) in property limited to a special class of heirs, as of the body.

estate in fee simple, an estate (*q.v.*) in property having all the rights in the property transferred free of any restriction, condition, or limitation. (2) Absolute ownership of real property.

estate in joint tenancy, an estate (*q.v.*) in property held by two or more persons and meeting the following requirements: each tenant has the same interest, the interest must accrue by the same instrument, the interest must commence at the same time, and each tenant must have undivided possession.

estate in remainder, an estate (*q.v.*) in property to take effect after another is determined.

estate in reversion, an estate (*q.v.*) in property remaining in the grantor of a particular estate.

estate tail, see *fee (c)* and *tail*.

estate tax, a tax on the value of property of a decedent.

estoppel, an admission or declaration by which a person is concluded, *i.e.*, prevented, from bringing evidence to controvert it, or to prove the contrary. It may be: by matter of record, which imports such absolute and incontrovertible verity that no person against whom the record is produced is permitted to deny it; by deed, because no person can dispute his own solemn deed, which is, therefore, conclusive against him, and those claiming under him, even as to facts recited in it; and by matter in pais, *e.g.*, a tenant cannot dispute his landlord's title. This includes estoppel by misrepresentation or negligence. See also, *equitable estoppel* and *promissory estoppel*.

estoppel in pais, see *pais*.

esto'vers, a right to take wood in reasonable quantities for house purposes or repairs. See also, *bote*.

estrays, valuable animals found wandering at large, whose owner is unknown.

estreat', to enforce a recognizance, *e.g.*, bond, by sending an extract (estreat), or copy, to the proper authority to be enforced.

estrepe (*ĕs strĕp*), to commit waste in lands to the damage of another.

estrepement, formerly a writ for the prevention of waste.

et, *l.*, and.

et al., or **et als.,** and others.

et cetera, and so forth.

et seq, "and the following."

et ux., or **et uxor,** and wife.

et vir., and husband.

Ethics in Government Act of 1978, an act to establish certain federal agencies, effect certain reorganizations of the federal government, to implement certain reforms in the operation of the federal government, and to preserve and promote the integrity of public officials and institutions, and for other purposes. 2 U.S.C. §§ 701 *et seq.*, 5 U.S.C. § 5316, 18 U.S.C. § 207, 28 U.S.C. §§ 49, 528, 529, 591-598, 1364.

Euclidean zoning, a zoning scheme based on district-and-use envisioning the specification of geographical areas separated according to zoning districts with the permitted uses for those districts set forth in ordinances. Village of Euclid v. Ambler Realty Co., 272 U.S. 365, 47 S.Ct. 114, 71 L.Ed. 303.

eviction, dispossession from land or buildings. See also, *constructive eviction* and *retaliatory eviction.* Cf. *ejectment.*

evidence, proof, either written or unwritten, of allegations at issue between parties. It may be (a) direct or indirect, which latter includes circumstantial evidence (*q.v.*); (b) substantive, *i.e.,* directed to proof of a distinct fact, or corroborative, *i.e.,* in support of previous evidence; (c) intrinsic, *i.e.,* internal, or extrinsic, *i.e.,* not derived from anything to be found in the document itself; (d) original or derivative, *i.e.,* which passes through some channel, *e.g.,* parol, as opposed to original documents or evidence. See also, *ambiguity, hearsay, primary evidence, relevancy,* and *relevant evidence.*

evidence in chief, proof which a party primarily relies upon in order to support his claim or defense.

Evidence Rules, see *Federal Rules of Evidence.*

ex, see *e.*

ex abundan'ti caute'la, out of abundant caution.

ex ae'quo et bo'no, in justice and fair dealing.

ex antecedentibus et consequentibus fit optima interpretatio, the best interpretation is made from the context.

ex cathe'dra, from the chair, *i.e.,* with authority.

ex contrac'tu, see *action.*

ex de'bito justi'tiae, from a debt of justice; as a matter of legal right.

ex delic'to, see *action.*

ex dolo malo non oritur actio, no right of action can arise out of a fraud.

ex gra'tia, as a matter of favor.

ex indus'tria, from fixed purpose.

ex malefi'cio, out of misconduct.

ex maleficio non oritur contractus, a contract cannot arise out of an illegal act.

ex me'ro mo'tu, of his own accord.

ex mo'ra, from delay or default.

ex mo're, according to custom.

ex necessita'te legis, from the necessity of the law.

ex necessita'te rei', from the necessity of the thing.

ex nihilo nihil fit, from nothing nothing comes.

ex nudo pacto non oritur actio, no right of action can arise from a contract not supported by consideration.

ex offi'cio, by virtue of his office.

ex par'te, of the one part; an action which is not an adverse proceeding against someone else.

ex par'te mater'na, or **pater'na,** from the mother's or father's side.

ex post fac'to, made after the occurrence, *e.g.,* penal and criminal legislation which has a retrospective application. (2) Every law which makes criminal an act which was innocent when done, or which inflicts a greater punishment than the law annexed to the crime when committed is an ex post facto law. The U.S. Congress is prohibited from passing ex post facto laws, U.S. Const. Art. I, Sec. 9. The states are prohibited from passing ex post facto laws, U.S. Const. Art. I, Sec. 10.

ex post facto law, see *ex post facto.*

ex pro'prio mo'tu, of his own motion.

ex pro'prio vigo're, of its own force.

ex rel., or **ex relatio'ne,** on relation or information.

ex tem'pore, from the time; without forethought.

ex turpi causa non oritur actio, no right of action can arise from a contract founded on an immoral consideration.

ex vi ter'mini, from the force of the term.

ex visitatio'ne De'i, from the visitation of God.

exaction, a wrong done by an officer or one in pretended authority, by taking a reward or fee contrary to law.

examination, the preliminary judicial investigation of the grounds for an accusation against a person arrested for crime, made by a magistrate, with a view to either discharging him or securing his commitment and appearance before the proper court for trial. It is sometimes called an examining trial. (2) An interrogation of a witness on oath. It may be oral or by written interrogatories (*q.v.*), by an attorney, a court, an officer called an examiner, or a commissioner.

examined copy, a copy of a record, public book, or register, which has been compared with the original.

examiner, an officer appointed by a court to take the testimony of witnesses under oath, and reduce it to writing. See also, *hearing examiner.*

examining trial, see *examination (1).*

excep'tio, *l.,* an exception; a plea; an objection.

exceptio firmat regulam in contrarium, an exception proves an opposite rule.

exceptio probat regulam de rebus non exceptis, an exception proves the rule concerning things not excepted.

excep'tio re'i judica'tae, a defense that the matter has been already decided in another cause between the same parties. Cf. *res judicata.*

exception, the express exclusion of something from the operation of a deed or contract. (2) A form of objection to a ruling or order of a trial court, which has as its purpose the preservation of the point at issue for adjudication on appeal. Under modern rules of civil procedure, formal exceptions to court rulings or orders are unnecessary. Fed. R. Civ. P. 46. See also, *bill of exceptions.*

excerp'ta, or **excerpts,** extracts.

excess, something which goes beyond what is right, proper or necessary, *e.g.,* undue violence in ejecting a trespasser from one's land, or a nonpaying passenger from a bus.

excess profits tax, an assessment or charge imposed by the United States government, at progressive rates, upon the net income in excess of a certain percentage of a corporation's invested capital. 64 Stat. 1137 (1951).

excessive verdict, an award of money damages, made by a jury, which in the absence of reasonable difference of opinion, is shocking to a sound judgment and a sense of fairness.

exchange, the transfer by one person to another of funds by means of a bill of exchange (*q.v.*). (2) The transfer of goods and chattels for other goods and chattels of like value, commonly called barter (*q.v.*). (3) A place where merchants and other persons engaged in trade meet to transact business. (4) A mode of conveyancing, by which mutual grants of real property are made, the one in consideration for the other, *e.g.,* in order to straighten a boundary line.

exchequer, an English government office which manages the public revenues. See also, *Court of Exchequer.*

excise, a form of tax, often imposed on merchandise produced or consumed within the country.

excited utterance, a statement (*q.v.*) relating to a startling event or condition made while the declarant (*q.v.*) was under the stress of excitement caused by the event or condition. It is not excluded from evidence as hearsay (*q.v.*) even though the declarant is available as a witness. Fed. R. Evid. 803(2). Cf. *res gestae.*

exclusion of witnesses, or **separation of witnesses,** at the request of a party the court shall order witnesses excluded so that they cannot hear the testimony of other witnesses, and it may make the order of its own motion. This does not authorize exclusion of (a) a party who is a natural person, (b) an officer or employee of a party which is not a natural person designated as its representative by its attorney, or (c) a person whose presence is shown by a party to be essential to the presentation of his cause. Fed. R. Evid. 615.

exclusive agency, a listing contract that assures the broker that as long as his employment continues no other broker will be hired.

exclusive right to sell, a listing contract that makes the broker the sole agent of the landowner for the sale of the property and also provides that the named broker will receive a commission in the event the property is sold by the named broker, the owner, or by anyone else.

exculpatory, exonerative; excusing; tending to clear from a charge of fault or guilt.

excusable homicide, see *homicide.*

excuss, to seize and detain by law.

execute, to accomplish, perform, complete. To execute a deed is to complete it by signing and delivery. (2) The English Statute of Uses was said to execute a use when it converted a use or trust estate into a legal one. (3) To exercise, *e.g.,* a power of appointment. (4) To enforce, *e.g.,* a judgment. (5) To put to death a convicted criminal in pursuance of his sentence.

executed, done; completed; performed; vested.

executed consideration, a consideration (*q.v.*) which is wholly past, and to be valid, must have been done or paid upon a request, express or implied.

executed contract, a contract that has fully adhered to the rights, obligations and formalities of the agreement. Leaving no matters undone or incomplete, the contract is fully performed or executed. Additionally, an executed contract also means that signatures, attestation requirements and appropriate filings have been fully completed, leaving no question as to the quality of the contract's formation.

executed estate, an estate (*q.v.*) in property, which is vested, whether possession and enjoyment be present or postponed.

executed remainder, a reversion (*q.v.*) to which someone is presently entitled. See also, *vested.*

executed trust, a trust (*q.v.*) in which the disposition or limitation of the beneficial estate is completely stated and precisely created.

executed use, a use (*q.v.*) in which the legal title and possession have been united.

execution, the writ, order, or process issued to a sheriff, directing him to carry out the judgment of a court, *e.g.,* to make the money due on the judgment out of the property of the defendant. See also, *execute.*

executive, that branch of the national, state, or local government which carries out and administers the laws, as distinguished from the legislative and judicial branches.

executor, a person nominated or designated by a testator in his will, or any codicil thereto, to administer and settle his estate. His duties are analogous to those of an administrator (*q.v.*) except as to matters specifically mentioned in the will. See also, *administration (2).*

executor de son tort (*dŭ sôn tôr*), a person who, without lawful authority, undertakes to act as the executor (*q.v.*) of a deceased person.

executory, something which is not completed, which requires something to be done or to happen, before it is perfect or assured; opposed to executed (*q.v.*).

executory consideration, something to be paid or done at a future time, in return for a promise presently made.

executory contract, a contract (*q.v.*) under which there are one or more obligations to be fulfilled; one in which some future act is to be done.

executory devise, or **bequest,** an estate in property which vests only on the happening of a future contingency. It differs from reversions, in that these, though deferred, have a present existence. An executory devise will, where it is possible, be construed as a contingent remainder.

executory trust, a trust (*q.v.*) in which the limitations are incomplete and in the form of general directions that must be supplemented; opposed to executed trust (*q.v.*).

executory use, sometimes called a shifting or springing use, a use (*q.v.*) which is to come into operation at a future date, or to pass from one person to another on the happening of a certain event, or the nonperformance of a condition.

exec'utrix, a woman who has been appointed to perform the duties of an executor (*q.v.*)

exempla illustrant non restringunt legem, examples illustrate, but do not restrain the law.

exemplary, or **punitive,** or **vindictive damages,** see *damages.*

exem'pli gra'tia, for the sake of example; for instance; commonly abbreviated, *e.g.*

exemplification, an attested or certified transcript or copy of an official record, sometimes under the seal of a particular court or public office.

exemption, an immunity or exception from the operation of the law, *e.g.,* freedom from levy or execution as to certain property or freedom from conscription. (2) An immunity from the imposition of an income tax, in an amount fixed by statute, which is allowed to a person for himself and for his dependents.

exe'quatur, the permission given by a government to a foreign consul to enter on his appointment.

exercise, to make use of. (2) To execute, *e.g.,* a power.

exer'citor ma'ris, *l.,* the managing owner of a vessel.

exer'citor na'vis, *l.,* (Rom.), the temporary owner or charterer of a ship.

exhibit, a concrete item of evidence, *e.g.,* a writing or object. (2) A document referred to in a pleading or an affidavit, and frequently therein identified by a letter or number.

exoneration, a flexible term for acquittal, release, of discharge, applied to criminal prosecutions, taxation, and civil actions. (2) Relieving an estate, or some part thereof, from liability or burden, by placing it on another estate or part, *e.g.,* a testator is said to exonerate his personalty from payment of his debts, if he charges them on another part of his estate, which is not primarily liable.

exonere'tur, an entry or notation of discharge of the bail, made on the bond when the condition is fulfilled.

exor'dium, the introductory part of a writing or a speech, *e.g.,* the exordium of a will identifies the testator, establishes his domicile, declares the instrument to be the testator's last will, and revokes all prior testamentary dispositions.

expatriation, the act and right of voluntarily forsaking one's own country and renouncing allegiance, with the intention of becoming a permanent resident and citizen of another country. See also, *naturalization.*

expectancy, the hope of an estate or interest in property which a person may obtain or enjoy in the future.

expectant heir, a person who has a prospect of obtaining property on the death of another person.

expedit reipublicae ne sua re quis male utatur, it is for public good that no one use his property badly.

expedit reipublicae ut sit finis litium, it is for the public good that there be an end of litigation.

experientia docet, experience teaches.

expert, a person who has acquired by special study, practice, and experience, peculiar skill and knowledge in relation to some particular science, art, or trade. (2) A witness who, because of such special knowledge, is called to testify or give his opinion in cases depending on questions peculiar to such science, art, or trade. Accord, Fed. R. Evid. 702. Cf. *skilled witness.*

express, descriptive of something which is stated in direct words and not left to implication, *e.g.,* an express promise or express trust.

express contract, a contract in which the parties are fully cognizant of its terms, conditions and overall requirements, and there is little dispute as to the legal rights and obligations of either of the parties. Mutual assent between the parties has been arrived at by outward expressions which may be "by the tongue, the eye, the hand or by all of them at once."

express trust, trusts generally evidenced by some written documentation, but oral trusts that can be verified or corroborated by other evidence are acceptable.

expressio eorum quae tacite insunt nihil operatur, the expression of those things which are tacitly implied has no effect.

expressio unius est exclusio alterius, the mention of one is the exclusion of another, *i.e.,* when certain persons or things are specified in a document, an intention to exclude all others from its operation may be inferred.

expressum facit cessare tacitum, what is expressed makes what is silent to cease, *i.e.,* where we find an express declaration we should not resort to implication.

expromis'sio (Rom.), a species of novation.

extend, in addition to its ordinary meanings, to value property. See also, *extent.*

extendi facias, see *extent.*

extension of time, additional or further time allowed, by way of indulgence, to perform an act, *e.g.,* pay a debt, file a pleading, or file a brief.

extent, or **exten'di fa'cias** (that you cause to be extended or appraised at their full value), the peculiar writ issued from the English exchequer, to recover debts of record due to the Crown.

extinguishment, the destruction or cessation of a right, either by satisfaction or by the acquisition of something which is greater, *e.g.,* a debt is extinguished by payment or by the creditor's acceptance of a security higher in the estimation of law, *e.g.,* a bond; an easement is extinguished by a release or by acquiring the tenement over which the easement existed. See also, *merger.*

extortion, formerly, narrowly defined as the unlawful taking, by color of office or of right, of money or anything of value which is not due.

Often defined by various state statutes. (2) Purposely obtaining property of another by threatening to: (a) inflict bodily injury on anyone or commit any other criminal offense; (b) accuse anyone of a criminal offense; (c) expose any secret tending to subject any person to hatred, contempt, or ridicule, or to impair his credit or business repute; (d) take or withhold action as an official, or cause an official to take or withhold action; (e) bring about or continue a strike, boycott, or other collective unofficial action, if the property is not demanded or received for the benefit of the group in whose interest the actor purports to act; (f) testify or provide information or withhold testimony or information with respect to another's legal claim or defense; or (g) inflict any other harm which would not benefit the actor. It is an affirmative defense to prosecution under (b), (c), or (d) that the property obtained by threat of accusation, exposure, lawsuit, or other invocation of official action was honestly claimed as restitution or indemnification for harm done in the circumstances to which such accusation, exposure, lawsuit, or other official action relates, or as compensation for property or lawful services. Model Penal Code § 223.4. See also, *blackmail.*

extra, *l.,* out of; beyond.

extra territorium jus dicenti non paretur impune, one exercising jurisdiction out of his territory cannot be obeyed with impunity.

extra vi'am, out of the way.

extra vires, see *ultra vires.*

extradition, or **interstate rendition,** the surrender by one nation or state, to another nation or state, of a person accused of crime committed in the latter, so that he may be tried there, pursuant to treaty or the Constitution and statutes of the United States. A person charged in any state with treason, felony, or other crime, who shall flee from justice and be found in another state, shall, on demand of the executive authority of the state from which he fled, be delivered up to be removed to the state having jurisdiction of the crime. U.S. Const., Art. IV, Sec. 2.

extrajudicial, outside of the regular course of court procedure, *e.g.,* self-help or an advisory opinion of law.

extraordinary, remarkable; in excess of the usual or ordinary.

extraordinary remedy, kinds of relief to which a court may resort in order to redress or prevent a wrong, but which are relatively seldom used, because other measures will usually afford relief, *e.g.,* habeas corpus and mandamus. See also, *prerogative writs.*

extraterritoriality, the quality of some laws which gives them operative force beyond the territory of the state or nation which enacted them, upon certain persons, *e.g.,* ambassadors, or upon certain rights.

extrinsic, external or from the outside. See also, *evidence.*

eyewitness, a person who gives evidence as to facts seen by himself. Cf. *earwitness.*

eyre, see *eire.*

eyre, justices in, formerly English judges who traveled a circuit. See also, *eire.*

F

fa'cias, *l.,* that you do, or cause.

fa'cio ut des, I do that you may give; a species of contract in which one agrees to do something for wages or an agreed sum of money.

fa'cio ut fa'cias, I do that you may do; a species of contract in which one agrees to do or forbear doing something in consideration of the other's doing or forbearing to do something, *e.g.,* a marriage contract.

fac si'mile (make it like), an exact copy. Cf. *duplicate.*

fact, a thing done or existing. (2) The events which are proven in the evidence heard by a court and upon which the law operates. Whether a thing was done or does exist, is a question of fact for the jury. What are the rights and liabilities of the parties, the facts being proven, is a matter of law for the court.

facta sunt potentiora verbis, deeds are more powerful than words.

factor, an agent employed to sell goods or merchandise consigned or delivered to him by or for his principal. See also, *broker.*

factorage, the compensation or commission which is paid to a factor (*q.v.*).

factory, a broad term for a building in which goods are manufactured.

factory acts, English laws regulating the hours of labor, the health and morals of those employed, and the education of young employees.

factum a judice quod ad ejus officium non spectat, non ratum est, an action of a judge, which relates not to his office, is of no force.

factum cuique suum, non adversario, nocere debet, a man's actions should injure himself, not his adversary.

factum unius alteri necere non debet, the deed of one should not hurt another.

failure, want; neglect; nonsuccess.

failure of consideration, the neglect, refusal, or inability of a contracting party to do, perform, or furnish, after making and entering into a contract, the consideration (*q.v.*) agreed upon.

failure of issue, dying without children.

failure of record, the neglect or inability of a defendant, who has pled a matter of record as a defense to an action, to produce such record.

faint pleader, a feigned action, or false plea.

fair, a flexible term for just, impartial, evenhanded, candid, or reasonable. (2) An event attended by persons having goods and chattels to exhibit and sell, held at stated intervals, or on special occasions.

fair cash value, the intrinsic value of shares of stock in a corporation, determined from the assets and liabilities of such corporation and considering every factor bearing on value. See also, *fair market value.*

Fair Credit Billing Act, title III of an act to increase deposit insurance, to establish a National Commission on Electronic Fund Transfers, and for other purposes. Its purpose is to protect the consumer against inaccurate and unfair credit billing and credit card practices. Among other things, it provides for disclosure of fair-credit billing rights, correction of billing errors, regulation of credit reports, and rights of credit-card customers. 15 U.S.C. §§ 1601, 1602, 1631, 1632, 1637, 1666-1666j.

Fair Credit Reporting Act, title VI of an act to amend the Federal Deposit Insurance Act to require insured banks to maintain certain records, to require that certain transactions be reported to the Department of the Treasury, and for other purposes. Among other things, it concerns permissible purposes of reports, obsolete information, disclosures to consumers, civil liability for noncompliance, and administrative enforcement. 15 U.S.C. §§ 1681 *et seq.*

Fair Debt Collection Practices Act, an act to amend the Consumer Credit Protection Act (*q.v.*) to prohibit abusive practices by debt collectors. Among other things, it deals with communication in connection with debt collection, harassment or abuse, false or misleading representations, unfair practices, legal actions by debt collectors, civil liability, and administrative enforcement. 15 U.S.C. §§ 1692 *et seq.*

fair hearing, a flexible term for a trial or interview which contemplates the taking of testimony, with the right of cross-examination assured to the parties, and the rendering of findings of fact supported by evidence. See also, *due process of law.*

Fair Housing Act, title VIII of an act to prescribe penalties for certain acts of violence or intimidation, and for other purposes. It concerns discrimination in the sale or rental of housing, discrimination in the financing of housing, discrimination in the provision of brokerage services, enforcement, and the like. 42 U.S.C. §§ 3601 *et seq.*

Fair Labor Standards Act of 1938, an act to provide for the establishment of fair labor standards in employment in and affecting interstate commerce. 29 U.S.C. §§ 201 *et seq.*

fair market value, a variable term for such sum as the sale of an article would bring in the market under ordinary conditions. (2) The coincidence of the price for which a willing seller, who does not have to sell, would sell, and at which a willing buyer, who does not have to buy, would buy. See also, *fair cash value.*

Fair Trade Act, formerly, an act to amend the Federal Trade Commission Act with respect to certain contracts and agreements which established minimum or stipulated resale prices and which were extended by state law to persons who were not parties to such contracts and agreements. 15 U.S.C. §§ 1, 45; 66 Stat. 631 (1952), repealed, 89 Stat. 801 (1975). See also, *fair trade laws.*

fair trade laws, formerly, various state statutes which allowed manufacturers or distributors of branded merchandise to fix a minimum retail price at which such merchandise may be sold. See also, *Fair Trade Act.*

fair use, the limited utilization which a person may make of a copyrighted book or other writing, without infringing the copyright. (2) Notwithstanding the provisions of 17 U.S.C. § 106, the fair use of a copyrighted work, including such use by reproduction in copies or phonorecords or by any other means specified by that section, for purposes such as criticism, comment, news reporting, teaching (including multiple copies for classroom use), scholarship, or research, is not an infringement of copyright, In determining whether the use made of a work in any particular case is a fair use, the factors to be considered include: (a) the purpose and character of the use, including whether such use is of a commercial nature or is for nonprofit educational purposes; (b) the nature of the copyrighted work; (c) the amount and substantiality of the portion used in relation to the copyrighted work as a whole; and (d) the effect of the use upon the potential market for or value of the copyrighted work. 17 U.S.C. § 107. See also, *copyright.*

fairness doctrine, a regulation of the Federal Communications Commission which imposes affirmative responsibilities on broadcasters that coverage of issues of public importance must be adequate and must fairly reflect differing viewpoints. In fulfilling this obligation, the broadcaster must provide free time for the presentation of opposing views if a paid sponsor is unavailable, and it must initiate programming on public issues if no one else seeks to do so.

fait *(fā)*, anything done. A deed lawfully executed.

fait accompli *(fā tăk kôm plē)*, an accomplished fact.

fait enrolle *(fā tôn rō lā)*, a deed enrolled.

fallow, land which has been plowed and left unsown; unused.

falsa demonstratio non necet, false description does not vitiate, *e.g.,* a legacy or devise.

falsa demonstratione logatum non perimi, a legacy is not to be destroyed by an incorrect description.

falsa orthographia, sive falsa grammatica, non vitiat concessionem, bad spelling or bad grammar does not vitiate a grant.

false, untrue or unjust.

false arrest, or **false imprisonment,** a tort consisting of restraint imposed on a person's liberty, without proper legal authority. (2) False imprisonment is a misdemeanor consisting of knowingly restraining another unlawfully so as to interfere substantially with his liberty. Model Penal Code § 212.3.

false pretenses, untrue statements made for the purpose of obtaining something of value, *e.g.,* money or goods, and to defraud the owner. Often defined by various state statutes which make it a criminal offense.

false return, a report made by a sheriff, constable, or other court officer, in which statements are made contrary to fact.

false swearing, in official matters, making a false statement under oath or equivalent affirmation, or swearing or affirming the truth of such a statement previously made, when he does not believe the statement to be true, if (a) the falsification occurs in an official proceeding, or (b) the falsification is intended to mislead a public servant in performing his official function. (2) Otherwise, making a false statement under oath or equivalent affirmation, or swearing or affirming the truth of such a statement previously made, when he does not believe the statement to be true, if the statement is one which is required by law to be sworn or affirmed before a notary *(q.v.)* or other person authorized to administer oaths. Model Penal Code § 241.2. Cf. *perjury.*

falsify, in taking accounts, to prove a debit or charge to be incorrect. See also, *surcharge.* (2) To make incorrect; to alter fraudulently, *e.g.,* a record.

falsifying judgments, occasionally used to mean reversing judgments.

falsus in uno, falsus in omnibus, false in one thing, false in all.

Family and Medical Leave Act, FMLA; an Act (1) to balance the demands of the workplace with the needs of families, to promote the stability and economic security of families, and to promote national interests in preserving family integrity; (2) to entitle employees to take reasonable leave for medical reasons, for the birth or adoption of a child, and for the care of a child, spouse, or parent who has a serious health condition; (3) to accomplish the purposes described in (1) and (2) in a manner that accommodates the legitimate interests of employers; (4) to accomplish the purposes described in (1) and (2) in a manner that, consistent with the Equal Protection Clause of the Fourteenth Amendment minimizes the potential for employment discrimination on the basis of sex by ensuring generally that leave is available for eligible medical reasons (including maternity-related disability) and for compelling family reasons, on a gender-neutral basis; (5) to promote the goal of equal employment opportunity for women and men. 29 U.S.C. §§ 2601 *et seq.*

family Bible, a Bible containing the family record of births, marriages and deaths. See also, *family records.*

family car doctrine, a principle recognized in some states, which holds the owner of an automobile liable for injury caused by its negligent use in the hands of members of the family.

family records, statements of fact concerning personal or family history contained in family Bibles (*q.v.*) genealogies, charts, engravings on rings, inscriptions on family portraits, engravings on urns, crypts, or tombstones, or the like. They are not excluded from evidence as hearsay (*q.v.*) even though the declarant (*q.v.*) is available as a witness. Fed. R. Evid. 803(13).

farm, a tract of land used for agricultural purposes. (2) Formerly, land let on lease under a rent, generally payable annually.

farmer, a person who cultivates a farm, whether he owns it, leases it, or is a cropper. (2) Formerly, the lessee of a tract of land.

F.A.S., price quoted by seller includes delivery of the goods along side an overseas vessel or on a dock designated by the buyer. U.C.C. § 2-319(2).

fasti dies, those days upon which legal business might be transacted, *i.e.,* lawful days.

fatetur facinus qui judicium fugit, he who flees judgment confesses his guilt.

favor, bias; partiality; prejudice.

fealty, formerly, the oath of fidelity to the lord taken by a tenant.

feasance (*fē´zans*), a performance.

feasant, doing or making.

feasor, doer or maker.

federal, pertaining to the national government of the United States. (2) Pertaining to an association of states or nations which have various relationships with a unified or general government. Often, the states or nations will operate within specific spheres and the unified or general government will concurrently operate within other spheres.

federal acts, or **federal laws,** statutes enacted by the Congress of the United States. They pertain to the matters which are within the legislative authority delegated to the national government by the United States Constitution, and permeate the laws of the states, insofar as they are applicable.

Federal Clean Air Act, see *Clean Air Act.*

Federal Coal Mine Health and Safety Act, see *Black Lung Benefits Act.*

Federal Deposit Insurance Act, see *Deposit Insurance Act.*

Federal Employers' Liability Act, statutes primarily applicable to carriers in interstate commerce, which abolished the major defenses formerly available to employers in lawsuits by their employees for personal injuries, and prohibited employers from limiting their liability by contract for injuries to employees. 45 U.S.C. §§ 51 *et seq.*

Federal Housing Act, an act to encourage improvement in housing standards and conditions and to provide a system of mutual mortgage insurance. 12 U.S.C. §§ 1701 *et seq.,* 18 U.S.C. §§ 433 *et seq.*

federal laws, see *federal acts.*

Federal Magistrate Act of 1979, an act to improve access to the federal courts by enlarging the civil and criminal jurisdiction of United States magistrates (*q.v.*), and for other purposes. 18 U.S.C. § 3401, 28 U.S.C. §§ 604, 631, 633-636, 1915.

federal question, an issue of law or controversy cognizable by the United States courts because it involves the construction of the Constitution, a federal law, or treaty.

federal question jurisdiction, federal jurisdiction can exist when a plaintiff or defendant can demonstrate a purely federal question. Federal district courts have original jurisdiction over civil actions arising under the constitution, laws and treaties of the United States.

Federal Reserve Act, an act to provide for the establishment of Federal reserve banks, to furnish an elastic currency, to afford means of rediscounting commercial paper, and to establish a more effective supervision of banking in the United States. 12 U.S.C. §§ 221 *et seq.*

Federal Reserve Bank, a banking corporation established under the Federal Reserve Act (*q.v.*) which is privately owned by member banks and serves the member banks, to the exclusion of public customers.

Federal Rules Act, the act which gave the Supreme Court of the United States authority to promulgate the Federal Rules of Civil Procedure. (*q.v.*). 28 U.S.C. § 2072; 48 Stat. 1064 (1934).

Federal Rules of Civil Procedure, rules (*q.v.*) which govern the procedure in the United States district courts in all suits of a civil nature whether cognizable as cases at law or in equity or in admiralty, with certain exceptions. They are to be construed to secure the just, speedy, and inexpensive determination of every action. They provide for one form of action to be known as a civil action. With modifications, they have been adopted by a large number of state courts. Adopted by order of U.S. Supreme Court December 20, 1937, transmitted to Congress of the U.S. January 3, 1938, effective September 16, 1938, and subsequently amended. Authorized by Federal Rules Act (*q.v.*).

Federal Rules of Criminal Procedure, rules (*q.v.*) which govern the procedure in all criminal proceedings in the U.S. courts, and whenever specifically provided for in one of the rules, to preliminary, supplementary, and special proceedings before U.S. magistrates and at proceedings before state and local judicial officers. They are intended to provide for the just determination of every criminal proceeding. They are to be construed to secure simplicity in procedure, fairness in administration, and the elimination of unjustifiable expense and delay. Effective in 1945; subsequently amended.

Federal Rules of Evidence, rules (*q.v.*) which govern proceedings in the United States courts and before United States magistrates. They are to be construed to secure fairness in administration, elimination of unjustifiable expense and delay, and promotion of growth and development of the law of evidence to the end that the truth may be ascertained and proceedings justly determined. Established by Pub. L. 93-595, effective July 1, 1975. Frequently followed by state courts.

Federal Trade Commission Acts, acts to create a Federal Trade Commission and to define its powers and duties. 15 U.S.C. §§ 41 *et seq.*; 38 Stat. 717 (1914); 52 Stat. 111 (1938).

Federal Youth Corrections Act, an act to provide a system for the treatment and rehabilitation of youth offenders, to improve the administration of criminal justice, and for other purposes. Among other things, it deals with sentencing, treatment, facilities, placement of youth offenders, their release, supervision of released youth offenders, apprehension of released offenders, and setting aside of convictions. 18 U.S.C. §§ 5005-5026.

fee, compensation for official or professional services. (2) An estate (*q.v.*) in property which goes to the heir of the owner, if he dies without disposing of it. Fees consist of three types: (a) Fee simple, or fee simple absolute, a freehold estate of inheritance, absolute and unqualified. This is the highest and most ample estate known to the law, out of which all others are carved. An owner in fee has absolute power of disposition. (b) Qualified, or base fee (*q.v.*). (c) Fee tail, a freehold estate of inheritance, limited to a person and particular heirs of his body, male or female.

fee farm, formerly land held in perpetuity by the tenant and his heirs at a yearly rent; a perpetual leasehold estate. Cf. *ground rent.*

fee simple, or **fee simple absolute,** see *fee (2)(a).*

fee tail, see *fee (2)(c).*

feigned issue, formerly, a proceeding whereby an important point could, by consent of the parties, be determined by a jury, without bringing an action, or raising it in pleadings.

fellow servant, formerly, a defense which could be raised by an employer, when sued by his employee for damages on account of personal injuries which he received in his employment, that the employer was not responsible for injuries to his employees which were caused by various other employees of the same employer. See also, *employers' liability acts* and *workers' compensation.*

felo de se (a felon with respect to himself), a person who commits suicide.

felonious assault, knowingly causing or attempting to cause serious physical harm to another by means of a deadly weapon or dangerous ordnance.

felonious homicide, killing a human creature without a legal justification or excuse. See also, *homicide.*

felony, a type of crime which is of a relatively serious nature; usually various offenses in various jurisdictions for which the maximum penalty can be death or imprisonment in the state penitentiary, regardless of such lesser penalty as may in fact be imposed. Occasionally defined by various state statutes. (2) Formerly, every offense at common law which caused a forfeiture of lands or goods, besides being punishable by death, imprisonment, or other severe penalty.

felony murder, rule stating that all killings perpetrated in the course of a felony constitute murder.

feme covert (*fĕm cō vĕrt*), a married woman. Cf. *Baron et feme.*

feme sole (*fĕm sōl*), an unmarried woman.

feoffment (*fĕf mant*), or **enfeoffment,** formerly, the transfer of possession of an English freehold estate by a ceremony called livery of seisin (*q.v.*), which consisted of a public delivery of the land by the transferor to the transferee. This was usually recorded in an instrument called a deed of feoffment.

fe'rae natu'rae, wild animals in their natural state.

fe'riae (Rom.), holidays.

ferme (*färm*), a farm; rent; a lease.

ferry, the franchise (*q.v.*) to carry persons or goods across a river for a toll.

feticide, or **foeticide,** criminal abortion.

fetus, or **foetus,** a flexible term for an unborn child. In some jurisdictions, the time which elapses after conception affects the definition.

feud, formerly, a grant of land made by a feudal superior or lord to a tenant in return for fealty (*q.v.*), military services, and other services. The lord in return was bound to protect the tenant. This was called the feudal system, which prevailed over the greater part of Europe in the Middle Ages.

feudal system, see *feud.*

fi. fa., abbreviation for fieri facias (*q.v.*).

fiat (*fī ăt*) (let it be done), a decree; an order or warrant by a judge or other constituted authority.

fiat justitia, ruat coelum, let right be done, though the heavens should fall.

fictio est contra veritatem, sed pro veritate habetur, fiction is against the truth, but it is to be esteemed truth.

fictio legis inique operatur alicui damnum vel injuriam, a legal fiction does not properly work loss or injury.

fictio legis neminem laedit, a fiction of law injures no one.

fictions, see *legal fiction.*

fictitious payee, a nonexistent person, who is not, and is not intended to be, a party to a negotiable instrument, but whose name is inserted as payee.

fidu'cia (Rom.), a contract by which a person transferred his property to another, on condition that it should be restored to him.

fiduciary, a broad term for someone who has a duty to act for the benefit of someone else. He must subordinate his personal interests to that duty in the event that there is a conflict. The duty requires fulfillment of trust and confidence, *e.g.,* trustee, executor, administrator, guardian, committee, assignee for the benefit of creditors, and public official. (2) Includes personal representative, guardian, conservator, and trustee. Uniform Probate Code § 1-201(13).

fiduciary relation, descriptive of the duties imposed upon persons who occupy a position of peculiar confidence toward others, *e.g.*, a trustee, executor, administrator, or director of a corporation. See also, *fiduciary*.

fief *(fēf)*, formerly, an English fee or manor.

fi'eri fa'cias, or **fi. fa.,** (that you cause to be made), an execution in a civil action, which is directed to the sheriff, via which a person who has recovered judgment for any debt or damages may obtain satisfaction from the personal property of the judgment debtor.

fi'eri fe'ci (I have caused to be made), a return made by a sheriff when he has executed a writ of fieri facias (*q.v.*) and levied the debt or part of it.

fieri non debet, sed factum valet, it ought not to have been done, but being done it is binding, *e.g.*, a marriage without proper consent.

fifty-five m.p.h. law, see *Emergency Highway Energy Conservation Act*.

file, see *filing*.

filiation, the relation of a child to its father.

filing, the act of delivering a deed, mortgage, financing statement, pleading, motion, court order, or other paper, to the officer who is authorized by law to receive it and preserve it for a particular purpose, *e.g.*, a court clerk or filing officer.

fi'lum, *l.*, a thread; a line; a boundary.

final, last; that which ends or concludes.

final decision, final judgment, or **final order,** a decree or judgment of a court which terminates the litigation in the court which renders it. Cf. *interlocutory*. (2) The United States Courts of Appeals have jurisdiction of appeals from certain final decisions of United States District Courts, 28 U.S.C. § 1291, but the courts have had difficulty defining final decision in that context. A decision may be final, even if it does not terminate the litigation, if the issue which is decided is fundamental to the further conduct of the case. (3) An order is a final judgment for purposes of United States Supreme Court jurisdiction if it involves a right separable from, and collateral to, the merits.

financial institution, any organization authorized to do business under state or federal laws relating to financial institutions, including without limitation banks and trust companies, savings banks, building and loan associations, savings and loan companies or associations, and credit unions. Uniform Probate Code § 6-101(3).

Financial Privacy Act, see *Right to Financial Privacy Act of 1978*.

financing statement, a document evidencing a secured transaction by outlining the obligation. A financing statement filed with the appropriate governmental bodies and authorities creates notice of a secured transaction to any parties.

finding, the determination of a court or jury as to a question of fact at issue, as distinguished from a court's conclusions of law. Fed. R Civ. P. 52(a). (2) The discovery and possession of that which belongs to, and was lost by another.

finding of no significant impact, FONSI; a document by a federal agency, as required by the National Environmental Policy Act (NEPA), briefly presenting the reasons why an action will not have a significant effect on the human environment and for which an environmental impact statement therefore will not be prepared; it shall include the environmental assessment or a summary of it. 40 C.F.R. § 1508.13.

fine, a form of punishment for the commission of a felony or misdemeanor, by which a sum of money is adjudged payable by the defendant to a public treasury. (2) Formerly, a sum of money paid by an English feudal tenant to his lord, usually on a change of estate, *e.g.*, in copyholds, on death or alienation.

firm, the persons composing a partnership, taken collectively. (2) The name or title under which a partnership transacts business.

firm offer, an offer (*q.v.*) by a merchant to buy or sell goods in a signed writing which by its terms gives assurance that it will be held open. It is not revocable for lack of consideration during the time stated, or if no time is stated, for a reasonable time, but in no event may such period of irrevocability exceed three months. Any such term of assurance on a form supplied by the offeree must be separately signed by the offeror. U.C.C. § 2-205. Cf. *option* (2).

first annuity mortgage, frequently, individuals have built up substantial equity in their property and as a result, a certain amount of money is taken out of the property and turned into an annuity with payments being made to service the debt but at the same time providing financial security to select individuals.

first impression, case of, a controversy which generates or raises a new question of law.

first instance, court of, the tribunal in which an action is first brought for trial, as contrasted with a court of appeal.

fiscal, a broad term pertaining to finance and often used with reference to the public treasury of a nation, state, county, or city.

fish royal, whale, porpoise, and sturgeon. They are so called because they belonged to the Crown, when they were washed ashore in England.

fishery, the right to catch fish. It may be public or common, *e.g.*, the right to catch fish in the sea and navigable rivers; or private, *e.g.*, the right to fish in nonnavigable streams, which belong to riparian owners.

fixed charges, expenses and allowances, such as rent, insurance premiums, and depreciation, which arise out of the existence of an enterprise, and which continue, regardless of whether business is conducted.

fixture, formerly, an article which was a personal chattel, but which, by being physically annexed to a building or land, became accessory to it and part and parcel of it. It was treated as belonging to the owner of the freehold, and passed with it to a vendee, and, though annexed by a tenant for his own convenience in the occupation of the premises, could not be removed by him. The rule has been modified by statute in many of the states, and is significantly relaxed in practice, especially as between landlord and tenant. Trade fixtures and ornamental fixtures may usually be removed by the tenant at the end of his term, provided he does no material injury to the freehold. Written leases often make specific provisions concerning the matter.

f.k.a., formerly known as.

flag, an emblem or symbol, usually rectangular and made of cloth, which designates a particular nation, state, city or other organization. The specific design of the United States flag has varied over the years. It was fixed by executive order of the President 10834, dated August 21, 1959, 3 C.F.R. The President 1959-1963 Compilation 367-370 (1964).

flagran'te delic'to, *l.*, in the very act of committing the crime.

floating capital, funds retained to meet current expenses.

floating indebtedness, unpaid obligations which grow out of current operations, which are not funded and for which there are no provisions for payment. Usually used to describe a public debt of such a nature.

floating zone, a special use district in which no specific location is assigned in the zoning ordinance. When the need for such a zone arises, the same public body that enacts the zoning ordinance enacts an amendment to the ordinance carving a new zone out of some existing zone.

floor plan rule, a principle which estops the owner of an article, placed by him on the floor of a retail dealer's showroom for sale, from denying the title of an innocent purchaser who has purchased from such dealer in the course of ordinary retail trade, without knowledge of any conflicting claim.

flotsam, goods cast overboard or lost from a vessel, which are found floating on the sea. Cf. *jetsam* and *ligan*.

FMLA, see *Family and Medical Leave Act*.

F.O.B., used in connection with a named place or vehicle, the price includes the cost of loading and delivery to that place or vehicle. U.C.C. § 2-319(1).

foe'nus nau'ticum, *l.*, marine interest. See also, *bottomry*.

foeticide, see *feticide*.

foetus, see *fetus*.

folc, or **folk,** the people.

FONSI, see *finding of no significant impact*.

food, anything and everything which human beings eat or drink to sustain life, including shortening, seasoning, candy, and confectionery.

Food, Drug and Cosmetic Act, an act to prohibit the movement in interstate commerce of adulterated and misbranded food, drugs, and cosmetics. 21 U.S.C. §§ 301-392

force, a flexible term for physical power, coercion, or unlawful violence. It may be (a) simple; (b) compound, *i.e.*, when some other crime is committed at the same time; (c) implied, as in every trespass. See also, *use of force*.

force and arms, with (vi et armis), words occasionally inserted in a declaration of trespass or indictment, though not absolutely necessary. See also, *force (c)*.

force majeure, a contract clause specifying that problems beyond the reasonable control of the parties will excuse performance.

forced heirs, in some jurisdictions, persons whom the testator cannot deprive of the part of his estate given them by law, except where he has just cause to disinherit them.

forcible entry, a taking possession of lands or buildings with force, threats, or actual violence (vi et armis), whether done by the actual owner or a stranger.

forcible detainer, the forcible keeping of possession of lands or buildings by one not the owner and not entitled to the possession. (2) Under some statutes, the refusal of a person, who is not entitled to possession, to give possession to the owner.

foreclosure, a procedure by which mortgaged property is publicly sold by order of court to the highest bidder, and the sum so generated, or so much of it as is necessary, is applied to the satisfaction of the mortgage debt. (2) Formerly, a proceeding, by which a mortgagor's right to redeem mortgaged property at any time, on payment of the debt secured, with interest, was barred.

foregift, a premium for a lease.

forehand rent, rent payable in advance.

foreign, something which belongs to another country or subject matter. Every nation is foreign to all the rest, and the several states are foreign to each other, with respect to their laws, although all are domestic in relation to the United States government and laws.

foreign bill of exchange, one drawn on a drawee residing in a different state or country from the drawer.

foreign corporation, a corporation (*q.v.*) created under the laws of another state or government.

Foreign Corrupt Practices Act of 1977, title I of an act to amend the Securities Exchange Act of 1934 (*q.v.*) to make it unlawful for an issuer of registered securities, or an issuer required to file reports, to make certain payments to foreign officials and other foreign persons, to require such issuers to maintain accurate records, and for other purposes. 15 U.S.C. §§ 78m, 78dd-1, 78dd-2, 78ff.

foreign judgment, a judgment (*q.v.*) rendered by a court of another state or country, than the one in which it is sought to enforce the judgment. The records and judicial proceedings of the courts of any of the states, when properly authenticated, are entitled to the same faith and credit in the courts of any other state as they have in the courts from whence the records are taken. U.S. Const. Art. IV, Sec. 1.

foreign laws, those enacted and in force in a foreign state or country.

foreign plea, a defense to a lawsuit in which the defending party objects to the court's jurisdiction.

forejudger, an English judgment by which a person is deprived of a thing or right.

forensic, belonging to, or applied in, courts of justice.

forensic medicine, the application of medical knowledge to the resolution of legal disputes; the influence of medical science on a lawsuit. (2) Sometimes used as a synonym for medical jurisprudence (*q.v.*).

foreseeable, capable of being known beforehand; descriptive of results, *e.g.*, some kind of harm, which should be anticipated will eventually occur from a particular condition of fact.

forestall, to head off or obstruct.

forestalling the market, buying merchandise or provisions on their way to market in such quantities as to destroy competition and enhance the price. Cf. *monopoly.*

forfeiture, occasionally, the loss of some right or property as a penalty for some illegal act.

forfeiture of a bond, an order of court that a bond be paid in cash to the public treasury because of the failure to perform the condition.

forfeiture of a lease, putting an end to the term for the nonpayment of rent or nonperformance of other conditions at the stipulated time. Courts tend to disfavor such acts.

forge, to make a false instrument for the purpose of fraud and deceit.

forged bill, forged check, or **forged draft,** an instrument on which the signatures are forged or otherwise falsely affixed.

forgery, the crimen falsi (*q.v.*) of the Roman law the false making or alteration of an instrument which purports on its face to be good and valid for the purposes for which it was created. (2) The false or unauthorized signature of a document, with a design to defraud. (3) With purpose to defraud or injure anyone, or with knowledge that he is facilitating a fraud or injury to be perpetrated by anyone, (a) altering any writing (*q.v.*) of another without his authority, (b) making, completing, executing, authenticating, issuing, or transferring a writing (*q.v.*) so that it purports to be the act of another who did not authorize the act, or to have been executed at a time or place or in a numbered sequence other than was in fact the case, or to be a copy of an original when no such original existed, or (c) uttering a writing (*q.v.*) which he knows to be forged in a manner specified in (a) or (b). Model Penal Code § 224.1(1).

form, the manner, *e.g.*, of a pleading, as opposed to the content. Often used as the opposite of substance. (2) A model to aid an attorney in drawing up an instrument, pleading, order, judgment, or other legal document.

forma dat esse, form gives being.

forma pauperis, see *in forma pauperis*.

formal contract, one, the legal operation of which is dependent upon the form in which it is made, the mode of expression, and not upon the sufficiency of the consideration that is given in return for it or upon any change of position by the promisee in reliance upon it.

formal party, or **nominal party,** a person who is not a real party in interest (*q.v.*), but is a party in name only, *e.g.*, someone who must be made a party for formal or representative reasons of guardianship or public office.

formal proceedings, those conducted before a judge with notice to interested persons. Uniform Probate Code § 1-201(15).

for'medon, formerly, an English writ for a person claiming a right to real property by virtue of a gift in tail (per formam doni), when out of possession.

former testimony, testimony (*q.v.*) given as a witness at another hearing of the same or a different proceeding, or in a deposition taken in compliance with law in the course of the same or another proceeding, if the party against whom the testimony is now offered, or in a civil action or proceeding, a predecessor in interest, had an opportunity and similar motive to develop the testimony by direct, cross, or redirect examination. It is not excluded by the hearsay (*q.v.*) rule if the declarant (*q.v.*) is unavailable as a witness. Fed. R. Evid. 804(b)(1).

formulary, a form; a precedent; a collection of forms; a collection of formulas.

fornication, a flexible term, often defined by various state statutes, for sexual intercourse by an unmarried person. It is usually punishable as a misdemeanor.

forprise, an exception or reservation. (2) An exaction.

forswear, to swear to a falsehood. (2) To reject or renounce upon oath.

forthcoming bond, a written obligation, taken by a sheriff, to secure the production of goods levied upon, when required.

forthwith, immediately; as soon as the nature of the case will permit.

fortior est custodia legis quam hominis, the custody of the law is stronger than man's.

fortuitous, accidental; happening by chance; unexpected; inevitable.

fo'rum, *l.,* a court of justice; the place where justice must be sought. (2) Formerly, an open space in Roman cities where the people assembled, markets were held, and the magistrates sat to transact their business.

fo'rum contrac'tus, the court of the place of making a contract.

fo'rum domici'lii, the court of a person's domicile.

forum non conveniens, an inconvenient court. (2) A doctrine which presupposes at least two forums in which a defendant is amenable to process. A court in such a situation may resist imposition upon its jurisdiction, even when jurisdiction is authorized by the letter of a general venue (*q.v.*) statute. It leaves much to the discretion of the court to which plaintiff resorts, but unless the balance is strongly in favor of the defendant, the plaintiff's choice of forum should rarely be disturbed. Factors to be considered: private interest of the litigant, *e.g.,* relative ease of access to sources of proof, availability of compulsory process for attendance of witnesses, cost of obtaining attendance of witnesses, possibility of view of the premises, and all other practical problems that make trial of a case easy, expeditious, and inexpensive;

public interest, *e.g.*, administrative difficulties in the court, burden of jury duty, and holding the trial in the view of the people whose affairs it touches.

fo'rum ori'ginis, the court of that place of which, at the time of his birth, a person's father was a citizen.

fo'rum re'i ges'tae, the court of the place where a thing was done.

fo'rum re'i si'tae, the court of the place where the thing, *e.g.*, real property, which is the subject of the action, is situated.

four corners, information or an intention which is apparent on the face of a deed, will, contract, or other instrument, without aid from extrinsic testimony, and by giving effect to the entire instrument, is said to be gleaned from its four corners.

fractionem diei non recipit lex, the law does not take notice of a portion of a day. When, therefore, a thing is to be done upon a certain day, all that day is allowed to do it.

franchise, a special privilege conferred by government, and vested in particular persons. In the United States, franchises are generally exercised by corporations created for the purpose, and deriving their powers under general or special laws, *e.g.*, telephone companies, transit systems, and power companies. (2) Elective franchise is the privilege of voting at an election of public officers. (3) The privilege of marketing the products and using the trade name, trademarks, and capitalizing on the good will of a manufacturer, merchant, or other business concern. It is usually conferred for a consideration.

franchise tax, revenue exacted from a corporation, for the privilege to do business in a state, and to own and use a part of its capital and property in that state. Often defined by various state statutes.

frank, free; the privilege of sending letters and other matters by the public mails without paying postage. (2) The signature placed on the envelope or wrapper by one having such a privilege, to indicate that it goes free.

frank-almoign (*moin*), free alms, the tenure by which English religious corporations hold land.

frank-fee, formerly, lands held by a man to himself and his heirs, free of service.

frank-tenement, an English freehold estate.

franking privilege, see *frank*.

fraud, a broad term for all kinds of acts which have as their objective the gain of an advantage to another's detriment, by deceitful or unfair means. It may be (a) actual, where there is deliberate misrepresentation or concealment, or (b) constructive, where the court implies it either from the nature of the contract or from the relation of the parties. Some courts are reluctant to define this term, because of the myriad forms which it can take. Fraud is a ground for setting aside a transaction, at the option of the person prejudiced by it, or for recovery of damages. See also, *deceit: misrepresentation; suppressio veri.* Cf. *mistake.*

fraud in the factum, getting one to sign a document through misrepresentation as to the nature of the document where the signer has no knowledge nor reasonable opportunity to obtain knowledge about the character of the document.

fraud in the inducement, misrepresentation of the terms, quality, etc. of a contractual relationship or other transaction that leads a person to agree to enter the transaction with a false understanding of the risks and obligations of the transaction.

Frauds, Statute of, various state legislative acts, patterned after a 1677 English act, known by the same name. *E.g.,* U.C.C. § 2-201. Because of the variations in each state, reference must be made to the specific state statutes. The main object was to take away the facilities for fraud, and the temptation to perjury, which arose in verbal obligations, the proof of which depended upon oral evidence. Its most common provisions are these: (a) all leases, excepting those for less than three years, shall have the force of leases at will only, unless they are in writing and signed by the parties or their agents; (b) assignments and surrenders of leases and interests in land must be in writing; (c) all declarations and assignments of trusts must be in writing, signed by the party (trusts arising by implication of law are, however, excepted); (d) no action shall be brought upon a guarantee, or upon any contract for sale of lands, or any interest in or concerning them, or upon any agreement which is not to be performed within a year, unless the agreement is in writing and signed by the party to be charged or his agent; (e) no contract for the sale of goods for a certain price or more, *e.g.,* $500.00, U.C.C. § 2-201, shall be good, unless the buyer accept part, or give something in part payment, or some memorandum thereof be signed by the parties to be charged or their agents.

fraudulent, descriptive of something which results in, or results from, a fraud (*q.v.*).

fraudulent conversion, theft offense in which the defendant has received into his possession the money or property of another person, firm, or corporation, and fraudulently withholds, converts, or applies the same to or for his own use and benefit, or to the use and benefit of any person other than the one to whom the money or property belonged.

fraudulent conveyance, a transfer of something of value, *e.g.,* property or money, to which creditors are entitled to look for the satisfaction of their claims, for the purpose of defeating the claims of those creditors. Often defined by various state statutes.

fraudulent misrepresentation, a misrepresentation (*q.v.*) which the maker (a) knows or believes is not as he represents it to be, (b) does not have the confidence in the accuracy of which that he states or implies, or (c) knows that he does not have the basis for that he states or implies. Restatement (Second) of Torts § 526. Accord, Restatement (Second) of Contracts § 162(1), if the maker intends his assertion to induce a party to manifest his assent (*q.v.*).

fraus est celare fraudem, it is fraud to conceal fraud.

fraus latet in generalibus, fraud lies hid in general expressions.

free, not bound; unrestricted; at liberty to act as one pleases.

free entry, egress, and regress, the right to go on and off land at will, *e.g.,* to take crops.

free ships, neutral ships. "Free ships make free goods," is a phrase often used to denote that goods on board a neutral ship shall be free from confiscation, even though belonging to an enemy.

Freedom of Information Act, an act relating to the organization and government of the United States and its civilian officers and employees, its agencies, and public information. 5 U.S.C. §§ 552 *et seq.;* 80 Stat. 383 (1966), as subsequently amended.

freehold, an estate in property, either in fee simple or tail, or for a person's life, whether his own or another person's.

freeholder, a person who owns a freehold (*q.v.*).

freeway, see *limited access highway.*

freight, the sum paid for the transportation of goods. (2) Goods which are being transported.

frequenter, a person who visits often. Occasionally defined by statute.

fresh, recent; not old, not stale.

fringe benefits, the residual part of total compensation provided by an employer to an employee, other than such direct elements of compensation as wage and salary, commission, bonus, overtime, and shift deferential payments, *i.e.,* employer contributions to social security, workers' compensation, unemployment compensation, health, life, and dental insurance, private pension plans, and cafeteria style benefit plans.

frolic of his own, an act of an employee, performed outside the scope of his employment, and with no intention of aiding his employer's business.

front foot, a measure used in apportioning and assessing the cost of public improvements, *e.g.,* streets, curbs, gutters, and sewer lines, in municipalities. By using this measure, the cost of the entire improvement is divided among abutting property owners, pro rata, according to the approximate benefit which each property receives from the improvement.

frontage, lands abutting upon a street or other improvement, frequently taken as the basis for levying assessments for improvements.

fruc'tus, *l.,* fruit; increase; that which results from a thing. See also, *fructus civiles.*

fruc'tus civi'les, all revenues which, though not strictly fruits, are recognized as such by law, *e.g.,* rent, interest, or profit.

fruc'tus industria'les, see *emblements.*

fruc'tus natura'les, products resulting from the powers of nature alone, *e.g.,* wool and milk.

fruc'tus penden'tes, fruits united with the thing which produced them.

frustra fit per plura, quod fieri potest per pauciora, that is needlessly done by many, *e.g.,* words, which can be done by less.

frustra probatur quod probatum non relevat, it is useless to prove that which, when proved, is not relevant.

fugitive, a person who runs away. (2) A person who, having committed a crime, flees from the jurisdiction within which it was committed, in order to escape punishment. See also, *extradition.*

full age, see *age (2).*

full faith and credit, the requirement that the public acts, records and judicial proceedings of every state shall be given the same effect by the courts of another state that they have by law and usage in the state of origin. U.S. Const., Art. IV, Sec. 1. Congress has prescribed the manner in which they may be proven. Cf. *comity* and *comity of nations.*

fully paid share, see *share.*

func'tus offi'cio, *l.,* having discharged his duty, *e.g.,* descriptive of an instrument, which once had life and power, but is no longer of value, because the power conferred by it has been exercised.

fund, a flexible term for something of value designated for a specific purpose, *e.g.,* cash for payment of debts. (2) Capital; hence, to fund is to capitalize.

fungible, with respect to goods or securities, those of which any unit is, by nature or usage of trade, the equivalent of any other like unit. U.C.C. § 1-201(17). *E.g.,* a bushel of wheat or other grain.

furiosi nulla voluntas est, a madman has no free will, *i.e.,* he is not criminally responsible.

further assurance, a covenant or promise made by a vendor or a grantor, to the effect that he will execute any additional conveyance or instrument, that may be required to perfect the vendee's or grantee's title.

furtum non est ubi initium habet detentionis per dominum rei, there is no theft where the origin of the possession was with the consent of the owner, *i.e.,* where the original possession is lawful, as in the case of a bailee.

future estate, an interest in property, the possession of which, is to commence at some future time. It includes remainders, reversions, and estates limited to commerce in futuro.

future goods, goods (*q.v.*) which are not both existing and identified. U.C. C. § 2-105(2).

futures, speculative contracts, which contemplate the delivery of the subject of the contract at some future time.

G

gabel', formerly, a rent, duty, tax, or service.

gage, (*l.,* vadium), a pawn or pledge.

gambling, see *gaming.*

game, birds and beasts of a wild nature that may be taken or killed by fowling and hunting. Often defined by various state statutes.

game laws, various national and state statutes concerning the preservation of game from useless and unreasonable destruction, and restricting their capture or killing to certain seasons of the year when it will interfere least with their propagation.

game of chance, an event, project, or contest which is determined entirely, or in part, by lot or luck, or fortuitously, and in which judgment, practice, skill, or adroitness have no office at all, or are thwarted. See also, *chance.*

gaming, or **gambling,** a broad and flexible term for the wagering of money, or something else of value, on the outcome or occurrence of an event. In some cases, the outcome of the event must result from chance, and in other cases, the event can be of any nature. Often defined by various national and state statutes. (2) In a narrow sense, playing at cards, dice, billiards, or other games for money, the winner taking the money of the loser.

ganancial property, a term for community property (*q.v.*).

gaol (*jāl*), see *jail.*

gaol delivery, an English commission for a judge to try prisoners and deliver them out of jail.

garnish, to attach via a garnishment (*q.v.*). See also, *attachment*.

garnishee, a person in whose hands a debt is attached, *i.e.*, who is warned not to pay money which he owes to another person, when the latter is alleged, or adjudged, to be indebted to the person warning or giving notice. See also, *attachment*.

garnishment, a form of attachment (*q.v.*), which has as its object the appropriation of money or credits in the hands of a third party.

gavelkind, land that yields rents. Formerly, a type of ancient English land tenure.

gemot', a moot (*q.v.*); meeting; public assembly.

general, common to many or all; extensive; not restricted; not special.

general acceptance, an unconditional acceptance by the drawee of a bill of exchange.

general agent, a person authorized to take charge of a particular line of business.

general appearance, a submission of the defendant to the jurisdiction of the court for all purposes.

general assembly, a body of legislators, *i.e.*, the senate and house of representatives.

general assignment, a transfer of all of a person's property which is subject to his debts to a fiduciary for the benefit of his creditors.

general average, see *average*.

general creditor, a person to whom a debt is owed, but who holds no security for the debt.

general damages, see *damages*.

general demurrer, see *demurrer*.

general issue, a response to a petition or a complaint filed in court, simply traversing the allegations in the petition or complaint, without offering any special matter to evade it, *e.g.*, the plea of not guilty. See also, *answer (1)* and *traverse*.

general jurisdiction, see *jurisdiction (5)*.

general legacy, bequest or devise, a gift of personal property which the testator intends to be satisfied from the general assets of the estate.

general partnership, a form of partnership under which the partners assume losses and liabilities of the business equally or decide by written agreement on another alternative.

general power of appointment, authority by which the donee of the power may appoint anyone. See also, *power of appointment*.

general ship, a vessel which is not chartered to any particular person, but which undertakes to carry for freight the goods of any one wishing to send them to any of the ports for which it is bound. The contract with each freighter is usually made by bill of lading.

general verdict, the decision of a jury, when they simply find for the plaintiff or defendant, without specifying the particular facts which they found from the evidence.

general warranty, a covenant or undertaking that a grantor and his heirs and personal representatives will forever warrant and defend real property for the grantee, his heirs, personal representatives, and assigns, against the claims and demands of all persons whatever. Cf. *special warranty.*

generale nihil certum implicat, a general expression implies nothing certain.

generalia specialibus non derogant, general words do not derogate from special.

generalis regula generaliter est intelligenda, a general rule is understood generally.

generation-skipping transfer tax, a provision of the 1986 Tax Reform Act which imposes such a tax on (a) transfers under trusts (or similar arrangements) having beneficiaries in more than one generation below that of the transferor, and (b) direct transfers to beneficiaries more than one generation below that of the transferor. Three taxable events trigger the imposition of the tax, (1) a taxable termination, (2) a taxable distribution, and (3) a direct skip (an absolute transfer for the benefit of a person at least two generations below that of the transferor.

Geothermal Energy Act of 1980, title VI of the Energy Security Act (*q.v.*), concerning loans, programs, use of geothermal energy, and regulations. 16 U.S.C. §§ 796, 824a-3, 824i, 824j; 30 U.S.C. §§ 1141, 1143, 1146, 1147, 1501 *et seq.*

gestation, the carrying of a child in the womb for the period which elapses between its conception and birth, usually about nine thirty-day months. This period is added, where gestation exists, to that which is allowed by the rule against perpetuities.

ges'tio, *l.,* behavior or conduct.

GI Bill of Rights, various acts which provide benefits and aid for returning war veterans. 38 U.S.C. §§ 693 *et seq.*

gift, a voluntary transfer of real or personal property, made without receiving a valid consideration; a gratuitous transfer of ownership; a gift proceeds from a detached and disinterested generosity out of affection, respect, admiration, charity or like impulses. See also, *donatio.*

gift causa mortis, a gift (*q.v.*), made by reason of, or in view of, death. Often revocable, if the donor (*q.v.*), does so during his lifetime.

gift inter vivos, a gift (*q.v.*) which is irrevocable and made while the donor (*q.v.*) is alive.

Gifted and Talented Children's Education Act of 1978, part A of title IX of an act to extend and amend expiring elementary and secondary education programs, and for other purposes, also known as the Education Amendments of 1978. 20 U.S.C. §§ 3311 *et seq.*

gist, the main point in question; the pith of a matter.

gist of action, the cause for which an action lies; the essential ground and foundation of a suit.

Glass-Steagall Act, provisions of the Banking Act of 1933 that mandated a separation of the commercial and investment banking industries. 12 U.S.C. §§ 377 *et al.;* 48 Stat. 162, §§ 16, 20, 21, 32 (1933).

good, not bad; adequate; sufficient; valid.

good behavior, conduct in conformity with law. When a person is suspected, on reasonable grounds, of an intent to commit a crime or misdemeanor, he may be required to give security for his good behavior for a stated time.

good consideration, a consideration (*q.v.*) founded on motives of generosity, prudence, and natural duty, *e.g.,* natural love and affection. See also, *meritorious consideration.*

good faith, honesty of purpose which negates an intent to defraud. A legal standard of motivation for a person's acts or conduct in dealing with his fellow men. (2) Honesty in fact in the conduct or transaction concerned. U.C.C. § 1-201 (19). (3) In the case of a merchant, honesty in fact and the observance of reasonable commercial standards of fair dealing in the trade. U.C.C. § 2-103(1) (b).

good samaritan law, a statute in derogation of the common law rule that anyone who voluntarily renders assistance to another in an emergency is liable for any negligence in providing assistance, limiting the liability of lay persons in such situations to willful and wanton misconduct.

good will, the intangible advantage or benefit which is acquired by a business, beyond the mere value of the capital or stock employed therein, in consequence of its having a body of regular customers and a favorable reputation.

goods, all things, including specially manufactured goods, which are movable at the time of identification to a contract for sale, other than the money in which the price is to be paid, investment securities, and things in action. It also includes the unborn young of animals and growing crops and certain other identified things attached to realty, *e.g.*, timber or minerals to be removed from realty upon severance by the seller. U.C.C. § 2-105.

goods and chattels, personal property, as distinguished from real property. The term includes, *e.g.*, merchandise for sale, household effects, office equipment, and jewelry. See also, *chattels.*

Government in the Sunshine Act, an act to provide that meetings of federal government agencies shall be open to the public, and for other purposes. 5 U.S.C. § 552b. See also, *open-meeting law.*

government survey, a way of describing land by a rectangular system of land surveys.

governmental function, a flexible term for various activities of a political entity or subdivision thereof, imposed or required for the protection and benefit of the general public, not having regard to any particular benefit to be derived as a corporate body, or to the citizens collectively, outside their relation to the state. *e.g.*, sewage disposal, law enforcement, fire protection, public education, and operation of public parks.

grace, days of, time of indulgence, usually three days, granted to an acceptor or maker for the payment of his bill of exchange or note.

graduated payment mortgage, a mortgage that has an initial lower rate affording first-time home buyers a lower payment option and gradually increasing payments.

graffer, formerly, a notary or scrivener.

grammatica falsa non vitiat chartam, false grammar does not vitiate a deed.

grand assize, formerly, a peculiar kind of English trial by jury, giving the alternative of trial by battle. See also, *assisa.*

grand cape, see *cape.*

grand jury, a body of persons, not less than twelve nor more than twenty-four, freeholders of a county, whose duty it is, on hearing the evidence for the prosecution in each proposed bill of indictment, to decide whether a sufficient case is made out, on which to hold the accused for trial. It is a body which is convened by authority of a court and serves as an instrumentality of the court. It has authority to investigate and to accuse, but it is not authorized to try cases. It is a creature of the common law which was instituted to protect the people from governmental oppression. In a few states, it has been partially abolished, but in others it exists by constitutional mandate. No person shall be held to answer for a capital or otherwise infamous federal crime, unless on a presentment or indictment of a grand jury, except in cases arising in the land or naval forces, or in the militia, when in actual service in time of war or public danger. U.S. Const., Amend. V. See also, *ignoramus* and *true bill.*

grand larceny, a more serious degree of larceny (*q.v.*), distinguished from petit larceny, and classified according to the value of the subject of the larceny, *e.g.*, $20.00 or more. Usually defined by statutes in the various states.

Granger Cases, six lawsuits, decided by the United States Supreme Court in 1876, growing out of the agitation for regulation of railroads and warehouses.

grant, to convey or transfer. The grantor is he who transfers, and the grantee is he who receives. (2) A license, right, or authority conferred, *e.g.*, grant of a patent, of probate, or of administration.

gratuitous, made without a legal consideration.

gratuitous licensee, any visitor, other than a business visitor, who is not a trespasser.

great care, that which a prudent person takes of his own property.

Great-Charter, see *Magna Charta.*

great seal, an emblem of sovereignty, used to authenticate public documents. Each state of the United States and the national government use unique emblems for this purpose.

grievance, a wrong which gives rise to a complaint because it is unjust, discriminatory and oppressive; typically used in the labor law context to describe a complaint filed by an employee or the employee's union representative against the employer.

gross, great, excessive, entire.

gross average, an average (*q.v.*) which falls on ship, cargo, and freight, as distinguished from particular average.

gross income, all income from whatever source derived, unless excluded by law; all undeniable accessions to wealth, clearly realized, and over which the taxpayer has complete dominion and control. Gross income includes the receipt of any financial benefit which is: (1) not a mere return of capital, and (2) not accompanied by a contemporaneously acknowledged obligation to repay, and (3) not excluded by a specific statutory provision. Gross income includes income realized in any form, whether in money, property, or services.

gross negligence, a flexible term for a high degree of negligence; such want of care as not even inattentive and thoughtless men are guilty of with respect to their own property.

gross profits, see *profit.*

gross sexual imposition, the act of a male who has sexual intercourse with a female not his wife, if: (a) he compels her to submit by any threat that would prevent resistance by a woman of ordinary resolution; or (b) he knows that she suffers from a mental disease or defect which renders her incapable of appraising the nature of her conduct; or (c) he knows that she is unaware that a sexual act is being committed upon her or that she submits because she mistakenly supposes that he is her husband. Model Penal Code § 213.1(2). Cf. *rape (2)*.

ground rent, a sum of money, or other thing of value, which is paid by a person for the use of land taken on lease.

ground water, in the context of interference with the use of water, water that naturally lies or flows under the surface of the earth. Restatement (Second) of Torts § 845.

growing crops, see *away-going* and *emblements*.

guarantee, a person to whom a guaranty is made by a guarantor. See also, *guaranty*.

guarantor, a person who makes a guaranty. See also, *surety*.

guaranty, or **guarantee,** a promise (*q.v.*) to a person to be answerable for the payment of a debt, or the performance of a duty by another, in case he should fail to perform his engagement. It may be for a single act, or be a continuing guaranty, covering all transactions of like kind and to a like amount, until revoked by the guarantor. (2) A promise (*q.v.*) to be surety (*q.v.*) for the performance of a contractual obligation made to the obligee. It is binding if the promise is in writing, signed by the promisor, and recites a purported consideration, the promise is made binding by statute, or the promisor should reasonably expect the promise to induce action or forebearance of a substantial character on the part of the promisee or a third person and the promise does induce such action or forebearance. Restatement (Second) of Contracts § 88.

guardian, a person appointed by a court to have the control or management of the person or property, or both, of another who is incapable of acting on his own behalf, *e.g.*, an infant or person of unsound mind (2) Guardians ad litem are appointed by the court to represent such persons, who are parties to a pending action. (3) A person who has qualified as a guardian of a minor or incapacitated person pursuant to testamentary or court appointment, but excludes one who is merely a guardian ad litem. Uniform Probate Code § 1-201(16). (4) A person who has qualified as a guardian of a minor or incapacitated person pursuant to parental or spousal nomination or court appointment, and includes a limited guardian, but excludes one who is merely a guardian ad litem. Uniform Probate Code § 5-103(6).

guardian ad litem, see *guardian*.

guest, a flexible term for various relationships between persons. (1) A person who is received at a hotel or motel. (2) A person who is given a gratuitous ride, for his own purposes, in a motor vehicle driven by another person.

guest statute, see *automobile guest statute.*

guilty, criminal, culpable. The status of a person who has violated the criminal laws, or has been found to have done so by due process of law.

H

ha'beas cor'pus, *l.* (that you have the body), words used in various writs, commanding one who detains another to have, or bring, him before the court issuing the same. See also, *habeas corpus ad subjiciendum.*

Ha'beas Cor'pus Act, the name given to the 1679 statute, which established the right of habeas corpus writs in cases of illegal detention. The right existed previously, but its efficiency had been impaired. This act gave it renewed force. See also, *habeas corpus ad subjiciendum.*

ha'beas cor'pus ad facien'dum et recipien'dum, or **cum causa,** a form of habeas corpus (*q.v.*), which issues when a person is sued in some inferior jurisdiction, and is desirous to remove the action into the superior court.

ha'beas cor'pus ad prosequen'dum, a form of habeas corpus (*q.v.*), which issued to remove a prisoner, in order that he might be tried in the proper jurisdiction.

ha'beas cor'pus ad responden'dum, a form of habeas corpus (*q.v.*), which issued in civil causes, to remove a person out of the custody of one court into that of another, so that he may be sued and answer in the latter.

ha'beas cor'pus ad satisfacien'dum, a form of habeas corpus (*q.v.*) which issued to remove a prisoner from one court to another, in order to charge him in execution upon a judgment of the last court.

ha'beas cor'pus ad subjicien'dum, the celebrated prerogative writ of American and English law, which is the usual remedy for a person deprived of his liberty. Its purpose is to test the legality of the restraints on a person's liberty, *i.e.,* whether he is restrained of his liberty by due process of law, not whether he is guilty or innocent. It is addressed to him who detains another in custody, and commands him to produce the body of the person in custody, with the day and cause of his caption and detention, and to do, submit to, and receive whatever the court shall think fit. This writ is guaranteed by U S. Const. Art. I, Sec. 9, and by the state constitutions. 28 U.S.C. §§ 2241-2255.

ha'beas cor'pus ad testifican'dum, a form of habeas corpus (*q.v.*), which issued to bring a witness into court, when he was in custody at the time of a trial.

habemus optimum testem, confidentem reum, we consider as the best witness a confessing defendant.

haben'dum, *l.,* a clause in a deed of conveyance which defines the extent of the interest conveyed.

habe're fa'cias, *l.,* (that you cause to have), words used in various writs of execution or in aid of execution.

habe're fa'cias possessio'nem, or **habe're fa'cias seisi'nam,** various writs issued for a successful plaintiff in ejectment, to put him in possession of the premises recovered.

habe're fa'cias vi'sum, a writ in divers real actions, where a view was required to be taken of the lands in controversy.

habita'tio, *l.,* (Rom.), the right of using a house as a dwelling.

habitual criminal statute, or **recidivist statute,** an act which imposes greater punishment for subsequent offenses than for the first. See also, *recidivism.*

hae'redes prox'imi, *l.,* (Rom.), heirs begotten by the person from whom they inherit; children.

hae'redes remotio'res, *l.,* (Rom.), heirs not begotten by him from whom they inherit, *e.g.,* grandchildren, descending in a direct line in infinitum.

haereditas, see *quaestus.*

haere'ditas ja'cens, *l.,* an estate in abeyance, *i.e.,* after the ancestor's death, and before the heir assumes possession.

hae'res, *l.,* an heir.

hae'res fac'tus (Rom.), an heir appointed by will.

hae'res legitimus est quem nuptiae demonstrant, he is the lawful heir whom the marriage proves to be so.

hae'res na'tus (Rom.), an heir by descent.

half blood, see *blood.*

half brother, see *brother.*

half sister, see *sister.*

hallucination, the perception by the senses of an object which has no existence; a symptom of insanity.

ham, or **hame,** formerly, a house.

hamlet, formerly, a small town.

hanaper office, formerly, an office in the common-law portion of the English Court of Chancery.

hand borrow, formerly, a kind of surety.

handhabend, a thief caught in the act, with the thing stolen in his hand.

Handicapped Individuals Act, see *Employment Opportunities for Handicapped Individuals Act.*

handsale, a sale confirmed by shaking hands, by which act the parties became bound.

handsel, earnest-money.

handwriting, anything written manually by a person, *e.g.*, with a pen or pencil.

harassment, with purpose to harass another: (a) making a telephone call without purpose of legitimate communication, (b) insulting, taunting, or challenging another in a manner likely to provoke violent or disorderly response, (c) making repeated communications anonymously or at extremely inconvenient hours, or in offensively coarse language, (d) subjecting another to an offensive touching, or (e) engaging in any other course of alarming conduct serving no legitimate purpose of the actor. Model Penal Code § 250.4.

harm, the existence of loss or detriment in fact of any kind to a person resulting from any cause. Restatement (Second) of Torts § 7(2).

harmless error, an error (*q.v.*) of a lower court or a defect in the proceeding of a lower court which does not affect the substantial rights of the parties. Fed. R. Civ. P. 61.

harriot, see *heriot.*

Hatch Act, an act to prevent pernicious political activities. 5 U.S.C. §§ 118i *et seq.*, 18 U.S.C. §§ 594 *et seq.*

hat money, primage; a small duty paid to the master and seamen of a ship.

hazardous employment, or **hazardous occupation,** a term used in worker's compensation statutes to mean work or service of a nature that incidentally occasions risks not present in other occupations. Occasionally defined by statutes in the respective states. (2) Similarly applied to statutes regulating the employment of minors.

head of the family, a person upon whom rests the legal or moral duty to support the members of the family. (2) A person who has accepted the responsibility of supporting the members of the family.

Head Start Act, subchapter B, subtitle A, tit. VI of an act to provide for reconciliation, also known as the Omnibus Budget Reconciliation Act of 1981. It provides for, among other things, financial assistance for

Head Start programs, appropriations, allotment of funds, designation of Head Start agencies, submission of plans to governors, administrative requirements and standards, appeals, notice and hearing, research, demonstration and pilot projects, and limitation with respect to certain unlawful activities. 42 U.S.C. §§ 9831 *et seq.*

headnote, see *syllabus.*

Health Insurance for the Aged and Disabled Act, unofficially called Medicare Act, title I of the Social Security Amendments of 1965, as subsequently amended; an act to provide a hospital insurance program for the aged under the Social Security Act with a supplemental medical benefits program, and an expanded program of medical assistance, to increase benefits under the Old-Age, Survivors, and Disability Insurance System, to improve the Federal-State public assistance programs, and for other purposes. 26 U S.C. § § 72 *et seq.*; 42 U.S.C. §§ 303 *et seq.*; 44 U.S.C. §§ 1395 *et seq.*; 45 U.S.C. §§ 228e, 231c, 231e-231l, 231n-231q and 231s.

Health Maintenance Organization Act, an act to amend the Public Health Service Act to provide assistance and encouragement for the establishment and expansion of health maintenance organizations, and for other purposes, as subsequently amended. 42 U.S.C. §§ 280c, 300e *et seq.*, 1320a-1, 1396a, 1396b.

hearing, a flexible term for a court proceeding or the trial of a suit. (2) The examination of witnesses incident to the making of a judicial determination as to whether an accused person shall be held for trial.

hearing examiner, a public official who is authorized by law to set times for hearings, summon witnesses, administer oaths, hear testimony, receive evidence, and make findings of fact or conclusions of law, or both, for various governmental administrative agencies. Analogous to a Commissioner (*q.v.*) of a court. Cf. *administrative law judge.*

hearsay, statements offered by a witness, based upon what someone else has told him, and not upon personal knowledge or observation. Usually, such evidence is inadmissible, but exceptions are made, *e.g.*, in questions of pedigree, custom, reputation, dying declarations, and statements made against the interest of the declarant. (2) A statement (*q.v.*), other than one made by the declarant (*q.v.*) while testifying at the trial or hearing, offered in evidence to prove the truth of the matter asserted. Fed. R. Evid. 801(c).

hedonic, value or satisfaction or pleasure; the non-earnings based value of life, the value we get from living as opposed to working.

hedonic damages, intangible damages for the lost pleasure of life, reduction of pleasure of life, and the loss of society and companionship; damages for the loss of value of life.

heir, a person who succeeds by operation of law, or via descent, to the estate (*q.v.*) of someone who dies intestate (*q.v.*). Such persons are identified by various statutes in the respective states. There can be no heir to a person who is living, but one whose right of inheritance is indefeasible, provided he outlive the ancestor, is an heir apparent. One who would be the heir if the ancestor should die immediately, but whose right of inheritance may be defeated by the birth of someone nearer to him, is an heir presumptive. (2) Occasionally limited to persons who succeed to real property. See also, *heirs.*

heir apparent, a person who is certain to inherit unless excluded by valid will.

heir presumptive, a person who will inherit if the potential intestate dies immediately, but who will be excluded if relatives closer in relationship to the intestate are born.

heirdom, succession by inheritance.

heirloom, occasionally, personal chattels which descend by special custom to the heir or devisee, instead of passing to the executor, *e.g.,* pictures, china, and jewels.

heirs, those persons, including the surviving spouse, who are entitled under the statutes of intestate succession to the property of a decedent. Uniform Probate Code § 1-201(17). See also, *heir.*

Heralds' College, an English corporation, established in 1483, empowered to make grants of arms and to permit change of names.

herbage, an English easement to pasture cattle on another's ground.

heredit'aments, a broad term for every kind of property that can be inherited. They are (a) corporeal, *e.g.,* lands and houses; and (b) incorporeal, *e.g.,* reversions, advowsons, and tithes. They are also (a) real *i.e.,* lands; (b) personal, *i.e.,* which are not connected with lands, *e.g.,* an annuity to a man and his heirs, or (c) mixed.

her'iot (Sc. herezeld), or **harriot,** an English tribute of money or the tenant's best animal, payable to the lord at the death of the tenant.

heriot service, an English form of rent.

heriot suit, an English right to chattels of a deceased tenant, reserved in a grant or lease.

heritable (Sc.), that which goes to the heir, usually all rights connected with land.

heritor, an owner of land.

hermaph'rodite, a person who has the physical characteristics of both sexes.

High Court of Admiralty, formerly, an English court of maritime jurisdiction, also called the Court of the Lord High Admiral. Its jurisdiction is now exercised by the Probate, Divorce, and Admiralty Division of the High Court of Justice (*q.v.*).

High Court of Justice, an English superior court established by the Judicature Act of 1873, which constitutes one of the two divisions of the Supreme Court of Judicature. For the purpose of organizing its work, but not for the purpose of Chancery, Queen's Bench or King's Bench, and Probate, Divorce and Admiralty. In addition, Judges of the Court may be specially commissioned to preside over the Courts of Assize.

high seas, a flexible term for the open and unenclosed portion of the oceans, which is not the territorial water of any particular nation. It usually begins three miles from a nation's coastline. (2) Occasionally, all of the unenclosed waters of the ocean beyond the low-water mark.

High Steward, Court of the Lord, an English tribunal for the trial of peers indicted for treason or felony, or for misprision of either.

high treason, see *treason.*

high-water mark, that part of the shore line of a river or an ocean which the water ordinarily reaches when the tide is highest.

Highway Energy Conservation Act, see *Emergency Highway Energy Conservation Act.*

highways, a broad term for public ways, either on land or water, which every person has a right to use. The term includes alleys, county roads, city streets, state and federal roads, and navigable rivers and streams.

hiring (Rom., locatio-conductio), a bailment (*q.v.*) for compensation.

HLA test, see *human leucocyte antigens test.*

hold, to possess or own as a tenant or grantee. (2) To bind under a contract, as an obligor is held and firmly bound. (3) To decide, adjudge, or decree, as a judge in disposing of a case.

holder, a person who is in possession of a document of title, or an instrument, or any investment security drawn, issued, or indorsed to him, or to his order, or to bearer, or in blank. U.C.C § 1-201(20).

holder for value, a holder (*q.v.*) who has given a valuable consideration for the document of title, instrument, or investment security which he has in his possession. A holder takes an instrument for value: (a) to the extent that the agreed consideration has been performed or that he acquires a security interest in, or a lien on, the instrument otherwise than by legal process; or (b) when he takes the instrument in payment of, or as security for, an antecedent claim against any person whether or not the claim is due; or (c) when he gives a negotiable instrument for it or makes an irrevocable commitment to a third person. U.C.C. § 3-303.

holder in due course, a holder (*q.v.*) who takes the instrument for value, in good faith, and without notice that it is overdue or has been dishonored or of any defense against or claim to it on the part of any person. A payee may be a holder in due course. A holder does not become a holder in due course of an instrument by purchase of it at a judicial sale or by taking it under legal process, or by acquiring it in taking over an estate, or by purchasing it as part of a bulk transaction not in regular course of business of the transferor. A purchaser of a limited interest can be a holder in due course only to the extent of the interest purchased. U.C.C. § 3-302.

holding, the principle which reasonably may be drawn from the decision which a court or judge actually makes in a case; the opposite of dictum (*q.v.*). (2) The resolution of the unique dispute which is before a judge or court in a specific case. (3) A broad term for something which a person owns or possesses.

holding company, a corporation, which is organized for the purpose of holding the stock of another, or other, corporations.

holding over, keeping possession of premises by a lessee after the expiration of his term.

holiday, a flexible term for a day specially designated by some governmental authority as a day of exemption from labor, or from the performance of legal business. Legal holidays often recognized in the United States are Sundays, New Year's Day, birthday of Martin Luther King, Jr., Presidents' Holiday, Memorial Day, Independence Day (Fourth of July), Labor Day, Veterans' Day, a day of National Thanksgiving, and Christmas Day.

hol'ograph, a document or instrument written entirely by the signer in his own handwriting, which, on account of the difficulty with which the forgery of such a document can be accomplished, is in some jurisdictions, and for certain purposes, held as valid without witnesses. The fact that it is entirely in the signer's handwriting must be proven by witnesses, however. See also, *holographic will*.

holographic will, a will (*q.v.*) which is written entirely by the signer in his own handwriting. See also, *holograph*.

Home Energy Assistance Act, see *Low-Income Home Energy Assistance Act of 1981*.

Home Loan Bank Act, an act to create Federal Home Loan Banks, and to provide for their supervision. 12 U.S. C. §§ 1421 *et seq.*

home rule charter, in some states, the organizational plan or framework of a municipal corporation, analogous to a constitution of a state or nation, drawn by the municipality itself and adopted by popular vote of its people.

homeowners' association, a form of private government that is a nonprofit corporation organized according to the declaration of restrictions, easements, liens, and covenants of a tract of land.

homestead, the place where a family resides. It usually includes the building which is the dwelling and the surrounding land which is used in connection with it. Occasionally defined by various state statutes, and occasionally limited by various state statutes to property of a value not exceeding a specified sum.

homicide, destroying the life of a human being; usually defined by various state statutes. It may be (a) excusable, as when committed by accident and without any intent to injure; (b) justifiable, if committed with full intent, but under such circumstances as to render it proper and necessary, as where the proper officer executes a criminal in strict conformity with his sentence, or kills a man when forcibly resisting an arrest, or where one kills another in defense of himself or his family, or to prevent him from committing an atrocious crime attempted with violence, *e.g.,* rape or robbery; (c) felonious, when committed wilfully and without sufficient justification. The latter includes (i) suicide; (ii) manslaughter, where one kills another in a sudden quarrel and without premeditation, or by accident while engaged in doing some unlawful act not amounting to a felony; (iii) murder, *i.e.,* wilful and premeditated killing with malice aforethought. This last offense is frequently divided by various state statutes into degrees, according to the atrociousness of the motives with which, or the circumstances under which, the crime is committed.

homologation (Sc.), the ratification of a deed that is defective. (2) (Rom.) Approbation or confirmation.

honor, to pay or accept and pay, or where a credit so engages to purchase or discount a draft complying with the terms of the credit. U.C. C. § 1-201(21). See also, *bill (2).*

honora'rium, a voluntary fee.

honorary trust, a trust to achieve a purely private objective but without benefit to specified persons, *i.e.,* a trust to maintain a grave or care for an animal.

hornbook, a one-volume work containing the elementary principles of law; a handbook.

hostile witness, a person who is called to give evidence and is unfriendly or inimical to the party whose attorney called him. Such a person is subject to cross-examination by the party calling him.

hotchpot (collatio bonorum), the taking into account advances (*q.v.*) made to children, in distributing the estate of a deceased person, who died intestate, so as to equalize the shares received by each.

house, a flexible term for a dwelling, an institution, a family, a mercantile firm, or a collection or persons.

house of correction, a place for the imprisonment of persons convicted of petty crimes.

house of ill fame, a house resorted to for purposes of lewdness and prostitution.

House of Representatives, the more numerous branch of the United States Congress, and of several state legislatures.

housebreaking, bursting or removing fastenings provided to secure doors or windows, with a view to entering a house. Obtaining entry by fraud, threats, or conspiracy is a constructive breaking. Cf. *burglary.*

household, a group of persons who dwell in the same house and constitute a family.

household furniture, or **household goods,** flexible terms for such personal property as was acquired for the furnishing and ornamentation of a person's home, and the use and convenience of his family in occupying it.

Houses of Parliament, the English House of Lords and the English House of Commons.

hue and cry, formerly, the common law process of pursuing a person accused of felony, without a warrant and with horn and voice.

human leucocyte antigens test, HLA; a paternity test which involves the drawing of blood and the typing of tissues.

hundred, a subdivision of an English county.

hundred court, an English court held for the inhabitants of a particular hundred (*q.v.*) Analogous to a court-baron (*q.v.*).

hung jury, a trial jury whose members are unable to agree upon a verdict. See also, *Allen charge.*

husband, a man who has a wife.

hush money, a bribe to hinder information being given.

hustings, a local or county court, principally in England.

hybrid statute of limitations, see *statute of repose.*

hypothecation, the deposit of stocks, bonds, or negotiable securities with another, to secure the repayment of a loan, with power to sell the same in case the debt is not paid, and to pay the loan out of the proceeds. (2) In an older and unusual sense, a species of pledge in which the pledgor retained possession of the thing pledged. Analogous to mortgage (*q.v.*) and security agreement (*q.v.*).

hypothetical question, an interrogatory or inquiry propounded to an expert witness, containing a statement of facts assumed to have been proven, and requiring the witness to state his opinion concerning them.

I

I.E., or **I.e.,** or **i.e.,** see *id est.*

ibid., or **ibi'dem,** *l.,* the same, *e.g.,* the same volume, case, page or place.

id., see *idem.*

id certum est quod certum reddi potest, that is certain which can be reduced to a certainty.

id est, that is.

i'dem, *l.,* the same.

idem agens et patiens esse non potest, it is impossible to simultaneously be the person acting and the person acted upon.

idem est nihil dicere et insufficienter dicere, it is the same thing to say nothing as it is not to say enough.

idem est non esse et non apparere, not to be and not to appear are the same, *i.e.,* the court will not presume any alleged fact to exist, unless it has been shown by competent testimony.

idem so'nans, sounding the same; used of names misspelled which yet would not mislead, because the variance is trifling, or because they would be pronounced the same if spelled correctly.

identification, the proof of the identity of a person or thing, *i.e.,* that he or it is the person or the item mentioned in the evidence. Cf. *personation.*

ides (ids), days in the months from which other days were reckoned.

idiocy, the condition of having been a person of unsound mind since birth; congenital mental deficiency. Cf. *lunatic.*

idiot, a person who is afflicted with idiocy (*q.v.*).

ignora'mus (we are ignorant), a word formerly written by a grand jury on a proposed bill of indictment, when the grand jury refused to return an indictment. It means that a sufficient prima facie (*q.v.*) case was not made out. The indorsement now used is, "not a true bill," or "not found."

ignorantia facti excusat; ignorantia juris non excusat, ignorance of the fact excuses; ignorance of the law excuses not.

illegal, contrary to law, or forbidden by law. (2) Occasionally, unlawful.

illegal conditions, provisions which are contrary to law, immoral, or repugnant to the nature of the transaction.

illegitimate, not authorized by law; often applied to describe children born out of lawful wedlock.

illicit, unlawful, or forbidden.

illusory, deceptive; having a false appearance.

illusory appointment, a concept recognized in some jurisdictions concerning the exercise of a power which in form carries out the wishes of the donor, but does not do so in spirit or reality, *e.g.,* where the donee of a power of appointment, who could not appoint exclusively to one or more of a class, does so practically by appointing a merely nominal sum to those he wishes to exclude.

illusory promise, a promise (*q.v.*) or apparent promise which is not consideration (*q.v.*), if by its terms the promisor or purported promisor reserves a choice of alternative performances, unless each of the alternative performances would have been consideration if it alone had been bargained for, or one of the alternative performances would have been consideration, and there is or appears to the parties to be a substantial possibility that before the promisor exercises his choice, events may eliminate the alternatives which would not have been consideration. Restatement (Second) of Contracts § 77.

imbecility, a flexible term for unsoundness of mind, which is characterized by the deficiency of the higher intellectual and moral facilities.

immaterial, unimportant; without weight or significance, in a particular context.

immaterial averment, or **immaterial evidence,** a claim, or proof which has no legal bearing on the point at issue.

immaterial issue, a question submitted for judicial resolution, which concerns a collateral matter, the decision of which will not settle the dispute between the parties.

immediate issue, children.

immemorial, beyond the memory of man.

Immigration and Nationality Act, various federal laws codified as ch. 12, tit. 8, U.S.C., concerning, among other things, immigration selection system, admission qualifications for aliens, travel control, deportation, alien crewmen, registration of aliens, nationality, naturalization, and refugee assistance. 8 U.S.C. §§ 1101-1524.

immoral contract, an agreement founded on an immoral consideration (contra bonos mores), *e.g.*, illicit cohabitation.

immovilia situm sequuntur, immovables follow the law of their locality.

immunity of witness law, see *witness immunity law.*

Immunized testimony, compelled testimony (*q.v.*) ordered by a federal court even though the witness has asserted his privilege against self-incrimination. No testimony or other information compelled under the order, or any information directly or indirectly derived from such testimony or other information, may be used against the witness in any criminal case. 18 U.S.C. §§ 6001-6005. See also, *witness immunity law.*

impanel, or **empanel,** to select a jury and record the names of its members.

imparl, to discuss a case with the opposite party, of his counsel, with a view to an adjustment of differences and an amicable settlement.

imparlance, time which the court allows either party to answer his opponent's pleading.

impeach, to charge a public official with crime or misdemeanor, or with misconduct in office. (2) To prove that a witness has a bad reputation for truth and veracity, and is therefore unworthy of belief. See also, *character evidence.*

impeachment of waste, a prohibition or restraint from committing waste (*q.v.*) upon lands and buildings; a demand for compensation for waste done by a tenant.

impediment, a legal hindrance or bar, *e.g.*, to making a contract or will, *e.g.*, infancy or unsoundness of mind.

impedimen'tum di'rimens, an impediment to marriage, which makes a purported marriage null and void.

imperative, obligatory. Cf. *directory statute.*

imperfect obligations, moral duties, such as charity or gratitude, which cannot be enforced by law.

imperfect trust, an executory trust. See also, *executory.*

imperitia culpae adnumeratur, want of skill in one professing to have it is accounted a fault.

impertinence, allegations in a court pleading, which are not responsive nor relevant to the issues, and which could not properly be put in issue or proven. Such matter may be ordered stricken from a pleading. Fed. R. Civ. P. 12(f).

implead, to bring a new party into a lawsuit that has been commenced earlier, on the ground that the new party is, or may be, liable to the party who brings him in, for all or part of the claim against the party who brings him in. Fed. R. Civ. P. 14. (2) Occasionally, to sue or prosecute.

impleader, the procedure by which a party to a lawsuit may implead (*q.v.*) a new party. Fed. R. Civ. P. 14.

implication, a necessary or possible inference of something not directly declared, which is generated by the things which are directly declared.

implied authority, power or permission which has been intentionally granted, but which has not been expressly declared to exist.

implied consent law, various state laws which provide that any person who operates a motor vehicle in the state is deemed to have given his consent to a chemical test, *e.g.*, of his blood, breath, urine, or saliva, for the purpose of determining the alcoholic content of his blood, if arrested for any offense arising out of acts alleged to have been committed while driving, or in physical control of, a motor vehicle in the state while under the influence of intoxicating beverages.

implied contract, a contract in which the agreement can only be shown by the acts and conduct of the parties, interpreted in light of the subject matter and of the surrounding circumstances.

implied easement, a privilege which may arise by operation of law under any of the following conditions: (1) a severance of unity of ownership in an estate; (2) continued use prior to separation, for so long, and so manifest or obvious, as to show that it was meant to be permanent; (3) reasonably necessary to beneficial enjoyment of land granted or retained; and (4) continuous servitude, as distinguished from temporary or occasional. See also, *easement.*

implied malice, an inference or conclusion of hate or ill will from the facts and circumstances proved.

implied power, such power as may be reasonably necessary to make an express power effective.

implied trust, a trust which results or comes about because of events or conditions where either the trust intent is not plain in literal meaning, by operation of law or due to an equitable finding.

implied warranty, a promise arising by operation of law, that something which is sold shall be merchantable, and fit for the purpose for which the seller has reason to know that it is required, *i.e.*, (a) unless excluded or modified, a warranty that the goods shall be merchantable is implied in a contract for their sale, if the seller is a merchant with respect to goods of that kind. The serving for value of food or drink to be consumed either on the premises or elsewhere is a sale for this purpose. U.C.C. § 2-314(1). (b) Where the seller, at the time of contracting, has reason to know any particular purpose for which the goods are required, and that the buyer is relying on the seller's skill or judgment to select or furnish suitable goods, there is, unless excluded or modified, an implied warranty that the goods shall be fit for such purpose. U.C.C. § 2-315.

impossibility, occasionally, an excuse for failure to perform a contract, when it cannot be done without unreasonable or extraordinary expense, or by unusual and extraordinary means.

impotence, or **impotency,** physical inability of a man or woman to perform the act of sexual intercourse. It is often a ground for a decree of nullity of marriage under various state statutes.

impotentia exusat legem, impossibility is an excuse at law.

impound, to place something in the custody of the law until a question affecting it is decided.

imprescriptible rights, those which cannot be lost or gained by prescription (*q.v.*).

imprisonment, confinement in a prison; restraint of a person's liberty. It may be for the purpose of detaining in custody one accused of crime, or for punishing one convicted of crime. Imprisonment for debt, not fraudulently contracted, is generally abolished by state constitutions and state statutes.

improbation (Sc.), the setting aside of deeds on the ground of falsehood or forgery.

improvement, a building erected on land, or other change for the better of the condition of the land or building, effected by the expenditure of labor and money. (2) A new and useful addition to, or modification of, an existing machine, article of manufacture, process, or composition of matter.

impunitas semper ad deteriora invitat, impunity always invites to worse faults.

imputed negligence, in some jurisdictions, the negligence (*q.v.*) which is chargeable to a person by reason of his relationship to the person who was actually negligent.

in, *l.,* in; within; at; upon; for; against.

in action, not in possession; applied to describe things which can only be recovered by an action (*q.v.*), unless voluntarily paid or delivered.

in adver'sum, against an adverse party.

in aequa'li ju're, in equal right.

in aequali jure melior est conditio possidentis, where the rights are equal the condition of the possessor is best.

in alie'no solo, on another's land.

in a'lio lo'co, in another place.

in alternativis electio est debitoris, in alternatives the debtor has the election.

in arti'culo mor'tis, at the point of death.

in autre droit, in another's right.

in banc, see *banc*.

in blank, without restriction. See also, *indorsement*.

in ca'mera, in chambers; secretly.

in ca'pite, in chief. See also, *tenure in capite*.

in chief, at first; direct. See also, *examination*.

in commen'dam, see *commandite*.

in commu'ni, in common.

in conjunctivis oportet utramque partem esse veram, in conjunctives, each part must be true.

in consimili casu, consimile debet esse remedium, in similar cases the remedy should be similar.

in contractibus tacite insunt quae sunt moris et consuetudinis, in contracts, matters of custom and general usage are implied.

in conventionibus contrahentium voluntas potius quam verba spectari placuit, in agreements, the intention of the parties should be regarded rather than the words actually used.

in criminalibus probationes debent esse luce clariores, in criminal cases the proof ought to be clear as day.

in custo'dia le'gis, see *custodia legis*.

in delic'to, in fault; guilty.

in dubio haec legis constructio quam verba ostendunt, in a doubtful case the construction which the words point out is the construction given by the law.

in dubio pars melior est sequenda, in a doubtful case the gentler course is to be pursued.

in dubio sequendum quod tutius est, in doubt, the safer course is to be adopted.

in durance vile, see *durance vile*.

in esse, in being; actually existing.

in exten'so, in its full extent; omitting nothing.

in extre'mis, at the very end; at the last gasp.

in fac'to, in fact.

in favo'rem liberta'tis, or **in favo'rem vi'tae,** in favor of liberty, or life.

in feo'do, in fee.

in fictione juris semper aequitas existit, in legal fictions there is always an inherent equity.

in fi'eri, in process of completion; still being done.

in flagran'te delic'to, see *flagrante delicto*.

in for'ma pau'peris, in the character of a poor man; applied to persons asking to have process and subpoenas issued gratis and counsel assigned, on account of poverty. Authorized in U.S. courts by 28 U.S.C. § 1915.

in fo'ro conscien'tiae, at the tribunal of conscience; applied to moral obligations as distinct from legal.

in frau'dem le'gis, in fraud of the law.

in futu'ro, in the future.

in generalibus versatur error, error dwells in generalities.

in ge'nere, in kind; of the same kind.

in good faith, see *good faith*.

in gre'mio le'gis, in the bosom of the law; in abeyance.

in gross, at large; not appurtenant or appendant.

in haec verba, in these words.

in initia'libus, in the preliminaries.

in invi'tum, against one unwilling.

in itin'ere, on a journey; on the way.

in judiciis minori aetati succurritur, in judicial proceedings infancy is favored.

in judi'cio, in a judicial proceeding.

in jure, in law; by right.

in jure, non remota causa, sed proxima spectatur, in law, the proximate, and not the remote, cause is to be regarded.

in lieu of, see *lieu*.

in li'mine, at the outset.

in litem, for a suit.

in lo'co paren'tis, in the place of a parent.

in maleficiis voluntas spectatur non exitus, in criminal acts the intention is to be regarded, not the result.

in misericor'dia, at the mercy.

in mitio'ri sen'su, in the milder sense.

in mo'ra, in delay.

in mor'tua ma'nu, in the dead hand; in mortmain (*q.v.*).

in nu'bibus, in the clouds; in abeyance.

in o'dium spoliatoris, in hatred of a despoiler, or wrongdoer.

in odium spoliatoris omnia praesumuntur, all things are presumed against one who destroys evidence.

in pais *(in pā´ ĭs)*, in the country; out of court; applied to simple words or acts, as opposed to deeds or records in court.

in pari delic'to, in equal fault.

in pari delicto, potior est conditio possidentis (or defendentis), where both parties are equally in the wrong, the possessor (or defendant), has the better position.

in pari mat'eria, upon the same matter or subject.

in perpe'tuam re'i memo'riam, for the perpetual remembrance of a thing, *e.g.,* a permanent record.

in perso'nam, against the person.

in pos'se, possible; opposed to *in esse (q.v.).*

in praesen'ti, at the present time; opposed to *in futuro (q.v.).*

in princi'pio, at the beginning.

in propria causa, nemo judex, no one should be a judge in his own case.

in pro'pria perso'na, in his own person, not by attorney.

in re, in the matter of; used in the name or style of court cases, other than actions between adverse parties.

in re communi potior est conditio prohibentis, in a partnership, the partner who forbids (a change) has the better right, *i.e.,* where the voices are equally divided.

in rem, against the thing; opposed to *in personam (q.v.).*

in restraint of trade, see *restraint of trade, in.*

in so'lido, in the whole; entirely.

in spe'cie, in the same form; in kind; in legal tender; formerly, in metal coin.

in sta'tu quo, in the same situation as.

in terro'rem, for a threat, or by way of.

in testamentis plenius voluntates testantium interpretantur, in testaments, the will of the testator should be liberally construed.

in toti'dem ver'bis, in just so many words.

in to'to, in the whole; altogether.

in toto et pars continetur, a part is included in the whole.

in trans'itu, in transit or movement from one place to another.

in va'dio, in pledge.

in ventre sa mere *(vôn tr sǎ mâr),* in his mother's womb, applied to a child who is begotten but not born.

in verbis non verba sed res et ratio quaerenda est, in words, not the words, but the thing and the meaning is to be inquired into.

inadequate, insufficient; not equal to full value.

inadequate consideration, a price or inducement which is less than would ordinarily be given or exacted, and if accompanied by fraud or deception, may operate to void a contract.

inadmissible, that which cannot be admitted or received, *e.g.*, parol evidence is inadmissible to vary the terms of a written contract.

inalienable, not transferable; not subject to being sold.

incapacitated person, any person who is impaired by reason of mental illness, mental deficiency, physical illness or disability, advanced age, chronic use of drugs, chronic intoxication, or other cause (except minority) to the extent of lacking sufficient understanding or capacity to make or communicate responsible decisions. Uniform Probate Code § 5-103(7).

incapacity, want of legal power or authority to do a thing.

incendiary, a person who maliciously sets fire to a building. See also, *arson.*

incentive zoning, zoning calculated to induce the landowner to introduce amenities the city deems desirable.

incerta pro nullis habentur, things uncertain are held for nothing.

incest, carnal knowledge of persons so related to each other that their marriage is prohibited by law, *e.g.*, of brother and sister, father and daughter, uncle and niece. Often defined by various state statutes. (2) Knowingly marrying or cohabiting or having sexual intercourse with an ancestor or descendant, a brother or sister of the whole or half blood, or an uncle, aunt, nephew, or niece of the whole blood. The relationships referred to include blood relationships without regard to legitimacy, and relationship of parent and child by adoption. Model Penal Code § 230.2.

inchoate right of dower, the claim or interest held by a wife in the lands of her spouse, contingent upon her surviving him.

incident, something which depends upon or appertains to another more important thing, termed the principal. (2) An event or occurrence.

incidental damages, resulting from a seller's breach of contract, include expenses reasonably incurred in inspection, receipt, transportation and care and custody of goods rightfully rejected, any commercially reasonable charges, expenses, or commissions in connection with effecting cover and any other reasonable expense incident to the delay or other breach. U.C.C. § 2-715(1).

inci'pitur, it is begun.

incite, to encourage, stimulate, or induce a person to commit a crime.

inclosure, or **enclosure,** a fence or similar device which surrounds or separates a parcel of land. (2) The English act of freeing land from rights of common (*q.v.*), by vesting it in some person as absolute owner.

inclusio unius est exclusio alterius, the inclusion of one is the exclusion of another. See also, *expressio unius, etc.*

incolas domicilium facit, residence makes domicile.

income, a flexible term for receipts or gains from services, business, sales, rents, royalties, investments, or other sources, but from which is usually excluded receipts of capital from inheritances. Often defined by various statutes.

income tax, a flexible term for various federal, state, and local duties or levies, established by various statutes and ordinances, and imposed upon or measured by the taxpayer's income (*q.v.*).

incommodum non solvit argumentum, inconvenience does not destroy an argument.

incompetent, a flexible term for disqualified, unable, or unfit. (1) A judge or juror is incompetent when from interest in the subject matter he is an unfit person to decide a controversy. (2) Testimony is incompetent when it is not such as by law ought to be admitted. (3) A witness is incompetent when by law he may not testify. See also, *competency.*

incorporated Law Society, an association of English attorneys and solicitors, analogous to an American bar association.

incorporation, the forming of a corporation.

incorporator, the person who joins with others to form a corporation and together execute the articles of incorporation.

incorporeal, not having a material body, intangible, invisible, existing only in contemplation of law.

incorporeal hereditaments, intangible rights issuing out of, or connected with, things corporate, *e.g.*, easements of light and air.

incumbent, a person who is occupying a public office.

incumbrance, a claim, lien, or liability attached to property, *e.g.*, a mortgage or a judgment.

indebitatus assumpsit, formerly one of the common counts (*q.v.*) in actions for debt, whereby the plaintiff alleged a debt and a subsequent promise on the part of the debtor to pay, founded on the consideration of the debt.

indecency, a flexible term for language or conduct which offends against modesty under the prevailing views of the times.

indecent, normally refers to nonconformance with accepted standards of morality; prurient appeal is not an essential component of indecent language.

indecent exposure, exposing one's genitals for the purpose of arousing or gratifying sexual desires of himself or of any person other than his spouse, under circumstances in which he knows his conduct is likely to cause affront or alarm. Model Penal Code § 213.5.

indefeasible, that which cannot be made void. Opposed to *defeasible.*

indefinite payment, money which a debtor transfers to his creditor, to whom the debtor owes several debts, without specifying the particular debt to which the money should be applied or credited. See also, *appropriation (2).*

indemnification, or **indemnity,** to make good another's loss caused by some particular act or omission.

indemnity, a payment or promise to pay which is given or granted, to a person to prevent his suffering damage.

indenture, a deed, mortgage, or other written instrument between two or more parties, so called because duplicates were once written on one piece of parchment, which was cut in half with a jagged edge.

independent contractor, a person who agrees with another to do something for him, in the course of his occupation, but who is not controlled by the other, nor subject to the other's right to control, with respect to his performance of the undertaking, and is thereby distinguished from an employee.

indeterminate sentence, a term of imprisonment, as a punishment for a crime, which leaves the exact period of punishment to be decided by executive authorities.

index animi sermo, speech is the index of the mind.

indicia, signs; marks.

indict, see *indictment.*

indictment, a written accusation that one or more persons have committed a crime, presented upon oath, by a grand jury. The person against whom the indictment is found is said to be indicted.

indigent person, see *pauper.*

indirect evidence, proof of collateral circumstances from which a fact in controversy, not directly attested by witnesses or documents, may be inferred. See *evidence.*

indirect tax, a tax paid primarily by a person who can shift the burden of the tax to someone else or who at least is under no legal compulsion to pay the tax, *e.g.,* a sales tax.

indispensable party, a person who has such an interest in the controversy pending in court that a final judgment or decree cannot be made, without either affecting that interest, or leaving the controversy in such a condition that its final determination may be wholly inconsistent with equity and good conscience.

indivi'sum, that which is held in common; not partitioned.

indorsee, a person in whose favor an indorsement (*q.v.*) is made.

indorsement, something written on an instrument in writing, and having relation to it. (2) Especially, the writing put on the back of a bill or promissory note and signed, by which the party signing, called the indorser, transfers the property in the bill or note to another, called the indorsee. Indorsement may, however, be in blank, *i.e.*, not specifying the name of the indorsee, in which case it may be transferred from hand to hand without further indorsement, and is payable to bearer. Indorsement may also be made without recourse, and thereby, the indorser relieves himself from liability in case the bill or note is not paid. Accord, U.C.C. §§ 3-201 to 3-206. (3) An indorsement must be written by or on behalf of the holder (*q.v.*) and on the instrument or on a paper so firmly affixed thereto as to become a part thereof. U.C.C. § 3-202(2). Words of assignment, condition, waiver, guaranty, limitation, or disclaimer of liability, and the like, accompanying an indorsement do not affect its character as an indorsement. U.C.C. § 3-202(4).

inducement, that which constitutes the motive for doing a thing.

indulgence, a favor granted, *e.g.*, forbearance to sue or to insist on payment of a debt at maturity.

inevitable, that which cannot be foreseen or prevented, *e.g.*, an accident (*q.v.*).

infamy, in some jurisdictions, the loss of character which results from conviction of a major crime, *e.g.*, treason, or other felony, and which, under the common law, rendered the person incompetent as a witness. (2) In jurisdictions in which such conviction does not render a person incompetent, it may be shown as affecting his credibility as a witness.

infant, a person who is not an adult (*q.v.*) or is not of age (*q.v.*). (2) Under the common law, a person under twenty-one years of age, without regard to sex. The rights, privileges, and disabilities of persons who are infants are defined by various state statutes.

infanticide, a type of homicide (*q.v.*), consisting of the killing of a child after it is born. The felonious destruction of the fetus is called feticide or criminal abortion.

infeoffment (*fěf*) (Sc.), the act or instrument of feoffment (*q.v.*), or investiture; synonymous with seisin, the instrument of possession.

inference, a rational conclusion deduced from facts proved.

inferior court, a flexible term for a tribunal whose judgments are subject to review by another tribunal. It is used to denote the position of a particular court, as it is related to another court, within the hierarchy of a court system. (2) All courts except the supreme court. (3) Courts of limited jurisdiction.

informal, deficient in legal form; lacking formality. An informality may, or may not, be of legal consequence. There is a tendency among courts to waive informality in some instances.

informal contract, any contract which is not recordable, not under seal and not governed by any specific statutory rule or standard. The nature of its enforceability does not depend upon its form but instead on the representations between the parties themselves.

information, communicated knowledge. (2) A formal accusation or complaint, filed by a prosecuting attorney or other law officer, charging a person or corporation with some crime or violation of law. In certain classes of criminal cases, it may be a substitute for an indictment or presentment by a grand jury. It is often used in civil cases, to exact penalties and forfeitures for violations of law, and in proceedings in quo warranto, to deprive a corporation of its franchise. The use of an information, as a form of procedure, is regulated by various federal and state statutes and constitutions.

informed consent rule, a knowing and voluntary consent given by a patient to medical treatment proposed by a physician which is sufficient to relieve the physician of any liability arising out of the treatment based on a theory of battery.

informer, a person who provides information concerning those who violate a law or penal statute, occasionally for the purpose of obtaining part, or the whole, of the penalty recoverable under the statute. See also, *common informer.*

in'fra, *l.,* below; under; within; occurring by itself in a book, it refers the reader to a subsequent part of the book, like post.

infra aeta'tem, within or under age.

infra cor'pus comita'tus, within the body of the county.

infra dignita'tem cu'riae, beneath the dignity of the court.

infra praesi'dia, within the walls, *i.e.,* completely within the power of the captors or those who have possession.

infringement, breach or violation of various intangible rights and privileges, *e.g.,* copyright (*q.v.*) or patent (*q.v.*).

ingress, egress, and **regress,** the right of a lessee, or other person having an interest in real property to enter, go upon, and return from, the property in question. See also, *emblements* and *free entry.*

ingrossing, writing an instrument for the formal execution of it by the parties thereto. See also, *engross.*

inhabitant, a flexible term, often used to indicate a person who has his residence or domicile in a particular place. Occasionally, but incorrectly, used as a synonym for citizen.

inheritance, something which descends to the heir on the intestate death of the owner. See also, *descent* and *heir.*

inheritance taxes, various state excises on the right and privilege to inherit or succeed to property. An analogous federal tax is called an estate tax.

inhibition, see *prohibition, writ of.*

iniquum est aliquem rei sui esse judicem, it is unjust for anyone to be judge in his own case.

initiative, a procedure occasionally authorized by statute, whereby laws may be adopted by popular vote, upon the petition of a certain number of electors.

injunction, a flexible, discretionary, process of preventive and remedial justice, which is exercised by courts that have equity powers. Courts issue injunctions when it appears that the ordinary remedy usually provided by the law is not a full, adequate, and complete one. Injunctions are preventive, if they restrain a person from doing something, or mandatory, if they command something to be done. They are preliminary, provisional, or interlocutory, if they are granted on the filing of a bill, or while the suit is pending, to restrain the party enjoined from doing or continuing to do the acts complained of, until final hearing or the further order of the court. They are final, perpetual, or permanent, if they are awarded after full hearing on the merits, and as a final determination of the rights of the parties.

injuria, injury, a wrong, or tort; an infringement of a right.

injuria absque (or sine) **damno,** a controversy in which no legal damage ensues from the wrong which was done.

injuria non excusat injuriam, one wrong does not justify another.

injuria non praesumitur, injury is not presumed.

injury, the invasion of a legally protected interest of another. Restatement (Second) of Torts § 7(1).

inland, within the same state or territory.

inmate, a person who dwells in a part of another's house or in a public institution.

inn, a generic term for a public house of entertainment, where all who choose to call may obtain food, lodging, and other accommodations necessary to a traveler, *e.g.*, a hotel or motel. Often defined by various state statutes.

innings, lands recovered from the sea.

innkeeper, a person who owns, or carries on the business of, an inn (*q.v.*), *e.g.*, the proprietor or operator of a hotel or motel. Such a person is characterized as one who seeks to make a profit by receiving guests. Often defined by various state statutes, which also establish the rights and duties of innkeepers.

innocent, not guilty. (2) A person who is not responsible for an event or occurrence. (3) A person who does not have knowledge of a particular fact which is material to a transaction.

innocent purchaser, someone who, in good faith (*q.v.*), gives a valuable consideration (*q.v.*) for the transfer of some particular item of personal or real property, and who does not know, or have reason to know, of any shortcoming in the seller's title. Cf. *bona fide purchaser* and *holder in due course.*

innominate contracts (Rom.), unnamed agreements, which failed to satisfy the definitions of particular technical classifications, but which were enforced whenever there had been performance by one party

innovation, a flexible term for something that is new or different. (2) (Sc.) An exchange of one obligation for another, so as to make the second come in place of the first. See also, *novation.*

innuendo (by hinting), an indirect statement. (2) The part of an indictment or pleading in an action for libel, which goes to explain a connection between what is expressly said in the alleged libel, and certain persons or things not named or explicitly stated therein, whereby it is made to appear that the actual statement is libelous.

Inns of Chancery, formerly, institutions at which English law students prepared themselves to be admitted to the Inns of Court (*q.v.*). There were nine: Clement's, Clifford's, Lyon's, Furnival's, Thavies', Symond's, New, Barnard's and Staples' Inn.

Inns of Court, colleges for English students of the common law. There are four of them, exercising the right of admitting persons to practice at the English bar: the Inner Temple, the Middle Temple, Lincoln's Inn, and Gray's Inn. They have a long and varied history, dating as early as the fifteenth century.

inops consi'lii, *l.*, destitute of counsel.

inquest, judicial inquiry. (2) Usually, an inquiry made by a coroner (*q.v.*) and jury concerning the cause of death of someone who has been killed, or has died suddenly, or under suspicious circumstances, or in prison. (3) Occasionally, an inquiry by a jury concerning someone's mental condition. (4) A jury.

inquest of office, an English inquiry made by a jury, before an officer of the Crown or commissioners, concerning some matter that entitles the Crown to possession of property, *e.g.*, escheat *(q.v.)*.

inquiry, writ of, a civil judicial process, addressed to the sheriff, and directing him to make inquiry with the assistance of a jury, as to the damages suffered by the plaintiff, and to return the inquisition *(q.v.)* into court. It is used in cases where judgment is taken by default, and the damages are unliquidated, and not ascertainable by mere calculation.

inquisition, an inquiry by a jury. (2) The document which records the results of the inquiry. See also, *inquest.*

insane, or **insanity,** a flexible term for various forms of mental unsoundness, aberration, or impairment. It implies disease or congenital defect of the brain, and embraces idiocy *(q.v.)*, lunacy, and a great many other afflictions of the mind, *e.g.*, mania *(q.v.)* in its various forms. (2) A person is not responsible [or criminal conduct if at the time of such conduct as a result of mental disease or defect he lacks substantial capacity either to appreciate the criminality or wrongfulness of his conduct or to conform his conduct to the requirements of law. The terms "mental disease or defect" do not include an abnormality manifested only by repeated criminal or otherwise anti-social conduct. Model Penal Code § 4.01. There must be a sufficient causal link between the defendant's mental disease or defect and his inability to control his behavior.

insolvency, a state of facts in which a debtor's available property cannot be liquidated for sufficient money to pay his debts. (2) The inability of a person to pay his debts as they become due in the ordinary course of business. (3) The condition of a person who either has ceased to pay his debts in the ordinary course of business or cannot pay his debts as they become due, or is insolvent within the meaning of the federal bankruptcy law. U.C.C. § 1-201(23). See also, *insolvent (2).*

insolvent, a person whose finances are in a condition of insolvency *(q.v.)*. (2) Under the Bankruptcy Reform Act *(q.v.)*, (a) with reference to an entity other than a partnership, financial condition such that the sum of such entity's debts is greater than all of such entity's property, at a fair valuation, exclusive of (i) property transferred, concealed, or removed with intent to hinder, delay, or defraud such entity's creditors, and (ii) property that may be exempted from property of the estate under law; (b) with reference to a partnership, financial condition such that the sum of such partnership's debts is greater than the aggregate, at a fair valuation, of, (i) all of such partnership's property, exclusive of property of the kind specified in (a)(i) above, and (ii) the sum of the excess of the value of each general partner's separate property, exclusive of property of the kind specified in (a)(ii) above, over such partner's separate debts. 92 Stat. 2549, tit. I, § 101 (1978); 11 U.S.C. § 101(26).

inspection, examination of goods or merchandise by officers, called inspectors, to see whether they conform to the standard required by law, and to grade them according to their true character and quality. (2) The right which a party to an action has, to examine and make copies of documents, and other objects, which are not privileged, and which constitute or contain evidence relating to the subject matter of the pending action. Fed. R. Civ. P. 34. See also, *discovery*.

inspection laws, various statutes designed to improve or maintain the standard or goods or merchandise produced or offered for sale.

inspex'imus, *l.*, we have seen. See also, *constat*.

installation, the ceremony of inducting into, or investing with, an office.

installment, something that is less than the whole. (2) A portion of something that is owing, *e.g.*, a debt or annuity.

installment contract, an agreement which requires or authorizes the delivery of goods in separate lots to be separately accepted, even though the contract contains a clause that each delivery is a separate contract, or its equivalent. U.C.C. § 2-612(1). (2) Occasionally used in the sense of installment note (*q.v.*).

installment note, an undertaking or promise to pay an indebtedness, by making periodic payments of a portion of the whole, according to a prearranged schedule, until the entire indebtedness is paid.

instance court, one of the two divisions of the Admiralty branch of the Probate, Divorce, and Admiralty Division of the English High Court of Justice (*q.v.*).

instan'ter, immediately; at once.

institor, *l.*, (Rom.), a clerk in charge of a shop or store.

institute, formerly, a type of law book or treatise, *e.g.*, Coke's Institutes, the Institutes of Gaius and Justinian, and Bouvier's Institutes of American Law.

institution, a flexible term for an incorporated or unincorporated association. (2) A society for the promotion of a public, charitable, or benevolent object.

instruct, to convey information. (2) The act of a trial judge in informing the jury concerning the law applicable to a case which the jury is to decide. See also, *jury instructions.* (3) To give orders or directions, as a principal does to his agent.

instructions, see *jury instructions.*

instrument, a formal legal writing. (2) A negotiable instrument (*q.v.*) U.C.C. § 3-102(1) (e). (3) A negotiable instrument (*q.v.*) or a security (*q.v.*), or any other writing which evidences a right to the payment of money, and is not itself a security agreement or lease, and is of a type, which is in ordinary course of business, transferred by delivery with any necessary indorsement or assignment. U.C.C. § 9-105(1) (g).

instrument of crime, anything specially made or specially adapted for criminal use, or anything commonly used for criminal purposes and possessed by the actor under circumstances which do not negative unlawful purpose. Model Penal Code § 5.06(1).

insufficiency, the condition or shortcoming of an answer or affidavit which does not reply specifically or directly to the charges made or the questions asked.

insurable interest, a genuine concern, on account of business, or title, or claim, or otherwise, in the subject of insurance, entitling the person possessing it to obtain insurance. In the absence thereof, the arrangement would be illegal because it would be a gaming, or gambling, contract.

insurance, the act of providing against a possible loss, by entering into a contract with a licensed corporation that is willing to bind itself to make good such loss, should it occur. The instrument by which the contract is made is called a policy; the consideration paid to the insurer, who is sometimes called an underwriter, is called a premium. Fire and marine insurance is usually by way of indemnity, *i.e.,* only such sum is paid by the insurer as is actually lost, and, on making such payment, he is entitled to stand in the place of the assured. (2) In the case of life or accident insurance, the insurer undertakes, in consideration of a premium, to pay a certain sum to the insured, or his legal representatives, on his death or injury by an accident. (3) There are many various types of insurance, each of which are defined by the respective policies which evidence the agreements between the parties, *e.g.,* automobile insurance, creditor life insurance, homeowner insurance, owner, landlord, and tenant insurance, and workers' compensation insurance.

insurance agent, or **insurance broker,** a person who is licensed for the purpose of soliciting and executing insurance contracts or policies on behalf of a license insurance corporation.

intangibles, a kind of property which is nonphysical and not subject to being sensed, *e.g.,* touched or felt, but which exists as a concept of people's minds, *e.g.,* promissory notes, bank accounts, and corporate stock.

integrated bar, a mandatory association of lawyers, who are licensed to practice in a particular jurisdiction.

integration, unification or bringing together; used especially regarding the various racial groups.

intendment, the true meaning.

intent, or **intention,** design; resolve; determination of the mind. (2) To render an act criminal, a wrongful intent must exist, but the wrongful intent may be presumed, if the necessary or probable consequences of the act were wrongful or harmful, and the act was deliberately committed. (3) Intent denotes the desire of an actor (*q.v.*) to cause consequences of his act or his belief that the consequences are substantially certain to result from it. Restatement (Second) of Torts § 8A. See also, *legislative intent.*

inten'tio, *l.* (Rom.), a count or charge.

intention, see *intent.*

intentional infliction of mental distress, a tort in which the plaintiff must prove the following elemental points: (1) conduct which is extreme and outrageous, (2) conduct which is intentional, and, (3) actual damages.

intentional tort, an act done with purpose, with knowledge, with a reckless disregard of result or with the gross disregard of the safety of others. Acts, commissions, omissions of responsibility or legal duty which are intentional in design, that is, a conscious choice with full realization of the probability of harm.

intentionally, or **with intent,** purposely. Model Penal Code § 1.13(12).

inter, *l.,* among; between.

inter a'lia, among other things.

inter a'lios, among other persons.

inter a'pices ju'ris, between the subtleties of the law.

inter arma silent leges, in time of war the laws are silent.

inter ca'nem et lu'pum, between dog and wolf; an expression for twilight, because then the dog seeks his rest and the wolf his prey.

inter par'tes, between the parties.

inter se, or **inter se'se,** among themselves.

inter vi'vos, between living persons.

interdict, an injunction.

interes'se ter'mini, *l.,* the right which a person acquires in real property, before he takes possession of it.

interest, an estate or right in property; (2) Money paid for the loan or use of another sum called the principal (*q.v.*). (3) The object of any human desire. Restatement (Second) of Torts § 1. See also, *compound interest.*

interest reipublicae ut sit finis litium, it is for the interest of the state that there should be an end of litigation.

interference, the condition which exists when one applicant for a patent claims to be the first inventor of something claimed by another applicant, or granted to a prior patentee. (2) The proceedings in the patent office, when opposing claimants are required to furnish proofs of their respective rights, and a public officer has to decide which is the prior inventor.

in'terim, *l.,* in the meantime; meanwhile.

interim order, a temporary court decree, which is put into effect until something else is one.

interlineation, writing between lines; the insertion of any matter in a written instrument, before or after its execution. If before, a memorandum thereof should be made at the time of the execution or attestation, or the parties should each place their initials adjacent to the insertion. The best practice is to scrupulously avoid interlineations in documents. An interlineation made by one party, after execution, and without the consent of the other party, if material, may invalidate the instrument.

interloc'utory, incident to a suit still pending. An order or decree, made during the progress of a case, which does not amount to a final decision, is interlocutory. See also, *decree* and *injunction.*

Internal Revenue Code, a consolidation of various acts concerning the taxes imposed by the federal government. U.S.C. tit. 26.

Internal Security Act of 1950, an act to protect the United States against certain un-American and subversive activities by requiring registration of Communist organizations. Repealed. See also, *Communist Control Act of 1954.*

international arbitration, the settlement of differences between states by judges of their own choice and on the basis of respect for law. See also, *arbitration.*

International Court of Justice, or **World Court,** the principal judicial organ of the United Nations (*q.v.*) composed of 15 judges elected by the General Assembly and Security Council two of whom may be citizens of the same nation. It sits at The Hague, Netherlands.

International law, is either public or private. (1) The former regulates the conduct of independent nations toward each other; (2) The latter decides the tribunal before which, and the law by which, private rights shall be determined. See also, *conflict of laws.*

Internet, an international network of computers linked together through the use of a standard protocol.

interpleader, a procedure by which persons having claims against another person may be joined as parties to a lawsuit and required to set up their claims, if their claims are such that the person initiating such procedure is, or may be, exposed to double or multiple liability. Fed. R. Civ. P. 22.

Interpleader Act, an act to confer alternative jurisdiction on United States district courts concerning bills of interpleader and bills in the nature of interpleader. 28 U.S.C. §§ 1335, 1397, 2361.

inter'polate, to insert words in a complete document.

interpretatio fienda est ut res magis valeat quam pereat, such an interpretation is to be adopted that the thing may rather stand than fall.

interpretatio talis (in) ambiguis semper fienda est, ut evitetur inconveniens et absurdum, in doubtful matters, such an interpretation is to be adopted that inconsistency and absurdity may be avoided.

interpretation, to construe; the assignment and declaration of the meaning of words or signs employed in a statute or instrument.

interrogatories, written questions propounded on behalf of one party in an action to another party, or to someone who is not a party, *e.g.*, a witness or potential witness, before the trial thereof. The person interrogated must give his answers in writing and upon oath. Fed. R. Civ. P. 26, 33. (2) Verbal questions put to a witness before an examiner and answered on oath. (3) Questions in writing annexed to a commission to take the deposition of a witness, to be put to and answered by the witness under oath, whose answers are to be reduced to writing by the commissioner.

interruption, the stopping, or breaking in upon, the running of a prescription, or of limitations, or the exercise of a right, by which the prescription or limitation is defeated, or the right lost.

intersection, the area embraced within the prolongation of the lateral boundary lines of two or more highways which join one another.

interstate agreement on detainers, a method available to participating states to obtain temporary custody of a defendant incarcerated in another jurisdiction and to constitute the exclusive means of transfer of a prisoner from one participating jurisdiction to another; an act to encourage expeditious disposition of charges outstanding against a prisoner and to provide cooperative procedures among member states to facilitate such disposition.

interstate commerce, trade, commerce, transportation, or communication among the states, or between any foreign country and any state, or between any state and anyplace or ship outside of the state.

Interstate Commerce Act, various acts of Congress codified as subtitle IV of tit. 49, U.S.C. It was revised, codified, and enacted into law without substantive change by 92 Stat. 1337 (1978), as subsequently amended.

interstate rendition, see *extradition.*

intervener, a party who enters a lawsuit via intervention (*q.v.*).

intervening force, a force (*q.v.*) which actively operates in producing harm to another after the actor's (*q.v.*) negligent act or omission has been committed. Restatement (Second) of Torts § 441(1).

intervention, the procedure by which a third person, not originally a party to the suit, but claiming an interest in the subject matter, comes into a case in order to protect his right or interpose his claim. The grounds and procedure are usually defined by various state statutes or modern rules of civil procedure, *e.g.*, Fed. R. Civ. P. 24.

inter vivos trust, a trust created and funded during the grantor's life.

intestate succession, if a decedent leaves no valid will, his or her property passes to his or her heirs as named by statute by operation of intestate succession. Intestate real property passes by descent and intestate personal property passes by distribution.

intestacy, the state or condition of a person who dies without leaving a valid will. (2) The condition of property which has not been disposed of by will, on the death of the owner. Cf. *testacy.*

intes'tate, a person who has died without leaving a valid will. A person dies intestate who either has made no will at all, or has made one not legally valid, or has made one, but revoked or canceled it, or if there is no one who can take under it.

intra vires, *l.*, within its powers, the opposite of ultra vires (*q.v.*).

intrusion, a technical term for the entry of a stranger on land at the termination of a particular estate, and before the heir, or person entitled in reversion or remainder, can enter. Cf. *trespass.*

inure, or **enure,** to take effect.

inval'id, not valid; of no binding force.

invention, the finding out, or contriving of something new; (2) The thing itself which has been invented, and which is the subject matter of a patent (*q.v.*).

in'ventory, an itemized list, or schedule, in writing, of personal property or goods, *e.g.*, belonging to the estate of an insolvent or deceased person. An inventory records or reflects the assets of an estate as of a particular date.

investiture, formerly, the open delivery of seisin or possession of real property under the feudal law. See also, *livery.*

investment, a flexible term for the employment of money in such a way as to produce an income, *e.g.*, loaning it on notes and mortgages, or purchasing income producing property or bonds.

investment contract, a contract, transaction or scheme whereby a person invests money in a common enterprise and is led to expect profits solely from the efforts of the promoter or third party. SEC v. W.J. Howey, 328 U.S. 293, 298-99 (1946).

invitee, a person who goes upon land or premises of another by invitation, express or implied; (2) Either a public invitee or a business visitor: (a) Public invitee is a person who is invited to enter or remain on land as a member of the public for a purpose for which the land is held open to the public; (b) Business visitor is a person who is invited to enter or remain on land for a purpose directly or indirectly connected with business dealings with the possessor of the land. Restatement (Second) of Torts § 332.

invito beneficium non datur, a benefit cannot be forced on one who is unwilling to receive it.

invi'to do'mino, *l.*, without the consent of the owner; a necessary element in the taking of goods or money, in order for the taking to constitute a larceny.

in vitro fertilization, the surgical removal of mature eggs from the female ovary through laparoscopy, examination of fluid removed from the ovary to confirm the presence of mature eggs, placement of a mature egg in a nourishing medium, introduction of a specimen of the husband's semen into the medium in a manner that encourages fertilization, incubation of the fertilized egg for several days in an environment that duplicates the female body, and reimplantation of the fertilized egg in the woman's uterus after several days.

invoice, a written account of goods sent or shipped, with the prices and other charges annexed.

involuntary manslaughter, the unlawful and unintentional killing of a human being, directly and proximately resulting from the commission of an unlawful act. Often defined by various state statutes. See also, *homicide.*

involuntary petition, a bankruptcy case commenced by creditors or other interested parties. Creditors whose claims total more than $5,000 must sign the involuntary petition.

ipsae leges cupiunt ut jure regantur, the laws themselves desire that they be governed by right.

ip'se, *l.,* a demonstrative pronoun, used for the sake of emphasis; myself, himself, itself; the very.

ip'se dix'it, he himself said it, a bare assertion, resting on the authority of an individual.

ipsis'simis ver'bis, *l.,* in the identical words, as opposed to substantially.

ip'so fac'to, by the very act itself, *i.e.,* as the necessary consequence of the fact or act.

ip'so ju're, by the law itself, *i.e.,* by the mere operation of law.

i're ad lar'gum, *l.,* to go at large; to be set at liberty.

irregular, done in the wrong manner, or without the proper formalities. Cf. *illegal.*

irrel'evant, not pertinent; not tending to aid or support, *e.g.,* evidence which does not tend to prove the fact at issue.

irreparable injury, a flexible term for a wrong or injustice in which the actual damage cannot be repaired by compensation in money.

irrepleviable, or **irreplevisable,** descriptive of something which cannot be replevied. See also, *replevin.*

irresistible impulse, an insanity defense holding that notwithstanding that one accused of committing a crime may have been able to comprehend the nature and consequences of his act, and to know that it was wrong, he may be excused if he was forced to its execution by an impulse which he was powerless to control in consequence of an actual disease of the mind.

irretrievable breakdown, a judicial determination after hearing concerning the condition of a marriage *(q.v.)* that there is no reasonable prospect of reconciliation, that the marriage has ended in fact; the no-fault basis on which a marriage may be dissolved. Uniform Marriage and Divorce Act § 305 and Commissioners' Note.

irrev'ocable, incapable of being revoked, *e.g.,* powers of appointment may be exercised so as to be irrevocable, and a power of attorney, in which the attorney has an interest for which he has given a valuable consideration, is irrevocable.

issuable, descriptive of a pleading which raises an issue.

issue, a flexible term for offspring or lineal descendants. (2) All of a person's lineal descendants of all generations, with the relationship of parent and child at each generation being determined by the definitions of child and parent. Uniform Probate Code § 1-201(21). (3) In the plural, the profits arising from real property. (4) The point or points which are left to be resolved by the jury or the court at the conclusion of the pleadings. Issues may be of fact or of law. (5) To join issue is a technical phrase for closing the pleadings. (6) To issue a writ or process is for the proper officer to deliver it to the party suing it out, or to the officer to whom it is directed. See also, *general issue.*

ita lex scripta est, the law is so written.

i'tem, also; an article, entry, or separate unit. (2) Any instrument for the payment of money, even though it is not negotiable, but not including money. U.C.C. § 4-104(1)(g).

i'ter, a footway or walkway; a right of passage.

itinerant, traveling or wandering.

J

jactitation, a false boast.

jactitation of marriage, untruthful boasting that one has married another.

jail, or **gaol,** a place for the confinement of prisoners. Often the place where city or county prisoners are confined while awaiting trial or as punishment for misdemeanors.

Jedburgh Justice, or **Lydford law,** punishment coming first and trial afterward. See also, *lynch law.*

jeofaile (*jĕf äl*) (corrupted from j'ai failli, *fr.*, I have failed), formerly an expression used to avow an oversight in pleading or other law proceedings.

jeopardy, peril; danger; the condition of a prisoner who is being tried for an alleged crime. See also, *double jeopardy.*

jetsam (Rom., *jactus mercium*), things which having been cast overboard and sunk, or thrown upon the shore. If the things float they are called flotsam (*q.v.*).

jettison, throwing something overboard to lighten a ship. (2) The things cast overboard to save the vessel. See also, *general average.*

Job Training Partnership Act, an act to provide for a job-training program, and for other purposes. Its purpose is to establish programs to prepare youth and unskilled adults for entry into the labor force and to afford job training to those economically disadvantaged individuals and other individuals facing serious barriers to employment, who are in special need of such training to obtain productive employment. 29 U.S.C. §§ 1501 *et seq., et al.*

jobber, a person who buys and sells for others.

John Doe, see *Doe, John.*

join issue, see *issue (5).*

joinder of causes of action, or **joinder of claims,** alleging two or more matters in the same suit or proceeding. Under modern rules of civil procedure, the plaintiff in his complaint, and the defendant in his counterclaim, may join, as independent or alternate claims, as many claims either legal or equitable or both, as he may have against an opposing party. Fed. R. Civ. P. 18(a).

joinder of parties, uniting all persons as plaintiffs or defendants, who have the same right, or against whom the same rights are claimed or relief is demanded. There is necessary joinder of parties, *e.g.,* Fed. R. Civ. P. 19, and permissive joinder of parties, *e.g., Id.* 20.

joint, united; coupled together in interest or liability; opposed to several (*q.v.*).

joint account, an account (*q.v.*) payable on request to one or more of two or more parties whether or not mention is made of any right of survivorship. Uniform Probate Code § 6-101(4).

joint action, a lawsuit brought by two or more as plaintiffs, or against two or more as defendants.

joint adventure, see *joint venture.*

joint and several liability, when one or more of the parties liable, or all of them, may be sued by the creditor at the creditor's option, there is a joint and several liability. Opposed to joint liability (*q.v.*).

joint bond, a bond (*q.v.*) executed by two or more obligors, who must be united in any action on the same, as opposed to a joint and several bond, on which any or all of the obligors may be sued at the option of the obligee.

joint contract, an agreement which two or more persons are bound to perform, or the benefits of which two or more must collectively demand.

joint enterprise, the prosecution of a common purpose, under such circumstances that each member of the enterprise has authority to act for all in respect to control of agencies employed to execute the common purpose. Cf. *joint venture.*

joint executors, or **trustees,** two or more persons united in the execution of a will or trust.

joint liability, an obligation for which two or more persons are liable, who must be united in any action brought on account of that liability, as opposed to a joint and several liability (*q.v.*). See also, *joint bond.*

joint stock company, a type of English partnership invested with some of the privileges of a corporation. It may also be created under various statutes of some of the states.

joint tenants, two or more persons to whom is transferred the same real property, via the same instrument, *e.g.,* deed or will, and who have the right to succeed to the entire property upon the death of the other person(s). The right of survivorship distinguishes joint tenancy from tenancy in common. Cf. *tenancy in common.*

joint venture, or **joint adventure,** an association of persons to carry out a single business enterprise for profit, for which purpose they combine their property, money, and effects. Cf. *joint enterprise.*

jointress, or **jointuress,** a woman who is entitled to jointure (*q.v.*).

jointure, a provision of property for a wife, made in lieu of dower, and established prior to marriage. (2) Formerly, a joint estate limited to husband and wife.

judex aequitatem semper spectare debet, a judge ought always to aim at equity.

judex non potest esse testis in propria causa, a judge cannot be a witness in his own cause.

judex non reddit plus quam quod petens ipse requirit, the judge does not give more than the plaintiff requires.

judge, a public official with authority to determine a cause or question in a court of justice and to preside over the proceedings therein.

judge advocate, a military legal officer. He may perform duties analogous to those of a civilian judge or civilian prosecutor or various other legal duties.

judge pro tem, a person who is temporarily authorized to perform the duties of a judge (*q.v.*).

judgment, the determination or decision of a court; the expression by a judge of the reasons for his decision. Judgments may be final, putting an end to the case; interlocutory, given in the progress of a case upon some matter which does not finally determine the case. They may be rendered on confession by the defendant; on default, when the defendant fails to appear, plead, or otherwise defend within the allotted time; or on the merits, after a full trial. See also, *summary judgment.*

judgment creditor, a person in whose favor a judgment for money has been entered, and is not satisfied.

judgment debtor, a person against whom a judgment determining that he should pay a sum of money stands unsatisfied.

judgment in rem, see *rem, judgment in.*

judgment non obstante veredicto, or **judgment N.O.V.,** see *non obstante veredicto.*

judgment note, see *cognovit note.*

judgment of previous conviction, evidence of a final judgment entered after a trial or upon a plea of guilty, but not upon a plea of nolo contendere (*q.v.*), adjudging a person guilty of a crime punishable by death or imprisonment in excess of one year, to prove any fact essential to sustain the judgment, but not including, when offered by the government in a criminal prosecution for purposes other than impeachment, judgments against persons other than the accused. It is not excluded from evidence as hearsay (*q.v.*) even though the declarant (*q.v.*) is available as a witness. The pendency of an appeal may be shown but does not affect admissibility. Fed. R. Evid. 803(22).

judgment on the merits, see *merits, judgment upon* and *judgment.*

judgment-proof, descriptive of all persons against whom judgments for money recoveries are of no effect, *e.g.,* persons who are insolvent, who do not have sufficient property within the jurisdiction of the court to satisfy the judgment, or who are protected by statutes which exempt wages and property from execution.

judgment record, the pleadings and proceedings in a court up to and including the judgment, made and kept by the clerk, or a transcript thereof.

judicandum est legibus, non exemplis, we should judge by the laws, not precedents.

Judicature Acts, statutes passed in England in 1873 and 1875 (36 and 37 Vict. c. 66; 38 and 39 Vict. c 77), which regulated the organization and powers of the courts, and the procedure therein; analogous to the various codes of civil procedure in the United States.

judices non tenentur exprimere causam sententiae suae, judges are not bound to explain the reason of their judgments.

judicia posteriora sunt in lege fortiora, the later decisions are the stronger in law.

judicial, relating to proceedings before a judge or in court.

judicial admission, or **confession,** a statement made in court or in due course of legal proceedings, and which is contrary to the interests of the person making it. It can be used for the purpose of deciding the lawsuit against the person making it.

judicial code, various federal laws enacted since 1789 concerning the judiciary and judicial procedure. They deal with, among other things, the organization of courts, the Department of Justice, court officers and employees, jurisdiction and venue, evidence, juries, fees, costs, executions, judicial sales, and particular proceedings. Codified as U.S.C. tit. 28.

judicial comity, the principle under which, out of deference and respect, the courts in one state or jurisdiction will give effect to the laws and judicial decisions of another. Cf. *full faith and credit.*

Judicial Councils Reform and Judicial Conduct and Disability Act of 1980, an act to revise the composition of the judicial councils of the federal judicial circuits, to establish a procedure for the processing of complaints against federal judges, and for other purposes. 28 U.S.C. §§ 153, 331, 332, 372, 604, *et al.*

judicial mortgage, the lien resulting from a judgment in favor of the person obtaining it.

judicial notice, the acceptance by the court of certain notorious facts without proof. (2) A judicially noticed adjudicative fact must be one not subject to reasonable dispute in that it is either (a) generally known within the territorial jurisdiction of the trial court, or (b) capable of accurate and ready determination by resort to sources whose accuracy cannot reasonably be questioned. Fed. R. Evid. 201 (b).

judicial sale, a transfer of the ownership of property, in exchange for a sum of money or a purchase money bond, made under the authority of some competent court, which conveys all the rights of the parties to the purchaser, without any warranty, other than that of the parties to the suit.

judicial separation, a judgment or decree of a divorce court, analogous to a divorce a mensa et thoro. See also, *divorce.*

judicial writs, all writs or process, subsequent to the original writ, which issued out of chancery. See also, *writ.*

Judiciary Act, the act of Congress of September 24, 1789, establishing federal courts. See also, *judicial code.*

judicis est judicare secundum allegata et probata, it is the duty of a judge to decide according to facts alleged and proved.

judicis est jus dicere non dare, it is for a judge to declare, not to make law.

judicium a non suo judice datum nullius est momenti, a judgment rendered by one not a proper judge is of no weight.

judi'cium De'i, *l.,* judgment of God; formerly, trial by ordeal.

judicium semper pro veritate accipitur, a judgment is always taken for the truth.

juncta juvant, in union there is strength.

junk bond, a debt instrument that is not of ordinary investment quality carrying a high rate of return. The expectation of a purchaser of such a bond is that the assets and cash flow of the acquired corporation will be used to satisfy these bonds.

jura eodem modo destituuntur quo constituuntur, laws are abrogated in the same manner in which they are made.

jura naturae sunt immutabilia, the laws of nature are unchangeable.

jura publica anteferenda privates, public rights are to be preferred to private ones.

ju'rat, a certificate or memorandum of the time, place, and person before whom an affidavit is sworn.

juration, the act of swearing; the administration of an oath.

juratores sunt judices facti, jurors are the judges of fact.

juridical, relating to the administration of justice.

juridical days, those on which courts are held and justice is administered; court days.

juris, *l.,* of law; of right.

Juris Doctor, the first, or lowest, professional degree in legal education.

ju'ris et de ju're, of law and from law.

juris praecepta sunt haec, honeste vivere, alterum non laedere, suum cuique tribuere, these are the precepts of the law, to live honorably, to hurt nobody, to render to everyone his due.

jurisconsul'ti, or **jurispruden'tes** (Rom.), formerly, persons who studied and expounded law.

jurisdiction, the authority of a court to hear and decide an action or lawsuit. (2) The geographical district over which the power of a court extends. (3) Subject-matter jurisdiction defines the court's authority to hear a given type of case. (4) Personal jurisdiction requires that the court personally summon the defendant within its geographical district, or that it summon the defendant under the authority of a long-arm statute (*q.v.*). This protects the individual interest that is implicated when a nonresident defendant is haled into a distant and possibly inconvenient court. (5) Jurisdiction is limited when the court has power to act only in certain specified cases; general or residual when it may act in all cases in which the parties are before it, except for those cases which are within the exclusive jurisdiction of another court; concurrent when the same cause may be entertained by one court or another; original when the court has power to try the case in the first instance; appellate when the court hears cases only on appeal, certiorari, or writ of error from another court; exclusive when no other court has power to hear and decide the same matter.

jurisincep'tor (Rom.), a student of the civil law.

jurisprudence, law. (2) A body of law. (3) Philosophy of law.

jurist, a judge; formerly a person versed in Roman law.

jury, a body of citizens sworn to deliver a true verdict upon evidence submitted to them in a judicial proceeding. They are respectively called jurymen or jurors. A grand jury is one summoned to consider whether the evidence, presented by the state against a person accused of crime, warrants his indictment. A petty or petit jury is the jury for the trial of cases, either civil or criminal. It usually consists of twelve persons, but by various statutes in many of the states, and in England, a lesser number may constitute a jury in some courts. A special jury or struck jury (*q.v.*) is one selected especially for the trial of a given cause, usually by the assistance of the parties.

jury box, a place in a courtroom where a jury sits. It is usually enclosed with a low rail.

jury charge, see *jury directions* and *charge (1)*.

jury directions, or **jury instructions,** a statement given by the judge, which sets forth the law applicable to a particular lawsuit, which has been heard by a jury and is about to be decided by the jury. Fed. R. Civ. P. 51.

jury nullification, occurs when a jury, based on its own sense of justice and fairness, refuses to follow the law and convict in a particular case even though the facts seem to allow no other conclusion but guilt.

jury of matrons, a group of women especially impaneled as a jury in two cases: (1) upon a writ de ventre inspiciendo (see also, *venter*); (2) where a female prisoner is condemned to be executed, and pleads pregnancy as a ground for postponing execution until after her confinement.

jury process, the writ for the summoning of a jury.

jury wheel, a revolving drum in which the names of persons subject to jury duty are placed, and from which the jury panels are drawn.

jus, *l.,* law; right; equity; authority.

jus abuten'di, the right of abusing, *i.e.,* complete ownership.

jus accrescen'di, the right of survivorship. See also, *joint tenants.*

jus accrescendi, inter mercatores locum non habet, pro beneficio commercii, the right of survivorship does not exist among merchants for the benefit of commerce.

jus accrescendi praefertur oneribus et ultimae voluntati, the right of survivorship prevails against incumbrances and the last will (of a joint tenant).

jus ad rem, an inchoate and imperfect right.

jus aquaeduc'tus, the right to bring water from or through the land of another.

jus civita'tis, the right of citizenship.

jus descendit, et non terra, a right descends, not the land.

jus dicere, et non jus dare, to declare the law, not to make it.

jus disponen'di, the right of disposing of property.

jus duplica'tum, a double right, *e.g.*, both title and possession.

jus est ars boni et aequi, the law is the science of what is good and just.

jus ex injuria non oritur, a right cannot arise out of wrongdoing.

jus gentium, the law of nations; international law; universal institution.

jus ima'ginis (Rom.), the right of using statutes of ancestors, resembling the right coat of arms.

jus in perso'nam, a right against another person.

jus in re, a complete and full right to a thing.

jus legi'timum, a legal right that may be enforced by due course of law.

jus ma'riti, formerly, the right of a husband to his wife's personal estate.

jus me'rum, a bare right.

jus natu'rae, the law of nature.

jus postlimi'nii, the right by which persons and things, taken by an enemy, are restored to their former state, on their coming again into the power of the nation to which they belong.

jus priva'tum, private law.

jus proprieta'tis, the right of property.

jus publicum privatorum pactis mutari non potest, a public right cannot be altered by the agreements of private persons.

jus re'rum, the law of things.

jus respicit aequitatem, law regards equity.

jus ter'tii, the right of a third person.

jus uten'di, the right to use property without destroying its substance.

jus'ta for'mam statu'ti, *l.*, according to the form of the statute.

justice, a flexible term, which is impossible to fully define in advance of the unique factual dispute which calls for its application. It is the pole star, or goal, of court decisions, but comes to light only under the influence of competing adversary arguments, in the context of the unique factual dispute. (2) The constant and perpetual disposition to render every man his due; fairness; conformity to law; merited reward or punishment. (3) A title sometimes given to judges, especially appellate judges, *e.g.*, Justices of the United States Supreme Court.

justice of the peace, in some jurisdictions, a minor judicial officer with specifically enumerated powers, *e.g.*, preventing breaches of the peace, and causing the arrest and commitment of persons violating the law. Under various state statutes, they may have limited jurisdiction to try certain cases.

justices in eyre, see *eyre, justices in.*

justiciability, a concept of uncertain meaning and scope. Its reach is illustrated by the various grounds upon which questions sought to be adjudicated in federal courts have been held not to be justiciable (*q.v.*). *E.g.*, no justiciable controversy is presented when the parties seek adjudication of a political question, when the parties ask for an advisory opinion, when the question has been mooted by subsequent developments, and when there is no standing to maintain the action. See also, *standing to sue.*

justiciable, a vague term descriptive of matters which a court will adjudicate. See also, *justiciability.*

justiciary, court of, the supreme criminal court in Scotland.

justifiable, lawful. See also, *justification.*

justifiable homicide, see *homicide.*

justification, a reason acceptable to a court as to why the defendant did what he is charged with having done, *e.g.*, in an action of libel, a defense showing the libel to be true, and in an action of assault, showing the violence to have been necessary. See also, *affirmative defense.*

justificator, see *compurgator.*

justify, see *justification.*

juvenile courts, tribunals specially created by various state statutes to supervise dependent, neglected, and delinquent children, *i.e.*, persons under a specified age.

K

kangaroo court, a mock court, *e.g.*, composed of fellow prisoners in a jail.

Keeper of the Great Seal, Lord, an English officer, through whose hands pass all charters, commissions, and grants of the Crown to be sealed. 5 Eliz. c. 13.

Keeper of the King's Conscience, the English Lord Chancellor.

Keeper of the Privy Seal, or **Lord Privy Seal,** a high English officer, through whose hands all charters pass before they reach the great seal.

kickback, the return of a part of one's compensation.

"kiddie tax," 1986 tax legislation aimed at preventing avoidance tactics of assignment of income to some minors. The rule applies to net unearned income (generally unearned income in excess of $1,000) of a child who is under the age of 14 at the close of the tax year. Previously, unearned income attributed to a child as a result of interest from bank accounts or notes, dividends from stocks, and other such unearned income was taxed at the child's applicable tax rate. Under this new legislation, net unearned income of a child under 14 is to be taxed at the higher of the child's regular rate or the rate at which it would be taxed if it were added to the parents income.

kidnapping, the forcible abduction or carrying away of a person from his, or her domicile, parents, or legal protector. Usually defined by various state statutes. (2) Unlawfully removing another from his place of residence or business, or a substantial distance from the vicinity where he is found, or unlawfully confining another for a substantial period in a place of isolation, with any of the following purposes: (a) to hold for ransom or reward, or as a shield or hostage; (b) to facilitate commission of a felony or flight thereafter; (c) to inflict bodily injury on, or to terrorize, the victim or another; or (d) to interfere with the performance of any governmental or political function. A removal or confinement is unlawful within the meaning of this definition if it is accomplished by force, threat or deception, or in the case of a person under the age of 14, or who is incompetent, if it is accomplished without the consent of a parent, guardian, or other person responsible for general supervision of his welfare. Model Penal Code § 212.1 See also, *Parental Kidnapping Prevention Act of 1980.*

kin, or **kindred,** blood relatives. They may be either (a) lineal, *i.e.,* in a direct line, either ascending, *e.g.,* a father or grandfather; or descending, *e.g.,* a son or grandson; or (b) collateral, *i.e.,* descended from a common ancestor, *e.g.,* a brother or cousin. The next of kin of a person is the person, or persons if there are more than one of the same degree, most nearly related to him. See also, *consanguinity.*

King's Bench, see *Court of King's or Queen's Bench.*

King's Counsel, or **Queen's Counsel,** the highest rank among English barristers. Such persons have unique rights and obligations.

king's evidence, see *state's evidence.*

kleptomania, an irresistible propensity to steal. In some jurisdictions, it is a defense to a charge of larceny.

knowingly, in criminal prosecutions, knowledge that one is acting in violation of some law or regulation; knowledge that the act done is illegal.

L

labor arbitration, the nonjudicial consideration and settlement of disputes between employers and employees. See also, *arbitration.*

Labor Management Relations Act of 1947, or **Taft-Hartley Act,** an act to amend the National Labor Relations Act, to provide additional facilities for the mediation of labor disputes affecting commerce, and to equalize legal responsibilities of labor organizations and employers. 29 U.S.C. §§ 141 *et seq.*

labor union, any one of various organizations composed of employed persons, which have as their objective the improvement of wages, hours, and working conditions.

laborer, a person who performs manual labor.

lach'es, negligence or unreasonable delay in pursuing a legal remedy, concurrent with a resultant prejudice to the opposing party, whereby a person forfeits his right. Cf. *acquiescence.*

LAER, see *lowest achievable emission rate.*

laesae majestatis crimen, see *leze majesty.*

land, soil. (2) Real property in general, including, *e.g.,* soil, buildings, water, and fences.

land contract, a contract for the sale of land that provides for a down payment, with the balance of the purchase price payable in monthly installments. The buyer receives his deed when all the installments have been paid or when the unpaid balance of the purchase price has been reduced to a certain agreed figure, whereupon the buyer is to receive a deed and give the seller a purchase money mortgage for the balance of the purchase price.

land office, formerly a government bureau, originally connected with the Treasury, and later with the Department of the Interior, which administers the public lands of the United States.

land patent, an instrument by which a government conveys or transfers the title of real property.

landlord, the person from, or under, whom lands or buildings are rented.

landmark, a natural barrier, monument, or marker, used to identify a boundary line, *e.g.,* between separate parcels of real property or separate states.

Lanham Act, ch. 22, tit. 15, U.S.C., concerning trademarks (*q.v.*). Among other things, it deals with registration, application, registrable marks, use by related companies, duration, renewal, assignment, cancelation, interference, remedies, and the like. 15 U.S.C. §§ 1051 *et seq.*

lapse, to slip away; to cease. In some jurisdictions, if a legatee or devisee dies before a testator, the legacy or devise is held to lapse and unite with the residue.

lapsed devise, or **lapsed legacy,** in some jurisdictions, a gift which is ineffective because of the death of the devisee or legatee before that of the testator.

larceny, the unlawful taking and carrying away of personal property, without color of right, and with intent to deprive the rightful owner of the same. Larceny is commonly classified as grand or petty, according to the value of the thing taken. Usually defined and classified by various state statutes. See also, *grand larceny.* Cf. *robbery* and *embezzlement.*

larceny by trick, inducing another to part with possession of his personal property by trick or artifice. See also, *larceny.*

last clear chance, a principle by which a plaintiff, who by his own fault has caused himself to be in a perilous situation, may recover damages, notwithstanding his own negligence, if the defendant did not exercise ordinary care to avoid injuring him after becoming aware of plaintiff's perilous situation.

last resort, see *resort, court of last.*

last will, or **last will and testament,** the will (*q.v.*) which a court accepts and records, *i.e.*, probates.

lata culpa dolo aequiparatur, gross negligence is equivalent to fraud.

latent, hidden. See also, *ambiguity.*

latent defect, a defect (*q.v.*) which is hidden and not discoverable by observation.

lateral support, the right to the support of one's land and buildings by the land adjoining.

law, a method for the resolution of disputes. (2) A rule of action to which people obligate themselves to conform, via their elected representatives and other officials. (3) The principles and procedure of the common law, as distinguished from those of equity.

law merchant, or **custom of merchants,** the general body of commercial usages which have become an established part of the law of the United States and England, and which relate chiefly to the transactions of merchants, mariners, and those engaged in trade. Unless displaced by the particular provisions of the U.C.C., the principles of law and equity, including, among other things, the law merchant, shall supplement its provisions. U.C.C. § 1-103.

Law-Related Education Act of 1978, part G of title III of an act to extend and amend expiring elementary and secondary education programs, and for other purposes, also known as the Education Amendments of 1978. It provided for grants and contracts to encourage state and local educational agencies, and other public and private nonprofit agencies, organizations, and institutions to provide education to equip nonlawyers with knowledge and skills pertaining to the law, the legal process and the legal system, and the fundamental principles and values on which they are based. 20 U.S.C. §§ 3001-3003; 92 Stat. 2216 (1978). Repealed, 95 Stat. 480 (1981).

lawful, legal; that which is sanctioned or permitted by law, or is compatible with law.

lawful age, see *age (2)*.

lawful representatives, legal heirs to real property.

Laws of Oleron', an ancient maritime code, on which the maritime law is largely founded.

lawsuit, any one of the various proceedings in a court of law. See also, *action*.

lay, or **layman,** one of the people; one not belonging to some particular profession.

lay corporations, English bodies politic composed of lay persons for lay purposes.

lay days, the period of time allowed by a charter-party for a ship to load or unload. See also, *demurrage*.

lay witness, any witness that is not an expert. A lay witness simply must have the general capacity to testify, record, recollect, narrate, attest to and affirm certain conditions and facts. Additionally, he or she must have the requisite level of mental capacity and emotional competency to outline in some logical and sensible sequence the facts, conditions and events before the trier.

le roy le veut *(lŭ rwå lŭ vŭ)*, or **le roy s'avisera** *(så vē rä)*, *fr.* the king assents, or the king will consider; the form of the royal assent or dissent to public bills passed by the English Parliament.

le salut du peuple est la supreme loi, the safety of the people is the supreme law.

lead counsel, or leader, see *leading counsel*.

leading, going before; guiding.

leading a use, formerly, descriptive of a deed made before a fine and recovery, specifying to whose use the fine should inure.

leading case, a precedent that has been so often followed as to establish a principle of law.

leading counsel, or **lead counsel,** or **leader,** the one of two or more attorneys employed in a case who has the principal care of the case.

leading question, an inquiry which suggests to a witness the answer which he is to make. It may be used in cross-examination. (2) Leading questions should not be used on the direct examination of a witness except as may be necessary to develop his testimony. Ordinarily leading questions should be permitted on cross-examination (*q.v.*). When a party calls a hostile witness (*q.v.*), an adverse party, or a witness identified with an adverse party, interrogation may be by leading questions. Fed. R. Evid. 611(c).

league, see *marine league.*

League of Nations, formerly (1920-1946), an international organization of separate states or nations for the purpose of preventing war and furthering other common interests. Its assets, and many of its powers and functions, were transferred to the United Nations (*q.v.*).

leap year, the calendar year, which occurs every fourth year, in which a day is added to the month of February.

learned treatises, to the extent called to the attention of an expert (*q.v.*) witness upon cross-examination (*q.v.*) or relied upon by him in direct examination, statements contained in published treatises, periodicals, or pamphlets on a subject of history, medicine, or other science or art, established as a reliable authority by the testimony or admission of the witness or by other expert testimony or by judicial notice. They are not excluded from evidence as hearsay (*q.v.*) even though the declarant is available as a witness. If admitted, the statements may be read into evidence but may not be received as exhibits. Fed. R. Evid. 803(18).

lease, a transfer of real or personal property for a period of time, *e.g.,* for years, or at will, or for life, by a person who has a greater interest in the property. The person transferring is called the landlord, or lessor; the rights or interest which he retains is his reversion; the person to whom the transfer is made is the tenant, or lessee. The consideration is usually the payment of a rent. A lease is usually drawn in duplicate, one copy being kept by the lessee, the other copy by the lessor. (2) Includes an oil, gas, or other mineral lease. Uniform Probate Code § 5-103(8).

lease and release, formerly, an English mode of conveyance. A lease was made for a year, and under the Statute of Uses, it gave seisin without entry or enrollment. Thereupon, the vendor released his reversion to the purchaser by ordinary deed of grant.

leasehold, land held under a lease.

leave and license, a defense to an action in trespass, setting up the consent of the plaintiff to the trespass.

legacy, a gift of personal property by will. It is subordinate to the claims of the creditors of the deceased. A legacy may be (a) simple, *i.e.*, of a specified thing, or part of a testator's estate, as opposed to (b) general, which comes out of any part of his assets; (c) demonstrative, which is a general legacy directed to be paid out of a specified fund. See also, *ademption* and *lapsed legacy*. Cf. *devise*.

legal, according, or relating, to law. (2) Historically, distinguished from *equitable (2), (3) (q.v.)*. See also, *lawful*.

legal aid society, any one of various organizations in the United States which provide legal representation, advice, and counsel, to persons who are financially unable to pay for the same.

legal assistant, see *paralegal*.

legal cause, the fact that the causal sequence by which an actor's *(q.v.)* tortious conduct has resulted in an invasion of some legally protected interest *(q.v.)* of another is such that the law holds the actor responsible for such harm *(q.v.)*, unless there is some defense to liability. Restatement (Second) of Torts § 9. An actor's negligent conduct is a legal cause of harm to another if his conduct is a substantial factor in bringing about the harm, and there is no rule of law relieving the actor from liability because of the manner in which his negligence has resulted in the harm. Id. § 431.

legal fiction, a factual assumption which a court makes and adopts to support its decision, in order to justify its resolution of a controversy, but which is not based on reality.

legal holiday, see *holiday*.

legal malice, constructive malice. or malice in law. See also, *malice*.

legal realism, a philosophy of law which critically analyzes judicial decision making with the objective of identifying the various psychological, sociological, economic, political, and other factors which influence the resolution of controversies.

Legal Services Corporation Act of 1974, an act to amend the Economic Opportunity Act of 1964 to provide for the transfer of the legal services program from the Office of Economic Opportunity to a Legal Services Corporation, and for other purposes. Among other things, it provides for financial assistance to qualified programs furnishing legal assistance to persons financially unable to afford it. 42 U.S.C. §§ 2996 *et seq.*

legal tender, the coin and paper money which are declared by statute to be good and sufficient for the payment of public and private debts.

legalize, to make lawful (*q.v.*).

legally competent, see *competency* and *competent*.

legatee, a person who is given personal property under a will. See also, *legacy*.

legem enim contractus dat, the contract makes the law.

leges posteriores priores contrarias abrogant, later laws abrogate prior contrary laws.

leges vigilantibus, non dormientibus subveniunt, the laws aid the vigilant, not those who sleep (on their rights).

legis interpretatio legis vim obtinet, the interpretation of law obtains the force of law.

legislative intent, frequently there is no such thing as a real legislative intent with reference to the particular facts at hand. This becomes especially so with the passage of time after the enactment of a statute. As most statutes proceed from and are supposed to reflect the public will, it is proper and necessary that they be given a construction that is likely to be regarded by the public in general as reasonable.

legislature, a body of public officials who collectively have the authority to make generalized law for future application. It usually consists of two branches, *i.e.*, the upper house, or Senate, and the lower house, or House of Representatives. The Senate is usually a much smaller body and each senator represents a much larger district, or constituency, than a representative. The United States Congress is a legislature, each state has its own legislature, and cities have legislatures called, variously, boards of aldermen, city commissions, city councils, or common councils.

legitimacy, the condition of persons who are born of lawfully married parents. (2) Lawfulness or legality.

legitimation, the act of making legitimate, children who were born out of wedlock, *e.g.*, by the subsequent marriage of the parents and acknowledgment of such children, or by legal proceedings.

lenity, see *rule of lenity*.

lesion, a bodily injury. (2) (Sc.) The degree of injury or duress sustained by a minor, or person of weak capacity, necessary to entitle him to avoid a deed.

lessee, see *lease*.

lesser included offense, a separate offense, all of the elements of which are alleged, among other elements, in an offense charged in an indictment.

lessor, see *lease*.

let, to make a lease (*q.v.*) of particular property. (2) To accept an offer for construction or for the furnishing of equipment or supplies, which has been competitively solicited.

letter, or **letters,** a written message or request; a written commission, sent to or issued to another, granting a privilege, or conferring an authority. (2) Letters includes letters testamentary (*q.v.*), letters of guardianship, letters of administration, and letters of conservatorship. Uniform Probate Code § 1-201(23); accord, § 5-103(9).

letter-missive, formerly analogous to a summons in an English civil action.

letter of advice, information, generally of some act done by the writer. (2) In international commercial transactions, a drawer's communication to the drawee that a described draft has been drawn. U.C.C. § 3-701(1).

letter of attorney, see *power of attorney.*

letter of credit, in sales, an irrevocable credit issued by a financing agency of good repute and, where the shipment is overseas, of good international repute. U.C.C. § 2-325(3). (2) Usually, an engagement by a bank or other person made at the request of a customer that the issuer will honor drafts or other demands for payment upon compliance with the conditions specified in the letter. It may be either revocable or irrevocable. The engagement may be either an agreement to honor or a statement that the bank or other person is authorized to honor. U.C.C. § 5-103(1)(a).

letter of license, an agreement between an English debtor and his creditors, whereby they grant him an extension of time to carry on his business. Cf. *composition.*

letters, see *letter.*

letters of marque (mark), commissions occasionally granted in time of war, authorizing private individuals to fit out vessels for the purpose of capturing the goods or subjects of a hostile nation.

letters of safe conduct, a passport or protection granted by a government to a subject of a hostile power, exempting him from seizure.

letters patent, an instrument issued by a government to the patentee, granting or confirming a right to the exclusive possession and enjoyment of land, or of a new invention or discovery. See also, *land patent* and *patent.*

letters testamentary, an instrument issued by a court empowering the person named in a will as executor to administer the estate of the testator. See also, *administration (2).*

leva'ri fa'cias, that you cause to be levied, formerly a common law writ of execution.

levitical degrees, degrees of kindred within which persons are prohibited to marry. Leviticus 18: 6-18.

levy, to assess, impose, or require a tax. (2) The act of a sheriff in subjecting property to the satisfaction of a court judgment. (3) The act of a sheriff in subjecting property to the lien of a court attachment.

lex, *l.,* a law; the law; occasionally used as synonymous with jus, right.

lex citius tolerare vult privatum damnum quam publicum malum, the law will more readily tolerate a private loss than a public evil.

lex commu'nis, the common law.

lex contrac'tus, the law of the contract.

lex de futuro, judex de praeterito, the law provides for the future, the judge for the past.

lex dilationes exhorret, the law abhors delays.

lex domici'lii, the law of the country where a person has his domicile (*q.v.*).

lex est dictamen rationis, law is the dictate of reason.

lex est norma recti, law is a rule of right.

lex fo'ri, or **lex ordinandi,** the law of the country where an action is brought. This regulates the forms of procedure and the nature of the remedy to be obtained.

lex judicat de rebus necessario faciendis quasi re ipsa factis, the law judges of things, which must necessarily be done, as if actually done.

lex lo'ci, the law of the place where a contract is made, *i.e.,* lex loci contractus; or thing is done, *i.e.,* lex loci actus; tort is committed, *i.e.,* lex loci delicti; or where the thing, *i.e.,* real estate, is situated, *i.e.,* lex loci rei sitae. It is usually applied in suits relating to such contracts, transactions, torts, and real estate.

lex loci contractus, the law of the place where the contract was formed.

lex mercatotria, the mercantile law or general body of established usages in commercial matters. See also, *law merchant.*

lex neminem cogit ad vana seu inutilia peragenda, the law forces no one to do vain or useless things.

lex nil facit frustra, nil lubet frustra, the law does nothing in vain; commands nothing in vain.

lex non cogit ad impossibilia, the law does not require impossibilities.

lex non curat de minimis, the law cares not about trifles.

lex non favet delicatorum votis, the law favors not the wishes of the dainty. In deciding whether an alleged nuisance should be restrained by injunction, the court considers whether it would materially inconvenience persons of ordinary, not fastidious, habits.

lex non scrip'ta, the unwritten law (*q.v.*).

lex ordinan'di, see *lex fori.*

lex posterior derogat priori, a prior statute gives place to a latter.

lex prospicit, non respicit, the law looks forward, not backward, *i.e.,* statutes are not as a rule retrospective.

lex reprobat moram, the law disapproves of delay.

lex respicit aequitatem, the law pays regard to equity.

lex scrip'ta, the written or statute law.

lex semper dabit remedium, the law will always furnish a remedy.

lex spectat naturae ordinem, the law regards the course of nature.

lex succurrit minoribus, the law assists minors.

lex ter'rae, the law of the land; the process of law.

lex uno ore omnes alloquitur, the law speaks to all in the same way.

LEXIS, a computer assisted legal research service provided by Lexis-Nexis, a member of the Reed Elsevier plc group which provides on-line access to legal information including cases, statutes, administrative regulations, and secondary material.

ley (*fr., loi*), law.

leze majesty (lēz măj ĕs tĭ), or laesae majestatis crimen, an offense against sovereign power; treason (*q.v.*).

liability, a duty, debt, obligation, or responsibility. (2) A present or potential duty, debt, obligation, or responsibility to pay or do something, which may arise out of a contract, tort, statute, or otherwise.

libel, defamatory writing; any published matter which tends to degrade a person in the eyes of his neighbors, or to render him ridiculous, or to injure his property or business. It may be published by writing, effigy, picture, or the like. Accord, Restatement (Second) of Torts § 568(1). (2) Broadcasting of defamatory matter by means of radio or television, whether or not it is read from a manuscript. *Id.* § 568A. Cf. *slander.* (3) In admiralty, the plaintiff's written statement of his case, analogous to a complaint (*q.v.*).

libellant, the party who files a libel (*q.v.*) in an admiralty court against another, who is called the libellee; analogous to a plaintiff.

libellee, see *libellant.*

libellus, *l.,* a little book.

libel'lus famo'sus, a libel; a defamatory writing, sign, or picture.

libelous per se, descriptive of various acts of libel (*q.v.*), which are actionable without proof of special damages. Usually, they are of three classes: (1) those imputing to the plaintiff criminal acts involving moral turpitude; (2) those imputing a contagious or offensive disease; and (3) those tending to injure plaintiff in his occupation or business.

li'ber, *l.,* book; a principal subdivision of a literary work.

liber assisa'rum, the book of assizes or pleas of the crown; part five of the Year Books (*q.v.*).

liber et leqa'lis ho'mo, a free and lawful man; one qualified to be a juryman.

liber ho'mo (Rom.), a free man.

li'bera batel'la (free boat), a right of fishing.

liberate, to set free.

liberty, a broad and flexible term for freedom, absence of restraint, or self-determination. (2) Authority to do something. (3) A franchise (*q.v.*).

li'berum marita'gium, land given as a dowry to a woman and her husband.

license, permission or authority to do something which would be wrongful or illegal to do if the permission or authority were not granted. The permission or authority may pertain to a public matter, *e.g.,* the privilege of driving a motor vehicle on the public highways, or to a private matter, *e.g.,* the privilege of manufacturing a patented article. In public matters, licenses are often required in order to regulate the activity. See also, *leave and license.*

licensee, a person who is privileged to enter or remain on land only by virtue of the possessor's consent. Restatement (Second) of Torts § 330.

licen'tia, *l.,* leave; a license.

licentiate, a person who is licensed to engage in an occupation.

licentiousness, ignoring moral restraints. (2) Doing what one pleases without regard to the rights of others.

Lidford, or **Lydford law,** see *Jedburgh justice* and *lynch law.*

liege (lēj), or **li'gius,** bound in allegiance. (2) Formerly, the relationship of a tenant to his landlord.

lien, a security device by which there is created a right (1) to retain that which is in a person's possession, belonging to another, until certain demands of the person in possession are satisfied; or (2) to charge property in another's possession with payment of a debt, *e.g.,* a vendor's lien (*q.v.*). It may be either (a) particular, arising out of some charge or claim connected with the identical thing; (b) general, in respect of all dealings of a similar nature between the parties; or (c) conventional, by express or implied agreement between the parties, *e.g.,* a mortgage; or (d) by operation of law, *e.g.,* a lien for taxes or an attorney's lien.

lien creditor, a creditor (*q.v.*) who has acquired a lien (*q.v.*) on the property involved, by attachment, levy, or the like, and includes an assignee for benefit of creditors from the time of assignment, and a trustee in bankruptcy from the date of the filing of the petition, or a receiver in equity from the time of appointment. U.C.C. § 9-301(3).

lieu *(lēu), fr.,* place. In lieu of, in the place, or stead, of.

life annuity, an annual payment during the continuance of a particular life or lives.

life estate, an interest in property which has a termination date concurrent with someone's death. The interest may be measured by the lifetime of the owner, who is called a life tenant, or by someone else's lifetime.

life insurance trust, a trust of life insurance policies set up during the owner's lifetime

life land, or **life hold,** land held on a lease for lives.

life rent (Sc.) a rent received for a term of life.

life tables, statistical charts showing the probable years of life remaining for people who attain certain ages, *e.g.,* United States Life Tables, published by the National Office of Vital Statistics of the Department of Health, Education and Welfare.

life tenant, see *life estate.*

li'gan, goods in the sea, tied to a buoy, so that they may be found again. See also, *jetsam.*

ligeance, allegiance.

light, in addition to the ordinary meanings, the direct, reflected, or diffused rays of the sun. (2) The medium through which light is admitted, *e.g.,* a window or a pane of glass. See also, *ancient lights.*

ligius, see *liege.*

li'gula, formerly, a copy or transcript of a court record or deed.

limitation, a restriction; a thing which limits or restrains. (2) Various periods of time, fixed by different state and federal statutes, called statutes of limitations, within which a lawsuit must be commenced, and after the expiration of which, the claimant will be forever barred from the right to bring the action. Generally, a statute of limitations is a procedural bar to a plaintiff's action which does not begin to run until after the cause of action has accrued and the plaintiff has a right to maintain a lawsuit. Cf. *statute of repose.* (3) A clause in a conveyance or will, which declares how long the estate transferred thereby shall continue, *e.g.,* "heirs," or "heirs of the body," are words of limitation which define the nature of the estate conveyed.

limited, restricted; circumscribed; not full.

limited access highway, or **freeway,** a highway especially designed for through traffic, and over which abutting property owners have no easement or right of access by reason of the fact that their property abuts on such highway.

limited administration, administration (*q.v.*) of the effects of a testator or intestate, which is limited either as to time or as to the assets to be administered.

limited divorce, a divorce (*q.v.*) a mensa et thoro (*q.v.*).

limited jurisdiction, see *jurisdiction (5)*.

limited liability, descriptive of the responsibility of a shareholder or investor in a corporation or other entity, whose liability is legally confined to his specific investment or guarantee in the capital of the company.

limited liability company, an unincorporated form of business organization, similar to a general or limited partnership but possessing a limited liability shield that protects its owners from liability to the same extent that stockholders of a corporation are insulated from its debts and obligations

limited owner, a tenant for life, in tail, or by courtesy, or other person not having a fee simple title to his property.

limited partnership, an unincorporated association or firm, in which one or more of the partners are, on compliance with the provisions of various state statutes regulating such partnerships, relieved from liability beyond the amount of the capital contributed by them. (2) A partnership (*q.v.*) formed by two or more persons under the provisions of the Uniform Limited Partnership Act, having as members one or more general partners and one or more limited partners. The limited partners, as such, are not bound by the obligations of the partnership. Uniform Limited Partnership Act § 1.

limited warranty deed, a deed in which the grantor covenants only against the lawful claims of all persons claiming by, through, or under the grantor.

Lindberg Act, an act to forbid the transportation of kidnapped persons in interstate commerce. 18 U.S.C. §§ 10, 1201, 1202.

linea recta semper praefertur transversali, the direct line is always preferred to the collateral.

lineal, in a direct line. See also, *kin*.

liquidated, fixed; ascertained.

liquidated damages, the exact amount which the parties to a contract expressly agree must be paid, or may be collected, in the event of a future default or breach of contract. Cf. *damages*.

liquidating, descriptive of a person or firm which is engaged in the primary purpose of settling, winding up, or closing out a business, as soon as circumstances permit.

liquidation, ascertaining and fixing the value of something, *e.g.*, a stock of goods, or the amount of damages. (2) Paying, settling, and discharging an indebtedness or liability. (3) Winding up the business of a person or firm.

liquidation price, the amount or portion of assets required by the articles to be distributed to the holders of the shares of any class upon dissolution, liquidation, merger, or consolidation of the corporation, or upon the sale of all or substantially all of its assets.

lis, *l.,* an action or dispute.

lis mota, a controversy begun.

lis pen'dens, a pending lawsuit. See also, *lis pendens notice.*

lis pendens notice, information or an announcement that a lawsuit is pending which has the purpose of affecting the title to particular property described therein. Such information or announcement is filed in the public records for the purpose of preventing any transactions which would thwart the purpose of the pending lawsuit.

listing contract, a written contract for the sale of property which contains the (1) names of the seller and broker, (2) a description of the property, usually by street address, (3) terms of sale, including sale price, whether sale is for cash or on terms, and so forth, (4) duration of the broker's employment, (5) commission to be paid, and (6) special agreements.

literal, written; adhering to the letter.

litigant, a person who is engaged in a lawsuit as a party.

litigation, a lawsuit; a contest in court.

littoral rights, the privileges which appertain to property which abuts on a lake or the ocean. Cf. *riparian rights.*

livery, delivery; formal transfer or investiture. (2) Formerly, a writ to obtain possession of lands on coming of age.

livery of seisin, formerly, the act by which real property was transferred. It was of two kinds: (a) when the grantor and the grantee both went on the premises, and the former delivered to the latter a turf, twig, or key, as symbolic of the whole; (b) when accomplished in sight of the land. See also, *feoffment.*

living, see *birth* and *death.*

living trust, a trust created by the settlor during the settlor's lifetime.

living will, a testamentary document in which the signer states his wishes for the withholding or withdrawal of life sustaining treatment in the event of an incurable or irreversible condition. Living wills are permitted by statute in most states.

loan, the furnishing of money to a person upon the agreement that the person will return a like sum of money to the person who furnished it, at a specified time or according to a schedule of repayment, usually with interest. (2) A bailment (*q.v.*) of personal property for consumption or use, which must be returned in kind or redelivered. (3) The money or personal property which is the subject of a loan.

loaned employee, or **loaned servant,** a person who is in the general employ of someone, but under the exclusive control of another, with respect to the performance of a particular work.

local, pertaining to a particular place or district.

local action, a lawsuit which must be brought in the county or district where the subject matter lies, or the cause of action arose, as distinguished from transitory action (*q.v.*).

local option, a legislative grant to the inhabitants of particular districts, *e.g.*, counties or precincts, to determine by ballot whether they wish to have licenses granted for the sale of intoxicants within their district.

local statutes, legislative acts, the effect of which is limited to a particular place, as distinguished from general statutes.

loca'tio, *l.* (Rom.), letting for hire.

loca'tio custo'diae, a deposit for safekeeping, for a reward.

loca'tio o'peris, the hiring of labor and services.

loca'tio o'peris facien'di, the bailment (*q.v.*) of things on which work is to be done.

loca'tio re'i, the hiring of a thing.

location, the act of selecting and designating lands or mining claims, which a person is authorized by law to enter and possess.

locative calls, references to physical objects in deed or mortgage descriptions, by which the boundaries of the tract conveyed may be ascertained, and the land be identified.

lockout, a cessation of the furnishing of work to employees, in an effort to obtain for the employer more desirable terms, Cf. *strike*.

lo'cus, *l.*, a place.

lo'cus contrac'tus, the place of the contract, *i.e.*, the place where it is made.

locus contractus regit actum, the place of the contract (*i.e.*, the law of the place) governs the act.

lo'cus delic'ti, the place where the tort or injury was committed.

lo'cus in quo, the place in which.

lo'cus poeniten'tiae, a place of repentance, *i.e.,* opportunity for withdrawing from an intended contract or act, or an impending liability, before one is bound, *e.g.,* by the act or acceptance of the other party.

lo'cus re'i si'tae, the place where the thing is situated.

lo'cus si'gilli, or **l.s.,** the place of the seal.

lodger, a person who occupies rooms in a house, the general control of which remains in the landlord.

loitering, wandering or remaining in a place, at a time, or in a manner not usual for law abiding individuals under circumstances that warrant alarm for the safety of persons or property in the vicinity.

long arm statute, various state legislative acts which provide for personal jurisdiction, via substituted service of process, over persons or corporations which are nonresidents of the state and which voluntarily go into the state, directly or by agent, or communicate with persons in the state, for limited purposes, in actions which concern claims relating to the performance or execution of those purposes, *e.g.,* transacting business in the state, contracting to supply services or goods in the state, or selling goods outside the state when the seller knows that the goods will be used or consumed in the state.

long-term debt, debt payable more that one year after date of issuance.

longa patientia trahitur ad consensum, long sufferance is construed as consent. See also, *acquiescence.*

lord, formerly, a person under whom real property was held by a tenant. (2) An English title of dignity.

Lord's Day, Sunday; the first day of the week.

loss, in insurance, the destruction of, or damage to, the subject of the insurance policy by the perils insured against, *e.g.,* the death of the person insured under a life policy, or injury suffered by a person insured under an accident policy. A loss may be total, where the whole subject matter is destroyed or so injured as to be valueless, or partial, not amounting to a total loss. In marine insurance, a loss not actually total may be constructively so, where the subject matter is so nearly destroyed or so situated that the cost of raising and repairing the vessel would be so great as to justify the owner in abandoning her to the underwriters, and claiming a complete loss. See also, *abandonment* and *insurance.*

lost or not lost, words used in a maritime insurance policy which enable the insured to recover, even if the subject of the insurance is already lost at the time of making the policy.

lost papers, writings which have been so mislaid that they cannot be found after diligent search. Secondary evidence of the contents of such writings is generally admissible.

lottery, a scheme for the distribution of prizes by lot, in which the elements of consideration, prize, and chance are present. See also, *gaming.*

Low-Income Home Energy Assistance Act of 1981, title XXVI of an act to provide for reconciliation, also known as the Omnibus Budget Reconciliation Act of 1981. Among other things, it provides for home energy grants to states to assist eligible households to meet the costs of home energy, and deals with applications, requirements, non-discrimination, and limitation on use of grants for construction. 42 U.S.C. §§ 8621 *et seq.*

low-water mark, that part of the shore to which the water recedes when the tide is lowest.

lowest achievable emission rate, LAER; the rate of emissions which reflects the most stringent emission limitation which is contained in the implementation plan of any State (unless the operator demonstrates that such limitations are not achievable) or, the most stringent emission limitation achieved in practice, whichever is more stringent. No new or modified major stationary source can be located in a non-attainment area unless, among other things, it can achieve LAER.

lowest responsible bidder, an offeror whose offer was competitively solicited, who offers the best price, is financially responsible, is capable of doing the work, has suitable equipment and facilities to do so, is prompt, and has previously done quality work.

l.s., see *locus sigilli.*

lucid interval, a period of sanity intervening between two attacks of insanity; a temporary cure or return of health.

lucri causa, *l.,* for the sake of gain; a term descriptive of the felonious intent with which property is taken.

lump sum alimony, alimony awarded as a payment of a definite sum or property in the nature of a final property settlement which serves a reasonable purpose such as rehabilitation or where the marriage's duration or the parties' financial position would make such an award advantageous to both parties.

lunatic, a person of unsound mind; an insane person. Occasionally defined by various state statutes. See also, *insanity.*

Lydford law, see *Jedburgh justice.*

lying by, acquiescence (*q.v.*).

lynch law, illegal summary punishment of real or suspected criminals by persons having no proper judicial authority to do so.

M

machine, a device or combination of devices by which energy can be utilized or an operation can be performed. When it is set in motion, it is capable of producing predetermined physical effects by its own operation.

MACT, see *maximum achievable control technology.*

magis de bono quam de malo lex intendit, the law favors a good, *i.e.,* lawful, rather than a bad construction.

magis'ter, *l.,* a master; ruler.

magister na'vis, master of a ship; he to whom the entire control of a vessel is committed.

magistrate, various public officials. (2) A term frequently employed to denote those who may issue warrants. (3) A public civil officer possessing such power—legislative, executive, or judicial—as the government appointing him may ordain. (4) An inferior judicial officer, *e.g.,* justice of the peace (*q.v.*). (5) "Magistrate" and "judicial officer" have been used interchangeably. See also, *Federal Magistrate Act of 1979.*

Magna Charta, *l.,* or Great Charter, a document which provided for the restitution of the ancient liberties of England, exacted by the barons from King John in 1215, and subsequently confirmed by over thirty different statutes, of which those of 9 Henry III and 25 Edward I are the most important. Among other things, it provided against abuses of the royal prerogative, and for the proper administration of justice.

magna culpa dolus est, gross negligence is equivalent to fraud.

Magnuson-Moss Warranty—Federal Trade Commission Improvement Act, an act to provide minimum disclosure standards for written consumer-product warranties; to define minimum federal content standards for such warranties; to amend the Federal Trade Commission Act(s) (*q.v.*) in order to improve its consumer protection activities; and for other purposes. 15 U.S.C. §§ 45, 46, 49, 50, 52, 56, 57a-57c, 2301 *et seq.*

mailbox rule, a rule of contract providing that an acceptance becomes effective upon proper dispatch; the offeree may be certain that the process of contract formation is completed, the offeror may be bound by such proper dispatch even before possessing actual knowledge of the acceptance.

maim, see *mayhem.*

mainpernable, an offense, or person charged therewith, that may be allowed bail.

mainpernors, formerly, persons to whom another person was delivered out of prison on their becoming bound to produce him whenever required. Similar to a person who serves as bail (*q.v.*).

mainprise, an old term for bail (*q.v.*).

mainsworn, forsworn. See also, *forswear.*

maintainor, a person who, without having an interest in the subject of an action, and not being retained as counsel or attorney, maliciously or officiously interferes and assists with money, or otherwise, to carry it on.

maintenance, the supply of necessaries to a person's wife and children, or to persons who are unable to provide for themselves. (2) The offense committed by a maintainor (*q.v.*). See also, *champerty.*

major continet in se minus, the greater contains the less.

majority, full age. See *age* (2). (2) The greater number.

majus dignum trahit ad se minus dignum, the more worthy draws to itself the less worthy.

maker, a person who signs a promissory note, and by so doing engages to pay it according to its tenor.

mal, a prefix meaning bad, wrong, fraudulent.

ma'la, or **malum,** *l.*, bad; wrong; fraudulent.

ma'la fi'des, bad faith, the opposite of bona fides.

mala grammatica non vitiat chartam, bad grammar does not vitiate a deed.

ma'la in se, acts which are wrong in themselves, whether prohibited by human laws or not, as distinguished from mala prohibita (*q.v.*).

ma'la prax'is, malpractice; bad or unskilled treatment by a physician, or other professional person, resulting in an injury to the person who employs him.

ma'la prohi'bita, acts which are prohibited by human laws, but not necessarily mala in se (*q.v.*), or wrong in themselves.

maledicta expositio quae corrumpit textum, it is a cursed exposition which corrupts the text

malefactor, a wrongdoer; a person convicted of a crime.

maleficia propositis distinguuntur, evil deeds are distinguished from evil purposes.

malfeasance, the commission of an unlawful act, particularly by a public official.

malice, hatred; ill will; a formed design to do an unlawful act, whether another may be prejudiced by it or not. If the known and necessary consequence of the act is injury to another, the law implies malice, but express malice, *i.e.*, actual ill feeling toward the person injured, may also be proved to exist.

malice aforethought, acting with one of the requisite states of mind necessary for the commission of the crime.

malicious, with malice; wrongful; wanton; without just cause.

malicious arrest, imprisonment, or **prosecution,** a malicious setting in motion of the law without probable cause, whereby someone is wrongfully and maliciously accused of a criminal offense or a civil wrong, and by reason of which that person sustains damage. See also, *malicious prosecution.*

malicious injuries, hurts wantonly inflicted on person or property, without just cause, *e.g.*, arson or destruction of property.

malicious prosecution, initiating or procuring the institution of criminal proceedings (*q.v.*) by a private person against another who is not guilty of the offense charged, if (a) he initiates or procures the proceedings without probable cause and primarily for a purpose other than that of bringing an offender to justice, and (b) the proceedings have terminated in favor of the accused. Restatement (Second) of Torts § 653. See also, *malicious arrest.* Cf. *wrongful civil proceedings.*

malin'gerer *(mə-lĭng'gər-ər),* a person who feigns illness or disease, especially in order to escape military duty or to obtain charity.

mali'tia praecogita'ta, *l.,* malice aforethought. See also, *malice.*

malitia supplet aetatem, malice supplies [the want of] age.

ma'lo gra'to, *l.,* in spite; unwillingly.

malpractice, the negligent, or otherwise improper, performance by a physician, attorney, or other professional person, of the duties which are devolved and incumbent upon him on account of his professional relations with his patient or client.

malum, see *mala.*

malum non praesumitur, evil is not presumed.

malus usus est abolendus, an evil custom should be abolished.

man of straw, see *men of straw.*

manager, a flexible term for a person appointed to have charge of the business of another or of a corporation. (2) A person appointed by the House of Representatives to prosecute an impeachment before the Senate.

manda'mus, we command; a prerogative writ issued by a court, addressed to a natural person or corporation, and not to the sheriff as are ordinary writs, requiring the person to whom it is addressed to do some act therein specified, which is generally one connected with his duty as a public official or as a corporation exercising public franchises. The writ may be alternative, *i.e.*, granted on ex parte affidavits, and requiring the person to do the thing or show cause why he should not be compelled to do it, or peremptory, *i.e.*, after final hearing, when there is nothing for the defendant to do but obey.

mandate, a judicial command. (2) A charge or commission. (3) Occasionally, a bailment (*q.v.*) of goods without reward, to have something done to them, not merely for safe custody.

mandatory, a person to whom a mandate or charge is given.

mania, various forms of mental disease, involving excitement. A person may be afflicted with a mania on certain subjects, or in certain directions, and be in all other respects mentally sound. See also, *lunatic*.

manifest, a document signed by the master of a ship, setting forth the description and destination of the goods shipped.

manifesto, a declaration of the reasons for the acts of one government toward another, made by the nation's constituted authorities.

Mann Act, an act to regulate interstate and foreign commerce, by prohibiting the transportation therein of women and girls for immoral purposes. 18 U.S.C. §§ 2421 *et seq.*

manor, formerly, an English estate in fee, granted by the Crown, to a person called the lord. A manor has various franchises appendant to it, *e.g.*, the right to hold a courtbaron (*q.v.*).

manslaughter, the unlawful killing of another, without malice (*q.v.*), express or implied. It is either voluntary, *i.e.*, upon sudden heat, or under strong provocation, or involuntary, *i.e.*, without intending the death of the person, upon the commission of some other unlawful act. (2) Criminal homicide (*q.v.*) which is committed recklessly, or a homicide (*q.v.*), which would otherwise be murder (*q.v.*), committed under the influence of extreme mental or emotional disturbance for which there is reasonable explanation or excuse. The reasonableness of the explanation or excuse is determined from the viewpoint of a person in the actor's situation under the circumstances as he believes them to be. Model Penal Code § 210.3 (1).

manufacture, to make goods (*q.v.*) by hand or by machinery. (2) An article produced by hand or by machinery.

march, a boundary.

margin, edge or boundary. (2) A sum of money deposited with a broker to secure him against loss in the stock bought or sold for the customer's account.

marine, or **maritime,** belonging or relating to the sea.

marine contract, an agreement relating to business done on the sea, or connected with vessels which sail thereon.

marine insurance, a contract of indemnity against losses by perils of the sea, *e.g.*, to ships or cargoes.

marine interest, a charge paid for the use of money on bottomry (*q.v.*) or respondentia (*q.v.*). It is usually large, and in proportion to the risk assumed.

marine league, a measure of distance equal to one-twentieth of a degree of latitude, or three nautical miles.

marital, pertaining to marriage, *e.g.*, marital rights or marital duties.

maritime, see *marine.*

maritime law, rules and decisions relating to harbors, ships, and seamen.

maritime lien, a device to secure a claim against a ship, *e.g.*, for wages, repairs, supplies furnished, or against goods transported in ships, for freight. See also, *lien.*

market, a public place for buying and selling at appointed times. (2) The demand for a particular article.

market overt, open market.

market value, see *fair market value.*

marketable title, see *title (1).*

marksman, a person who cannot write and therefore makes only an X mark in executing instruments, another writing his name on each side of the mark.

marriage, the status of a man and woman who have engaged in due form of law to live together, and to discharge toward each other the duties of husband and wife. (2) A personal relationship between a man and a woman arising out of a civil contract to which the consent of the parties is essential. A marriage licensed, solemnized, and registered as provided in the law is valid in the state. A marriage may be contracted, maintained, invalidated, or dissolved only as provided by law. Uniform Marriage and Divorce Act § 201. (3) The solemnity by which married persons are united. The consent of both parties is essential to its validity. The age of consent, and therefore of legal capacity for marrying, at common-law, was fourteen in males and twelve in females. In the United States, the age of consent and the capacity to marry are strictly regulated by various state statutes. See also, *common-law marriage.*

marriage articles, occasionally, articles of agreement between parties contemplating marriage, and preliminary to a settlement. See also, *marriage settlement.*

marriage by proxy, or **proxy marriage,** a marriage (*q.v.*) in which a party to the marriage is unable to be present at the solemnization and authorizes in writing a third person to act as his proxy (*q.v.*). If the person solemnizing the marriage is satisfied that the absent party is unable to be present and has consented to the marriage, he may solemnize the marriage by proxy. If he is not satisfied, the parties may petition a court for an order permitting the marriage to be solemnized by proxy. Uniform Marriage and Divorce Act § 206(b).

marriage license, in most jurisdictions statute requires that couples apply for and obtain a marriage license as an essential prerequisite to the lawful solemnization of a marriage.

marriage settlement, (a) antenuptial, an arrangement in writing, made before marriage, and in consideration of it, whereby the property rights of the future marriage partners are modified from those which they would have enjoyed if they had married without such an arrangement. *E.g.,* in the case of a second marriage, such an arrangement might limit or abrogate the rights of the parties in the respective property of the other, both during life and after death, and secure for the respective children of the parties, the inheritance of the individual property of the parties. (b) Postnuptial, or after marriage, an arrangement analogous to (a), but which is only voluntary and unenforceable.

marshal, an officer of the United States, whose duty it is to execute the process of the United States courts. His duties are similar to those of a sheriff. (2) In some jurisdictions, an officer of a city or town, whose duties are analogous to those of a chief of police.

marshaling, arranging in a certain or suitable order.

marshaling of assets, an equitable requirement that if two or more creditors have a claim against the same debtor, a creditor who may resort to two funds for the satisfaction of his claim must first satisfy his claim from such fund as the other creditor(s) cannot resort to. Usually applied when the debtor is insolvent.

martial law, temporary control of an area and the population thereof, which is imposed by a military commander under the authority of his civilian chief. It may be imposed in the territory of an enemy in war, or in the home territory when normal authority is unable to function. When it is imposed in the territory of an enemy in war, it must be exercised in accordance with international law and the conventions of civilized warfare. When it is imposed in the home territory, its justification may be reviewed by the courts.

Mary Carter agreement, an agreement by the plaintiff and some, but not all, of the defendants whereby limitations are placed on the financial responsibility of the agreeing defendants.

master, an officer of a court appointed to assist the court, *e.g.,* in taking and reporting testimony, examining and stating accounts, computing damages, and executing the decrees of the court. (2) The commander, or first officer, of a merchant ship. (3) Formerly, an employer. (4) A principal who employs an agent to perform service in his affairs and who controls or has the right to control the physical conduct of the other in the performance of the service. Restatement of Agency, Second § 2.

master of the rolls, the president of the English Court of Appeal.

ma'ter fami'lias, *l.,* the mother of a family.

material, important; relevant; substantial; capable of properly influencing the result of a lawsuit. (2) As it concerns perjury (*q.v.*), falsification is material, regardless of the admissibility of the statement under rules of evidence, if it could have affected the course or outcome of the proceeding. It is no defense that the declarant mistakenly believed the falsification to be immaterial. Whether a falsification is material is a question of law. Model Penal Code § 241.1(2).

material fact, or **material facts,** in an application for insurance, information which is substantial and which, if communicated to the insurer, would influence the insurer in deciding to make the contract or fixing the premium rate. (2) The portion of the unique facts of a dispute, on which a court elects to base its decision.

material misrepresentation, a misrepresentation (*q.v.*) that would be likely to induce a reasonable person to manifest his assent (*q.v.*), or that the maker knows would be likely to induce the recipient to do so. Restatement (Second) of Contracts §162(2).

materialmen, persons, firms, or corporations who furnish material used in building ships, houses, or other construction. Occasionally defined by various state statutes. See also, *mechanics' and materialmen's lien.*

matrimonia debent esse libera, marriages ought to be free.

matrimonial causes, lawsuits for divorce, judicial separation, nullity of marriage, restitution of conjugal rights and for jactitation of marriage.

matron, see *jury of matrons.*

matter in pais, see *pais.*

matter of course, see *of course.*

maturity, ripeness; full development; the time when a promissory note (*q.v.*) becomes due.

maxim, an axiom; a general or leading principle.

maximum achievable control technology, MACT; the basis upon which the EPA must set emission standards for sources of HAPs. For categories of existing sources, EPA must set the standard at least as stringent as the best performing 12%. For categories of new sources, MACT can be no less stringent that the best performing source. MACT can be more stringent than these standards.

mayhem, at common law, the deprivation of a member of the body proper for defense in a fight, *e.g.*, an arm, leg, eye, or foretooth, or of those parts. The loss of which abates a man's courage; but not a jawtooth, ear, or nose, because they were supposed to be of no use in fighting. Often defined by various state statutes, which may make no distinction between one member and another with regard to the offense of cutting or wounding.

mayor, the chief magistrate of a city, town, or village. The state statutes or municipal charters.

mayor's court, in some jurisdictions, a court with limited authority, similar to the court of a Justice of the Peace (*q.v.*) or of a Magistrate (*q.v.*).

McCarran Act, an act to protect the United States against certain un-American and subversive activities, by requiring registration of Communist organizations. 50 U.S.C. §§ 781 *et seq.* Repealed.

McGuire Act, an act to amend the Federal Trade Commission Act, with respect to certain contracts and agreements which establish minimum or stipulated resale prices and which are extended by state law to persons who are not parties to such contracts and agreements. 15 U.S.C. §§ 1, 45.

McNaghten Rule, *M'naghten Rule.*

meander, to wander or wind; descriptive of the banks or course of a stream.

meander lines, imaginary lines run in surveying lands bordering on rivers or other streams, to ascertain the quantity of land.

measure of damage, various rules for the determination of the sum of money which will fairly compensate a person for loss to his person, to his property, or on account of breach of contract, under the facts of each unique lawsuit.

mechanics' and **materialmen's lien,** a statutory lien (*q.v.*) which is created in favor of a person who furnishes labor or material for an improvement, either on funds in the owner's hands or on the property improved, *e.g.*, a building, a motor vehicle, or a swimming pool.

mediate, to settle by mediation (*q.v.*); indirect; intervening.

mediation, the settlement of disputes by the amicable intervention of an outside party who is a stranger to the controversy.

medical jurisprudence, the influence of law on medicine and its practice. Sometimes used as a synonym for forensic medicine (*q.v.*).

Medicare Act, see *Health Insurance for the Aged and Disabled Act.*

medieta'tis lin'guae, or **de medietatis linguae,** *l.,* of the half tongue; a term applied to a jury composed one-half of persons who speak English and one-half of persons who speak a foreign language.

melior est conditio possidentis, the condition of the party in possession is the better one, *i.e.,* where the right of the parties is equal.

meliorations, improvements to real property.

melius est petere fontes quam sectari rivulos, it is better to go to the fountain head than to follow streamlets from it. This applies especially to quotations, extracts, and conclusions deduced from precedent cases and authorities.

me'lius inquiren'dum, *l.,* formerly, a writ for a second inquiry.

memorandum, an informal record of some fact or agreement. (2) In the law of contract, a writing which evidences a contract so as to make it enforceable under the Statute of Frauds. The writing must be signed by or on behalf of the party to be charged, reasonably identify the subject matter of the contract, sufficiently indicate that a contract with respect thereto has been made between the parties or offered by the signer to the other party, and state with reasonable certainty the essential terms of the unperformed promises in the contract. Restatement (Second) of Contracts § 131. (3) In marine insurance, a clause limiting the liability of the insurer. (4) A typewritten instrument analogous to a brief (*q.v.*), which is submitted to a trial court.

memorial, a petition or representation by one or more individuals to a legislative body or chief executive.

men of straw, formerly, persons who frequented the courts for the purpose of giving false evidence. (2) Worthless persons, those without means. See also, *straw man.*

mens rea, criminal intent; evil intent; guilty intent. See also, *actus non fact reum, nisi mens sit rea.*

mens testatoris in testamentis spectanda est, in wills the intention of the testator is to be regarded.

mensa et thoro, from bed and board; a type of divorce or judicial separation of husband and wife.

mental cruelty, habitually behaving in such a cruel and inhuman manner as to indicate a settled aversion to a person's spouse, or to destroy permanently his or her peace or happiness. Often defined by various state statutes.

mental reservation, a silent exception from the general words of a promise or agreement.

mercantile law, that branch of law which deals with matters affecting trade, *e.g.,* bills of exchange and insurance. See also, *commercial law.*

merchant, a person who deals in goods of the kind, or otherwise by his occupation holds himself out as having knowledge or skill peculiar to the practices or goods, involved in the transaction, or to whom such knowledge or skill may be attributed by his employment of an agent or broker or other intermediary, who by his occupation holds himself out as having such knowledge or skill. U.C.C. § 2-104(1). See also, *between merchants.*

merchantable, descriptive of goods which are at least such as: (a) pass without objection in the trade under the contract description; and (b) in the case of fungible goods, are of fair average quality within the description; and (c) are fit for the ordinary purposes for which such goods are used; and (d) run, within the variations permitted by the agreement, of even kind, quality and quantity within each unit and among all units involved; and (e) are adequately contained, packaged and labeled as the agreement may require; and (f) conform to the promises or affirmations of fact made on the container or label, if any. U.C.C. § 2-314(2).

meretricious, descriptive of a relationship with a prostitute (*q.v.*).

merger, in real property, an absorption by operation of law, of a lesser right or estate in a greater right or estate, upon the union of their ownership in the same person. It takes place independently of the will of the party. See also, *extinguishment.* (2) A consolidation of corporations, in which only one of two or more former corporations survives the consolidation, or which brings into existence a new corporation and destroys the former corporations.

merger of offenses, where commission of one crime necessarily involves commission of a second, the offense so involved is said to be merged in the offense of which it is part.

meritorious consideration, a consideration (*q.v.*) founded upon some moral obligation, *e.g.,* natural love and affection. See also, *good consideration.*

merits, judgment upon, a final resolution of a lawsuit, rendered after a hearing of the entire case on the pleadings and evidence.

mesne (men), middle; intermediate.

mesne process, all process (*q.v.*) which intervenes in the progress of a lawsuit, between its beginning and end, as distinguished from primary and final process.

mesne profits, the gain or income from real property realized during a specific period of time, particularly that derived while the possession has been improperly withheld.

messuage, a dwelling house with outbuildings, garden, and the curtilage (*q.v.*).

metes, measures of length, such as inches, feet, yards, and rods.

metes and bounds (mēts), the boundary lines of land with courses, distances, terminal points, and angles. See also, *courses and distances.*

middleman, an agent between two parties, who has no fiduciary duty towards either party.

mileage, compensation allowed by law to witnesses, sheriffs, and other public officers, for their expenses in traveling on public business.

military law, a system for the government of persons in military service; distinguished from martial law (*q.v.*), which affects all persons within the scope of military operations or occupation, whether they are in the service or not. See also, *uniform code of military justice.*

Military Selective Service Act, various federal laws enacted since 1863, currently the act of June 24, 1948, as amended. It provides for, among other things, registration of male citizens and every other male person residing in the U.S. between the ages of 18 and 26, liability for training and service, manner of selection for training and service, and the like. 10 U.S.C. § 2535a.

military testament, a nuncupative will (*q.v.*).

Miller-Tydings Act, an act to amend the antitrust laws of the United States, to provide for the establishment of contracts for resale price maintenance in states where such contracts are lawful in intrastate transactions. 15 U.S.C. § 1. See also, *McGuire Act.*

minatur innocentibus qui parcit nocentibus, he threatens the innocent who spares the guilty.

mineral, in its widest sense, includes any part of the earth which can be obtained from underneath its surface for the purpose of profit, whether (a) by mines, or underground workings, or (b) by quarries or open workings, *e.g.,* ore, coal, gas, and oil.

minima poena corporalis est major qualibet pecuniaria, the smallest bodily punishment is greater than any pecuniary one.

minime mutanda sunt quae certam habuerunt interpretationem, things which have a certain interpretation are to be altered as little as possible.

minimus, the smallest. See also, *de minimus non curat lex.*

mining right, the privilege to enter upon a specific piece of ground and occupy it for the purpose of working it, either by underground excavations or open workings, to obtain from it the mineral or ores which may be deposited therein.

ministerial, descriptive of official duties or acts of an official or administrator, who is bound to follow instructions; opposed to judicial or discretionary.

ministerial functions, activities which are absolute, fixed, and certain and in the performance of which there is no discretion. (2) Occasionally, private corporate functions of a municipality, as distinguished from public and governmental functions. Cf. *governmental function.*

minor, a person who is under a particular number of years of age, which number varies from state to state. Frequently the number is 18 to 21. Uniform Probate Code §§ 1-201(24), 5-103(10).

minor ward, a minor *(q.v.)* for whom a guardian *(q.v.)* has been appointed solely because of minority. Uniform Probate Code § 5-103(22).

minority, descriptive of a person or group of persons who do not predominate in numbers within the nation, electorate, or other group to which they belong, *e.g.,* Black persons or persons of Mexican descent in the United States. (2) The status of a person who is of less than full age. See also, *age (2)* and *minor.*

minutes, notes or records of a transaction, meeting, or other event. (2) A memorandum of what takes place in court, made by authority of the court, from which the final record is afterward made up.

Miranda rights, in the absence of other effective measures, the following procedures to safeguard the privilege against self-incrimination must be observed, *i.e.,* a person in police custody must, prior to interrogation, be clearly informed that he has the right to remain silent, and that anything he says will be used against him in court; he must be clearly informed that he has the right to consult with a lawyer and to have the lawyer with him during interrogation, and that, if he is indigent, a lawyer will be appointed to represent him.

mirror image rule, a rule of contract providing that the acceptance must conform precisely to the terms of the offer.

misadventure, an accident or misfortune by which an injury occurs to another, without negligence and while performing a lawful act.

misappropriation, the act of misapplying funds or property to an unauthorized purpose.

misbehavior, improper or unlawful conduct; misconduct.

miscarriage, a failure of justice. (2) Abortion (*q.v.*).

miscegenation, formerly, an offense under various state statutes, consisting of intermarriage of persons belonging to the White and Black races.

misdemeanor, any crime or offense not amounting to a felony (*q.v.*).

misdemeanor manslaughter, in some jurisdictions, proof that a death was caused by even an unintentional misdemeanor would be sufficient to obtain a conviction for involuntary manslaughter.

misdirection, an error in law made by a judge in instructing or charging a trial jury.

misera est servitus ubi jus est vagum aut incertum, wretched is the slavery where the law is changeable or uncertain.

misfeasance, the improper performance of some lawful act. (2) A wrongful act.

misjoinder, the improper union of parties, claims, or causes of action in one lawsuit.

misnomer, the giving of the wrong name to a person in legal documents or judicial proceedings.

misprision, of treason, the offense of not giving information concerning an act of high treason of which one is aware; (2) of felony, to conceal, or aid in concealing, a felony.

misrepresentation, a false statement which may variously constitute grounds for the rescission of a contract or for the recovery of damages for losses caused thereby. Accord, Restatement (Second) of Contracts § 159. See also, *fraudulent misrepresentation*.

mistake, error; a fault in judgment or conduct; an act done or omitted, by reason of ignorance of law or facts, which a party would not have committed if he had rightly understood the law or facts. (2) In the law of contract, a belief that is not in accord with the facts. Restatement (Second) of Contracts § 151.

mistrial, an erroneous trial. Descriptive of a trial at which an event supervenes, that causes the judge to terminate the proceedings because he believes that a fair verdict cannot be obtained on account of that event.

misuser, abuse of a privilege or right.

mitigation, reduction of damages or of punishment. Circumstances which do not amount to a defense, justification, or excuse for an act, may properly be considered in mitigation of the punishment, or of the damages which a person injured by the act might otherwise recover.

mitter *(mĭt tā̆), fr.,* to put, to send, or to pass.

mitter a large *(à lãrzh)*, to put or set at large.

mitter le droit *(lǔ drwä)*, to pass a right. See also, *release.*

mitter l'estate, to pass the estate.

mit'timus (we send), a written court order directed to the keeper of a prison, directing that he receive and safely keep an offender. (2) A form of process to transfer records from one court to another.

mixed, blended; confused; united; compound; not pure or simple.

mixed action, a lawsuit pertaining to both real property and damages, *e.g.,* where possession is demanded of real property and damages are demanded for its unjust detention. Cf. *personal action* and *real action.*

mixed contract, (Rom.), an agreement in which one of the parties confers a benefit on the other, and requires of the latter something of less value than what he has given.

mixed larceny, or **compound larceny,** the offense of larceny *(q.v.)* which is combined with circumstances of aggravation, or violence to the person, or taking from a dwelling house.

mixed property, property which is not classifiable as real or personal, but which is a compound of both, *e.g.,* emblements, fixtures, heirlooms, or title deeds.

mixed questions of law and fact, controversies in which a jury finds the particular facts, and the court decides upon the legal result of those facts.

M'Naghten Rule, test applied in some states for the defense of insanity; states that the proper standard or test for criminal responsibility is whether the accused was laboring under such a defect of reason, from disease of the mind, as not to know the nature and quality of the act he was doing, or, if he did know it, he did not know that what he was doing was wrong.

Mobile Home Construction Safety Act, see *National Manufactured Housing Construction and Safety Standards Act of 1974.*

mobilia non habent situm, movables have no situs.

mobilia sequuntur personam, movables follow the person. In accordance with this maxim, personal assets of an intestate are distributed according to the laws of the state where he was domiciled, not of that where they are situated.

model, in sales transactions, an object which is offered for inspection when the subject matter is not at hand and which has not been drawn from the bulk of the goods. Any sample or model which is made part of the basis of a bargain creates an express warranty that the whole of the goods shall conform to the sample or model. U.C.C. § 2-313(1)(c) and Official Comment 6. Cf. *sample* (2).

Model Penal Code, or **Penal and Correctional Code,** a proposal by the American Law Institute approved May 24, 1962, concerning general principles of criminal liability, general principles of jurisdiction, responsibility, inchoate crimes, authorized disposition of offenders, authority of the court in sentencing, offenses involving danger to the person, offenses against property, offenses against the family, offenses against public administration, offenses against public order and decency, treatment and correction, and organization of correction. New Jersey and Pennsylvania have adopted major provisions of it, and other jurisdictions have used it, or parts of it, as a pattern for their local state codes.

Model Rules of Professional Conduct, proposed rules to govern the legal profession, consisting of seven topics, rules and comments. Adopted by the House of Delegates of the American Bar Association on August 2, 1983. Research notes were prepared to compare counterparts in the Model Code of Professional Responsibility (*q.v.*) and to provide selected references to other authorities; they have not been adopted and do not constitute part of the Rules.

Model Uniform Product Liability Act, a proposal by the U.S. Department of Commerce for voluntary use by the states. It is intended to help to assure that persons injured by unreasonably unsafe products receive reasonable compensation for their injuries, to help stabilize product liability insurance rates, and to introduce uniformity and stability into the law of product liability. 44 Fed. Reg. 62714-62750 (1979).

modify, to effect some change in form or qualities, powers or duties, purposes or objects.

modo et forma, *l.,* (in the manner and form mentioned), formerly a response to a prior pleading, which put the opposite party on proof of his allegations in every detail.

mo'dus, *l.,* manner; means; way.

modus et conventio vincunt legem, the form of the agreement and consent of the parties overrule the law.

modus operandi, manner of operation.

moiety, variously, a half or any equal share, e.g., a third.

molestation, the offense of annoying a person for the purpose of controlling his actions. (2) The offense of disturbing children, accompanied by abnormal sexual motivations.

mol'liter matnus impo'suit, *l.,* (he laid hands gently on him), a defense in an action of battery, that the defendant used only the necessary force, and for a justifiable reason.

money, a medium of exchange, authorized or adopted by a domestic or foreign government as a part of its currency. U.C.C. § 1-201(24).

money counts, formerly, the common counts (*q.v.*) in an action of assumpsit (*q.v.*), founded on an alleged promise to pay money in consideration of a precedent indebtedness, *e.g.*, indebitatus assumpsit, quantum meruit, and quantum valebant.

monition, in admiralty practice, an order of a court analogous to a summons (*q.v.*).

monomania, insanity (*q.v.*) only upon a single subject, and with a single delusion of the mind.

monopoly, an exclusive privilege of buying, selling, making, working, or using a particular thing. (2) The absolute and exclusive control by a person, or combination of persons, of the sale of, a particular commodity. (3) A combination of producers or dealers to raise commodity prices via the more or less exclusive control of the supply or the purchasing power.

month, calendar, one of the twelve divisions of the year by which we reckon time, consisting of an unequal number of days. The word month, in commercial dealings and statutes, means a calendar month.

monuments, permanent landmarks established or used for the purpose of indicating boundaries and corners of land. They may be natural, *e.g.*, rivers and streams, or artificial, *e.g.*, steel pins or posts set in the ground.

moot, descriptive of something which is not genuine or concrete, something which is pretended. (2) A meeting, especially for the purpose of arguing points of law by way of exercise.

moot case, or **moot point,** an issue before a court which is not genuine, has already been disposed of, or the resolution of which cannot be implemented.

moot court, a pretended court, usually held in law schools, where moot cases are argued and decided. See also, *moot* and *moot case.*

moot point, see *moot case.*

moral certainty, the degree of probability which would induce a person to act in the ordinary affairs of life as if the thing were certain. (2) That degree of certainty which leaves room for no reasonable doubt.

moral turpitude, a flexible term for an act of baseness, vileness, or depravity, contrary to the accepted and customary rule of right and duty between human beings.

moratorium, the lawful suspension of legal remedies against debtors during times of financial distress.

mo'ratur in le'ge, *l.,* he demurs.

more or less, words in a description of land, meaning that the quantity is uncertain and not warranted, and that no right of either party shall be affected by any ascertained excess or deficiency, which is less than a certain percentage, *e.g.,* 10%.

mortality tables, various statistical charts showing the expectancy of life. See also, *life tables.*

mortgage (môr gāg), (a dead pledge), a conveyance of real or personal property to a person called the mortgagee, to secure the payment of money by the mortgagor and to become void upon the performance of such act. At common law, such conveyances became absolute upon failure to perform the condition, but in equity, the mortgagor is permitted to redeem. The manner in which the equity of redemption may be barred is regulated by various state statutes. A legal mortgage is one created by the conveyance or assignment of the property to the mortgagee. An equitable mortgage is one in which the mortgagor does not actually convey the property, but does some act by which he manifests his intention to bind it as security. (2) Any conveyance, agreement, or arrangement in which property is used as security or collateral. Uniform Probate Code §§ 1-201 (25), 5-103 (11). Cf. *lien* and *security agreement.*

mor'tis causa, in prospect of death.

mortmain, a state of ownership of real property which makes it inalienable, whence it is said to be in a dead hand. See also, *Mortmain Act.*

Mortmain Act, various state statutes restricting or prohibiting the gift of lands in perpetuity (*q.v.*) to religious and charitable corporations, which are patterned after various English acts.

mortuary, a place where dead bodies are kept and prepared, previous to interment. (2) Formerly, a gift left by a person at his death to his parish church.

mortuary tables, see *mortality tables.*

Most Favored Nation Clause, a provision of a treaty guaranteeing to the citizens of the contracting states the privileges granted by either party to the citizens of other favored nations.

mote (mōt), a meeting or assemblage. See also, *gemot* and *moot.*

mother hubbard clause, an all-inclusive clause in a lease whose purpose is to prevent leaving small unleased strips of land which may exist without the knowledge of either party when the grantor is uncertain about the precise area that he owns.

motion, an application to a court, by the parties or their counsel, for a rule or order, either in the progress of a lawsuit, or summarily, *e.g.,* a motion for a writ of habeas corpus. A motion may be made either ex parte (*q.v.*), or on notice to the other side, and when based on facts not found in the record, must be supported by an affidavit, a deposition, or testimony in open court, that such facts are true.

motion day, a time specifically designated by the court for the hearing of motions and other nonjury matters.

motion in li'mine, a motion (*q.v.*) at the outset; a pretrial motion for an order prohibiting introduction of evidence regarding or reference in trial to matters specified in the motion.

motive, the purpose underlying a defendant's conduct; that which leads or tempts the mind to indulge in a criminal act.

motor vehicle, a flexible term for various devices for the transportation of persons or property over or upon the public highways. It commonly does not include construction equipment, farm tractors, muscular powered conveyances, and conveyances propelled by electric power from overhead wires. Usually defined by various state statutes. Cf. *automobile.*

Motor Vehicle Air Pollution Control Act, title I of an act to amend the Clean Air Act (*q.v.*) to require standards for controlling the emission of pollutants from certain motor vehicles, to authorize a research and development program with respect to solid-waste disposal, and for other purposes. 42 U.S.C. §§ 1857f-1 *et seq.*

Motor Vehicle and Schoolbus Safety Amendments of 1974, an act to amend the National Traffic and Motor Vehicle Safety Act of 1966 (*q.v.*) to, among other things, provide for the remedy of certain defective motor vehicles without charge to the owners, and to require that schoolbus safety standards be prescribed. 15 U.S.C. §§ 1391-1393, 1397-1399, 1401, 1402, 1408, 1410a-1420, 1424.

Motor Vehicle Safety Act, see *National Traffic and Motor Vehicle Safety Act of 1966.*

movables, a classification of property which includes goods, furniture, chattels, and things which may be carried from place to place.

mulct, occasionally, a fine of money or a penalty.

multa non vetat lex, quae tamen tacite damnavit, the law does not forbid many things which it has silently condemned.

multifariousness, under older codes of procedure, the joinder in one bill of complaint of several distinct and independent causes of action, which was a ground for demurrer.

multipartite, divided into several parts.

multiple listing, a means by which brokers in a given area pool their efforts to sell properties listed with any member of the pool.

multiple-party account, any of the following types of account (*q.v.*): a joint account (*q.v.*), a P.O.D. account (*q.v.*), or a trust account (*q.v.*). It does not include accounts established for deposit of funds of a partnership, joint venture, or other association for business purposes, or accounts controlled by one or more persons as the duly authorized agent or trustee for a corporation, unincorporated association, charitable or civic organization or a regular fiduciary or trust account where the relationship is established other than by deposit agreement. Uniform Probate Code § 6-101(5).

multiplicity of actions, or **suits,** the improper bringing of more than one action or lawsuit for what might be determined in a single action.

multitude, a vague term for an assembly of persons. There is no consensus as to how many persons constitute a multitude.

multitudo imperitorum perdit curiam, a multitude of ignorant practitioners destroys a court.

municipal, commonly, that which relates to a city; more generally, that which pertains to the state or nation.

municipal corporation, see *city.*

municipal law, jurisprudence which pertains to a particular state or nation, as distinguished from international law (*q.v.*).

muniments, writings which constitute evidence of title to real property, *e.g.,* deeds, wills, and affidavits of inheritance.

murder, the wilfull killing of a human being with malice aforethought, either express or implied. Under various state statutes, murder is divided into degrees, depending upon the amount of malice and deliberation exhibited by the murderer, and whether the act was committed in the perpetration of some other crime, *e.g.,* arson, rape, burglary, or robbery. (2) Criminal homicide (*q.v.*) which is committed purposely or knowingly, or is committed recklessly under circumstances manifesting extreme indifference to the value of human life. Such recklessness and indifference are presumed if the actor is engaged or is an accomplice in the commission of, or an attempt to commit, or flight after committing or attempting to commit robbery, rape, or deviate sexual intercourse by force or threat of force, arson, burglary, kidnapping, or felonious escape. Model Penal Code § 210.2. See also, *homicide.* But cf. *manslaughter (2).*

muta'tis mutan'dis, with the necessary changes in points of detail.

mute, a defendant who abstains from pleading to an indictment. Under various state and federal rules of criminal procedure, if a defendant refuses to plead, the court shall enter a plea of not guilty.

mutiny, the unlawful resistance of a superior officer, on board a ship or in the army. (2) The disobedience of orders, accompanied with force, commotion, threats, or other violent disturbances.

mutual, reciprocal; interchanged; common.

mutual credits, notations of amounts owing to the other, given by each of two persons to the other.

mutual insurance, a form of insurance (*q.v.*) in which the person insured becomes a member of the company, which is the insurer, and all members of the company assume responsibility to indemnify each other against loss.

mutual mistake, a misunderstanding shared in by both parties to a contract, which warrants reformation of the contract, or other judicial relief. See also, *mistake.*

mutual promises, engagements or assurances which are made simultaneously by two parties to each other, each of which is the consideration for the other.

mutual rescission, see *rescission.*

mutual testament, or **mutual will,** the testamentary disposition of property by two persons, in which each makes reciprocal devices and bequests. Under some circumstances, it may constitute a binding contract.

mutuality, reciprocity of obligation; the state in which, one person being bound to perform some act for the benefit of another, that other is bound to do something for the benefit of the former. (2) The condition of being mutual (*q.v.*).

mu'tuum (Rom.), a loan whereby the absolute property in the thing lent passes to the borrower, and he is obligated to restore an equivalent in things of the same kind. See also, *fungible.*

N

NAA, see *nonattainment area.*

NAAQS, see *national ambient air quality standards.*

naked, incomplete; not clothed with power.

naked contract, see *nudum pactum.*

name, one or more words used to designate a particular person, corporation, or other entity. Personal names are either Christian, *i.e.*, first names commonly given at baptism, or surnames, *i.e.*, names derived from one's parents or ancestors (the family name).

narra'tio, *l.,* a count; a declaration.

nascitu'rus, not yet born.

national ambient air quality standards, NAAQS; primary and secondary air quality standards are established for all criteria pollutants. Primary standards are considered the minimum standards necessary to maintain public health with an adequate margin of safety. Secondary standards are those necessary to promote the public welfare.

national bank, a bank (*q.v.*) created and governed under the provisions of the laws of the United States. Cf. *state bank.*

National Conference of Commissioners on Uniform State Laws, the outgrowth of the American Bar Association's appointment in 1889 of a Special Committee on Uniform State Laws. In 1890 the American Bar Association recommended the passage by each state of a law providing for the appointment of state commissioners to confer with commissioners from other states on the subject of uniformity in legislation, which was accomplished by 1892. Its object is to promote uniformity in state laws on all subjects where uniformity is deemed desirable and practicable. Following an extensive process of selection of subjects and drafting, the uniform acts were approved by the Conference and recommended for general adoption throughout the United States.

national emission standards for hazardous air pollutants, NESHAP; special standards established to control emissions of those air pollutants which might reasonably be expected to result in an increase in mortality or other irreversible or incapacitating illness.

National Energy Conservation Policy Act, an act to provide for the regulation of interstate commerce, to reduce the growth in demand for energy in the United States, and to conserve nonrenewable energy resources produced in the U.S. and elsewhere, without inhibiting beneficial economic growth. U.S.C. tit. 12, tit. 15, tit. 42.

National Environmental Policy Act of 1969, NEPA; an act to establish a national policy for the environment, to provide for the establishment of a Council on Environmental Quality, and for other purposes. 42 U.S.C. §§ 4321, 4331-4335, 4341-4347.

National Manufactured Housing Construction and Safety Standards Act of 1974, formerly known as National Mobile Home Construction and Safety Standards Act of 1974, title VI of an act to establish a program of community development block grants, to amend and extend laws relating to housing and urban development, and for other purposes. Among other things, its purpose is to reduce the number of personal injuries and deaths, and the amount of insurance costs and property damage resulting from mobile home accidents, and to improve the quality and durability of mobile homes. 42 U.S.C. §§ 5401 *et seq.*

national maximum speed limit, see *Emergency Highway Energy Conservation Act.*

National School Lunch Act, an act to provide assistance to the states in the establishment, maintenance, operation, and expansion of school-lunch programs, and for other purposes. 42 U.S.C. §§ 1751-1760.

National Traffic and Motor Vehicle Safety Act of 1966, an act to provide for a coordinated national safety program and establishment of safety standards for motor vehicles in interstate commerce to reduce accidents involving motor vehicles and to reduce the deaths and injuries occurring in such accidents. 15 U.S.C. §§ 1381 *et seq.*

nationality, the political status acquired by belonging to a nation or state. It arises by birth or by naturalization, and determines the allegiance (*q.v.*) of a person. See also, *citizen* and *citizen of the United States.* (2) The nationality of ships depends upon that of their owners, and is indicated by the flag they carry.

natura appetit perfectum, ita et lex, nature aspires to perfection; so does the law.

natural, according to nature; not artificial.

natural allegiance, see *allegiance.*

natural and probable consequences, those effects or results which a person of average competence and knowledge, in the situation of a person whose conduct is in question, having the same opportunities of observation, is expected to foresee as likely to follow on such conduct.

natural-born citizens, persons who are born within the jurisdiction of a national government, *i.e.*, in its territorial limits, or those born of citizens temporarily residing abroad. See also, *citizen* and *citizen of the United States.*

natural child, the child of one's body, not necessarily illegitimate. (2) Occasionally, equivalent to bastard.

Natural Gas Policy Act of 1978, an act concerning wellhead pricing, incremental pricing, emergency authorities and other authorities, natural gas curtailment policies, administration, enforcement, review, and effect on state laws. 15 U.S.C. §§ 3301 *et seq.*, 42 U.S.C. § 7255.

natural law, a philosophy concerning the law of nature and the dictate of right reason, in contradistinction to positive or statute law.

natural love and affection, words used in deeds of conveyance to express a meritorious consideration (*q.v.*), being that love which one has for his kindred.

natural person, a human being, as distinguished from an artificial person, *i.e.,* a corporation (*q.v.*) which has a legal, though not actual, existence.

natural presumption, a presumption (*q.v.*) of fact, which derives its force from observation and experience.

naturalization, the legal act of investing aliens with the privileges and obligations of a citizen (*q.v.*). See also, *citizen of the United States.*

navigable, capable of being traveled upon. A river, estuary or other body of water is so called, when the public has a right of navigation thereon, *e.g.,* to use it as a highway for shipping.

ne, *l.* and *fr.,* not; lest; that not.

ne admit'tas, do not admit.

ne distur'ba pas (nŭ dĭs tûr bä′ på), the defendant did not obstruct.

ne ex'eat, or **ne exeat repub'lica,** a prerogative writ issued by a court to prevent a defendant from going away and evading the jurisdiction.

ne un'ques, never.

ne unques accouple, never lawfully married.

ne unques administrator, or **ne unques executor,** a denial that a party was the personal representative of the deceased.

necessaries, a flexible term for various goods and services which are required to sustain life, and are suitable to the rank and position of the person concerned.

necessary easement, an easement (*q.v.*) which arises by implication from the sale of the servient estate, and without which there could be no reasonable manner of enjoying the dominant estate.

necessitas non habet legem, necessity has no law.

necessitas publica major est quam privata, public necessity is stronger than private.

necessitas quod cogit, defendit, necessity defends what it compels, *e.g.,* acts necessary for self-preservation.

necessitas sub lege non continetur, quia quod alias non est licitum necessitas facit licitum, necessity is not limited by law, since what otherwise is not lawful, necessity makes lawful.

necessitas vincit legem, necessity overcomes law.

necessity, variously defined as pressing need, overruling power, compulsion, or irresistible force, depending upon the context in which it is used and the facts to which it is applied.

negative pregnant, in civil procedure, a denial which implies or carries with it an affirmative; a denial in form which is not a denial in substance.

negligence, a flexible term for the failure to use ordinary care under the particular factual circumstances revealed by the evidence in a lawsuit. (2) Conduct which falls below the standard established by law for the protection of others against unreasonable risk of harm. It does not include conduct recklessly disregardful of an interest of others. Restatement (Second) of Torts § 282. See also, *comparative negligence, concurrent negligence, contributory negligence, gross negligence, slight negligence,* and *reasonable man.*

negligence per se, negligence (*q.v.*) of itself or as a matter of law, *e.g.,* the violation of a statute passed for the protection of the public.

negligent conduct, either (1) an act which the actor (*q.v.*) as a reasonable man (*q.v.*) should recognize as involving an unreasonable risk of causing an invasion of an interest of another, or (2) a failure to do an act which is necessary for the protection or assistance of another and which the actor is under a duty to do. Restatement (Second) of Torts § 284.

negligent homicide, criminal homicide (*q.v.*) which is committed negligently. Model Penal Code § 210.4(1). See also, *negligence.*

negotiability, that quality of certain written instruments by which a transferor may convey to an innocent transferee a better title than he has himself. See also, *negotiable instrument* and *negotiation (1).*

negotiable instrument, a writing which is signed by the maker or drawer, and contains an unconditional promise or order to pay a sum certain in money and no other promise, order, obligation or power given by the maker or drawer, except as authorized by law, which is payable on demand or at a definite time, and which is payable to order or bearer. U.C.C. § 3-104(1). See also, *negotiability* and *negotiation (1).*

negotiate, to perform a negotiation (*q.v.*).

negotiation, the transfer of an instrument (*q.v.*) in such form that the transferee becomes a holder (*q.v.*). If the instrument is payable to order, it is negotiated by delivery with any necessary indorsement; if payable to bearer, it is negotiated by delivery. U.C.C. § 3-202(1). See also, *negotiability* and *negotiable instrument.* (2) Preliminary communications between parties, which seek to determine whether the parties can make a mutually agreeable sale, purchase, bargain, or contract.

negotio'rum ges'tor (Rom.), a person who spontaneously, and without the knowledge or consent of the owner, intermeddles with property with the object of benefiting the owner.

neighboring, adjacent to or adjoining.

neminem laedit qui jure suo utitur, he who stands on his own rights injures no one.

nemo agit in seipsum, no one can sue himself.

nemo contra factum suum venire potest, no one can go against his own deed. See also, *estoppel.*

nemo dat quod non habet, no one can give that which he has not, *i.e.,* no one can give a better title to a thing than he possesses himself.

nemo de domo sua extrahi potest, no one can be dragged out of his own house. Every man's house is his castle.

nemo debet aliena jactura locupletari, no one ought to gain by another's loss.

nemo debet bis puniri pro uno delicto, no one ought to be punished twice for the same offense.

nemo debet esse judex in propria causa, no one should be judge in his own cause.

nemo debet locupletari aliena jactura, no one ought to be enriched at another's expense.

nemo est haeres viventis, no one is the heir of a living person, *i.e.,* strictly speaking, the determination of heirship occurs only at the death of the owner.

nemo est supra leges, no one is above the law.

nemo ex suo delicto meliorem suam conditionem facere potest, no one can make his condition better by his own tort.

nemo patriam, in qua natus est, exuere nec ligeantiae debitum ejurare possit, no man can disclaim his native land nor abjure the bond of allegiance.

nemo potest esse simul actor et judex, no one can be at once suitor and judge. Cf. *nemo debet esse judex, etc.*

nemo potest esse tenens et dominus, no man can be at the same time tenant and landlord.

nemo potest facere per alium, quod per se non potest, no one can do through another what he cannot do himself.

nemo potest plus juris ad alium transferre quam ipse habet, no one can transfer a greater right to another than he himself has. Cf. *nemo dat, etc.*

nemo praesumitur ludere in extremis, no one is presumed to trifle at the point of death, *i.e.,* an expression in a will is not to be taken as meaningless or absurd if this can be avoided.

nemo praesumitur malus, no one is presumed to be bad.

nemo tenetur ad impossibile, no one is bound to [perform] an impossibility.

nemo tenetur edere instrumenta contra se, no one is obliged to produce instruments which tell against himself.

nemo tenetur seipsum accusare, no one is bound to incriminate himself.

NEPA, see *National Environmental Policy Act of 1969.*

nephew, the son of a brother or sister.

ne'pos, and **nep'tis** (Rom.), a grandson and a granddaughter.

NESHAP, see *national emission standards for hazardous air pollutants.*

net profits, see *profit.*

neutrality, the policy of a nation which takes no part, directly or indirectly, in a war between other nations.

never indebted, in civil procedure, a plea by which the defendant denies the existence of the contract, or the facts on which the plaintiff relied.

new assignment, under older codes of civil procedure, a restatement of the plaintiff's cause of action with more particularity and certainty, analogous to the amendment (*q.v.*) of a court pleading.

new for old, in insurance, the deduction made from the insurer's payment, in cases of partial loss, because of the increased value of new materials substituted for old in making repairs, usually one-third of the cost, after deducting the value of the old materials used in reconstruction.

new matter, various facts not previously alleged in the pleadings, by either party to a lawsuit.

new source performance standards, NSPS; emission standards for new or modified stationary sources. They must also include a percentage reduction in emission limitation and percentage reduction achievable through the application of the best technological system of continuous emission reduction which the EPA determines has been adequately demonstrated, taking into account costs, other health and environmental impact and energy requirements.

new servitude, see *additional servitude.*

new style, the modern system of computing time by the Gregorian year, formulated in 1582 and introduced into Great Britain in 1752.

new trial, a rehearing of a lawsuit before another jury, granted by the court on motion of the party dissatisfied with the result of a previous trial, upon a proper showing that substantial justice requires it. In United States courts, and in state courts which have analogous rules, a new trial may be granted in an action in which there has been a trial by jury, for any of the reasons for which new trials were historically granted in actions at law, and in an action tried without a jury, for any of the reasons for which rehearings were historically granted in suits in equity. Fed. R. Civ. P. 59(a). The usual grounds for a new trial are errors of the court in rulings during the trial or in charging the jury, misconduct of the jury or witnesses, newly discovered evidence which the party seeking a new trial could not with reasonable diligence have discovered and produced at the trial, surprise which prevents the party or his counsel from adequately presenting his case, and irregularities which render it probable that an impartial trial has not been had. See also, *trial*.

newly discovered evidence, proof which could not have been discovered with reasonable diligence and produced at the trial; not newly recollected evidence. See also, *new trial*.

newspaper, a flexible term for any one of various regularly publishedand disseminated daily, semiweekly, or weekly publications, containing current information and other articles of interest to its readers. Often defined by various state statutes concerning legal notices.

next friend, a person who, without having been regularly appointed guardian, brings suit and acts for an infant or other person who is under a legal disability (*q.v.*). The next friend is usually a relative, and is responsible for the propriety of the proceedings and the court costs.

next of kin, see *kin*.

niece, the daughter of a brother or sister.

nient (nyôn), *L. fr.*, nothing.

nient comprise, (kôm prēz), not included.

nient culpable (kül păbl), not guilty; a plea to a criminal charge or an allegation of tort.

nient dedire (dā dēr), to say nothing; to suffer judgment by default.

nient le fait (lu fā), the same as non est factum; a plea that the instrument sued on is not defendant's deed.

night, or **nighttime,** the time of darkness between sunset and sunrise. Occasionally defined by various state statutes.

ni'hil, or **nil,** *l.*, nothing.

ni'hil ca'piat per bre've, or **bil'lam,** that he take nothing by his writ or bill; an old form of judgment against the plaintiff.

ni'hil di'cit, he says nothing; an old form of judgment by default.

ni'hil ha'bet, he has nothing; a return made by the sheriff, when he has not been able to take anything on an execution (*q.v.*).

nihil habet forum ex scena, the court has nothing to do with what is not before it.

nihil quod est inconveniens est licitum, nothing that is inconvenient is allowed.

nil, see *nihil.*

nil agit exemplum litem quod lite resolvit, an example does no good which settles one question by another.

nil consensui tam contrarium est quam vis atque metus, nothing is so opposed to consent as force and fear.

nil de'bet, he owes nothing; formerly, a general denial in a lawsuit for debt on a simple contract.

nil ha'buit in tenemen'tis, he has no interest in the tenements or real property.

nimia subtilitas in jure reprobatur, too much subtlety in law is reprehensible.

nimium altercando veritas amittitur, by too much altercation truth is lost.

1983, 42 U.S.C. § 1983; originally section 1 of the 1871 Civil Rights Act, also known as the Ku Klux Klan Act. It added civil remedies to the criminal penalties imposed by the 1866 Civil Rights Act. The section states as follows: Every person who, under color of any statute, ordinance, regulation, custom, or usage, of any State or Territory or the District of Columbia, subjects, or causes to be subjected, any citizen of the United States or other person within the jurisdiction thereof to the deprivation of any rights, privileges, or immunities secured by the Constitution and laws, shall be liable to the party injured in an action at law, suit in equity, or other proper proceeding for redress. For the purposes of this section, any Act of Congress applicable exclusively to the District of Columbia shall be considered to be a statute of the District of Columbia.

ni'si, *l.,* unless. (2) A decree, rule, or order of the court is described as nisi when it is not to be of force unless the party against whom it is made fails within a certain time to show cause against it, *i.e.,* a good reason why it should not be made. See also, *decree nisi* and *rule nisi.*

nisi pri'us, unless before, formerly, words in an English writ, directing the sheriff to summon jurors. In the United States, the term is descriptive of the trial of civil cases before a single judge, with a jury; a trial court; a court of first instance. See also, *courts of assize* and *nisi prius.*

no contest, see *nolo contendere.*

no-fault divorce, see *Uniform Marriage and Divorce Act*

no-fault insurance, various statutory plans concerning automobile insurance which are intended to provide a method of compensating automobile accident victims without regard to fault. The plans vary in the extent to which the method of compensation provided for eliminates the ordinary tort system. Such plans are in effect in a minority of the states.

No Net Cost Tobacco Program Act of 1982, an act to provide for the operation of the tobacco price support and production adjustment program in such a manner as to result in no net cost to taxpayers, to limit increases in the support price for tobacco, and for other purposes. 7 U.S.C. §§ 1314 *et seq.*, 1445 *et seq., et al.*

Noise Control Act of 1972, an act to control the emission of noise detrimental to the human environment, and for other purposes. It provides for federal programs, identification of major noise sources, information on control technology, noise emission standards, control and abatement of aircraft noise, enforcement, citizen suits, and the like. 42 U.S.C. §§ 4901-4918; 49 U.S.C. § 1431 as subsequently amended. See also, *Quiet Communities Act of 1978.*

nol. pros., abbreviation for *nolle prosequi (q.v.).*

no'lens vo'lens, *l.,* whether willing or unwilling.

nol'le prose'qui, *l.,* or **nol. pros.,** unwilling to prosecute; an entry made on the court record by which the plaintiff or prosecutor declares that he will proceed no further.

no'lo conten'dere, no contest; a plea in criminal cases whereby the defendant tacitly admits his guilt by throwing himself on the mercy of the court.

nomina sunt notae rerum, names are the marks of things.

nominal, existing in name only; unimportant.

nominal damages, see *damages.*

nominal partner, a person who has no actual interest in the trade or business of a partnership or its profits, but by allowing his name to be used, holds himself out as apparently having an interest therein.

nominal party, see *formal party.*

nominal plaintiff, a person whose name is used in prosecuting an action, but who has no real interest in the matter in controversy. See also, *formal party.*

nominate contracts, formerly, undertakings or agreements which were distinguished by particular names, the use of which determined the rights of the parties.

nomina'tim, by name; expressed one by one.

nomination, the act of mentioning by name; presenting the name of a candidate for an office or appointment. Cf. *election.*

non, *l.,* not.

non accipi debent verba in demonstrationem falsam quae competunt in limitationem veram, words which admit of a true, *i.e.,* intelligible or consistent, meaning ought not to be received in a false sense.

non aliter a significatione verborum recedi oportet quam cum manifestum est aliud sensisse testatorem, it behooves us not to depart from the literal meaning of words, unless it is evident that the testator intended some other meaning.

non assump'sit, he did not promise.

non ce'pit, he took not.

non com'pos men'tis, descriptive of a person who is not of sound mind, *e.g.,* a lunatic, idiot, or drunken person.

non conces'sit (he did not grant), formerly, a plea by which the defendant denied that the plaintiff had received a grant, *e.g.,* letters patent, as he claimed.

non con'stat, it is not certain; it does not follow.

non culpa'bilis, not guilty.

non damnifica'tus (not injured), formerly, a plea in defense of an action of debt on an indemnity bond.

non debet cui plus licet, quod minus est non licere, he who is allowed to do the greater should not be prohibited from doing the lesser.

non decipitur qui scit se decipi, he is not deceived who knows himself to be deceived.

non demi'sit, he did not demise.

non deti'net, he does not detain.

non est fac'tum, the deed on which plaintiff sues is not the defendant's deed; the instrument was not executed by the defendant.

non est inven'tus, not found; a sheriff's return when the defendant is not found in his territorial jurisdiction.

non est regula quin fallat, there is no rule which may not fail, *i.e.,* every rule has its exceptions.

non facias malum ut inde veniat bonum, you are not to do evil that good may come of it.

non fe'cit, he did not make it.

non impedi'vit, he has not impeded.

non infre'git conventio'nem, he has not broken the covenant.

non li'quet, it does not appear clear.

non obstan'te, notwithstanding.

non obstan'te veredic'to, notwithstanding the verdict. A type of judgment which is entered by the court for legal cause, despite a contrary or different verdict rendered by the jury. Abbreviated N.O.V.

non omne damnum inducit injuriam, not every loss works an injury.

non omne quod licet honestum est, not everything which the law allows is honorable.

non possessori incumbit necessitas probandi possessiones ad se pertinere, a person in possession is not bound to prove that the possessions belong to him.

non potest adduci exceptio ejus rei cujus petitur dissolutio, an exception [or plea in bar] cannot be founded on the very thing the avoidance of which is sought. For example, the fact that the contract exists is no answer to a suit to avoid the contract for fraud or illegality.

non potest probari quod probatum non relevat, that may not be proved which, if proved, is immaterial.

non pros., or **non prose'quitur,** the plaintiff does not pursue his action. A judgment of dismissal granted on motion of the defendant, upon the plaintiff's failing to take the proper steps at the proper time. Cf. *nolle prosequi.*

non quod dictum est, sed quod factum est, inspicitur, regard is to be had, not to what is said, but to what is done.

non refert an quis assensum suum praefert verbis, aut rebus ipsis et factis, it matters not whether a man gives his assent by his words or by his acts and deeds.

non refert quid notum sit judici, si notum non sit in forma judicii, it matters not what is known to the judge, if it be not known in a judicial form.

non remota causa sed proxima spectatur, the immediate, not the remote, cause is to be considered.

non se'quitur (it does not follow), used to indicate a fallacious conclusion.

non valet donatio nisi subsequatur traditio, a gift is not valid unless accompanied by possession.

non videntur qui errant consentire, they are not considered to consent who act under a mistake.

nonaccess, nonexistence of sexual intercourse between husband and wife.

nonage, not of full age; infancy. Cf. *age* (2).

nonattainment area, NAA; air quality control regions, or portions thereof, for which one or more of the ambient air quality standards have not been met.

nonclaim, the omission or neglect to assert a right. See also, *claim.*

nonconforming use, a use which was lawful prior to the passage of a zoning ordinance, but which fails to conform to the requirements of the zoning ordinance.

nonfeasance, the failure to perform a positive duty which is imposed by law upon a public official. Cf. *malfeasance* and *misfeasance.*

nonissuable plea, a response to a claim raised in a lawsuit, upon which a decision would not determine the action upon its merits, *e.g.,* a plea in abatement.

nonjoinder, or **non-joinder,** the omission to make someone a party to an action who should have been so joined.

non-profit corporation, a corporation that is not formed for the pecuniary gain or profit of, and whose net earnings or any part of them is not distributable to, its members, trustees, officers, or other private persons.

nonresidence, the condition of a person who is a nonresident (*q.v.*).

nonresident, a flexible term for a person who does not live within some geographical area. See also, *residence.*

nonresident decedent, a decedent (*q.v.*) who was domiciled in another jurisdiction (*q.v.*) at the time of his death. Uniform Probate Code § 1-201 (26).

nonsuit, a judgment against the plaintiff, when he fails to prove his case or neglects to appear at the trial. Cf. *directed verdict.*

nonuser, a failure or ceasing to exercise a right or privilege.

Norris-La Guardia Act, an act to define and limit the jurisdiction of courts sitting in equity, in matters involving or growing out of labor disputes. 18 U.S.C. § 3692; 29 U.S.C. §§ 101-115.

noscitur ex sociis, qui non cognoscitur, ex se, he who cannot be known from himself may be known from his associates, *e.g.,* the meaning of a word may be ascertained from the context.

NSPS, see *new source performance standards.*

not found, words indorsed on a bill of indictment by a grand jury when it does not have sufficient evidence to return an indictment. See also, *ignoramus.* (2) Words indorsed on a summons by a sheriff when he is unable to find the person for whom the summons is issued within his territorial jurisdiction.

not guilty, in criminal proceedings, a general denial of the accusation, which puts the prosecutor to the proof of every material fact alleged.

(2) Formerly, the general issue in actions of trespass, trover, and other actions founded on tort. (3) The verdict of acquittal.

not proven, a verdict allowed in criminal trials in some jurisdictions, *e.g.,* Scotland.

notary, or **notary public,** a public official whose duties, powers, and manner of appointment vary in the different states. Commonly authorized to administer oaths, to take affidavits, acknowledgments and depositions, and to protest notes and bills of exchange for nonpayment.

note, a promissory note (*q.v.*). (2) A memorandum. (3) To note a dishonored bill is for a notary public to initial it, giving the date and the reason assigned for its not being paid.

note of hand, occasionally a promissory note (*q.v.*).

notice, information given to a person of some act done, or about to be done; knowledge. Notice may be actual, when knowledge is brought home to the party to be affected by it; or constructive, when certain acts are done in accordance with law, from which, on grounds of public policy, the party interested is presumed to have knowledge. It may be written, or oral, but written notice is preferable as avoiding disputes as to its terms. (2) A person has notice of a fact when he has actual knowledge of it, or he has received a notice or notification of it, or from all the facts and circumstances known to him at the time in question, he has reason to know that it exists. U.C.C. § 1-201(25).

notice in pais, information received other than from the record or writing.

notice of dishonor, concerning commercial paper, oral or written knowledge or notification given in a reasonable manner, in terms which identify the instrument and state that it has been dishonored. A misdescription which does not mislead the party notified does not vitiate the notice. Sending the instrument bearing a stamp, ticket, or writing stating that acceptance or payment has been refused or sending a notice of debit with respect to the instrument is sufficient. U.C.C. § 3-508(3). See also, *dishonor.*

notice of lis pendens, see *lis pendens notice.*

notice of protest, concerning commercial paper, a certificate of dishonor, which is normally forwarded with the notice of dishonor (*q.v.*), made under the hand and seal of a United States consul or vice consul or a notary public or other person authorized to certify dishonor by the law of the place where dishonor occurs. The protest must identify the instrument and certify either that due presentment has been made or the reason why it is excused and that the instrument has been dishonored by nonacceptance or nonpayment. It must also certify that notice of dishonor has been given to all parties or to specified parties. U.C.C. § 3-509. See also, *protest (3)*.

notice to produce, under some codes of practice, if a party to an action has in his possession a document which would be evidence for the other party if produced, the latter may give his adversary notice to produce it at the trial, and, in default of production, may give secondary evidence of it. See also, *inspection*. Cf. *discovery*.

notice to quit, a request from a landlord to his tenant, to vacate the premises leased and give possession to the landlord, at a time therein specified. It should be in writing, giving sufficient description of the premises, and should be served the required length of time before the tenant is requested to move out. Often defined and governed by various state statutes.

noting bills of exchange, see *note (2)*.

notorious, well known; obvious; apparent. Occasionally, such facts are not required to be proven.

notorious possession, such open occupation of real property, by an adverse claimant as to establish a presumption of knowledge thereof in the owner.

N.O.V., see *non obstante veredicto*.

novatio non praesumitur, novation is not presumed.

novation, the substitution of a new obligor or obligation for an old one, which is thereby extinguished, *e.g.*, the acceptance of a note of a third party in payment of the original promisor's obligation, or the note of an individual in lieu of that of a corporation. Accord, Restatement (Second) of Contracts § 280. Cf. *substituted contract*.

now, at the time when such word is employed. Cf. *forthwith*.

Nuclear Waste Policy Act of 1982, an act to provide for the development of repositories for the disposal of high-level radioactive waste and spent nuclear fuel, to establish a program of research development and demonstration regarding the disposal of high-level radioactive waste and spent nuclear fuel, and for other purposes. 42 U.S.C. §§ 10101 *et seq*.

nuda pactio obligationem non parit, a naked promise, *i.e.*, one without consideration, does not create a legal obligation.

nu'dum pac'tum, *l.*, or **naked contract,** a bare contract, *i.e.*, one made without consideration (*q.v.*), upon which, therefore, no action will lie.

nudum pactum ex quo non oritur actio, no action arises from a naked promise.

nuisance, a flexible and imprecise term for various activities which annoy, harm, inconvenience, or damage other persons, under the particular facts and circumstances proven in a lawsuit or criminal prosecution. It may be (a) private, as where one uses his property so as to damage another's or to disturb his quiet enjoyment of it; or (b) public or common, where the whole community is annoyed or inconvenienced by the offensive acts, *e.g.*, where a person obstructs a highway, or carries on a business that fills the air with noxious and offensive fumes. Accord, Restatement (Second) of Torts §§ 821A, 821B(1), 821D. Cf. *qualified nuisance.*

nul, *fr.,* no or none.

nul'la bo'na (no goods), a return made by a sheriff to an execution in a civil action, or other writ commanding him to seize the goods of a person, when he finds no property to act upon.

nulla emptio sine pretio esse potest, there can be no sale without a price.

nulla pactione effici potest ut dolus praestetur, by no contract can one effect that a fraud shall be maintained.

nulla terre sans seigneur, no lands without a lord.

nullity of marriage, or **annulment of marriage,** a state of facts with regard to an ostensible marriage which renders it cancelable, void, or voidable, at the will of one of the parties to it. Thus, among other things, fraud or duress in bringing about the marriage or the prior subsisting marriage of one of the parties are grounds for declaring a marriage a nullity. Usually, such a lawsuit is prosecuted in the same court and governed by the same rules of procedure as a suit for divorce (*q.v.*). It differs from a suit for divorce, however, because it claims that the marriage was cancelable, void, or voidable from the beginning, while a suit for divorce seeks severance for causes occurring after the marriage. (2) A declaration of invalidity of a marriage, in lieu of the traditional annulment of a marriage, is provided for by Uniform Marriage and Divorce Act § 208. Some of the common grounds for annulment, *e.g.*, fraud, have been abolished completely; others have been restated to avoid unnecessary overlap with dissolution sections. Uniform Marriage and Divorce Act § 208, Commissioners' Note.

nulli'us fi'lius (a son of nobody), a bastard.

nullum simile est idem nisi quatuor pedibus currit, no like is identical, unless it runs on all fours.

nullum tempus occurrit reipublicae, no time can prejudice the commonwealth, *i.e.*, the statute of limitations does not run against the state.

nullus commodum capere potest de injuria sua propria, no one can obtain an advantage by his own wrong.

nunc pro tunc, *l.,* (now for then), occasionally, a court will allow the entry of an order or judgment or other act so as to have retroactive effect which is so described.

nuncu'pative will, an oral disposition of property intended to take effect upon death, made during a final illness in the presence of witnesses. It usually disposes of personal property only. Regulated by various state statutes, which may require that it be reduced to writing.

nunquam crescit ex post facto praeteriti delicti aestimatio, the heinousness of a past offense is never increased by what happens afterward.

nun'quam indebita'tus, *l.,* never indebted.

nuptial, pertaining to, or constituting, marriage.

nuptias non concubitus sed consensus facit, not cohabitation but consent makes the marriage.

nurture, the care and education of children.

O

oath, various solemn affirmations, declarations or promises, made under a sense of responsibility to God, for the truth of what is stated or the faithful performance of what is undertaken. Under various statutes, different forms of affirmation or solemn declaration are allowed in lieu of oaths, where an oath is not binding on the conscience of the individual, or the witness has conscientious scruples against making oaths. Oaths are judicial, *i.e.,* made in the course of judicial proceedings, or extrajudicial, *i.e.,* voluntary or outside of judicial proceedings, evidentiary, *i.e.,* relating to past facts, or promissory, *i.e.,* relating to the future performance of acts or duties, *e.g.,* those of a judge, corporate director, or other official.

oath of office, various declarations or promises, made by persons who are about to enter upon the duties of a public office, concerning their performance of that office. An oath of office is required by federal and state constitutions, and by various statutes to be made by major and minor officials, *e.g.,* President of the United States, governor, judge, notary public, juror, executor, administrator, guardian, and court commissioner. The oath of office required of the President of the United States is prescribed by U.S. Const., Art. II, Sec. 1.

oath purgatory, a solemn affirmation, declaration, or promise, made by a person who is in contempt of court, concerning facts which tend to excuse his default.

obedientia est legis essentia, obedience is the essence of the law.

ob'iter dic'tum, see *dictum.*

objection, a resistance or protest on legal grounds, *e.g.,* to the admissibility of evidence, or to the entry of an order or judgment.

obligation, a flexible term for various undertakings or events which bind a person, usually to do or abstain from doing a certain act. A perfect obligation, as distinguished from an imperfect obligation, is one which can be enforced by the law. (2) A bond. (3) The operative part of a bond.

obligee, a person to whom an obligation (*q.v.*) is due.

obligor, a person who is bound to perform an obligation (*q.v.*).

obscene, a flexible term, descriptive of language, literature, and other forms of communication, which are indecent and calculated to promote corruption of sexual morals. The definition varies from time to time and from place to place. (2) State statutes designed to regulate obscene materials are confined to works which depict or describe sexual conduct. That conduct must be specifically defined by the applicable state law as written or authoritatively construed. A state offense must be limited to works which, taken as a whole, appeal to the prurient interest in sex, which portray sexual conduct in a patently offensive way, and which taken as a whole do not have serious literary, artistic, political, or scientific value. The material can be regulated without a showing that it is utterly without redeeming social value. Obscenity is to be determined by applying contemporary community standards, not national standards. (3) Material is obscene if, considered as a whole, its predominant appeal is to prurient interest, *i.e.,* a shameful or morbid interest, in nudity, sex, or excretion, and if in addition it goes substantially beyond customary limits of candor in describing or representing such matters. Predominant appeal is to be judged with reference to ordinary adults unless it appears from the character of the material or the circumstances of its dissemination to be designed for children or other specially susceptible audience. Model Penal Code § 251.4(1). See also, *pornography.*

obscene material, see *pornography (3).*

obscenity, conduct which is objectionable or offensive to accepted standards of decency and that tends to corrupt the public morals by its indecency and lewdness. Material is obscene if, considered as a whole, its predominant appeal is to prurient interest, that is, a shameful or morbid interest, in nudity, sex or excretion, and if in addition it goes substantially beyond customary limits of candor in describing or representing such matters. Model Penal Code § 251.4.

obstruction of justice, the offense of intentionally hindering or obstructing the arrest, conviction, and punishment of accused persons, including all proper and necessary proceedings for administering justice. Often defined by various state statutes.

obvious, easily discovered, seen, or understood; plain, manifest, evident, palpable.

occupancy, physical presence on real property. (2) Occasionally, taking possession of real property which before did not belong to anybody.

occupant, a person who has the actual use or possession of something, *e.g.,* a house or a room.

occupation, actual possession, use, and enjoyment of real property, *e.g.,* land or houses. (2) Taking temporary possession of an enemy's country. (3) A profession, trade, or business, which takes a person's time or attention.

occupational license, a charge or fee assessed by a governmental unit, *e.g.,* a city, for the privilege of engaging in a certain occupation within the geographical boundary of that unit.

Occupational Safety and Health Act of 1970, an act to assure safe and healthful working conditions by authorizing enforcement of standards developed under the act, by assisting and encouraging the states in their efforts to assure safe and healthful working conditions, by providing for research, information, education, and training in the field of occupational safety and health, and for other purposes. 29 U.S.C. §§ 651 *et seq.*

odiosa et inhonesta non sunt in lege praesumenda, odious and dishonest things are not to be presumed in law.

of course, descriptive of acts which may be done in legal proceedings without leave of court, or which the court will grant, on application, without further inquiry.

offense, a violation of criminal law; a crime or misdemeanor.

offer, a proposition to do a thing, which becomes an obligation or contract if unconditionally accepted by the person to whom it is made, before it is withdrawn. (2) The manifestation of willingness to enter into a bargain, so made as to justify another person in understanding that his assent to the bargain is invited and will conclude it. Restatement (Second) of Contracts § 24.

off-going crop, see *away-going crops.*

office, a position or appointment entailing particular rights and duties. Often defined by various state constitutions or statutes. (2) The room or place in which an officer transacts public business, and keeps the papers, records, and documents committed to his care.

officer, a flexible term, which varies with the context in which it is used, for a person who performs an agency function for a public entity, *e.g.,* nation, state, county, city or court, or for a private corporation. He may be elected or appointed. If he is a public officer, he will usually have specific duties assigned to him by law, *i.e.,* the performance of a portion of the sovereign power of his government.

official, pertaining to a public charge or office. (2) An officer (*q.v.*).

official detention, arrest, detention in any facility for custody of persons under charge or conviction of crime or alleged or found to be delinquent, detention for extradition or deportation, or any other detention for law-enforcement purposes; it does not include supervision of probation or parole, or constraint incidental to release on bail. Model Penal Code § 242.6(1).

offici'na justi'tiae, *l.,* the workshop or business place of justice.

officious will, (Rom.), a testamentary disposition, by which a testator leaves his property to his family.

officium nemini debet esse damnosum, an office ought to be injurious to no one [employed in it].

offsets, the principle which prohibits the construction of major new sources of air pollution in nonattainment areas unless the proponent of the new source can obtain reductions in pollution within the area that will more than compensate for the pollution contributions to be made by the new source.

Old Age and Survivors Insurance Benefits Act, an act to establish a system of Federal old age benefits, and to enable the several States to make more adequate provision for aged persons, blind persons, dependent and crippled children, maternal and child welfare, public health, and the administration of their unemployment compensation laws; to establish a Social Security Board; to raise revenue; and for other purposes. 42 U.S.C. §§ 301 *et seq.*

old style, the system of computing time which was in effect prior to the new style (*q.v.*).

Older Americans Act of 1965, an act to provide assistance in the development of new or improved programs to help older persons, through grants to the states for community planning and services, and for training, through research, development, or training project grants, and to establish an operating agency to be designated as the Administration on Aging, as subsequently amended. 20 U.S.C. § 1087-2; 42 U.S.C. §§ 3001 *et seq.*, 8622, 9902, 9904, 9911.

olograph, an instrument written entirely by the party whose name is signed to it. See also, *holograph* and *holographic will.* Cf. *allograph.*

omissio eorum quae tacite insunt nihil operatur, the omission of those things which are understood without special mention is of no consequence.

omission, the neglect to perform what the law requires. (2) A failure to act. Model Penal Code § 1.13(4).

omne majus continet in se minus, the greater contains the less.

omne quod solo inaednicatur solo cedit, everything which is built upon the soil belongs to the soil.

omnia praesumuntur contra spoliatorem, all things are presumed against a spoliator, *e.g.*, if he wrongfully withholds or destroys evidence in his possession, it will be presumed to be adverse to him.

omnia praesumuntur rite et solemniter esse acta donec probetur in contrarium, all things are presumed to have been done properly and with due formalities until it be proved to the contrary.

Omnibus Crime Control Act of 1970, an act to amend the Omnibus Crime Control and Safe Streets Act of 1968 (*q.v.*), and for other purposes. 5 U.S.C. §§ 5108, 5313-5316; 18 U.S.C. §§ 351, 924, 1752; 42 U.S.C. §§ 3711, 3723, 3731, 3733, 3735, 3746-3748, 3750-3750d, 3756, 3763, 3764, 3769, 3791, 3793, 3795.

Omnibus Crime Control and Safe Streets Act of 1968, an act to assist state and local governments in reducing the incidence of crime, to increase the effectiveness, fairness, and coordination of law enforcement and criminal justice systems at all levels of government, and for other purposes. 5 U.S.C. §§ 5314-5316, 7313; 18 U.S.C. §§ 921-928, 2510-2513, 2515-2520, 3103a, 3501, 3502, 3731; 18 U.S.C. App. §§ 1201-1203; 42 U.S.C. §§ 3334, 3711, 3721-3723, 3731-3733, 3735, 3741, 3742, 3750-3766, 3769, 3791, 3793, 3795; 47 U.S.C. § 605; 82 Stat. 197, 638, 1236 (1968), as amended. See also, *Omnibus Crime Control Act of 1970.*

omnis ratihabitio retrotrahitur et mandato priori aequiparatur, every ratification has a retrospective effect, and is equivalent to a previous request.

omnium contributione sarciatur quod pro omnibus datum est, that which is given for all should be made good by the contribution of all. A principle of the law of general average. See also, *average.*

onerous, burdensome; importing a valuable consideration, as opposed to gratuitous. A transaction or undertaking is said to be onerous when the liabilities it entails outweigh the benefits.

onus, *l.,* a burden.

o'nus proban'di, *l.,* the burden of proof (*q.v.*).

open, to commence, *e.g.,* the trial of a case. The right to open a case rests with him who has the affirmative of the issue, or against whom judgment must be rendered if no proof is offered. (2) To make public, *e.g.,* sealed depositions, verdicts, or orders. (3) To vacate, or subject to re-examination, *e.g.,* judgments or public bids.

open account, a running or unsettled account (*q.v.*).

open court, court proceedings held in a public place, to which all persons who conduct themselves properly have free access. Opposed to court in chambers.

open end mortgage, a present mortgage (*q.v.*) to secure a present loan and future advances; a security device by which real property is appropriated or encumbered to secure a specific concurrent loan, and any additional indebtedness to such extent as is expressly authorized by the mortgage instrument. Occasionally regulated by various state statutes.

open-fields doctrine, a rule of law that an individual may not legitimately demand privacy, and consequently the guarantee and protection from searches and seizures without a warrant or probable cause, for activities conducted out of doors in fields, except in the area immediately surrounding the home. Only the curtilage (*q.v.*) is included with the home for Fourth Amendment purposes. No expectation of privacy legitimately attaches to open fields.

open listing, a listing contract which contains no provision forbidding the landowner from selling the land himself or to hire other brokers.

open-meeting law, or **sunshine law,** various federal and state statutes that require that all meetings of governmental bodies held to conduct decision-making business be open to the public and the press. Federal law generally applies to agencies but not departments headed by a single officer, nor to the President. State laws generally apply to state agencies and local governmental bodies, *e.g.,* city councils and county boards. See also, *Government in the Sunshine Act.*

open policy, an insurance contract in which the value of the subject insured is left to be ascertained in case of loss. Cf. *valued.*

open shop, an employer who employs union and nonunion workmen without discrimination.

opening statement, an informative and nonargumentative recital to a judge and jury, concerning counsel's case and the facts which he intends to establish in support thereof, given before any evidence is offered in a trial.

operation of law, the manner in which a person acquires rights or liabilities without any act of his own, usually arising from the happening of events, *e.g.,* an heir's right to real property left by a person who dies intestate.

operative, a workman; a person employed to perform labor for another, chiefly mechanical.

operative part, those clauses in a conveyance or other instrument which carry out its main object, especially the clause in a deed which contains the words of grant.

opinion, an inference or a conclusion, formed or entertained by a witness, as opposed to facts directly seen, heard, or perceived by him. Usually, a person's opinions are not competent testimony in a case. (2) If the witness is not testifying as an expert (*q.v.*), his testimony in the form of opinions or inferences is limited to those opinions or inferences which are (a) rationally based on the perception of the witness and (b) helpful to a clear understanding of his testimony or the determination of a fact in issue. Fed. R. Evid. 701. See also, *expert.* (3) A judge's statement of the reasons for the decision which the court pronounces. (4) An attorney's statement, usually in writing, of what he believes the law to be as to a particular question, or state of facts, or proposed line of conduct, about which a client asks his advice.

oppression, the abuse of authority by a public officer.

optimus legum interpres consuetudo, custom is the best interpreter of the laws.

option, a power or right to choose. (2) An offer to sell something at a definite price and according to definite terms and conditions, which if accepted would constitute a binding contract to sell and buy, and which cannot be revoked or withdrawn for a specific period of time, because the offeree has given a valuable consideration for the collateral agreement that the offer should not be revoked before that period of time. Accord, Restatement (Second) of Contracts § 25; to avoid ambiguity, the phrase "option contract" is used in the Restatement. Cf. *firm offer.*

option contract, see *option (2).*

oral, delivered by word of mouth; verbal. See also, *parol evidence rule.*

orator, or **oratrix** (one who prays), occasionally, a petitioner or a plaintiff.

ordeal, formerly, a method of criminal trial founded on superstition. It was of four kinds, *i.e.,* by combat, by fire, by hot water, and by cold water.

order, a mandate or direction by an individual or by judicial authority. Orders of a court, as distinguished from judgments (*q.v.*), are decisions or directions concerning summary or interlocutory matters. (2) In commercial paper transactions, a direction to pay which is more than an authorization or request. It must identify the person to pay with reasonable certainty. It may be addressed to one or more such persons jointly or in the alternative but not in succession. U.C.C. § 3-102(1)(b).

order of delivery, see *replevin*.

Order of the Coif, an honorary scholastic legal society, named for the custom of wearing a white lawn coif or headdress when admission was granted to the English order of sergeants. American law students are elected to the Order of the Coif upon their graduation, if they are in the top ten percent of their class. At the option of the local chapter, it may also be required that candidates for the Order of the Coif engage in activities that contribute directly to legal education, such as legal research and writing.

ordinance, a law, statute, or legislative enactment, particularly the legislative enactments or statutes of a municipal corporation.

ordinary, occasionally, a judge with limited jurisdiction, *e.g.,* probate, and administration and supervision of estates.

ordinary and necessary expense, in federal income taxation, an expenditure for such a purpose as is a common and accepted occurrence in the field of business. An expenditure made in good faith with the intention of benefiting the business with respect to which it is made.

ordinary care, see *reasonable care*.

ore leave, the right to dig and take ore from land.

o're te'nus, *l.,* by word of mouth.

organization, a corporation, government, or governmental subdivision or agency, business trust, estate, trust, partnership, or association, two or more persons having a joint or common interest, or any other legal or commercial entity. U.C.C. §1-201(28). Accord, Uniform Probate Code §§ 1-201(27), 5-103(12).

Organization of American States, an international organization between the republics of the Western Hemisphere, established in 1948. Its measures of enforcement are subordinated to the obligations of its members to the United Nations.

Organized Crime Control Act of 1970, an act relating to the control of organized crime in the United States. Among other things, it seeks the eradication of organized crime in the United States by strengthening the legal tools in the evidence-gathering process, by establishing new penal prohibitions, and by providing enhanced sanctions and new remedies to deal with the unlawful activities of persons engaged in organized crime. 18 U.S.C. §§ 841-848, 1511, 1623,1826, 1955, 1961-1968, 2516, 3148, 3503, 3504, 3331-3334, 3661-3664, 6001-6005. See also, *Racketeer Influenced and Corrupt Organizations Act.*

original, first; primary as opposed to secondary; not derived from any other source, or authority, *e.g.,* original jurisdiction. (2) An authentic instrument, as distinguished from a copy. (3) An original of a writing or recording is the writing or recording itself or any counterpart intended to have the same effect by a person executing or issuing it. An original of a photograph includes the negative or any print therefrom. If data are stored in a computer or similar device, any printout or other output readable by sight, shown to reflect the data accurately, is an original. Fed. R. Evid. 1001(3).

original jurisdiction, the authority of a court to hear and determine a lawsuit when it is initiated, as contrasted with appellate jurisdiction.

original package, the container in which goods, transported from one place to another, are shipped, kept, handled and delivered.

original writ, formerly, the mode of beginning English lawsuits. See also, *writ.*

orphan, a minor who has lost both parents. The term is sometimes applied to an infant who has lost but one.

orphan's court, a tribunal in some states, which has jurisdiction over the persons and estates of orphans.

ostensible, apparent, declared, or avowed.

ostensible partner, a person whose name appears in a firm name, and is held liable as a partner, whether he is so or not. See also, *nominal partner.*

oust, ouster, to dispossess; dispossession.

out of court, not before the court, *e.g.,* a settlement between the parties made out of court. (2) The situation of a plaintiff who has been nonsuited or is otherwise unable to maintain his lawsuit.

out of the state, descriptive of a person who is a nonresident *(q.v.)* of the state or is temporarily outside of the state and beyond the reach of its process.

outer barrister, see *utter barrister.*

outlawry, formerly, an English procedure, by which a person was put out of the protection of the law for wilfully avoiding the execution of the process of the courts.

outrage, a tort, by extreme and outrageous conduct intentionally or recklessly causing severe emotional distress to another. Liability has been found only where the conduct has been so outrageous in character, and so extreme in degree as to go beyond all possible bounds of decency and to be regarded as atrocious and utterly intolerable in a civilized community. Restatement (Second) of Torts § 46, Comment d. Cf. *emotional distress.*

over, above; beyond. In conveyancing, a gift or limitation which is to come into existence upon the termination of preceding estate.

overdraw, to draw bills or checks upon a bank, for a greater amount than one has on deposit, or is entitled to draw.

overdue, the condition of a note or bill, after the time of payment has passed, without its being paid.

overplus, that which is left beyond a certain amount; surplus.

overrule, to set aside the authority of a former decision, *e.g.,* so that it will not have precedent value. (2) The act of a court, in rejecting a motion or objection made by a party to a lawsuit.

overt, visible, open, public.

owing, unpaid, *e.g.,* a debt, whether due or not.

owner, a flexible term for a person who has the right of dominion or title concerning something that is subject to ownership. (2) A person who has control over a thing with the right to use it or dispose of it as he sees fit. The term is properly applied only to one who has absolute ownership, as distinguished from special ownership, or the right to possess and enjoy, which a bailee may have.

oyer (ō'yer), *L. fr.,* to hear.

oyer and terminer, a commission directed to English judges to hear and determine treasons and all manner of felonies and trespasses. See also, *Court of Oyer and Terminer.*

oyez, occasionally, hear ye, usually pronounced oh! yes!

P

pacta privata juri publico derogare non possunt, private compacts cannot derogate from public right.

pacta quae turpem causam continent non sunt observanda, contracts founded upon an immoral consideration are not to be observed.

pac'tum (Rom.), an agreement.

pain and suffering, various kinds of distress and discomfort, *e.g.,* aches, hurts, and soreness, for which a court or jury may award damages.

pais (*pā*), the country, outside the court. Matter in pais is fact which is not a matter of record. Estoppel in pais is an estoppel (*q.v.*) by words spoken or acts done, as distinguished from an estoppel by deed or record. Trial per pais is trial by jury.

palimony, a popular term for money paid by one person to another person with whom the first person lived out of wedlock, analogous to alimony (*q.v.*), adjudged by a court on the theory that (a) the courts should enforce express contracts between nonmarital partners except to the extent that the contract is explicitly founded on the consideration of meretricious (*q.v.*), sexual services, or (b) in the absence of an express contract, the courts should inquire into the conduct of the parties to determine whether that conduct demonstrates an implied contract (*q.v.*), agreement of partnership (*q.v.*), or joint venture (*q.v.*), or some tacit understanding between the parties. (2) The courts may also employ the doctrine of quantum meruit (*q.v.*), or equitable remedies, *e.g.*, constructive (*q.v.*) or resulting trusts (*q.v.*), when warranted by the facts of the case.

Pan American Union, the permanent secretariat of the Council of the Organization of American States, established in 1948.

Pandects, or **The Digest,** an abridgment or compilation of the civil law, which was promulgated A. D. 533.

panel, a division or portion of the members of a court, which has the authority and powers of the entire court. (2) The group of persons summoned to act as jurors at a particular term of court, or for the trial of a particular action.

paper book, an appendix to an appellate court brief; an abstract of the evidence and pleadings necessary to the full understanding of a case.

paper money, the promissory notes of the government which pass as money. See also, *legal tender*.

paper patent, a term of derision, applied to patents which have never been used commercially, or been recognized by the trade.

paper title, documentary or record evidence of the ownership of real property, which may or may not be valid.

papers, a flexible term for various documents, pleadings, court orders and judgments, motions, notices, exhibits, instruments, and records.

Paperwork Reduction Act of 1980, an act to reduce paperwork and enhance the economy and efficiency of the federal government and the private sector by improving federal information policymaking, and for other purposes. 44 U.S.C. §§ 2904, 2905, 3501 *et seq.*

par, equal. Bills of exchange, notes, stocks, and bonds, among other things, are said to be at par when they sell for their face value, and above or below par when they sell for more or for less than their face value.

par in parem imperium non habet, an equal has no power over an equal.

par value, the face value of a share of stock or bond.

parage, equality of blood or dignity; coheirs are said to hold by parage.

paralegal, or **legal assistant,** a person who assists a lawyer under the lawyer's direction and control, and can do anything permitted by the lawyer except appear in court and advise clients concerning the law. His duties may encompass such diverse tasks as interviewing clients, marshaling facts, making recommendations, and drafting forms. Persons qualify as paralegals by education, formal training, experience, or a combination of them. (2) A person under the supervision and direction of a licensed lawyer, who may (a) apply knowledge of law and legal procedures in rendering direct assistance to lawyers engaged in legal research; (b) design, develop, or plan modifications or new procedures, techniques, services, processes, or applications; (c) prepare or interpret legal documents and write detailed procedures for practicing in certain fields of law; (d) select, compile, and use technical information from such references as law digests, legal encyclopedias, or practice manuals; and (e) analyze and follow procedural problems that involve independent decisions. Ky. Sup. Ct. Rule (SCR) 3.700.

paramount, superior.

parapherna'lia, the personal ornaments of a married woman.

parcel, a lot, tract, boundary, or portion of land.

parcenary, or **parceners,** see *coparcenary.*

pardon, the remission by the chief executive of a state or nation of a punishment which a person convicted of crime has been sentenced to undergo.

pa'rens pa'triae, *l.* (father of his country), a doctrine by which the government supervises children and other persons who are under a legal disability. It often takes the form of supervision which is analogous to that of a parent.

parent, the lawful father or mother of a person. (2) Any person entitled to take, or who would be entitled to take if the child died without a will, as a parent under the Uniform Probate Code by intestate succession from the child whose relationship is in question and excludes any person who is only a stepparent, foster parent, or grandparent. Uniform Probate Code § 1-201(28); accord, § 5-103(13).

parent corporation, a domestic or foreign corporation which owns and holds a majority of record shares of another corporation, domestic or foreign, entitling the holder of the shares to exercise a majority of the voting power and as a result has control of that corporation (the subsidiary corporation).

Parental Kidnapping Prevention Act of 1980, sections 6-10 of an act to amend tit. XVIII of the Social Security Act. It concerns cooperation between state courts, promotion and expansion of the exchange of information between states, enforcement of custody and visitation decrees of sister states, deterrence of interstate abductions and other unilateral removals of children to obtain custody and visitation awards, and the like. 28 U.S.C. § 1738A; 42 U.S.C. §§ 654, 655, 663.

parenticide, a person who murders a parent, or the act of doing so.

pa'res, a person's peers or equals.

pa'ri delic'to, in equal fault; guilty to the same extent.

pa'ri mate'ria, in the same matter; on the same subject.

pa'ri pas'su (with equal step), equally; without preference.

paribus sententiis reus absolvitur, where the opinions are equal, *i.e.,* the votes or judges are equally divided, judgment is for the defendant.

parish, in Louisiana, a civil division, corresponding to the county in other states.

park, public grounds kept for purposes of adornment and popular resort for recreation, exercise and pleasure.

parking, the storing or stationing of automobiles or other vehicles.

parliament, the legislative branch of the government of England. See also, *Houses of Parliament.*

Parliamentary law, the body of regulations which govern procedure in legislatures and similar organizations.

parol, by word of mouth.

parol evidence rule, a significant provision in American law, that when dealings between parties are reduced to an unambiguous written instrument, *e.g.,* a deed, contract, or lease, the instrument cannot be contradicted or modified by oral evidence. The rule is subject to various limitations and exceptions, however.

parole, supervised suspension of the execution of a convict's sentence, and release from prison, conditional upon his continued compliance with the terms of parole. (2) A regular part of the rehabilitative process. Assuming good behavior, it is the normal expectation in the vast majority of cases. Statutes generally specify when a prisoner will be eligible to be considered for parole and detail the standards and procedures applicable. Cf. *commutation (1), (2).*

parricide, or **patricide,** a person who kills his father, or the act of doing so.

pars rationa'bilis, *l.,* a reasonable part.

part, a share; less than the whole, *e.g.*, part payment or part performance. (2) Organs, tissues, eyes, bones, arteries, blood, other fluids, and any other portions of a human body. Uniform Anatomical Gift Act § 1(e).

part owners, persons who have title to something together or in common, *e.g.*, a vessel. See also, *cotenancy, joint tenants* and *tenancy in common.* Cf. *partnership.*

partial dependent, a person who has income, which is in an amount insufficient for his or her support, and who looks to another person as a source of supplementary support.

par'ticeps criminis, *l.* a partner in crime. Cf. *accomplice.*

particular average, see *average.*

particular estate, an interest in real property which is granted out of a larger interest in real property. The larger interest then becomes an expectancy, either in reversion (*q.v.*) or in remainder (*q.v.*).

particular lien, a right to detain a chattel from the owner, until a certain claim against it is satisfied. See also, *lien.*

particularity, in pleading, the allegation of details.

particulars, see *bill of particulars.*

partition, the act of dividing. (2) A right of action, by which real property belonging to two or more joint owners, *e.g.*, joint tenants or tenants in common, may be divided by a court, into two or more separate parcels of proportionate value, which become the respective properties of the individual owners. (3) Voluntary conveyances by which the same is accomplished without court action.

partnership, an association of two or more persons to carry on as co-owners of a business for profit. Uniform Partnership Act § 6(1). It is usually the result of a contract to combine property or labor, or both, for the purpose of a common undertaking and the acquisition of a common profit. A partnership is dissolved by the death of any of the partners, but this and other rules applicable thereto are often modified by the agreement entered into by the partners at the outset of their undertaking.

partus sequitur ventrem, the offspring follows the dam. This maxim applies to the status of animals.

party, a person who takes part in a legal transaction, *e.g.*, a person with an immediate interest in an agreement or deed or a plaintiff or a defendant in a lawsuit. (2) As distinct from third party, a person who has engaged in a transaction or made an agreement. U.C.C. § 1-201(29).

party wall, an upright structural support erected on the line between adjoining lots of different owners, for the use of both.

pass, in sales and conveyancing, to transfer or to become transferred. (2) To decide upon or allow.

passage, or **passageway,** a right of way.

passenger, a person who has taken a place in a public conveyance for the purpose of being transported from one place to another; a person who is so transported.

passive, inactive or permitted.

passive debt, a debt (*q.v.*) upon which no interest is payable.

passive trust, a trust (*q.v.*) concerning which the trustee has no active duty to perform. See also, *bare trustee.*

passive use, see *permissive use.*

passport, a document identifying a citizen, in effect requesting foreign nations to allow the bearer to enter and to pass freely and safely, recognizing the right of the bearer to the protection of American diplomatic and consular officers. (2) A license for safe passage from one place to another.

pasture, the right of grazing cattle. (2) Land employed for grazing purposes.

patent, a flexible term for a grant of some privilege, property, or authority, by the government or sovereign to one or more individuals. (2) An instrument by which the state or national government conveys its lands. (3) An instrument granting to original inventors the exclusive right for a period of years to manufacture, sell, and use the invention described therein. Congress may enact patent laws, U.S. Const. Art. I, Sec. 8. See also, *land patent* and *paper patent.*

patent ambiguity, see *ambiguity.*

patent office, a bureau of the United States Department of Commerce at Washington, D.C., to which all applications for invention patents must be made. The office is headed by a Commissioner of Patents and it is charged with the administration of the laws concerning the granting of patents and related activities.

pater est quem nuptiae demonstrant, he is the father whom the marriage points out.

paterfami'lias (Rom.), a person who is sui juris or is the head of a family.

pathometer, an instrument commonly known as a lie detector.

Patient Antidumping Act, a provision in the Consolidated Omnibus Budget Reconciliation Act of 1986 (COBRA) prohibiting hospitals from refusal to admit or improper transfer of emergency patients in unstable condition based on apparent inability to pay.

pa'tria potes'tas (Rom.), the power of a paterfamilias (*q.v.*) over his family.

patricide, see *parricide.*

pauper, or **indigent person,** an economically poor, destitute, or helpless person; a person who is unable to provide for and maintain himself or his family from his income or his other resources. Occasionally defined by various statutes.

pawn, a security device, *i.e.,* the deposit by a debtor of personal property with a lender for the purpose of pledging the personal property as security for the debt. (2) The item of personal property so deposited.

pawnbroker, a person engaged in the business of lending money on the security of a pawn (*q.v.*). Often closely regulated and supervised under various state statutes and city ordinances, which may also define the term.

payable, descriptive of something which ought to be paid, usually at once.

payable on demand, see *demand instrument.*

payee, a person to whom a promissory note, check, or bill of exchange is made payable.

payment, the satisfaction of a debt, or obligation to pay money. It may be made in money, or anything of value which is unconditionally accepted by the payee as a substitute therefor.

payment into court, the deposit of a sum of money with the proper officer of a court by a party to a lawsuit, (a) when he cannot safely pay it to either of several persons claiming it and desires them to interplead and have the court determine who shall receive it; (b) when he desires to relieve himself from the responsibility of administering a fund in his hands as trustee for others; or (c) when he admits the plaintiff's claim only to the extent of the amount paid in and disputes the rest. The usual effect of such payment is to relieve the party paying from liability for court costs, unless a judgment is rendered against him for a larger amount than the sum so paid in. Cf. *interpleader* and *Interpleader Act.*

payment under protest, see *protest (2).*

peace, public order; freedom from war, violence, or public disturbance.

peace, bill of, see *bill of peace.*

peace bond, a bond (*q.v.*) for good behavior; bail (*q.v.*) in a reasonable sum, conditioned on the defendant keeping the peace and on his good behavior for a fixed period of time, *e.g.,* one year, which may be required by a court if there are reasonable grounds to believe that the release of a defendant would endanger persons or property. Regulated by various state statutes and rules of criminal procedure.

pecuniary, relating to money.

pecuniary legacy, a testamentary gift of money.

peddler, a person who carries merchandise from place to place and sells it or offers to sell it. Often defined by various state statutes and city ordinances.

pedigree, lineage, genealogy. See also, *hearsay.*

peer, an equal.

pen register, an aural interception device attached to a telephone line, usually at the telephone company's central office, which records on paper the date, time, and number of all outgoing calls dialed from a particular telephone, and cuts off without determining whether the call was completed and without monitoring the conversation. Issuance of a warrant is not mandated by the U.S. Constitution before it is used.

penal, pertaining to or respecting punishment.

penal action, a lawsuit to recover a statutory penalty.

Penal and Correctional Code, see *Model Penal Code.*

penal bill, formerly, a bond to do a certain act, or in default thereof, pay a certain sum of money by way of penalty.

penal code, penal laws, or **penal statutes,** various legislative acts which prohibit particular behavior and impose a penalty for the commission of it. The United States penal code is tit. 18 U.S.C., Crimes and Criminal Procedure. See also, *Model Penal Code.*

penalty, punishment. The consequence imposed upon the perpetrator, for the violation of a penal law or the violation of a personal right, *e.g.,* the requirement of payment of a sum of money into the public treasury, or an extraordinary payment to an aggrieved person, which exceeds actual damages.

penden'te li'te, *l.,* while the suit is pending. See also, *administration* and *alimony.*

pendente lite nihil innovetur, during litigation, no change in the position of things, or of the parties, should be made.

pendent jurisdiction, this is a type of jurisdiction that exists in cases where a plaintiff has both a federal and state law claim. In deciding whether to exercise pendent jurisdiction, the court must construe whether a series of events or a singular transaction may be said to constitute a single cause of action.

pension, a stated allowance granted by a government or a private employer to an individual or his representative, for services previously performed.

Pension Benefit Guaranty Corporation, see *Employee Retirement Income Security Act of 1974.*

peppercorn, the berry or fruit of the pepper plant; something of insignificant value.

per, *l.*, by; through; during.

per an'num, by the year.

per autre vie (*ō tr vē*), during the life of another.

per ca´pita, by the head, *i.e.* by the number of individuals; opposed to per stirpes (*q.v.*).

per con'tra, on the other hand.

per cu'riam, by the court.

per di'em, by the day.

per for'mam do'ni, by the form of the gift.

per frau'dem, through fraud.

per incu'riam, through want of care.

per infortu'nium, by misadventure.

per mi'nas, by threats.

per my et per tout (mē ã pär tōō), by share and by whole.

per pais, trial, see *pais*.

per quod, whereby.

per se, by itself; alone.

per stir'pes, by the number of families; opposed to per capita (*q.v.*).

per to'tam cu'riam, by the full court.

per ver'ba de futu'ro, by words of the future, *i.e.*, a promise.

per ver'ba de praesen'ti, by words of the present, *i.e.*, a declaration.

perambulation, a walking of boundaries.

perception, the taking possession of, *e.g.*, crops by harvesting, or money by counting it out and accepting it in payment of a debt. (2) Seeing, or otherwise detecting or comprehending.

percolating waters, water diffusing through the ground beneath the surface, either without a definite channel or in an unknown and not readily ascertainable course. It is an appurtenance to the land in which it is found.

perdurable, lasting long or forever.

peremptory, absolute; final; admitting of no excuse for non-performance, *e.g.*, an order or mandamus. See also, *challenge*.

perfect, complete; descriptive of contracts and obligations which can be enforced by law, and of trusts which have been executed. Cf. *imperfect obligations* and *imperfect trust*. (2) To take all of the applicable steps required by law, *e.g.*, filing, concerning a security interest (*q.v.*), which has attached. U.C.C. § 9-303(1). Such steps are specified in U.C.C. §§ 9-302, 9-304, 9-305, and 9-306.

performance, the act of doing something, especially something required by a contract or condition, which relieves a person from all further liability thereunder.

peril, danger; risk; that which threatens or causes a loss, *e.g.,* the subject of insurance.

perils of the sea, fortuitous action of the sea or extraordinary risks or occurrences from without, *e.g.,* storms, violence of the elements, shipwreck, or collision. (2) In bills of lading, causes of loss or injury for which carriers will not hold themselves liable. (3) In policies of marine insurance, those risks for which the insurer is liable.

perjury, a false statement under oath or affirmation, wilfully made in regard to a material matter of fact. Usually defined by various statutes. (2) Making a false statement under oath or equivalent affirmation, or swearing or affirming the truth of a statement previously made, in an official proceeding when the statement is material (*q.v.*) and he does not believe it to be true. Model Penal Code § 241.1(1). Cf. *false swearing.*

permanent, lasting, continuing, durable.

permanent disability, a disablement or incapacity, which in reasonable probability, will continue for an indefinite period of time, without any present indication of recovery therefrom. See also, *disability.*

permissive, suffered, or allowed.

permissive use, or **passive use,** formerly, a subterfuge to evade the laws of mortmain, forfeiture and other English acts, in which one person held the title to real property for the use of another.

permissive waste, the neglect to repair a building.

perpetual injunction, see *injunction.*

perpetuating testimony, a court proceeding for the purpose of giving, taking, and recording in writing, the testimony of a party or a witness to be used in a lawsuit which has not yet been commenced, when by reason of, *e.g.,* the witness's age, or infirmity, or going abroad, the testimony is likely to be lost. Authorized by various state statutes and rules of civil procedure. Fed. R. Civ. P. 27.

perpetuity, the tying up or disposing of property, so that it is never at the absolute disposal of any person or group of persons. This is contrary to public policy, and the rule against perpetuities forbids any executory interest to come into being later than a life or lives in being, and 21 years thereafter, allowing for gestation where it exists. The rule is subject to occasional variations and exceptions, and is occasionally modified by various state statutes. See also, *wait-and-see doctrine.*

person, a human being or a corporation. Often defined by various federal and state statutes. (2) An individual or an organization. U.C.C.

§ 1-201(30). (3) An individual, a corporation, an organization, or other legal entity. Uniform Probate Code § 1-201(29); accord, § 5-103(14). (4) Individuals, partnerships, corporations, and other associations. Uniform Partnership Act § 2.

persona, a personality or person.

persona designata, *l.* a person described as an individual, as distinguished from one described merely as a member of a class.

personal, appertaining to a person, or to the person.

personal action, a lawsuit brought to recover personal property, or for damages for the breach of a contract, or injuries to person or property, as distinguished from real action (*q.v.*).

personal chattels, movable things which may be attached to the person and carried about with him from one place to another, as distinguished from chattels real, *i.e.,* interests in land which do not amount to a freehold.

personal contract, an agreement relating to personal property.

personal injury, a hurt or wrong, either to the physical body of a person, or to the reputation of a person, or to both.

personal jurisdiction, see *jurisdiction (4).*

personal property, the right or interest which a person has in things movable, or in any estate in real property which is less than a freehold. (2) Anything which is subject to ownership and which is not a freehold in real property.

personal representative, the executor or administrator of a deceased person. (2) Includes executor, administrator, successor personal representative, special administrator, and persons who perform substantially the same function under the law governing their status. General personal representative excludes special administrator. Uniform Probate Code § 1-201(30).

personal rights, the privileges of personal security, comprising those of life, limb, reputation, and liberty.

personalty, personal property (*q.v.*).

personam, see *in personam.*

personation, the offense of pretending to be another person, whether real or fictitious.

persuasion, influencing another by request, argument, or representation. When carried to such an extent as to deprive the person influenced of freedom of will, it is a ground for setting aside a will or other instrument made in pursuance thereof. Cf. *undue influence.*

pertinent, relevant; tending to prove or disprove the allegations of the parties.

petit, see *petty.*

petit jury, see *jury.*

petition, a request made to a public official or public body that has authority to act concerning it. The right to Petition the government for a redress of grievances is secured to the people. U.S. Const., Amend. I. (2) Under some codes and rules of civil procedure, the written statement of the plaintiff's case which initiates a lawsuit. (3) A written request to the court for an order after notice. Uniform Probate Code § 5-103(15).

petition for rehearing, a request to a court by a party adversely affected by a final decision in a particular appeal or lawsuit, that the court reconsider its earlier decision, upon particular grounds, *e.g.*, the court has overlooked a material fact in the record or a controlling statute or decision. Usually defined and regulated by various rules of court, codes of civil procedure, and statutes.

petitory action, a lawsuit in which the title to property is liquidated, as distinguished from a possessory action, in which possession is sought.

petty, or **petit,** small; trifling; of little importance.

petty average, see *average.*

petty bag office, formerly an office in the common law portion of the English Court of Chancery.

petty cash, money set aside for the provision of making change or immediate payments of comparatively small amounts.

petty jury, see *jury.*

petty larceny, see *larceny.*

petty offenses, minor offenses triable summarily by a magistrate without a jury.

petty treason, formerly, a term for the act of a servant killing his master or of a wife killing her husband.

physical harm, the physical impairment of the human body or of land or chattels. Restatement (Second) of Torts § 7(3).

picketing, to attempt to influence someone by patrolling, a particular area, usually with placards or signs. When it is peaceful, it is a legal form of communication. Usually regulated by various statutes and court decisions. (2) Formerly, an offense.

"piercing the corporate veil," "disregarding the separate existence of the corporation"; "disregarding the corporate entity"; ignoring the existence of the corporation so as to impose liability for the corporation's obligations on its individual or corporate shareholders; imposition of liability on other corporations owned by the same shareholders;

imposition of liability on a successor corporation for obligations of a predecessor.

pillory, formerly, a wooden frame with boards and holes, through which the head and hands of a convicted criminal were put to punish him.

pilotage, the compensation of a pilot for conducting a vessel into, or out of, port. (2) The office or employment of a pilot.

pin money, an allowance given to a person's wife to defray her personal expenses.

piracy, the commission on the sea of such acts of robbery and violence as would amount on land to a felony. Defined by various federal statutes. Congress is empowered to define and punish piracies and felonies committed on the high seas and offenses against the law of nations. U.S. Const., Art. I, Sec. 8. (2) Infringement of copyright.

pis'cary, the right to fish in someone else's waters.

pla'cita commu'nia, *l.,* the common pleas, *i.e.,* civil actions between individual persons. (2) The court where they were tried.

plain-view doctrine, a rule of law creating an exception to the requirement that police officers have a search warrant, when the police, while conducting themselves lawfully, *e.g.,* while patrolling the streets or executing a search warrant for something else, inadvertently come upon incriminating evidence, and it is immediately apparent to the police that they have evidence of a crime. In such a situation, the evidence may be seized without a warrant.

plaint, formerly, a written statement of a cause of action, analogous to a complaint (*q.v.*) or a petition (*q.v.*), which was used to initiate a lawsuit.

plaintiff, a person who initiates a lawsuit.

planned unit development, PUD; a development consisting of town houses, homes, apartments, or combinations of such buildings, all with common open areas and some with private recreation facilities. The developer is permitted to construct more units per acre than is allowed under a standard lot and block subdivision. This more efficient land use results in lower prices for buyers.

plea, the formal response of a defendant to the charge in an indictment or to a civil lawsuit. See also, *pleadings.* (2) In England, a legal proceeding, hence (a) pleas of the Crown, criminal prosecution, and (b) common pleas, civil causes.

plea agreement, or **plea bargain,** an agreement (*q.v.*) reached by the attorney for the government and the attorney for a defendant in a criminal case, or the defendant when acting pro se (*q.v.*), that upon entering of a plea of guilty or nolo contendere (*q.v.*) to a charged offense or to a lesser or related offense, the attorney for the government will (a) move for dismissal of other charges, (b) make a recommendation, or agree not to oppose the defendant's request, for a particular sentence, with the understanding that such recommendation or request shall not be binding upon the court, or (c) agree that a specific sentence is the appropriate disposition of the case. The court is not permitted to participate in such discussions. Fed. R. Crim. P. 11(e)(1).

plead, to answer the opponent's plea in an action. (2) To file a pleading in a court. (3) To make a plea, *e.g.,* not guilty. (4) Occasionally, to argue a cause in court.

pleader, a party who files a pleading.

pleading, or **pleadings,** the alternate and opposing written statements of the parties to a lawsuit. Under the Federal Rules of Civil Procedure, and analogous state rules of civil procedure, the pleadings consist of a Complaint and an Answer; a Reply to a Counterclaim denominated as such; an Answer to a Cross-claim, if the Answer contains a Cross-claim; a Third-party Complaint, if a person who was not an original party is summoned; and a Third-party Answer, if a Third-party Complaint is served. No other pleadings shall be allowed, except that the court may order a Reply to an Answer or a Third-party Answer. Fed. R. Civ. P. 7(a). Pleadings consist of simple, concise, and direct averments of claims for relief, defenses, and denials. Matters which constitute an avoidance or affirmative defense must be set forth affirmatively. *Id.* 8.

plebiscite (plĕb ĭ sĭt), a vote of the people.

pledge, a pawn or thing delivered to another as security for the payment of a debt, or for the performance of an obligation. (2) The transaction by which the pawn is given and the money obtained. The vital characteristic of such a transaction is that the creditor or secured party takes and holds actual possession of the pawn or collateral. (3) In a nontechnical sense, to make a paper transaction for security purposes, in which the creditor does not obtain actual possession.

plena et celeris justitia fiat partibus, let full and speedy justice be done to the parties.

plenary, full, conclusive.

plenary proceedings, or **plenary suits,** lawsuits in which the conduct of business is full and formal, as opposed to summary proceedings, in which the conduct of business is brief and informal.

ple'ne administra'vit, *l.,* he has fully administered. The defense of an executor or administrator, when sued for a debt of his testator, which he has no assets to satisfy.

plurality, a greater number. A plurality of votes is a larger number of votes cast for one candidate than any other candidate has received. It may be less than a majority, which is more than half of all votes cast.

pluries, (often), process that issues in the third instance, after the first and the alias have been ineffectual. Cf. *alias* (2).

plus peccat auctor quam actor, the instigator of a crime offends more than the doer of it.

poaching, unlawfully taking or destroying game.

P.O.D. account, an account (*q.v.*) payable on request to one person during his lifetime and on his death to one or more P.O.D. payees (*q.v.*), or to one or more persons during their lifetimes and on the death of all of them to one or more P.O.D. payees. Uniform Probate Code § 6-101(10).

P.O.D. payee, a person designated on a P.O.D. account (*q.v.*) as one to whom the account is payable on request after the death of one or more persons. Uniform Probate Code § 6-101(11).

poinding, the detention of cattle found trespassing. See also, *pound*.

police, the collective and various law enforcement officers appointed by a state, county, or city, to care for various portions of the public safety under the supervision on a case-by-case basis of the courts, *e.g.,* prevent crimes and protect the public, investigate crimes and allegations thereof, make arrests, patrol the streets and highways, and maintain public order.

police power, a flexible term for the authority of federal and state legislatures to enact laws regulating and restraining private rights and occupations for the promotion of public health, safety, welfare, and order.

policy, of a statute, its objective or intention, sometimes distinguished from its letter. See also, *legislative intent.* (2) The written contract or instrument by which insurance is effected.

policy, public, see *public policy.*

political, variously, pertaining to government, its policies, its theories, or its conduct. (2) Descriptive of the influences which citizens attempt to exert on their government. (3) Descriptive of orderly conduct of government, as opposed to revolution by force.

poll, the head, whence poll tax, a capitation tax; to poll a jury, *i.e.,* to question the members one by one in open court as to their verdict; to poll, *i.e.,* to take votes. See also, *deed poll.*

poll tax, see *tax.*

pollution, contamination, corruption, or defilement. See also, *air pollution* and *water pollution.*

polyandry, the state of a woman who has several husbands.

polygamy, plurality of wives or husbands. (2) Marrying or cohabiting with more than one spouse at a time in purported exercise of the right of plural marriage. The offense is a continuing one until all co-habitation and claim of marriage with more than one spouse terminates. Exempted are parties to a polygamous marriage, lawful in the country of which they are residents or nationals, while they are in transit through or temporarily visiting the jurisdiction. Model Penal Code § 230.1(2). (3) Contracting or purporting to contract marriage with another, knowing that the other is thereby committing polygamy. Model Penal Code § 230.1(3). Cf. *bigamy.*

pontage, a payment for crossing, or for repair of, a bridge.

pool, an aggregation of the interests or property of various persons, to further a joint end, by subjecting them to centralized control and common liability.

pooling agreement, a contract between various persons to submit their interests to joint control and common liability, for their mutual advantage.

popular action, a lawsuit initiated by a member of the public, to recover a penalty. Occasionally authorized by various statutes. See also, *qui tam.*

popular election, election by the people as a whole rather than by a select group.

pornography, pictures and other forms of communication which are intended to arouse sexual desire or create sexual excitement. (2) Works which have as their object material gain via appeal to sexual curiosity and appetite. (3) Pornography or pornographic material which is obscene (*q.v.*) forms a subgroup of all obscene expression, but not the whole, at least as the word "obscene" is now used in our language. The words "obscene material" have a specific judicial meaning, *i.e.*, obscene material which deals with sex. (4) Hard-core pornography may be difficult to define, "But I know it when I see it." Jacobellis v. Ohio, 378 U.S. 184, 197 (1964) (Stewart, J., concurring).

port, a harbor or place for taking in or discharging cargo, especially one where customs are levied.

portion, that part of a person's estate which is given or left to a child. See also, *distribution* and *heir.*

positive, actual; express; absolute; not doubtful; direct, as opposed to negative, *e.g.*, evidence. (2) Laid down; made by men, *e.g.*, positive law, as opposed to natural law.

posito uno oppositorum negatur alterum, when one of two opposite positions is affirmed, the other is denied.

pos'se, a possibility. Something is in posse when it may possibly exist; in esse when it actually exists. See also, *posse comitatus.*

posse comita'tus, the power of a county, which includes all able-bodied men therein who may be called on by the sheriff to assist him in preserving the peace.

posse comitatus law, a federal statute that provides for punishment of whoever, except in cases and under circumstances expressly authorized by the Constitution or Act of Congress, willfully uses any part of the Army or Air Force as a posse comitatus (*q.v.*) or otherwise to execute the laws. 18 U.S.C. § 1385; 70A Stat. 626, § 18(a), (1956), amended, 73 Stat. 144, § 17(d) (1959).

posses'sio (Rom.), detention or possession.

possession, having a thing in one's own power or control. It may be (a) actual; (b) constructive, or in law, *i.e.*, without actual personal occupation; (c) apparent, as where land descends to the heir of a disseisor; (d) naked, *i.e.*, without color of right. (2) A person who is in possession of land includes only one who (a) is in occupancy of land with intent to control it, or (b) has been, but no longer is, in occupancy of land with intent to control it, if after he has ceased his occupancy without abandoning the land, no other person has obtained possession as stated in (a), or (c) has the right as against all persons to immediate occupancy of land, if no other person is in possession as stated in (a) and (b). Restatement (Second) of Torts § 157. Accord, *Id.* § 328E. (3) A person who is in possession of a chattel is one who has physical control of the chattel with the intent to exercise such control on his own behalf, or on behalf of another. *Id.* § 216. (4) Seisin (*q.v.*). (5) Occupation, *e.g.*, by a lessee. (6) The thing possessed. See also, *adverse possession.*

possession vaut titre, possession is equivalent to title; a principle under which a good faith purchaser of goods is generally protected against the original owner.

possessory actions, lawsuits relating to, or arising out of, the possession of real or personal property. Cf. *petitory action.*

possibility, a future event which may or may not happen. (2) An interest in property depending on the occurrence of an uncertain event.

post, after; a later page or line.

post di'em, after the day.

post dissei'sin, a writ for him who, having recovered lands, was again dispossessed by the former disseisor.

post entry, a subsequent or additional entry of goods at a custom house to make up the original entry to the proper total.

post li'tem mo'tam, after the dispute has arisen.

post obit gift, a rudimentary form of will in which the landholder made a gift of his freehold estate to a distributor. It was stipulated that the gift was to take effect at the landholder's death and that the land should then be distributed according to the instructions which the landholder had given. The landholder reserved the equivalent of a modern life estate.

post office, an official government office for the receipt and delivery of mail. Congress is empowered to establish post offices. U.S. Const., Art. I, Sec. 8.

postage, the fee charged by law for delivering letters, newspapers, packages, and other items through the mail.

postdate, to date an instrument as of a day later than the one on which it is made.

poste'a, formerly, a statement of the proceedings in a common law action, indorsed by the judge before whom the trial was had.

posterity, all of the descendants of a person in a direct line.

posthumous child, a person born after his or her father's death or taken out of the body of a dead mother.

postmaster, a government officer who is in charge of a post office (*q.v.*).

Postmaster General, the chief officer of the United States Postal Service.

post-mortem, after death. (2) An examination of a human body after death. See also, *autopsy.*

postnatus, born after.

post-notes, bank notes payable in the future and not on demand.

postnuptial settlement, a settlement (*q.v.*) made after marriage.

postremo geniture, see *borough-English.*

potentia non est nisi ad bonum, power is not conveyed but for the public good.

potior est conditio defendentis, or **possidentis,** the condition of one defending or possessing is the better.

pound, an enclosure in which stray or unclaimed cattle or other animals are placed. (2) A place where distrained goods are kept.

pound-breach, the offense of breaking open a pound to take cattle.

poundage, occasionally, the fee allowed to a sheriff or other officer as a commission on the money made by virtue of an execution. Regulated by various state statutes.

pour over will, a will that pours assets, usually the residue of the testator's estate, into a trust. The trust provisions are not included in the will, rather, the trust agreement is created separately, either by the testator during his or her lifetime, or by another settlor.

poverty affidavit, a sworn statement in writing, filed by a party to a lawsuit, asserting that he is unable to furnish security for court costs. See also, *in forma pauperis.*

power, authority to act, which one person gives to another. It may authorize the donee to do something on his own behalf, or to act for the donor, either generally or in a particular matter. A power is naked, when the donee has no interest in the subject matter and, coupled with an interest, when the donee has an interest in the subject matter. The former may be revoked at the will of the donor; the latter, not without the consent of the donee. A power may be conferred by a power of attorney (*q.v.*).

power of appointment, authority conferred by deed or will, to make a gift or distribution of property, or to dispose of an interest in real property. It may be (a) appendant, *i.e.*, appurtenant, to be exercised out of the estate limited to the donee; (b) in gross, *i.e.*, to create an estate which will take effect upon the expiration of his own estate; (c) collateral, *i.e.*, with reference to an estate in which the donee takes no interest; (d) general, when the donee is at liberty to appoint to whom he pleases; (e) special, when he is restricted to a particular class, or particular individuals or objects.

power of attorney, or **letter of attorney,** a written grant of a power (*q.v.*) or authority, in precise terms, which identifies the agent (*q.v.*) and is signed by the principal (*q.v.*). Often regulated, as to contents and formalities, by various state statutes. See also, *durable power of attorney.*

practicable, that which may be done or accomplished; that which is feasible or possible.

practice, see *procedure.*

practice court, a course of study in legal education in which law students engage in pretended trials. (2) See *bail court.*

practice of law, any service rendered, which involves legal knowledge or legal advice, *e.g.*, representation, counsel, advocacy, or drafting of instruments, which is rendered in respect to the rights, duties, obligations, liabilities, or business affairs of someone requiring the services. Often defined by various rules of court, and occasionally by various state statutes. See also, *attorney at law.*

prae'cipe, command. A note on which the particulars of the process which a person wishes to have issued are written. It is lodged in the office out of which the required writ is to be issued.

prae'dial, that which grows from the ground, *e.g.*, grain, hay, fruit, and herbs.

prae'dium (Rom.), an estate; a farm.

praemuni're, to forewarn; formerly, the offense of submitting to or maintaining the authority of a foreign power in England.

praestat cautela quam medela, caution or prevention is better than cure.

prayer, the portion of a pleading, usually at the end, which makes a specific demand for judgment for the relief to which the pleader (*q.v.*) deems himself entitled. Relief in the alternative, or of several different types may be demanded. Fed. R. Civ. P. 8(a). See also, *pleading*.

preamble, introduction or preface. (2) The introduction of a legislative resolution or act, which states its intent and the mischiefs to be remedied.

precarious right, the privilege to enjoy the use of something at the will of another.

preca'rium, (Rom.), a form of permissive use or occupancy, the duration of which depends on the owner's will.

precatory words, not mandatory; language in a will which expresses a suggestion, wish, request, recommendation, or advice, and which is not shown by the other portions of the will to be mandatory.

precedence, priority; the right to go before another.

precedent, or **precedent case,** see *case*.

precedent condition, or **condition precedent,** a qualification, restriction, or limitation, which suspends or delays the vesting or enlargement of an estate in property, or a right, until a specified event has occurred. This terminology is not used in the Restatement (Second) of Contracts; Topic 5, Conditions and Similar Events, Introductory Note.

precept, a command given by a person in authority.

precinct, a police district. (2) A political subdivision of a county or city.

predecessor, a person who precedes another; the correlative to successor, as ancestor is to heir.

preemption, the right to purchase something before, or in preference to, any other person.

preemptive rights, preemptive rights enable the holders of shares of any class, other than shares which are limited as to dividend or distribution rate and liquidation price, on the offering or sale of shares of the same class for cash, to purchase those shares in proportion to their respective holdings of shares of that class at a fixed price.

preference, the receiving by a creditor of a greater proportion of the indebtedness due him from the assets of an insolvent (*q.v.*) debtor, than is received by other creditors of the same class, *e.g.*, unsecured creditors.

preferential voting, systems of election, under which the voter is permitted, or required, to express more than one choice for the same office.

preferred shares, shares that are entitled to a preference or priority in payment as against holders of common shares.

preferred stock, the shares of capital stock of a corporation, which under its bylaws have priority as to payment of dividends, up to a fixed amount, over the common stock, preferred stock does not have priority over debts due creditors, however.

pregnancy, the condition of a woman who is with child.

pre-incorporation agreements, an agreement entered into by those who are to be the initial shareholders of a corporation.

prejudice, a prejudgment, or bias which interferes with a person's impartiality and sense of justice.

prejudicial error, error (*q.v.*) committed during trial, which is of sufficient importance, that it will be grounds for new trial, or for reversal, on appeal.

preliminary, something which precedes, *e.g.*, something which is introductory or preparatory.

preliminary proof, see *proof of claim.*

premarital agreement, see *prenuptial agreement.*

premeditation, a design or intention, formed to commit a crime or do an act, before it is done.

premises, real property, *i.e.*, land or buildings or both. (2) Something which has been previously stated. (3) That part of a deed which precedes the habendum (*q.v.*).

premises liability, the liability of owners or occupiers of real property for personal injury sustained by entrants (including tenants) upon the land.

premium, the consideration paid for the issuance or renewal of a policy of insurance.

premium note, a promissory note given in payment of the premium due on a policy of insurance.

prenuptial agreement, an agreement between prospective spouses made in contemplation of marriage and to be effective upon marriage.

prepense, aforethought. Cf. *premeditation* and *malice.*

preponderance of evidence, the greater weight of the evidence, in merit and in worth. (2) Sufficient evidence to overcome doubt or speculation.

prerogative, special powers and privileges, *e.g.*, of the government.

prerogative writs, orders or process, the issuance of which is discretionary with the court, as opposed to writs of right. They are the writs of procedendo, mandamus, prohibition, quo warranto, habeas corpus, and certiorari, which are extraordinary remedies. See also, *extraordinary remedy.*

prescribe, to order or direct; to lay down rules. (2) See also, *prescription.*

prescribed by law, authorized by legislative enactment.

prescription, (Usucapio, Rom.), the transfer of rights in, or title to, real property by enjoying it peaceably without interruption, openly, and as if it were of right, over a long period of time, *e.g.*, 15 years or 21 years. The period of time required for prescription was originally time out of mind, but is now the time after which a person is prevented by the statutes of limitation from recovering real property or an interest therein.

present sense impression, a statement (*q.v.*) describing or explaining an event or condition made while the declarant (*q.v.*) was perceiving the event or condition, or immediately thereafter. It is not excluded from evidence as hearsay (*q.v.*) even though the declarant is available as a witness. Fed. R. Evid. 803(1).

presentation, see *presentment.*

presentment, in commercial paper transactions, occasionally called presentation, a demand for acceptance or payment made upon the maker, acceptor, drawee, or other payor by or on behalf of the holder. It may be made by mail, or through a clearing house, or at the place of acceptance or payment specified in the instrument, or if there be none, at the place of business or residence of the party to accept or pay. U.C.C. § 3-504(1), (2). (2) The report by a grand jury of an offense brought to its notice.

presents, a document, legal instrument, or other writing.

president, the chief executive officer or presiding officer of a corporation, society, or other body.

President of the United States, the officer in whom the executive power of the United States is vested. U.S. Const., Art. II, Sec. 1.

Presidential Electors, see *Electors, Presidential.*

presumption, a conclusion or inference drawn from the proven existence of some fact or group of facts. Presumptions may be either (a) juris et de jure (of law and by the principles of law), such as the presumption of incapacity in a minor to act, which are conclusive and irrebuttable; (b) juris (of law), which may be disproved or rebutted by evidence; or (c) judicis, or facti, *i.e.*, presumptions of fact drawn by a judge from the evidence. (2) In certain civil actions, a presumption imposes on the party against whom it is directed the burden of going forward with evidence to rebut or meet the presumption, but does not shift to that party the burden of proof in the sense of the risk of nonpersuasion, which remains throughout the trial upon the party on whom it was originally cast. Fed. R. Evid. 301. See also, *circumstantial evidence*.

presumptive, descriptive of something which may be inferred or presumed.

presumptive title, a right or claim which is presumed from mere possession; an appearance of ownership.

pretense, see *false pretenses*.

pretensed, pretended or claimed.

preterition, (Rom.), the entire omission of a child's name from the father's will.

pretermitted child, a person born after the execution of his or her parent's will, and not mentioned therein. Such persons are usually allowed to inherit, despite the provisions of the will, under various state statutes.

pre'tium affectio'nis, *l.*, an imaginary value set on a thing by one peculiarly desirous of possessing it.

pre-trial conference, or **pre-trial hearing,** a meeting between the judge and counsel for the parties, preliminary to the trial of a lawsuit. Under modern rules of civil procedure, in any lawsuit the court may in its discretion direct the attorneys for the parties to appear before it for a conference to consider any matters that may aid in the disposition of the lawsuit. Fed. R. Civ. P. 16.

Pretrial Services Act of 1982, an act concerning the establishment of pretrial services, its organization and administration, its functions and powers, and annual reports. It deals with information for pretrial release hearings, recommendations of appropriate release conditions for persons charged with offenses, supervision of persons released, the operation of facilities for the custody or care of persons released, *e.g.*, halfway houses, addict and alcoholic treatment centers, and counseling services, and the like. 18 U.S.C. §§ 3152-3155; 28 U.S.C. § 604.

prevarication, equivocation; deceitfully seeming to undertake a thing, with the purpose of defeating or destroying it.

prevention of significant deterioration, PSD; a federal policy established to protect the quality of those areas of the country that currently meet or exceed national ambient air quality standards.

price, the consideration, usually money, given for the purchase of something.

price discrimination, as prohibited by the Robinson-Patman Act (*q.v.*), the making of a distinction in price between customers for reasons which do not reflect differences in cost of manufacture, transportation, or sale.

pri'ma fa'cie (prī mã fa shĭe), *l.*, at first view; on the first aspect.

prima facie evidence, proof of a fact or collection of facts which creates a presumption of the existence of other facts, or from which some conclusion may be legally drawn, but which presumption or conclusion may be discredited or overcome by other relevant proof. Cf. *circumstantial evidence* and *presumption.*

pri'mage, formerly, a payment by a merchant or consignee to the master and sailors of a ship or vessel.

primage and average, see *average.*

primary, first or principal.

primary caretaker presumption, a presumption that the best interests of the child in child custody determinations are best served by awarding them to the primary caretaker parent. In determining who is the primary caretaker the courts look to which parent (1) prepares and plans meals; (2) bathes, grooms and dresses; (3) purchases, cleans and cares for clothes; (4) provides medical care, including nursing and trips to physicians; (5) arranges for social interaction among peers; (6) arranges alternative care; (7) puts the child to bed at night; (8) disciplines; (9) educates; and, (10) teaches elementary skills.

primary election, balloting by the members of a political party for the purpose of choosing candidates or delegates.

primary evidence, the best proof of which the case in its nature is susceptible; original, as opposed to secondary or derivative; used especially of documents. See also, *best evidence.*

primary obligation, a duty or responsibility which is the correlative of a primary right (*q.v.*).

primary right, a privilege, either in rem or in personam, the breach of which gives rise to a secondary right, *e.g.,* the breach of the primary right of driving on the highways free from negligent interference by other persons, gives rise to the secondary right of damages.

primer election, first choice.

primogeniture, the English right of the eldest born to succeed to the inheritance, to the exclusion of younger children.

principal, the leading, or most important; the original. (2) A person, firm, or corporation from whom an agent derives his authority. (3) A person who is first responsible, and for whose fulfillment of an obligation a surety becomes bound. (4) The chief or actual perpetrator of a crime, as distinguished from the accessory (*q.v.*), who may assist him. (5) The important part of an estate, as distinguished from incidents or accessories. (6) A sum of money loaned, as distinguished from the interest paid for its use.

principal challenge, a challenge (*q.v.*) of a juror for cause.

principal in the first degree, the immediate perpetrator of the crime.

principal in the second degree, abettor; one actually or constructively present at the scene of the crime who aided or encouraged its commission without directly participating.

principia probant, non probantur, principles prove, they are not proven.

principle, an abstract generalization. (2) That which constitutes the essence of a matter, *e.g.*, a new discovery or invention.

principle of law, a rule; a doctrine; an abstract generalization concerning the legal consequences which should be assigned as the result of facts. Courts decide unique factual disputes, and in doing so, either apply former generalizations or generate new ones.

prior tempore, potior lure, first in time, strongest in law.

priority, a precedence or prior right. Often used to denote the relative rights of creditors and lienholders to be paid out of the assets of an insolvent estate, or the liquidation of particular property, in the order of securing their liens.

prisoner, a person who is held in confinement against his will, usually to answer for a crime with which he is charged, or as punishment for a crime of which he has been convicted. When unlawfully confined, he may secure his release by a writ of habeas corpus ad subjiciendum (*q.v.*).

privacy, see *right to privacy.*

Privacy Act of 1974, an act to safeguard individual privacy from the misuse of federal records, to provide that individuals be granted access to records concerning them which are maintained by federal agencies, and to establish a Privacy Protection Study Commission. 5 U.S.C. § 552a.

Privacy Protection Act of 1980, an act to limit governmental search and seizure of documentary materials possessed by persons, and to provide a remedy. 42 U.S.C. § 2000aa *et seq.*

Privacy Protection for Rape Victims Act of 1978, an act to amend the Federal Rules of Evidence (*q.v.*) to provide for the protection of the privacy of rape victims. It deals with the relevance of the victim's past behavior. Fed. R. Evid. 412; 92 Stat. 2046 (1978).

private, affecting or belonging to individuals, as distinguished from the public generally, *e.g.,* private acts or private nuisances.

private carrier, a person who transports merchandise only for those with whom he may choose to contract, and not for anyone in the public at large who may desire to employ him. See also, *carrier.*

private corporation, a corporation incorporated by private individuals for private purposes which has no political or governmental franchises or duties.

private express trust, the relationship under which one person, called the trustee, holds legal title to property for the benefit of one or more other persons, each called the beneficiary or cestui que trust. The person creating the trust is called the settlor. The property held by the trustee is called the corpus, the subject matter of the trust, the trust property, the principal or the res.

private nuisance, see *nuisance.*

private prosecutor, see *prosecutor.*

private waters, in the context of interference with use of water, watercourses (*q.v.*) or lakes whose channels or beds are privately owned, and are not public waters (*q.v.*). Restatement (Second) of Torts § 847A(2).

privateer, a vessel owned by one or more private individuals, armed and equipped at his or their expense, for the purpose of carrying on maritime war under the authority of a belligerent nation.

privatorum conventio juri publico non derogat, the agreement of private individuals cannot derogate from the rights of the public.

privatum commodum publico cedit, private advantage must yield to public.

priv'ies, persons who have an interest in something because of their peculiar relationship to another person. Thus, *e.g.,* an heir is privy in blood to the ancestor; an executor or administrator, privy in representation to the deceased; the lessee privy in estate to the lessor; a person having an interest derived from a contract to which he is not a party is privy to one of the parties.

privilege, an exceptional right or exemption. It is either (a) personal, attached to a person or office; or (b) attached to a thing, sometimes called real. The exemption of ambassadors and members of Congress from arrest while going to, returning from, or attending to the discharge of their public duties, is an example of the first. (2) The fact that conduct which, under ordinary circumstances, would subject an actor (*q.v.*) to liability, under particular circumstances does not subject him to liability. A privilege may be based upon (a) the consent of the other affected by the actor's conduct, or (b) the fact that its exercise is necessary for the protection of some interest of the actor or of the public which is of such importance as to justify the harm caused or threatened by its exercise, or (c) the fact that the actor is performing a function for the proper performance of which freedom of action is essential. Restatement (Second) of Torts § 10. (3) An ordinary right.

privileged communication, see *confidential communications.*

privile'gium, a law relating to or directed against an individual person. (2) A privilege.

privilegium non valet contra rempublicam, a privilege avails not against the interest of the public.

privity, participation in knowledge or interest. Persons who so participate are called privies (*q.v.*). Privity in deed, *i.e.*, by consent of the parties, is opposed to privity in law, *e.g.*, tenant by courtesy.

privy, see *privies.*

priv'y council, a relatively inactive English body, which is theoretically the King's or Queen's private counsel. It has a statutory judicial committee, which hears appeals from ecclesiastical courts, prize courts, colonial courts and from courts in some of the independent countries of the commonwealth.

prize, a vessel or goods captured at sea, from a public enemy in time of war, and which after condemnation becomes the property of the captors.

prize court, a tribunal which adjudicates cases of maritime captures made in time of war, and other matters connected with international law. In the United States, the United States District Courts have exclusive jurisdiction of prize cases.

pro, *l.*, for; as; on account of; according to.

pro bono, or **pro bo'no pu'blico,** for the public or general good.

pro confes'so, as confessed; a judgment (*q.v.*) taken when the defendant in a lawsuit fails to appear or make answer.

pro for'ma, as a matter of form.

pro hac vi'ae, for this occasion.

pro indivi'so, as undivided; descriptive of the possession of lands by joint or co-owners before partition.

pro interes'se su', according to his interest.

pro ra'ta, in proportion.

pro se, for himself or herself.

pro tan'to, for so much; to that extent.

pro tem, or **pro tem'pore,** for the time being.

probable cause, a reasonable ground for suspicion, supported by circumstances sufficiently strong to warrant a cautious person to believe that an accused person is guilty of the offense with which he is charged. (2) Concerning a search, probable cause is a flexible, common-sense standard. It merely requires that the facts available to the officer would warrant a person of reasonable caution in the belief that certain items may be contraband or stolen property or useful as evidence of a crime; it does not demand any showing that the belief is correct or more likely true than false. A practical, nontechnical probability that incriminating evidence is involved is all that is required.

probandi necessitas incumbit illi qui agit, the necessity of proving rests upon him who sues.

probate, proof to a judge of a court which has jurisdiction that an instrument, offered as the last will and testament of a deceased person, is his last will and testament. When proved to the satisfaction of the judge, it is received, filed, and recorded, and is then said to be admitted to probate or probated.

probate court, various state courts which have jurisdiction in the matter of proving wills, appointing executors and administrators, and supervising the administration of estates. See also, *surrogate.*

probate, divorce, and admiralty division, a portion of the English High Court of Justice (*q.v.*).

probation, the delay of the imposition of punishment which has been imposed upon a person who has been convicted of a crime. It is often granted by a court on specific conditions concerning the person's future activities. Ordinarily regulated by various federal and state statutes.

probatis extremis, praesumitur media, the extremes being proved, the mean is presumed.

problem case, see *case.*

proceden'do, a prerogative writ addressed by a superior court to an inferior court, directing the latter to proceed forthwith to judgment. See also, *extraordinary remedy* and *prerogative writs.*

procedure, the manner in which litigants proceed in the adversary conduct of a lawsuit, including the various steps by which the parties go about the litigation process. Occasionally called practice. Usually codified by rules or in codes, *e.g.*, Federal Rules of Civil Procedure (*q.v.*), Federal Rules of Criminal Procedure (*q.v.*), analogous state rules of procedure, and various state codes of practice. See also, *pleadings*.

proceeding, an action at law or a suit in equity. Uniform Probate Code §§ 1-201(32), 5-103(16).

process, the means whereby a court enforces obedience to its orders. Process is termed (a) original, when it is intended to compel the appearance of the defendant; (b) mesne, when issued pending suit to secure the attendance of jurors and witnesses; and (c) final, when issued to enforce execution of a judgment. (2) In patent law, the art or method by which any particular result is produced, *e.g.*, the smelting of ores or the vulcanizing of rubber.

proces-verbal, *fr.*, (*prō sa vǎr bål´*), an authenticated statement of official acts or transactions, made by an official cognizant of them. Cf. *transcript*.

prochein, next.

prochein ami (*prōō shǎn´âmē´*), next friend (*q.v.*).

proclamation, a public announcement made by authority of a chief executive, *e.g.*, President, Governor, or Mayor. (2) The declaration of a bailiff (*q.v.*), made by authority of the court, of what is about to be done.

proctor, an attorney practicing law in an admiralty court.

procuration, agency; the act by which one person authorizes another to act in his place; a letter of attorney.

procurator, a person who acts for another by virtue of a procuration (*q.v.*).

product liability, the portion of American law which deals with the responsibility of a manufacturer or seller of merchandise, to the buyer and other persons affected by the merchandise, concerning the quality of the merchandise and the consequences resulting from a lack of quality in the merchandise.

profert, *l.*, he produces; a declaration in the record of a lawsuit that a party alleging a deed in his pleadings produces it in court.

professional association, a group of professional people organized to practice their profession together, but not necessarily in corporate or partnership form.

professional privilege, see *confidential communications*.

professional service corporation, a corporation (*q.v.*) which is organized by individuals who are licensed to render a professional service, *e.g.*, attorneys, dentists, or physicians, for the purpose of rendering those professional services to the public via the corporate organization, and not as individual practitioners. Usually authorized and regulated, and often defined, by various state statutes.

proffer, to offer, present, or propose.

profit, gain; income of money or land, in which latter sense it is generally used in the plural. By gross profits, it is frequently meant the difference between the price at which goods are sold and that paid for their purchase. By net profits is understood the real profit, or gain, ascertained by deducting from gross profits all expenses of handling, storing, selling and delivery.

profit a prendre (*prō fē tå prôn dr'*), the right to take something, *e.g.*, minerals, gravel, or soil, from the land of another.

progressive tax, a tax that increases in percentage as taxpayers' income levels increase; a high income taxpayer will pay a higher percentage of his/her income than would a low-income taxpayer.

prohibition, formerly, national laws prohibiting the manufacture and sale of intoxicating liquors in the United States. Cf. *local option.* See also, *prohibition, writ of.*

prohibition, writ of, an order or mandate from a superior court to prevent an inferior court from taking cognizance of, or determining, a matter which is outside of its jurisdiction.

pro'licide, the destruction of human offspring; it includes feticide and infanticide.

prolix'ity, a long and unnecessary statement of facts in a pleading or affidavit.

promise, an engagement or undertaking for the performance or non-performance of a particular thing. (2) In commercial paper transactions, an undertaking to pay, which is more than an acknowledgment of an obligation. U.C.C. § 3-102(1)(c). (3) A manifestation of intention to act or refrain from acting in a specified way, so made as to justify a promisee (*q.v.*) in understanding that a commitment has been made. Restatement (Second) of Contracts § 2(1).

promisee, a person to whom a promise is made. Accord, Restatement (Second) of Contracts § 2(3).

promisor, a person who makes or gives a promise. Accord, Restatement (Second) of Contracts § 2(2).

promissory estoppel, a promise by which the promisor should reasonably expect to induce action or forebearance of a definite and substantial character on the part of the promisee, and which does induct such action or forebearance. Such a promise is binding if injustice can be avoided only by enforcement of the promise. See also, *contracts*.

promissory note, an unconditional promise in writing, made by one person to another, signed by the maker, engaging to pay on demand or at a definite time, a sum certain in money, to the order of such other, or to bearer. U.C.C. § 3-104(1), (2).

promoter, one who, acting alone or in conjunction with one or more other persons, directly or indirectly takes initiative in founding and organizing the business or enterprise of an issuer.

proof, the establishing of the truth of an allegation by evidence (*q.v.*). (2) The evidence itself. The person claiming the affirmative of an allegation ordinarily has the necessity of proving it; this is called the onus probandi, or burden of proof. (3) The affidavits made to support a claim or statement of fact, which is doubted or disputed or of which a person acting in a representative capacity requires evidence under oath.

proof of claim, the sworn statement of a claimant under an insurance contract, or of a principal witness, as to the time and manner of a loss. Usually required by insurers as a prerequisite to a demand for payment of a loss. Occasionally called a preliminary proof. (2) Various official forms for the purpose of asserting the rights of creditors in bankruptcy proceedings.

proper, genuine, suitable, or correct. (2) Occasionally, that which is one's own.

property, a very extensive and flexible term for various rights of ownership; this may be (a) general or absolute; (b) special or qualified, as in the case of a bailee for a special purpose. (2) Everything that is owned. In this sense it is (a) real, or (b) personal. (3) Anything that may be the subject of ownership. Uniform Probate Code § 1-201(33); accord, § 5-103(17).

property tax, a tax conditioned on ownership of property and measured by the value of such; this form of tax includes general property taxes related to property as a whole in addition to real and personal tangible, whether taxed at a single rate or classified rates. Real property includes all lands, buildings, and fixtures thereon and appurtenances thereto. Personal property is not included as part of the real estate and pertains only to inventories and other properties owned by commercial enterprises. Property taxation represents a system of uniform taxation of real and personal property when such is not exempt by provision of law.

propinquity, relationship; near kindred.

proportional tax, a tax that exacts the same percentage of family income regardless of the income level.

proposal, a formal offer to do something.

pro'pria perso'na, see *in propria persona.*

proprietary functions, acts which are performed by a municipality for the improvement of the territory within the corporate limits. (2) The doing of such things as inure to the benefit, pecuniarily or otherwise, of the municipality.

proprietor, a person who has property rights in something; an owner.

proprietorship, or **sole proprietorship,** occasionally, an unincorporated business owned solely by one person.

prop'ter, *l.*, for; on account of.

prop'ter affec'tum, formerly, a challenge to a juror on account of some bias or affection.

prop'ter defec'tum, formerly, a challenge to a juror on account of some defect or incapacity.

prop'ter delic'tum, formerly, a challenge to a juror on account of crime.

prorogation, a putting off to another time, or postponement. Cf. *continuance.*

prosecutor, a person who brings an action against another in the name of the government. A public prosecutor is an officer appointed or elected to conduct all prosecutions in behalf of the government. A private prosecutor is an individual who, not holding office, conducts an accusation against another. Occasionally, an aggrieved person will employ a private attorney to serve as a private prosecutor.

prospective heir, an heir who may inherit but who may be excluded. A prospective heir includes an heir apparent and an heir presumptive. An heir apparent is one who is certain to inherit unless excluded by valid will. An heir presumptive is a person who will inherit if the potential intestate dies immediately, but who will be excluded if relatives closer in relationship to the intestate are born.

prospectus, a document issued and distributed with the objective of interesting prospective investors, *e.g.,* in a corporation, setting forth the objects of the proposed undertaking and inviting persons to subscribe for shares.

prostitute, a woman who indiscriminately engages in sexual intercourse, usually for hire.

prostitution, engaging in sexual activity for hire.

protected person, a minor or other person for whom a conservator has been appointed or other protective order has been made. Uniform Probate Code § 5-103(18).

Protection of Children Against Sexual Exploitation Act of 1977, an act concerning punishment of persons who employ, use, persuade, induce, entice, or coerce a minor to engage in sexually explicit conduct for the purpose of producing a visual or print medium depicting such conduct, certain activities relating to material involving the sexual exploitation of minors, and the transportation of minors. 18 U.S.C. §§ 2251-2253.

protective proceeding, a proceeding (*q.v.*) under the provisions of Part 4 of Article V of the Uniform Probate Code. Uniform Probate Code § 5-103(19).

protest, a solemn declaration of opinion, usually of dissent. (2) An express reservation, whereby a person protects himself against the effects of any admission that might be implied from his act, *e.g.*, payment under protest. (3) In commercial paper transactions, a certificate of dishonor (*q.v.*), made under the hand and seal of a United States consul or vice consul or a notary public or other person authorized to certify dishonor by the law of the place where dishonor occurs. It may be made upon information satisfactory to such person. U.C.C. § 3-509(1). (4) A document drawn by the master of a ship, and formally attested, stating the circumstances under which damage has happened to the ship or her cargo.

prothonotary, occasionally, a court clerk or the chief clerk of a court.

pro'tocol (prō tō cōl), in international law, a record of preliminary negotiations. (2) Prescribed formalities.

province, a territorial division or a colony of a country. (2) Duty; power; responsibility; *e.g.*, it is the province of the court to judge the law, that of the jury to decide the facts.

provisional, temporary; made or existing for a time or until something further is done, *e.g.*, provisional orders or appointments.

provisional director, a temporary director appointed by the court with the same rights and duties as other directors.

provi'so, it being provided; a condition or stipulation, *e.g.*, a proviso for redemption.

proximate cause, something which produces a result, and without which the result could not have occurred. (2) Any original event which in natural unbroken sequence produces a particular foreseeable result, without which the result would not have occurred.

proxy, a person appointed by another to represent him, usually at a meeting, *e.g.*, of stockholders in a corporation or of creditors. (2) The writing by which the appointment is made.

proxy marriage, see *marriage by proxy.*

PSD, see *prevention of significant deterioration.*

psychological parent, one who on a continuing, day-to-day basis, through interaction, companionship, interplay, and mutuality, fulfills the child's psychological needs for a parent, as well as the child's physical needs. The psychological parent may be a biological, adoptive, foster, or common-law parent, or any other person. ·

puberty, the age of fourteen in males and twelve in females.

public, the whole body politic; all of the citizens of a nation, state, city, or community. (2) That which affects, or is open or related to, all persons, as distinguished from private. (3) As it relates to disorderly conduct (*q.v.*), affecting or likely to affect persons in a place to which the public or a substantial group has access, *e.g.,* highways, transport facilities, schools, prisons, apartment houses, places of business or amusement, or a neighborhood. Model Penal Code § 250.2(1).

public charity, a benevolence or philanthropy, in which there is a benefit conferred on the public at large, or some portion thereof, or upon an indefinite class of persons. See also, *charitable use.*

public corporation, a corporation created by the state for political or governmental purposes.

public figure, in the law of libel and slander, a person who has assumed a role of special prominence in the affairs of society, *e.g.,* persons occupying positions of such persuasive power and influence that they are deemed public figures for all purposes, and persons who have thrust themselves to the forefront of particular public controversies in order to influence the resolution of the issues involved.

public invitee, see *invitee* (2).

public nuisance, see *nuisance.*

public officer, see *officer.*

public policy, a highly flexible term of imprecise definition, for the consideration of what is expedient for the community concerned. (2) The principle of law which holds that no person can do that which has a tendency to be injurious to the public, or against the public good. (3) The statutes and precedents, and not the general considerations of public interest.

public prosecutor, see *prosecutor.*

public service corporation, a business organization which supplies the public with utilities, *e.g.,* gas, water, and electricity.

public use, the justification to acquire property by eminent domain (*q.v.*). (2) In some jurisdictions, strictly and narrowly, use by the public. (3) In other jurisdictions, including U.S. Supreme Court, public advantage. (4) What is public use frequently and largely depends on various facts and circumstances surrounding the proposed acquisition.

public waters, in the context of interference with use of water, navigable (*q.v.*) waters of the United States, watercourses (*q.v.*) and lakes navigable under the law of the state in which they are located, and watercourses and lakes that are open to public use or subject to public protection and control by virtue of state law. Restatement (Second) of Torts § 847A(1).

publication, a making public. (2) Of a libel or other defamatory matter, bringing it to the knowledge or notice of a third person. Accord, Restatement (Second) of Torts §§ 577, 630. (3) Of a will, its acknowledgment by the testator, in the presence of witnesses, as his last will.

pu'blici ju'ris, *l.,* of public right.

PUD, see *planned unit development.*

puff, a general estimate, loosely given as a matter of opinion. See also, *puffing.*

puffer, a person who attends an auction by arrangement with the vendor for the purpose of bidding and thereby raising the price. See also, *by-bidding.*

puffing, the expression by a seller of an opinion which is favorable to the item he is selling.

puis darrein continuance (*pwē då rān´*), *fr.,* since the last adjournment.

puisne (*pū´ nĭ*), (*L. fr.*) see *pur,* later born. (2) Later in date, *e.g.,* an incumbrance. (3) Lower in rank.

punitive damages, see *damages.*

pur (purpose), *L. fr.,* by; for; during.

pur autre vie, see *per autre vie.*

purchase money mortgage, any mortgage given by the vendor to secure the payment of all or a portion of the purchase price.

purchaser, a person who acquires by buying. (2) A person who acquires real property otherwise than by descent. (3) A person who takes by sale, discount, negotiation, mortgage, pledge, lien, issue or re-issue, gift, or any other voluntary transaction creating an interest in property. U.C.C. § 1-201(32), (33).

purchaser for value, a person who acquires property in exchange for a valuable consideration. Such a consideration may be the complete satisfaction and discharge of an antecedent debt.

purge, to clear one's self of a criminal charge or a contempt.

purposely, descriptive of an act of the will, of an act by intention, or of an act by design.

pursuit of happiness, an imprecise term for personal freedom or liberty, *e.g.,* privileges of family and home, right to own property, or right to pursue any occupation or profession without restrictions that are not imposed upon others in a similar situation.

purview, the body of a statute, as distinguished from the preamble. (2) The general scope or object of a statute.

put, an option which permits a holder to sell a certain stock at a fixed price for a stated quantity and within a stated period.

putative, supposed; reputed.

putative marriage, a doctrine allowing a putative spouse to acquire the same rights as a legal spouse. Its purpose is to try to safeguard the economic interests of a party to a void or voidable marriage who cohabits in good faith belief that the marriage was valid.

putative spouse, a person who has cohabited with another to whom he is not legally married, in the good faith belief that he was married to that person, until knowledge of the fact that he is not legally married terminates his status and prevents acquisition of future rights. Uniform Marriage and Divorce Act § 209.

pyramiding, trading on margin, in which the trader uses his profits from one transaction to buy or sell additional amounts.

Q

qdro, see *qualified domestic relations order.*

QTIP trust, refers to qualified terminal interest property trust; a trust that affords surviving spouses some declaration options on whether they wish to take full advantage of the marital deduction under most estate distribution schemes. Requirements of a QTIP trust include, (1) property must pass to surviving spouse from decedent, (2) income must be distributed at least on an annual basis, (3) no power of appointment in surviving spouse or others to benefit anyone except surviving spouse during surviving spouse's lifetime, (4) donor must direct and/or executor must irrevocably elect on return, and (5) property will be included in surviving spouse's estate for federal tax purposes.

qua, in the character of.

quacum'que vi'a (data), *l.,* whichever way it is taken.

quae communi legi derogant stricte interpretantur, those things which derogate from the common law are to be strictly construed.

quae contra rationem juris introducta sunt, non debent trahi in consequentiam, things introduced contrary to the spirit of the law ought not to be drawn into a precedent.

quae est ea'dem, *l.,* which is the same.

quae in curia regis acta sunt rite agi praesumuntur, things done in court are presumed to be rightly done.

quae non valeant singula, juncta juvant, things which may not avail singly are effective when united.

quaecumque intra rationem legis inveniuntur, intra legem ipsam esse judicantur, those things which are within the reason of a law are considered to be within the law itself.

quaelibet concessio fortissime contra donatorem interpretanda est, every grant is to be construed most strongly against the grantor.

quaere, *l.,* inquire; meaning that the question or proposition, to which the word is appended is a doubtful one. Cf. *quare.*

quaestus (Rom.), the estate which a person has by acquisition or purchase, in contradistinction to haereditas, which he has by descent.

qualification, that which makes a person fit or eligible for an office or position or to exercise a franchise, *e.g.,* voting. See also, *qualify.* (2) A limitation; diminution.

qualified, limited.

qualified domestic relations order, qdro; an award to the nonemployee spouse of a specific share of the periodic pension benefits the employee spouse will receive in the future based on the percentage of future pension payments attributable to the period of the marriage prior to the commencement of the divorce action.

qualified indorsement, a writing put on the back of a bill or promissory note, without recourse, *i.e.,* giving no right to resort to the indorser for payment. See also, *indorsement* (2).

qualified nuisance, as distinguished from absolute nuisance, something lawfully, but so negligently or carelessly, done or permitted as to create a potential and unreasonable risk of harm which in due course results in injury to another. See also, *nuisance.*

qualify, to take the oath of an office to which a person has been appointed or elected and execute any necessary bond.

quality, the nature of an estate (*q.v.*) in property, as regards the time of its commencement or the certainty of its duration. (2) The state or condition of persons or goods.

quamdi'u se be'ne ges'seret, *l.,* as long as he shall conduct himself properly, *i.e.,* during good behavior.

quan'do acci'derint, *l.,* a judgment against an executor or administrator, to be enforced when assets come into his hands.

quando aliquid mandatur, mandatur et omne per quod pervenitur ad illud, when anything is commanded, everything by which it can be accomplished is commanded.

quando aliquid prohibetur ex directo, prohibetur et per obliquum, when a thing is forbidden to be done directly, it is also forbidden to be done indirectly.

quando aliquis aliquid concedit, concedere videtur et id sine quo res uti non potest, when a person grants a thing, he is supposed to grant also that without which the thing cannot be used.

quando lex aliquid alicui concedit, concedere videtur et id sine quo res ipsa esse non potest, when the law gives a man anything, it gives him also that without which the thing cannot exist.

quando res non valet ut age valeat quantum valere potest, when any instrument does not operate in the way I intend, let it operate as far as it can.

quando verba statuti sunt specialia, ratio autem generalis, generaliter statutum est intelligendum, when the words of a statute are special, but its object general, it is to be construed as general.

quantity, a characteristic which is ascertained by weighing or measuring. (2) The duration of an estate (*q.v.*) in property or degree of an interest.

quan'tum, *l.,* how much; as much as.

quan'tum damnifica'tus, under older rules of practice, an issue out of chancery to be tried at common law, asking how much the plaintiff was damaged.

quan'tum me'ruit, as much as he has earned; a theory of recovery in which one party to a contract sues the other, not on the contract itself, but on an implied promise to pay for so much as the party suing has done. If one party refuses to perform his part, the other may rescind and sue on a quantum meruit.

quan'tum vale'bant, as much as they were worth; a theory of recovery for goods which have been supplied and no price for which was mentioned, *e.g.,* by an innkeeper to a guest, or where they are not supplied as ordered and are yet not returned.

quarantine, enforced detention, which is authorized by various federal and state statutes, for the purpose of preventing the spread of contagious diseases.

qua're, *l.,* wherefore; why. Cf. *quaere.*

qua're clau'sum fre'git, trespass (*q.v.*), consisting of an unauthorized entry on the land of another.

qua're eje'cit in'fra ter'minum, formerly, a writ against a person who ejected another during the currency of a term created by the former.

qua're obstrux'it, formerly, a writ which lay for a person who was obstructed in his right to pass over another person's land.

quarter days, Lady day, March 25th; Midsummer day, June 24th; Michaelmas day, September 29th; Christmas day, December 25th.

quarter sessions, general, an English court of record held by justices of the peace for the finding of indictments by the grand jury, the trial of enumerated major and minor offenses, and the hearing of certain appeals.

quash, to annul or suppress, *e.g.,* an indictment, a conviction, or an order.

qua'si, *l.,* as if; almost. Often used to indicate significant similarity or likeness to the word that follows, while denoting that the word that follows must be considered in a flexible sense.

quasi contract, an obligation which arises without express agreement between the parties; an implied contract. Cf. *unjust enrichment.*

quasi in rem, proceedings, the purpose of which is to affect the interest of the defendant in specific real property within the state, which at the outset of the proceeding has been brought within the control of the court.

quasi partner, a joint owner; a tenant in common; a person who has an undivided interest in property.

quasi personalty, items which are personal property in law, though appertaining to real property, *e.g.,* emblements or fixtures.

quasi realty, property which in law appertains to, and passes as, realty, though it is actually personal property, *e.g.,* heirlooms and title deeds.

quasi trustee, a person who reaps a benefit from a breach of trust, and therefore becomes answerable to the beneficiary of the trust as if he were the trustee. See also, *trust.*

que estate (kwē), *l.,* whose estate.

queen's counsel, see *king's counsel.*

question, an interrogatory. (2) An issue to be decided in a court of law. It may be a question of law, or a question of fact.

qui approbat non reprobat, he who accepts [in part] cannot reject.

qui bene interrogat, bene docet, he who interrogates well, teaches well.

qui destruit medium, destruit finem, he who destroys the means destroys the end.

qui facit per alium facit per se, *l.*, he who acts through another acts by or for himself; the doctrine of respondeat superior in the law of agency.

qui haeret in litera, haeret in cortice, he who sticks at the letter sticks in the bark, *i.e.*, does not get at the solid substance of the law.

qui in jus dominiumve alterius succedit jure ejus uti debet, he who succeeds to the right or property of another should also perform his duties, *e.g.*, the heir is subject to the debts of his ancestor to the extent of any property coming to his hands as such.

qui in utero est pro jam nato habetur, quoties de ejus commodo quaeritur, he who is in the womb is held as already born, whenever his benefit is in question.

qui jure suo utitur, nemini facit injuriam, he who uses his legal rights harms no one.

qui male agit, odit lucem, he who acts badly hates the light.

qui mandat ipse fecisse videtur, he who gives the order is taken to be himself the doer. Cf. *qui facit per alium, etc.*

qui nascitur sine legitimo matrimonio, matrem sequitur, he who is born out of wedlock follows the condition of his mother.

qui non habet in aere luat in corpore, ne quis peccetur impune, he who cannot pay with his purse must suffer in his person, lest he who offends should go unpunished.

qui non improbat, approbat, he who does not disapprove approves.

qui non prohibet quod prohibere potest, assentire videtur, he who does not forbid what he can forbid is understood to assent.

qui parcit nocentibus, innocentes punit, he who spares the guilty punishes the innocent.

qui per fraudem agit, frustra agit, what a man does fraudulently, he does in vain [because the courts will give relief against him].

qui prior est tempore, potior est jure, he who is first in time is stronger in law.

qui rationem in omnibus quaerunt, rationem subvertunt, he who seeks a reason for everything subverts reason.

qui sentit commodum, sentire debet et onus, he who receives the advantage ought also to bear the burden.

qui tacet, consentire videtur, he who is silent is understood to consent.

qui tam, an action in which the plaintiff states that he is suing for the state as well as himself.

qui tam action, a lawsuit on a penal statute, which is partly for the benefit of the state and partly for the benefit of an informer.

qui tardius solvit, minus solvit, he who pays too late pays too little.

qui vult decipi decipiatur, let him be deceived who wishes to be deceived, *i.e.,* the court will not relieve a person who has been guilty of negligence so gross as to invite deception.

qui'a, *l.,* because.

qui'a ti'met, because of fears; a form of lawsuit which originated in equity, and which is filed to protect property from future injury. *E.g.,* a lawsuit which seeks the cancellation of an instrument that serves to cloud the title to real property.

quicquid plantatur solo, solo cedit, whatever is affixed to the soil passes with a grant of the soil.

quicquid solvitur, solvitur secundum modum solventis, whatever is paid is paid according to the direction of the payer, *i.e.,* the debtor may state, at the time of payment, which of two or more debts he intends to liquidate.

quid pro quo, *l.,* something for something; a consideration.

Quiet Communities Act of 1978, an act to extend provisions of the Noise Control Act of 1972 (*q.v.*) for one year, and for other purposes. It provides for public information and research to promote the development of noise control programs and grants to states, local governments, and regional planning agencies. 42 U.S.C. §§ 4901, 4905, 4910, 4913, 4918.

quiet enjoyment, the name of a covenant in a lease, by which the lessor warrants that the lessee shall not be disturbed in his possession. It does not amount to a warranty of title.

quie'tus, freed or acquitted; a written discharge or release, which is given to a public officer when he faithfully accounts for the public funds which he has collected and turns them over to the public treasury.

quilibet potest renunciare jure pro se introducto, anyone may give up a right introduced for his own benefit.

quitclaim, to release a claim or right of action.

quitclaim deed, a written instrument that transfers a party's rights or claims concerning particular property, whatever those rights or claims might be. It is usually used to voluntarily divest a party of his or her undetermined rights and claims, and to merge them into the title of an owner who desires to perfect his title to the property.

quittance, an acquittance or release.

quo a'nimo, *l.,* (with what mind), the intent.

quo ligatur eo dissolvitur, as an obligation is contracted, so it must be dissolved, *e.g.,* a deed by a deed.

quo warran'to, by what authority; a proceeding by which the court inquires into the right of a person or corporation to hold an office or to excercise a franchise.

quo'ad, as far as.

quoad hoc, as to this.

quod ab initio valet, in tractu temporis non convalescet, that which is invalid in its commencement gains no strength by lapse of time.

quod compu'tat, an interlocutory judgment or decree that the defendant account.

quod contra legem fit, pro infecto habetur, what is done contrary to law is considered as not done, *i.e.,* no one can derive lawful advantage from it.

quod datum est ecclesiae, datum est Deo, what is given to the church is given to God.

quod dubitas, ne feceris, when you doubt about a thing, do not do it.

quod fieri debet, facile praesumitur, that which ought to be done is easily presumed.

quod fieri non debet, factum valet, that which ought not to be done is [sometimes] valid when done, *e.g.,* a marriage without the proper consents.

quod necessitas cogit, excusat, that which necessity compels she excuses, *i.e.,* a person is not held criminally responsible for actions which he or she is forced to commit.

quod nullius est, est domini regis, that which is the property of nobody belongs to our lord the King.

quod per me non possum, nec per alium, what I cannot do myself, I cannot do by another, *i.e.,* a person cannot delegate a power he does not himself possess.

quod pure debetur, praesenti die debetur, that which is due unconditionally is due at once.

quod recu'peret, that he do recover the debt or damages; a final judgment for plaintiff in a personal action.

quod semel placit in electione, amplius displicere non potest, when election is once made it cannot be revoked.

quod tacite intelligitur, deesse non videtur, what is tacitly assumed does not appear to be wanting.

quod ultra, as to the rest.

quod vanum et inutile est, lex non requirit, the law does not require what is vain and useless.

quorum, the minimum number of members, *e.g.,* directors on a board of directors or members of a legislative body, which is necessary to be present in order to constitute a meeting capable of transacting business.

quoties in verbis nulla est ambiguitas, ibi nulla expositio contra verba fienda est, where there is no ambiguity in the words of an instrument, no interpretation should be given to it contrary to the words, *i.e.,* parol evidence to contradict or vary the clear words of a written instrument is inadmissible.

R

Racketeer Influenced and Corrupt Organizations, or **RICO, Act,** title IX of the Organized Crime Control Act of 1970, (*q.v.*). Among other things, it deals with prohibited racketeering activities, criminal penalties, civil remedies, venue and process, expedition of actions, evidence, and demands by the Attorney General for documentary materials relevant to a racketeering investigation. 18 U.S.C. §§ 1961-1968.

RACT, see *reasonably available control technology.*

Railway Labor Act, an act to provide for the prompt disposition of disputes between carriers and their employees. 45 U.S.C. §§ 151 *et seq.;* 44 Stat. 577 (1926).

raised crops, various cultivated plants or fruit grown to maturity, but as yet unharvested.

rape, the act of having sexual intercourse with a woman by force and against her will. Often defined by various state statutes. (2) The act of a male who has sexual intercourse with a female not his wife, if: (a) he compels her to submit by force or by threat of imminent death, serious bodily injury, extreme pain or kidnapping, to be inflicted on anyone; or (b) he has substantially impaired her power to appraise or control her conduct by administering or employing without her knowledge, drugs, intoxicants, or other means for the purpose of preventing resistance; or (c) the female is unconscious; or (d) the female is less than 10 years old. Model Penal Code § 213.1(1). Cf. *gross sexual imposition.*

Rape Victims Privacy Act, see *Privacy Protection for Rape Victims Act of 1978.*

rasure, see *erasure.*

rate, the amount which a public regulatory agency authorizes a public utility to charge for its products or services. (2) The valuation which is assigned to a decedent's estate, for purposes of taxation.

rate of exchange, the price at which a bill of exchange (*q.v.*), drawn in one country upon a person resident in another country may be sold in the former.

ratification, the act of adopting or confirming an act or undertaking, done or made by another without authority, or by the person himself at a time when he was legally incompetent to do so. Cf. *recognition*.

ratihabitio mandato aequiparatur, ratification is equivalent to a command.

ra'tio deciden'di, *l.*, the reason for the decision in a unique lawsuit. (2) The determining factor in a court's decision, variously identified as being what judges said, or what they did, in precedent cases.

ratio legis est anima legis, the reason of the law is the life of the law.

ratio'nes, formerly, the pleadings in a lawsuit.

rattening, the taking away or hiding of the tools, clothes, or other property of a workman, in order to compel him to join a union or to cease working.

ravish, to rape (*q.v.*).

ravishment, occasionally, the taking away of a wife from her husband or a ward from his guardian. See also, *ravish*. Cf. *abduction*.

ready, willing, and able, descriptive of a person who, although he does not have the cash in hand, is able to command the necessary funds to complete his obligations under a contract within the time allowed.

real, pertaining to land or buildings, as opposed to personal property (*q.v.*). Cf. *chattels*.

real action, a lawsuit initiated for the specific recovery of lands, buildings, and hereditaments.

real contract, an agreement concerning real property.

real covenant, a promise or obligation in a conveyance of real property, by which the grantor binds himself and his heirs to do, or to refrain from doing, something with reference to the estate conveyed.

real estate, see *real property*.

Real Estate Settlement Procedures Act, an act to further the national housing goal of encouraging home ownership by regulating certain lending practices and closing and settlement procedures in federally related mortgage transactions, and for other purposes. Among other things, it deals with uniform settlement statements, special information booklets, kickbacks, unearned fees, title companies, and liability of the seller. 12 U.S.C. §§ 2601 *et seq*.

real fixture, personal property which has become a part of the land by reason of the annexor's intention at time of annexation. See also, *fixture*.

real party in interest, a person who, under the provisions of substantive law, owns the rights which are sought to be enforced in a lawsuit.

real property, real estate, or **realty,** all land and buildings, including estates and interests in land and buildings which are held for life, but not for years, or some greater estate therein. (2) Real property includes land and any interest or estate in land. Uniform Partnership Act § 2.

real right (Sc.), a privilege concerning property, entitling the owner to initiate a lawsuit for possession, as opposed to a right against a person or personal right.

real things, property which is substantial and immovable, and the rights and profits annexed to or issuing out of them.

realty, see *real property.*

reasonable accommodation, a term used in the Americans with Disabilities Act of 1990 which means (a) making existing facilities used by employees readily accessible to and usable by individuals with disabilities; and (b) job restructuring, part-time or modified work schedules, reassignment to a vacant position, acquisition or modification of equipment or devices, appropriate adjustment or modifications of examinations, training materials or policies, the provision of qualified readers or interpreters, and other similar accommodations for individuals with disabilities.

reasonable belief, see *reasonably believes.*

reasonable care, or **ordinary care,** an imprecise term for the conduct of a reasonably prudent person under similar circumstances. See also, *negligence* and *reasonable man.*

reasonable certainty, or **reasonable medical certainty,** descriptive of the quality of proof necessary to authorize recovery for permanent personal injuries; a qualified medical opinion, based on reasonable probability, which takes the fact of damages out of the area of speculation.

reasonable doubt, a doubt based on reason which arises from the evidence or lack of evidence. (2) The state of mind of jurors in which, after the comparison and consideration of all the evidence, they cannot say that they feel an abiding conviction to a moral certainty of the truth of a criminal charge against a defendant.

reasonable man, a person exercising those qualities of attention, knowledge, intelligence, and judgment which society requires of its members for the protection of their own interests and the interests of others. A fictitious person who is never negligent, and whose conduct is always up to standard. Restatement (Second) of Torts § 283, Comments b & c.

reasonable medical certainty, see *reasonable certainty.*

reasonable time, any time fixed by agreement, which is not manifestly unreasonable. What is a reasonable time for taking any action depends on the nature, purpose, and circumstances of such action. U.C.C. § 1-204(1), (2).

reasonably available control technology, RACT; devices, systems, process modifications, or other apparatus or techniques, the application of which will achieve emission limitations established by the EPA, taking into account the necessity of imposing such limitations to maintain air quality standards, the social and economic impacts of imposing such limitation and alternative means available for achieving the air quality standards.

reasonably believes, or **reasonable belief,** designates a belief which an actor is not reckless or negligent in holding. Model Penal Code § 1.13(16).

rebate, discount; a deduction from a payment.

rebut, to disprove; answer. (2) To repel or bar, *e.g.,* a claim.

rebuttal evidence, see *rebutting evidence.*

rebutter, under old forms of pleading, the response of a defendant to a plaintiff's surrejoinder. Cf. *pleadings.*

rebutting evidence, or **rebuttal evidence,** proof which is given by one party in a lawsuit to explain or disprove evidence produced by the other party.

recall, in some states, a procedure by which a popularly elected official may be retired from office before the expiration of his term, as the result of a subsequent vote of the people.

recaption, self-help; the right of a person who has been deprived of his goods, wife, or child by another, to retake them, provided he does so without a breach of the peace.

recapture, the recovery by force of property captured by an enemy.

receipt, an acknowledgment in writing of having received a sum of money or an article. It is presumptive evidence that the person signing it has received the money or articles described therein, but it is not conclusive and the party may show that it was obtained by fraud or through mistake.

receiver, or **receiver pendente lite,** a person appointed by order of court to receive the rents and profits of property where it is desirable that they should come into the hands of a responsible and impartial person, *e.g.,* in actions for dissolution of partnership and foreclosure of mortgage. Cf. *commissioner (1)* and *trustee in bankruptcy.*

receivership, a proceeding in which a person or entity, called a receiver, is appointed to preserve the assets of an insolvent corporation, partnership, or individual for the benefit of creditors.

receiving, acquiring possession, control, or title, or lending on the security of the property. Model Penal Code § 223.6.

receiving stolen goods, the offense of knowingly accepting, buying, or concealing goods and chattels (*q.v.*) which were illegally obtained by another person. Often defined by various state statutes.

receiving stolen property, purposely receiving (*q.v.*), retaining, or disposing of movable property of another, knowing that it has been stolen, or believing that it has probably been stolen, unless the property is received, retained, or disposed with purpose to restore it to the owner. Model Penal Code § 223.6.

recession, see *rescission.*

recidivism, the act of committing an offense, or various offenses, repeatedly; the practice of being a career criminal. See also, *habitual criminal statute.*

reciprocal contract, an agreement by which the parties enter into mutual engagements, *e.g.,* sale or partnership.

reciprocity, mutuality (*q.v.*); specially applied to treaty dealings between nations.

recital, a statement in a written instrument of something which has occurred. Recitals lead up to, and explain, the operative part, and are either introductory or narrative. Recitals in a deed are binding upon the party making them, and his privies.

reckless disregard of safety, an actor's (*q.v.*) conduct, if he does an act or intentionally fails to do an act which it is his duty to the other to do, knowing or having reason to know of facts which would lead a reasonable man (*q.v.*) to realize, not only that his conduct creates an unreasonable risk of physical harm to another, but also that such risk is substantially greater than that which is necessary to make his conduct negligent. Sometimes called wanton or willful misconduct. Restatement (Second) of Torts § 500.

reckless driving, various offenses pertaining to the operation of a motor vehicle in such a manner as to indicate a wilful disregard for the lives or safety of the public. Usually defined by various state statutes.

recklessness, careless, heedless, indifferent, wanton conduct; a state of mind which disregards the possibility or probability of injurious consequences, or although foreseeing such consequences continues in spite of them.

recklessly endangering, recklessly engaging in conduct which places or may place another person in danger of death or serious bodily injury. Recklessness and danger are presumed where a person knowingly points a firearm at or in the direction of another, whether or not the actor believes the firearm to be loaded. Model Penal Code § 211.2.

reclaim, to demand again; to claim anew or repossess. (2) To put waste or wild lands, or lands injured by incursions of rivers or the sea, in a cultivated and fruitful condition.

recognition, an express or implied acknowledgment that an act done for a person, by another, was done by authority of the former, Cf. *ratification.*

recognitors, formerly, a jury.

recognizance, or **recognizance bond,** an obligation or acknowledgment of a debt in a court of law with a condition that the debt shall be void on the performance of a stipulated undertaking, *e.g.,* to appear before the proper court, to keep the peace, or to pay the debt, interest, and costs that the plaintiff may recover.

reconven'tio (Rom.), a counterclaim or cross-action.

reconversion, the return to its original condition, in contemplation of law, of property which has been constructively converted. Cf. *conversion (3)(b).*

reconveyance, the act or instrument by which real property, which has been transferred to someone, is transferred back to the original grantor. (2) Occasionally, the act or instrument by which a mortgagee, on being paid off, conveys the mortgaged property back to the mortgagor.

record, a written memorial of the actions of a legislature or of a court. (2) The copy of a deed or other instrument relating to real property, officially preserved in a public office.

record, court of, see *court.*

record, debts of, sums certain in money, which appear to be due by the evidence of a court of record, *e.g.,* judgments. See also, *debt.*

recorder, in some states, a public officer who has charge of the records of deeds and instruments relating to real property, and other legal instruments required by law to be recorded.

recoupment, a form of set-off or counterclaim; the right of the defendant to set up a claim for damages against the plaintiff in the same lawsuit, because of the plaintiff's violation of some obligation growing out of the contract on which he sues, or for some failure of consideration.

recourse, the right of a holder of a negotiable instrument to look to the original payee, or a previous indorser, for its payment, in case it is not paid by the maker. See also, *indorsement.*

recovery, the obtaining of an object or money via a lawsuit.

recreational use statute, a statute in partial derogation of the common law rule rendering owners and occupiers of property liable to persons permitted to enter as "licensees," imposing on them an affirmative duty to inspect for and remedy or warn of hazards. Under typical recreational use statutes, owners or occupiers who permit access for specified recreational uses have no affirmative duty to keep the premises safe for entry or use, and are not responsible for injuries caused by the act of a recreational user.

recrimination, a defense in a lawsuit for divorce, by which it is established that the complaining party is guilty of misconduct equal to the misconduct of the defendant. In such a case, the court has discretion to deny a divorce for that reason.

rectification, see *reformation.*

recto, breve de, see *breve de recto.*

recuperatores (Rom.), judges.

recurrent insanity, insanity (*q.v.*) which is temporary in character and which returns from time to time.

recusal, the process by which a judge is disqualified from a case on the objection of either party or on his own motion because of self interest, bias or prejudice.

recusation, civil law term to the effect that a judge is disqualified from hearing a case because of interest or prejudice; a method by which an heir declares he will not be heir.

redden'do sing'ula sing'ulis, *l.,* by applying each term to its correlative; a rule of construction.

redden'dum, the clause in a lease reserving rent.

redeemable bonds, or **callable bonds,** instruments of indebtedness which are issued by governments and corporations, and which, although due and payable at a specified time, can be paid at any time before maturity at the option of the issuing body.

redemise, a regranting of land demised or leased.

redemption, a buying back; the paying off of a debt, upon which a transfer of real property, as security, becomes void. See also, *equity of redemption.*

redemption of shares, a corporation's reacquisition of shares pursuant to a provision in the security that specifies the terms on which such reacquisition may be made; usually redemption is at the option of the corporation, but it may be required at a particular time or on the happening of a particular event.

redemption price, the amount required by the articles of incorporation to be paid on redemption of the shares.

reduc'tio ad absur'dum, *l.,* the method of disproving an argument by showing that it leads to an absurd consequence.

reduction into possession, the act of converting a chose in action *(q.v.)* into a chose in possession *(q.v.), e.g.,* by obtaining money.

reentry, or **re-entry,** the act of resuming possession of land or a building, in pursuance of a right reserved by the owner on parting with the possession. Leases usually contain a clause providing that the lessor may terminate the lease and reenter on nonpayment of rent, or on breach of any of the covenants by the lessee.

reeve (rēv), formerly, an English officer appointed to execute process, make arrests, and keep the peace. There were several kinds of reeves, *e.g.,* the shire-reeve or sheriff.

re-examination, a second interrogation; one that follows and relates to the cross-examination. See also, *examination (2).*

re-exchange, the difference in the value of a bill of exchange, including damages, caused by its being dishonored in a foreign country in which it is payable. This depends on the rate of exchange between the two countries.

referee, a person to whom something is referred for arbitration. (2) An administrative officer appointed to hear and determine claims and disputes, *e.g.,* in workers' compensation cases.

referee in bankruptcy, formerly, a judicial and administrative officer of the United States District Court with jurisdiction to hear and determine bankruptcy matters; now called bankruptcy judge.

reference, the submission of a controversy to a referee *(q.v.).* (2) The proceedings before a referee.

referen'dum, in some jurisdictions, and in some particular cases, the practice of referring measures passed by the legislative body to the voters for their approval or rejection. (2) A popular election held pursuant to such a practice.

reformation, or **rectification,** the correction of a written instrument, via a lawsuit, so as to make it express the true agreement or intention of the parties.

refresh the memory, or **refresh the recollection,** to refer a witness to something while he is testifying, in order to bring facts within the recall of the witness. Subject to certain conditions, a witness may use a writing to refresh his memory for the purpose of testifying. Accord, Fed. R. Evid. 612.

regalia, the royal rights of a sovereign.

register, a book in which facts of a public or quasi public character, *e.g.,* marriages, births, or deaths, are officially recorded.

registrar, a public or private officer whose business is to keep various official or corporate records.

regrant, a second conveyance or transfer of real property by the same person.

regress, a going back; re-entry. See also, *ingress.*

regressive tax, a tax that does not increase in direct proportion to the increase in taxpayer income; a high income taxpayer will pay a lower percentage of his/her income than would a low income taxpayer.

regular on its face, descriptive of process from a court having authority to issue it, and which is legal in form, containing nothing to apprise anyone that it is issued without authority.

Rehabilitation Act of 1973, prohibits covered employers from discriminating in employment against persons with handicaps

rehabilitative alimony, alimony awarded to supplement means already available in an amount reasonably required during the post-marriage period to maintain a spouse until he or she in the exercise of reasonable efforts and endeavors is in a position of self support.

rehearing, a second trial of a lawsuit after judgment has been pronounced. (2) A second consideration of argument in a court of appeal. Usually authorized in only a few enumerated instances, pursuant to various rules of court or rules of civil procedure.

reinsurance, the act of an insurer in making a contract of insurance with another insurer to protect himself against some, or all, of the risks that he has assumed by the original insurance. See also, *insurance.*

reissuable notes, formerly, bank notes which could be put back in circulation after their payment.

rejection, in the law of contract, a manifestation of intention not to accept an offer, unless the offeree manifests an intention to take it under further advisement. Restatement (Second) of Contracts § 38(2).

rejoinder, formerly, a common-law pleading. Cf. *pleadings.*

relation, or **relation back,** retroactive application. When an act is done, or an order or adjudication made, and it operates upon the subject matter as if done at an earlier date, it is said to do so by relation. See also, *relator* and *kin.*

relative, a person who would receive the property of a deceased person under a statute of descent and distribution in case of intestacy (*q.v.*). See also, *kin.*

relator, the person who furnishes the knowledge or facts on which an information (*q.v.*), or a proceeding in quo warranto (*q.v.*), is based. Such proceedings are usually in the name of the state, ex rel. (ex relatione) the relator.

release, the giving up or surrender of a claim or right of action. It may be to the person against whom the claim exists, or the right may be enforced, which operates as a discharge of the claim or extinguishment of the right, or in the case of release of an interest in real estate, it may be by conveyance to another who already has some interest in the real estate. (2) A writing providing that a duty owed to the maker of the release is discharged immediately or on the occurrence of a condition (*q.v.*). Restatement (Second) of Contracts § 284(1).

release, lease and, see *lease and release.*

releasee, a person in whose favor a release is made.

releasor, a person who gives or makes a release.

rel'evancy, the connection between a fact tendered in evidence and the issue to be proved. Cf. *irrelevant.*

relevant evidence, evidence (*q.v.*) having any tendency to make the existence of any fact that is of consequence to the determination of the action more probable or less probable than it would be without the evidence. Fed. R. Evid. 401.

relict, a surviving spouse.

relief, the redress or assistance which a court grants to a person on account of the wrongs which another person has done to the former. See also, *remedy.* (2) Formerly, a payment which a tenant made to the lord on coming into possession of an estate.

religious liberty, the privilege of worshiping according to the dictates of a person's conscience, without annoyance or harassment. Guaranteed by U.S. Const., Amend. I, XIV, Sec. 1, and various state constitutions.

relinquishment, a forsaking or abandonment of something, *e.g.,* a claim in a lawsuit.

relocation (Sc.), the renewal of a lease.

rem, action in, a lawsuit initiated for the purpose of affecting a specific item, or several items, of property. See also, *action* and *in rem.*

rem, judgment in, a determination or decision by a court which affects a specific item, or several items, of property. See also, *judgment.*

remainder, an expectant portion, or residue, of interest in real property, which on the creation of a particular estate is at the same time limited to another person who is to enjoy it after the termination of such particular estate. A contingent remainder is one which is limited to take effect on an event or condition which may not happen or be performed. A vested remainder is one by which a present interest passes to the party, but the right of possession is postponed until after the termination of the particular estate.

remainderman, a person who is entitled to a remainder (*q.v.*).

remand, to recommit a person to jail or prison. (2) To send a lawsuit back to the same court from which it came, for trial or other action.

remedy, the legal means to declare or enforce a right or to redress a wrong. (2) Any remedial right to which an aggrieved party is entitled, with or without resort to a tribunal. U.C.C. § 1-201(34). See also, *relief* (*1*).

remise, release, and quitclaim, to part with or convey title without warranty. See also, *quitclaim.*

remission, a release or discharge of a debt or fine. (2) Pardon of an offense or crime.

remit, to pay money. (2) See also, *remission.*

remittance draft, a check drawn by the payor bank on another bank to the order of the presenting bank.

remitting bank, any payor or intermediary bank remitting, *i.e.,* paying, for an item (*q.v.*). U.C.C. § 4-105(f).

remittitur, in some states, a form of decision made by appellate courts in which a lawsuit is disposed of on appeal by ordering a new trial, unless a party agrees to accept a specified lesser amount of damages than that awarded in the trial court. Cf. *additur.*

remit'titur dam'num, the damage is remitted.

remoteness, distance; a lack of connection between a wrong and an injury, sufficiently close to entitle the party injured to claim compensation from the wrongdoer.

removal of cause, a change of venue; a transfer of a lawsuit from one state court to another or from a state court to a federal court.

Renewable Energy Resources Act of 1980, title IV of the Energy Security Act (*q.v.*) concerning coordinated dissemination of information on renewable energy resources and conservation, establishment of life-cycle energy costs for federal buildings, energy self-sufficiency initiatives, photovoltaic amendments, and small-scale hydropower initiatives. 16 U.S.C. §§ 2705, 2708; 42 U.S.C. §§ 7371-7374, 8255, 8271, 8274-8276.

renewal, the replacement of something old with something new. (2) An extension of the term of a lease or the time for payment of a promissory note.

renounce, to reject or give up something.

rent, the consideration given in exchange for the use of real property. (2) A periodic payment, usually made in money, but which may be in kind or in service, due by a tenant of land, a building, or other real property, to his landlord.

rent strike, an organized refusal of tenants to pay their rent to their landlord, for the purpose of persuading their landlord to comply with the housing laws or to grant some concession.

renunciation, a refusal to accept a testamentary transfer.

reparable injury, a wrong or an injustice that has already been done, and in which the actual damage can be substantially repaired by compensation in money.

repatriation, the recovery of a person's rights as a citizen, *e.g.*, the return of a civilian or soldier, captured during war, to his or her own nation.

repeal, to annul or set aside a legislative act by another legislative act. Repeals may be express, *i.e.*, declared by direct language in the new act, or implied, *i.e.*, when the new act contains provisions contrary to, or irreconcilable with, those of the former act.

repleader, to plead again. Formerly, a procedure when the pleadings (*q.v.*) in a lawsuit failed to raise a definite issue. Cf. *amendment (1)*.

replevin, a form of lawsuit which is used to recover possession of specific chattels which have been unlawfully taken from, or withheld from, the plaintiff. It may be brought by a general owner who has the right to immediate possession, or by someone who has a special property in the chattel, *e.g.*, a creditor whose claim is secured by the chattel. Usually defined by various state statutes. Occasionally called claim and delivery or order of delivery.

replication, formerly, a common law pleading, *i.e.*, the plaintiff's response to the defendant's plea or answer. Analogous to a reply (*q.v.*). See also, *pleadings.*

reply, under modern rules of civil procedure, the plaintiff's response to a counterclaim denominated as such, or a response, ordered by a court, to an answer or third-party answer. Fed. R. Civ. p. 7(a). See also, *pleadings.* (2) Under some codes of civil practice, a pleading which is the plaintiff's response to the defendant's answer.

reporter, a court official responsible for recording the proceedings in trials, including the questions propounded to, and answers made by, witnesses. (2) A court official responsible for compiling, indexing, and publishing the opinions of an appellate court. See also, *reports*.

reports, or **reports of cases,** various bound books in which are published the courts' opinions in precedent cases which have been judicially argued and determined. Occasionally called Reporters. See *Table of Abbreviations*, post.

repose, see *statute of repose*.

representation, a statement made by either of the parties to a contract, *e.g.*, of insurance, to induce the other to enter into it. See also, *misrepresentation*. (2) The legal standing of a person who acts for, or in place of, another or who succeeds to his rights and duties, *e.g.*, an agent, executor, devisee, or heir.

representative, a person who acts for another, usually applied to someone who is elected as a member of Congress or of some legislative body from a particular district. (2) An agent, an officer of a corporation or association, and a trustee, executor or administrator of an estate, or any other person empowered to act for another. U.C.C. § 1-201(35).

representative action, see *class action*.

reprieve (rē prēv), to suspend the execution of a sentence for a time.

reprisals, the taking or doing of one thing, in satisfaction for another. They are occasionally resorted to between nations when no other means of obtaining redress are available.

republican form of government, a government by representatives chosen by the people. The United States shall guarantee to every state in the union a republican form of government. U.S. Const., Art. IV, Sec. 4.

republication, a second execution of a will or a ratification of it, *e.g.*, by a codicil, after cancellation or revocation.

repudiation, in the law of contract, a statement by the obligor (*q.v.*) to the obligee (*q.v.*) indicating that the obligor will commit a breach that would of itself give the obligee a claim for damages for total breach of contract (*q.v.*), or a voluntary affirmative act which renders the obligor unable or apparently unable to perform without such a breach. Restatement (Second) of Contracts § 250.

repugnancy, an inconsistency or incompatibility, *e.g.*, between two or more clauses of the same written instrument.

repugnant, that which is inconsistent with, or incompatible with, something else.

reputation, the opinion of a person's character generally entertained by those who know him best. Accord, Fed. R. Evid. 803(21). See also, *hearsay* and *libel*.

request, a demand or notice of a desire on the part of one of the parties to a contract that the other party should perform his part.

requirements contract, an agreement wherein the amount of the commodity needed by the purchaser is not definitely ascertainable at the time of making. In sales transactions, a term which measures the quantity by the output of the seller or the requirements of the buyer means such actual output or requirements as may occur in good faith, except that no quantity unreasonably disproportionate to any stated estimate, or in the absence of a stated estimate to any normal or otherwise comparable prior output or requirements, may be tendered or demanded. U.C.C. § 2-306(1).

requisition, a formal demand for something which one has a right to receive. (2) The demand made by the governor of one state on the governor of another state for the return of a fugitive from justice.

res., *l.*, a thing, or things.

res commu'nes, things which cannot be appropriated to the exclusive use of an individual, *e.g.*, light, air, and flowing water.

res ges'tae, all of the things done, including words spoken, in the course of a transaction or event. Cf. *excited utterance.*

res in'tegra, a subject or point not yet decided.

res inter alios acta, alteri nocere non debet, a transaction between other persons should not prejudice one who was not a party to it.

res inter alios judicatae nullum allis praejudicium faciunt, matters adjudged in a cause do not prejudice those who were not parties to it.

res ip'sa lo'quitur, the thing speaks for itself; a doctrine in negligence law, which is occasionally invoked when the court holds that no further proof of negligence is needed than the incident itself. (2) It may be inferred that harm suffered by a plaintiff is caused by negligence of the defendant when (a) the event is of a kind which ordinarily does not occur in the absence of negligence, (b) other responsible causes, including the conduct of the plaintiff and third persons, are sufficiently eliminated by the evidence, and (c) the indicated negligence is within the scope of defendant's duty to the plaintiff. Restatement (Second) of Torts § 328D(1).

res judica'ta, a controversy already judicially decided. The decision is conclusive until the judgment is reversed. In litigation, the judgment of a court of competent jurisdiction on the merits of a case is a bar to a new lawsuit involving the same cause of action (*q.v.*) between the same parties, before the same court or any other court, because it is in the interest of the state and individuals that there should be some end to litigation. Cf. *collateral estoppel.*

res judicata pro veritate accipitur, a thing adjudged is taken as true.

res nullius naturaliter fit primi occupantis, a thing which has no owner naturally belongs to the first finder.

res sua nemini servit, no one can have an easement over his own property.

resale, a second sale of the same thing.

rescission, the cancellation of, or putting an end to, a contract by the parties, or one of them, *e.g.,* for any reason mutually acceptable to the parties, or on the ground of fraud. See also, *agreement of rescission.*

rescissory action *(Sc.),* a lawsuit initiated to rescind or annul a written instrument, *e.g.,* a deed or contract.

rescue, the offense of forcibly taking a person or thing out of the custody of the law, *e.g.,* a prisoner or property.

reservation, in a grant, the withholding of something or a stipulation for the return to the grantor of something, *e.g.,* rent, out of the thing granted.

residence, a flexible term for a permanent place of abode or of carrying on business. Cf. *domicile.*

residence of a foreign corporation, the state or nation under the laws of which the corporation was organized.

residual jurisdiction, see *jurisdiction* (5).

residuary, relating to the residue, or that which is left after certain portions or interests are disposed of.

residuary clause, the portion of a will which disposes of all the property remaining after previous bequests and devises are satisfied.

residuary devisee, the person who takes the surplus real property under the residuary clause *(q.v.)* of a will.

residuary estate, whatever property remains in the estate after all testamentary gifts have been analyzed and provided for, after payment of debts and all expenses have been accounted for and taxes have been calculated and remitted.

residuary legacy, bequest or devise, a gift of the estate remaining when claims against the estate and specific, general, or demonstrative legacies and bequests have been satisfied.

residuary legatee, the person who takes the surplus personal property under the residuary clause *(q.v.)* of a will.

resignation, the act of voluntarily declining to serve longer in an office, and renouncing its rights and privileges.

resolution, the expression of an intention or an opinion by a legislative assembly. (2) The annulment of a contract by consent of the parties or by the decision of a competent court.

resort, court of last, a tribunal from which there is no further appeal.

Resource Conservation and Recovery Act of 1976, see *Solid Waste Disposal Act.*

respite, a temporary suspension of the execution of a sentence. (2) The grant by creditors to a debtor of additional time within which to pay debts.

respon'deat ous'ter, *l.,* let him answer or plead over, formerly, a form of interlocutory judgment entered when a defendant failed in substantiating a dilatory plea, so that the case had to be gone into on the merits.

respon'deat supe'rior, let the principal be held responsible; the responsibility of an employer or a principal for the acts of his employees or agents.

respondent, a party against whom a motion is filed in the course of a lawsuit; analogous to a defendant or an appellee.

responden'tia, a loan of money for maritime interest on goods laden on a vessel, with the understanding that if the goods are lost, the money shall not be repaid; seldom used. It differs from bottomry (*q.v.*), in being a hypothecation of the cargo only.

respon'sa pruden'tum, *l.,* formerly, the opinions of learned lawyers which formed a part of the Roman laws.

responsible bidder, in public contracts, financial responsibility, integrity, skill, ability, and the likelihood of the bidder's doing faithful and satisfactory work.

Restatement (Second) of Contracts, a written summary of the common law of contract (*q.v.*) as it has developed in the American courts, adopted and promulgated in 1979 by the American Law Institute. It has been followed and adopted in large part by the American courts.

Restatement (Second) of Torts, a written summary of the common law of tort (*q.v.*) as it has developed in the American courts, adopted and promulgated 1963-1977 by the American Law Institute. It has been a major influence on the shape and direction of modern American tort law and has been followed and adopted in large part by the American courts.

Restatements, or **Restatements of the Law,** various written summaries of the common law concerning various topics as it has developed in the American courts, adopted and promulgated by the American Law Institute. The Restatements continue to be developed from time to time; there is the original group of Restatements and the second edition of the Restatements concerning some of the topics treated in the original group. The Restatements have been followed and adopted in large part by the American courts.

restitu'tio in in'tegrum, *l.,* the rescinding of a contract or transaction, so as to restore the parties to their original positions.

restitution, the restoring of property or a right to a person who has been unjustly deprived of it. A writ of restitution is the process by which a successful appellant may recover something of which he has been deprived under a prior judgment.

restraining order, a temporary directive by a court, to preserve the status quo pending a full hearing, entered in a lawsuit, without notice if necessary, on a summary showing of its necessity to prevent immediate and irreparable injury.

restraint of marriage, conditions attached to a gift to a person who has never been married, which are designed to prevent marriage by the donee. Such conditions are void. This usually does not apply to conditions against a second marriage or a marriage with a particular person.

restraint of trade, in, descriptive of unreasonable acts or contracts which prevent a person from carrying on, or engaging in, commerce. (2) A promise is in restraint of trade if its performance would limit competition in any business or restrict the promisor in the exercise of a gainful occupation; it is unenforceable on grounds of public policy if it is unreasonably in restraint of trade. Restatement (Second) of Contracts § 186.

restrictive indorsement, an indorsement (*q.v.*) which either is conditional, or purports to prohibit further transfer of the instrument, or includes the words "for collection," "for deposit," "pay any bank," or like terms signifying a purpose of deposit or collection, or otherwise states that it is for the benefit or use of the indorser or of another person. U.C.C. § 3-205.

resulting trust, a trust that arises by operation of law rather than the result of any intentional act by the settlor where it appears that the settlor, in conveying away property, did not make an effective disposition of beneficial interests or did not intend that the person taking or holding title should have beneficial interest.

retail enterprise, a business which sells in small quantities and deals directly with the ultimate consumer. Cf. *resale.*

retainer, the employment of an attorney by a client, to give his professional services. (2) The fee paid for such employment. (3) Occasionally, the right of an executor or administrator to pay his own debt out of the assets of his testator, in priority over all other debts of equal degree.

retaliatory eviction, a defense by a tenant (*q.v.*) to an action for eviction (*q.v.*) that the eviction was solely caused by the desire of the landlord (*q.v.*) to avenge the tenant's reporting of a violation of the building code, or the like.

retired shares, shares which are restored to the status of an authorized but unissued share.

retorsion, retaliation against the citizens of a nation by another nation, because of similar treatment of its citizens by the former.

retract, to withdraw, *e.g.*, a damaging statement or an offer before it has been accepted.

retrax'it, formerly, a proceeding analogous to a nolle prosequi (*q.v.*), except that it barred any future action.

retroactive statute, a legislative act which imposes a new or additional burden, duty, obligation, or liability concerning a past transaction or event.

return, an indorsement or report by an officer, recording the manner in which he executed the process or order of a court.

return day, the date named in a court order, or other court process, or which is fixed by statute or court rule, by which an officer must report the manner in which he executed the order or process.

reverse, to set aside a judgment, order, or other decision, on appeal or by the same court, and enter a contrary or different order or decision.

reverse discrimination, unfair treatment or bias exercised against a person or class for the purpose of correcting a pattern of discrimination against another person or class; majority groups are discriminated against in an effort to equalize minority groups, usually by way of affirmative action programs.

reversion, or **reverter,** the residue of an estate in property left in the grantor after a grant of a particular estate, less than the whole, to another. The reversion arises by operation of law, and is a vested interest which can be presently conveyed or devised, although the possession cannot be enjoyed until after the termination of the particular estate.

reversionary interest, an estate in property which is to be enjoyed at a future time, after the determination of an intermediate estate.

reversionary lease, a lease (*q.v.*) which is intended to take effect in the future. (2) A second lease which is intended to commence after the expiration of a former lease.

reverter, a reversion (*q.v.*).

review, a second examination of a determination, *e.g.*, an appeal or a writ of certiorari. See also, *bill of review.*

revival, the restoration or revitalization of something that has lost its legal significance due to intervening facts or the passage of time, *e.g.*, a will or a lawsuit.

revive, to give new life to a right of action once barred, *e.g.*, by acknowledging or promising to pay a debt barred by the statute of limitations. (2) To restore to its original force a judgment which has become dormant.

revivor, see *bill of revivor.*

revocation, the recalling or withdrawing of a grant, e.g., an unaccepted offer, a gift by will, or an agency. (2) The making void of a deed, will, or other instrument. A will may often be revoked by another will, by burning or other act done with the intention of revoking, by the disposition of the property during the testator's lifetime, or by marriage. The revocation of wills is usually regulated by various state statutes.

rex non potest peccare, the king (government) can do no wrong.

RICO Act, see *Racketeer Influenced and Corrupt Organizations Act.*

rider, an unrelated enactment or provision included in a proposed legislative measure.

rien (*ryăn*), *fr.*, nothing.

rigging the market, enhancing the quoted value of shares of stock by creating the false impression that the stock is in great demand.

right, a legally protected privilege or relationship of a person; a well-founded claim; the correlative of obligation. It may be (a) personal or public; (b) primary or secondary; (c) in rem or in personam; (d) absolute as that of an owner, or qualified as that of an agent or bailee.

right of action, a claim which a person may enforce via a lawsuit.

right of privacy, see *right to privacy.*

right of survivorship, see *survivor.*

right of way, an easement (*q.v.*) for the purposes of a passageway.

right to begin, or **right to open,** the privilege of the party in a lawsuit who has the burden of the affirmative of the issue, and consequently the right to be the first to address the court and jury.

Right to Financial Privacy Act of 1978, title XI of the Financial Institutions Regulatory and Interest Rate Control Act of 1978. It deals with confidentiality of records, customer authorizations, administrative subpoenas and summons, search warrants, judicial subpoenas, the use of information, civil penalties, injunctive relief, and grand-jury information. 12 U.S.C. §§ 3401 *et seq.*

right to privacy, the right (*q.v.*) to be let alone by other people. The protection of the general right to privacy is, like the protection of life and property, left largely to the law of the individual states. U.S. Const. Amend. IV, protects individual privacy against certain kinds of governmental intrusion, but its protections go further and often have nothing to do with privacy at all. Other provisions of the U.S. Const. protect personal privacy from other forms of governmental invasion, *e.g.,* Amend. I imposes limitations upon governmental abridgement of freedom to associate and privacy in one's associations, Amend. III prohibits the unconsented peacetime quartering of soldiers, and to some extent Amend. V reflects concern for the right of each individual to a private enclave where he may lead a private life.

right-to-work laws, state laws which consist of constitutional or statutory prohibitions on union security agreements.

rights, see *Miranda rights.*

riot, a tumultuous disturbance of the peace by three or more persons assembled of their own authority. Often defined by various state statutes. (2) Participating with two or more others in a course of disorderly conduct (*q.v.*): (a) with purpose to commit or facilitate the commission of a felony or misdemeanor; (b) with purpose to prevent or coerce official action; or (c) when the actor or any other participant to the knowledge of the actor uses or plans to use a firearm or other deadly weapon. Model Penal Code § 250.1(1). See also, *unlawful assembly.*

riparian owner, an owner of property who has rights to, or connected with, the banks of a flowing stream.

riparian rights, the privileges which appertain to property which abuts on a flowing stream of water, *e.g.,* a river or creek. Cf. *littoral rights.*

ripe, or **ripeness doctrine,** a principle which has the basic rationale to prevent the courts, through avoidance of premature adjudication, from entangling themselves in abstract disagreements over administrative policies, and also to protect the agencies from judicial interference until an administrative decision has been formalized and its effects felt in a concrete way by the challenging parties.

risk, the danger or hazard insured against, *e.g.,* in a life policy, death; in a fire policy, fire; in a marine policy, perils of the sea. See also, *insurance.*

robbery, theft from a person, accompanied by violence or threats putting the person in fear. Usually defined by various state statutes. (2) Inflicting serious bodily injury upon another, threatening another with, or purposely putting him in fear of, immediate serious bodily injury, or committing or threatening immediately to commit a felony, in an attempt to commit theft or in flight after the attempt or commission. Model Penal Code § 222.1(1).

Robinson-Patman Act, an act to amend the Clayton Anti-Trust Act, to prevent price discrimination (*q.v.*) and other discriminatory practices. 15 U.S.C. §§ 13 *et seq.*

roll, see *rolls.*

rolling stock, the engines and cars of a railroad employed in the transportation of passengers and goods.

roll-over mortgage, a short-term mortgage to which a lender will commit by rolling it over one or more times for additional periods at then existing rates of interest.

rolls, or **roll,** formerly, a court record entered on parchment which could be rolled up; hence, any records of a court or office.

Roman law, see *civil law.*

rout, a lesser form of a riot (*q.v.*) in which the purpose is not carried out.

royal fish, whale and sturgeon.

royalty, a payment made to a holder of a patent, or to an author or composer, for the privilege of making, selling or using patented articles, books, plays, or music. (2) Payment to the owner of mineral lands, varying according to the amount of the mineral which is removed.

ru'bric, formerly, the title of a legislative act.

rule, an order of a court or other competent legal authority. (2) A principle of law.

rule absolute, see *absolute* (2).

rule against perpetuities, see *perpetuity.*

rule day, a particular day or days of the month, regularly set aside by a court for the purpose of announcing decisions. Often held concurrently with motion day (*q.v.*).

Rule in Shelley's case, a principle of the common law that where the ancestor takes a freehold, and by the same conveyance, deed, or devise, it is limited, either mediately or immediately, to his heirs, the word "heirs" is a word of limitation, not of purchase, and he is thereby vested with the fee simple title. Abolished or modified by various state statutes.

Rule in Wild's case, see *Wild's case, rule in.*

rule nisi, *see nisi* (2).

rule of lenity, when choice has to be made between two readings of what conduct Congress has made a crime, it is appropriate, before the court chooses the harsher alternative, to require that Congress should have spoken in language that is clear and definite. (2) Ambiguity concerning the ambit of criminal statutes should be resolved in favor of mildness.

rules of court, various orders established by a court for the purpose of regulating the conduct of the business of the court. Among other things, they usually regulate licensing for the practice of law, civil procedure, criminal procedure, and appellate procedure. See also, *Federal Rules of Civil Procedure, Federal Rules of Criminal Procedure,* and *Federal Rules of Evidence.*

run, to pass by; to take effect. The statute of limitations runs against a claim when the time has passed within which it can be enforced by an action at law.

run with the land, see *covenant.*

Runaway and Homeless Youth Act, title III of an act to provide a comprehensive, coordinated approach to the problems of juvenile delinquency, and for other purposes. Among other things, it provides for grants to develop local facilities to deal with the immediate needs of runaway youth, reports to Congress, and a statistical survey. 42 U.S.C. §§ 5701 *et seq.*

Runaway Pappy Act, various state laws modeled after the Uniform Reciprocal Enforcement of Support Act, a proposal by the National Conference of Commissioners on Uniform State Laws (*q.v.*) concerning the interstate enforcement of family support.

S

sabotage (så bō tăzh'), the act of intentionally damaging the machinery or otherwise injuring the property of an employer, or of a nation at war.

safe-conduct, a permit enabling an enemy subject to travel to a particular place for a particular purpose.

safe place to work, a location in which an employee is directed to work, at which all the safeguards and precautions which ordinary experience, prudence, and foresight would suggest, have been taken to prevent injury to the employee, while he is himself exercising reasonable care.

said, a term used to designate with certainty the person previously mentioned in a deed, contract, pleading, or other legal writing.

sale, a transfer of the property rights in something for a price in money. (2) The passing of title to goods from the seller to the buyer for a price. U.C.C. § 2-106(1). See also, *bargain and sale, bill of sale,* and *sales.*

sale note, see *bought and sold notes.*

sale on approval, unless otherwise agreed, a transaction in which goods are delivered primarily for use, and in which they may be returned by the buyer, even though they conform to the contract. U.C.C. § 2-326(1)(a).

sale or return, unless otherwise agreed, a transaction in which goods are delivered primarily for resale, and in which they may be returned by the buyer, even though they conform to the contract. U.C.C. § 2-326(1)(b).

sales, transactions in goods (*q.v.*) (U.C.C. § 2-102), as contradistinguished from transactions in real property (*q.v.*). See also, *sale.*

salus populi (or **respublicae**) **suprema lex,** the safety of the community (or state) is the highest law.

salus ubi multi consiliarii, where there are many counsellors there is safety.

salvage, compensation made to persons, called salvors, by whose skill and exertion ships or goods are saved from imminent peril.

salvage loss, in marine insurance, the loss (*q.v.*) sustained by the necessary sale of goods at a port short of the port of destination, in consequence of perils by the sea. The amount realized from the sale of the goods is credited on the amount payable under the policy.

salvor, see *salvage.*

sample, a small quantity of a substance or merchandise, exhibited as a fair specimen of the whole. (2) In sales transactions, an object actually drawn from the bulk of goods which is the subject matter of the sale. Any sample or model which is made part of the basis of a bargain creates an express warranty that the whole of the goods shall conform to the sample or model. U.C.C. § 2-313(1)(c) and Official Comment 6. Cf. *model.*

sanction, the power of enforcing a statute, or inflicting a penalty for its violation. (2) Consent.

sane, descriptive of a person who has sufficient judgment, intelligence, reason, and mental power to observe and know the difference between right and wrong, or one who, having such, has sufficient will power to refrain from doing the wrong.

sans (*sän*), *fr.*, without.

satisfaction, the payment of money owing.

satisfaction, entry of, a notation or indorsement made on the margin of the official record, or elsewhere, that constitutes notice and a record that a legal obligation, *e.g.*, a judgment or mortgage, has been paid.

satius est petere fontes quam sectari rivulos, it is better to seek the source than to follow the streamlets, *i.e.,* it is better to examine original reports, and other original material, than to trust quotations.

savings bank trust, see *Totten Trust.*

scandal, a libelous statement or action. (2) In pleading, unnecessary allegations which reflect cruelly on the moral character of an individual, or state anything in repulsive language which detracts from the dignity of the court.

schedule, any one of various forms or lists which are annexed to official documents, *e.g.,* petition in bankruptcy or income tax return, for the purpose of providing detailed information.

schedule I, II, III, IV, or **V drug** or **substance,** see *controlled substance.*

Schoolbus Safety Amendments, see *Motor Vehicle and Schoolbus Safety Amendments of 1974.*

scien'ter (knowingly; wilfully), an element in crime and some civil wrongs descriptive of the perpetrator's guilty knowledge.

scilicet, "that is to say"; a word used in pleadings as an introduction to a more detailed statement of matters previously mentioned in general terms.

scintilla (*sĭn tĭl' ȧ*) **of evidence,** the slightest bit of evidence tending to support a material issue in a lawsuit. In some jurisdictions, only such an amount of evidence is necessary in a civil action to justify a jury verdict.

scire debes cum quo contrahis, you ought to know with whom you are dealing.

scire et scire debere aequiparantur in lege, knowledge, and the duty to know, are held for the same in law, *i.e.,* the law considers a person cognizant of that which they ought to know.

sci're fa'cias (cause to know), in some jurisdictions, a judicial writ founded on some record and requiring the person against whom it is brought to show cause why the party bringing it should not have advantage of such record, or why the record should not be annulled and vacated.

scire feci, the sheriff's return on a scire facias (*q.v.*) that he has given notice to the party against whom it was issued.

scope of employment, the act of a servant of the kind he is employed to perform, done substantially within the authorized time and space limits, and actuated, at least in part, by a purpose to serve the master. Restatement of Agency § 228.

scribere est agere, to write is to act, *e.g.,* an overt act of treason may consist of writing.

scrip, or **scrip certificate,** a written acknowledgment by a corporation that the holder is entitled to a specified number of shares therein.

scrivener, formerly, a person who drew contracts or other legal documents (Cf. *draftsman*), or loaned money at interest for his clients, receiving a commission.

scroll, formerly, a mark made with a pen, intended to take the place of a seal (*q.v.*).

seal, an impression on wax, paper, or other substance capable of being impressed, made for the purpose of authenticating the document to which it is attached. (2) In the law of contract, a manifestation in tangible and conventional form of an intention that a document be sealed. It may take the form of a piece of wax, a wafer, or other substance affixed to the document, or an impression made on the document. By statute or decision in most states in which the seal retains significance, a seal may take the form of a written or printed seal, word, scrawl, or other sign. Restatement (Second) of Contracts § 96. (3) The metal die or other device with which the impression is made. Cf. *scroll.*

search, an exploration or inspection of a person's house, premises, automobile, truck, or person, by a public officer, *e.g.,* a policeman, for the purpose of discovering evidence of crime or a person who is accused of a crime. Cf. *seizure* (2). (2) The use of electronic devices to capture conversation is a search within the meaning of U.S. Const., Amend. IV. (3) The exposure of luggage located in a public place to a trained drug-sniffing dog does not constitute a search within the meaning of same.

search warrant, a written order, issued by a court for probable cause (*q.v.*), specifying the place where a search is to be made and the things to be looked for, and directing that when found, they should be brought before the court.

search, right of, the privilege of a warship to examine the papers of a merchant ship in time of war, in order to ascertain whether the ship searched or her cargo is liable to seizure. See also, *contraband* (3).

seasonal employment, work in occupations which can be carried on only at certain seasons or during fairly definite portions of the year.

seaworthiness, the sufficiency of a vessel's materials, construction, equipment, officers, men, and outfit, for the voyage or service in which it is employed. It is an implied condition of all policies of marine insurance, unless otherwise expressly stipulated, that the vessel shall be seaworthy.

secondary boycott, variously, a combination to refrain from dealing with a person, or to advise or by peaceful means persuade his customers so to refrain, or to exercise coercive pressure upon such customers, actual or prospective, in order to cause them to withhold or withdraw patronage.

Secondary meaning, Doctrine of, a provision of law that where a name has acquired a secondary meaning through the business of a prior user of that name, the prior user will be protected against a subsequent user of that name in the same business.

secondary obligation, a duty or responsibility which is the correlative of a secondary right. See also, *primary right.*

secondary right, see *primary right.*

secret trust, a gift by a testator upon a trust not committed to writing.

secta, followers.

section, division, *e.g.,* of a legislative act, statute, or book, less than a chapter and greater than a clause. (2) A subdivision of a township (*q.v.*) under United States survey, one mile square and containing 640 acres.

secured creditor, a creditor (*q.v.*) who holds security (*q.v.*) which assures him that a debtor's promise to pay will be performed. Cf. *secured party.*

secured party, a lender, seller, or other person in whose favor there is a security interest (*q.v.*), including a person to whom accounts, contract rights, or chattel paper have been sold. When the holders of obligations issued under an indenture of trust, equipment trust agreement, or the like are represented by a trustee or other person, the representative is the secured party. U.C.C. § 9-105(1)(i).

Securities Exchange Act of 1934, an act to provide for the regulation of securities exchanges and of over-the-counter markets operating in interstate and foreign commerce and through the mails, and to prevent inequitable and unfair practices on such exchanges and markets. 15 U.S.C. §§ 78a *et seq.*

Securities Investor Protection Act of 1970, an act to provide greater protection for customers of registered brokers and dealers and members of national securities exchanges. 15 U.S.C. §§ 78aaa, *et seq.*

security, goods or an item of property which assures the performance of a contract, *e.g.,* a pledge or mortgage. (2) The personal obligation of another which assures the performance of a contract. (3) An instrument (*q.v.*) which is issued in bearer or registered form, and is of a type commonly dealt in upon securities exchanges or markets or commonly recognized in any area in which it is issued or dealt in as a medium for investment, and is either of a class or series or by its terms is divisible into a class or series of instruments, and evidences a share, participation of other interest in property, or in an enterprise or evidences an obligation of the issuer. U.C.C. § 8-102(1)(a). (4) Any note, stock, treasury stock, bond, debenture, evidence of indebtedness, certificate of interest or participation in an oil, gas or mining title or lease or in payments out of production under such a title or lease, collateral trust certificate, transferable share, voting trust certificate or, in general, any interest or instrument commonly known as a security, or any certificate of interest or participation, any temporary or interim certificate, receipt or certificate of deposit for, or any warrant or right to subscribe to or purchase, any of the foregoing. Uniform Probate Code §§ 1-201(37), 5-103(20).

security agreement, an agreement (*q.v.*) which creates or provides for a security interest (*q.v.*). U.C.C. § 9-105(1)(h).

security interest, an interest in personal property of fixtures which secures payment or performance of an obligation. The term also includes any interest of a buyer of accounts, chattel paper, or contract rights. U.C.C. § 1-201(37).

se'cus, *l.* (otherwise), to the contrary effect.

sedition, stirring up ill will against the lawful government.

seduction, the offense of a man deceitfully inducing a woman to have unlawful sexual intercourse with him. Often defined by various state statutes.

seisin (*sē´ zĭn*), possession. (2) Formerly, feudal possession.

seizure, the act of taking possession of property, *e.g.,* for a violation of law or by virtue of an execution. (2) The act of a law-enforcement officer who by means of physical force or show of authority in some way restrains the liberty of a person. Cf. *search*.

Selective Service Act, see *Military Selective Service Act*.

self-dealing, a contract, action or transaction between or affecting a corporation and: (a) one or more of its directors or officers; or (b) any person in which one or more of its directors or officers (i) are directors, trustees or officers or (ii) have a financial or personal interest.

self-defense, the protection of one's person and property from injury. A person may defend himself when attacked, repel force by force, and even commit homicide in resisting an attempted felony, *e.g.,* murder, rape, robbery, burglary, and the like.

self-executing provision, in constitutions, a clause which supplies the means by which the right given may be enforced or protected, or by which a duty enjoined may be performed.

self-serving, descriptive of statements made in the interest of the person who makes them.

seller, a person who sells or contracts to sell goods. U.C.C. § 2-103(1)(d).

semble, *fr.,* it seems; occasionally used in legal writing to denote that a point is not decided directly but may be inferred.

semper in dubiis benigniora praeferenda sunt, in doubtful matters, the more liberal construction is to be preferred.

sem'per para'tus, *l.,* always ready (to perform).

semper praesumitur pro matrimonio, the presumption is always in favor of the validity of a marriage.

semper praesumitur pro negante, the presumption is always in favor of the negative.

senate, the less numerous of the two bodies constituting the Congress of the United States, or the legislature of one of the states. A member of this body is called a senator.

senility, the effects of extreme age on the mind.

sensus verborum est anima legis, the meaning of words is the soul of the law.

sentence, a judgment of punishment in a criminal proceeding.

separate estate, property belonging to a married woman for her separate use, independently of her husband and his debts.

separate maintenance, distinct and independent support for the wife, provided by her husband, without a dissolution of the marriage.

separation, the living apart of husband and wife in pursuance of a mutual agreement. Cf. *judicial separation.*

separation agreement, a written agreement between a couple about to be legally separated or divorced that provides for child support, child custody, alimony, and property division.

separation of witnesses, see *exclusion of witnesses.*

sequester, to separate or set apart.

sequi debet potentia justitiam, non praecedere, power should follow justice, not precede it.

sergeant-at-arms, an officer appointed by a legislative body to carry out its orders, analogous to a bailiff or a sheriff.

sergeant at law, or **sergeant of the coif,** formerly, an English barrister of superior degree.

seria'tim, *l.,* severally and in order.

servant, an agent employed by a master to perform service in his affairs whose physical conduct in the performance of the service is controlled or is subject to the right to control by the master. Restatement of Agency, Second § 2.

service, the act of bringing a judicial proceeding to the notice of the person affected by it, *e.g.,* by delivering to him a copy of a written summons or notice. (2) The relationship of an employee or servant to his employer or master. (3) Formerly, the duty which an English tenant owed to his lord by reason of his estate, *e.g.*, rent.

servient tenement, a parcel of land over which an easement runs.

servitude, the right of an owner of real property to use a portion of the real property of another owner in conjunction with his own. See also, *easement.* (2) Slavery.

session, a term; the sitting of a court or legislature for the transaction of business.

set, several parts of the same bill (*q.v.*) of exchange, given by a drawer to a payee, any one of which being paid, the others are void.

set-off, a counterclaim or cross-claim. It arises as a result of a transaction which is unrelated to the facts which created the original cause of action.

settled land, real property, the succession to which is limited to a person other than the one for the time being entitled to the beneficial enjoyment of it, who is called a limited owner (*q.v.*).

settlement, a deed, will, or other instrument, whereby real property becomes settled land (*q.v.*). The principal kinds of settlements are: (a) marriage or antenuptial, (b) postnuptial, and (c) family settlements, also called resettlements. (2) A mutual accounting by which the parties come to an agreement as to what is due from one to the other; payment in full. (3) In reference to a decedent's (*q.v.*) estate, includes the full process of administration, distribution, and closing. Uniform Probate Code §1-201(38).

settlor, a person who furnishes, either directly or indirectly, the consideration (*q.v.*) or corpus (*q.v.*) for a trust (*q.v.*).

sever, to divide. A joint tenancy is severed when one joint tenant conveys his share to a stranger. (2) To remove, *e.g.*, growing crops or fixtures. (3) Defendants sever their defenses when they plead independently.

several, distinct; separate; opposed to joint (*q.v.*). Thus, a several covenant is a promise made by two or more separately, each binding himself for the whole.

several liability, separate and distinct liability from that of another to the extent that an independent action may be brought without joinder of others.

severalty, the quality of ownership of persons who are sole owners of ascertained shares of real property.

Sexual Exploitation of Children Act, see *Protection of Children Against Sexual Exploitation Act of 1977.*

sexual imposition, see *gross sexual imposition.*

sham pleading, a written pleading (*q.v.*) which, while in good form, is patently false and made in bad faith (*q.v.*).

share, a portion of something; in a corporation, a certain portion of the capital entitling the shareholder to a proportionate part of the surplus profits, otherwise called a dividend. A fully paid share is one for which the whole nominal amount has been paid.

shareholder, a person whose name appears on the books of a corporation as the owner of shares of that corporation.

Shelley's case, see *Rule in Shelley's case.*

sheriff, the chief executive officer of a county. It is usually his duty to keep the peace, make arrests, execute the process of the courts, and perform such other duties as may be prescribed by various state statutes. Formerly called shire-reeve in England.

Sherman Act, or **Sherman Anti-Trust Act,** an act to protect trade and commerce against unlawful restraints and monopolies. 15 U.S.C. §§ 1 *et seq.*

shifting use, see *use.*

ship's husband, a person appointed by the owners of a ship to manage all matters connected with the employment thereof on shore, such as repairs and affreightment. He is the general agent of the owners in relation to the ship, and is usually, though not necessarily, a part owner.

ship's papers, documents required to prove the ownership of a ship and her cargo. They include her certificate of registry, charter party, passport, and bill of health.

shire, a geographical division in England, analogous to a county in the United States.

shire-gemot, formerly, the Saxon county court.

shire-reeve, see *sheriff.*

shop right, a privilege of an employer, which the law recognizes, to practice and use, without compensation, an invention developed by an employee.

short sale, a sale of capital stock which the vendor does not possess at the time of sale, but which he expects to acquire subsequently for delivery under his contract.

short-term debt, interest-bearing debt, payable within one year from the date of issuance; obligations having no fixed maturity date if payable from a tax levied for collection in the same year as that of issuance.

shyster, a derogatory term for a person who carries on a business, or practices law, dishonestly.

sic utere tuo ut alienum non laedas, use your own so as not to injure another's property.

signature, the name or mark of a person, subscribed or printed by himself, or by his direction. See also, *marksman.* (2) In commercial paper transactions, a signature is made by use of any name, including any trade or assumed name, upon an instrument, or by any word or mark used in lieu of a written signature. U.C.C. § 3-401(2). (3) In the law of contract, the signature to a memorandum (*q.v.*) may be any symbol made or adopted with an actual or apparent intention to authenticate the writing as that of the signer. Restatement (Second) of Contracts § 134.

simil'iter, *l.,* in like manner.

similitude rule, a provision of the tariff laws, whereby imported articles which are not enumerated and which are similar in material, quality, texture, or use, to any article enumerated as chargeable with duty, are subject to the same rate of duty which is levied on the enumerated article which it most resembles.

simple, plain; unconditional; not under seal nor of record; not combined with anything else. See also, *fee* (2).

simple assault, see *assault* (3).

simple negligence, negligence (*q.v.*) which is neither gross nor wanton, but merely a failure to exercise ordinary care.

simple trust, a vesting of property in one person for the use and benefit of another, in which the nature of the trust is not further declared by the settlor (*q.v.*).

simple will, a will that does not include trust provisions within the will and does not pour assets into a trust that was created during the testator's life.

simplex commendatio non obligat, mere recommendation does not bind [like a warranty].

si'ne, *l.,* without.

si'ne di'e, without day, *i.e.,* indefinitely; descriptive of a final adjournment of a legislative body.

sine possessione usucapio procedere non potest, there can be no prescription without possession.

si'ne pro'le, without issue.

sinecure (*sī ne cūr*), an office which has revenue without any employment.

SIP, see *state implementation plan.*

sister, a woman who has the same father and mother as another person, or has one of them only. In the latter case, she is called a half-sister.

skilled witness, a person who is allowed to give evidence on matters of opinion and abstract fact, because he has knowledge, training, and experience which is not acquired by ordinary persons. Cf. *expert.*

slander, the malicious defamation of a person in his reputation, profession, or business, by spoken words. To impute a criminal offense or misconduct in business is actionable without proof of special damage, but in any case, proof of special damage arising from the false and malicious statements of another is a sufficient ground of action. Usually, the truth of the words spoken is a defense. Occasionally defined by various state statutes. (2) Publication of defamatory matter by spoken words, transitory gestures, or any form of communication other than written or printed words or embodiment in physical form or any other form of communication that has the potentially harmful qualities characteristic of written or printed words. Restatement (Second) of Torts § 568(2). Cf. *libel (1), (2).*

slander of title, falsely and maliciously making an oral or written statement regarding the plaintiff's title to specific property or property rights, if special damages result therefrom. Cf. *disparagement (1).*

slight negligence, an absence of that degree of care and vigilance which persons of extraordinary prudence and foresight are accustomed to use, or in other words, a failure to exercise great care.

slip-and-fall, an accident in which a customer in a business establishment (usually a supermarket) slips on a foreign substance or on a slick floor surface or trips over an obstruction and is injured; can also involve slipping on an icy patch in a parking lot or on a sidewalk.

smart money, damages (*q.v.*) awarded beyond the actual injury, by way of punishment and example, in cases of gross misconduct on the part of the defendant. Cf. *exemplary damages.*

Smith Act, an act to prohibit certain subversive activities; to amend certain provisions of law with respect to the admission and deportation of aliens; and to require the fingerprinting and registration of aliens. 18 U.S.C. §§ 2385, 2387.

Smokey Bear law, a statute prohibiting manufacturing, reproducing, or using the character "Smokey Bear," or any facsimile thereof, or the name "Smokey Bear," knowingly and for profit, except as authorized by the Secretary of Agriculture. 18 U.S.C. § 711.

smuggling, the offense of knowingly and intentionally importing or exporting prohibited articles, or of defrauding the revenue by importing or exporting goods, without paying duty on them.

soc (sŏk, sōk), jurisdiction.

socage (*sŏk aj*), formerly, English tenure by any certain or determinate service.

Social Security Act, see *Old Age and Survivors Insurance Benefits Act.*

societe anonyme (*so sē ā tā' ă nō nēm'*), *fr*, a private business corporation.

socii mei socius, meus socius non est, the partner of my partner is not my partner.

sociological jurisprudence, a philosophy of law which regards law as one of the agencies of social welfare.

sodomy (*sŏd'ə-mē*), carnal copulation between human beings, or between man and animal, contrary to nature.

Solar Energy and Energy Conservation Act of 1980, title V of the Energy Security Act (*q.v.*) concerning the Solar Energy and Energy Conservation Bank, utility program, residential energy efficiency program, energy conservation for commercial buildings and multi-family dwellings, weatherization program, energy auditor training and certification, industrial energy conservation, and coordination of federal energy conservation factors and data. 42 U.S.C. §§ 6862-6965, 6869, 6872, 8211 *et seq.*

Solar Energy Research, Development, and Demonstration Act of 1974, an act to authorize a vigorous federal program of research, development, and demonstration to assure the utilization of solar energy as a viable source for national energy needs, and for other purposes. 42 U.S.C. §§ 5551 *et seq.*

Solar Heating and Cooling Demonstration Act of 1974, an act to provide for the early development and commercial demonstration of the technology of solar heating and combined solar heating and cooling systems. 42 U.S.C. §§ 5501 *et seq.*

sola'tium (*Sc.*), damages allowed in certain lawsuits in addition to the actual loss suffered, as consolation for wounded feelings.

sold note, a written instrument, given by a broker to a buyer, stating that the goods therein mentioned were sold to him. Cf. bought and sold notes and *bill of sale.*

Soldiers' & Sailors' Civil Relief Act of 1940, an act to promote and strengthen the national defense by suspending enforcement of certain civil liabilities of certain persons serving in the Military and Naval establishments, including the Coast Guard. 50 U.S.C. Appendix §§ 501 *et seq.*

sole, single. See also, *feme sole.*

sole proprietorship, see *proprietorship.*

solicitation, the offense of asking or enticing another to engage in illegal conduct for hire.

solicitor, an attorney at law.

Solicitor General, an officer of the United States Department of Justice, who determines which lawsuits involving the federal government will be appealed, and who briefs and argues all cases before the United States Supreme Court, in which the federal government is a party.

Solid Waste Disposal Act, also known as the **Resource Conservation and Recovery Act of 1976,** an amendment to provide technical and financial assistance for the development of management plans and facilities for the recovery of energy and other resources from discarded materials and for the safe disposal of discarded materials, and to regulate the management of hazardous waste. 42 U.S.C. ch. 82, §§ 6901 *et seq.*

Solomon Amendment, Section 1113 of the Department of Defense Authorization Act, 1983, which provides, among other things, that any person who is required by law to submit to registration under the Military Selective Service Act (*q.v.*), and fails to do so, shall be ineligible for any form of assistance or benefit provided under tit. IV of the Higher Education Act of 1965. 50 U.S.C. App. § 462(f).

solvent, the condition of a person who has sufficient money or property, or both, with which to pay his debts in full. Cf. *insolvency.*

son assault demesne (*sôn ăs sōl´ dŭ măn´*), *fr.,* his own assault; the plea of self-defense in an action of assault.

sounding in damages, descriptive of a lawsuit which is initiated for the recovery of unascertained damages (*q.v.*).

sovereign immunity, a rule of law holding that a nation or state, or its political subdivisions, is exempt from being sued, without its consent in its own courts or elsewhere. Often criticized as being erroneously conceived, anachronistic, and unjust. Occasionally modified by court decisions and various state and federal statutes, *e.g.,* Tort Claims Act (*q.v.*).

sovereignty, the supreme authority of an independent nation or state. It is characterized by equality of the nation or state among other nations or states, exclusive and absolute jurisdiction and self-government within its own territorial limits, and jurisdiction over its citizens beyond its territorial limits.

speaking demurrer, a demurrer (*q.v.*) which alleges new matter in addition to that contained in the pleading to which the demurrer is filed.

special, distinctive; that which relates to a particular act, thing, or person; opposed to general.

special acceptance, the acceptance (*q.v.*) of a bill of exchange with the qualification that it is payable in one place, and there only.

special agent, a representative whose authority is confined to a particular or individual instance. See also, *agent*.

special assumpsit, an action of assumpsit (*q.v.*) brought on express contract.

special damages, see *damages*.

special demurrer, see *demurrer*.

special deposit, the placing of a particular thing in the custody of another, which is to be returned in specie.

special indorsement, in commercial paper transactions, an indorsement (*q.v.*) which specifies the person to whom or to whose order it makes the instrument payable. U.C.C. § 3-204(1).

special issue, in pleading, a denial of some particular material allegation, and thus in effect denying the right of action, though not traversing the whole declaration.

special jury, see *jury*.

special matters, in court pleadings, allegations concerning capacity, fraud, mistake, condition of the mind, conditions precedent, official documents or acts, judgments, time and place, and special damage. Fed. R. Civ. P. 9.

special partner, a member of a limited partnership (*q.v.*) whose liability is limited to the amount contributed by him to the business of the firm, and who does not have the powers of a general partner.

special pleaders, English lawyers who devote themselves mainly to the drawing of court pleadings.

special pleading, the allegation of new matter to avoid the effect of the previous allegations of the other party, as distinguished from a direct denial of them.

special property, a right in property, as distinguished from general ownership, which entitles a person to obtain or retain its possession for a particular time or purpose.

special session, an extra sitting of a court, grand jury, or legislative body, which is held at a time other than the time regularly scheduled for its sittings.

special tail, an estate tail which is limited to the children of two given parents, *e.g.*, to A and the heirs of his body by B. See also, *fee 2(c)*.

special trust, a trust (*q.v.*), by terms of which the trustee is required to do a thing particularly pointed out.

special verdict, the finding by a trial jury of particular facts in a lawsuit, usually in answer to questions submitted, leaving to the court the application of the law to the facts thus found.

special warranty, a covenant or undertaking that a grantor and his heirs and personal representatives will forever warrant and defend real property for the grantee, his heirs, personal representatives, and assigns, against the claims and demands of the grantor and all persons claiming by, through, or under him. Cf. *general warranty.*

special warranty deed, a deed in which the grantor covenants only against the lawful claims of all persons claiming by, through, or under the grantor.

specialty, a writing sealed and delivered, containing an agreement, usually for the payment of money. In many jurisdictions, unsealed writings stand on the same footing with sealed writings, they have the same effect, and the same actions may be brought thereon.

specie, see *in specie.*

specific legacy, a gift of property which can be distinguished with reasonable accuracy from other property which is part of the testator's estate.

specific performance, the actual carrying out of a contract in the particular manner agreed upon. Courts of equity will compel and coerce specific performance of a contract in many cases, where damages payable in money, the usual remedy at law, would not adequately compensate for its nonperformance, *e.g.,* in the case of contracts concerning land or for the sale of a unique chattel.

specifica'tio (Rom.), a form of accession (*q.v.*), by which he who by his labor converted the material of another into a new product became the owner of the product; he was, however, liable to compensate the owner.

specifications, various detailed descriptions or statements, *e.g.,* in contracts, in applications for patents, or in prosecutions.

Speedy Trial Act of 1974, and **Speedy Trial Act Amendments of 1979,** an act to assist in reducing crime and the danger of recidivism (*q.v.*) by requiring speedy trials and by strengthening the supervision over persons released pending trial, and for other purposes. 18 U.S.C. §§ 3152 *et al.,* 3161 *et al.*

Speluncean Explorers, The Case of the, a fictional case on appeal by Fuller. 62 Harv. L. Rev. 616-645 (1948-1949).

spendthrift trust, in some jurisdictions, a trust (*q.v.*) created to provide a fund for an improvident or unthrifty beneficiary. In jurisdictions where it is enforced by the courts, such a fund may not be aliened by the beneficiary, nor reached by his creditors.

spite fence, a barrier erected by a landowner for the sole purpose of shutting off light and air from the windows of buildings on the adjoining premises.

spoliation, the mutilation or destruction of something, *e.g.*, the erasure or alteration of a writing.

spoliatus debet ante omnia restitui, a person who has been robbed ought, first of all, to have his goods restored.

spot zoning, zoning in which a political subdivision, by amendment of its laws, singles out and reclassifies one piece of property in a particular zone without any apparent basis for such distinction.

spring gun, a booby trap; a firearm set as a trap for intruders and discharged upon contact with a hidden wire or cord.

springing durable power of attorney, a power of attorney that does not take effect unless and until a specified later time is reached or a certain event occurs.

springing use, see *use*.

sprinkling trust, a trust held for the benefit of children or children and the surviving spouse in which the trustee is empowered to expend the amounts of principal and/or income to or for the benefit of any one or more of the beneficiaries to the exclusion of other beneficiaries, as the trustee in discretion determines.

spurious, not genuine; false.

squatter, a person who settles on public lands or the private lands of others, without any legal authority.

stabit praesumptio donec probetur in contrarium, a presumption stands until the contrary is proved.

"stacking," an insurance term which refers to the ability of an insured who is insured by more than one insurance coverage to recover under more than one insurance policy or coverage under the same policy.

stakeholder, a person with whom property is deposited, pending the settlement of a dispute between two or more others. (2) A person who initiates an interpleader (*q.v.*).

stale demand, a claim or cause of action which has not been asserted for so long that the courts will not enforce it. Cf. *laches* and *limitation* (2).

stalking, engaging in a pattern of conduct that will knowingly cause another to believe that the offender will cause physical harm to the other person or cause mental distress to the other person.

standard policy, a form of insurance contract which is required, or recommended, to be issued in a particular state. Regulated by various state statutes and administrative officials.

standing mute, see *mute.*

standing to sue, whether a party to a lawsuit has a sufficient stake in an otherwise justiciable (*q.v.*) controversy to obtain judicial resolution of it. Where the party does not rely on any specific statute authorizing invocation of the judicial process, the question of standing depends upon whether the party has alleged such a personal stake in the outcome of the controversy as to ensure that the dispute sought to be adjudicated will be presented in an adversary context, and in a form historically viewed as capable of judicial resolution. See also, *justiciability.*

star chamber, see *Camera Stellata.*

sta're deci'sis, *l.,* to stand by decided cases, to follow precedent. A flexible doctrine of Anglo-American law that when a court expressly decides an issue of law, which is generated by the facts of a unique dispute, that decision shall constitute a precedent which should be followed by that court and by courts inferior to it, when deciding future disputes, except when the precedent's application to a particular problem case is unsuitable to the character or spirit of the people of the state or nation, and their current social, political, and economic conditions.

stare decisis, et non quieta movere, adhere to precedents and do not unsettle things established.

state bank, a banking corporation organized and operated under the laws of a particular state Cf. *national bank.*

state implementation plan, SIP; plans developed by the state subject to EPA approval for achieving and maintaining the national ambient air quality standards for that state. If a state fails to adopt an adequate SIP, EPA must devise and implement a SIP for that state.

stated account, see *account (2).*

stated capital, the amount of capital contributed to a corporation by its stockholders; the capital or equity of a corporation.

statement, an oral or written assertion or nonverbal conduct of a person, if it is intended by him as an assertion. Fed. R. Evid. 801(a).

statement against interest, a statement (*q.v.*) which was at the time of its making so far contrary to the declarant's (*q.v.*) pecuniary or proprietary interest, or so far tended to subject him to civil or criminal liability, or to render invalid a claim by him against another, that a reasonable man in his position would not have made the statement unless he believed it to be true. It is not excluded by the hearsay (*q.v.*) rule if the declarant is unavailable as a witness. A statement tending to expose the declarant to criminal liability and offered to exculpate an accused is not admissible unless corroborating circumstances clearly indicate the trustworthiness of the statement. Fed. R. Evid. 804(b) (3).

statement under belief of impending death, see *dying declaration.*

state's evidence, an accomplice in the commission of a crime, who testifies against those with whom he committed the offense.

stating part, under older codes of practice, the narrative in a bill in equity, setting out all of the essential facts on which plaintiff relies.

status, the condition of a person or thing in the eyes of the law.

status quo, the existing state of things at any given date.

statute, a law enacted by the legislative body of a nation or a state for prospective application. It may be (a) declaratory, *i.e.,* one which does not alter the existing law, as opposed to remedial or amending; (b) enabling, *i.e.,* removing restrictions, as opposed to disabling. Statutes may also be either public or private, the latter including those which have a special application to particular persons or places. (2) Includes the Constitution and a local law or ordinance of a political subdivision of the state. Model Penal Code § 1.13(1).

statute of frauds, see *Frauds, Statute of.*

statute of limitations, see *limitations (2).*

statute of repose, sometimes called hybrid statute of limitations, a statute which bars a right of action even before injury has occurred, if the injury occurs subsequent to a specified time period. It is a substantive, as distinguished from a procedural, limitation. As applied to, *e.g.,* products liability actions, a statute of repose limits a manufacturer's potential liability by limiting the time during which a cause of action can arise. Cf. *limitations (2).*

statute of uses, see *use.*

statutes, see *code.*

Statutes at Large, the laws enacted by the Congress of the United States for prospective application. They are originally compiled in the chronological order of their enactment. They are subsequently reorganized into the United States Code. See also, *code (1).*

statutory, created by, or depending upon, a statute, as distinguished from equitable or common-law rules.

statutory agent, a corporate agent upon whom may be served any process, notice or demand which may be required or permitted by statute to be served on a corporation.

statutory construction, the act of a court in determining the meaning of a statute (*q.v.*) as it relates to a particular factual dispute before it. See also, *legislative intent.*

statutory intent, see *legislative intent.*

stay of execution, a delay in issuing an execution (*q.v.*), or suspension of the authority to levy one already issued, until a future time; generally allowed in cases of appeal, or proceedings in error, on the filing of a sufficient bond for the satisfaction of the judgment, or decree, if affirmed.

stay of proceedings, the suspension of a lawsuit, *e.g.,* where a plaintiff is wholly incapacitated from suing, or ought not to be allowed to plead; or pending appeal, or where there is an action pending elsewhere to determine the same question, or one which should be first determined, or until the plaintiff, if a nonresident, shall furnish security for costs.

stealing, larceny (*q.v.*).

step-brother, see *brother.*

stet proces'sus, *l.,* an order of the court to stay proceedings. See also, *stay of proceedings.*

stevedore, a person whose occupation is to undertake the stowage and discharge of cargoes.

stint, limit.

stipendiary estate, an estate in property granted in return for services.

stipulation, an agreement; a bargain, proviso, or condition, *e.g.,* an agreement between opposing litigants that certain facts are true. It is binding without consideration (*q.v.*) if it complies with an applicable statute or rule of court. Accord, Restatement (Second) of Contracts § 94. (2) In admiralty practice, a recognizance in the nature of bail for the appearance of a defendant.

stirpes, *l.,* the person from whom a family is descended. Cf. *per capita* and *per stirpes.*

stock, the capital of a merchant or other person engaged in business, including his merchandise, money, and credits. (2) The goods which a merchant keeps for sale. (3) The capital of a corporation, usually divided into equal shares of a fixed nominal value, the ownership of which is evidenced by certificates. (4) A family.

stock certificate, or **certificate of stock,** written evidence of the ownership of stock (*q.v.*) in a corporation (*q.v.*).

stock company, an insurance company in which the shareholders contribute all the capital, share all the losses, and divide all the profits.

stock dividend, a corporate dividend payable to the stockholders of the corporation in shares of the corporation's stock, instead of money.

stock exchange, an association of stockbrokers organized for the purpose of trading in shares of corporate stock and other investment securities. See also, *security (3), stock (3),* and *stockbroker.* (2) The building in which the business of a stock exchange is carried on.

stockbroker, a person who buys and sells shares of corporate stock and other investment securities for and on behalf of other persons. See also, *security (3)* and *stock (3).*

stoppage in transit, or **stoppage in trans'itu,** the right of a seller to stop delivery of goods in the possession of a carrier or other bailee when he discovers the buyer to be insolvent, and to stop delivery of carload, truckload, planeload, or larger shipments of express or freight when the buyer repudiates or fails to make a payment due before delivery, or if for any other reason the seller has a right to withhold or reclaim the goods. U.C.C. § 2-705(1).

stowage, the manner or method of loading a ship.

straight-line depreciation, a method of depreciation under which the depreciation deduction is spread evenly over the life of the property.

stranding, the running of a ship on shore accidentally or voluntarily. When accidental, or done voluntarily to avoid a worse fate, the loss is one within the terms of an ordinary policy of marine insurance.

stranger, a person who is neither a party (*q.v.*), nor in privity (*q.v.*) with a party, in a legal transaction.

straw man, a person who is only a nominal party to a transaction. See also, *men of straw.*

strict liability, certain types of conduct and activity are deemed so inherently dangerous, so controversial and so threatening to the community at large that any resulting damages to any party will result in a finding of strict tortious liability. Strict liability is liability without requiring proof of fault.

strict scrutiny test, a test for determining whether a denial of equal protection exists; where a statute or regulation is found to adversely affect a fundamental right it is subject to a strict scrutiny test which requires the government to establish that it has a compelling interest justifying the law and that such measures are necessary to further a governmental purpose.

strictis'simi ju'ris, *l.,* of the most strict law, *i.e.,* to be most strictly applied.

strike, an organized refusal of workers to work, which takes place for the purpose of generating economic pressure which will cause an employer to grant improved wages or working conditions. See also, *rent strike.*

struck jury, in some jurisdictions, a trial jury obtained by striking names from a list of potential jurors furnished by the court, or a proper officer thereof. See also, *jury.*

structured settlement, a settlement in which the defendant agrees to pay damages to the plaintiff over some period; commonly consists of a lump-sum payment followed by periodic payments funded with an annuity.

style, the name of a lawsuit or precedent case, *e.g.,* Smith v. Jones. See also, *new style.*

sua sponte, upon its own responsibility or motion, *e.g.,* an order made by a court without prior motion by either party.

sub, *l.,* under.

sub modo, under condition or restriction.

sub nom, under the name; in the name of.

sub nomine, see *sub nom.*

sub potesta'te, under the power or protection of another.

sub sigil'lo, under seal.

sub silen'tio, in silence.

subagent, an under agent; a person employed by an agent to perform some, or all, of the business relating to the agency.

Subchapter S corporation, a legal hybrid often selected by small business interests, the S corporation is a mix of a partnership and a C corporation, legislatively invented to permit smaller, less capitalized businesses to be taxed at regular rates rather than corporate rates. An S corporation cannot have more that 35 shareholders. Shareholders must be individuals, estates or qualifying trusts. An S corporation must not have more than one class of outstanding stock. An S corporation has simply filed a tax election that results (1) in the corporation being exempt from income tax (with certain technical exceptions), and (2) the taxable income being allocated directly to the shareholders much as in a partnership or limited partnership.

subcontract, an agreement made by a contractor with a third person, for the third person to perform a part, or all, of the work that the contractor has undertaken.

subinfeudation, formerly, the act by which an inferior English lord carved out an estate from that held by him of a superior, and granted it to another who held directly of him.

subject matter, the object under discussion or consideration or in dispute.

subject-matter jurisdiction, see *jurisdiction (3)*.

sublease, see *underlease*.

submission, a yielding. (2) The agreement or court decision by which matters in dispute are referred to someone, *e.g.*, a judge, jury, referee, or arbitrators, for decision.

subornation, the offense of procuring another person to commit a crime, *e.g.*, perjury.

subpoena (sŭb pēnå), a court order or writ commanding attendance in a court under a penalty for the failure to do so. A subpoena ad testificandum is personally served upon a witness to compel him to attend a trial or deposition and give evidence. (2) A subpoena duces tecum is personally served upon a person who has in his possession a book, instrument, or tangible item, the production of which in evidence is desired, commanding him to bring it with him and produce it at the trial or deposition. Cf. *citation* and *summons*.

subrogation, the substitution of a person to the rights of another person concerning a debt or claim which the former person has paid.

subscribe, to write one's name under, or at the end, *i.e.*, to attest or authenticate a writing, deed, or instrument, by one's signature. (2) To agree in writing to purchase and pay for something, *e.g.*, shares of stock in a corporation.

subscriptions for shares, a written agreement to purchase capital stock of a corporation.

subsequent, following after. A condition subsequent is a condition (*q.v.*) which, if not performed, defeats or diverts a right or estate existing or vested; this terminology is not used in the Restatement (Second) of Contracts. Topic 5, Conditions and Similar Events, Introductory Note.

subsequent remedial measures, measures which are taken after an event, which if taken previously, would have made the event less likely to occur. Evidence of the subsequent measures is not admissible to prove negligence (*q.v.*) or culpable (*q.v.*) conduct in connection with the event. This does not require the exclusion of evidence of subsequent measures when offered for another purpose. Fed. R. Evid. 407.

subsidiary corporation, a domestic or foreign corporation in which another corporation, domestic or foreign, (the parent corporation) owns a majority of its shares and thus exercises control.

subsidy, governmental aid in establishing, or carrying on, private enterprises which are found to be of great public importance, *e.g.*, airlines and urban mass transportation systems, and which cannot be self-supporting.

substantial damages, see *damages.*

substantial evidence, a flexible term for more than a mere scintilla of evidence (*q.v.*); such relevant evidence as a reasonable mind might accept as adequate to support a conclusion.

substantive law, the positive law of duties and rights. Cf. *adjective law.*

substitute, a person who is put in the place of another person, or an object which is put in the place of another object. (2) To put one person or thing in the place of another person or thing.

substituted contract, a contract (*q.v.*) that is accepted by an obligee in satisfaction of an obligor's existing duty, *e.g.*, an earlier contract. Restatement (Second) of Contracts § 279(1). Cf. *novation.*

substituted performance, in the law of contract, (a) the acceptance by an obligee of a performance offered by the obligor that differs from what is due, in satisfaction of the obligor's duty, and (b) the acceptance by an obligee of a performance offered by a third person, in satisfaction of the obligor's duty. Restatement (Second) of Contracts § 278.

subtenant, a person who rents from a tenant.

succession, the event of following, or coming into, the rights of another; used particularly concerning the right of an heir to the possession of, and beneficial interest in, the estate of a deceased ancestor. (2) The mode of acquiring the rights of persons who constitute a corporation, by someone who becomes a stockholder in the corporation.

successor, or **successors,** a person who replaces another person, *e.g.*, in a public office, as heir to particular property, or as a subsequent owner of particular property. (2) Successors means those persons, other than creditors, who are entitled to property of a decedent (*q.v.*) under his will or the Uniform Probate Code. Uniform Probate Code § 1-201(42). See also, *succession.*

Sudden Infant Death Syndrome Act of 1974, an act to provide financial assistance for research activities for the study of sudden infant death syndrome, and for other purposes. 42 U.S.C. § 300C-11.

sudden passion, in manslaughter, an intense and vehement emotional excitement, leading to violent and aggressive action, *e.g.*, rage, hatred, furious resentment, or terror.

sue, to initiate a civil lawsuit or civil action.

suffrage, vote; elective franchise.

sugges'tio fal'si, misrepresentation (*q.v.*).

sui generis, of its own kind; peculiar to itself.

su'i ju'ris, of his own right; descriptive of a person who is neither a minor nor insane, nor subject to any other disability, and is therefore able to make contracts and act in his own right.

suicide, a felo de se (*q.v.*); a person who kills himself.

suit, a lawsuit or civil action.

sum of the years-digits depreciation, a depreciation method under which the annual allowance is computed by applying a changing fraction to the taxpayer's cost of the property reduced by the estimated salvage value. The denominator of the fraction is the sum of the numbers representing the successive 12-month periods in the estimated life of the property and the numerator of which is the number of 12-month periods, including that for which the allowance is being computed, remaining in the estimated useful life of the property.

summary, short; speedy; unceremonious; opposed to plenary or regular.

summary judgment, a decision of a court concerning the merits of a lawsuit, which is rendered on the motion of a party, when the pleadings, depositions, answers to interrogatories, and admissions on file, together with any affidavits, show that there is no genuine issue as to any material fact and that the party who made the motion is entitled to a judgment as a matter of law. An interlocutory summary judgment may be rendered on the issue of liability alone, although there is a genuine issue as to the amount of damages. Fed. R. Civ. P. 56.

summary jurisdiction, the authority of a court to make an order without further preliminaries, *e.g.*, committing for trial.

summing up, in a trial, the argument made by counsel at the close of the evidence. (2) In some jurisdictions, a concise review of the evidence in a trial, made by a judge, in charging the jury.

summons, a court order or writ, commanding the sheriff to notify a party named therein to appear in court on or before a specified date, and defend the complaint in an action commenced against him. It should also notify the party that, in case of his failure to do so, judgment by default will be rendered against him for the relief demanded in the complaint.

summum jus summa injuria, the strictest administration of the law sometimes works the greatest injustice.

Sunday law, or **Blue law,** a legislative act requiring the cessation from labor and business on the Sabbath day.

Sunset law, a legislative device to force review of a regulatory program by enacting a law that says that a particular governmental program, agency, or function, will expire as of a certain date unless there is enacted in the meanwhile a statute reauthorizing it.

Sunshine law, see *open-meeting law.*

supercargo, an agent employed by the owner of a cargo to sell merchandise shipped, to purchase returning cargoes, and to receive freight.

superse'deas, a court order or writ by which proceedings are stayed.

supersedeas bond, an undertaking or promise, with a surety, made in a court proceedings for the purpose of obtaining a suspension of the judgment of a court and a delay in execution thereon, pending the outcome of an appeal. See also, *bond (1).*

superseding cause, an act of a third person or other force which by its intervention prevents the actor from being liable for harm to another which his antecedent negligence is a substantial factor in bringing about. Restatement (Second) of Torts § 440.

superstitious uses, in England, money or property given for religious purposes not recognized by law, as opposed to charitable uses. Cf. *charitable use.*

supplemental bill, under older codes of procedure, an addition to an original bill in equity in order to supply some defect, or to allege facts which have occurred since the filing of the original bill. Cf. *amendment (1).*

supplica'vit, an English writ directing justices to require security to keep the peace from a person named. Cf. *peace bond.*

support, to argue in favor of, *e.g.,* a proposition, rule, or order. (2) Concerning land or a building, the right not to have it let down by the act of an adjoining or underlying owner.

suppres'sio ve'ri, *l.,* a wilful concealment of material facts.

suppressio veri, expressio falsi, suppression of the truth is [equivalent to] a false representation.

supr a protest, after protest.

supra, above; occurring by itself in a book or article, it refers the reader to a previous part.

Supreme Court of Judicature, an English court consisting of two divisions, *i.e.,* the High Court of Justice and the Court of Appeal.

surcharge, to prove that items have been omitted from an account, which ought to be allowed and credited to the party surcharging.

surcharge and falsify, to rectify an account, by inserting credits and striking out charges which have been wrongfully omitted, or inserted, to the detriment of the party seeking relief.

surety, a person who makes himself responsible for the fulfillment of another's obligation, in case the latter, who is called the principal, fails himself to fulfill it. It includes a guarantor. U.C.C. § 1-201(40). See also, *guarantor* and *guaranty.*

Surface Mining Control and Reclamation Act of 1977, an act to provide for the cooperation between the Secretary of the Interior and the states with respect to the regulation of surface coal mining operations, and the acquisition and reclamation of abandoned mines, and for other purposes. 30 U.S.C., ch. 25, §§ 1201 *et seq.*

surface water, fallen rain and melted snow which is diffused over the top of the ground until it reaches some well defined channel in which it is accustomed to, and does, flow with various other waters. Accord, Restatement (Second) of Torts § 846.

surname, the family name; a name added to the Christian name.

surplus, the amount by which a corporation's assets exceed its liabilities plus stated capital, if any.

surplusage, in court pleadings, the allegation of unnecessary matter which may be ordered stricken by the court. Upon motion made by a party, the court may order stricken from any pleading any insufficient defense, or any redundant, immaterial, impertinent, or scandalous matter. Fed. R. Civ. P. 12(f).

surprise, an occurrence by which a party to a contract or a lawsuit is taken unaware, and through no fault of his own, is put in a position which will be injurious to his interests. Courts will sometimes relieve parties from the obligation of contracts which they were surprised into making, and will frequently grant new trials or continuances on the ground of surprise.

surrebutter, and **surrejoinder,** formerly, two of the court pleadings used in common-law practice. Cf. *pleadings.*

surrender, to relinquish or forego; the yielding up of an estate for life or years, *e.g.,* a lease, so that it merges in the fee or reversion. It may occur by deed or by operation of law.

surrogate, in some jurisdictions, a judge who has authority in the matter of probating wills, granting letters of administration, and the settlement of estates. Analogous to the judge of a probate court (*q.v.*).

surrogate parenting, process whereby a third party conceives a child through artificial insemination, carries it to term, and then relinquishes the child to the sperm donor and his wife in accord with a contract executed before the child's conception. Ordinarily a surrogate receives a fee or honorarium from the sperm donor, who also pays for all of the expenses of the procedure.

surviving spouse, the spouse who outlives the other spouse.

survivor, one of two or more persons who lives longer than the other or others. In England, and in some of the United States, when one of two or more joint tenants (*q.v.*) survives the other or others, he becomes vested with the whole estate by virtue of the right of survivorship.

survivorship, see *joint tenants* and *survivor.*

survivorship tenancy, a type of tenancy where in the event of the death of one of the survivorship tenants, the decedent's interest passes at death to the surviving tenants by virtue of the language in the survivorship deed.

suspension, an interruption, stay, or delay. (2) Concerning estates or rights, a temporary extinguishment which may be followed by a revival.

syllabus, or **headnote,** an abstract; a written summary of a point of law which was decided or stated in a precedent case.

syllabus rule, a rule for the analysis of precedent cases, peculiar to the Supreme Court of Ohio, providing that the official syllabus (*q.v.*) of a precedent case, as printed in the official state reports, alone constitutes the law of the case. The syllabus must be read in view of the facts which are found in the precedent case, however.

symbolic delivery, the transfer of possession of something, as a representative of another thing, of which actual delivery cannot be conveniently made on account of its bulk or situation.

T

tacit, inferred, silent, implied from silence.

tack, to add or append. (2) A lease.

tacking, adding together or attaching together, *e.g.*, successive periods of adverse possession of the same real property by different persons.

Taft-Hartley Act, see *Labor Management Relations Act of 1947.*

tail, a limitation, *e.g.*, an estate tail is a freehold (*q.v.*) of inheritance, limited to a person and the heirs of his body in general, or some of them in particular.

take, to be entitled to or receive, *e.g.*, a devisee takes under a will; to lay hold upon; to carry away.

tala'gium, formerly, taxes.

Talented Children's Education Act, see *Gifted and Talented Children's Education Act of 1978.*

ta'les (*l., talis*), or **talesmen,** jurors summoned to fill vacancies existing in the regular panel.

tales de circumstan'tibus, jurors selected from bystanders.

talesman, see *tales*.

tangible, descriptive of something which may be felt or touched; corporeal.

tariff, a tax. (2) A schedule or tabulated list, *e.g.*, of import duties or rates of charge by public utilities.

tax, a sum of money assessed against, and collected from, a person for the support of the government. An income tax is one proportioned to the amount of his income. A poll tax is one which is assessed on all individuals alike, *i.e.*, by the head, without reference to the value of his property or the amount of his income. Indirect taxes are those levied on articles manufactured or imported, *e.g.*, excise and customs, so called because the tax is not levied on the consumer directly, but is in reality paid by him in the enhanced price of the article. (2) To fix or determine, *e.g.* the amount of court costs to be paid by the losing party.

tax abatement, a tax reduction or "forgiveness" of real estate and/or personal property taxes. A tax abatement is sometimes granted for a limited time to a business or industry's commercial property. An abatement is intended to encourage the business or industry to locate or expand within a community since the economic growth of the community will be naturally fostered by the location or expansion therein.

tax anticipation notes, notes that are issued in anticipation of the collection of taxes. The proceeds from such are treated as current or short-term loans and paid back from the anticipated tax collection with the issuance of the note. The notes are retirable only from the tax collections and frequently only from the tax collections anticipated with their issuance.

tax avoidance, a legitimate organizing of a taxpayer's affairs so as to minimize the amount of taxes which he must pay, *e.g.*, electing to take advantage of the alternatives which are offered to a taxpayer within the framework of the revenue laws. Cf. *tax evasion.*

tax base, the taxable value of real and tangible personal property from which a community can raise tax revenue.

tax burden, the percentage of income which is consumed by a tax or tax system; typically the term is used in reference to the income of an individual or a family. The term is frequently applied in conjunction with the determination of whether a particular tax burden is progressive, proportional, or regressive. Across the nation, taxes which are progressive seem to find better acceptance than those which are proportional or regressive.

tax deed, a written instrument or document evidencing the conveyance of title to real property sold for the nonpayment of taxes assessed thereon.

tax duplicate, a copy of a public auditor's book or tax assessor's book, showing the names of taxpayers, the value of their taxable property, and other relevant tax information, made for the use of the tax collector in collecting taxes.

tax evasion, a deceit consisting of a breach of law, by which the revenue laws' application to a particular taxpayer are frustrated. Cf. *tax avoidance.*

tax exempt property, specific classes of property not subject to property taxation, *i.e.,* properties owned by the government, schools, colleges, and churches.

tax levy, an issue placed on the ballot which seeks voter approval for a specified amount of revenue to be raised by a particular millage rate; an imposition by a governmental unit as agreed to by the voting public for the provision of tax revenues or special assessments for specific purposes.

taxable income, "gross income" less certain authorized deductions.

taxi, or **taxicab,** a motor vehicle (*q.v.*) which is offered or held out to the public for hire, with a driver, and which does not follow a regular route or observe a regular schedule. Often defined and regulated by various state statutes and city ordinances.

telegram, a message transmitted by radio, teletype, cable, any mechanical method of transmission, or the like. U.C.C. § 1-201(41).

teller, a person who keeps tally; an employee of a bank who receives or pays out money; a person appointed to count votes.

temple, two English inns of court (*q.v.*), called Inner and Middle.

temporary injunction, an injunction (*q.v.*), which is effective only until the trial of the lawsuit in which it was issued.

temporary restraining order, see *restraining order.*

tenancy, the condition or estate of a person who is a tenant (*q.v.*). (2) The term for which a tenant (*q.v.*) holds. (3) The real property which a tenant (*q.v.*) holds.

tenancy by sufferance, when a tenant initially had a rightful possessory right, and upon expiration of that right holds over wrongfully, tenancy by sufferance comes into being. The tenancy at sufferance exists only as long as the landlord fails to indicate whether he will treat the occupier as a tenant or a trespasser.

tenancy from month to month, a type of tenancy created where no definite term of letting is specified by the parties and the rent is payable monthly. A tenant who pays rent monthly and has no lease is a tenant from month to month. This tenancy cannot be terminated except by giving notice.

tenancy in common, the holding of distinct but undivided shares in real property by two or more persons. Upon the death of a tenant in common, his share goes to his heirs or devisees, and not, as in the case of a joint tenancy in some jurisdictions, to the survivors. Cf. *joint tenants.*

tenant, a person who holds or has possession of real property, *e.g.,* a lessee.

tenant at sufferance, a person who holds over at the end of his term as a tenant of real property, without any contract, express or implied, that he may do so.

tenant at will, a person who holds real property at the will of the lessor. A tenancy at will may be terminated by either party at any time, and the death of either party terminates the tenancy. The lessee cannot transfer his estate.

tenant for life, a person who has the right to real property for his own or another's life.

tenant for years, a person who holds real property for a term of years, *e.g.,* a lessee.

tenant from year to year, a person whose tenancy can only be terminated at the end of a complete year, or by number of years, from the commencement of his holding, and upon due notice. A lease at an annual rent, under which no certain term is fixed, creates a tenancy from year to year.

tenant in fee, see *fee (2).*

tenant in tail, see *tail.*

tenants by entireties, see *entireties, tenants by.*

tender, an offer; the offer to deliver money or specific personal property in pursuance of a contract, and in such a way as to leave nothing further to be done to fulfill the obligation of the party tendering. See also, *legal tender.*

tender offer, a offer to purchase shares announced by a company or individual which indicates that it will pay a price above the current market price for any shares tendered of a company which it wants to take control of.

tender years doctrine, a presumption that holds that a mother of young children will generally be given preference for child custody if the other factors are evenly balanced.

tenement, everything that may be possessed or owned, provided it be of a permanent nature, whether it be corporeal (*q.v.*) or incorporeal (*q.v.*). (2) A house or building. See also, *easement.*

tenendum, to be held; a clause in a deed (*q.v.*) wherein the tenure of the land is stated.

tenor, the meaning and intent of a written document, as opposed to its actual words. (2) Occasionally, a correct copy.

Tenterden's Act, Lord, (9 Geo. IV. c. 14), the English predecessor of various state statutes which supplement the statute of frauds and require the following, among other things, to be in writing: (a) acknowledgments of debts that are barred by statute; (b) representations as to a person's character or solvency, made in order to obtain credit for him; (c) executory contracts for the sale of goods.

tenure, a broad term for any of the various ways in which a person holds property or an office. See also, *hold (1).*

tenure in capite, formerly the holding of land directly from the sovereign or head of the nation.

ter tenant, see *terre tenant.*

term, a word, or expression; a condition, *e.g.*, the terms of a promise, agreement, or contract. (2) That portion of an agreement which relates to a particular matter. U.C.C. § 1-201(42). Accord, Restatement (Second) of Contracts § 5. (3) An end or limit, *e.g.*, a period of time limited for the payment of a note, the performance of a contract, or the enjoyment of an estate. (4) The period of time during which a court holds a session.

ter'minus, *l.*, a limit or boundary, either of space or time.

terminus a quo, the starting point.

terminus ad quem, the destination.

terre tenant (tar), or **ter tenant,** a person who holds, or has the seisin of, land.

terrier, an English register or survey of land.

territorial waters, usually, the portion of the ocean which is within three miles from the coast of a nation. By international law, they are within the jurisdiction of that country. Cf. *high seas.* See also, *three-mile limit* and *twelve-mile limit.*

territory, a portion of a nation which is subject to a particular jurisdiction, *e.g.*, municipal, judicial, or military. (2) A division of land belonging to the United States, which is not within the boundaries of any particular state, and which is governed by United States officers.

terroristic threat, a threat to commit a crime of violence with purpose to terrorize another or to cause evacuation of a building, place of assembly, or facility of public transportation, or otherwise to cause serious public inconvenience, or in reckless disregard of the risk of causing such terror or inconvenience. Model Penal Code § 211.3.

testacy, the state or condition of leaving a valid will. Cf. *intestacy.*

testament, a will or disposition of personal property.

testamentary, relating to a will, *e.g.*, capacity or disposition. (2) Given or appointed by will, *e.g.*, a testamentary gift or guardian.

testamentary capacity, to make a valid will a testator must have the ability to understand the general nature of the testamentary act, to know the nature and extent of his property, and the natural objects of his bounty, and be able to interrelate these factors.

testamentary causes, court proceedings relating to wills and administration of decedents' estates.

testamentary trust, a trust created and funded in a will. The testamentary trust accomplishes the preservation of accumulated assets, affords the opportunity for expert financial management and gives greater economic flexibility to both surviving spouse and issue.

testamentum omne morte consummatum, every will is perfected by death.

testate, the condition of a person who dies, having made a valid will.

testator, a man who makes a will.

testatrix, a woman who makes a will.

testa'tum, the witnessing part of a deed (*q.v.*) or other formal instrument. It follows the recitals, if there are any, and introduces the operative part of the instrument by the words, "Now this indenture witnesseth," or similar words.

testatum writ, a court order or summons issued into a county other than that in which the venue of a lawsuit is established.

teste (*test*), the witnessing part of a writ, warrant, or other process, indicating by whose authority it is issued.

testes ponderantur non numerantur, witnesses are weighed, not numbered, *i.e.*, the mere number of the witnesses brought forward to prove any fact is not so important as their credibility and judgment.

testimonium clause, the attesting clause in a will.

testimony, statements made by a witness under oath or affirmation. Cf. *evidence.*

theft, larceny (*q.v.*).

theft by deception, purposely obtaining property of another by (1) creating or reinforcing a false impression, including false impressions as to law, value, intention, or other state of mind; (2) preventing another from acquiring information which would affect his judgment of a transaction; (3) failing to correct a false impression which the deceiver previously created or reinforced, or which the deceiver knows to be influencing another to whom he stands in a fiduciary or confidential relationship; or (4) failing to disclose a known lien, adverse claim, or other legal impediment to the enjoyment of property which he transfers or encumbers in consideration for the property obtained, whether such impediment is or is not valid, or is or is not a matter of official record. Deception as to a person's intention to perform a promise may not be inferred from the fact alone that he did not subsequently perform the promise. Deceive does not include falsity as to matters having no pecuniary significance, or puffing by statements unlikely to deceive ordinary persons in the group addressed. Model Penal Code § 223.3.

theft by failure to make required disposition, purposely obtaining property upon agreement, or subject to a known legal obligation to make specified payment or other disposition, whether from such property or its proceeds or from his own property to be reserved in equivalent amount, and dealing with the property obtained as his own and failing to make the required payment or disposition. Model Penal Code § 223.8.

theft by unlawful taking or disposition, unlawful taking or exercising unlawful control over movable property of another with purpose to deprive him thereof. (2) Unlawful transfer of immovable property of another or any interest therein with purpose to benefit himself or another not entitled thereto. Model Penal Code § 223.2.

theft of services, purposely obtaining labor, professional service, transportation, telephone or other public service, accommodation in hotels, restaurants or elsewhere, admission to exhibitions, use of vehicles or other movable property, which he knows are available only for compensation, by deception or threat, or by false token or other means to avoid payment therefor. (2) Knowingly diverting the services of others, over which he has control but to which he is not entitled, to his own benefit or the benefit of another not entitled thereto. Model Penal Code § 223.7.

third degree, various illegal methods which might be employed by police to extort confessions from accused persons.

third party, a person who is a stranger (*q.v.*) to a transaction, contract, or proceeding.

thoroughfare, a street or way open at both ends and free from all obstructions.

three-mile limit, an imaginary line three miles from the shore, which marks the boundary of a nation's control over the waters of the ocean. See also, twelve-mile limit. Cf. *high seas* and *territorial waters.*

throw into bankruptcy, adjudication of bankruptcy by a court of competent jurisdiction.

ticket of leave, an English license to be at large, granted to a convict for good behavior and recallable for misconduct.

tidewater, inlets of the sea, bays, coves, and rivers, in which the water, whether salt or not, rises and falls with the tide.

timber, oak, ash, elm, and other trees used for building. It is real property until severed, when it becomes personal property. See also, *waste.*

time, the measure of duration, *e.g.*, days, months, or years. (2) The particular minute, hour, or day, when an act is dove or a crime committed. See also, *day, essence,* and *Uniform Time Act of 1966.*

timesharing condominiums, condominiums found in vacation areas where ownership of the unit for an entire year is unnecessary, expensive, and burdensome for many people. The timesharing concept allows the buyer to purchase a time slot of ownership.

tipstaff, an English, and occasionally an American, officer of a court whose duty it is to arrest persons guilty of contempt, and to take charge of prisoners.

tithing, formerly, an English subdivision containing ten families, forming part of a hundred (*q.v.*).

title, ownership; a valid claim of right. In this sense, it may be original, as in the case of an inventor's title to a patent, or derivative, where the owner takes from a predecessor. A marketable title to land is one which the courts will force on an unwilling person who has contracted to purchase it. A bad title is one which gives the holder no legal estate. A doubtful title is one which may not be bad, yet not so free from doubt that a court will force a purchaser to take it pursuant to his contract. The usual covenants of title given by vendors and mortgagors are: (a) for right to convey, (b) for quiet enjoyment, (c) for freedom from incumbrances, and (d) for further assurance when called on. Under various state statutes, these covenants may be implied in a conveyance and need not be expressly inserted. (2) The distinguishing name of a writing, *e.g.*, an act of a legislature or a book. (3) An appellation of honor or dignity. No title of nobility may be granted by the United States or any state. U.S. Const., Art. I, Secs. 9 and 10. No person holding any office of profit or trust under the United States shall, without the consent of Congress, accept of any present, emolument, office, or title from any king, prince, or foreign state. U.S. Const., Art. I, Sec. 9.

title bond, occasionally, a written contract to buy and sell real property.

title deed, a written instrument which transfers the ownership of real property from one person to another. It is evidence of the ownership of real property. The form and formalities are often regulated by various state statutes.

title insurance, insurance which shifts or transfers to a responsible insurer the risks of defective title, *i.e.,* forgery, insanity and minority, marital status incorrectly given, defective deeds, *etc.* The insurer agrees, subject to the terms of its policy, to indemnify such person against any loss he may sustain by reason of any defects in title not enumerated in the policy and to defend at its own expense any lawsuit attacking the title where such lawsuit is based on a defect in title against which the policy insured.

title state, a state in which statutes have been enacted saying that the sale of a motor vehicle has not taken place until the certificate of title is properly transferred by a public official and delivered to the purchaser; the seller is regarded as the owner of the vehicle until the certificate of title is so transferred and delivered.

Tobacco Program Act, see *No Net Cost Tobacco Program Act of 1982.*

toft, a place where a house has formerly stood.

toll, a payment for passage, *e.g.,* over a road or ferry. (2) To stop, delay, or suspend, *e.g.,* the running of the statute of limitations. (3) To bar or take away, *e.g.,* a writ of entry.

tonnage, the carrying capacity of a ship or vessel. (2) A tax or duty paid on such capacity.

tontine, in some jurisdictions, a system of life annuities with benefit of survivorship among the annuitants.

torrens system, in some jurisdictions, proceedings authorized by statute for the registration and guaranty of land titles.

tort, any one of various, legally recognized, private injuries or wrongs which do not arise as the result of a breach of contract.

Tort Claims Act, an act to establish a procedure for suits on tort claims against the United States. 28 U.S.C. §§ 1291 *et seq.*

tortfeasor, a person who commits a tort (*q.v.*); a wrongdoer; a trespasser.

tortious (*tor shus*), wrongful; descriptive of an act which generates a tort (*q.v.*). (2) The fact that conduct, whether of act or omission, is of such a character as to subject the actor (*q.v.*) to liability under the law of torts. Restatement (Second) of Torts § 6.

torture, bodily pain; the act of inflicting bodily pain.

total disability, in insurance policies, such physical inability as will render the insured unable to perform all substantial and material acts necessary to the prosecution of his business or occupation in the customary or usual manner. See also, *disability (2), (3).*

total loss, a phrase used in insurance, to designate a loss (*q.v.*) which is either actually or constructively complete, as distinguished from a partial loss.

toti'dem ver'bis, *l.,* in so many words.

to'ties quo'ties, *l.,* as often as occasion shall arise.

Totten trust, the standard trust relationship entered into when the depositor makes a deposit of cash into a bank or financial institution; a savings account trust where the named beneficiary is entitled to the balance of the account remaining at the death of the depositor. It is a tentative trust revocable at will until the depositor dies or completes the gift in his lifetime by some unequivocal act or declaration such as delivery of the passbook or notice to the beneficiary.

tout temps prist et encore est (*too ton pre e on cor e*), *L. fr.,* formerly, a plea in an action for a breach of contract that defendant always has been, and still is, ready to fulfill it.

to wit, to know; that is to say; namely.

town, variously, a civil division less than a county, a small collection of houses, or a village. Occasionally defined by various state statutes concerning municipal corporations. Cf. *city.*

township, a division of the public lands of the United States into tracts of six miles square, containing thirty-six sections (*q.v.*), of 640 acres each. (2) In some states, a subdivision of a county.

trade, restraint of, see *restraint of trade, in.*

trade-mark, see *trademark.*

trademark, or **trade-mark,** a distinctive mark, signature, or device, affixed to an article or to its wrapper, package, or container, to show that it is manufactured, grown, or selected by a particular person, firm, or corporation. In a case of infringement, courts will enjoin the wrong-doer from using an imitation of a trademark.

Trademark Act, see *Lanham Act.*

trade-name, or **trade name,** the name under which a business is carried on.

trade secret, a plan, process, tool, mechanism, or compound, known only to its owner and those of his employees to whom it is necessary to confide it, in order to apply it to the uses intended. It is distinguishable from a patent in that it may be used by anyone who is able to discover its nature.

trade union, or **trade-union,** an association of workmen in any trade. See also, *labor union.*

trade usage, see *usage of trade.*

trader, a person who buys and sells goods and chattels with the purpose of making a profit. A person who merely sells what he has raised, *e.g.,* a farmer or gardener, is not a trader.

trading stamps, coupons given with purchases of goods, redeemable for goods or cash.

traditio loqui facit chartam, delivery makes a deed speak, *i.e.,* come into operation.

transaction, an item of business; a broad term for an act by one party which affects another party, and out of which a lawsuit might potentially arise.

transactional immunity, a type of witness immunity that protects a witness from prosecution for offenses to which the compelled testimony relates.

transcript, a verbatim written record of a lawsuit, hearing, or testimony; a copy, especially an official copy.

transfer, to pass from one person to another; to convey.

transfer tax, a tax (*q.v.*) on succession, or the right to receive a bequest, based on the value of the succession and assessed against and paid by the recipient.

transferred intent, doctrine holding that if the defendant shoots or strikes at A, intending to wound or kill him, and unforeseeably hits B instead, he is held liable to B for an intentional tort. The intent to commit a battery upon A is pieced together with the resulting injury to B; it is "transferred" from A to B.

transhipment, the act of taking a cargo out of one ship and loading it on another.

transire, an English warrant or certificate that a ship has paid customs dues and may therefore sail.

transit terra cum onere, the land passes with its incumbrance.

transitory action, a lawsuit, the venue of which may be established in any county. Statutes in the various states often require that all lawsuits or actions shall be brought in the county where the defendants, or some of them, or the subject matter of the action, may be found.

transitus, see *stoppage in transit.*

transportation, various means of moving persons or goods from one place to another. Defined by various federal and state statutes. (2) The punishment of sending a convicted criminal beyond the seas, or into exile.

trauma, or **traumatic injury,** a bodily hurt or injury produced by violence.

traverse, in older forms of pleading, the denial of some matter of fact alleged. A traverse is either general, denying all that was alleged in the last pleading of the adverse party, or special, meeting the exact words of that portion of the pleading which it is intended to deny.

treason, or **leze majesty,** an offense against the duty of allegiance; levying war against the United States, or adhering to their enemies, giving them aid and comfort. 18 U.S.C. § 2381. A person can be convicted of treason only on the testimony of two witnesses to the same overt act, or confession in open court. U.S. Const., Art. III, Sec. 3.

Treasurer of the United States, an officer whose duty it is to receive and keep the moneys of the United States; to disburse them only on warrants drawn by the Secretary of the Treasury and countersigned by the proper officer; to take receipts, and to keep and render accurate accounts to the comptroller.

treasure-trove, money, plate, or bullion found hidden in the earth, or any private place, the owner of which is unknown.

treasury notes, promissory notes (*q.v.*) issued by the United States Treasury Department, which are receivable in payment of debts due the government.

treasury shares, shares belonging to the corporation and not retired, that have been either issued and thereafter acquired by the corporation, or paid as a dividend or distribution in shares of the corporation on treasury shares of the same class; such shares are deemed to be issued, but are not considered an asset or liability of the corporation, or as outstanding for dividend or distribution, quorum, voting, or other purposes.

treaty, a written agreement between nations. On the part of the United States, it may be made by the President, by and with the advice and consent of the Senate, two-thirds of those present concurring. U.S. Const., Art. II, Sec. 2.

trespass, any transgression of the law less than treason, felony, or misprision of either. (2) Especially, trespass quare clausum fregit, *i.e.,* entry on another's close (*q.v.*), or land without lawful authority. (3) Trespass on the case, or Case, was formerly a general name for torts which had no special writ or remedy. (4) Criminal trespass is entering or surreptitiously remaining in a building or occupied structure, or separately secured or occupied portion thereof, knowing that he is not licensed or privileged to do so. Model Penal Code § 221.2(1). (5) Defiant trespass is entering or remaining in any place as to which notice against trespass is given, knowing that he is not licensed or privileged to do so. The notice against trespass must be given by actual communication to the actor, posting in a manner prescribed by law or reasonably likely to come to the attention of intruders, or fencing or other enclosure manifestly designed to exclude intruders. Model Penal Code § 221.2(2). See also, *de bonis asportatis.*

trespasser, a person who commits a trespass (*q.v.*). (2) A person who enters or remains upon land in the possession of another without a privilege to do so created by the possessor's consent or otherwise. Restatement (Second) of Torts § 329.

trespasser ab initio, in some jurisdictions, a person who, having lawfully entered, does something he is not entitled to do; his trespass or wrong then relates back and he is a trespasser from the beginning.

trial, the examination of the issues in a civil or criminal lawsuit by an authorized tribunal; the presentation and decision of the issues of law or fact in an action. It may be by a judge or judges, with or without a jury (*q.v.*). See also, *new trial.*

trial per pais, see *pais.*

tribunal, a court. (2) The place in which a session of court is held.

triers, see *triors.*

trino'da neces'sitas, *l.,* the threefold necessity; formerly descriptive of the taxes for which all lands were liable.

triors, or **triers,** in some jurisdictions, persons appointed by the court to decide on challenges (*q.v.*) to a jury.

tripartite, divided into three parts; descriptive of a deed or contract to which there are three distinct parties.

trover, or **trover and conversion,** formerly, a special form of trespass (*q.v.*) on the case, based on the finding (actual or fictitious) by the defendant of goods lost by the plaintiff.

true bill, an indictment or bill of indictment; the indorsement which the grand jury (*q.v.*) makes upon a bill of indictment when, having heard the evidence, they are satisfied that there is a prima facie case against the accused. Cf. *ignoramus.*

trust, a right in property held by one person, called the trustee, for the benefit of another, called the beneficiary, or cestui que trust. Trusts are divided into active, where the trustee has some duty to perform, so that the legal estate must remain in him or a successor, or the trust be defeated; passive, where the trustee simply holds the title in trust for the beneficiary, and has no duties to perform; express, where it is created by express terms in a deed, will, or other instrument; implied, including precatory, constructive, and resulting trusts, where a court will presume, from the nature of the transaction, the relations of the parties and the requirements of good faith, that a trust was intended, though no express words be employed to create it. See also, *quasi trustee.*

trust account, an account (*q.v.*) in the name of one or more parties as trustees for one or more beneficiaries where the relationship is established by the form of the account and the deposit agreement with the financial institution (*q.v.*) and there is no subject of the trust other than the sums on deposit in the account. It is not essential that payment to the beneficiary be mentioned in the deposit agreement. Does not include a regular trust account under a testamentary trust or a trust agreement which has significance apart from the account, or a fiduciary account arising from a fiduciary relation, *e.g.*, attorney-client. Uniform Probate Code § 6-101 (14).

trust receipt, a security device consisting of an instrument representing a three party transaction, wherein the seller of goods conveys title, not to the buyer, but to the lender, who is the holder of the trust receipt. Cf. *security agreement.*

trustee, a person who holds property for the benefit of another. See also, *trust.*

trustee in bankruptcy, an officer of a bankruptcy court who administers the estate of a bankrupt under the direction of the court. He holds the title to the bankrupt's estate for the benefit of the creditors of the bankrupt, and investigates the affairs of the estate and the activities of the bankrupt.

Truth in Lending Act, title I of the Consumer Credit Protection Act (*q.v.*). 15 U.S.C. §§ 1601-1608, 1610-1613. Among other things, it requires the disclosure of finance charges, including disclosure in the advertisement of credit transactions.

tur'pis cau'sa, a base or immoral consideration on which no contract or lawsuit can be founded.

tutor, a guardian (*q.v.*), of an infant.

twelve-mile limit, an imaginary line established under an agreement between England and the United States, by which the latter is permitted to search the ships of the former for illicit liquor within twelve miles of the shore line. Cf. *three-mile limit, high seas* and *territorial waters.*

two-issue rule, in some jurisdictions, if a case presents two separate issues, and if one issue, complete in itself as a cause of action or defense, is submitted to the jury free from error, and the jury returns a general verdict and there is nothing to indicate upon which issue the general verdict is grounded, the issue which presents the claimed error may be disregarded. This rule does not apply where one of the issues submitted to the jury is entirely unsupported by the evidence.

U

uber'rima fi'des, *l.,* utmost good faith. Contracts made between persons in a particular relationship of confidence, *e.g.,* guardian and ward or attorney and client, require the fullest information to be given beforehand by the person in whom the confidence is reposed, to the person confiding, and perfect fairness in dealing, or the court will refuse to enforce the contract on behalf of the former.

ubi aliquid conceditur, conceditur et id sine quo res ipsa esse non potest, when anything is granted, that also is granted without which it could not exist. See, *e.g., way of necessity.*

ubi eadem ratio, ibi eadem lex, where the same reason exists, there the same law prevails.

ubi jus, ibi remedium, where there is a right, there is a remedy.

ubi jus incertum, ibi jus nullum, where the law is uncertain, there is no law.

ubi lex est specialis, et ratio ejus generalis, generaliter accipienda est, where the law is special and the reason of it is general, it ought to be taken as being general.

ubi non est principalis, non potest esse accessorius, where there is no principal, there can be no accessory.

ultimate facts, the final and resulting facts reached by processes of logical reasoning from the detailed or probative facts. Distinguished from evidence and legal conclusions. See also, *fact.*

ultimatum, a final offer, especially one made by either of the parties in a diplomatic negotiation.

ul'timus hae'res, *l.,* the ultimate heir.

ul'tra vi'res, *l.,* beyond their powers. Descriptive of the acts of a corporation when it exceeds the authority granted to it in its articles of incorporation or charter, *e.g.,* by making a contract concerning a particular subject.

umpire, a referee; a person who decides a question in dispute; especially one who is chosen by arbitrators to finally determine a point on which they are unable to agree.

un ne doit prise advantage de son tort demesne, one ought not to take advantage of his own wrong.

unavoidable accident, an occurrence which was not intended, and which, under all the circumstances, could not have been foreseen or prevented by the exercise of reasonable precautions.

uncertainty, vagueness, indefiniteness. A gift by will is void for uncertainty if it is impossible to ascertain the testator's intention with regard to it.

uncertificated security, shares which are not represented by an instrument and the transfer of which is registered on books maintained for that purpose by or on behalf of the issuer.

unclean hands, see *clean hands.*

unconscionable, a flexible term concerning contracts, used without definition in the U.C.C. and the Uniform Consumer Credit Code. The principle is one of the prevention of oppression and unfair surprise. The basic test is whether, in light of the general commercial background and the commercial needs of the particular trade or case, the clause involved is so one-sided as to be unconscionable under the circumstances existing at the time of the making of the contract. U.C.C. § 2-302, Official Comment 1. If a court finds a sales contract or clause of a sales contract to have been unconscionable at the time it was made, it may refuse to enforce the contract, or it may disregard the clause, or it may limit the application of the clause so as to avoid any unconscionable result. U.C.C. § 2-302(1). Accord, Restatement (Second) of Contracts § 208.

unconstitutional, see *constitutional.*

uncore prist (*ôn cŏr prē*), *L. fr.,* always ready. See also, *tout.*

un'de nil ha'bet, *l.,* formerly, a writ providing a remedy for a widow to whom no dower had been assigned within the period limited by law.

underinsured motorist coverage, insurance providing for situations in which the offending motorist does not carry enough coverage to pay the claim and the injured party has a higher coverage limit for such instances.

underlease, or **sublease,** a grant by a lessee to another of a part of his interest under the original lease, reserving to himself a reversion. The lessee is then called an underlessor or sublessor, and his assignee an underlessee or sublessee. An underlease for the whole term, not reserving any part to the lessee, is an assignment (*q.v.*). A lessee continues liable to his lessor on the covenants contained in the lease, whether he assigns, or underleases; a sublessee is not liable to the original lessor; an assignee of a lease is.

undertaking, a promise. (2) A promise formally given in the course of a legal proceeding, which may be enforced by attachment or otherwise.

undertenant, one who holds by an underlease (*q.v.*).

underwriter, an insurer.

undisclosed principal, a person whose agent acts without disclosing the fact of his agency and without the third party's knowledge of the existence of the principal. If the third party knows of the agency relationship, but not of the identity of the principal, the principal is then partially disclosed.

undue influence, improper persuasion (*q.v.*) which results in a person, *e.g.*, a testator, acting otherwise than according to his free will. (2) In the law of contract, unfair persuasion (*q.v.*) of a party who is under the domination of the person exercising the persuasion, or who by virtue of the relation between them is justified in assuming that that person will not act in a manner inconsistent with his welfare. Restatement (Second) of Contracts § 177(1).

unenforceable contract, a contract (*q.v.*) for the breach of which neither the remedy of damages nor the remedy of specific performance is available, but which is recognized in some other way as creating a duty of performance, though there has been no ratification. Restatement (Second) of Contracts § 8. Cf. *voidable contract*.

uniform acts, or **uniform laws,** various proposals for legislation to be consistently adopted by all of the legislatures of the states of the United States, made by the National Conference of Commissioners on Uniform State Laws (*q.v.*).

Uniform Anatomical Gift Act, a proposal drafted by the National Conference of Commissioners on Uniform State Laws and approved by the American Bar Association in August, 1968, for an act authorizing the gift of all or part of a human body after death for specific purposes. It has been enacted into law with variations in 50 states and the District of Columbia.

Uniform Code of Military Justice, chapter 47 of an act to revise, codify, and enact into law, titles 10 and 32 of the U.S.C., concerning punishment for offenses committed by military personnel. 10 U.S.C. §§ 801-940.

Uniform Commercial Code, a proposal by the American Law Institute and the National Conference of Commissioners on Uniform State Laws for comprehensive legislation relating to commercial transactions, *i.e.*, sales, commercial paper, bank deposits and collections, letters of credit, bulk transfers, warehouse receipts, bills of lading, other documents of title, investment securities, and secured transactions. It has been adopted in each of the states of the United States, except Louisiana, where it has been adopted in part, and in the District of Columbia and the Virgin Islands.

Uniform Determination of Death Act, a proposal by the National Conference of Commissioners on Uniform State Laws, approved in 1980, intended to provide a comprehensive basis for determining death (*q.v.*) in all situations. It has been substantially adopted in 13 states and the District of Columbia.

uniform laws, see *uniform acts.*

Uniform Marriage and Divorce Act, a proposal by the National Conference of Commissioners on Uniform State Laws approved in 1970, amended in 1971 and 1973, and recommended for adoption by the states. It relates to marriage, dissolution of marriage without reference to fault (popularly called "no-fault divorce"), and custody of children. It has been substantially enacted into law, at least in part, in Arizona, Colorado, Illinois, Kentucky, Minnesota, Missouri, Montana, and Washington.

Uniform Partnership Act, a proposal by the National Conference of Commissioners on Uniform State Laws, approved in 1914, and recommended for adoption to the legislatures of all the states. It relates to the nature of partnership, the relations of partners to persons dealing with the partnership, the relations of partners to one another, the property rights of a partner, and the dissolution and winding up of a partnership. It has been enacted into law in 48 states, the District of Columbia, Guam, and the Virgin Islands.

Uniform Probate Code, a proposal drafted by the National Conference of Commissioners on Uniform State Laws, approved in August, 1969, and recommended for adoption in all states. It relates to affairs of decedents, missing persons, protected persons, minors, incapacitated persons, and certain others. It has been enacted into law in Alaska, Arizona, Colorado, Florida, Hawaii, Idaho, Maine, Michigan, Minnesota, Montana, Nebraska, New Mexico, North Dakota, and Utah. A portion of it, Article VII, Part 1, has been enacted into law in Kentucky.

Uniform Product Liability Act, see *Model Uniform Product Liability Act.*

Uniform Time Act of 1966, an act to promote the observance of a uniform system of time (*q.v.*) throughout the U.S. Among other things, it provides for advancement of time or changeover dates, superseding of state laws, enforcement, zones for standard time, and the designation of zone standard time. 15 U.S.C. §§ 260 *et seq.*

Uniformed Services Former Spouses' Protection Act, title X of the Department of Defense Authorization Act, 1983. It concerns payment of retired or retainer pay in compliance with court orders, annuities under the survivor benefit plan, medical benefits, and commissary and exchange privileges. 10 U.S.C. §§ 1408 *et al.*

unilateral contract, a one-sided contract (*q.v.*); an agreement in which only one party makes a promise and on the other side of which the consideration has been fully performed, *e.g.*, a promise to repay a loan of money. (2) Occasionally, an agreement which is void because only one party is bound by it and it therefore lacks mutuality of obligation.

uninsured motorist, a person who is an owner or operator of an uninsured motor vehicle, a person of doubtful financial responsibility, or someone whose identity cannot be determined who causes personal injury or death resulting from the ownership, maintenance, or use of a motor vehicle. Some motor vehicle liability insurance policies provide for payment to the policyholder in the event of such losses.

uninsured motorist coverage, insurance providing for situations in which the offending motorist carries no insurance which guarantees that the injured insured will be in the same position as if he were injured through the negligence of an insured motorist.

Union, the United States of America. See also, *labor union.*

union security agreements, provisions in the union contract which seek to make membership one hundred percent in occupational groups they represent.

union shop, a factory, store or other place of employment that requires all nonunion employees to become members of the union within a prescribed period after initial employment.

United Nations, a world organization of sovereign equal nations with the primary purpose of maintaining international peace and security. Its charter has been in force since October 24, 1945. It acts through six principal organs, *i.e.*, General Assembly, Security Council, Economic and Social Council, Trusteeship Council, International Court of Justice, and Secretariat.

United States Commissioners, formerly, judicial officers appointed by the United States District Courts under the provisions of 28 U.S.C. § 631, who performed preliminary and examining functions analogous to those performed by a justice of the peace. See also, *examination (1)*. Cf. *United States Magistrates.*

United States Court of Appeals, formerly called Circuit Court of Appeals, United States courts of any of 12 circuits or judicial divisions of the United States, including the District of Columbia, which are second in rank to the United States Supreme Court. They have appellate jurisdiction over decisions of the United States district courts, except where a direct review may be had in the United States Supreme Court.

United States Magistrates, judicial officers appointed by the United States District Courts for the purpose of performing the duties formerly performed by United States Commissioners (*q.v.*) and to render assistance to the Court, *e.g.*, by serving as special masters in civil actions, conducting pretrial or discovery proceedings, and preliminary review of applications for post-trial relief made by individuals convicted of criminal offenses. 28 U.S.C. §§ 631-639. See also, *Federal Magistrate Act of 1979.*

United States of America, the contiguous states bounded on the north by Canada and the Great Lakes, and on the south by Mexico and the Gulf of Mexico, and extending from the Atlantic to the Pacific Ocean, and the states of Alaska and Hawaii, united under one national government, having a national constitution adopted in 1787, and amended from time to time since. At present there are 50 states.

unity, oneness; agreement in particulars.

unity of interest, the characteristic of a joint tenancy by which none of the tenants has a greater interest in the subject of tenancy than the others have. See also, *joint tenants.*

unity of possession, the possession (*q.v.*) by one person of several different estates or rights in the same real property, *e.g.*, where land subject to an easement comes into the hands of the person entitled to the easement, or where a lessee of lands afterwards buys the fee simple. By this unity of possession the lesser right is extinguished. See also, *merger.* (2) The characteristic of joint tenancy by which each tenant has the entire possession of the whole real property. See also, *joint tenants.*

unity of title, the characteristic of a joint tenancy by which the estate is transferred to all of the tenants by the same instrument or event. See also, *joint tenants.*

universal, unlimited; without exception; relating to the whole or all.

universal agent, a person who is appointed to do all acts which his principal can do, and which he has the power to delegate.

universal legacy, a bequest of the whole of the testator's property to one or more persons.

universal partnership, a partnership (*q.v.*) in which the partners agree to hold all their property in common.

universal representation (Sc.), the doctrine by which the heir is held to represent the ancestor as to all things, and therefore to be responsible for his debts.

unjust enrichment, the doctrine which places a legal duty of restitution upon a defendant who has acquired something of value at the expense of the plaintiff. Cf. *quasi contract.*

unlawful, contrary to law.

unlawful assembly, a gathering of three or more persons with the intent of committing a crime with force. (2) A generic term comprehending, among other things, riot and affray. Often defined by various state statutes. See also, *riot.*

unlawful force, force (*q.v.*) including confinement, which is employed without the consent of the person against whom it is directed and the employment of which constitutes an offense or actionable tort or would constitute such offense or tort except for a defense (*e.g.,* absence of intent, negligence, or mental capacity; duress; youth; or diplomatic status) not amounting to a privilege to use the force. Assent constitutes consent within the meaning of this definition, whether or not it otherwise is legally effective, except assent to the infliction of death or serious bodily harm. Model Penal Code § 3.11(1).

unliquidated, variously, unsettled, unpaid, not converted into money, or not ascertained. See also, *damages.*

u'no fla'tu, *l.* (with one breath), at the same moment.

unreasonable risk, a condition which occurs when an act is one which a reasonable man (*q.v.*) would recognize as involving a risk of harm to another. Restatement (Second) of Torts § 291.

unsound mind, a generic term for a defective, impaired, or diseased intellect, including lunacy and idiocy. Often defined by various state statutes.

untenantable, not fit to be rented or occupied by a tenant.

unwritten law, a supposed rule that the murder of a wife's paramour or a daughter's seducer is not a criminal offense.

upset price, the amount of money at which property sold by auction is put up, or under which it cannot be sold.

urban renewal, city planning and improvement undertaken by various official agencies, including city governments and the United States government. It comprehends slum clearance, redevelopment, remedying unsanitary, deficient, and obsolete housing, correction of inadequate transportation, sanitation, and other facilities and services, random land use, and traffic congestion.

ure (*ūr*), custom. (2) Effect; operation. See also, *inure.*

usage, practice long continued. (2) Habitual or customary practice. Restatement (Second) of Contracts § 219.

usage of trade, any practice or method of dealing having such regularity of observance in a place, vocation, or trade as to justify an expectation that it will be observed with respect to the transaction in question. The existence and scope of such a usage are to be proved as facts. If it is established that such a usage is embodied in a written trade code or similar writing, the interpretation of the writing is for the court. U.C.C. § 1-205(2). Accord, Restatement (Second) of Contracts § 222(1), (2).

usance, the time at which a bill of exchange, drawn in one country, on another country, is usually made payable. See also, *bill (2).*

use, a trust (*q.v.*) in which the person who has the possession for the benefit of another also has an active duty to perform concerning the subject matter. (2) Before the Statute of Uses, a use was in its nature equitable, being a right enforced by the court of chancery to the beneficial ownership of an estate, the possession of which was vested in confidence in another, called feoffee to uses, the beneficiary being the cestui que use. The effect of this separation of the legal and beneficial ownership being to enable secret transfers of land to be made, and also the rights of the Crown and of the lord to forfeiture, escheat, and the like to be evaded, the Statute of Uses (27 Hen. VIII. c. 10) was passed, enacting, in effect, that where any person was seised to the use, confidence, or trust of another, the latter should take a legal estate coextensive with the equitable one which he would have had prior to the statute. The statute does not apply to leaseholds or copyholds, nor does it execute (*i.e.,* operate on) a second use, otherwise called a use upon a use, or upon a use or trust which has active duties attached to it, called an active use. Common-law uses are those last mentioned, which were unaffected by the statute. (3) A springing use is one which is to come into operation at a future date. (4) A shifting use is one which shifts from one person to another on the happening of a certain event, or nonperformance of a condition. (5) Enjoyment; application to one's service.

use and derivative use immunity, a type of witness immunity that protects the witness from the use of compelled testimony and evidence derived therefrom.

use and occupation, a cause of action which may be brought by the owner of real property against a person using or occupying it, on an implied agreement to pay the reasonable value of his use and occupation.

use immunity, a type of witness immunity that only prevents the prosecution from using the compelled testimony in any criminal proceeding; it does not prevent prosecuting authorities from making derivative use of the fruits of the witness' compelled testimony by obtaining investigatory leads from it.

use of force, conduct which invades any of another's interests (*q.v.*) of personality and thus is, unless privileged, a battery (*q.v.*), assault (*q.v.*), or false imprisonment (*q.v.*). Restatement (Second) of Torts § 117.

useful, descriptive of an invention which is capable of performing a beneficial function.

user, use; enjoyment. Cf. *nonuser*.

Uses, Statute of, see *use*.

usuarius, *l.,* one who had the mere use of a thing belonging to another for the purpose of supplying his daily want.

usuary, see *usuarius*.

usuca'pio (Rom.), title by prescription (*q.v.*).

usufruct (Rom.), the right to the beneficial ownership of something, the proprietorship of which is in another.

usufructuary, a person who enjoys the usufruct (*q.v.*).

usurpation, a taking and holding of property or a public office without right.

usury, interest on money which is in excess of the legal maximum. Often defined by various state statutes. (2) Formerly, all interest on money.

usury laws, various state statutes fixing the rate of interest which may be charged, and prescribing penalties for taking interest in excess of the lawful rate.

uterine, born of the same mother.

u'ti posside'tis, as you possess.

utile per inutile non vitiatur, the useful is not vitiated by the useless, *e.g.,* clear words are not affected by words which are superfluous.

utter, to offer; to publish; to attempt to pass off a forged document or counterfeit coin as genuine.

utter barrister, or **outer barrister,** an English attorney who is neither King's counsel nor a sergeant at law, but who tries cases in court.

u'xor (*ü ksoir*), *l.,* a lawful wife. Cf. *et ux*.

ux'oricide (*ūksōrĭsīd*), the murder of a wife by her husband. (2) A person who murders his wife.

V

vacant, empty; not occupied.

vacant succession, an inheritance, the heir to which is unknown.

vacan'tia bo'na (Rom.), things without an owner; the goods of someone dying without successors.

vacate, to cancel, annul, or render of no effect, *e.g.*, a judgment or order. (2) To move out of, *e.g.*, a house.

vacation, the period of time between the end of one term of court and the beginning of another.

vagabond, or **vagrant,** a wanderer; an idle person who, being able to maintain himself by lawful labor, either refuses to work or resorts to unlawful practices, *e.g.*, begging, to gain a living.

valid, good; effectual; of binding force.

valid enforceable contract, a contract which is not defective as to parties, content or structure, that is, not lacking in specific language or required clauses and which has parties who are competent and willing participants in the contractual process and whose subject matter is not outlawed by statute or other regulatory authority.

valuable consideration, a consideration (*q.v.*) which has a money value.

value, the utility or worth of an object. (2) Except as otherwise provided with respect to negotiable instruments and bank collections, a person gives value for rights if he acquires them: (a) in return for a binding commitment to extend credit or for the extension of immediately available credit whether or not drawn upon and whether or not a charge-back is provided for in the event of difficulties in collection; or (b) as security for, or in total or partial satisfaction of, a pre-existing claim; or (c) by accepting delivery pursuant to a pre-existing contract for purchase; or (d) generally, in return for any consideration sufficient to support a simple contract. U.C.C. § 1-201(44). See also, *holder for value.*

value added tax, VAT; a tax levied against a product as it is produced and distributed because each step adds value to the product.

value received, a phrase denoting that a consideration has been given.

valued, descriptive of an insurance policy in which the value of the thing insured is settled at the time of making the insurance and is inserted in the policy. It is distinguished from an open policy, in which the value is left to be afterwards ascertained.

valuer, a person who appraises property.

vandalism, willful and malicious acts committed with the intent to damage or destroy property of another.

variance, under some codes of civil practice, a disagreement between successive pleadings by the same party. (2) A disagreement between the statements in the pleadings and the evidence adduced in proof thereof.

vassal, formerly, a person obligated to render feudal service to an English lord.

vehicle, every contrivance capable of being used as a means of transportation on land. (2) Every contrivance capable of being used as a means of transportation on land, water, or in the air. Occasionally defined by various state and federal statutes.

vehicular assault, recklessly causing serious physical harm to another while operating or participating in the operation of a motor vehicle, motorcycle, snowmobile, locomotive, watercraft, or aircraft.

vehicular homicide, intentionally or negligently causing the death of another while operating or participating in the operation of a motor vehicle, motorcycle, snowmobile, locomotive, watercraft, or aircraft.

vendee, a buyer; a person to whom something is sold.

venditio'ni expo'nas, *l.,* that you expose for sale; a writ or order directing a sheriff to sell goods which he has taken under a fieri facias (*q.v.*).

vendor, a seller; a person who sells something.

vendor's lien, the right of a seller whose sale price, or any part of it, is unpaid, to charge the land sold with payment thereof, even after he has conveyed or delivered possession of it to the purchaser. In some jurisdictions, the lien is not valid unless expressly reserved in the deed. Analogous to a mortgage given to secure purchase money.

vendor's privilege, in La., the vendor has a privilege on something sold, *i.e.,* he is paid from the proceeds of the thing in preference to all other creditors.

vendue (*vĕn du*), an auction.

veni're fa'cias (make to come), a writ to the sheriff to summon a jury.

venire facias ad responden'dum, a writ of summons to answer an indictment for misdemeanor.

venire facias de novo, a writ to summon a jury for a new trial.

venter (*vĕn 'têr*), or **ventre** (von tr), the womb. See also, *de ventre inspiciendo, in ventre sa mere* and *jury of matrons.*

venue (*ven 'u*), or **visne** (*ven*), the neighborhood; the county in which a particular lawsuit should be tried; the county from which the jury is taken for the trial of a lawsuit. Often regulated by various state and federal statutes. A change of venue is the sending of a lawsuit to be tried before a jury of another county, *e.g.,* when circumstances render it impossible to have an impartial trial in the county where the cause of action arose.

verba accipienda sunt secundum subjectam materiam, words are to be understood with reference to the subject matter.

verba aliquid operari debent, words ought to be interpreted in such a way as to have some operation.

verba chartarum fortius accipiuntur contra proferentem, the words of a grant are to be taken most strongly against the person employing them.

verba cum effectu accipienda sunt, words ought to be construed so as to give them effect.

verba generalia restringuntur ad habilitatem rei vel aptitudinem personae, general words must be narrowed to the nature of the subject or the capacity of the person, *e.g.*, of the grantor.

verba illata, vel relata, inesse videntur, words implied or referred to are considered to be incorporated.

verba intentioni debent inservire, words ought to be made subservient to the intent.

verba ita sunt intelligenda, ut res magis valeat guam pereat, words are to be so understood that the object may be carried out rather than fail. See also, *benigne, etc.*

verbal, made by word of mouth; oral (*q.v.*).

verdict, the decision of a jury concerning the matters submitted to it in the trial of a lawsuit. It may be general, *i.e.*, for plaintiff, fixing the amount to be recovered, or for defendant without more, or special, the latter giving the facts found, and leaving the conclusion of law to the court. See also, *special verdict.*

verification, the affidavit of a party, *e.g.*, in a court pleading, or of his agent or attorney, that certain statements of fact, *e.g.*, the allegations of a pleading, are true.

veritas demonstrationis tollit errorem nominis, correctness of the description removes the error of the name, *e.g.*, in a will, if the identity of a legatee is established, a mere error in his name is unimportant.

veritas habenda est in juratore; justitia et judicium in judice, truth is the thing that is needed and wanted in a juror, justice and judgment in a judge.

veritas nihil veretur nisi abscondi, truth fears nothing but concealment.

veritas nimium altercando amittitur, by too much altercation truth is lost.

versus, *l.*, against.

vested, established; fixed. A right or estate is vested in a person when he becomes entitled to it. It may be vested in possession when he has a right to present enjoyment, or vested in interest when he has a present fixed right of future enjoyment, *i.e.*, a right to an estate, the possession of which is postponed to a fixed time or the happening of a certain event. See also, *reversion.*

vested remainder, see *remainder.*

ve'tera statu'ta, *l.,* ancient statutes; statutes commencing with Magna Charta (*q.v.*) and ending with those of Edward II.

ve'to, *l.* (I forbid), the refusal of an executive officer, whose assent is necessary to the validity of an act passed by a legislative body, to concur therein. The veto power is given to the President of the United States, U.S. Const., Art. I, Sec. 7, and to the governors of many of the states.

vexa'ta quaes'tio, *l.,* an undetermined point which has often been discussed.

vexatious, annoying; harassing; oppressive.

vexatious suit, a lawsuit which is initiated without probable cause, for purposes of annoyance or oppression.

vi et ar'mis, *l.,* with force and arms.

vi'a, by way of. (2) (Rom.) A right of way (*q.v.*).

via antiqua via est tuta, the old way is the safe way.

via trita est tutissima, the trodden path is the safest.

viability, a capability of living after birth.

vicarious liability, substituted or indirect responsibility, *e.g.,* the responsibility of an employer for the torts committed by his employee within the scope of his employment.

vicarius non habet vicarium, a substitute cannot have a substitute. See also, *delegatus, etc.*

vice, in the place of; instead of. (2) Immorality or evil. (3) A defect.

vice chancellor, a judge of the English court of chancery.

vice comes, *l.,* the sheriff.

Vice-President of the United States, the second officer in point of rank in the United States. He is elected at the same time and for the same term as the President. He is President of the Senate, but has no vote unless the Senate is equally divided. In case of the removal from office, death, resignation, or inability of the President, the duties of the President devolve on the Vice-President. U.S. Const., Art. I, Sec. 3; Art. II, Sec. 1; and Amend. XII.

vice versa, *l.,* reversing the order; on the contrary.

vicinage, neighborhood; proximity.

Victim and Witness Protection Act of 1982, an act to provide additional protections and assistance to victims and witnesses in federal cases. It concerns victim impact statements, protection of victims and witnesses from intimidation, restitution, guidelines for fair treatment of crime victims and witnesses, profit by a criminal from sale of his story, and bail. 18 U.S.C. §§ 1503, 1505, 1510, 1512-1515, 3146, 3663, 3664.

vi'de, see; a word of reference. Vide ante or supra refers to a previous passage; vide post or infra refers to a subsequent one.

vide'licet, or **viz.,** to wit; formerly used to precede a specification of particulars in a deed, contract, or court pleading.

viduity, widowhood.

view, an inspection of property mentioned in evidence in a trial, or a site where a crime has been committed, by the jury or certain persons called viewers, under an order of court.

viewer, see *view*.

vigilantibus non dormientibus jura subveniunt, laws come to the assistance of the vigilant, not of the sleepy. See also, *laches*.

vill, formerly, a manor, village, or town.

vin'culo matrimo'nii, *l.*, from the bond of matrimony. See also, *divorce*.

vindictive damages, see *damages*.

violation, an act which contravenes the provisions of a statute or administrative regulation. (2) An act contrary to another's right, committed with force. (3) A rape.

violence, physical force used against law, private rights, or public liberty; an assault or intimidation by a display of force.

vis, *l.*, force.

vis impres'sa, direct force; original force.

vis ma'jor, inevitable accident; irresistible force.

visa, the recognition by one nation of the validity of a passport issued by another nation; the concurrence by one nation in the request which is implied by the issuance of a passport by another nation. See also, *passport* and *vise*.

vise' (*vē zā* ´), the countersignature of an official, *e.g.*, that of a consul of one nation affixed to a passport issued by another nation. See also, *visa*.

visitor, a person appointed in a guardianship or protective proceeding (*q.v.*) who is trained in law, nursing, or social work, is an officer, employee, or special appointee of the court, and has no personal interest in the proceeding. Uniform Probate Code § 5-103(21).

visne (*vēn*), see *venue*.

vital statistics, public records of births, diseases, marriages, and deaths. Usually defined and regulated by various state statutes.

vitiation (Sc.), material alteration in an instrument.

vi'va vo'ce, *l.*, by word of mouth. See also, *evidence*.

vivary (*vī va rē*), formerly, an English park, warren, or fishery.

viz., see *videlicet*.

VOC, see *volatile organic compounds*.

void, of no force or effect; absolutely null. Cf. *voidable*.

void ab initio, a contract null from its inception.

void contract, a contract which possesses no legal effect or influence. A void contract never existed by operation of law. Void contracts are those bargained for exchanges which are plainly illegal–such as "hit man" organized crime contract—contrary to a serious public policy determination or other statutory interpretation or guideline.

void for uncertainty, see *uncertainty*.

void marriage, a marriage offending some strong public policy of the state and needs no formal judicial action or declaration to establish its invalidity.

voidable, descriptive of an imperfect obligation which may be legally annulled or cured or confirmed, at the option of one of the parties, *e.g.*, the contract of an infant with an adult. See also, *voidable contract*. Cf. *void*.

voidable contract, a contract (*q.v.*) where one or more parties have the power, by a manifestation of election to do so, to avoid the legal relations created by the contract, or by ratification of the contract to extinguish the power of avoidance. Restatement (Second) of Contracts § 7. Cf. *unenforceable contract*.

voidable marriage, a marriage that can be ratified by conduct of the parties after removal of the legal impediment that made it vulnerable, and unless it is judicially annulled in timely fashion (before ratification or death of a party, or the tolling of the action under an applicable statute of limitation). A valid union from its inception.

voir dire (*vwär dẽr*) (*ventatem dicere*), a preliminary examination of a prospective juror, in order to determine his or her qualifications to serve as a juror. (2) Occasionally, a preliminary examination of a witness in order to determine his or her competency to speak the truth.

volatile organic compounds, hydrocarbon substances that mix with NOx and sunlight to form ozone. EPA has recently promulgated rules defining VOC for purposes of ozone pollution control.

volenti non fit injuria, no injury is done [in the eye of the law], when the person injured consents.

Volstead Act, formerly, a legislative act passed by Congress, regulating the traffic in intoxicating liquors under U.S. Const., Amend. XVIII.

voluntary, acting without compulsion; done by design. (2) When applied to a gift, promise, or conveyance, descriptive of an act which is done either without consideration (*q.v.*) or for only a good consideration (*q.v.*).

voluntary manslaughter, the unlawful killing of another human being without malice aforethought; malice aforethought will be negated if, and only if the provocation was legally sufficient and was determined by the jury to be adequate to cause a reasonable person to act rashly and without due consideration.

voluntary petition, a way of commencing a bankruptcy in which the debtor requests an order of relief for the determination that he or she or the entity is bankrupt.

voluntary waste, the spoiling or destroying of real property which is the result of the deliberate act of the tenant, *e.g.,* where he pulls down a wall or cuts timber. Opposed to permissive waste (*q.v.*).

voluntas in delictis, non exitus spectatur, in crimes the intention, and not the consequence, is looked to.

voluntas reputatur pro facto, the will is to be taken for the deed.

voluntas testatoris est ambulatoria usque ad extremum vitae exitum, the will of a testator is revocable until the latest moment of life.

volunteer, a person who injects himself into affairs which do not legally or morally concern him, or which do not affect his interests. (2) A person who receives a gift, promise, or conveyance without giving a valuable consideration therefor. (3) A person who offers his services to his country in time of war.

voting trust, an arrangement by which shares of stock in a corporation are held in trust for the purpose of voting them at stockholders' meetings. The shareholders in the corporation who contribute their shares of stock to the voting trust receive in exchange shares of stock in the voting trust.

vouch, to rely on; to quote. (2) To call on a person who has made a warranty of title to real property to defend the title.

voucher, any one of various documents which evidence a transaction, *e.g.,* a receipt.

vouching to warranty, see *vouch* (2).

vox emissa volat; litera scripta manet, the spoken word flies away; the written one remains.

voyeurism, committing trespass or otherwise surreptitiously invading the privacy of another, to spy or eavesdrop on another, for the purpose of sexually arousing or gratifying oneself.

W

wad'set (Sc.), a kind of mortgage.

wage earners' plan, or **Chapter XIII proceedings,** a statutory remedy for insolvent debtors, under the Bankruptcy Reform Act (*q.v.*), by which the debtor's future earnings are paid to a trustee, who pays them to the creditors. The plan for such an arrangement must be submitted to the Court and to the creditors for their approval. Debtors who utilize such a remedy are relieved from garnishment, attachment and execution for debt during the term of the proceedings.

wager, a bet; a promise by one person to pay a sum of money to another person in case a certain thing happens or does not happen. A wager is distinguishable from insurance (*q.v.*), because in insurance there must be an insurable interest (*q.v.*).

Wager of Battel, see *battel.*

wager of law, see *compurgator.*

wager policy, a contract of insurance in which the insured has no interest in the subject of the insurance. See also, *wager.*

wages, the agreed compensation paid by an employer to an employee for work done.

Wagner Act, an act to diminish the causes of labor disputes burdening or obstructing interstate and foreign commerce, and to create a National Labor Relations Board. 29 U.S.C. §§ 151 *et seq.*

waifs, goods found, but claimed by nobody. (2) Goods stolen, but waived (*waviata*) or thrown away by the thief in his flight.

wait-and-see doctrine, or law, various state laws concerning perpetuities which provide that in determining whether an interest would violate the rule against perpetuities, the period of perpetuities shall be measured by actual rather than possible events, provided however, the period shall not be measured by any lives whose continuance does not have a causal relationship to the vesting or failure of the interest. Any interest which would violate the rule as thus modified must be reformed, within the limits of the rule, to approximate most closely the intention of the creator of the interest. See also, *perpetuity.*

waive, to forego; to decline to take advantage of, *e.g.*, a legal right or an omission or irregularity. (2) See also, *waifs.*

waiver, a positive act by which a legal right is relinquished.

Walsh-Healey Act, an act to provide conditions for the purchase of supplies and the making of contracts by the United States. 41 U.S.C. §§ 35-45.

want of consideration, the lack of any legally valid consideration (*q.v.*) for a contract.

wanton misconduct, such behavior as manifests a disposition to perversity. It must be under such circumstances and conditions that the party doing the act, or failing to act, is conscious that his conduct will, in all common probability, result in injury. See also, *reckless disregard of safety.*

ward, an infant who is under guardianship (*q.v.*). (2) A person for whom a guardian has been appointed. A minor ward is a minor for whom a guardian has been appointed solely because of minority. Uniform Probate Code § 5-103(22). (3) A subdivision of a city, borough, county, or parish for election purposes. See also, *watch.*

ward of the court, an infant who is under the protection of a court, *e.g.*, a juvenile court or a court of equity.

warden, a guardian or keeper; the title given to various public officers who perform such functions as part of their official duties.

wardship, the condition of a person who is a ward (*q.v.*).

warehouse, a place for the receiving and storing of goods and merchandise for hire.

warehouse receipt, a receipt (*q.v.*) issued by a person engaged in the business of storing goods for hire. U.C.C. § 1-201(45). By the terms of the warehouse receipt, the warehouseman (*q.v.*) agrees to deliver the goods to the person depositing them or his assignees. The assignment of such a receipt, and its presentation to and acknowledgment by the warehouseman, operates as a delivery of the goods described.

warehouseman, a person who is engaged in the business of storing goods for hire. U.C.C. § 7-102(1)(h).

warrant, written authority. (2) A written order from a court to an officer, directing the officer to arrest a person. Accord, Restatement (Second) of Torts § 113.

warrant of attorney, in some jurisdictions, written authority to an attorney by which it is intended that a judgment shall be entered, authorizing the attorney to appear on behalf of the person giving the authority and to confess judgment. See also, *cognovit note.*

warranty, a guarantee concerning goods or land which is expressly or impliedly made to a purchaser by the vendor. See also, *implied warranty.*

warranty deed, a deed containing certain assurances or guarantees by the grantor that the deed conveys a good and unencumbered title.

warranty of goods, an undertaking that goods (*q.v.*) are of a certain quality. See also, *implied warranty.*

warranty of fitness, see *implied warranty (b)*.

warranty of land, see *general warranty* and *special warranty*.

warranty of merchantability, see *implied warranty (a)*.

warren, in England, a place for the keeping of wild beasts or fowl. See also, *game*.

waste, the spoil or destruction of houses, gardens, trees, or other portions of real property, by a tenant, to the prejudice of the inheritance. It is either (a) permissive, consisting of mere neglect or omission to do what is necessary to prevent injury; or (b) voluntary *(q.v.)*. Sometimes a tenant, by the terms of the instrument creating his estate, holds his lands without impeachment of waste, *i.e.*, with general permission to commit waste of any ordinary character.

"wasting asset" corporation, a corporation organized to exploit a specific asset such as a mine, an oil field, a piece of land, or a patent, with no intention of continuing in business after such exploitation.

watch, a body of police officers on duty at night; ward being chiefly applied to those on duty by day.

water bailiff, an English officer whose duty it is to search ships.

water pollution, the making of the drinkable water, and water on which fish and wildlife depend for their existence, unclean or impure for those purposes by a concentration of material, *e.g.*, human excreta, organic industrial wastes, infectious agents, plant nutrients, organic pesticides, industrial waste, chemicals, and sediment, or by heat.

Water Quality Act of 1965, an act to amend the Federal Water Pollution Control Act to establish a Federal Water Pollution Control Administration, to provide grants for research and development, to increase grants for construction of sewage treatment works, to require establishment of water quality criteria, and for other purposes. 33 U.S.C. §§ 1151 *et seq.*

watercourse, an artificial or natural stream. (2) A right to the flow of water over one's own land or to discharge water onto one's neighbor's land. (3) In the context of interference with the use of water, it is limited to a stream of water of natural origin; it includes springs, lakes, and marshes in which a stream originates or through which it flows. Restatement (Second) of Torts § 841.

watered stock, capital stock issued by a corporation which is not fully paid up.

way, a passage. (2) A right of passage. Ways are either public or private; those which are public being usually called highways. A private way, or right of way, may be founded on grant, license, or prescription, being either an easement or customary right.

way of necessity, a way (*q.v.*) which arises by operation of law, *e.g.,* where a person grants to another a piece of land which can only be reached by crossing other remaining land of the grantor.

waybill, a document containing the names of passengers or the description of goods, carried in a public conveyance. Cf. *bill* (**4**).

way-going crops, see *away-going.*

ways and means, the name often given to a committee appointed in legislative bodies to determine the manner of raising funds for the use of the government.

weapon, a flexible term for any one of various objects used, or intended to be used, as an instrument for fighting. Often defined by various state statutes. (2) Anything readily capable of lethal use and possessed under circumstances not manifestly appropriate for lawful uses which it may have. The term includes a firearm which is not loaded or lacks a clip or other component to render it immediately operable, and components which can readily be assembled into a weapon. Model Penal Code § 5.06(2).

Welsh mortgage, in England, a conveyance of an estate in property, redeemable at any time by the mortgagor, on payment of the loan; the rents and profits being in the meantime received by the mortgagee in satisfaction of interest, subject to an account. The mortgagee cannot foreclose.

wergild, formerly, a fine imposed for homicide or grave injury.

WESTLAW, a computer-assisted legal research service provided by West Publishing Company which provides on-line access to legal information including cases, statutes, administrative regulations, and secondary material.

wetlands, there are two types of wetlands: (1) inland wetlands are marshes and (2) coastal wetlands which are estuarian lands (salt marshes).

wharfage, money paid for landing goods upon, or loading them from, a wharf.

wharfinger, a person who owns or keeps a wharf for the purpose of receiving and shipping goods.

Wharton's Rule, when a plurality of offenders is necessary to the idea of an offense, *e.g.,* adultery, bigamy, or dueling, conspiracy (*q.v.*) cannot be charged because it would evade the statutory limitation on the punishment for the offense. It is a judicial presumption to be applied in the absence of legislative intent to the contrary.

whereas, in view of the following facts; a word which introduces a recital of a fact.

whistle blower, an employee who refuses to participate in and/or reports illegal activities of his employer or fellow employees.

whistle blower action, statutes designed to protect whistle blowers from the retaliation of their employers.

white acre, a term used to signify a hypothetical parcel of land.

white rents, rent payable in silver. Cf. *black rents.*

white slavery, the interstate transportation of females for immoral purposes. See also, *Mann Act.*

whole blood, see *blood.*

wife, a woman who has a husband.

wild animal, see *animal.*

Wild's case, rule in, a devise to B and his children or issue, B having no issue at the time of the devise, gives him an estate-tail; but if he has issue at the time, B and his children take as joint tenants or as tenants in common, according to the other words of the will.

wilful, see *willful.*

wilful misconduct, see *reckless disregard of safety.*

will, the final declaration of the disposition which a person desires to have made of his or her property after death. It is revocable during the testator's or testatrix's lifetime. It usually must be in writing. Infants under the age of discretion and persons of unsound mind have no legal capacity to make a will. Usually regulated by various state statutes. (2) Includes codicil (*q.v.*) and any testamentary (*q.v.*) instrument which merely appoints an executor or revokes or revises another will. Uniform Probate Code § 1-201(48).

will contest, see *contest of will.*

willful, or **wilful,** intentional; deliberate. (2) A voluntary, intentional violation of a known legal duty; a finding of bad purpose or evil motive is not required. See also, *reckless disregard of safety.*

Wind Energy Systems Act of 1980, an act to provide for an accelerated program of wind energy research, development and demonstration, to be carried out by the Department of Energy with the support of the National Aeronautics and Space Administration and other federal agencies. 42 U.S.C. §§ 9201 *et seq.*

winding up, the process of collecting and distributing the assets of a corporation which is bankrupt, or unable or unwilling to carry on its business any longer. (2) The liquidation of a partnership.

with force and arms, see *force and arms.*

with intent, see *intentionally.*

withdrawal of juror, the removal of a member of a trial jury from the jury box, in order to put an end to the proceedings.

without day, indefinitely. See also, *sine die.*

without prejudice, see *prejudice.*

without recourse, (*sans recours*), see *indorsement* (2).

without reserve, descriptive of an auction (*q.v.*) at which the auctioneer makes an offer to sell the goods at any price bid by the highest bidder. After the auctioneer calls for bids, the goods cannot be withdrawn unless no bid is made within a reasonable time. Restatement (Second) of Contracts § 28(1) (b).

witness, a person who sees an act or event occur, *e.g.,* the execution of a deed. (2) A person who testifies in the trial of a lawsuit.

witness immunity law, title II of an act relating to the control of organized crime in the U.S. It provides, among other things, that whenever a federal witness refuses, on the basis of his privilege against self-incrimination, to testify or provide other information in particular proceedings, and an order is communicated to the witness, the witness may not refuse to comply with the order on the basis of the privilege against self-incrimination, but no testimony or other information compelled under the order, or information directly or indirectly derived from the testimony or other information, may be used against the witness in any criminal case, except a prosecution for perjury, giving a false statement, or otherwise failing to comply with the order. 18 U.S.C. §§ 6001 *et seq.*

Witness Protection Act, see *Victim and Witness Protection Act of 1982.*

Woodsy Owl law, a statute prohibiting knowingly and for profit manufacturing, reproducing, or using the character, "Woodsy Owl," the name, "Woodsy Owl," or the slogan, "Give a Hoot, Don't Pollute." 18 U.S.C. § 711a.

woolsack, the seat of the lord chancellor in the English House of Lords.

words of limitation, see *limitation* (3).

workers' or **workmen's compensation,** various state remedies provided for by statute, by which indemnity for injuries or death arising out of private employment is furnished to employees and their dependents. The liability of the employer is usually in a limited amount, and is determined independently of the fact of negligence or lack of negligence.

World Court, see *International Court of Justice.*

World Wide Web, WWW; a hypertext-based system of connected network servers that access Internet resources globally.

wounding, see *battery* and *mayhem.*

wreck, any portion of a shipwreck or her cargo which is recovered on shore or at sea, including flotsam (*q.v.*), jetsam (*q.v.*), and ligan (*q.v.*).

writ, a written court order or a judicial process. It is issued by authority of a court, and directed to the sheriff or other officer authorized by law to execute it. He must return it with a brief statement of what he has done in pursuance of it, to the court or officer who issued it. Writs are either (a) prerogative, when the granting of them is in the discretion of the court, as in the case of habeas corpus; or (b) of right, when the applicant is entitled as of course. The latter class includes original writs by which an action is commenced, *e.g.*, a summons, and judicial writs under which classification almost all writs at present fall, *e.g.*, writs in aid (*q.v.*), and writs of execution. (3) An action, *e.g.*, the writs of waste and partition.

writ coram nobis, see *coram nobis*.

writ in aid, a court order or process issued after a writ of execution has failed.

writ of assistance, see *assistance, writ of*.

writ of attaint, see *attaint (2)*.

writ of entry, in some jurisdictions, a real action by a person disseised, to recover possession.

writ of error, an original writ, directing an inferior court to send the record of proceedings before it to a superior court for review. Analogous to an appeal.

writ of inquiry, see *inquiry, writ of*.

writ of restitution, see *restitution*.

writing, or **written,** printing, typewriting, or any other intentional reduction to tangible form. U.C.C. § 1-201(46). (2) Writing includes printing or any other method of recording information, money, coins, tokens, stamps, seals, credit cards, badges, trademarks, and other symbols of value, right, privilege, or identification. Model Penal Code § 224.1(1).

wrong, the infringement of a right.

wrongful civil proceedings, taking an active part in the initiation, continuation, or procurement of civil proceedings by a person against another, if (a) he acts without probable cause, and primarily for a purpose other than that of securing the proper adjudication of the claim in which the proceedings are based, and (b) except when they are ex parte (*q.v.*), the proceedings have terminated in favor of the person against whom they are brought. Restatement (Second) of Torts § 674. Cf. *malicious prosecution*.

wrongful death, a separate and independent action from the decedent's action for the benefit of relatives of the decedent, for compensable losses suffered by them as a result of his death.

Y

year, variously, the period in which the earth makes one complete revolution around the sun, twelve calendar months, three hundred and sixty-five days. See also, *bissextile* and *new style*.

year books, annual reports of cases in a regular series from the time of King Edward II to Henry VIII.

year to year, see *tenant from year to year*.

yielding and paying, the first words of the reddendum clause in a lease, constituting a covenant to pay rent.

Youth Corrections Act, see *Federal Youth Corrections Act*.

Z

zoning, the division of a city or county into separate areas, and the application to each area of regulations which limit the various purposes to which the land and buildings therein may be devoted.

TABLE OF ABBREVIATIONS

EXPLANATIONS OF ABBREVIATIONS AND REFERENCES TO REPORTS OF CASES AND OTHER LEGAL PUBLICATIONS

There are a great many sources of legal abbreviations, one of the most commonly used of which is *A Uniform System of Citation*, published by the Harvard Law Review Association, fifteenth edition, 1991. *A Uniform System of Citation* has received wide acceptance, but many publishers refuse to observe its rules, and instead use their own abbreviations. Such publishers often decipher their abbreviations in a legend near the front of their books. Many courts prescribe their own forms of abbreviation for use in briefs and opinions in those courts. Writers have used various abbreviations over the years. The abbreviations established by *A Uniform System of Citation* have changed in the various editions. These facts cause some abbreviations for the same reference to vary from one publication to another. Those variations are, to a significant extent, included herein.

Anyone who compares the various catalogs of law reports must be impressed by the wide discrepancies between them. They differ greatly, not only as to the number of reports included and the form of abbreviation to be adopted in citing, but also as to the spelling of the reporters' names, the style of the courts whose decisions are reported, and the period covered by the reports. They cannot all be correct, and it is possible that not one of them is so in every particular. Many of these errors are due to careless proofreading.

It may not be out of place to point out the reasons for many discrepancies, and the liabilities to error to which original explorers are subjected.

(1) Many of the old English Reports were hastily published, and at a time when the art of printing was extremely crude. Typographical errors abounded on every page, and even the name of an author, or editor, would be spelled several different ways in as many different places. Thus, the name of one reporter is spelled *Benloe* (now commonly accepted on account of its brevity), *Bendloe, Benlowe, Bendlow, Benloes, Benloos, Bendloes* and *Benlowes*. In our own country, the name of a South Carolina reporter is spelled *Spears* in the first volume of his law reports; *Speers* in the second volume of the law reports and in the original edition of his equity reports; and *Spears* in a reprint of the latter. The *s*, which should be separated from the name of the reporter by an apostrophe, frequently becomes incorporated with it, and *vice versa*. The printers who make such errors in spelling proper names are, of course, still more liable

to err in the matter of figures, and it is no unusual thing to find two or three different dates to the same case.

(2) Prior to the eighteenth century, cases were seldom arranged in chronological order, and the earliest case in point of time was quite as likely to appear at the end of a volume as at the beginning. Anyone who tries to ascertain the period covered by the reports, by looking at two or three cases in the beginning and two or three at the end, is almost sure to be deceived. The title pages themselves are frequently deceitful, as cases of both earlier and later dates than those mentioned are often incorporated in the volume, apparently after the title page has been printed. Our American reporters are not free from this fault, and one may have to look through not only an entire volume, but even an entire series of volumes, to find the earliest case reported. *E.g.*, the earliest case reported in *Bland's Chancery (Md.)* is found in vol. 2, p. 89; in *Johnson's Cases (N.Y.)*, vol. 3, p. 415; *Grant's Cases (Pa.)*, vol. 3, p. 1; *Wheeler's Criminal Cases (N.Y.)*, vol. 2, p. 586; *Cowen's Reports (N.Y.)*, vol. 9, p. 655; *Giffard's Chancery Reports (England)*, vol. 5, p. 13.

(3) The regnal do not correspond strictly with the calendar years, and when the former only are mentioned it is easy to err in stating the latter. A case decided in 10th Eliz., may have been decided in 1567 or 1568, and often it is impossible to say which, from anything found in the reports themselves. A common error is to add the year of the reign to the year A.D. when the reign began, which is like adding 10 to 1, and concluding that the tenth year fell on the eleventh. Another common error is to reckon the regnal years of Charles II from 1660, the year of his restoration, instead of from 1649, the year of his father's death and his own succession, as maintained by the royalists and all reporters since the restoration.

(4) Some catalogs designate the "period covered" by the years from and to which the cases run, both dates being exclusive. In others, both dates are inclusive, and in others still the first is inclusive and the last exclusive.

The dates given herein are those of the earliest and latest cases reported, except in a few instances where one or two cases of an earlier or later date are inserted in an appendix or prefixed to the regular series of reports, or are incorporated as exhibits to the cases reported in the volume.

A. Atlantic Reporter; Association.

A.2d Atlantic Reporter, Second Series.

A. & E. Adolphus and Ellis, Queen's Bench, Eng., 1834-1841.

A. & E. Cas. American and English Annotated Cases, 1906-1912.

A. & E. Ency. American and English Encyclopedia of Law.

A. & E. (N.S.). Adolphus and Ellis, Queen's Bench, Eng., New Series, 1841-1852.

A.B.A. American Bar Association.

A.B.A.J. American Bar Association Journal.

A.B.A. Rep. American Bar Association Reports.

A.B.F. American Bar Foundation.

A.C. Court of Appeal in Chancery, Eng.; Appellate Court; Appeal Court, Chancery.

A.D., A.D.2d New York Appellate Division Reports, since 1896.

ADEA Age Discrimination in Employment Act of 1967.

A.F.T.R. American Federal Tax Reports.

A.F. JAG L. Rev. Air Force JAG Law Review.

A.G. Attorney General.

A.K. Marsh. A.K. Marshall, Kentucky Court of Appeals, 1817-1821.

A.L.I. American Law Institute.

ALJ or **A.L.J.** Administrative Law Judge.

A.L.R. American Law Reports [First Series].

A.L.R.2d American Law Reports, Second Series.

A.L.R.3d American Law Reports, Third Series

A.L.R.4th American Law Reports, Fourth Series.

A.L.R.5th American Law Reports, Fifth Series.

A.L.R. Fed. American Law Reports, Federal.

A.M.A. American Medical Association.

A.M.C. American Maritime Cases.

APA Administrative Procedures Act.

A.T.L. L.J. Journal of the American Trial Lawyers Association.

Abb. Adm. Abbott's Admiralty, U.S. District Court, Southern District of New York, 1847-1850.

Abb. App. or **Abb. App. Dec.** Abbott's New York Court of Appeals Decisions.

Abb. Dec. Abbott's Decisions, New York.

Abb. N.C. Abbott's New Cases, Practice, New York, 1874-1894.

Abb. Pr. Abbott's Practice Cases, New York Courts, 1854-1865.

Abb. Pr. (N.S.) Abbott's Practice Cases, New Series, New York, 1863-1875.

Abb. U.S. Abbott, U.S. Circuit and District Courts, 1865-1871.

Abr. Abridged; Abridgment.

Abr. Ca. Eq. Abridgment of Cases in Equity, Eng.

Act. Acton's Prize Causes, Privy Council, Eng., 1809-1811.

Act. Can. Acta Cancellaria, Reports and Entries in Chancery, Monro, Eng., 1545-1625.

Act. Reg. Acta Regia. Royal Acts.

Ad. Administrative.

Ad. & E. See A. & E.

Ad. L. Bull. Administrative Law Bulletin.

Ad. L. Rev. Administrative Law Review.

Add. Addison, Pennsylvania County Courts and Court of Errors, 1791-1799.

Add. E.R. Addams' Ecclesiastical Reports, Eng., 1822-1826.

Adm. Admiralty.

Adv. Adversus; Against. Used to cross-index; indicates that the names of the parties in a case have been reversed.

Aik. Aikens, Vermont Supreme Court, 1825-1827.

Al. Aleyn, King's Bench, Eng., 1646-1648.

Ala. Alabama Reports, Supreme Court, 1840-1976. For earlier reports, see also, Minor, Stew., Stew. & P., and Port.

Ala. App. Alabama Appellate Court Reports, 1910-1976.

Ala. L.J. Alabama Law Journal, Montgomery, 1882-1884.

Ala. L. Rev. Alabama Law Review.

Ala. Sel. Cas. Alabama Select Cases, Supreme Court, 1861-1863.

Alas. Alaska Reports, 1900-1959 (nonstandard).

Alb. L.J. Albany Law Journal, Albany, N.Y., since 1870.

Alb. L. Rev. Albany Law Review.

Alc. & N. Alcock and Napier, King's Bench, Ireland, 1831-1833.

Alc. R. Cas. Alcock's Registry Cases, Ireland, 1832-1837.

Ald. or **Alden** Alden's Condensed Reports, Pennsylvania.

Allen. Massachusetts Supreme Court, vols. 83-96, 1861-1867.

Allen (N.B.) New Brunswick Reports, 1848-1866.

Am. American.

Am. & E. Corp. Cas. American and English Corporation Cases (ex-cepting Railway), Northport, N.Y.

Am. & E. Ry. Cas. American and English Railway Cases, Northport, N.Y.

Am. & Eng. Ann. Cas. American and English Annotated Cases, 1906-1912.

Am. Bankr. L.J. American Bankruptcy Law Journal.

Am Bankr. R. American Bankruptcy Reports.

Am. Bankr. Rev. American Bankruptcy Review.

Am. B.A. American Bar Association Annual Reports.

Am. Cor. Cas. American Corporation Cases, Chicago.

Am. Cr. Rep. American Criminal Reports, Chicago.

Am. Dec. American Decisions, from earliest period to 1869, San Francisco.

Am. Fed. Tax R. American Federal Tax Reports.

Am. Hist. Rev. American Historical Review.

Am. J. Comp. L. American Journal of Comparative Law.

Am. J. Int'l L. American Journal of International Law.

Am. J. Legal Hist. American Journal of Legal History.

Am. Jur. American Jurist, Boston, 1829-1843; American Jurisprudence, [First Edition].

Am. Jur. 2d. American Jurisprudence, Second Edition.

Am. Lab. Leg. Rev. American Labor Legislation Review.

Am. L.C. American Leading Cases, Hare and Wallace.

Am. L.J. American Law Journal, Philadelphia, 1808-1810, 1813-

1814, 1817; New Series, 1848-1852. Another periodical of same name, Columbus, Ohio, 1 8 8 4 - 1885.

Am. L. Mag. American Law Magazine, Philadelphia, 1843-1846.

Am. L. Rec. American Law Record, Cincinnati.

Am. L. Reg. American Law Register, Philadelphia.

Am. L. Reg. (N.S.) American Law Register, New Series.

Am. L. Rev. American Law Review.

Am. L.T. American Law Times, Washington, 1868-1877.

Am. Prob. Rep. American Probate Reports, New York.

Am. R. or **Am. Rep.** American Reports, Albany, N.Y., 1871-1888.

Am. Ry. Cas. American Railway Cases, Boston, 1854-1856.

Am. Ry. Rep. American Railway Reports, New York, 1873-1881.

Am. St. R. or **Am. St. Rep.** American State Reports, San Francisco, 1888-1911.

Am. Tr. M. Cas. American Trade Mark Cases, Cincinnati, from earliest period to 1871.

Am. U.L. Rev. American University Law Review.

Amb. Ambler Chancery, Eng., 1737-1783 (some earlier cases in an appendix) .

Ames, Cas. B. & N. Ames, Cases on Bills and Notes, Boston, 1881.

And. Anderson Common Pleas, Eng., 1534-1604.

Andr. Andrews, King's Bench, Eng., 1737-1738.

Ann. Annual; Annaly, King's Bench, Eng., 1733-1738. See also, Lee, t.H.

Annals Annals of the American Academy of Political and Social Science.

Anno. Cas. American and English Annotated Cases.

Annot. Annotation.

Anst. Anstruther, Exchequer, Eng., 1792-1797.

Anth. Anthon, New York Supreme Court, Nisi Prius Cases, 1807-1851.

Ap. C. Appeal Cases, Law Reports.

App. Appendix; Appleton (Me.); Appellate Reports.

App. D.C. Appeal Cases, District of Columbia, 1893-1941.

App. Div., App. Div. 2d Appellate Division, New York Supreme Court (nonstandard).

App. & S. Appleton and Shepley (Me.).

Arb. J. Arbitration Journal.

Arch. Court of Arches, England.

Arch. P.L. Cas. Archbold, Poor Law Cases, England, 1842-1858.

Ariz. Arizona Reports, Supreme Court, since 1866.

Ariz. App. Arizona Appeals Reports, 1965-1976.

Ariz. L. Rev. Arizona Law Review.

Ariz. St. L.J. Arizona State Law Journal.

Ark. Arkansas Reports, Supreme Court, since 1837.

Ark. L. Rev. Arkansas Law Review.

Arkley Judiciary Reports, Scotland, 1846-1848.

Arm. M. & O. Armstrong, Macartney and Ogle, Nisi Prius, Ireland, 1840-1842.

Arn. Arnold, Common Pleas, Eng., 1838-1839.

Arn. & H. Arnold and Hodges, Queen's Bench, Eng., 1840-1841.

Ash. Ashmead, Pennsylvania,

various courts, 1808-1841.

Asp. (N.S.) Aspects; Aspinall, Maritime Cases, New Series, Eng., 1870- 1878.

Ass. Liber Assisarum, Book of Assizes, Queen's Bench, Eng., 1327-1377.

Ass'n. Association.

Atk. Atkyns, Chancery, Eng., 1736-1754.

Atl. Atlantic Reporter.

Att'y Gen. Attorney General.

Austr. L.J. Australian Law Journal.

Av. Cas. Aviation Cases.

B. Bar; Bench; Boston.

B. & A. Barnewall and Alderson, King's Bench, Eng., 1817-1822.

B. & Ad. Barnewall and Adolphus, King's Bench, Eng., 1830-1834.

B. & B. Broderip and Bingham, Common Pleas, Eng., 1819-1822.

B. & C. Barnewall and Cresswell, King's Bench, Eng., 1822-1830.

B. & L. Browning and Lushington, Admiralty, Eng., 1863-1866.

B. & P. Bosanquet and Puller, Common Pleas, Eng., 1796-1804.

B. & P. (N.R.) Bosanquet and Puller, New Reports, Common Pleas, Eng., 1804-1807.

B. & S. Best and Smith, Queen's Bench, Eng.

B.C. Bail Court, Eng.

B.C.C. Bail Court Cases, Eng., Lowndes and Maxwell, 1852-1854.

B.C. Ind. & Com. L. Rev. Boston College Industrial and Commercial Law Review.

B.C.L. Rev. Boston College Law Review.

B.C.R. Bail Court Reports, Eng., Saunders and Cole, 1842-1848.

B.J. Bar Journal.

B. Mon. Ben Monroe, Kentucky Court of Appeals, 1840-1857.

B.R. Bancus Regis; King's Bench, Eng., Bankruptcy Reports; Bankruptcy Reporter, since 1979 (nonstandard).

B.R. or **B. Reg.** National Bankruptcy Register, United States Courts, 1867-1879.

B.T.A. Board of Tax Appeals Reports (U.S.), 1924-1942.

B.U.L. Rev. Boston University Law Review.

B.Y.U. L. Rev. Brigham Young University Law Review.

Bac. Abr. Bacon's Abridgment.

Bail. Bailey, South Carolina, Superior Courts and Court of Appeals, 1828-1832.

Bail. Eq. Bailey, South Carolina, Equity Cases, 1830-1831.

Bald. or **Bald. C.C.** Baldwin, U.S. Circuit Court, Third Circuit, 1827-1833.

Ball & B. Ball and Beatty, Chancery, Ireland, 1807-1814.

Balt. L.T. Baltimore Law Transcript, 1868-1870.

Ban. & A. Banning and Arden, Patent Cases, U.S. Courts.

Bank. Bankruptcy (nonstandard).

Bank. C.T. Rep. Bankrupt Court Reporter, New York, 1867-1868.

Bank. & Ins. Bankruptcy and Insolvency Reports, English Courts, 1853-1855.

Bankr. Bankruptcy Reporter, since 1979; Bankruptcy.

Bar. & Arn. Barron and Arnold, Election Cases, Eng., 1843-1846.

Bar. & Aust. Barron and Austin, Election Cases, Eng., 1842.

Barb. Barbour, New York Supreme Court, 1847-1877.

Barb. Ch. Barbour, New York Chancery Cases, 1845-1848.

Barn. Barnardiston, King's Bench, Eng., 1726-1734.

Barn. Ch. Barnardiston, Chancery, Eng., 1740-1741.

Barnes Notes of Cases, Common Pleas, Eng., 1732-1756.

Barr Pennsylvania State Reports, vols. 1-10.

Batty King's Bench, Ireland, 1825-1826.

Baxt. Baxter, Tennessee Supreme Court, 1871-1878.

Bay South Carolina Superior Courts, 1783-1804.

Beasl. Beasley, New Jersey Equity, vols. 12-13, 1858-1861.

Beat. Beatty, Chancery, Ireland, 1813-1830.

Beav. Beavan, Roll's Court, Eng., 1838-1866.

Beav. & W. Beavan and Walford, Parliamentary Cases, 1846.

Bee Admiralty Cases, U.S. District Courts, 1792-1808. (An appendix contains some earlier decisions. See Hopk. Adm.)

Bel. Bellewe, King's Bench, Eng., 1378-1400.

Bell. App. Scotch Appeals, House of Lords, 1842-1850.

Bell, C.C. Crown Cases, Reserved, Eng., 1858-1860.

Bell, Com. Commentaries on the Laws of Scotland.

Bell, Dec. Decisions, Court of Session, Scotland, 1794-1795.

Bell, Dict. of Dec. Bell's Dictionary of Decisions, Court of Sessions, Scotland, 1808-1833.

Bell, Sess. Cas. Bell, Session Cases, Scotland, 1790-1792.

Belt Supplement to Vesey, Sr., Chancery, Eng., 1845-1855.

Ben. Benedict, U.S. District Court, Southern Dist. of N.Y., 1865-1879.

Ben. Benloes, Bendloes, or Benlowes. Different spellings appear in different places in the same volume, called "New Benloes." King's Bench, Eng., 1530-1627.

Bench and Bar Law Periodical, Chicago, 1869-1874.

Benl. & D. Benloe or Bendloe, called "Old Benloe," and Dalison, separate reports bound together. Com. Pleas, Eng., 1512-1579. Four cases, 1357-1512, inserted.

Benn. Bennett (California).

Benn. F.I. Cas. Bennett, Fire Insurance Cases, New York, 1872-1877.

Benn. & H. Bennett and Heard, Leading Criminal Cases, Boston,

Bent. Bentley, Chancery, Ireland, 1831.

Bert. Berton, New Brunswick, 1835-1839.

Best & S. See B. & S.

Bibb Kentucky Court of Appeals, 1808-1817.

Big. Cas. Bigelow's Cases, King's Bench, Eng., 1066-1195.

Big. Cas. B. & N. Bigelow's Leading Cases, Bills and Notes, Boston, 1880.

Big. Cas. Torts Bigelow's Cases in Torts, Boston, 1875.

Big. L. & A. Ins. Cas. Bigelow's Life and Accident Insurance Cases, New York, 1872-1877.

Bing. Bingham, Common Pleas, Eng., 1822-1834.

Bing, N.C. Bingham, New Cases, Common Pleas, Eng., 1834-1840.

Binn. Binney, Pennsylvania Supreme Court, 1799-1814.

Biss. Bissell, U.S. Circuit Court, Seventh Circuit, 1851-1883.

Bitt. Pr. Cas. Bittleston, Practice Cases, Eng., 1875-1876.

Bitt. W. & P. Bittleston, Wise and Pamell, New Magistrate's Cases, Eng., 1844-1850.

Bkcy. Bankruptcy (nonstandard).

Bkcy. & Ins. R. Bankruptcy and Insolvency Reports, Eng., 1853-1855.

Bkg. L.J. Banking Law Joumal (nonstandard).

Bl. C. C. Blatchford's Circuit Court Reports.

Bl. Com. Blackstone, Commentaries on the Laws of England.

Bl. H. Henry Blackstone, Common Pleas, Eng., 1788-1796.

Bl. R., or **Bl. W.** Sir William Blackstone, King's Bench, 1746-1779.

Black U.S. Supreme Court, vols. 66-67.

Black., D. & O. Blackham, Dundas and Osborne, Nisi Prius, Ireland, 1846-1848.

Black., W. Sir Wm. Blackstone's Reports, K.B.

Blackf. Blackford, Indiana Supreme Court, 1817-1847.

Bland Maryland High Court of Chancery, 1797-1832.

Blatch. Blatchford, U.S. Circuit Court, Second Circuit.

Blatch. & H. Blatchford and Howland, U.S. District Court, Southern Dist. of N.Y., 1827-1837.

Blatch. Pr. Blatchford, Prize Cases, U.S. Courts, Southern Dist. of N.Y., 1861-1865.

Bli. Bligh, House of Lords, Eng., 1819-1821.

Bli. (N.S.) Bligh, House of Lords, Eng., New Series, 1827-1837.

Bond U.S. Courts, Southern Dist. of Ohio, 1856-1871.

Bos. & Pul. Bosanquet and Puller's Reports, C.P.

Bos. & P.N.R. Bosanquet and Puller's New Reports, C.P.

Bosw. Bosworth, New York City Superior Court, vols. 14-23, 1856-1863.

Bott. Poor Law Cases, Eng., 1768-1827.

Boyce Boyce's Report, Delaware.

Br. & F. Brodrick and Fremantle, Ecclesiastical Cases, Eng., 1695-1864.

Br. & G. Brownlow and Goldesborough, Common Pleas, Eng., 1558-1625.

Br. & Mac. Browne and Macnamara, Railway and Canal Cases, Eng.

Br. N.C. Brooke, New Cases, King's Bench and Chancery, Eng., 1515-1558.

Br. N.C. Brooke's New Cases, K.B.

Brac. Bracton De Legibus et Consuetudinibus Angliae.

Bradf. Bradford, New York Surrogate's Court, 1849-1857.

Bradw. Bradwell, Illinois Appellate Courts, 1877-1886.

Brain. Leg. Pr. Brainard's Legal Precedents, Land and Mining Cases, Washington.

Branch Branch (Florida).

Brayt. Brayton, Vermont Supreme Court, 1815-1819.

Breese Illinois Supreme Court, vol. 1.

Brev. Brevard, South Carolina Constitutional and District Court, 1793-1816.

Brews. Brewster, Pennsylvania, various courts, 1856-1873.

Bridg. Sir J. Bridgman, King's Bench, Eng., 1613-1633.

Bridg. O. Orlando Bridgman, Common Pleas, Eng., 1660-1667.

Bright. Brightly, Court of Nisi Prius, at Philadelphia, and Pennsylvania Supreme Court, 1809-1851.

Brod. & B. Broderip and Bingham's Reports, C.P.

Bro. Ch. Brown (William), Chancery Cases, Eng., 1778-1794.

Bro. P.C. Brown, House of Lords (Parliamentary) Cases, Eng., 1702-1778.

Bro. P.C. Brown, Parliament Cases.

Bro. Sup. Brown's Supplement to Morison's Dictionary of Decisions, Scotland, 1620-1768.

Bro. Syn. Brown's Synopsis of Decisions, Court of Session.

Brock. Brockenbrough, U.S. Circuit Court, Fourth Circuit, 1802-1836. See also, Va. Cas.

Brock. & H. Brockenbrough and Holmes, Virginia General Court, 1789-1826.

Broun Justiciary Cases, Scotland, 1842-1845.

Brown, Adm. Admiralty, U.S. Courts, Western Districts.

Brown, N.P. Nisi Prius Cases, Michigan.

Browne Pennsylvania Common Pleas, First Judicial District, 1801-1814.

Brownl. Brownlow and Goldes-borough's Reports, C.P.

Bruce Court of Session, Scotland, 1714-1715.

Brunner Collected Cases, U.S. Courts, 1791-1880.

Buck Reports in Bankruptcy, Eng., 1816-1820.

Bull. Bulletin; Weekly Law Bulletin, Ohio.

Bulst. Bulstrode, King's Bench, Eng., 1609-1638.

Bunb. Bunbury, Exchequer, Eng., 1713-1741.

Burn. Burnett, Wisconsin Territory, Supreme Court, 1842.

Burr. Burrow, King's Bench, Eng., 1756-1772.

Burr. S.C. Burrow, Settlement Cases, King's Bench, Eng., 1732-1776.

Bus. Law. Business Lawyer.

Busb. Busbee, North Carolina Supreme Court, 1852-1853.

Busb. Eq. Busbee, North Carolina Cases in Equity, 1852-1853.

Bush Kentucky Court of Appeals, 1866-1879.

C. Cases; Chancellor; Chancery; Chapter; Codex (Juris Civilis) Justinian; College; Common; Court. See also, Cow.

C.A. Court of Appeals; California Appellate Reports (nonstandard).

C.A.A. Civil Aeronautics Authority Reports.

C.A.B. Civil Aeronautics Board Reports.

C. & E. Cababe and Ellis, Queen's Bench, Eng., 1882-1885.

C. & J. Crompton and Jervis, Exchequer, Eng., 1830-1832.

C. & K. Carrington and Kirwan, Nisi

Prius, Eng., 1843-1853.

C. & L.C.C. Cave and Leigh, Crown Cases, Eng.

C. & M. Crompton and Meeson. Exchequer, 1832-1834.

C. & P. Carrington and Payne, Nisi Prius, Eng., 1823-1841.

C.B. Chief Baron of the Exchequer; Common Bench; Common Bench Reports, Eng., 1845-1856.

C.B. (N.S.) Common Bench Reports, New Series, Eng., 1856-1865.

C.C. Chancery Cases; Circuit Court; County Court; Crown (or Criminal) Cases.

C.C.A. Circuit Court of Appeals; County Court Appeals.

CCH Commerce Clearing House.

C.C. (N.S.) Circuit Court Reports, New Series.

C.C.P. Court of Common Pleas.

C.C.P.A. Court of Customs and Patent Appeals.

C.C.R. Crown Cases Reserved.

C.E. Canada East.

C.F.R. Code of Federal Regulations.

C.J. Chief Judge; Chief Justice; Corpus Juris.

C.J.B. Chief Judge in Bankruptcy.

C.J.C. Cowper's Justiciary Cases.

C.J.S. Corpus Juris Secundum.

C.L. Mag. Criminal Law Magazine and Reporter, Jersey City, N.J.

C.L.P. Act Common Law Procedure Act, 1871, Eng.

C.L.R. Common Law Reports, 1853-1855; California Law Review (nonstandard); Columbia Law Review (nonstandard).

C.M.A. United States Court of Military Appeals Reports, 1951-1975.

C.M.R. United States Court-Martial Reports, 1951-1977.

C.M. & R. Crompton, Meeson and Roscoe, Exchequer, Eng., 1834-1835.

C.P. Common Pleas.

C.P.D. Common Pleas Division, Law Reports, Eng.

C.R. Carolous Rex; King Charles I.

C.S. Court of Session, Scotland; Custos Rotulorum; Keeper of the Rolls.

C.S.C.A. Court of Session Cases, Scotland, 1821-1875.

C.S.C.R. Cincinnati Superior Court Reporter, 1870-1873.

C.W. Canada West.

Ca. or **Cas.** Cases t. (tempore) F., in time of Finch; t. Holt, in time of Holt; t. H., in time of Hardwicke; t. K., in time of King; t. N., in time of Northington; t. Talb., in time of Talbot; B.R., or t. Wm. III., in time of William III. (12 Mod.).

Cai. Caines, New York Supreme Court, 1803-1805.

Cai. Cas. Caines' Cases, New York Court of Errors, 1796-1805.

Caines Caines, New York.

Caines' Cas. See Cai. Cas.

Cal. California Reports, Supreme Court, since 1850.

Cal. App. California Appellate Reports, since 1905.

Cal. App. Supp. California Appellate Reports Supplement, since 1929.

Cal. L.J. California Law Journal, San Francisco, 1862-1863.

Cal. L.R. California Legal Record, San Francisco, 1878-1879.

Cal. L. Rev. California Law Review (nonstandard).

Cal. Rptr. California Reporter, since

1959.

Cal. St. B.J. California State Bar Journal.

Cal. Unrep. California Unreported Cases, 1855-1910.

Cal. W. L. Rev. California Western Law Review.

Cald. Caldecott, Settlement Cases and Justice of the Peace, Eng., 1776-1785.

Calif. L. Rev. California Law Review.

Call Call's Reports, Virginia Court of Appeals, 1796-1818; U.S. Circuit Court, 1793-1825.

Calth. Calthrop, King's Bench, Eng., 1609-1618.

Cam. & N. Cameron and Norwood, North Carolina Court of Conference, 1800-1804.

Cam. Scacc. Camera, Scaccarii, Exchequer Chamber.

Camb. L.J. Cambridge Law Journal.

Campb. Campbell, Nisi Prius, Eng., 1807-1816.

Can. Canada Supreme Court Reports.

Can. B. Rev. Canadian Bar Review.

Can. L.J. Canada Law Journal, 1855-1864.

Can. L.J. (N.S.) Canada Law Journal, New Series.

Can. L.T. Canadian Law Times.

Cap. U. L. Rev. Capital University Law Review.

Car. & K. See C. & K.

Car. & M. Carrington and Marshman, Nisi Prius, Eng., 1841-1842.

Car. & P. See C. & P.

Car. H. & A. Carrow, Hamerton and Allen, Magistrate's Courts, 1844-1847. See also, New Ses. Cas.

Car. L.R. or **Car. L. Rep.** Carolina Law Repository, N.C., 1811-1816.

Carp. Carpmael, Patent Cases, Eng., 1602-1842.

Carr. & Kir. Carrington and Kirwan's Reports, N.P.

Carr. & P. Carrington and Payne's Reports, N.P.

Cart. Carter, Common Pleas, Eng., 1664-1675.

Carth. Carthew, King's Bench, Eng., 1686-1700.

Cary Chancery, Eng., 1557-1604.

Cas. Casualty; Cases.

Cas. B.R. Cases in King's Bench t. Wm. III. (12 Mod.).

Cas. C.L. Cases in Crown Law.

Cas. C.R. Cases temp. Wm. III. (12 Mod.) .

Cas. Eq. Abr. Abridgment of Cases in Equity, Eng.

Cas. L. & Eq. Cases in Law and Equity (10 Mod.).

Cas. P. Cases in Parliament.

Cas. Pr. C.P. Cases of Practice, Common Pleas, Eng., 1706-1740; with rules and orders, 1457-1741.

Cas. Pr. K.B. Cases of Practice, King's Bench, Eng., 1732-1760.

Case & Com. Case and Comment.

Case W. Res. L. Rev. Case Western Reserve Law Review.

Casey Pennsylvania State Supreme Court, vols. 25-36.

Cath. U.L. Rev. Catholic University of America Law Review.

Cent. Central.

Cent. Dig. Century Digest.

Cent. L.J. Central Law Journal.

Cent. Rep. Central Reporter, Rochester.

Ch. Chancery.

Ch. C.R. Chancery Chambers Reports, Canada, 1858-1872.

Ch. Cas. Chancery Cases, Eng., 1660-1688.

Ch. Cas. Ch. Choyce Cases in Chancery, Eng., 1557-1606.

Ch. Cas. Sp. Special Cases in Chancery, Eng., 1669-1693.

Ch. Pre. Precedents in Chancery, Eng., 1689-1723.

Ch. R. Reports in Chancery, Eng., 1625-1710.

Chand. Chandler, Wisconsin Supreme Court, 1849-1852; Chandler New Hampshire Reports.

Chap. Chapter.

Charlt. Charlton, T.U.P., Georgia Superior Courts, 1805-1810.

Charlt. Charlton, R.M., Georgia Superior Courts, 1811-1837.

Chas. Charles I., Eng.

Chase's Dec. Chase's Decisions, U.S. Circuit Court, Fourth Circuit, 1865-1869.

Chem. Chemical.

Chest. Co. R. Chester County (Pa.) Reports, 1866-1885.

Cheves South Carolina Court of Appeals, at Law, 1839-1840.

Cheves, Ch. or **Eq.** South Carolina Court of Appeals, in Equity, 1839-1840.

Chi.-Kent L. Rev. Chicago-Kent Law Review.

Chi. L.J. Chicago Law Journal, 1878-1879.

Chi. L.N. Chicago Legal News.

Chi. L. Rec. Chicago Law Record.

Chip. D. D. Chipman, Vermont Supreme Court, 1789-1824.

Chip. N. N. Chipman, Vermont Supreme Court, 1789-1791.

Chip. (N.B.) Chipman, New Brunswick Supreme Court, 1825-1827.

Chit. Chitty, Bail Court Reports, Eng., 1770-1882.

Cin. L.B. Cincinnati Law Bulletin.

Cin. L. Rev. University of Cincinnati Law Review (nonstandard).

Cin. Super. Ct. or **Cin. Superior Ct.** Superior Court of Cincinnati.

Cir. Ct. Circuit Court.

City Ct. R. City Court Reports, New York.

City H. Rec. City Hall Recorder, New York, Criminal, 1816-1821.

Civ. App. Court of Civil Appeals.

Civ. Lib. Rev. Civil Liberties Review.

Civ. Pro. Rep. Civil Procedure Reports, New York, various courts.

Cl. & F. Clark and Finnelly, House of Lords, Eng., 1831-1846.

Clark Clark, Ala. and Pa.

Clarke Ch. New York Court of Chancery, 1839-1841.

Clarke (Ia.) Iowa Supreme Court, vols. 1-8.

Clarke & H. Clarke and Hall, Contested Election Cases, in Congress, 1789-1834.

Clay. Clayton, York Assize, Nisi Prius, Eng., 1631-1650.

Clev. B.J. Cleveland Bar Association Journal.

Clev. L. Rec. Cleveland Law Record, 1855-1856.

Clev. L. Rep. Cleveland Law Reporter, 1878-1879.

Clev.-Mar. L. Rev. Cleveland-Marshall Law Review.

Clev. St. L. Rev. Cleveland State Law Review.

Cliff. Clifford, U.S. Circuit Court, First Circuit, 1858-1878.

Cliff. & S. Clifford and Stephens, Referee's Court in Parliament, Eng., 1867-1872.

Co. County; Coke, King's Bench and other courts, Eng., 1572-1616.

Co. Ct. Cas. County Court Cases, Eng., 1844-1846.

Co. Ct. Chr. County Courts Chronicle, London, 1847-1884.

Co. Ct. Rep. County Courts Reports, London, 1860-1880.

Co. Inst. Coke's Institutes, 1, 2, 3, and 4.

Co. Lit. Coke on Littleton.

Co. M.C. Coke's Magna Charta.

Co. on Court. Coke's 4th Inst.

Co. P.C. Coke's Pleas of the Crown (3rd Inst.).

Coch. Cochran, Nova Scotia Law Reports (N.S.), 1859.

Cock. & R. Cockburne and Rove, Election Cases, Eng., 1833.

Cod. Jur. Civ. Codex Juris Civilis.

Code Rep. The Code Reporter, New York, various courts, 1848-1851.

Code R. (N.S.) Code Reports, New Series, New York, various courts, 1850-1852.

Col. & C. Coleman and Caines' Cases, New York Supreme Court, 1794-1805.

Col. Cas. Coleman's Cases, New York Supreme Court, 1793-1800.

Col. C.C. Collyer's Chancery Cases, 1844-1846.

Col. J. Columbian Jurist, New York, 1885-1886.

Cold. Coldwell, Tennessee Supreme Court, 1860-1870.

Coll. Colles, Cases in Parliament, House of Lords, Eng., 1697-1713.

Colo. Colorado Reports, Supreme Court, since 1864.

Colo. App. Colorado Court of Appeals Reports, since 1891.

Colo. L.R. Colorado Law Reporter, Denver, 1880-1884.

Colo. Law. Colorado Lawyer.

Colt. Coltman, Registration Cases, Eng.

Colum. J.L. & Soc. Probs. Columbia Journal of Law & Social Problems.

Colum. J. Transnat'l L. Columbia Journal of Transnational Law.

Colum. L. Rev. Columbia Law Review.

Com. Comment; Commerce; Commercial; Common; Commentaries; Communication.

Com. L.J. Commercial Law Journal.

Comb. Comberbach, King's Bench, Eng., 1685-1698.

Comm. Committee.

Comm'n Commission.

Comm'r Commissioner.

Comp. Comparative.

Comst. Comstock, New York Court of Appeals, vols. 1-4.

Comyn King's Bench, Eng., 1695-1739.

Con. & L. Conner and Lawson, Chancery, Ireland, 1841-1843.

Con. Sur. Connoly, New York Surrogate's Courts.

Conf. Conference.

Cong. Congress; Congressional.

Cong. Dig. Congressional Digest.

Conn. Connecticut Reports, Supreme Court of Errors, since 1814. See also, Kirby, Root, and Day.

Conn. B.J. Connecticut Bar Journal.

Conn. Cir. Ct. Connecticut Circuit Court Reports, 1961-1974.

Conn. L. Rev. Connecticut Law

Review.

Conn. Supp. Connecticut Supplement, since 1935.

Consist. Consistory Reports, Haggard.

Consol. Consolidated.

Const. Constitution; Constitutional.

Const. (S.C.) Treadway's S.C. Constitutional Reports.

Const. (N.S.) (S.C.) Mills' S.C. Constitutional Report, New Series.

Constr. Construction.

Cont. Contract, Contracts.

Contemp. Contemporary.

Conv. (N.S.) Conveyance & Property Lawyer.

Cooke Tennessee, various courts, 1811-1814.

Cooke & A. Cooke and Alcock, King's Bench, Ireland, 1833-1834.

Cooke, Pr. Ca. Practice Cases in Common Pleas Court, Eng., 1706-1747.

Coop. Pr. C. Cooper's Practice Cases in Chancery, Eng., 1837-1838; miscellaneous cases, 1820-1838.

Coop. Ch. Cooper, Tennessee, Court of Chancery, 1872-1878.

Coop. t. Br. Cooper, Cases in Chancery t. Lord Brougham, 1833-1834.

Coop. t. Cott. Cooper, Cases in Chancery, t. Lord Cottenham, 1846-1847; miscellaneous cases, 1557-1847.

Coop t. Eld. Cooper, Cases in Chancery t. Lord Eldon, 1792-1815.

Corb. & D. Corbett and Daniell, Election Cases, Eng., 1819.

Corp. J. Corporation Journal.

Cosm. Cosmetic.

Coup. (S.C.) Couper, Scotch Justiciary, 1868-1885.

Cow. Cowen, New York Supreme Court and Court of Errors, 1821-1829.

Cow. Cr. Rep. Cowen's Criminal Reports, State Courts and U.S. Supreme Court, 1860-1874.

Cowp. Cowper, King's Bench, Eng., 1774-1778.

Cox, C.C. Cox's Criminal Cases, Eng.

Cox, Ch. Chancery, Eng., 1783-1796.

Cox, M. & H. Cox, Macrae and Hertslet, County Courts, Eng., 1847-1852.

Cox, Mag. Cas. Cox's Magistrate Cases, 1859-1882.

Coxe New Jersey Law, vol. 1, 1790-1795.

Cr. & Ph. Craig and Phillips, Chancery, Eng., 1840-1841.

Cr. & St. Craigie and Stewart, Scotch Appeals, House of Lords, 1726-1821. Last three vols. by Paton. See also, Pat. App.

Crabbe Crabbe's Reports, U.S. District Court, Eastern District of Pennsylvania, 1836-1846.

Cranch Cranch's U.S. Supreme Court Reports, vols. 5-13, 1801-1815.

Cranch, C.C. Cranch, U.S. Circuit Court for District of Columbia, 1801-1840.

Cranch Pat. Dec. (N.S.) Cranch's Patent Decisions, New Series.

Craw. & D. Crawford and Dix, Circuit Cases, Ireland, 1839-1846.

Craw. & D., Ab. C. Crawford and Dix, Abridged Cases, Ireland, 1837-1838.

Crim. Criminal.

Crim. App. Court of Criminal Appeals.

Crim. Def. Criminal Defenses, Select American Cases, St. Louis.

Crim. L. Mag. Criminal Law Magazine, Jersey City, N.J.

Crim. L. Rep. or **Crim. L. Rptr.** Criminal Law Reporter.

Cripps Ecclesiastical Courts, Eng., 1846-1849.

Cro. Croke, Queen's Bench and King's Bench, Eng., 1582-1641; occasionally, Keilwey's Reports, published by Serjeant Croke.

Cromp. Crompton's Courts.

Cromp. & J. Crompton and Jervis' Reports, Ex.

Cromp. & M. Crompton and Meeson's Reports, Ex.

Ct. Cl. U.S. Court of Claims.

Ct. Cust. App. U.S. Court of Customs Appeals.

Ct. Mil. App. U.S. Court of Military Appeals.

Ct. of Cl. See Ct. Cl.

Cum. Bull. Cumulative Bulletin, U.S. Treasury Department.

Cum. L. Rev. Cumberland Law Review.

Cum.-Sam. L. Rev. Cumberland-Samford Law Review.

Cunn. Cunningham, King's Bench, Eng., 1734-1835.

Cur. Com. Current Comment and Legal Miscellany, Philadelphia.

Current Med. Current Medicine for Attorneys.

Curt. Curtis, U.S. Circuit Court, First Circuit, 1851-1856.

Curt. E.R. Curteis, Ecclesiastical Reports, Eng., 1834-1844.

Cush. Cushing, Massachusetts Supreme Court, vols. 55-66, 1848-1853.

Cushm. Cushman, Mississippi High Court of Errors and Appeals, vols. 23-29.

Cust. Ct. Customs Court Reports.

Cyc. Cyclopedia of Law and Procedure.

D. U.S. District Court; Davis; Defendant; Digest (Juris Civilis); District; Division; Disney.

D. & C. Deacon and Chitty, Bankruptcy, Eng., 1832-1835; Pennsylvania District and County Reports (nonstandard).

D. & C. 2d, D. & C. 3d Pennsylvania District and County Reports, Second Series and Third Series (nonstandard).

D. & L. Dowling and Lowndes, various courts, Eng., 1843-1849.

D. & M. Davison and Merivale, Queen's Bench, Eng., 1843-1844.

D. & R. Dowling and Ryland, King's Bench, Eng., 1822-1827.

D. & R. Mag. Cas. Dowling and Ryland, Magistrates' Cases, Eng., 1822-1827.

D. & R. (N.P.C.) Dowling and Ryland, Nisi Prius Cases, Eng., 1822-1823.

D.C. District Court; District of Columbia; District of Columbia Reports, 1801-1893. See also, MacArth.

DEA Drug Enforcement Administration.

D.L.R. Dominion Law Reports, Can.

D.L.R.2d Dominion Law Reports, Second Series, Can.

D.L.R.3d Dominion Law Reports, Third Series, Can.

D.P. Domus Procerum; House of Lords.

D.P.R. Decisiones de Puerto Rico, since 1899.

D.T., or **Dak.** Dakota Territory Supreme Court.

Dakota Dakota Reports, Supreme Court of Dakota, 1867-1889.

Dal. Dalison, Common Pleas, Eng., 1546-1574.

Dall. Dallas, U.S. Courts and Courts of Pennsylvania, 1754-1806.

Dall. (Tex.) Dallam, Supreme Court of Texas, before annexation, 1840-1844.

Dallas Dallas Styles, Scotland.

Dalr. Dalrymple's Decisions, Court of Session, Scotland, 1698-1720.

Daly New York Court of Common Pleas.

Dan. Daniell, Exchequer, Equity, Eng., 1817-1820.

Dana Kentucky Court of Appeals, 1833-1840.

Dan. & Ll. Danson and Lloyd's Mercantile Cases, King's Bench, Eng., 1828-1829.

Dav. Davies, Common Law Reports, Ireland, 1604-1612, See also, Daveis.

Daveis U.S. District Court, Maine, 1839-1849 (cited as 2 Ware).

Day Connecticut Supreme Court of Errors, 1802-1813.

D. Chip. D. Chipman (Vermont)

Dea. Deane, Admiralty and Ecclesiastical Courts, Eng., 1855-1857.

Dea. & Sw. Deane and Swabey, Probate and Divorce, Eng., 1855-1857.

Deac. Deacon, Bankruptcy, Eng., 1835-1840.

Deac. & Chit. Deacon and Chitty, Bankruptcy, Eng., 1832-1835.

Deady U.S. Courts, Oregon and California, 1861-1869.

Dears. & B. Dearsley and Bell, Crown Cases Reserved, Eng., 1856-1858.

Dears. C.C. Dearsley, Crown Cases, Eng., 1852-1856.

Deas & A. Deas and Anderson, Court of Session, Scotland, 1829-1832.

Dec. Dig. Decennial Digest.

Dec. Eng. J.J. Decisions of English Judges, Court of Session, Scotland, during the usurpation, 1655-1661.

De G. De Gex, Bankruptcy, Eng., 1844-1848; 1839-1850.

De G. & J. De Gex and Jones, Chancery and Bankruptcy Appeals, 1857-1859.

De G. & Sm. De Gex and Smale, Chancery and Bankruptcy Appeals, 1846-1852.

De G., F. & J. De Gex, Fisher and Jones, Chancery and Bankruptcy Appeals, 1859-1862.

De G., J. & S. De Gex, Jones and Smith, Chancery and Bankruptcy Appeals, 1862-1865.

De G., M. & G. De Gex, Macnaghten and Gordon, Chancery and Bankruptcy Appeals, 1851-1857.

Def. Defense.

Del. Delaware Reports, Supreme Court, 1832-1966. See also, Har. and Houst.; Delane, Election Cases, Eng., 1832-1835.

Del. Cas. Delaware Cases, 1792-1830.

Del. Ch. Delaware Chancery Reports, 1814-1968.

Del. Co. R. Delaware County (Pa.) Reports.

Delinq. Delinquency.

Dem. Demarest, Surrogate's Court, N.Y., 1882-1888.

Den. C.C. Denison, Crown Cases, Eng., 1844-1852.

Den. L.J. Denver Law Journal.

Denio New York Supreme Court and Court of Errors, 1845-1848.

Dep. or **Dep't** Department.

Dep't State Bull. U.S. Department of State Bulletin.

Desau. Desaussure, South Carolina Court of Chancery and Court of Appeals, 1784-1817.

Det. C.L. Rev. Detroit College Law Review.

Dev. Development; Devereux, North Carolina Supreme Court, at Law, 1826-1834.

Dev. & B. Devereux and Battle, North Carolina Supreme Court, at Law, 1834-1839.

Dev. & B. Eq. Devereux and Battle, North Carolina Supreme Court, in Equity, 1834-1839.

Dev. Ct. Cl. Devereux, U.S. Court of Claims, 1856

Dev. Eq. Devereux, North Carolina Supreme Court, in Equity, 1826-1834.

Dick. Dickens, Chancery, Eng., 1559-1797.

Dick. Dickinson (N.J.).

Dick. L. Rev. Dickinson Law Review.

Dict. Dictionary.

Dict. of Dec. Dictionary of Decisions, Court of Session, Scotland (Morison and others), from beginning to 1822.

Dig. Digest.

Dill. Dillon, U.S. Circuit Court, Eighth Circuit, 1870-1880.

Dipl. Diplomacy.

Dirl. Dirleton, Court of Session, Scotland, 1665-1677.

Dis. or **Disney** Disney's Cincinnati Superior Court Reports, 1854-1859.

Dist. District.

Distrib. Distributor or Distributing.

Div. Division.

Dod. Dodson, Admiralty, Eng., 1811-1822.

Dom. Proc. Domus Procerum; House of Lords, Eng.

Don. Ch. Donnelly, Chancery, Eng., 1836-1837.

Don. Ir. L. Cas. Donnell, Irish Land Cases, 1871-1876.

Doug. Douglas, King's Bench, Eng., 1778-1785.

Doug, E.C. Douglas, Election Cases, Eng., 1775-1776.

Doug. (Mich.) Douglass, Michigan Supreme Court, 1843-1847.

Dow House of Lords, Eng., 1812-1818.

Dow & C. Dow and Clark, House of Lords, Eng., 1827-1832.

Dow. & Ry. N.P. Dowling and Ryland's K.B. Reports; Dowling and Ryland's Nisi Prius.

Dowl. Dowling's Practice Cases, various courts, Eng., 1830-1841.

Dowl. (N.S.) Dowling's Practice Cases, various courts, Eng., New Series, 1841-1843.

Drap. Draper, King's Bench, Upper Canada, 1829-1831.

Drew. Drewry, Chancery, Eng., 1852-1859.

Drew. & Sm. Drewry and Smale, Chancery, Eng., 1859-1865.

Drink. Drinkwater, Common Pleas, Eng., 1840-1841.

Dru. Drury, Chancery, Ireland, t. Ld. Sugden, 1843-1844.

Dru. t. Nap. Drury, Chancery, Ireland t. Ld. Napier, 1858-1859.

Dru. & Wal. Drury and Walsh, Chancery, Ireland, 1837-1840.

Dru. & War. Drury and Warren, Chancery, Ireland, 1841-1843.

Dru. Sel. Cas. Drury, Select Cases in Chancery, Ireland, 1858-1859. Same as Dru. t. Nap.

Dud. (Ga.) Dudley, Georgia Superior Courts, 1830-1833.

Dud. (S.C.) Dudley, South Carolina Court of Appeals, at Law, 1837-1838.

Dud. Eq. Dudley, South Carolina Court of Appeals, in Equity, 1837-1838.

Duer New York City Superior Court, 1852-1857.

Dunl., B. & M. Dunlop, Bell and Murray, Court of Session, Scotland, 1838-1862.

Duq. L. Rev. Duquesne Law Review.

Durie (also called Dury), Court of Session, Scotland, 1621-1642.

Durn. & E. Durnford and East, Term Reports, King's Bench, Eng., 1785-1800.

Dury See Durie.

Dutch. Dutcher, New Jersey Law Reports, vols. 25-29, 1855-1862.

Duv. Duvall, Kentucky Court of Appeals, 1863-1866.

Duv. (Can.) Duval, Canada Supreme Court.

Dy. Dyer, King's Bench, Eng., 1513-1582.

E. East; Eastern.

E. & A. Ecclesiastical and Admiralty Division, Law Reports.

E. & Ir. App. Cas. English and Irish Appeal Cases, House of Lords, Eng.

EAJA Equal Access to Justice Act.

E.D. Eastern District.

EEOC Equal Employment Opportunity Commission.

ERISA Employee Retirement Income Security Act of 1974, as amended.

E. Rep. Eastern Reporter, Albany, N.Y.

Eag. & Y. Eagle and Younge, Tithe Cases, Exchequer, Eng., 1204-1825.

East King's Bench, Eng., 1800-1812.

Ecc. or **Eccl.** Ecclesiastical.

Ecc. or **Eccl. & Adm.** See E. & A.

Ecc. & Mar. Ecclesiastical and Maritime Cases, Eng., 1841-1850.

Econ. Economic, Economics or Economy.

Ed. Edition; Editor; Edward.

Eden Chancery, Eng., 1757-1766.

Edg. Edgar, Court of Session, Scotland, 1724-1725.

Edin. L.J. Edinburgh Law Journal, 1832-1833.

Edm. Edmond's Select Cases, New York Courts, 1834-1848.

Educ. Education or Educational.

Edw. Edward I. of England.

Edw. Admr. Edwards, Admiralty, Eng., 1808-1812.

Edw. Ch. Edwards, New York Vice-Chancellor's and Supreme Court, 1831-1850.

El. & B. Ellis and Blackburn, Queen's Bench, Eng., 1852-1858.

El. & E. Ellis and Ellis, Queen's Bench, Eng., 1858-1861.

El., B. & E. Ellis, Blackburn and Ellis, Queen's Bench, Eng., 1858-1860.

El., B. & S. Ellis, Best and Smith's Reports, Q.B.

Elchies Faculty Collection, Court of Session, Scotland, 1733-1754.

Elec. Electric; Electrical; Electricity.

Em. Ct. App. Emergency Court of Appeals.

Eng. England; English; English's Reports (Arkansas).

Eng. Ch. English Chancery Reports, American Reprint, 1821-1865.

Eng. Com. L. English Common Law Reports, American Reprint, 1813-1865.

Eng. Ex. English Exchequer Reports, American Reprint, 1853-1869.

Eng. J.J. See Dec. Eng. J.J.

Eng. Rep. English Reports—Full Reprint.

Env't Environment.

Envtl. or **Envt'l** Environmental.

Eq. Equity; Equity Division, Law Reports and Law Journal.

Eq. Ca. Abr. Equity Cases Abridged, Anonymous, Eng., 1732-1769.

Eq. R. Equity Reports, Eng., 1853-1855.

Equip. Equipment.

Er. Error.

Esp. Espinasse, Nisi Prius, Eng., 1793-1810.

Est. Estate or Estates.

Et al. (Et alii, aliae, alios) And others.

Et. seq. (Et sequentes, sequentia) And the following.

Et ux., or **Et uxor.** And wife.

Et vir. And husband.

Ex. Exchequer; Exchequer Reports by Welsby, Hurlstone and Gordon, Eng., 1847-1856.

Ex. Ch. Exchequer Chamber.

Ex. D. Exchequer Division, High Court of Justice, Eng.

Exch. Exchange.

Exr. or **Ex'r** Executor.

Ex rel. Ex relatione; at the instance of; on behalf of; on relation of.

Exrx. Executrix.

Ex'x. Executrix.

F. Federal Reporter, since 1880; Forum.

F.2d Federal Reporter, Second Series.

F. & F. Foster and Finlayson, Nisi Prius, Eng., 1856-1867.

F.C.A. Federal Code Annotated.

F. Cas. Federal Cases, 1789-1880.

FOIA Freedom of Information Act.

F.R.D. Federal Rules Decisions, since 1938.

F. Supp. Federal Supplement, since 1932.

F.T.C. Federal Trade Commission Decisions; Federal Trade Commission

Fac. Dec. fo. Faculty Decisions, Court of Session, Scotland, folio edition, 1752-1825.

Fac. Dec. 8vo. Faculty Decisions, Court of Session, Scotland, 8vo. edition, 1825-1841.

Fairf. Fairfield, Maine Supreme Court, vols. 10-12, 1833-1835.

Falc. Falconer, Court of Session, Scotland, 1681-1686, (Pt.2nd. of Gilmour and Falconer).

Falc. & F. Falconer and Fitzherbert, Election Cases, 1835-1838.

Falc. D. David Falconer, Court of

Session, Scotland, 1744-1751.

Fam. Family.

Far. Farresley, King's Bench, Eng. (7 Modern Reports), 1702-1703, with additions in Leach's Edition, 1733-1744.

Fed. Federal; Federal Reporter (nonstandard).

Fed. B.J. Federal Bar Journal.

Fed. Com. B.J. Federal Communications Bar Journal.

Fed. Cas. Federal Cases (nonstandard).

Fed. R. App. P. Federal Rules of Appellate Procedure.

Fed. R. Civ. P. Federal Rules of Civil Procedure.

Fed. R. Crim. P. Federal Rules of Criminal Procedure.

Fed. R. Evid. Federal Rules of Evidence.

Fed. Reg. Federal Register.

Fed'n Federation.

Ferg. Ferguson, Consistorial Court, Scotland, 1811-1817.

Fiduc. or **FIduciary** Pennsylvania Fiduciary Reporter, since 1951.

Fin. Finance.

Finch, H. Chancery, Eng., 1673-1680.

Finch, T. Chancery, Eng., 1689-1722. See Prec. Ch.

Fish. Fisher's Patent Cases, U.S. Circuit and Supreme Courts, 1848-1873.

Fish. Dig. Fisher's Digest, all courts, Eng.

Fish. Pat. Rep. Fisher's Patent Reports (U.S.).

Fish. Pr. Fisher, Prize Cases, U.S. Courts, 1812-1813.

Fish. (W.H.) Wm. H. Fisher, Patent Reports, 1821-1851.

Fitz G. Fitz Gibbons, King's Bench and other courts, Eng., 1728-1732.

Fla. Florida Reports, Supreme Court, 1846-1948.

Fla. St. U.L.Rev. Florida State University Law Review.

Fla. Supp. Florida Supplement, since 1948.

Flan. & K. Flanagan and Kelly, Rolls Court, Ireland, 1840-1842.

Flippin U.S. Circuit Court, Sixth Circuit, 1859-1880.

Fo. or **Fol. Dict.** Folio Dictionary of Decisions, Court of Session, Scotland, 1540-1808. See also, Kames & W.

Fogg New Hampshire Supreme Court, vols. 32-37.

Foley Poor Law Cases, Eng., 1601-1730.

Fonbl. Fonblanque, Bankruptcy, Eng., 1849-1852.

Food Drug Cosm. L.J. Food Drug Cosmetic Law Journal.

For. Forensic; Forrester, Cases, time of Talbot, Eng., 1734-1738.

Forb. Forbes, Court of Session, Scotland, 1705-1713.

Forrest Exchequer, Eng., 1800-1801.

Forst. Forster, Crown Cases, Ireland, 1767.

Fort. Fortnightly; Fortescue, various courts, Eng., 1695-1736.

Forum The Forum, Law Review, Baltimore, 1874-1875.

Fost. Foster, Crown Cases, Eng., 1708-1760.

Fost. (N.H.) Foster, New Hampshire Supreme Court, vols. 21-31.

Found. Foundation or Foundations.

Fount. Fountainhall, Court of Session, Scotland, 1678-1712.

Fox & S. Fox and Smith, King's

Bench, Ireland, 1822-1824.

Fras. Fraser, Election Cases, Eng., 1790-1792.

Freem. Freeman, King's Bench, Eng., 1670-1704.

Freem. Ch. Freeman, Chancery, Eng., 1660-1706.

Freem. (Ill.) Freeman, Illinois.

Freem. (Miss. Ch.) Freeman, Mississippi Superior Court of Chancery, 1839-1843.

G. & D. Gale and Davison, Exchequer, Eng., 1841-1843.

G. & J. Glyn and Jameson, Bankruptcy, Eng., 1815-1828.

Ga. Georgia Reports, Supreme Court, since 1846. See also, Charlt., Charlt. R.M., Dud., and Ga. Dec.

Ga. App. Georgia Appeals Reports, since 1907.

Ga. Dec. Georgia Decisions, Superior Courts, 1842-1843.

Ga. L.R. Georgia Law Reporter, Atlanta, 1885-1886.

Ga. L. Rev. Georgia Law Review.

Gaii Institutionum Commentarii, IV.

Gal. & Dav. Gale and Davidson's Reports, K.B.

Gale Exchequer, Eng., 1835-1836.

Gall. Gallison, U.S. Circuit Court, First Circuit, 1812-1815.

Gaz. Weekly Law Gazette.

Gaz. Bkcy. Gazette of Bankruptcy, Eng., 1862-1863.

Gen. General.

Geo. George; Georgetown; King George, Eng.

Geo. L.J. Georgetown Law Journal.

Geo. Wash. L. Rev. George Washington Law Review.

George Mississippi Supreme Courts, vols. 30-39.

Gibbs Michigan Supreme Court, vols. 2-4.

Giff. Giffard, Chancery, Eng., 1854-1865.

Giff. & H. Giffard and Hemming, Chancery, Eng., 1731-1736.

Gil. Gilfillan (Minn.).

Gilb. Gilbert, Chancery and Exchequer, Eng., 1706-1725.

Gilb. Q.B. Gilbert, Queen's Bench, Eng., 1713-1714.

Gill Maryland Court of Appeals, 1843-1851.

Gill & J. Gill and Johnson, Maryland Court of Appeals, 1829-1842.

Gilm. Gilmour, Court of Session, Scotland, 1661-1666.

Gilm. (Ill.) Gilman, Illinois Supreme Court, vols. 6-10.

Gilm. (Va.) Gilmer, Virginia Court of Appeals, 1820-1821.

Gilp. Gilpin, U.S. District Court Pennsylvania, 1828-1836.

Glanv. Glanville, Tractatus De Legibus et Consuetudinibus Regni Angliae.

Glanv. P.C. Glanville, Parliamentary Cases, Eng., 1623-1624.

Glasg. Reg. Glasgow Registration Appeal Court, 1835-1843.

Glass. Glasscock, all courts, Ireland, 1831-1832.

Glyn & J. Glyn and Jameson, Bankruptcy, Eng., 1815-1828.

Godb. Godbolt, King's Bench, Eng., 1575-1638.

Godol. Godolphin, King's Bench, Eng.

Gonz. L. Rev. Gonzaga Law Review.

Gosf. Gosford, Court of Session, Scotland.

Goulds. Gouldsborough, all courts, Eng., 1585-1601.

Gov. Governor.

Gov't Government.

Gow Nisi Prius, Eng., 1818-1820.

Grant Cas. Grant's Cases, Pennsylvania Supreme Court, 1814-1863.

Grant, (U.C.) Upper Canada Error and Appeal Reports, 1846-1866.

Grant, (U.C.) Ch. Grant, Chancery, Upper Canada, 1849-1882.

Gratt. Grattan, Virginia Court of Appeals, 1844-1880.

Gray Massachusetts Supreme Court, vols. 67-82, 1854-1860.

Green New Jersey Law Reports, vols. 13-15, 1831-1836.

Green, Ch. New Jersey Court of Chancery, vols. 2-4.

Green, C.E. New Jersey Chancery Reports, vols. 16-27.

Green Bag Law Magazine, Boston.

Green, Cr. Law R. Green, Criminal Law Reports, N.Y.

Green, J.S. Green, J.S., N.J.

Green, Tr. Green's Trials for High Treason, Scotland, 1820.

Greene Iowa Supreme Court, 1847-1854.

Greenh. P. P. Greenhood's Public Policy.

Greenl. Greenleaf, Maine Supreme Court, vols. 1-9.

Guar. Guaranty.

Guild Prac. Guild Practitioner.

Guthrie Sheriff Court Cases, Scotland, 1854-1878.

Gwil. Gwillim, Tithe Cases, Eng., 1224-1824.

H. Handy's Reports (Ohio).

H. & C. Hurlstone and Coltman, Exchequer, Eng., 1862-1866.

H. & G. Hurlstone and Gordon, Exchequer, Eng., 1854-1857.

H. & H. Horn and Hurlstone, Exchequer, Eng., 1838-1839.

H. & N. Hurlstone and Norman, Exchequer, Eng., 1856-1862.

H. & P. Hopwood and Philbrick, Election Cases, Eng., 1863-1867.

H. & R. Harrison and Rutherford, Common Pleas, Eng., 1866-1868.

H. & T. Hall and Twells, Ld. Chancellor and Appeal, Eng., 1849-1850.

H. & W. Hurlstone and Walmsley, Exchequer, Eng., 1840-1841.

H.Bl. Henry Blackstone, Common Pleas, Eng., 1788-1796.

H.L. House of Lords, Eng.

H.L.C. House of Lords Cases, Clark and Finnelly, Eng., 1847-1866.

H.L.R. (N.S.) House of Lords Reports, New Series, Eng.

H.R. House of Representatives; House of Representatives bill.

H.R. Rep. House of Representatives Report.

Had. Earl of Haddington, Court of Session, Scotland, 1592-1624.

Hagg. Adm. Haggard, Admiralty, Eng., 1822-1838.

Hagg. Con. Haggard, Consistory, Eng., 1752-1821.

Hagg. Eccl. Haggard, Ecclesiastical, Eng., 1827-1833.

Hailes Court of Session, Scotland, 1766-1791.

Hall New York City Superior Court 1828-1829.

Hall & T. Hall and Twells, Chancery, Eng., 1849-1850.

Hall's J. of Jur. The Journal of

Jurisprudence, Philadelphia, 1821.

Halst. Halstead, New Jersey Law, vols. 6-12, 1821-1831.

Halst. Ch. Halstead, New Jersey Chancery, vols. 5-8, 1845-1853.

Ham. Hammond, Ohio Reports, vols. 1-9.

Han. (N.B.) Hannay, New Brunswick Supreme Court, 1867-1871.

Hand Hand (N.Y.).

Handy Handy's Cincinnati Superior Court Reports, 1854-1856.

Hanm. Hanmer's Lord Kenyon's Notes, K. B.

Har. (Del.) Harrington, Delaware Superior Court, 1832-1854.

Har. (Mich.) Harrington, Michigan Court of Chancery, 1836-1842.

Har. (N.J.) Harrison, New Jersey Law, vols. 16-19, 1837-1842.

Har. & G. Harris and Gill, Maryland Court of Appeals, 1826-1829.

Har. & H. Harrison and Hodgin, Municipal Courts, Upper Canada, 1845-1851.

Har. & J. Harris and Johnson, Maryland Court of Appeals, 1800-1826.

Har. & McH. Harris and McHenry, Maryland Provincial Court and Court of Appeals, 1658-1799.

Har. & R. Harrison and Rutherford, Common Pleas, Eng., 1865-1866.

Har. & W. Harrison and Wollaston, King's Bench, Eng., 1835-1836.

Harc. Harcarse, Court of Session, Scotland, 1681-1691.

Hard. Hardres, Exchequer, Eng., 1655-1669.

Hardin Kentucky Court of Appeals, 1805-1808.

Hare Chancery, Eng., 1841-1853.

Harp. Harper, South Carolina Constitutional Court, 1823-1824.

Harp. Eq. Harper, South Carolina Court of Appeals, in Equity, 1824.

Harris Pennsylvania State Supreme Court, vols. 13-24.

Hart, Pat. Dec. Hart's Patent Decisions Digest.

Harv. C.R.-C.L. L. Rev. Harvard Civil Rights-Civil Liberties Law Review.

Harv. Int'l L. J. Harvard International Law Journal.

Harv. J. on Legis. Harvard Journal on Legislation.

Harv. L. Rev. Harvard Law Review.

Harv. Women's L.J. Harvard Women's Law Journal.

Hask. Haskell (U.S.).

Hastings L.J. Hastings Law Journal.

Haw. Hawaii Reports, Supreme Court, since 1847 (nonstandard).

Hawk. P.C. Hawkin's Pleas of the Crown.

Hawks North Carolina Supreme Court, 1820-1826.

Hay. & Haz. Hayward & Hazelton (D.C.), 1841-1862.

Hayes Exchequer, Ireland, 1830-1832.

Hayes & J. Hayes and Jones, Exchequer, Ireland, 1832-1834.

Hayw. (N.C.) Haywood, North Carolina Superior Courts, 1789-1806.

Hayw. (Tenn.) Haywood, Tennessee Court of Errors and Appeals, 1816-1818; 1813-1818 in appendix.

Head Tennessee Supreme Court, 1858-1859.

Heisk. Heiskell, Tennessee Supreme Court, 1870-1874.

Hem. & M. Hemming and Miller,

Chancery, Eng., 1862-1865.

Hemp. Hempstead, U.S. Courts, Ninth Circuit, 1820-1855.

Hen. & M. Hening and Munford, Virginia Court of Appeals and Superior Court of Chancery, 1806-1810.

Het. Hetley, Common Pleas, Eng., 1627-1631.

Hill (N.Y.) New York Supreme Court and Court of Appeals, 1841-1845.

Hill (S.C.) South Carolina Court of Appeals, 1833-1837.

Hill (S.C.) Ch. South Carolina Court of Appeals in Chancery, 1833-1837.

Hill & D. Hill and Denio (Lalor's Supplement), New York Supreme Court, etc., 1842-1844.

Hilly. Hillyer (Cal.).

Hilt. Hilton, New York Court of Comman Pleas, 1855-1860.

Hist. Historical; History.

Hob. Hobart, King's Bench, Eng., 1603-1625.

Hodges Common Pleas, Eng., 1835-1837.

Hoff. Ch. Hoffman, New York Assistant Vice-Chancellor's Court, 1839-1840.

Hoff. L.C. Hoffman's Land Cases, U.S. District Court, Cal., 1853-1858.

Hog. Hogan, Rolls Court, Ireland, 1816-1834.

Holmes U.S. Circuit Court, First Circuit, 1870-1875.

Holt, Adm. Admiralty Court Cases, Eng., 1863-1867.

Holt, Eq. Holt's Equity Reports, Eng., 1845.

Holt (K.B.) Sir John Holt, King's Bench, Eng., 1688-1710.

Holt (N.P.) Holt's Nisi Prius Reports, Eng., 1815-1817.

Home Court of Session, Scotland, 1735-1744. See also, Kames.

Home, Dict. of Dec. Home, Dictionary of Decisions, Court of Session, Scotland, 1540-1791.

Hop. & C. Hopwood and Coltman, Registration Cases, Eng., 1868-1878.

Hope Court of Session, Scotland.

Hopk. Hopkins, New York Court of Chancery, 1823-1826.

Hopk. Adm. Hopkinson, Admiralty Decisions, 1779-1805. Published also as an appendix to Bee.

Hosp. Hospital.

Hous. L. Rev. Houston Law Review.

Houst. Houston; Houston, Delaware Superior Court, 1855-1879.

Houst. C.C. Houston, Delaware Criminal Cases, 1856-1879.

How. Howard, U.S. Supreme Court, vols. 42-65, 1843-1860.

How. App. Cas. Howard's Court of Appeals Cases, N.Y., 1847-1848.

How. L.J. Howard Law Journal.

How. Miss. Howard, Mississippi Supreme Court, vols. 2-8, 1834-1843.

How. Pr. Howard, Practice Reports, New York Courts, 1844-1884.

How. Pr. (N.S.) Howard, Practice Reports, New York Courts, New Series.

Hud. & B. Hudson and Brooke, Irish Common Law Reports, 1827-1831.

Hugh. C.C. Hughes, U. S. Circuit Court, Fourth Circuit, 1792-1883.

Hughes Kentucky Court of Appeals,

1785-1801.

Hum. Human.

Hume Court of Session, Scotland, 1781-1822.

Humph. Humphreys, Tennessee Supreme Court, 1839-1851.

Hun New York Supreme Court.

Hut. Hutton, Common Pleas, Eng., 1584-1638.

I. & N. Dec. Immigration and Nationality Decisions.

I.C.C. Interstate Commerce Commission Reports.

ICC Prac. J. ICC Practitioners' Journal.

Ia. Iowa Reports, Supreme Court, 1855-1968 (nonstandard).

Ib. or **Ibid.** Ibidem; In the same place, volume, or case.

Id. Idem; The same.

Ida. Idaho Reports, since 1866 (nonstandard).

Ill. Illinois Reports, Supreme Court, since 1819. See also, Breese, Scam., and Gilm.

Ill. App. Illinois Appellate Court Reports, since 1877.

Ill. B.J. Illinois Bar Journal.

Ill. Ct. Cl. Illinois Court of Claims Reports, since 1889.

Ill. L.F. University of Illinois Law Forum.

Ill. L. Rev. Illinois Law Review.

Ind. Indiana Reports, Supreme Court, since 1848. See also, Blackf., Smith.

Ind. App. Indiana Court of Appeals Reports; Indiana Appellate Court Reports, since 1891.

Ind. L.J. Indiana Law Journal.

Ind. L.M. Indiana Law Magazine, Indianapolis, 1883-1885.

Ind. L. Rev. Indiana Law Review.

Indem. Indemnity.

Indian Terr. Indian Territory Reports (Oklahoma), 1896-1907.

Indus. Industrial; Industries; Industry.

Ins. Insurance.

Ins. Counsel J. Insurance Counsel Journal.

Ins. L.J. Insurance Law Journal.

Inst. Institute; Institutes, Coke's or Justinian's.

Int. Com. Interstate Commerce Commission Reports (nonstandard).

Int. Rev. Bull. Internal Revenue Bulletin.

Int. Rev. Rec. Internal Revenue Record, New York.

Int'l International.

Int'l Aff. International Affairs.

Int'l & Comp. L. Q. International and Comparative Law Quarterly.

Intra. Intramural.

Inv. Investment.

Ir. Ireland; Irish.

Ir. App. Cas. Irish Appeal Cases, House of Lords, Eng., 1726-1740.

Ir. C.L.R. Irish Common Law Reports, 1850-1866.

Ir. Ch. Irish Chancery Reports, 1850-1866.

Ir. Eq. Irish Equity Reports, 1838-1851.

Ir. J. Irish Jurist, 1849-1866.

Ir. L. Rec. Irish Law Recorder, 1827-1831; New Series, 1833-1838.

Ir. L. Rep. Irish Law Reports, Dublin, 1838-1850.

Ir. L.T. Irish Law Times and Solicitors' Journal.

Ir. R. (C.L.) Irish Reports, Common Law, 1867-1878.

Ir. R. (Eq.) Irish Reports, Equity, 1867-1878.

Ired. Iredell, North Carolina Supreme Court at Law, 1840-1852.

Ired. Eq. Iredell, North Carolina Supreme Court, in Equity, 1840-1852.

Irv. Irvine's Justiciary Cases, Scotland, 1852-1867.

J. Journal; Judge; Justice.

J. & W. Jacob and Walker, Chancery, Eng., 1819-1821.

J.A. Judge Advocate.

JAG J. JAG [Judge Advocate General] Journal.

J.A.M.A. Journal of the American Medical Association.

J. Air L. & Com. Journal of Air Law and Commerce.

J. Am. Jud. Soc'y Journal of American Judicature Society.

J. Am. Soc'y C.L.U. Journal of American Society of Chartered Life Underwriters.

J. Bus. L. Journal of Business Law.

J. Crim. L.C. & P.S. Journal of Criminal Law, Criminology and Police Science.

J. Fam. L. Journal of Family Law.

J. For. Sci. Journal of Forensic Sciences.

J.J. Marsh. J.J. Marshall, Kentucky Court of Appeals, 1829-1832.

J. Law & Econ. Journal of Law and Economics.

J. Legal Ed. or **J. Legal Educ.** Journal of Legal Education (**Ed.** nonstandard).

J. Mar. J. Prac. & Proc. John Marshall Journal of Practice and Procedure.

J.P. Justice of the Peace; The Justice of the Peace, and County, Borough, Poor Law Union, and Parish Law Recorder, London.

J.P. Ct. Justice of the Peace's Court.

J. Pat. Off. Soc'y Journal of Patent Office Society.

J. Plan. L. Journal of Planning Law.

J. Pub. L. Journal of Public Law.

J. Tax. or **J. Tax'n** Journal of Taxation.

Jac. Jacob, Chancery, Eng., 1821-1822.

James Nova Scotia Law Reports, 1853-1855.

Jebb & B. Jebb and Bourke, King's Bench, Ireland, 1841-1842.

Jebb & S. Jebb and Symes, King's Bench, Ireland, 1838-1841.

Jebb, C.C. Jebb's Crown Cases, Reserved, Ireland, 1822-1840.

Jeff. Jefferson, Virginia General Court, 1730-1740, 1768-1772.

Jenk. Jenkins, Exchequer, Eng., 1220-1623.

Johns. Johnson, Chancery, Eng., 1858-1860.

Johns. Johnson, New York Supreme Court, etc., 1806-1823.

Johns. & H. Johnson and Hemming, Chancery, Eng., 1860-1862.

Johns. Cas. Johnson's Cases, New York Supreme Court, etc., 1794-1803.

Johns. Ch. Johnson, New York Court of Chancery, 1814-1823.

Jones Jones (Pa.)

Jones (Ir.) Exchequer. Ireland, 1834-1838.

Jones (N.C.) North Carolina Supreme Court, at Law, 1853-1862.

Jones (N.C.) Eq. North Carolina Supreme Court, in Equity,

1853-1863.

Jones & C. Jones and Cary, Exchequer, Ireland, 1838-1839.

Jones & L. Jones and Latouche, Chancery, Ireland, 1844-1846.

Jones & McMurtie Jones and McMurtie (Pa.).

Jones & S. Jones and Spencer, New York City Superior Court, vols. 33-41.

Jones, T. King's Bench, Eng., 1667-1685.

Jones, W. King's Bench, Eng., 1620-1640.

Jour. of Jur. Journal of Jurisprudence and Scottish Law Magazine, Edinburgh.

Jour. of L. Journal of Law, Philadelphia, 1830-1831.

Jud. Judicature; Judicial.

Jur. Juridical; Jurist; The Jurist, Reports all courts, Eng., 1837-1854.

Jur. (N.S.) The Jurist, New Series, all courts, Eng., 1855-1866.

Jur. Sc. The Scottish Jurist, Court of Session, 1829-1873.

Jur. St. Judicial Styles, Scotland.

Jurid. Juridical.

Jurid. Rev. Juridicial Review.

Juris. Jurisprudence.

Just. Justice; Justinian Institutes.

Just. Cas. Justiciary Cases, Scotland.

Just. P. Justice of the Peace and Local Government Review.

Juv. Juvenile.

K. King.

K.B. Court of King's Bench.

K.C. King's Counsel.

K. & G. Keane and Grant, Registration Appeal Cases, Eng., 1854-1862.

K.C.R. Reports in time of King, Chancellor, 1724-1734.

K.L.S. Kentucky Law Summary (nonstandard).

Kames Court of Session, Scotland, 1716-1768.

Kames & W. Kames and Woodhouslee, Dictionary of Decisions, Court of Session, Scotland, 1540-1804.

Kames, R.D. Kames' Remarkable Decisions, Court of Session, Scotland, 1716-1752.

Kames, S.D. Kames' Select Decisions, Court of Session, Scotland, 1752-1768.

Kan. Kansas Reports, Supreme Court, since 1862. See also, McCa.

Kan. App. Kansas Court of Appeals Reports, 1895-1901.

Kan. App. 2d Kansas Court of Appeals Reports, since 1977.

Kan. L.J. Kansas Law Journal, Topeka.

Kan. L. Rev. University of Kansas Law Review (nonstandard).

Kay Chancery, Eng. (V.C. Wood), 1853-1854.

Kay & J. Kay and Johnson, Chancery, Eng. (V.C. Wood), 1854-1858.

Keb. Keble, King's Bench, Eng., 1661-1678.

Keen Rolls Court, Eng., 1836-1838.

Keilw. Keilwey, King's Bench, 1496-1530.

Kel. Sir John Kelyng, King's Bench, Eng., 1662-1669.

Kel. 1, 2 Wm. Kelynge's Reports, Eng., two parts—Chancery, 1730-1732; King's Bench, 1731-1734.

Kelly Georgia Supreme Court.

Ken. Kenyon, Notes of Cases, King's Bench and Chantery, Eng.,

1753-1759.

Kent Kent's Commentaries on American Law.

Kern. Keman, New York Court of Appeals, vols. 11-14.

Kerr New Brunswick, 1840-1848.

Keyes New York Court of Appeals, 1863-1868.

Kilk. Kilkerran, Court of Session, Scotland, 1738-1752.

Kirby Connecticut Superior Court, 1785-1788.

Kn. Knapp, Privy Council, Eng., 1829-1836.

Kn. & O. Knapp and Ombler, Election Cases, Eng., 1834-1837.

Kulp Kulp (Pa.)

Ky. Kentucky Reports, Court of Appeals, 1785-1951. See also, Hughes, Sneed, Hardin, Bibb, A.K. Marsh., Litt., T.B. Mon., B. Mon., J.J. Marsh., Dana, Met., Duv., and Bush.

Ky. Ct. App. Kentucky Court of Appeals, since 1976.

Ky. L.J. Kentucky Law Journal.

Ky. L.R. or **Ky. L.Rep.** or **Ky. L. Rptr.** Kentucky Law Reporter, 1880-1908 (Ky. L.R. & Ky. L.Rep. nonstandard).

Ky. Op. Kentucky Opinions, 1864-1886.

Ky. St. B.J. Kentucky State Bar Journal.

L. Law; Lord.

L. 5, (Long quinto.) One of the parts of the Year Books.

L. & A. Ins. Cas. Life and Accident Insurance Cases, New York, 1872-1877.

L. & Bk. Bull. Law and Bank Bulletin, Cincinnati, 1857-1858.

L. & C.C.C. Leigh and Cave, Crown Cases Reserved, Eng., 1861-1865.

L. & C.P. Law and Contemporary Problems (nonstandard).

L. & M. Lowndes and Maxwell, Bail Court, Eng., 1852-1854.

L.A. Los Angeles.

L.C. Library of Congress; Lord Chancellor; Lower Canada.

L.C. Adm. Lower Canada Admiralty Courts, 1873-1884.

L.C. Jur. Lower Canada Jurist.

L.C.L.J. Lower Canada Law Journal, Montreal, 1865-1868.

L.C.R. Lower Canada Reports, 1850-1867.

L. Cent. The Law Central, Washington, D.C., 1881.

L. Ct. Law Court.

L. Div. Law Division.

L. Ed. Lawyer's Edition, United States Supreme Court Reports, 1754-1956.

L. Ed. 2d Lawyers' Edition, United States Supreme Court Reports, Second Series, since 1956.

L.I.L. Lincoln's Inn Library.

L. Inst. J. Law Institute Journal.

L.J. Law Journal; Lord Justice.

L.J. Notes of Cas. Law Journal Notes of Cases, London.

L.J. (N.S.) Law Journal (New Series), Eng., Reports of all courts.

L. Lib. J. or **L. Libr. J.** or **L. Library J.** Law Library Journal (nonstandard).

L.M. & P. Lowndes, Maxwell and Pollock, Bail Court, Eng., 1850-1851.

L. Mag. The Law Magazine, London, Eng., 1828-1856.

L. Mag. & R. The Law Magazine and Review, London, Eng.

L.Q. Law Quarterly.

L.Q.R. or **L.Q.Rev.** Law Quarterly Review (nonstandard).

L.R. Law Reports, all courts, London, Eng.

L.R.A. Lawyers' Reports Annotated.

L.R. & Q.J. Law Review and Quarterly Journal, London, 1844-1856.

L.R. (Ir.) Law Reports, Ireland.

L.S. Mag. The Law Students' Magazine, London, 1844-1853.

L. Rep. The Law Reporter, Boston, 1838-1866; The Law Reporter, all courts, Eng.

L. Rev. Law Review.

L.T. The Law Times, all courts, Eng.

L.T. (N.S.) The Law Times (New Series), all courts, Eng.

La. Louisiana Reports, Supreme Court, 1830-1841, 1900-1972. See also, Mart., Rob.

La. Ann. Louisiana Annual Reports, Supreme Court, 1846-1900.

La. App. Louisiana Courts of Appeal Reports, 1924-1932.

La. L.J. Louisiana Law Journal, New Orleans, 1841-1842, 1876-1878.

La. L. Rev. Louisiana Law Review.

La Them. La Themis, Law Periodical, Lower Canada.

Lab. L.J. Labor Law Journal.

Lalor Supplement to Hill and Denio, New York Supreme Court, 1842-1844.

Lanc. Bar The Lancaster (Pa.) Bar, Law Periodical.

Land Econ. Land Economics.

Lane Exchequer, Eng., 1605-1612.

Lang. & T. Langfield and Townsend, Exchequer, Ireland, 1841-1842.

Lang. Con. Langdell's Select Cases on Contracts.

Lang. Sales Langdell's Select Cases on Sales of Personal Property.

Lans. Lansing, New York Supreme Court, 1869-1873.

Lans. Ch. Lansing's Chancery (N.Y.).

Latch King's Bench, Eng., 1625-1628.

Law. Lawyer; Lawyers; Lawyers'; Lawyer's.

Law. & Banker Lawyer and Banker and Central Law Journal.

Law & Contemp. Prob. or **Probs.** Law and Contemporary Problems (Prob. nonstandard).

Law & Eq. Rep. Law and Equity Reporter, New York, 1876-1877 (merged into The Reporter).

Law Chr. The Law Chronicle, or Journal of Jurisprudence, Edinburgh, 1829-1832; The Law Chronicle, London, 1833-1835.

Law Dig. The Law Digest, London, 1845-1856.

Law. Guild Rev. Lawyers' Guild Review.

Law Int. The Law Intelligencer, Providence, 1829-1831.

Law L. The Law List, London.

Law Lib. J. Law Library Journal (nonstandard).

Law Libr. J. Law Library Journal.

Law Q. Rev. Law Quarterly Review.

Law Rec. The Law Recorder, all courts, Ireland, 1827-1836.

Law Rep. Law Reporter (Mass.); Law Repository, North Carolina Supreme Court, 1811-1816.

Law Rep. News Law Report News.

Law, The Monthly Law Journal, London, 1874-1875.

Lawy. Rep. Lawyers' Reports, all cases of general interest in State and U.S. courts, Rochester.

Lea Lea (Tenn.).

Leach, C.C. Leach, Crown Cases, Eng., 1730-1814.

Lee Ecclesiastical Courts, Eng., 1752-1758; Lee (Cal.).

Lee, t. H. Lee's Reports in time of Hardwicke, King's Bench, Eng., 1733-1738.

Leg. Adv. The Legal Adviser, Chicago.

Leg. Chr. Legal Chronicle, Pottsville, Pa.

Leg. Exam. The Legal Examiner, and Law Chronicle, London, 1831-1833, 1869-1872.

Leg. Gaz. Legal Gazette, Philadelphia, various courts, 1869-1876.

Leg. & Ins. Rep. Legal and Insurance Reporter.

Leg. Int. Legal Intelligencer, Philadelphia.

Leg. N. Legal News, Montreal.

Leg. Obs. Legal Observer, Eng., 1830-1857.

Leg. Rep. The Legal Reporter, Dublin, 1840-1841.

Legal Intell. Legal Intelligencer.

Legis. Legislation.

Lehigh Va. Law Rep. Lehigh Valley Law Reporter.

Leigh Virginia Court of Appeals and General Court, 1829-1842.

Leon. Leonard, King's Bench, Eng., 1582-1615.

Lev. Levinz, King's Bench, and other courts, Eng., 1660-1696.

Lew. C.C. Lewin's Crown Cases, Eng., 1822-1838.

Ley King's Bench, Eng., 1608-1629.

Lib. Liberties; Library (nonstan-

dard).

Lib. Ass. Liber Assissarum; Book of Assizes, King's Bench, 1327-1377. Year Book, pt. 5.

Libr. Library; Librarian.

Lilly Nisi Prius Reports, Eng., 1688-1693.

Lit. Littleton, Common Pleas and Exchequer, Eng., 1626-1631.

Litt. Littell, Kentucky Court of Appeals, 1822-1824.

Litt. Sel. Cas. Littell's Select Cases, Kentucky Court of Appeals, vol. 16 Kentucky Reports, 1795-1821.

Liv. L. Mag. Livingston's Law Magazine, New York, 1853-1856.

Liv. L. Reg. Livingston's Law Register, New York, 1849-1868.

Ll. & G. Lloyd and Goold, Chancery, Ireland, 1834-1839.

Ll.& W. Lloyd and Welsby, Queen's Bench, Eng., 1829-1830.

Lock. R.C. Lockwood's Reversed Cases, New York Court of Errors, 1799-1847.

Lofft King's Bench, Eng., 1772-1774.

Longf. & T. Longfield and Townsend, Exchequer, Ireland, 1841-1842.

Low. Lowell, U.S. Circuit Court, District of Massachusetts, 1865-1877.

Loy. L. Rev. Loyola of New Orleans Law Review.

Loy. L.A. L. Rev. Loyola of Los Angeles Law Review.

Loy. U. Chi. L.J. Loyola University of Chicago Law Journal.

Lud. Luders, Election Cases, Eng., 1784-1787.

Lum. Lumley's Poor Law Cases, various courts, Eng., 1834-1842.

Lush. Lushington, Admiralty, Eng.,

1860-1863.

Lutw. Lutwyche, Common Pleas, Eng., 1682-1704.

Lutw. R.C. Lutwyche, Registration Cases, Eng., 1843-1853.

Luz. L. Obs. Luzerne Legal Observer, Carbondale (Pa.), 1860-1864.

Luz. L.R. Luzerne Legal Register, Wilkesbarre (Pa.), 1872-1888.

M. & C. Mylne and Craig, Chancery, Eng., 1835-1841.

M. & G. Manning and Granger, Common Pleas, Eng., 1840-1845.

M. & M. Moody and Malkin, Nisi Prius, Eng., 1826-1830.

M. & P. Moore and Payne, Common Pleas, Eng., 1827-1831.

M. & R. Manning and Ryland, King's Bench, Eng., 1827-1830.

M. & R. Mag. Cas. Manning and Ryland, Magistrate's Cases, Eng., 1827-1830.

M. & Rob. Moody and Robinson, Nisi Prius, Eng., 1830-1844.

M. & S. Maule and Selwyn, King's Bench, Eng., 1813-1817.

M. & Scott Moore and Scott, Common Pleas, Eng., 1831-1834.

M. & W. Meeson and Welsby, Exchequer, Eng., 1836-1847.

M.C. Magistrates' Cases; Master Commissioner; Member of Congress; Municipal Court (non-standard).

M.C.C. Moody's Crown Cases, Eng., 1824-1844.

M.J. Military Justice Reporter, since 1975.

M.R. Master of the Rolls, Eng.

Mac. Mackey, District of Columbia Supreme Court.

Mac. & G. Macnaghten and Gordon, Chancery, Eng., 1849-1852.

Mac. & H. Macrae and Hertslet, Insolvency Cases, Eng., 1840-1852.

MacArth. MacArthur, District of Columbia, Supreme Court, 1873-1879.

MacArthur & M. MacArthur and Mackey (D.C.).

MacArthur's Pat. Cas. MacArthur's Patent Cases, U.S.

Mac F. Mac Farland, Jury Courts, Scotland, 1838-1839.

Mac. P.C. Macrory's Patent Cases, 1841-1856.

Mach. Machine; Machinery.

Macl. & R. Maclean and Robinson, Scotch Appeals, House of Lords, 1839.

Macl. R. Cas. Maclaurin, Remarkable Criminal Cases, Scotland, 1670-1773.

Macph. Macpherson and others, Court of Session, Scotland, 1862-1873

Macq. Macqueen, Scotch Appeals, House of Lords, 1849-1865.

Macq. L.C. Macqueen, Leading Cases of Parliamentary Divorce, Eng., 1669-1842.

Madd. Maddock, Chancery, Eng., 1815-1822.

Madd. & G. Maddock and Geddart, Chancery, Eng., 1821; Maddock and Geldart, Chancery, Eng., 1821.

Mag. Magistrate.

Magis. Ct. Magistrate's Court.

Man. Manhattan; Manitoba Reports, 1875-1883; Manning (Mich.).

Man. L.J. Manitoba Law Journal, 1884-1885.

Man. L.R. Manitoba Law Reports.

Man. Unrep. Cas. Manning's Unreported Cases (La.).

Manson Manson English Reports.

Mar. Marine; Maritime.

Mar. L.C. (N.S.) Maritime Law Cases, New Series, Eng.

Mar. L.R. Maritime Law Reports, Admiralty, Eng., 1860-1871.

March King's Bench, Eng., 1639-1642.

Marq. L. Rev. Marquette Law Review.

Marr. Marriage; Marriott, Admiralty, Eng., 1776-1779.

Marsh. Marshall, Common Pleas, Eng., 1813-1816.

Marsh. A.K. Marshall, A.K., Kentucky Court of Appeals, 1817-1821.

Marsh. Dec. Chief Justice Marshall's Decisions, by Brockenbrough, 1802-1836.

Marsh. J.J. Marshall, J. J., Kentucky Court of Appeals, 1829-1832.

Mart. (La.) Martin, Louisiana Supreme Court, 1809-1823.

Mart. (La. N.S.) Martin, Louisiana Supreme Court, New Series, 1823-1830.

Mart. (N.C.) Martin, various courts, North Carolina, 1778-1797.

Mart. & Y. Martin and Yerger, Tennessee Supreme Court, 1825-1828.

Marvel Marvel (Del.).

Mas. Mason, U. S. Circuit Court, First Circuit, 1815-1830.

Mass. Massachusetts Reports, Supreme Judicial Court, since 1804. See also, Quin., Wms., Tyng, Pick., Met., Cush., Gray, Allen.

Mass. App. Ct. Massachusetts Appeals Court Reports, since 1967.

Mass. App. Dec. Massachusetts Appellate Decisions, since 1941.

Mass. App. Div. Massachusetts Appellate Division Reports, 1936-1950.

Mass. L. Rev. Massachusetts Law Review.

Mat. Matrimonial and Divorce Division, Eng.

McAll. McAllister, U. S. District Court, California, 1855-1859.

McCa. McCahon, U.S. Courts, Kansas, 1858-1868 (nonstandard).

McCart. McCarter, New Jersey Ecuity, vols. 14, 15, 1861-1862.

McCl. McCleland, Exchequer, Eng., 1824.

McCl. & Yo. McCleland and Younge, Exchequer, Eng., 1824-1825.

McCord South Carolina Constitutional Court and Court of Appeals, 1821-1828.

McCord, Ch. South Carolina Court of Appeals, in Chancery, 1825-1827.

McCra. McCrary, U.S. Circuit Court, Eighth Circuit, 1874-1883.

McGloin Louisiana Courts of Appeal, 1880.

McLean U. S. Circuit Court, Seventh Circuit, 1829-1855.

McMull. McMullan, South Carolina Court of Appeals, at Law, 1835-1842.

McMull. Eq. McMullan, South Carolina Court of Appeals, in Equity, 1827-1837, 1840-1842.

Md. Maryland Reports, Court of Appeals, since 1851. See also, Har. & McH., Har. & J., Gill. & J., Gill., Bland.

Md. App. Maryland Appellate

Reports, since 1967.

Md. Ch. Maryland High Court of Chancery Reports, 1847-1854.

Md. L. Rec. Maryland Law Record, Baltimore.

Md. L. Rep. Maryland Law Reporter, Baltimore, 1871-1872.

Md. L. Rev. Maryland Law Review.

Me. Maine Reports, Supreme Court, 1820-1965.

Me. L. Rev. Maine Law Review.

Med. Media (nonstandard); Medical; Medicine.

Med. L.J. Medico-Legal Journal, New York. 1884-1886.

Med. Trial Tech. Q. Medical Trial Technique Quarterly.

Megone Cases under the Companies Acts, Eng., 1888-1890.

Meigs Tennessee Supreme Court, 1838-1839.

Melb. Melbourne.

Mem. Memorandum; Memoranda; Memphis.

Mem. L.J. Memphis Law Journal, 1878-1879.

Mem. St. U. L. Rev. Memphis State University Law Review.

Mer. Merivale, Chancery, Eng., 1815-1817.

Met. Metcalf, Massachusetts Supreme Court, vols. 42-54, 1840-1847.

Met. (Ky.) Metcalfe, Kentucky Court of Appeals, 1858-1863.

Mfg. Manufacturing.

Mfr. Manufacturer.

Mich. Michigan Reports, Supreme Court, since 1847. See also, Doug., Har., and Walk.

Mich. App. Michigan Appeals Reports, since 1965.

Mich. Ct. Cl. Michigan Court of Claims Reports, 1938-1942.

Mich. L.J. Michigan Law Journal.

Mich. L. Rev. Michigan Law Review.

Mich. N.P. Michigan Nisi Prius Reports, Circuit Courts, 1869-1871.

Mil. L. Rev. Military Law Review.

Miles Philadelphia District Court, 1835-1842.

Miller Miller (La.).

Miller's Dec. Miller's Decisions, U.S. 8th Circuit Ct.

Mills South Carolina Constitutional Court, 1817-1818.

Milw. Milward, Ecclesiastical, Ireland, 1819-1843.

Min. Mineral.

Min. Rep. Mining Reports, State and U.S. Courts, Chicago.

Minn. Minnesota Reports, Supreme Court, 1851-1977.

Minn. L. Rev. Minnesota Law Review.

Minor Alabama Supreme Court, 1820-1826.

Misc. or **Misc.Rep.** N.Y. Miscellaneous Reports.

Misc. 2d N.Y. Miscellaneous Reports, Second Series.

Miss. Mississippi Reports, 1818-1966. See also, Walk., How., Sm. & M., Freem.

Miss. L.J. Mississippi Law Journal.

Mkt. Market.

Mkts. Markets.

Mo. Missouri Reports, Supreme Court, 1821-1956.

Mo. App. Missouri Appeal Reports, 1876-1951.

Mo. Jur. Monthly Jurist, Bloomington, Ill., 1877-1878.

Mo. L. Mag. Monthly Law Magazine, London, 1838-1841.

Mo. L. Rev. Missouri Law Review.

Mo. W.J. Monthly Western Jurist, Bloomington, Ill., 1875-1877.

Moak English Reports, American reprint of all cases of value in the U.S.

Mod. Modern; Modern Reports, King's Bench, Eng., 1663-1732.

Mod. C.L. & Eq. Modern Cases in Law in Equity.

Mod. L. Rev. Modern Law Review, London.

Mol. Molloy, Chancery, Ireland, 1807-1832.

Mon. Monroe, T. B., Kentucky Court of Appeals, 1824-1828.

Mon. B. B. Monroe, Kentucky Court of Appeals, 1840-1857.

Monag. Monaghan (Pa.).

Mont. Montana Reports, Supreme Court, since 1868.

Mont. & A. Montagu and Ayrton, Bankruptcy, Eng., 1833-1838.

Mont. & B. Montagu and Bligh, Bankruptcy, Eng., 1832-1833.

Mont. & Ch. Montagu and Chitty, Bankruptcy, Eng., 1838-1840.

Mont. & Mac. Montagu and MacArthur, Bankruptcy, Eng., 1828-1830.

Mont. Bkcy. Montagu, Bankruptcy Reports, Eng., 1830-1832.

Mont. Co. Law Repr. or **Rptr.** Montgomery County (Pa.) Law Reporter.

Mont. D. & D. Montagu, Deacon & De Gex, Bankruptcy, Eng., 1840-1844.

Mont. L.R. Montreal Law Reports, (Q.B.) Queen's Bench, (S.C.) Supreme Court.

Mont. L. Rev. Montana Law Review.

Month. Law. Bul. Monthly Law Bulletin, N.Y.

Moo. & R. Moody and Robinson's Reports, N. P.

Moo. & S. Moore and Scott's Reports, C. P.

Moody Crown Cases Reserved, Eng., 1824-1844.

Moore J. B. Moore, Common Pleas, Eng., 1817-1827.

Moore, Sir F. Queen's Bench, Eng., 1512-1621.

Moore, Ind. Ap. Moore's Indian Appeals, Privy Council, 1836-1872.

Moore, P.C.C. Moore's Privy Council Cases, 1836-1862.

Moore, P.C.C. (N.S.) Moore's Privy Council Cases (New Series), 1862-1873.

Mor. Dict. of Dec. Morison, Dictionary of Decisions, Court of Session, Scotland, 1540-1808.

Mor. Syn. Morison, Synopsis of Decisions, Court of Session, Scotland, 1808-1816.

Morr. Morris, Iowa Supreme Court, 1839-1846.

Morr. Bkcy. Morrell, Reports of Cases under English Bankruptcy Act of 1883, 1884-1890.

Morr. Min. R. Morrison's Mining Reports.

Mos. Mosley, Chancery, Eng., 1726-1730.

Mun. Municipal.

Mun. Ct. Municipal Court.

Munic. L.J. Municipal Law Journal (nonstandard).

Munf. Munford, Virginia Court of Appeals, 1810-1820.

Mur. & H. Murphy and Hurlstone, Exchequer, Eng., 1837.

Murph. Murphey, North Carolina

Supreme Court, 1804-1819.

Murr. Murray, Jury Courts, Scotland, 1815-1830.

Mut. Mutual.

My. Fed. Dec., Myer, Federal Decisions, all U.S. Courts, from organization to 1882, arranged by subjects.

Myl. & C. Mylne and Craig, Chancery, Eng., 1835-1841.

Myl. & K. Mylne and Keen, Chancery, Eng., 1832-1835.

Myrick Probate Court Reports, San Francisco, 1872-1879.

N. North; Northern.

N.A. North America.

NACCA L.J. National Association of Claimant's Counsel of America Law Journal.

N. & M. Neville and Manning, King's Bench, Eng., 1832-1836.

N. & P. Neville and Perry, Queen's Bench, Eng., 1836-1838.

N.B. New Brunswick Reports. See also, Chip., Bert., Kerr, Allen, Han., Pugs., Pugs. & B.

N.B.R. National Bankruptcy Register, 1867-1879.

N. Benl. New Benloe, King's Bench. Eng., 1509-1625.

N.C. North Carolina Reports, Supreme Court. See also, Mart., Hayw., Tayl., Conf., Cam. & N., Murph., Car. L. R., N.C.T.R., Hawks, Dev., Dev. & B., Ired., Busb., Jones, Winst., Phil.

N.C. App. North Carolina Court of Appeals Reports, since 1968.

N.C.C.A. Negligence & Compensation Cases Annotated (nonstandard).

NCCUSL National Conference of Commissioners on Uniform State Laws.

N.C.L.Rev. North Carolina Law Review.

N.C.T.R. North Carolina Term Reports, 1816-1818.

N.D. North Dakota Reports, Supreme Court, 1890-1953; Northern District.

N.D.L.Rev. North Dakota Law Review.

N.E. North Eastern Reporter.

N.E.2d North Eastern Reporter, Second Series.

NEPA National Environmental Policy Act of 1969.

N.Eng. Rep. New England Reporter, Rochester.

N.F. Newfoundland.

N.H. New Hampshire Reports, Supreme Court, since 1816. See also, Smith.

N.Ir.L.Q. Northern Ireland Legal Quarterly.

N., H. & C. Nichol, Hare and Carrow, English Railway Cases, 1835-1855.

N.J. New Jersey Reports, Supreme Court, since 1948.

N.J. Eq. New Jersey Equity Reports, Court of Chancery and Supreme Court in Equity, since 1830. See also, Sax., Green, Halst., Stockt., Beasl., McCart., Green, C.E., Stew.

N.J.L. New Jersey Law Reports, Supreme Court and Court of Errors and Appeals, Cases at Law, 1790-1948. See also, Coxe, Pen., South., Halst., Green, Har., Spenc., Zab., Dutch., Vroom.

N.J.L.J. New Jersey Law Journal.

N.J. Misc. New Jersey Miscellaneous Reports, 1923-1949.

N.J. Super. New Jersey Superior Court Reports, since 1948.

N.L. Nelson's Lutwyche Reports, C.P.

N.M. New Mexico Reports, Supreme Court and Court of Appeals, since 1890.

N.M. L.Rev. New Mexico Law Review.

N.P. Nisi Prius; Ohio Nisi Prius Reports (nonstandard).

N.R. New Reports (Bosanquet and Puller), Common Pleas, Eng., 1804-1807; New Reports, all courts, Eng., 1862-1865.

N.R. (N.S.) New Reports (New Series), Queen's Bench, Eng., 1862-1873.

N.S. or **n.s.** New Style; New Series; N.S. Nova Scotia Law Reports.

N.S. Dec. Nova Scotia Decisions, Supreme Court, 1866-1875.

N.S. Eq. Nova Scotia Equity Reports, 1873-1882.

N.W. North Western Reporter.

N.W. 2d North Western Reporter, Second Series.

N.Y. New York Reports, Court of Appeals, since 1847. See also, Comst., Seld., Kern.

N.Y. Ann. Cas. New York Annotated Cases.

N.Y.C. Rep. or **Rptr.** New York Code Reporter, 1848-1851.

N.Y. Civ. Pro. R. New York Civil Procedure Reports.

N.Y. Cr. R. New York Criminal Reports, Albany.

N.Y.L.F. New York Law Forum.

N.Y.L.J. New York Law Journal.

N.Y.L. Sch. L. Rev. New York Law School Law Review.

N.Y. Leg. N. New York Legal News.

N.Y. Leg. Obs. New York Legal Observer, 1842-1854.

N.Y. Mo. L.B. New York Monthly Law Bulletin.

N.Y.S. New York Supplement, since 1938.

N.Y.S.2d New York Supplement, Second Series.

N.Y. St. R. New York State Reporter, Albany.

N.Y. Sup. Ct. New York Supreme Court Reports, 1873-1896.

N.Y. Super. New York City Superior Court. See also, Hall, Sandf., Duer, Bosw., Rob., and Sweeney.

N.Y. Supp. New York Supplement (nonstandard).

N.Y. Supr. New York Supreme Court Reports, 1873-1896. See also, Barb., Lans., Hun, Thomp. & C.

N.Y. Tr. New York Transcript.

N.Y. Tr. (N.S.) New York Transcript, New Series.

N.Y.U.L.Q.Rev. New York University Law Quarterly Review.

N.Y.U.L.Rev. New York University Law Review.

N.Y.W.Dig. The New York Weekly Digest.

Nat. Natural; National (nonstandard).

Nat'l or **Natl.** National.

Nat'l B.J. National Bar Journal.

Nat'l Bk. Cas. National Bank Cases, Albany and San Francisco, 1864-1889.

Nat'l B.R. National Bankruptcy Register, New York, 1867-1879.

Nat'l Corp. Rep. National Corporation Reporter.

Nat'l Munic. Rev. National

Municipal Review (nonstandard).

Nat'l Tax J. National Tax Journal.

Neb. Nebraska Reports, Supreme Court, since 1860. Some Territorial cases added.

Neb. L.J. Nebraska Law Journal.

Neb. L. Rev. Nebraska Law Review.

Negl. & Comp. Cas. Ann. Negligence & Compensation Cases Annotated.

Negl. & Comp. Cas. Ann. (N.S.). Negligence & Compensation Cases Annotated, New Series.

Negl. & Comp. Cas. Ann.3d Negligence & Compensation Cases Annotated, Third Series.

Negl. & Comp. Cas. Ann. 4th Negligence & Compensation Cases Annotated, Fourth Series.

Nels. Nelson, Chancery, Eng., 1625-1695.

Nev. Nevada Reports, Supreme Court, since 1865.

New Benl. New Benloe, King's Bench, Eng., 1509-1625.

New Eng. New England.

New L.J. New Law Journal.

New Mag. Cas. New Magistrates' Cases, Eng., Brittleston, Wise and Parnell, 1844-1850.

New Ses. Cas. New Session Cases, Carron, Hamerton and Allen, and others, all courts, Eng., 1844-1851.

New T.R. New Term Reports, all courts, Eng., 1835-1841.

Newb. Adm. Newberry, U.S. District Courts in Admiralty, 1842-1857.

1983 42 U.S.C. § 1983, concerning civil actions for deprivation of rights.

Nolan King's Bench, Magistrates' Cases, Eng., 1791-1792.

North. Northington, Chancery (by Eden), Eng., 1757-1766.

Northam. Law Rep. or **Rptr.** Northampton Law Reporter.

Notre Dame Law. Notre Dame Lawyer.

Nott & H. Nott and Huntington, U.S. Court of Claims, vols. 1-7.

Nott & McC. Nott and McCord, South Carolina Constitutional Court, 1817-1820.

Noy King's Bench, Eng., time of Elizabeth, James and Charles.

Nw. U. L. Rev. Northwestern University Law Review.

O. Ohio Reports, Supreme Court, 1821-1851 (nonstandard).

O.A.G. Opinions of the Attorney General (nonstandard).

O.Benl. Old Benloe, Common Pleas, Eng., 1486-1580.

O.C.C. Ohio Circuit Court Reports (nonstandard).

O.C.D. Ohio Circuit Decisions (nonstandard).

O.D. Ohio Decisions (nonstandard).

O.G. or **O.G. Pat. Off.** Official Gazette, U.S. Patent Office.

O.L.A. Ohio Law Abstract (nonstandard) .

O.L.D. Ohio Lower Court Decisions (nonstandard).

O.L.J. Ohio Law Journal, Columbus, 1880-1884 (nonstandard).

O.L.R. Ohio Law Reporter (nonstandard).

O.O. Ohio Opinions (nonstandard).

O.R. Ohio Reports, Supreme Court, 1821-1851 (nonstandard).

O.S. Ohio State Reports, Supreme Court, since 1852 (nonstandard).

OSHA Occupational Safety and

Health Act of 1970, as amended.

O.S.L.J. Ohio St. L.J. (nonstandard).

O. Supp. Ohio Supplement (non-standard).

Off. Office.

Ohio. App. Ohio Appellate Reports.

Ohio App.2d, 3d Ohio Appellate Reports, Second Series and Third Series.

Ohio C.C., Ohio C.C.(n.s.) Ohio Circuit Court Reports, 1885-1917.

Ohio C.C.R. Ohio Circuit Court Reports, 1885-1901.

Ohio C. Dec. Ohio Circuit Decisions, 1885-1901.

Ohio Dec. Ohio Decisions.

Ohio L. Abs. Ohio Law Abstract.

Ohio L.Bull. Ohio Law Bulletin.

Ohio Leg. N. Ohio Legal News.

Ohio Misc. Ohio Miscellaneous Reports, since 1965.

Ohio Misc. 2d Ohio Miscellaneous Reports, Second Series.

Ohio N.P., Ohio N.P. (n.s.) Ohio Nisi Prius Reports, 1894-1934.

Ohio N.U.L.Rev. Ohio Northern University Law Review.

Ohio Op. Ohio Opinions.

Ohio Op.2d, 3d Ohio Opinions, Second Series and Third Series.

Ohio S. & C.P. Dec. Ohio Superior and Common Pleas Decisions.

Ohio St. Ohio State Reports. Supreme Court, since 1852.

Ohio St. 2d, 3d Ohio State Reports, Second Series and Third Series.

Ohio St. L. J. Ohio State Law Journal.

Oil & Gas Tax Q. Oil and Gas Tax Quarterly.

Okla. Oklahoma Reports, Supreme Court, 1890-1953.

Okla. B.J. Journal of the Oklahoma Bar Association.

Okla. Crim. Oklahoma Criminal Reports, 1908-1953.

Okla. L. Rev. Oklahoma Law Review.

Olc. Adm. Olcott, Admiralty, U.S. District Court, Southern District of New York, 1843-1847.

Old. Oldright, Nova Scotia Law Reports, 1860-1866.

Old Ben. See O. Benl. and Benl. & D.

O'm. & H. O'Malley and Hardcastle, Election Cases, 1869-1880.

Ont. Ontario High Court of Justice.

Ont. App. Ontario Appeal Reports.

Ont. Pr. Ontario Practice Reports.

Op. Att'y Gen. Opinions, U.S. Attorney General, since 1791. For state Attorney General Opinions, add in parenthesis the abbreviation for the state, *e.g.*, Op. Att'y Gen. (Ky.).

Ord. Order.

Or. Oregon Reports, Supreme Court, since 1853.

Or. App. Oregon Reports, Court of Appeals, since 1969.

Or. L. Rev. or **Ore. L. Rev.** Oregon Law Review.

Or. T.R. Oregon Tax Reporter, since 1962.

Otto U.S. Supreme Court, vols. 91-107.

Outerbridge Outerbridge (Pa.).

Over. Overton, Tennessee, various courts, 1791-1817.

Owen King's Bench, Eng., 1556-1615.

Oxley Young's Admiralty Decisions, Canada, 1865-1880.

P. Pacific Reporter; Plaintiff; Probate

Division, Law Reports, Eng.; Parliament; Pleas.

P.2d Pacific Reporter, Second Series.

P. & D. Perry and Davison, Queen's Bench, Eng., 1838-1841.

P. & K. Perry and Knapp, Election Cases, Eng., 1833.

P.C. Privy Council, Law Reports, Eng.; Pleas of the Crown; Probate Court.

P.C.C. Penal and Correctional Code (Model Penal Code).

P. Ct. Probate Court.

P-H Prentice-Hall.

P.J. Presiding Judge or Presiding Justice.

P.L. Mag. Poor Law Magazine, Glasgow and Edinburgh.

P.R.R. Puerto Rico Reports, 1899-1972.

P.U.R. Public Utilities Reports, Annotated.

P.U.R. (n.s.) Public Utilities Reports, New Series.

P.U.R.3d, 4th Public Utilities Reports, Third Series and Fourth Series.

P.W. or **P. Wms.** Peer Williams, Chancery, Eng., 1695-1735.

Pa. Pennsylvania Reports, Supreme Court, 1829-1832; Pennsylvania State Reports, since 1845. See also, Add., Yeates, Binn., Bright., Serg. & R., Rawle, Pen. & W., Pa. St., Watts, Whart., Watts & S., Grant Cas., Barr, Jones, Harris, Casey, Wright, Smith.

Pa. C., Pa. Co. Ct. or **Pa. County Ct.** Pennsylvania County Court Reports, 1885-1921.

Pa. Commw. Pennsylvania Commonwealth Court Reports, since 1970.

Pa. D. Pennsylvania District Reports, 1892-1921.

Pa. D. & C. Pennsylvania District and County Reports, since 1921.

Pa. D. & C.2d, 3d Pennsylvania District and County Reports, Second Series and Third Series.

Pa. Dist. R. Pennsylvania District Reports, 1892-1921.

Pa. Fiduc. Pennsylvania Fiduciary Reporter, since 1951.

Pa. L.J. Pennsylvania Law Journal, 1842-1848.

Pa. L.J. Rep. Pennsylvania Law Journal Reports, Clarke, 1842-1861.

Pa. L. Rec. Pennsylvania Law Record, Philadelphia, 1879-1880.

Pa. St. Pennsylvania State Supreme Court, since 1845 (nonstandard).

Pa. Super. or **Pa. Super. Ct.** Pennsylvania Superior Court Reports, since 1895.

Pac. Pacific; Pacific Reporter.

Pac. C. L.J. Pacific Coast Law Journal, San Francisco, 1878-1882.

Pac. L. Mag. Pacific Law Magazine, San Francisco, 1867.

Pac. L.R. or **L. Rptr.** Pacific Law Reporter, San Francisco, 1870-1878.

Pagin Pagin's Federal Precedents and Forms.

Paige New York Court of Chancery, 1828-1845.

Paine U.S. Circuit Court, Second Circuit, 1810-1840.

Palm. Palmer, King's Bench, Eng., 1619-1629.

Park. Parker, Exchequer, Eng., 1743-1766.

Park. C.C. Parker, Criminal Cases, various courts of New York,

1823-1868.

Pars. Eq. Cas. Parsons' Equity Cases, First Judicial District, Pennsylvania, 1841-1851.

Pat. Patent.

Pat. App. Patterson, Scotch Appeals, House of Lords, 1851-1873.

Pat. & H. Patton, Jr., and Heath, Virginia Special Court of Appeals, 1855-1857.

Pat. & T.M. Rev. Patent and Trade Mark Review.

Pat. L. Ann. Patent Law Annual.

Pat. Off. Ga. Official Gazette, U.S. Patent Office.

Paton Scotch Appeals, House of Lords, Eng., 1753-1821.

Pea. Peake's Reports, K.B., Eng.

Peake Nisi Prius, Eng., 1790-1812.

Peake Add. Cas. Peake's Additional Cases, Nisi Prius, Eng., 1795-1812. (Cited as 2nd Peake).

Pears. Pearson's Decisions, Twelfth Judicial District, Pennsylvania, 1851-1880.

Peck Tennessee Supreme Court, 1821-1824.

Peck (Ill.) Illinois Supreme Court, vols. 11-30.

Peckw. Peckwell, Election Cases, Eng., 1802-1806.

Pen. Pennington, New Jersey Laws, vols. 2 and 3, 1806-1813.

Pen. & W. Penrose and Watts, Pennsylvania Supreme Court, 1829-1832.

Pennewill Pennewill (Del.).

Pennyp. Pennypacker, Pennsylvania Supreme Court, cases omitted from regular reports, 1881-1884.

Pers. Personal.

Pet. Peters, U.S. Supreme Court,

vols. 26-41, 1828-1842.

Pet. Adm. Peters' Admiralty Decisions, U.S. District Court, Eastern District of Pennsylvania, 1780-1807.

Pet. C.C. Peters, U.S. Circuit Court, 1803-1818.

Phil. Ch. Phillips, Chancery, Eng., 1841-1849.

Phil. E.C. Phillips, Election Cases, Eng., 1780-1781.

Phil. Ecc. Phillimore Ecclesiastical Courts, Eng., 1809-1821.

Phil. L.J. Philippine Law Journal.

Phil. (N.C.) Phillips, North Carolina Supreme Court, at Law, 1866-1868.

Phil. (N.C.) Eq. Phillips, North Carolina Supreme Court, in Equity, 1866-1868.

Phil. R. Ecc. Robert Phillimore, Ecclesiastical Judgments, Eng., 1867-1875.

Phila. Reports of various courts in Philadelphia.

Pick. Pickering, Massachusetts Supreme Court, vols. 18-41, 1822-1840.

Pickle Pickle's Reports (Tenn.).

Pig. & R. Piggott and Rodwell, Election Cases, Eng., 1843-1845.

Pike Arkansas Supreme Court, vols. 1-5.

Pinn. Pinney, Wisconsin Supreme Court, 1839-1852.

Pitc. Pitcairn, Criminal Trials, Scotland, 1488-1624.

Pitt. Pittsburgh.

Pitts. Various courts, Pittsburgh, Pa., 1853-1873.

Pitts. L.J. Pittsburgh Legal Journal.

Pl. Pleas.

Plan. Planning.

Plow. Plowden, various courts, Eng., 1550-1579.

Pol. Political; Politics; Pollexfen, King's Bench, Eng., 1669-1684.

Pol. Sci. Q. Political Science Quarterly (nonstandard).

Police J. Ct. Police Justice's Court.

Pol'y Policy.

Poph. Popham, King's Bench, Eng., 1592-1627.

Port. Porter, Alabama Supreme Court, 1834-1839.

Port. Ind. Porter, Indiana.

Pow., R. & D. Power, Rodwell and Dew, Election Cases, Eng., 1848-1856.

Pr. Ed. Prince Edward's Island Reports, 1850-1882.

Pr. R. Practice Reports, Upper Canada.

Prac. Practical; Practice; Practitioners.

Prac. Law. Practical Lawyer.

Pratt Contraband Cases in High Court of Admiralty, Eng., 1740-1751. Appendix of Treaties, 1604-1827.

Pratt P.L. Cas. Bott's Poor Law Cases edited by Pratt, Eng., 1768-1827.

Prec. Ch. Precedents in Chancery, Eng., 1689-1722 (edited by T. Finch).

Price Exchequer, Eng., 1814-1824.

Price Pr. Cas. Price, Notes of Practice Cases, Exchequer, Eng., 1830-1831.

Pro., or **Prob.** Probate Division, Law Reports, Eng.

Prob. Probate; Problems (nonstandard).

Probs. Problems.

Proc. Procedures; Proceedings.

Prod. Product; Production.

Prop. Property.

Psych. Psychiatry; Psychology.

Pub. Public.

Pub. Doc. Public Documents.

Pub. L. Public Law.

Pugs. Pugsley, New Brunswick, Supreme Court, 1872-1876.

Pugs. & B. Pugsley and Burbidge, New Brunswick Supreme Court, 1877-1881.

Pyke Quebec, King's Bench, 1809-1810.

Q. Quarterly; Queen; Quebec (nonstandard).

Q.B. Queen's Bench.

Q.B. (N.S.) Adolphus and Ellis, Queen's Bench, New Series, 1841-1852.

Q.B. Div. Queen's Bench Division, Law Reports, Eng.

Q.L.J. Quarterly Law Journal, Richmond, Va., 1856-1859.

Q.L.R. Quebec Law Reports.

Que. Quebec.

Queb. Q.B. Quebec Queen's Bench Reports.

Quin. Quincy, Massachusetts, various courts, 1761-1772.

R. Reports; Reporter; Review; Rex; Regina; King; Rolls Court.

R. & M. Ryan and Moody, Nisi Prius, Eng., 1823-1826.

R. & R.C.C. Russell and Ryan's Crown Cases, Eng., 1800-1823.

R.C.L. Ruling Case Law.

RESPA Real Estate Settlement Procedures Act.

R.I. Rhode Island Reports, Supreme Court, since 1828.

RICO Racketeer Influenced and

Corrupt Organizations Act.

R.M. Charlt. R.M. Charlton, Georgia.

R.R. Railroad.

Railw. Cas. Railway Cases, Eng., by Nicholl, Hare, Oliver, Beavan, etc., all courts, 1835-1854.

Rand. Randolph, Virginia Court of Appeals, 1821-1828.

Rawle Pennsylvania Supreme Court, 1828-1835.

Raym. Lord Raymond, King's Bench and Common Pleas, Eng., 1694-1732.

Raym., T. T. Raymond, various courts, Eng., 1660-1682.

Rayner Tithe Cases, Eng., 1575-1782.

Real Pr. Cas. Real Property Cases, all courts, Eng., 1842-1847.

Rec. Record.

Rec. A.B. City N.Y. Record of the Association of the Bar of the City of New York.

Record of N.Y.C.B.A. Record of the Association of the Bar of the City of New York (nonstandard).

Redf. Redfield, New York Surrogate's Court, 1846-1882.

Redf. & B. Redfield and Bigelow, Leading Cases on Bills and Notes.

Reev. E.L. Reeve's English Law.

Ref. Referee; Referees; Referee's; Refining; Reform.

Ref. J. Referees' Journal; Journal of the National Association of Referees in Bankruptcy.

Reg. Register; Regulation.

Rel. Relations.

Reorg. Reorganizations.

Rep. Reporter (nonstandard for reports of cases); Reports; Representative; Coke's Reports; The Reporter, Boston.

Rep. Ch. Reports in Chancery, Eng., 1625-1710.

Res. Reserve.

Rev. Review; Revised.

Rev. Leg. Revue Legale, Montreal.

Rice South Carolina Court of Appeals and Errors, at Law, 1838-1839.

Rice Ch. South Carolina Court of Appeals and Errors, in Equity, 1838-1839.

Rich. Richmond; Richardson, South Carolina Court of Appeals and Errors, at Law, 1844-1868.

Rich. & W. Richardson and Woodbury (N.H.).

Rich. Cas. Richardson Cases, South Carolina Court of Appeals and Errors, 1831-1832; 1828-1834.

Rich. Eq. Richardson, South Carolina Court of Appeals and Errors, in Equity, 1844-1868.

Ridg. App. Ridgeway's Irish Appeals, 1784-1796.

Ridg., L. & S. Ridgeway, Lapp and Schoales, Ireland, 1793-1795.

Ridg. t. Hard. Ridgeway, King's Bench, Eng., 1733-1736; Chancery, in time of Hardwicke, 1744-1745.

Riley South Carolina Court of Appeals, etc., at Law, 1836-1837.

Riley Ch. South Carolina Court of Appeals, etc., in Equity, 1836-1837.

Ritchie Equity Decisions, Nova Scotia, 1873-1882.

Rob. Adm. Robinson, High Court of Admiralty, Eng., 1798-1808.

Rob. Eccl. Dr. Robertson, Ecclesiastical Courts, Eng., 1844-1853.

Rob. (La.) Robinson, Louisiana Supreme Court, 1841-1846.

Rob. (N.Y.) Robertson, New York City Superior Court, vols. 24-30,

1863-1868.

Rob. (Va.) Robinson, Virginia General Court and Court of Appeals, 1842-1844.

Rob., W. Dr. W. Robinson, Admiralty, Eng., 1838-1852.

Robb Pat. Cas. Robb's Patent Cases, U.S. Courts, 1789-1850.

Robert. Sc. App. Robertson, Scotch Appeals, House of Lords, Eng., 1707-1727.

Robin. Sc. App. Robinson, Scotch Appeals, House of Lords, Eng., 1840-1841.

Robt. Robertson, New York City Superior Court.

Rocky Mt., or **Mtn., L. Rev.** Rocky Mountain Law Review (**Mt.** nonstandard).

Rog. Rec. Rogers, New York City Hall Recorder.

Rolle King's Bench, Eng., 1614-1624.

Rom. Cas. Romilly, Notes of Cases, Eng., 1767-1787.

Root Connecticut Supreme Court, 1764-1797.

Rose Bankruptcy, Eng., 1810-1816.

Rot. Cur. Rep. Rotuli Curiae Regis. Rolls of the King's Bench, Eng., 1194-1199.

Rowe Law Courts, England and Ireland, 1798-1810.

Rptr. Reporter (reports of cases).

Russ. Russell, Chancery, Eng., 1823-1829.

Russ. & M. Russell and Mylne, Chancery, Eng., 1829-1833.

Rut.-Cam. L. Rev. Rutgers-Camden Law Review.

Rut., or **Rutgers, L. Rev.** Rutgers Law Review (**Rut.** nonstandard).

Ry. Railway.

Ry. & Can. Cas. Railway and Canal Cases, Eng., Neville and Macnamara; Brown and Macnamara.

Ry. & Cor. L.J. Railway and Corporation Law Journal, New York.

S. Section; Series; South; Southern.

S. & D. Shaw and Dunlop, Court of Session, Scotland, 1800-1862.

S. & R. See Serg. & R.

S. & S. Simon and Stewart. Chancery, Eng., 1822-1826.

S. & Sm. Searle and Smith, Probate and Divorce, Eng.

S. & T. Swabey and Tristram, Probate and Divorce, Eng.

S.C. South Carolina Reports, since 1868. For prior reports, see also, Bay, Brev., Desau., Const., Nott & McC., McCord, Harp., Bail., Hill, Riley, Dud., Rice, Cheves, McMull., Speers, Strobh., Rich.

S.C. Eq. South Carolina Equity Reports, 1784-1868.

S.C.L. South Carolina Law Reports, 1783-1868.

S.C.L.Q. South Carolina Law Quarterly.

S.C. L. Rev. South Carolina Law Review.

S. Cal. L. Rev. Southern California Law Review.

S. Ct. Supreme Court Reporter, since 1882.

S.D. South Dakota Reports, Supreme Court, 1890-1976; Southern District.

S.D. L. Rev. South Dakota Law Review.

S.E. South Eastern Reporter.

S.E.2d South Eastern Reporter, Second Series.

S.F. San Francisco.

SIPA Securities Investor Protection

Act of 1970.

S.L.T. Southern Law Times, Chattanooga, Tenn.

S. Tex. L.J. South Texas Law Journal.

S.W. South Western Reporter.

S.W.2d South Western Reporter, Second Series.

S.W.L.J. Southwestern Law Journal and Reporter, Nashville, 1844.

Sadler Sadler, Penn.

Salk. Salkeld, King's Bench, Eng., 1689-1712.

San Fern. V. L. Rev. San Fernando Valley Law Review.

Sandars' Just. Sandars, Justinian.

Sandf. Sandford, New York City Superior Court, vols. 3-7, 1847-1852.

Sandf. Ch. Sandford, New York Court of Chancery, 1843-1847.

Saund. Saunders, King's Bench, Eng., 1666-1672.

Saund. & C. Saunders and Cole, Bail Court, Eng., 1846-1848.

Saus. & Sc. Sausse and Scully, Chancery, Ireland, 1835-1840.

Sav. Savile, Common Pleas, Eng., 1580-1594.

Saw. Sawyer, U.S. Courts, Ninth Circuit.

Sax. Ch. Saxton, New Jersey Court of Chancery, 1830-1832.

Say. Sayer, King's Bench, Eng., 1751-1756.

Sc. Scotch.

Sc. Jur. The Scottish Jurist, Court of Sessions, 1829-1873.

Sc. L.J. Scottish Law Journal, Glasgow, 1858-1861.

Sc. L.M. Scottish Law Magazine, Edinburg, 1862-1867.

Sc. L.R. Scottish Law Reporter.

Scam. Scammon, Illinois Supreme Court, vols. 2-5.

Sch. School.

Sch. & L. Schoaler and Lefroy, Chancery, Ireland, 1802, 1809.

Sci. Science; Sciences; Scientific.

Sco. Scott, Common Pleas, Eng., 1834-1840.

Sco. (N.R.) Scott's New Reports, Common Pleas, Eng., 1840-1845, 1859-1860.

Scot. Scotland.

Scot. L. Rev. Scottish Law Review and Sheriff Court Reports.

Scots L.T. Scots Law Times.

Sec. Section; Securities.

Sel. Cas. Select Cases t. King; cases published anonymously under this title, Chancery, Eng., 1724-1733.

Seld. Selden, New York Court of Appeals, vols. 5-10.

Seld. Notes. Selden's Notes, N.Y.

Sen. Senator.

Ser. Series.

Serg. & R. Sergeant and Rawle, Pennsylvania Supreme Court, 1814-1828.

Serv. Service.

Ses. Cas. Sessions Cases, King's Bench, Eng., 1710-1846. See also, New Ses. Cas.

Ses. Cas. Sc. Court of Session Cases, Scotland.

Shaw Court of Session, Scotland, 1821-1838.

Shaw & D. Shaw and Dunlop, Court of Session, Scotland, 1800-1862.

Shaw & McL. Shaw and McLean, Scotch Appeals, House of Lords, 1835-1838.

Shaw App. Shaw's Scotch Appeals,

House of Lords, 1821-1824.

Shaw, J. Justiciary Cases, Scotland, 1848-1852.

Shaw, P. Justiciary Cases, Scotland, 1819-1831.

Shaw, T. Court of Teinds, Scotland, 1821-1831.

Shep. (Me.) Shepley, Maine Supreme Court, vols. 13-30, 1836-1849.

Shep. Sel. Cas. Shepherd's Select Cases, Alabama Supreme Court, 1861-1863.

Shep. Touch. Sheppard's Touchstone.

Show. Shower, King's Bench, Eng., 1678-1694.

Show. P.C. Shower's Parliamentary Cases, Eng., 1694-1698.

Sid. Siderfin, King's Bench and Exchequer, Eng., 1657-1670.

Silv. Silvernail, N.Y. Supreme Court.

Sim. Simons, Chancery, Eng., 1826-1852.

Sim. & St. Simons and Stuart, Chancery, Eng., 1822-1826.

Sim. (N.S.) Simons, Chancery, Eng., New Series, 1850-1852.

Skin. Skinner, King's Bench, Eng., 1681-1697.

Sm. & G. Smale and Gifford, Chancery, Eng., 1852-1858.

Sm. & M. Smedes and Marshall, Mississippi High Court of Errors and Appeals, 1843-1850.

Sm. & M. (Ch.) Smedes and Marshall, Mississippi Superior Court of Chancery, 1840-1853.

Sm. Eq. Manual Smith's (Jos. W.) Manual of Equity.

Smith King's Bench and Chancery, Eng., 1803-1806.

Smith & B. Smith and Batty, King's Bench, Ireland, 1824-1825.

Smith, E.D. New York Common Pleas, 1850-1858.

Smith (Ind.) Indiana Supreme Court, 1848-1849.

Smith, L.C. Smith's Leading Cases (Hare and Wallace).

Smith (N.H.) Superior and Supreme Courts, New Hampshire, 1796-1816.

Smith (Pa.) Pennsylvania State Supreme Court, vols. 51-81.

Smythe Common Pleas and Exchequer, Ireland, 1839-1840.

Sneed (Ky.) Printed Decisions, Kentucky Court of Appeals, 1801-1805.

Sneed (Tenn.) Tennessee Supreme Court, 1853-1858.

So. Southern Reporter.

So.2d Southern Reporter, Second Series.

Soc. Social; Sociological; Sociology.

Soc'y Society.

Sol. Solicitor (nonstandard).

Sol. J. Solicitors' Journal (nonstandard).

Sol. J. & R. Solicitors' Journal and Reporter, London.

Solic. Solicitors; Solicitors'; Solicitor's.

Sou. L.J. Southern Law Journal, Tuscaloosa, Ala., 1878-1879.

Sou. L.J. & R. Southern Law Journal and Reporter, Nashville, 1879-1882.

Sou. L.R. Southern Law Review, Nashville, 1872-1874.

Sou. L.R. (N.S.) Southern Law Review, New Series.

South. Southard, New Jersey Law, vols. 4 and 5, 1816-1820.

Speers South Carolina Court of Appeals, etc., at Law, 1842-1844.

Speers Eq. South Carolina Court of Appeals, etc., in Equity, 1842-1844.

Spenc. Spencer, New Jersey Law, vol. 20, 1842-1846.

Spinks Ecclesiastical and Admiralty, Eng., 1853-1855.

Spinks Pr. Cas. Spinks Prize Cases, Eng., 1854-1856.

Spot. Spottiswoode, Court of Session, Scotland.

Spr. Sprague (U.S.).

Sprague Admiralty Decisions, U.S. District Court, Massachusetts, 1841-1864.

St. Saint; State; Street.

St. Tr. State Trial, Eng., 1163-1820.

St. Tr. (N.S.) State Trial, New Series, Eng., 1820-1831.

Stair Court of Session, Scotland, 1661-1681.

Stan. L. Rev. Stanford Law Review.

Stark. Starkie, Nisi Prius, Eng., 1814-1822.

Starr & Curtis Starr and Curtis' Illinois Statutes.

Stat. United States Statutes at Large; Statute; Statutes.

Staunt. St. P.C. & Pr. Staunforde Pleas and Prerogative.

Stew. Stewart, Alabama Supreme Court, 1827-1831.

Stew. Adm. Stewart, Vice-Admiralty Reports, Nova Scotia, 1803-1813.

Stew. & P. Stewart and Porter, Alabama Supreme Court, 1831-1834.

Stew. (N.J.) Stewart, New Jersey Equity, vols. 28-45, 1877-1889.

Stiles Stiles (Iowa).

Stockt. Stockton, New Jersey

Equity, vols. 9-11, 1853-1858.

Story U.S. Circuit Court, First Circuit, 1839-1845.

Stra. Strange, all courts, Eng., 1715-1747.

Strobh. Strobhart, South Carolina Court of Appeals, etc., at Law, 1843-1850.

Strobh. Eq. Strobhart, South Carolina Court of Appeals, etc., in Equity, 1846-1850.

Stu. Stuart, King's Bench, Lower Canada, 1810-1835.

Stu. Adm. Stuart, Vice-Admiralty Reports, Lower Canada, 1836-1874.

Stu., M. & P. Stuart, Milne and Peddie, Court of Session, etc., Scotland, 1851-1853.

Stud. Studies.

Sty. Style, King's Bench, Eng., 1645-1655.

Sumn. Sumner, U.S. Circuit Court, First Circuit, 1829-1839.

Sup. Ct. Supreme Court (state).

Sup. Jud. Ct. Supreme Judicial Court.

Super. Ct. Superior Court.

Supra. Above; Before.

Sur. Surety.

Sur. Ct. Surrogate's Court.

Sw. L.J. Southwestern Law Journal.

Swa. Adm. Swabey, Admiralty, Eng., 1855-1859.

Swa. & Tr. Swabey & Tristram, Probate and Divorce, Eng., 1858-1865.

Swan Tennessee Supreme Court, 1851-1853.

Swans. Swanston, Chancery, Eng., 1818-1819.

Sweeney New York City Superior Court, vols. 31 and 32, 1869-1870.

Swin. Swinton, Justiciary Court, Scotland, 1835-1841.

Swin. Reg. Swinton, Registration Appeals, Scotland, 1835-1843.

Syme Justiciary Court, Scotland, 1826-1829.

Symp. Symposium.

Sys. System.

T. Territory; Term; **t.** during the time of.

T.B. Mon. T.B. Monroe, Kentucky Court of Appeals, 1824-1828.

T. & M. Temple and Mew, Criminal Appeal, Eng., 1848-1851.

T.C. Tax Court of U.S., since 1942.

T.D. Treasury Decisions.

T.L.R. The Times Law Reports, London.

T.M. Trademark.

T.R. Term Reports (Durnford and East), King's Bench, Eng., 1785-1800.

Tam. Tamlyn, Rolls Court, Eng., 1829-1830.

Taney U.S. Circuit Court, Fourth Circuit, 1836-1861.

Tanner Tanner (Ind.).

Tapp. Tappan, Ohio Common Pleas, Fifth Circuit, 1816-1819.

Taunt. Taunton, Common Pleas, Eng., 1807-1819.

Tax. or **Tax'n** Taxation.

Taxes Taxes: The Tax Magazine.

Tayl. (N.C.) Taylor, North Carolina Superior Courts, 1798-1802.

Tayl. (N.C.T.R.) Taylor, North Carolina Term Reports, Supreme Court, 1816-1818.

Tayl. (U.C.) Taylor, King's Bench, Upper Canada, 1823-1827.

Tchrs. Teachers.

Tech. Technical; Technique; Technology.

Tel. Telegraph; Telephone.

Temp. L.Q. Temple Law Quarterly.

Tenn. Tennessee Reports, Supreme Court, 1791-1971. See also, Over., Cooke, Hayw., Peck, Mart. & Y., Yerg., Meigs, Humph., Swan, Sneed, Head, Cold., Baxt., Heisk., and Lea.

Tenn. App. Tennessee Appeals Reports, 1925-1971.

Tenn. Cas. Tennessee Cases (Shannon).

Tenn. Ch. Tennessee Chancery Reports, 1872-1878. See also, Coop.

Tenn. Crim. App. Tennessee Criminal Appeals Reports, 1967-1971.

Tenn. L. Rev. Tennessee Law Review.

Tex. Texas Reports, Supreme Court, 1846-1962. See also, Dall.

Tex. App. Texas Appeals Reports, 1873-1892.

Tex. Civ. App. Texas Civil Appeals Reports, 1892-1911.

Tex. Civ. Cas. Texas Court of Appeals Decisions, Civil Cases, 1876-1892.

Tex. Cr. R. or **Tex. Crim.** Texas Criminal Reports, 1876-1963. (**Cr.R.** nonstandard).

Tex. L.J. Texas Law Journal, Tyler, 1877-1882.

Tex. L.R. Texas Law Review, Austin, 1883-1886. Cf. **Tex. L. Rev.** Texas Law Review, University of Texas, School of Law, Austin.

Tex. Supp. Texas Supplement.

Tex. Tech L. Rev. Texas Tech Law Review.

Thac. Thacher, Criminal Cases,

Boston Municipal Court, 1823-1843.

Thomp. & C. Thompson and Cook; New York Supreme Court, 1874-1875.

Thomp. Tenn. Cas. Thompson's Unreported Tennessee Cases.

Thoms. Thomson, Nova Scotia Decisions, 1834-1851; 1856-1859.

Tiffany Tiffany (N .Y.) .

Tinw. Tinwald, Court of Session, Scotland.

Tit. Title.

Tol. Toledo.

Toth. Tothill, Chancery, Eng., 1559-1646.

Tr. Trust; Trusts.

Transnat'l Transnational.

Transp. Transport; Transportation.

Tread. Treadway, South Carolina Constitutional Court, 1810-1816.

Tuck. Tucker, New York Surrogate's Court, 1862-1869.

Tuck. S.C. Tucker's Select Cases, Newfoundland.

Tud. L.C. Tudor's Leading Cases.

Tul. L. Rev. Tulane Law Review.

Turn. Turner (Ark.).

Turn. & R. Turner and Russell, Chancery, Eng., 1822-1824.

Tyler Vermont Supreme Court, 1800-1803.

Tyng Tyng's Reports, Massachusetts Supreme Court, vols. 1-17, 1806-1822.

Tyr. Tyrwhitt, Exchequer, Eng., 1830-1835.

Tyr. & G. Tyrwhitt and Granger, Exchequer, Eng., 1835-1836.

U. University(ies).

U. Balt. L. Rev. University of Baltimore Law Review.

U.C. Upper Canada.

UCC or **U.C.C.** Uniform Commercial Code.

U.C.C.C. Uniform Consumer Credit Code.

U.C. (C.P.) Upper Canada, Common Pleas.

U.C.C. L.J. Uniform Commercial Code Law Journal.

UCCRS or **UCC Rep. Serv.** Uniform Commercial Code Reporting Service.

U.C.D.L.Rev. University of California-Davis Law Review.

U.C.E. & A. Upper Canada, Error and Appeals, 1846-1866.

U.C. Jur. Upper Canada Jurist, 1844-1848.

U.C. (K.B.) Upper Canada, King's Bench, 1823-1830.

U.C.L.A. Law Review University of California at Los Angeles Law Review.

U.C.L.J. Upper Canada, Law Journal, Toronto, 1855-1864. See also, Can. L.J.

U.C.M.J. Uniform Code of Military Justice.

U.C. (Q.B.) Upper Canada, Queen's Bench, 1832-1843.

U.C. (Q.B.N.S.) Upper Canada, Queen's Bench, New Series.

U. Chi. L. Rev. University of Chicago Law Review.

U. Cin. L. Rev. University of Cincinnati Law Review.

U. Colo. L. Rev. University of Colorado Law Review.

U. Det. J. Urb. L. University of Detroit Journal of Urban Law.

U. Det. L.J. University of Detroit Law Journal.

U. Fla. L. Rev. University of Florida

Law Review.

U. Ill. L. F. University of Illinois Law Forum.

U. Kan. City L. Rev. University of Kansas City Law Review.

U. Kan. L. Rev. University of Kansas Law Review.

UMKC L. Rev. University of Missouri at Kansas City Law Review.

U. Mich. J.L.Ref. University of Michigan Journal of Law Reform.

U. Mo. Bull. L. Ser. University of Missouri Bulletin Law Series.

U.N. United Nations.

U.P.A. Uniform Partnership Act.

U.P.C. Uniform Probate Code.

U. Pa. L. Rev. University of Pennsylvania Law Review.

U. Pitt. L. Rev. University of Pittsburgh Law Review.

URESA Uniform Reciprocal Enforcement of Support Act.

U. Rich. L. Rev. University of Richmond Law Review.

U. Tol. L. Rev. University of Toledo Law Review.

U. West L.A. L. Rev. University of West Los Angeles Law Review.

U.S. United States; United States Reports, since 1790. See also, Dal., Cranch, Wheat., Pet., How., Black., Wal., and Otto.

U.S. App. D.C. United States Court of Appeals Reports, District of Columbia, since 1941.

U.S.C. United States Code.

U.S.C.A. United States Code Annotated.

U.S.C.C. United States Circuit Court.

U.S.C.C.A. United States Circuit Court of Appeals.

U.S.C.M.A. United States Court of Military Appeals Reports (non-standard).

U.S.C.S. United States Code Service.

U.S.D.C. United States District Court (nonstandard).

U.S.F. L. Rev. University of San Francisco Law Review.

U.S. Jur. United States Jurist, Washington, 1871-1873.

U.S.L.J. United States Law Journal, New York and New Haven, 1822-1826.

U.S.L. Mag. United States Law Magazine, New York, 1850-1852.

U.S.L. Rev. United States Law Review.

U.S.L.W. United States Law Week, since 1933.

U.S.P.Q. United States Patent Quarterly.

U.S.R.S. United States Revised Statutes.

Univ. University (nonstandard).

Urb. Urban.

Utah Utah Reports, Supreme Court, 1855-1974.

Util. Utilities; Utility.

v. Versus; Volume.

V.C. Vice-Chancellor.

V.I. Virgin Island Reports, since 1917.

V.P. Vice-President.

Va. Virginia Reports, Supreme Court and Supreme Court of Appeals, since 1790. See also, Jeff., Wash., Call, Hen. & M., Gilm., Rand., Leigh, Rob., Gratt.

Va. Cas. Virginia Cases, General Court, 1789-1826.

Va. J. Int'l L. Virginia Journal of

International Law.

Va. L.J. Virginia Law Journal, Richmond.

Va. L. Reg. (N.S.) Virginia Law Register, New Series.

Va. L. Rev. Virginia Law Review.

Val. U. L. Rev. Valparaiso University Law Review.

Van Ness Prize Cases, U.S. District Court, New York, 1814.

Vand. L. Rev. Vanderbilt Law Review.

Vaugh. Vaughan, Common Pleas, Eng., 1666-1674.

Vent. Ventris, King's Bench, Eng., 1668-1691.

Vern. Vernon, Chancery, Eng., 1680-1719.

Vern. & S. Vernon and Scriven, King's Bench, Ireland, 1786-1788.

Ves. Vesey, Chancery, Eng., 1746-1755.

Ves. Jr. Vesey, Jr., Chancery, Eng., 1789-1817.

Ves. & B. Vesey and Beames, Chancery, Eng., 1812-1814.

Ves. Sr. See Ves.

Vict. Victoria.

Vill. L. Rev. Villanova Law Review.

Vin. Abr. Viner's Abridgment, English Law.

Vroom New Jersey Law, vols. 30-85.

Vt. Vermont Reports, Supreme Court, since 1826. See also, Chip. N., Chip. D., Tyler, Brayt., and Aik.

W. West; Western; Wright (Ohio) (nonstandard).

W. & S. Wilson and Shaw, Scotch Appeals, House of Lords, 1825-1834.

W. & T. White and Tudor's Leading Cases, Equity.

W. Bl. Sir Wm. Blackstone, various courts, Eng., 1746-1779.

W.C.R. West Coast Reporter, San Francisco.

W.D. Western District.

W., H. & G. Welsby, Hurlstone and Gordon, Exchequer, 1847-1856.

W.L.B. Weekly Law Bulletin, Cincinnati.

W.L.G. Weekly Law Gazette, Cincinnati, 1857-1860.

W.L.J. Western Law Journal, Cincinnati, 1843-1853.

W.L.M. Western Law Monthly, Cleveland, 1859-1863.

W.N. Weekly Notes, all courts, Eng.

W.N. Cas. Weekly Notes of Cases, all courts, Pennsylvania, Philadelphia.

W.P.C. Wollaston's Practice Cases, all courts, Eng., 1840-1841.

W.R. Weekly Reporter, all courts, Eng.

W. Res. L. Rev. Western Reserve Law Review.

W. Va. West Virginia Reports, Supreme Court of Appeals, 1863-1973.

W. Va. L. Rev. West Virginia Law Review.

W., W. & D. Willmore, Wollaston and Davison, Queen's Bench, Eng., 1837.

W., W. & H. Willmore, Wollaston and Hodges, Queen's Bench, Eng., 1838-1839.

Wal. See Wall.

Wal. C.C. Wallace, U.S. Circuit Court, Third Circuit, 1801.

Wal., Jr. Wallace, Jr., U.S. Circuit Court, Third Circuit, 1842-1862.

Walk. Ch. Walker, Michigan Court

of Chancery, 1842-1845.

Walk. (Miss.) Walker, Supreme Court of Mississippi, 1818-1832.

Walk. (Pa.) Walker, Pennsylvania Supreme Court, cases omitted from regular reports, 1853-1884.

Wall. Wallace, U.S. Supreme Court, vols. 68-90, 1863-1874.

Wallis Chancery, Ireland, 1766-1791.

Ware U.S. District Court, Maine, 1822-1866. Includes Daveis.

Wash. Washington; Washington Reports, Supreme Court, since 1889.

Wash. App. Washington Appellate Reports, since 1969.

Wash. C.C. Washington, U.S. Circuit Court, Third Circuit, 1803-1827.

Wash. (Va.) Washington, Virginia Court of Appeals, 1790-1796.

Wash. & Lee L. Rev. Washington and Lee Law Review.

Wash. L. Rev. Washington Law Review, Seattle.

Wash. Terr. Washington Territory Reports, 1854-1888.

Wash. U.L.Q. Washington University Law Quarterly, St. Louis.

Watts Pennsylvania Supreme Court, 1832-1840.

Watts & S. Watts and Sergeant, Pennsylvania Supreme Court, 1841-1845.

Web. P.C. Webster's Patent Cases, Eng., 1601-1855.

Welsh Registry Cases, Ireland, 1832-1840.

Wend. Wendell, New York Supreme Court and Court of Errors, 1828-1841.

Went. Off. Exor. Wentworth's Office of Executor.

West House of Lords, Eng., 1839-1841.

West. Jur. Western Jurist, Des Moines, 1867-1883.

West t. H. West's Reports, time of Hardwicke Chancery, 1736-1739.

Western Res. L. Rev. Western Reserve Law Review (non-standard).

Whart. Wharton, Pennsylvania Supreme Court, 1835-1841.

Whart. St. Tr. Wharton's State Trials. U.S.

Wheat. Wheaton, U.S. Supreme Court, vols. 14-25, 1816-1827.

Wheel. C.C. Wheeler's Criminal Cases, New York Courts, 1791-1824.

Whit. Pat. Cas. Whitman, Patent Cases, U.S., 1810-1874.

White Justiciary Cases, Scotland, 1885-1888.

Wight. Wightwick, Exchequer, Eng., 1810-1811.

Willes Various courts, Eng., 1737-1758.

Williams Williams (Vt.).

Wilm. Wilmot's Notes and Opinions, King's Bench, Eng., 1757-1770.

Wils. Wilson, King's Bench and Common Pleas, Eng., 1742-1774.

Wils. & S. Wilson and Shaw, Scotch Appeals, House of Lords, 1825-1834.

Wils. Ch. Wilson, Chancery, Eng., 1818-1819.

Wils. Ex. Wilson, Exchequer, Eng., 1805-1817.

Wils. Super. or **Sup. Ct.** Wilson, Superior Court of Marion County, Indiana, 1871-1874.

Winch Common Pleas, Eng.,

1622-1625.

Winst. Winston, North Carolina Supreme Court at Law, 1863-1864.

Winst. Eq. Winston, North Carolina Supreme Court, in Equity, 1863-1864.

Wis. Wisconsin; Wisconsin Reports, Supreme Court, since 1853; Court of Appeals, since 1978. See also, Burn., Chand., and Pinn.

Wis. L.N. Wisconsin Legal News, Milwaukee, 1878-1882.

Wis. L. Rev. Wisconsin Law Review.

Withr. Withrow (Iowa).

Wm. & Mary L. Rev. William & Mary Law Review.

Wm. Mitchell L. Rev. William Mitchell Law Review.

Wms. Peere Williams, Chancery, Eng., 1695-1735.

Wms. (Mass.) Williams, Massachusetts Supreme Court, vol. 1, 1804-1805.

Wol. Pr. Wollaston, Practice Cases, Eng., 1840-1841.

Wolf. & B. Wolferstan and Bristowe, Election Cases, Eng., 1859-1864.

Wolf. & D. Wolferstan and Dew, Election Cases, Eng., 1857-1858.

Wood. & M. Woodbury and Minot, U.S. Circuit Court, First Circuit, 1845-1847.

Wood T. Cas. Wood, Tithe Cases, Eng., 1650-1798.

Woods U.S. Circuit Court, Fifth Circuit, 1867-1883.

Woodw. Dec. Woodward's Decisions (Pa.).

Woolw. Woolworth, U.S. Circuit Court, Eighth Circuit, 1863-1869.

Wright Ohio Supreme Court, 1831-1834, 1 vol.

Wright (Pa.) Pennsylvania State Supreme Court, vols. 37-50.

Wyo. Wyoming Reports, Supreme Court, 1870-1959.

Wyo. L.J. Wyoming Law Journal.

Wythe Virginia High Court of Chancery, 1788-1799.

Y. & C. Younge and Collyer, Exchequer, Eng., 1834-1840.

Y. & C. Ch. Younge and Collyer, New Chancery Cases, Eng., 1841-1843.

Y. & J. Younge and Jervis, Exchequer, Eng., 1826-1830.

Y.B. Yearbook; Year Books, King's Bench, Eng., 1307-1537.

Y.B. Ed. I. Year Books, King's Bench, Eng., during reign of Edward I., 1272-1307.

Yates Select Cases, New York Courts, 1811.

Yeates Pennsylvania, various courts, 1791-1808.

Yel. Yelverton, King's Bench, Eng., 1602-1612.

Yerg. Yerger, Tennessee Supreme Court, 1818-1837.

You. Younge Reports, Exchequer.

Young Admiralty Decisions, Nova Scotia, 1865-1880.

Younge Exchequer, Equity, Eng., 1830-1832.

Zab. Zabriskie, New Jersey Law, vols. 21-24, 1845-1855.